Australian Poets
& Their Works   A Reader's Guide
William Wilde

Melbourne

OXFORD UNIVERSITY PRESS

Oxford   Auckland   New York

OXFORD UNIVERSITY PRESS AUSTRALIA

Oxford   New York
Athens   Auckland   Bangkok   Bombay
Calcutta   Cape Town   Dar es Salam   Delhi
Florence   Hong Kong   Istanbul   Karachi
Kuala Lumpur   Madras   Madrid   Melbourne
Mexico City   Nairobi   Paris   Singapore
Taipei   Tokyo   Toronto

and associated companies in
Berlin   Ibadan

OXFORD is a trade mark of Oxford University Press

National Library of Australia
Cataloguing-in-Publication data:

Wilde, W.H. (William Henry).
Australian poets and their works : a reader's guide

ISBN 0 19 553769 6.

1. Australian poetry—Dictionaries. 2. Poets,
Australian—Biography—Dictionaries. I. Title.
(Series : Oxford paperback reference).

A821.009

Edited by Venetia Somerset
Cover design by Design Argonauts
Typeset by Abb-typesetting Pty Ltd, Victoria
Printed by McPhersons Printing Group, Australia
Published by Oxford University Press,
253 Normanby Road, South Melbourne, Australia

PREFACE

Australian Poets and Their Works: A Reader's Guide has its origins in *The Oxford Companion to Australian Literature* (William H. Wilde, Joy Hooton and Barry Andrews). The *Companion*, first published in 1985 and issued in a revised and expanded edition in 1994, contains more than 400 entries on individual authors whose published works consist mainly of poetry, and a further 150 entries on authors who have published some poetry but who are mainly recognised for their achievements in other genres. The *Companion* also includes some 200 entries on individual volumes of poetry, individual poems, folk-songs and ballads, and numerous entries on poetry movements, societies, controversies, magazines, anthologies, critical works, and prizes. The *Companion* thus contains the largest single body of writing on Australian poetry produced in this country. It offers a comprehensive account of the poetry published in Australia from the earliest days of settlement to the mid-1990s. It seems appropriate, then, both in the interest of the general reader wishing to become better acquainted with the history and diversity of Australian poetry and of the student seeking more detailed knowledge of individual poets, to provide all this information in a discrete, convenient, inexpensive source. This *Reader's Guide* attempts to satisfy these and associated needs.

Central to the *Guide* are the alphabetical entries on individual poets. Not every Australian writer who has published a book of poetry has been included. In contemporary times the publication of poetry has proceeded at an astonishing rate; each year produces several new writers with claims to be included in works of this kind. Because of exigencies of space and cost some selectivity has been necessary. Generally, only those poets with more than one collection have been included. There will certainly be, among the readers and critics and writers who peruse this book, some disagreement with my inclusions and omissions. In the long term, however, any deficiencies in my assessments will be self-remedying. The entries on individual books of poetry and individual poems have been included among the same alphabetical organisation. Readers will also find analyses of many individual works in the author entries themselves, along with full biographical information and complete lists of publications.

Some entries include assessment of individual poets' achievements and status. Where a poet's work has long been exposed to critical judgment (e.g. nineteenth- and early twentieth-century poets), the assessments in the *Guide* mirror, in the main, accepted literary opinion. In the case of contemporary writers on whom judgments are only now being formed. assessments attempt to incorporate both existing opinions and my own judgments, the latter stemming from my study and experience in the field. Where there are differences between my perceptions of individual writers and those formed by others I certainly make no claim of superiority for my judgments. Poetry is the most esoteric, personal and individual of literary genres; such qualities virtually assure a wide variation of reader response.

The *Reader's Guide* introduces several younger poets not included in the Second Edition of the *Companion*, as well as a number of recent publications. These include *Selected Poems*, and important new collections, from some of Australia's leading poets. A new feature is the Introduction, which traces the development of Australian poetry in the two centuries since White settlement and evaluates the poets within the context of their historical periods.

As with both editions of *The Oxford Companion to Australian Literature*, I acknowledge my indebtedness to all those writers, critics, academics, bibliographers and interested observers who have contributed over 200 years to the body of knowledge about Australian literature. The preface to each edition of the *Companion* acknowledges specific individuals, but I would like to reiterate that indebtedness here. I am grateful to Alexa Burnell for her painstaking categorisation of the *Companion* entries to ascertain their credentials for inclusion in the *Reader's Guide*, and to Peter Rose, who not only conceived the idea of deriving *Reader's Guides* from the *Companion* (*Australian Novelists and Their Works* will appear in due course) but who has also, in a copy-editor's role, adapted many of the original *Companion* entries to fit the context of the *Reader's Guide*. It has been a contribution much beyond what might have been expected from him. My principal debt, of course, is to my co-authors on the *Companion*, Joy Hooton and the late Barry Andrews.

BILL WILDE

TWO CENTURIES OF
AUSTRALIAN POETRY

The Early Colonial Period

First Fruits of Australian Poetry, written by Englishman Barron Field and produced by government printer George Howe in 1819, was the first book of poetry published in the Australian colony. Appointed by patronage to the Supreme Court of New South Wales, Field had a brief and rather turbulent legal career in the new settlement. Contemporary reaction to his poetry was positive if none too complimentary. One opinion was that the name bestowed on him at birth had proved to be remarkably appropriate.

> Thy poems, Barron Field, I've read,
> And thus adjudge their meed:–
> So poor a crop proclaim thy head
> A *barren field* indeed.
>
> (Anon)

Not short on egotism, Field claimed, by inference on the title page of the book, to be the 'first Austral harmonist', thus underlining the poetic priority that he had already appropriated in the title itself. *First Fruits of Australian Poetry* contained just two poems, 'Botany Bay Flowers' and 'The Kangaroo'. Field objected, in 'Botany Bay Flowers', to the scientific labelling of the strange but often brilliant colonial flora with dull and obscure botanical names ('barbarous Latin tags'). He felt that such natural beauty as the long-flowering heath so abundant on Port Jackson's headlands ought to be clothed in the more descriptive language of poetry. In keeping, however, with the customary patronising attitude adopted by those who had been exiled in the colony, any semblance of an admiring response to the local scene was invariably accompanied by a counterbalancing recital of antipodean shortcomings. 'Botany Bay Flowers' was no exception. For all its spectacular flora, Australia was seen as a desolate, even grotesque land, bedevilled by natural disasters such as bushfires, droughts and floods and inhabited by the most unattractive human and animal species that the Creator had been able to imagine, chief of which were the hapless Blacks and the bizarre kangaroo. Australia proved to be, for its first 'harmonist', a land devoid of pleasant associations, and he left it with no regrets.

> Lastly a ship is poetry to me
> Since piously I trust, in no long space
> Her wings shall bear me from this prose-dull land.

Poetry, in the Antipodes, had made an unpromising beginning.

In spite of his claim to be the first Australian poet, Field was the contemporary of three other writers, one of whom was Michael Massey Robinson. An Oxford-educated lawyer, transported to New South Wales in 1798 for blackmail and pardoned in 1811, Robinson was the first poet to receive royalties in Australia, two cows from the government herd being his reward for composing odes to celebrate the birthdays of their majesties, George III and Queen Charlotte, in the years 1810–21. The celebratory odes, couched in the flowery language that marked the public-poem genre, conveyed even less of the real nature of the country or the colony than Field's verses did, a point clearly not lost on Field, as his decision to ignore Robinson's poetry indicates. The Great South Land lay, in Robinson's opinion, 'unprofitably idle' until the coming of his countrymen.

> But when Britannia's sons came forth, to brave
> The dreary perils of the length'ning wave,
> When her bold Barks with swelling Sails unfurl'd
> Traced these rude Coasts, and hail'd a new found world,
> Soon as their footsteps press'd the yielding Sand
> A Sun more genial brighten'd on the Land.

The implications are interesting, particularly in view of this present generation's emphasis on conservation. Only the inhabited, colonised land was seen by Robinson as worthwhile. Without the civilisation brought by English discoverers and settlers the primitive land had no function, not even, apparently, for the poetic imagination. It is illuminating to contrast this attitude to Nature with that of Wordsworth in English poetry or William Cullen Bryant in American. The two other contemporaries of Field, although his *First Fruits* preceded their writings by some years, were William Charles Wentworth and Charles Tompson. Wentworth was the first of our poets who could be said to be more Australian than English in origin, having been born on a ship between Sydney and Norfolk Island in 1790. Later a newspaper publisher, landowner and politician, Wentworth first studied law in England. While at Cambridge he submitted a poem, 'Australasia', in the Chancellor's 1823 poetry competition. The opening words, 'Land of my birth!', marked the first occasion that an Australian writer had laid claim, publicly, to that special relationship. Although 'Australasia' was, like Robinson's odes, filled with the traditional poetic flourishes of the day, it did convey a real sense of its author's pride in his native land and his confidence in its prospects of future greatness. The poem concludes with the well-known lines,

> May this – thy new born infant – then arise
> To glad thy heart, and greet thy parent eyes;
> And Australasia float, with flag unfurl'd
> A new Britannia in another world.

Charles Tompson, born in Sydney in 1806 of convict parents, was the first Australian-born poet to have a book of poetry, *Wild Notes, from the Lyre of a Native Minstrel*, published here (1826). A self-declared 'native minstrel', Tompson, having known no other land, found the familiar Australian landscape picturesque, even romantic, qualities that transplanted English eyes had rarely perceived. And, unlike Michael Massey Robinson, who saw the primitive, uncolonised land as neither use nor ornament, Tompson protested against the despoiling of so much natural beauty by 'the rude invasions of the falling axe' of civilisation. He was possibly, then, the first Australian 'greenie'.

The Later Colonial Period

The second phase of Australia's colonial history, extending from about the 1830s to the 1880s, brought a huge surge of expansion and growth. With the crossing of the Blue Mountains and the development of the other colonies much of the continent was made available for settlement. The gold discoveries of the 1850s precipitated almost open immigration, changing forever the British racial and cultural homogeneity that had characterised the population of the first half-century. The rapidly growing population's character was further changed by the ever-increasing numbers of native-born and the gradual 'Australianisation' of earlier immigrants. Opportunities for social and economic advancement in the developing country began to appear unlimited, depending not on class or family background but on an individual's energy, initiative and ambition.

The three poets who dominated the middle decades of the nineteenth century were Charles Harpur, Adam Lindsay Gordon and Henry Kendall. Gordon, highly esteemed in his own day and lionised for decades after his death (there is a bust of him in Poet's Corner in Westminster Abbey), is now remembered more for his colourful and tragic life than for his poetry. Kendall, too, was well thought of by contemporary critics yet today is chiefly associated in the minds of most Australians with the one favourite schoolroom poem, 'Bell Birds'. Paradoxically, Charles Harpur, largely ignored as a poet in his own lifetime, is now widely judged to have been the only substantial poet of the whole colonial century. Harpur, like Tompson, was born of convict (emancipist) parents. He spent most of his boyhood in the picturesque Hawkesbury valley of New South Wales: the influence of its beauty and serenity on him is reflected in his occasional use of the pseudonym 'A Hawkesbury Lad'. His later life was to prove stormy, unfulfilled and tragic; not a little of the blame for that lay in his own abrasive personality which alienated him from many who were originally well disposed towards him. Harpur's strongest impulse was to poetry; his ambition was to be the first person to 'tune the harp Australian'. In his poem 'The Dream by the Fountain' he expresses a sense of his poetic destiny.

> I know that 'tis mine 'mid the Prophets to stand!
> I feel like a Monarch of Song in the Land!

That dream was not fulfilled in his own lifetime and he died embittered and unrecognised. Of those who had thus far in Australia's history contributed to its store of poetry Harpur was the only devoted student of the poetic craft. He took as his mentors the English Romantics Wordsworth and Shelley. From Wordsworth he drew an awareness of the fundamental link between man and nature, from Shelley an intense radicalism that drove him to struggle for the creation of a more equitable society. The only widely anthologised Harpur poems have been the nature lyrics 'A Midsummer Noon in the Australian Forest' and 'Dawn and Sunrise in the Snowy Mountains'. Effective though they are, with their characteristically Australian images of light, space and distance, of vast skies and impressive mountains and of the heat-hushed somnolence of the bush, these lyrics would not have raised Harpur's poetic achievement above that of Kendall. The more substantial Harpur poems include several based on pioneer experiences, 'The Creek of the Four Graves', 'Lost in the Bush', 'The Bush Fire', and 'A Storm in the Mountains', the last being reminiscent of parts of Wordworth's *The Prelude*. Harpur also wrote several long, complex philosophical and intellectual poems which are beyond anything achieved by the other poets of the period – 'The Tower of the Dream', 'The World and the Soul', 'The Witch of Hebron' and 'Genius Lost', a series on the English poet Thomas Chatterton.

Adam Lindsay Gordon, sent out in disgrace to South Australia in 1853 at the age of 20 because of several rather harmless youthful escapades, joined the Mounted Police and soon became known as a daring horseman and a dashing if sometimes foolhardy steeplechase rider. A legacy from his mother allowed him to become a landowner and he was, briefly and unspectacularly, a member of Parliament. He fell upon hard times, suffered badly from old head injuries received in race falls, published two books of poetry and the day after receiving the second volume (and an account for its publication) committed suicide on Brighton Beach, Melbourne. In that volume, *Bush Ballads and Galloping Rhymes* (1870), was 'The Sick Stockrider', a poem widely accepted as the progenitor of the bush ballad, soon to become a highly popular verse form. Although its imagery, language and tone seem more in keeping with English gentlemen riding in the hunt than Australian horsemen in pursuit of bushrangers or droving cattle, 'The Sick Stockrider' led Marcus Clarke to attribute to Gordon the beginning of a school of national Australian poetry.

More substantial but less remarked poems of Gordon in his day are the narrative 'From the Wreck' and 'The Rhyme of Joyous Garde', the latter a story about Sir Lancelot and Queen Guinevere.

It is difficult to reconcile the few Australian emphases in Gordon's poetry with the adulation of him that persisted for several decades after his death. Obviously the outburst of nationalist spirit that rose to a peak in the 1890s and early in the twentieth century would have benefited from the existence, real or imagined, of a poetic figurehead, a national poet, who could be seen to be representative of the movement. Later poets such as Lawson and Paterson were not then available and Gordon was virtually the only suitable figure at hand. His qualifications lay partly in his apparent rejection of his aristocratic English background in favour of the more egalitarian Australian way of life, and partly in his particular acclaim in 'The Sick Stockrider' of the bush-based component of that life, the nationalists believing that the bush ethos should properly be at the heart of the new Australian character and identity. Inherent in that way of life were several characteristics exhibited by Gordon's dying stockman – a laconic acceptance of one's lot, a refusal to brood over life's disappointments and lost opportunities and a fatalistic shrug of the shoulders over the question mark of a life hereafter. At the heart of his poem, however, was the code of mateship, a vital ingredient of bush life where survival depended on both sturdy, individual independence and a willingness to help others.

> Life is mostly froth and bubble
> Two things stand like stone
> Kindness in another's trouble
> Courage in your own.

Writing in the *Melbourne Review* in October 1882, only two months after the death of Henry Kendall, Alexander Sutherland, who edited the first posthumous collections of Kendall's poetry (1886 and 1890), expressed the hope 'that a few of Kendall's pieces will find their way into Australian schoolbooks and so become known to the rising generation', for he believed Kendall to have been the first poet 'to have woven the beauties of Australian skies and seas, rivers and mountains, into verse'.

Sutherland has had his wish, for Kendall has, down the years, been mostly labelled a 'schoolroom' poet. Such Kendall lyrics as 'Bell Birds', 'September in Australia' and 'The Song of the Cattlehunters' have been taught to successive generations of schoolchildren by patriotic schoolmasters for much of the past century. Contemporary literary opinion still largely views Kendall as a landscape poet. In many Kendall lyrics, against the landscape is set the wistful, melancholy figure of the poet himself ('Often I sit, looking back to a childhood/ Mix't with the sights and the sounds of the wildwood') and the landscape that he describes becomes suffused with the emotional glow that rises from him. For generations of readers the sad, pensive air that clings to such poems (certainly his own life was sad enough) has a special attraction. Thus they remain something like the old songs 'Danny Boy' and 'The Rose of Tralee' – perennial sentimental favourites. But there is more to Kendall than being merely the poet 'of sweet and melancholy confidences'. His narrative poetry, with Australian backgrounds such as 'A Death in the Bush' and 'The Glen of Arrawatta' and on biblical subjects such as 'King Saul at Gilboa', reveals a fine selective judgment of theme and a controlled yet fluent narrative skill. His ironic portraits of such Australian bush characters as the legendary 'Bill the Bullock Driver' and 'Jim the Splitter' only partly conceal, beneath their superficially good-natured tone, his distaste for the narrow-mindedness, parochialism, roguery and insensitivity (especially to the natural beauty through which they plod) of such bush types. As several of his predecessors had done, Kendall sought to establish his identity as an *Australian* poet. Field, the first 'Austral harmonist', Tompson, 'a native minstrel', Harpur, 'the bard of his country' – with Kendall it was NAP, initials frequently attached to his poems to signify his standing as a 'Native Australian Poet'. Kendall had much the same poetic ambition as Harpur – to become 'the Monarch of Song in the Land'. It is possible to see, in retrospect, that that ambition was within his grasp. The fragments of a work which he called 'The Australian Shepherd' show that there was, in the mind of the young poet in the 1860s, the idea of a series of poems linked by the theme of life in the Australian bush. If poems such as 'A Death in the Bush', and 'The Glen of Arrawatta' and shorter poems in which the shepherd was involved, 'The Curlew Song', 'Morning in the Bush' and 'A Death Scene in the Bush', had been integrated with the many others he planned, but which remained unwritten, they would possibly have comprised our first national epic. But the character of Kendall himself and the circumstances of his life would have made the production of such a *magnum opus* virtually impossible. Kendall was closer in time to the rising tide of nationalism (he died in 1882) than Harpur or Gordon, but he could never have satisfied the nationalists' criteria for a national poet. His lyric poetry, his romantic diction, his sentimentality and his obsession with the lush coastal landscape seemed to them more colonialist (read 'English') in character and flavour than Australian. For them, therefore, Kendall had little appeal.

The End of Colonialism and the Rise of Nationalist Radicalism

As is evident from the foregoing comments on the colonial century, neither nationalism nor radicalism were new movements that suddenly sprang into life in the 1890s. Nationalism began with the 'currency lads and lasses', the first generation of native-born Australians who shared few of the sentimental ties that linked their parents to England. They saw their lives as bound to the new land; its future was their future. With each succeeding generation their numbers were greater, their influence more marked; by the 1890s the population balance had shifted dramatically in their favour with three in every four of the people living here being Australian-born. Regular outbursts of nationalist feeling had occurred throughout the middle decades of the colonial century but by 1887 William Lane, in the first issue of the *Boomerang*, was indicating that a climax was near.

> We are for this *Australia*, for the nationality that is creeping to the verge of being, for the progressive people that is just plucking aside the curtain that veils its fate.

Radicalism, on the other hand, had its first spectacular explosion in Australia with the Eureka Stockade in 1854, while the loosely organised craft unions of Melbourne won an Eight-Hour Day victory in 1856. The growth of trade unions became so rapid in the following decades that by 1886 there was a nationwide Miners' Association and the following year a federal Shearers' Union. As it turned out the 1890s were economically difficult times. The financial crisis of 1891–93 and a prolonged drought brought large-scale unemployment in the cities and the foreclosure by banks and pastoral companies, which had financed the pastoral and mining expansion of the 1880s, on the properties encumbered to them. The shearers' paper, the *Hummer* (later the *Worker*), and the *Boomerang*, operated on unashamedly, offensively Australian and strongly radical lines but it was around the *Bulletin* with its nationalist-radical banner and its masthead motto 'Australia for the Australians' that the twin movements really gathered. Founded in 1880 by J.F. Archibald and John Haynes, the *Bulletin* had, by the beginning of the Nineties, become one of the country's most popular magazines. Its most conspicuous stance was the cultural chauvinism that it encouraged among its writers and its most conspicuous creation – in a magazine identified by many regular and idiosyncratic features – was the idealised bushman stereotype. Late in its first decade it had christened itself the Bushman's Bible, largely, one suspects, because of Archibald's own personal enthusiasm for the Bush and Bush life, an enthusiasm not fully shared by all his writers. The *Bulletin*'s celebration was of the bushman rather than the Bush, the Bush being mostly seen as the testing environment in which the fine qualities of the bushman were brought out. But, spelt with a capital B, allegedly because of Henry Lawson's insistence, the Bush began to appear as more than a mere geographic entity, a place on the map. It took on the personality of a living thing, often harsh and unforgiving, but something uniquely Australian nevertheless. Almost all the writers of the period who have passed into Australian literary legend were published in the *Bulletin* in the Nineties and the first decade of the twentieth century – Henry Lawson, A.B. Paterson, 'Breaker Morant', Will Ogilvie, Barcroft Boake, Edward Dyson, 'Steele Rudd', Joseph Furphy, Barbara Baynton, Mary Gilmore. But the pride of its stable were undoubtedly Lawson and Paterson, two writers who had contrary views about the Bush and Bush life but whose contribution to the nationalist-radical cause was immeasurable.

Neither Lawson nor Paterson were accomplished poets. Paterson was comfortable with the bush ballad, Lawson more at ease when his fiery radicalism inflamed his verse. At his best in stories of horses and horsemanship, Paterson bequeathed to Australian literature and folklore a classic tale of skill, daring and courage, both animal and human, 'The Man from Snowy River'. More than any other poet Paterson created Australian Arcadia ('Old Australian Ways', 'In the Droving Days', 'Clancy of the Overflow', 'On Kiley's Run', 'The Travelling Post Office' and 'The Road to Gundagai') and he peopled it with legendary characters (The Man from Ironbark, Mulga Bill, Saltbush Bill, Stingy Smith and countless shearers, drovers, squatters, bush jockeys, jackaroos, 'new chums' and swagmen). His nationalist enthusiasm informs 'Song of the Federation' and 'Song of the Future' and his radical sentiments are emphatic in 'A Bushman's Song' with its criticism of scab labour and 'On Kiley's Run', where absentee English landlords are regarded with contempt. Much more gifted as a short-story writer, Lawson gloried, nevertheless, in the title 'The People's Poet'. His chief contribution was to stimulate the growing mood of social disenchantment of the day, especially with his poems 'Faces in the Street' and 'The Army of the Rear'; his indignation against an inequitable and uncaring social system in those and other writings struck a responsive chord in many Australians. Lawson's picture of the hardship, pain and futility of bush life is explicit in 'Past Carin'', 'Out Back' and 'The Great Grey Plain', while his espousal of mateship, the only worthwhile aspect (as he saw it) of bush life, is at the heart of 'Shearers', 'Bill' and 'The Never Never Land'.

A contemporary of Lawson and Paterson, Bernard O'Dowd took the nationalist-radical theme out of the popular arena of the bush ballad and into the realm of more complex and serious poetry. Born in Ballarat with its echoes of the Eureka Stockade and the son of Irish immigrants, therefore inherently predisposed to radicalism, O'Dowd was a schoolteacher-turned-lawyer and for more than two decades was the chief draftsman for the Victorian crown solicitor's office. Too radical even for the renowned socialist organisation the Progressive Lyceum, he published his strong views on social injustice in the well-disposed *Bulletin* and in his own magazine, *Tocsin*. In his address to the Literature Society of Melbourne in 1909 O'Dowd prescribed 'Poetry Militant', that is, poetry devoted to sociological and political purposes, as the only path for the radical poet to take. His first book of poems, *Dawnward?* (1903), addressed to 'Young Democracy', voiced his discontent with the existing social, economic and political structure of Australia and outlined his suggestions for a better future. O'Dowd's finest poem, *The Bush*, was the most influential of the nationalist-radical statements of the period. He visualised the Australia of the future as a world force for justice and equality. At the heart of its greatness would be the Bush, which would come to be a maternal and religious source of strength for the nation. The moulding of this Great Australia would also depend on radical idealism. Australia, O'Dowd warned, had to root out from its society all that was unjust and oppressive – the 'ugly towns and cities', the 'joyless factories', 'the mephitic mines and lanes of pallid woe', all of which represented EVIL in 'full malignant flower'. When all that foulness was replaced by 'Truth, Liberty, Equality'

> Love-lit her chaos shall become Creation:
> And dewed with dream, her silence flower in song.

O'Dowd did more than merely describe, as the bush balladists had done, picturesque aspects of life in Australia in the new nationalist-radical age. He pointed to the idealism at the heart of the twin philosophies and demanded that all Australians take it into their lives.

The First World War and Its Aftermath

Whether the Nineties was as legendary a decade as it is represented by writers such as Vance Palmer, A.W. Jose, G.A. Taylor and Randolph Bedford in their books on the period, or a myth conjured up by the rosy glow of retrospection is still a matter of some controversy. The following decades, however, from 1900 to the end of the First World War and beyond, witnessed what historian Geoffrey Serle has described as 'a curious hesitation in development towards nationhood'. That hiatus was brought about by the combination of a domestic recession, intense industrial strife, an awareness of Australia's isolation in the Pacific and the possible threat to its security, increasing urbanisation which diminished the strength of the nationalistic bush ethos, and a strong sentimental attachment, especially among the conservative (and Protestant) middle class, to the old ties with Britain. Although the bush ballad continued to exert its attraction over the country as a whole (*The Man from Snowy River* is still the most successful volume of verse ever published in Australia) there were some poets in the new century who had little affinity with the bush ethos and no relish at all for the intensity of Poetry Militant. Two lyric writers, linked in the so-called 'Celtic Twilight' because of their backgrounds, were Victor Daley, born in Ireland in 1858 and Roderic Quinn, born in Sydney of Irish parents in 1867. Another Celt by background was John Shaw Neilson, born in South Australia in 1872 of Scottish parents. Neilson has long been considered Australia's greatest literary enigma. While the poetry of the minor lyrists Daley and Quinn has struggled to survive into modern times, Neilson's almost ethereal verse has received more and more recognition down the years. The apparent incongruity between the grace and delicacy of his poetry and his poor background and hard life of manual labour has long puzzled and fascinated students of Australian literature. Published in the *Bulletin* as early as 1896 and assisted throughout his career by A.G. Stephens, Neilson became well known with his first volume, *Heart of Spring*, in 1917. His wistful 'Love's Coming' and the haunting 'The Orange Tree' are two of his more memorable lyrics.

Christopher Brennan also stood remote from the popular literary scene in Australia in the early 1900s – in the words of fellow poet Hugh McCrae, 'a star in exile, unconstellated at the south'. His milieu was German romanticism, French symbolism and the work of English poets Milton, Keats, Patmore, Tennyson and Swinburne. In his own poetry he took himself and the universe, not Australia, as his subject matter. Brennan's stature and achievements remain, even today, the subject of considerable scholarly debate. Seldom does a discussion of Australian writers ever venture into the field of comparative literature. Harpur is never measured against Wordsworth, Kendall against Tennyson. Their worth is estimated only in Australian literature; it is not simply that any other estimate would depreciate their achievements but that it would be largely unrealistic, even valueless. With Brennan, however, there comes, for the first time in Australian poetry, a suggestion of universal merit. Pioneer literary critic H.M. Green made such an assessment: 'he is among the very best poets of his day or of our day in at least the English-speaking world', and R.G. Howarth, an eminent literary scholar, spoke of 'the monumental writings of our finest poet'. It is impossible to find, in a century and a half of Australian literary criticism, another example of the serious application of the word 'monumental' to an Australian poetic work. The complexity of Brennan's work has made him largely inaccessible to the general reader, but his influence on later poets such as 'William Baylebridge', R.D. FitzGerald, Kenneth Slessor and Judith Wright was considerable. The list may well be much longer. No serious poet of the period 1930 to 1970 and beyond would have been unaware of the great shadow Brennan had thrown across the Australian literary scene.

With the outbreak of the First World War there were some Australians (especially of Irish ancestry) who felt that the argument was none of our affair but the overall response was that Australia, because of its historical ties and its membership of the Empire, should go to the assistance of Britain and her allies. Ultimately, and particularly on the issue of conscription for overseas service, the war was to divide the country. The most significant poetry of the war came as a reaction to its horror. Mary Gilmore's *The Passionate Heart* (1918) was a mixture of compassion for those who were its victims ('O sweet, O young, O unaccounted Dead'), repugnance at the idea of war itself and anger at Australia's participation in it. No great Australian poet came out of the First World War, certainly no Rupert Brooke, but Mary Gilmore's poignant, tender 'Gallipoli' is a perfect cameo of a poem. The bitterest expression of repugnance to the war was 'To God: From the Weary Nations' by Frank Wilmot ('Furnley Maurice') in 1916. It was a powerful condemnation of war and of mankind for resorting to its brutality. Wilmot, who had published his first poetry in Bernard O'Dowd's radical journal *Tocsin*, lumped friend and foe into one huge 'sinners brotherhood' responsible for the war. He particularly criticised Australians for being part of it for they were abandoning the great nationalist dream of the Nineties of moulding for this country a future untainted by the evil influences of the older civilisations of Europe. Wilmot, with 'The Gully' (1925) and *Melbourne Odes* (1934), was the chief spokesman for the nationalist-radical cause, now much diminished, in the period between the wars, as well as an advocate for modernism in Australian poetry. The strong Digger tradition, born in the Gallipoli campaign and on the battlefields of France, was responsible for a surge of popular verse. Its emphasis on mateship and other attitudes inherent in the bush ethos guaranteed it a widespread appeal. C.J. Dennis, successful with *Backblock Ballads* (1913) and *The Songs of a Sentimental Bloke* (1915, the year in which it sold 67 000 copies), sacrificed one of his larrikin heroes, Ginger Mick, at Gallipoli. It was said that most Australian soldiers serving in France had their own pocket editions of *The Sentimental Bloke*. The Digger tradition was also actively cultivated by *Aussie: The Australian Soldiers' Magazine*, which began in France in 1918 but, in the face of diminishing enthusiasm for the parochial type of patriotism that was needed to sustain it, ceased in 1931.

By the 1920s the infatuation with the ballad had run its course, except for 'John O'Brien' (Father P.J. Hartigan) whose *Around the Boree Log*

(1921), with its captive Irish-Australian Catholic congregations, went into a new edition almost annually for several decades. A significant new literary movement began in Sydney in 1923 centred on the magazine *Vision*. Its inspiration came mainly from Norman Lindsay and Hugh McCrae, although the young poets Kenneth Slessor and R.D. FitzGerald were also involved, together with Lindsay's son Jack, and Frank Johnson. The 'Visionists' opposed both the modernist poetry emanating from Europe and the nationalist strain of Australian writing. Speaking some forty years later, A.D. Hope commended them on departing 'from the stock-rail and bowyangs school, the great mateship picnic and the literary canons of Clancy's Thumbnail Dipped in Tar' but was less impressed with their bizarre use of classical mythology, Renaissance, medieval and Regency French paraphernalia to create an Australian *vie de bohème*. Such *Vision* exotica, he commented, 'smelt of theatrical effects and fancy dress balls rather than any serious concern with man and his world; there was a forced raffishness about its doctrine of the Life Force that made it both absurd and tawdry'. It did not appear that way at the time, however. Norman Lindsay was the most influential cultural figure of the period; artists and writers stood in awe of him and he commanded a veneration that persisted for some time. Hugh McCrae, who had already indicated, with *Satyrs and Sunlight* (1909), that his own disposition was towards Poetry Triumphant (poetry of beauty and ornamentation, the reverse of O'Dowd's Poetry Militant), came to Sydney to join with Lindsay in *Vision*'s attempt 'to find truth by responding to the image of beauty, to vitality of emotion'. An exuberant and imaginative lyrist, McCrae peopled his poems with satyrs, fauns, nymphs and other fantasy creatures. His delight in language, his delicate fancy and his whimsy appealed to such contemporaries as Slessor, H.M. Green, Judith Wright and, more particularly, Mary Gilmore, who idolised him but who would herself have been more emotionally drawn to Poetry Militant.

Mary Gilmore is the first woman poet to gain a place in this historical outline. *Annals of Australian Literature* lists only three women poets in its nineteenth-century publications: Fidelia Hill, whose *Poems and Recollections of the Past* (1840) was the first book of verse written by a woman to be published in Australia, Ada Cambridge, who wrote religious and confessional poetry including *Unspoken Thoughts* (1887), and Mary Hannay Foott, whose poem 'Where the Pelican Builds Her Nest' provided the title for her small book of poems in 1885. Mary Gilmore became the best-known literary figure of the decades between the wars, publishing six books of verse and three of prose in that period. A poet who benefits from 'selection' rather than 'collection', she is best remembered for some exquisite lyrics – 'Gallipoli', 'Eve-Song', 'The Tenancy', 'The Passionate Heart', 'The White Swan', 'Nurse No Long Grief' – and the stirring patriotic poems she wrote during the Second World War – 'No Foe Shall

Gather Our Harvest' and 'Singapore'. For many the poem that most characterises her and her affirmation of her country is the magnificent 'Old Botany Bay'.

Vision's influence lasted somewhat longer than its mere four copies of 1923–24 might suggest, but by the mid-1930s the dalliance was over. Kenneth Slessor's early poetry, *Thief of the Moon* (1924) and *Earth-Visitors* (1926), reflect the vitalist *Vision* aesthetic. With later lyrics such as 'The Night Ride', 'A City Nightfall' and 'Winter Dawn', the surrealist landscape of Elizabethan taverns and the Gods flying in for a tryst with maidens is abandoned by him in favour of the more realistic environment of Sydney and the Australian countryside. The most significant of Slessor's poems are 'Captain Dobbin', 'Five Visions of Captain Cook' and 'Five Bells'. Romance and realism are blended in them to produce poetry of exceptional quality. 'Five Bells', in which the poet laments memory's failure to wholly recall his dead friend Joe Lynch, is one of the true high points of Australian poetry. With its inherent admission of the near futility of human existence it reduced Slessor's poetic voice to silence. His poetic reputation, however, continues to grow and he is clearly one of the finest Australian poets of any period.

With the Jindyworobak movement the late 1930s saw an attempt to revive the fading fortunes of extreme nationalism. In 1938 Rex Ingamells founded the Jindyworobak Club in Adelaide and published *Conditional Culture*, a prose manifesto which directed Australian writers to what the Jindyworobaks saw as their proper material, that is, typically Australian environment values enshrined in language peculiarly suited to them. Applauding the way in which their art, law and customs provided a culture for the Aborigines which was closely bound with their environment, the Jindyworobaks urged a similar regime for all Australians. Many writers felt attracted, some strongly, others less so and only briefly. Its chief poets were Ingamells, Roland Robinson, William Hart-Smith, Ian Mudie and Flexmore Hudson. They, and others, were represented in the annual Jindyworobak anthologies which persisted until 1953.

The 1940s to the 1970s

The four decades from the beginning of the 1940s to the end of the 1970s can be conveniently separated into two distinct if somewhat overlapping periods. The 1940s and 1950s were dominated by a small group of exceptional poets, R.D. FitzGerald, A.D. Hope, Douglas Stewart, James McAuley and Judith Wright, who have come to be referred to as the 'mainstream' poets and whose work provided Australia with the most sustained poetic period it had thus far witnessed. The 1960s and 1970s produced many new poetic voices. Many of them, both 'mainstream' and 'second wave', are still writing in the 1990s.

The 1940s and 1950s

R.D. FitzGerald, born 1902 and the oldest of the 'mainstream' poets, had a brief flirtation in his twenties with Lindsay's *Vision* group. He won the Australian Literature Society's Gold Medal in 1938 for his volume *Moonlight Acre*, and the Sesquicentenary Prize for the long poem 'Essay on Memory'. His best work came after the Second World War with several significant volumes, *Heemskerck Shoals* (1949), *Between Two Tides* (1952) and *This Night's Orbit* (1953). He continued to publish both poetry and prose until the late 1970s. 'Essay on Memory' declares FitzGerald's belief in the interconnection of the past and the present, thus the impact on the present of all life that has preceded it. Such a belief affirms the importance, therefore, of virtually every individual existence, brief though each may be, as brief, for example, as the interval 'between two tides'. Because his life is important each individual should try to fashion a meaningful existence through his achievements. This positivist philosophy, the need to 'advance in action', is at the heart of FitzGerald's poetry. Never popular or widely read because of his difficult themes and dense, sometimes awkward style (once referred to as 'an arthritic goosestep'), FitzGerald is a poet's poet; he exerted a major influence on his contemporaries, most of whom admired, even if they did not always emulate it, his credo that worthwhile poetry should concern itself with complex philosophical and intellectual concepts. One of his most successful poems, the historical 'The Wind at Your Door', based on an early convict flogging, is both an absorbing narrative and a sensitive appraisal of the meaning to the individual and the nation of Australia's convict heritage.

A.D. Hope was prominent as poet and critic from the early 1930s but did not publish his first volume of poetry until *The Wandering Islands* in 1955. The most gifted and individualistic of the 'mainstream' poets, Hope has always had a deep conviction of the innate worth of poetry and of the vital role that the poet played. He established an early reputation as a satirist, being quick, for example, to attack the meretricious posturing, as he saw it, of the Angry Penguins, preferring (hence his 'academic' reputation) the traditional techniques and time-honoured themes that had served the poet so long and well. His many poetry volumes, including several Collected and Selected editions, and his numerous collections of aggressively perceptive literary criticism won him Australian and international literary awards, including, in 1965, the Britannica-Australia award. No other Australian poet has produced so many memorable individual poems – 'The Death of the Bird', 'The Double Looking Glass', 'Meditation on a Bone', 'Pyramis', 'Moschus Moschiferus', 'Imperial Adam', 'William Butler Yeats', 'On an Engraving by Casserius', and even 'Australia' in which Hope, the anti-nationalist, while despising the cultural wasteland that his homeland is and has been, anticipates, in much the same way that O'Dowd had, that ultimately 'from the deserts' the 'prophets' will come. Internationally acclaimed, Hope is, in the opinion of many, Australia's finest poet of the twentieth century.

Douglas Stewart, poet, dramatist, essayist, short-story writer and literary editor, was the complete man of letters of the 'mainstream' period. His greatest contribution to Australian literature, however, came from his twenty years of editing the *Bulletin* Red Page and his decade as literary editor of Angus & Robertson. For thirty years he guided the development of Australian literature, nurturing the talents of dozens of writers. Such a domination of the Australian publishing scene led, inevitably, to the criticism that Stewart was moulding a pattern of poetry that was becoming too inward-looking, too insulated from literary developments in Europe and America. His own poetry lacks the commitment to philosophical themes that characterised FitzGerald's work and avoids the astringent, controversial edge so frequent in Hope. Its gently ironic, good-natured tone, its relaxed language and its accessibility have, however, won Stewart more satisfied readers than either FitzGerald or Hope could ever have had. A meticulous observer of nature with a readily admitted spiritual indebtedness to its wonder and beauty, Stewart is at his most appealing in lyrics such as 'Brindabella', 'Spider Gums' and 'Snow Gums'. He is not, nevertheless, devoid of moral and intellectual curiosity, as 'The Silkworms' and 'Rutherford' indicate, the latter providing a sensitive insight into the moral dilemma that confronts the nuclear scientist. Deeply attracted to the 'voyager' theme, Stewart contributed to it with his remarkably successful verse drama of Scott's Antarctic odyssey, *Fire on the Snow*, and with 'Terra Australis' and 'Worsley Enchanted'.

James McAuley instigated (with Harold Stewart) the Ern Malley Hoax in 1944 because he felt that the 'immense deviation' of the Angry Penguins would lead to 'the gradual decay of meaning and craftsmanship in poetry', and thus the ultimate loss of tradition and conservatism. His highly regarded first volume of poetry, *Under Aldebaran* (1946), which established him immediately as a 'mainstream' poet, contained both intensely personal and more widely philosophical poetry. The personal poems are filled with his disquiet about the unbridgeable gap between actuality and what the mind and soul aspire to; the philosophical indicate his conviction that traditional moral and intellectual values provide the only means of countering the galloping ills of modern civilisation. *A Vision of Ceremony* (1956), published after his conversion to Roman Catholicism, brought a new note of personal joy and a somewhat more optimistic view of society at large. The early poem 'Henry the Navigator' pointed the way to the later long narrative *Captain Quiros* (1964), which described that Portuguese explorer's search for the Great South Land and itself became part of the store of 'voyager' poetry in our literature. McAuley returned in his later poetry to more personal themes: his religious preoccupations, memories of his early life, reflections on his new life in Tasmania (he became professor of English at Hobart), his delight in the natural beauty of the island, and, finally, his response to the certainty of his imminent death from cancer. Although no 'nationalist' in the then contemporary use of the word, McAuley, in 'Envoi', expressed similar sentiments to those of Hope in 'Australia' – frustration with Australian attitudes ('the faint sterility that disheartens and derides') but an admission of his inescapable heritage ('I am fitted to that land as the soul is to the body'). In his long career as editor of *Quadrant* McAuley published what he saw as the best of contemporary Australian poetry.

Published in 1946, the same year as McAuley's *Under Aldebaran*, Judith Wright's first book, *The Moving Image*, reinforced the opinion of many at the time that, with those two books, the first Golden Age of Australian poetry had begun. Typical of the excitement of the day was mentor Douglas Stewart's verdict on Judith Wright's first book: 'These poems promise anything, everything, the world!' *The Moving Image* established Judith Wright, especially with 'South of My Days', as the poet of her 'blood's country', the New England Tablelands of New South Wales. She also wrote perceptively and affectionately from the intuition and understanding inherited from her family background, of themes and characters from Australia's past. 'Bullocky', for example and in spite of her later rejection of it because she felt that it had come to be wrongly interpreted as a hymn of praise, is a classic pioneer poem. *Woman to Man* (1949), the second Wright volume, explored in archetypal rather than personal fashion, and in brilliant poetry, the simple immensity of the life forces of sexual and maternal love. *The Gateway* (1953) and *The Two Fires* (1956) revealed that the poet's emotional and intellectual maturity had brought a complex vision of an interdependent world incorporating nature in all its forms and man. Later work, *Fourth Quarter* (1976), *Phantom Dwelling* (1985) and *The Human Pattern*, a selected volume published in 1990 when she was 75, shows her creative power undiminished, the familiar themes now being renewed and reviewed from the perspective and equanimity of age. Creator of the finest poetry that this country has yet received from a woman, she became the first Australian to be awarded the Queen's Gold Medal for poetry (1992). Now in her eightieth year she occupies, as poet and seer, a highly revered place in Australian literary history.

Although the 1940s–1960s were dominated by these five 'mainstream' poets there were others who began writing during that period and continued into recent decades. David Campbell, in his early poems, attempted to mythologise characters from, and elements of, the Australian tradition. His later, more meditative and beautifully descriptive lyrics took on a more universal aspect while his final work saw him moving into a more experimental phase. Rosemary Dobson, a lover of art, mythology and antiquity, achieved her best work towards the end of the 'mainstream' period and beyond, creating a body of lucid, highly crafted poetry which has received increasing recognition with time. Francis Webb, who came through the Red Pages of the *Bulletin* in the 1940s, was a disturbed and tragic schizophrenic. An extraordinarily gifted if esoteric writer and a cult figure to many of the new generation of poets of the 1970s, he stands apart from the 'mainstream' stereotype.

The 1960s and 1970s

Throughout the 1960s a number of changes occurred in major literary editorships. Vincent Buckley took over from Douglas Stewart on the Red Page in 1961, to be followed by R.A. Simpson in 1963. R.F. Brissenden, David Campbell and Rodney Hall came on to the *Australian*, and emerging poets Bruce Beaver, Les Murray and Robert Adamson were involved in the rapid changes occurring around *Poetry Australia*, *Poetry Magazine* and *New Poetry*. Those editorship changes and others, combined with a growing demand for the appearance of more experimental poetry in literary magazines and the rapid rise of many new small poetry magazines and publishing outlets, let to much greater variety after 1960. The hierarchy of the 1940s and 1950s of a few major poets surrounded by a coterie of lesser lights gave way to a much more numerous second wave of writers whose individuality of technique and theme was soon apparent. Some idea of the poetic riches emanating from those decades can be gauged from the fact that it would be possible to name almost forty writers whose reputations have continued to build into the present time. It would be impossible to establish an agreed order of merit among them, but clearly Peter Porter and Les Murray would have to be regarded as outstanding. They have both established international as well as Australian reputations. Committed, almost inevitably, because of his voluntary expatriatism, to a public assessment of Australian culture and character, Porter used, in 'On First Looking into Chapman's Hesiod', a comparison between the new urban Athens of the sixth century BC and the older rural Boeotia to somewhat disadvantage Australia by comparison with Britain and Europe. Les Murray, stung by the implied criticism of his 'vernacular republic', replied in 'On Sitting Back and Thinking About Porter's Boeotia'. Little of Porter's poetry, however, is directed at Australia, to which he has increasingly returned in recent years. The chief message of his finely articulated poetry is that the poet's art provides the most effective means of sustaining significance and meaning in life. Largely ignored in Australia during the 1960s when he commenced publishing and regarded as an outsider in Britain in the same period, Porter, with more than a dozen major books of poetry, has now become recognised as one of the finest poets currently writing in English.

By contrast with Porter, Les Murray has never been drawn away, physically or spiritually, from his origins. His poetry is a continual reverencing of what he sees as the real Australia. Varied and rich as his poetry undoubtedly is, there is at its core a commitment to the ideals and values that he sees represented in Australia's rural-centred history and in the Australian character that was formed out of the bush ethos. A modern 'nationalist', Murray echoes the kind of response to Australia that was at the heart of the 1890s and is still obviously alive and well today, as the irresistible movement towards a republic indicates. Poet, anthologist, essayist, editor and critic, Murray has been an outstanding literary figure in Australia in the past twenty years.

Bruce Beaver holds a respected place in recent Australian literary history, both as a poet and as an influential poetic innovator. The 34-poem series *Letters to Live Poets* (1969) provided a form of 'spiritual biography' that both in form and content pointed the way for the recent generation of poets to follow.

Bruce Dawe is a tremendously vital poet. Armed with satirical barbs disguised in contemporary Australian idiom, he fights verbal battles on behalf of all the ordinary individuals who, unable to speak adequately for themselves, are oppressed by life and the harsh forces that shape it. His remarkable contribution as a poet is that while dressing it up in trendy, modern, colloquial gear, he has managed to give poetry back its traditional bardic role, much to the delight of many readers who had grown weary of it being appropriated, often in incomprehensible symbolism and obscure language, for a variety of esoteric personal/intellectual/ philosophical causes.

Revolution in the 1960s–1970s

The influence on Australian poets of the American poetry published in such books as Donald Allen's *New American Poetry* (1960) and Donald Hall's *Contemporary American Poetry* (1962) became pronounced during the middle and late 1960s. Although there was little agreement among poets about the specific changes required so that Australian poetry would reflect the modernity of attitude and technique seen in American verse, there was a growing dissatisfaction with existing Australian poetry and a sense that a new and more adventurous direction was at least worth exploring. The forces seeking such a change were gathered around the Monash University poetry readings 1967–69, the La Mama poetry workshops 1968–69, the Balmain group in Sydney and the fragmentation of the Poetry Society of Australia, not to mention dozens of unnamed poetry groups operating in universities, community halls, cafés and pubs all around the nation. Complementary forces helping the revolution to full expression included those already mentioned – the myriad small and often short-lived magazines that had emerged in the 1960s and new publishing 'houses' such as Grace Perry's South Head Press, Outback Press, Wild and Woolley, Rigmarole of the Hours as well as the more substantial University of Queensland Press, which produced the Paperback Series devoted to new poets, and Angus & Robertson, who published the innovatory Poets of the Month series. Anthologies devoted to the new poetry included Thomas Shapcott's *Australian Poetry Now* (1970) and *Contemporary American and Australian Poetry* (1976), the latter providing a yardstick to measure the progress Australian poets had made towards 'liberation'. Although almost all of the poets who published in the period were touched to some extent by the experimentalist movement, those who played significant roles included Shapcott, Rodney Hall, Robert Adamson, John Tranter, John A. Scott, Kris Hemensley, Michael Dransfield and Alan Wearne.

Thomas Shapcott, like many others who advocated the need for change in Australian poetry at the time, was able to use the new experimentalism without becoming its permanent slave. It was with his late 1960s volumes, *A Taste of Salt Water*, *Inwards to the Sun* and *Fingers at Air*, that innovatory techniques were first allowed full scope. Later works such as the highly regarded *Shabbytown Calendar* (1975), *Turning Full Circle* (1979) and several *Selected* volumes indicate new and further dimensions to his art, dimensions which he continues to explore and expand. A versatile man of letters and an experienced literary administrator, Shapcott has received most of this country's accolades as well as several international awards including the Struga Golden Wreath for poetry in 1989.

John Tranter has made a similarly prolific contribution to the Australian literary scene in the past two decades as poet, anthologist, editor, publisher, teacher, reviewer and producer of cultural and arts radio programmes. His Introduction to *The New Australian Poetry* (1979) stressed the need for a drastic change. His early collections display his remarkable technical ingenuity and illustrate his belief that the language of a poem is its only 'reality'. In later collections, notably *Under Berlin: New Poems 1988*, post-modernism mixes with poetry that resumes its more traditional role of communicator with the reader. As the 'graying of the underground' (Mark O'Connor's phrase) of 1968 has gradually eventuated (Tranter and Adamson were only 25 at the time, Shapcott and Hall 33) many of the anti-establishment forces of those days have become the establishment of these days. Tranter, however, continues his personal quest for the ultimate limits to which poetry may be extended.

Robert Adamson also contributed to the rise of the 'New Australian Poetry'. He edited the magazine *New Poetry* and, partly as a result of his link with the American Black Mountain poets and Robert Duncan in particular, wrote 'The Rumour', an experimental poem which was one of the foundation stones of post-modernism in Australia. Adamson has long shed any labels that might once have been attached to his poetry. He is now a versatile writer combining, as his latest volumes, *The Clean Dark* and *Waving to Hart Crane*, indicate, both simple, meditative personal poetry and freewheeling variations of form and language. He is also an exceptionally uninhibited, amusing and ironic reader of his own verse.

John A. Scott won poetry awards at Monash in the lively late 1960s. His long narrative poem 'St Clair', which he had begun in the 'underground' days, appeared with 'Preface' and 'Run in the Stocking' in *St Clair: Three Narratives*. These poems, with their varied techniques and puzzling shifts of narrative, have extended the boundaries of contemporary Australian poetry.

Poets of Today – and Tomorrow

With a few unusual exceptions, and allowing for such external intervention as disease (Keats, Byron, Francis Webb), accidents (T. Harri Jones, Michael Dransfield), suicides (Adam Lindsay Gordon, Sylvia Plath) and war (Rupert Brooke), poetry and human longevity have not proved incompatible. Most poets are long livers and seldom fall silent while a stanza remains to be written. Exuberant early poetry usually gives way to the sober reflections of maturity, which are ultimately enhanced by the wisdom that sometimes comes as a reward of, and panacea for, old age. The poets of today, then, include many of the poets of yesterday. Contemporary Australian poetry is still occasionally enriched by the voices of elder poets Judith Wright, A.D. Hope and Rosemary Dobson. Most of the poets of the 1960s–1970s have also continued to write into the 1990s. Some, like Gwen Harwood, Chris Wallace-Crabbe, Robert Gray and Geoff Page, have, like good wine, been enriched by time and age, providing new generations of readers with ever-increasing pleasure. Most of the rising poets of today, however, were born in or about the 1950s and 1960s. Some have already distinguished themselves. Jennifer Maiden published the first of her dozen volumes of poetry when she was 25 and has already won numerous prizes. Her early, extremely complex work created a poetic terrain dubbed 'Maidenland' by one critic. In more recent times, with *The Winter Baby* and *Acoustic Shadows*, she has settled into a confident and controlled pattern of writing that suggests she will also be a poet of tomorrow. Philip Salom, a West Australian, nurtured as so many young WA writers have been by the busy Fremantle Arts Centre Press, has published six books of poetry. In a little over a decade Alan Gould has published seven volumes of poetry, much of it deriving from his interest in Norse mythology and his obsession with the sea and its history. Kevin Hart, an academic who has written extensively on literary theory and poetry, has published five books of poetry, four of which have won awards. John Forbes has gained a reputation for compressed lyric poetry filled with skilful symbolism and acute observation of the nuances of contemporary life. Peter Rose, whose two books of poetry have appeared since 1990, has won several awards; complex, innovative and stylishly poetic, Rose will be a major voice of tomorrow. Philip Hodgins, only in his mid-thirties, is a widely anthologised poet and has published five books of poetry, much of which is a brilliant if sometimes ironic analysis, based on his childhood and later experiences, of the traditional Australian pastoral experience. John Foulcher is steadily building a reputation as a sensitive observer of the seemingly ordinary but utterly significant experiences that life brings. The list of today's many fine poetic voices could be stretched beyond the limits of the reader's patience. It would certainly include Alan Alexander, Jamie Grant, Susan Hampton, Stephen K. Kelen and Christopher Kelen, Anthony Lawrence, Rhyll McMaster, Jean Kent, Jan Owen and Dorothy Porter.

Fostered by many supportive poetry organisations which regularly publish the work of their members, by a seemingly endless round of literary festivals where both novice and expert practitioners can hear and be heard, by an abundance of poetry readings in cities and towns all over the country, by the increasing popularity of performance poetry in clubs, pubs and even gaols, and by the infusion of new poets from a variety of ethnic backgrounds, poetry today would have to be said to be remarkably alive and extraordinarily well. It is certainly not now, as it was in those first years, a 'barren field'.

A'BECKETT, Sir, William (1806–69), born London, had a career in law and literature before coming to Australia in 1837. He was appointed resident judge of Port Phillip in 1845 and chief justice of the newly created Supreme Court of Victoria in 1852. A'Beckett, who had published a book of verse in England at the age of 18, edited the weekly *Literary News* in NSW in 1837, published *Lectures on the Poets and Poetry of Great Britain* in 1839, contributed articles to the *Port Phillip Herald* under the pseudonym 'Malwyn', wrote a poem on Ludwig Leichhardt in that newspaper (later reprinted in Edmund Finn's *The Chronicles of Early Melbourne*, 1888), and published a long verse narrative, *The Earl's Choice*, in 1863. He was the great-grandfather of Martin Boyd.

ADAMS, A.H. (Arthur Henry) (1872–1936), born in NZ, graduated from Otago University and tried law and journalism before coming to Australia, where he became secretary to the theatrical entrepreneur J.C. Williamson. In 1900 he left for China to cover the Boxer Rebellion, and after some further visits to London, Australia and NZ returned to Australia and established himself as a leading journalist, editing, in succession, the Red Page of the *Bulletin*, the *Lone Hand* and the Sydney *Sun*. His verse, which includes the collections *Maoriland: And Other Verses* (1899), *London Streets* (1906) and *The Collected Verses of Arthur H. Adams* (1913), avoids the rawness of the contemporary Australian ballads but also lacks their verve and intensity. Of his novels, which include *Tussock Land* (1904), *Galahad Jones* (1910), *A Touch of Fantasy* (1911), *The Knight of the Motor Launch* (1913), *Double Bed Dialogues* (1915), *Grocer Greatheart* (1915), *The Australians* (1920), *Lola of the Chocolates* and *A Man's Life* (1929), *Galahad Jones* and *The Australians* are the best. Australia, or more often Sydney, frequently figures in his work as a partly known rather than a fully felt landscape and although both his fiction and poetry are crafted to a degree, the tone of his work oscillates between romantic sentimentality and cynicism or worldly wisdom.

ADAMS, Francis (1862–93) was born at Malta, son of an army surgeon and well-known novelist, Bertha Jane Grundy Adams. Educated in England, Adams studied languages in Paris with a diplomatic post in mind but was compelled by tuberculosis to come to Australia in 1884. In 1887 he turned to journalism and leader-writing with the *Brisbane Courier* and with William Lane's radical weekly, the *Boomerang*; he also became a prolific contributor of poems, short fiction and critical articles to the *Bulletin*. Although initially enthusiastic about Australia ('a true republic'), in 1890 Adams returned ('mind-sick of Australia') to England where in 1893, with his health much deteriorated, he committed suicide.

Although he spent less than six years in Australia, Adams's influence was considerable, for he brought a sophisticated intellect, born partly of his European experiences and background, to contemporary Australian social, cultural and political

1

problems. His major effect was on the developing radicalism of the day. His intensely radical collection of poetry, *Songs of the Army of the Night* (1888), violent in its outbursts against privilege, oppression and exploitation of the poor and lowly, encouraged radicalism in this country by predicting a successful democracy here. The local scene was further scrutinised in the prose works, *Australian Essays* (1886) and *The Australians* (1893), the latter contrasting the two Australias, the lush, populated, coastal fringe and the dry, sparsely peopled interior. In a judgment that expressed a belief close to the heart of the developing nationalism of the time, Adams assessed the bushman as 'the one powerful and unique national type yet produced in Australia'.

Interest in Francis Adams has remained high since the 1890s and continues to increase, a recognition not so much of his own creative writing as of the impact of his intellectual modernity and revolutionary zeal, qualities which helped to sound the death knell of colonialism in Australia. Adams is the subject of Clive Turnbull's biographical essay, *These Tears of Fire* (1949), which was included in *Australian Lives* (1965).

ADAMSON, Bartlett (1884–1951), born Ringarooma in north-eastern Tasmania, was a journalist with the *Sunday News* and *Smith's Weekly* in Sydney from 1919 to 1950. His smoothly lyrical poetry includes *Twelve Sonnets* (1918); *These Beautiful Women* (1932); *Bringer of Light: An Allegorical Fantasy* (1945), a long poem on a romantic medieval theme that was judged in the *Bulletin's* Red Page (16 January 1964) to be 'a swoon of romantic nonsense' with versification 'unusually capable'; *Comrades All and Other Poems for the People* (1945), which attests to Adamson's political attitudes (he was a member of the Communist Party); and *For Peace and Friendship* (1952), a posthumous selection from his poetry. His fiction includes *Mystery Gold* (1925) and *Nice Day for a Murder and Other Stories* (1944). An influential member of the FAW, Adamson challenged that organisation's conservative attitudes. He was president three times over a twenty-year period. Len Fox gave the address, *Bartlett Adamson*, published in 1963, to commemorate his achievements.

ADAMSON, Robert (1943–), born Sydney of Scottish and Irish ancestry, spent his boyhood in Neutral Bay and the environs of the Harbour but often visited the Hawkesbury River district where his paternal grandfather was a fisherman. Boyhood unruliness, culminating in several semi-criminal misdemeanours, sent him to the Gosford Boys' Home for juvenile offenders and he was seldom out of corrective institutions until his mid-twenties. He educated himself while in gaol and developed an interest in poetry. After he became part of the Sydney literary scene in the late 1960s, Adamson was instrumental in the rise of the so-called New Australian Poetry, editing Grace Perry's magazine, *New Poetry*, and establishing Prism Books where such poetry was published. For more than two decades he has been an influential literary personality, successfully combining careers in writing, editing and publishing. He was editor-director, with Dorothy Hewett, of Big Smoke Books, editing, designing and publishing several collections of Hewett's poetry as well as his own. He launched Paper Bark Press to publish Hewett's *Alice in Wormland* (1987); Paper Bark (Adamson's wife, photographer, Juno Gemes, and writer, Michael Wilding, are also part of the Press, which has published the work of Terry Gillmore and Tim Thorne and Adamson's own *The Clean Dark*), has been praised for its quality design and presentation.

Adamson now lives on the Hawkesbury River ('I doubt I could live without the river') close to where he spent his time as a boy, fishing with his grandfather and exploring the river environment. Adamson's books of poetry include *Canticles on the Skin* (1970), *The Rumour* (1971), *Swamp Riddles* (1974), *Theatre I–XIX* (1976), *Cross the Border* (1977), *Where I Come From* (1979), *Selected Poems* (1977, for which many of the earlier poems were rewritten and which won the Grace Leven Prize for Poetry), *The*

Law at Heart's Desire (1982), *The Clean Dark* (1989), *Selected Poems 1970–1989* (1990) and *Waving to Hart Crane* (1994).

The Clean Dark has been Adamson's chief poetic triumph, winning the NSW and Victorian State Literary Awards and the National Book Council's Banjo Award. He also published *Zimmer's Essay* (1974) in collaboration with Bruce Hanford, an experimental fictional work, which, partly narrative, partly discursive and with a concluding poetry section, critically examines the prison experience. His autobiographical collection of prose and poetry, *Wards of the State*, was published in 1992.

Recognised as one of Australia's best contemporary poets, Adamson has recorded in his poetry the depths and achievements of his personal and professional life. His early poetry (*Canticles of the Skin* and *Swamp Riddles*) recounts reform school, prison and drug experiences and highlights the growing importance to him of the Hawkesbury River and its landscape. Both themes recur in much of his later poetry. Adamson's links with the American Black Mountain poets, particularly Robert Duncan, and his revolutionary ambitions for Australian poetry led to 'The Rumour', a complex poem which, in terms of experimental form and preoccupation with the craft of poetry, can now be seen as one of the foundation stones of post-modernism in Australian poetry. It has been seen, too, as 'a manifesto of the new romanticism' (James Tulip), the 'romantic' label being one that has long attached to Adamson. Some of the later volumes such as *Where I Come From* and *The Law at Heart's Desire* are autobiographically based, recording painful periods of Adamson's boyhood as well as the destructive break-up of his first marriage. *The Clean Dark* celebrates the Hawkesbury as his soul-country. The river's physical and spiritual influences coalesce:

> The river / is like a blank page
> you enter it / differently: shape
> it as you would
> a new thought / first vaguely
> with phrases / then sentences
> until finally / its language
> starts talking

The Clean Dark, among the most significant volumes of poetry of the late 1980s, also contains poems critical of both political and community apathy about the environment, violence and intolerance e.g. 'Canticle for the Bicentennial Dead', 'Wild Colonial Boys', 'Phasing Out the Mangroves', 'Remembering Posts', 'No River No Death'. Among the more personal poems are those that recall lost friends such as Robert Duncan and Francis Webb, others with new hope ('Songs for Juno'), and yet others with the inescapable Adamson burden of old griefs and uneasy memories ('The Difference Looking Back', 'Dreaming Up Mother', 'What's Slaughtered's Gone').

In *Waving to Hart Crane* the elegiac note is stronger , not least because several poems are dedicated *in memoriam* (e.g. Robert Harris, Brett Whiteley) or recall dead poets (e.g. Christopher Brennan, Francis Webb). A sense of life diminishing comes through strongly; the comment from 'Autumn Highway' that 'our poems/ become thinner/ sadder, less/ tense' is borne out in 'Through the Coddling Night', 'The Kingfisher', 'The Written Moon' and 'Love on Ice'. In the long poem 'The Sugar Glider', from Part Five, with its particular praise of American poet Michael Palmer, there is a partial return to optimism about poetry's role in the new millennium, a role much questioned in earlier poems in the book. There is still 'The joy of being/ a modern poet/ to skip time and space/ looking for the perfect reader'. With its shifting shapes and forms, its profusion of 'thinner' poems (single-word lines), language pared to the ultimate, and above all its 'pure contemplation' (often rising from customary river settings), *Waving to Hart Crane* is Adamson's most dramatic – and emphatic – work.

Wards of the State, while autobiographically based, is not the complete key to the enigma of Adamson's early life but it does, more so than the rest of his writings, reveal something of the detail of the experiences of reform school, prison and young manhood. Adamson has always had to contend with the publicly perceived image of *persona* in lieu of person. It is unlikely that *Wards of the State* will change that situation. He has also edited (with Manfred Jurgensen) the anthology *Australian Writing Now* (1988).

ADAMSON, Walter (1911–), born Königsberg, Germany, came to Australia in 1939 and worked at various jobs until he joined the Australian Army in 1944 as an Italian language interpreter. In 1949 he went to Bolivia, where he taught English, but returned to Australia in 1953. Since 1969 he has been a full-time writer, contributing short stories, poems and articles to Australian and German magazines and newspapers. His publications include two fictionalised accounts of his experiences of Australia published in German in 1973 and 1974; a novel, *The Institution* 1974; a collection of light verse, *Adamson's Three Legged World* (1985); and a collection of short stories, *The Man with the Suitcase* (1989).

AFTERMAN, Allen (1941–), born Los Angeles, USA, a graduate in arts and law, was associated with the La Mama poetry workshops and lectured in law at the University of Melbourne before resigning in 1973 to become a full-time writer. Afterman has published two books of poetry, *The Maze Rose: Poems, 1970–1973* (1974) and *Purple Adam: Poems 1974–1979* (1980); much of the latter volume stems from Afterman's reaction to the genocide of the Jews in Europe and the Aborigines in Tasmania.

AFTERMAN, Susan (1947–), born Dandenong, Victoria, was educated at the University of Melbourne and has worked as an architect in Australia, England and Israel. She has published two collections of poetry, *Rites* (1979, under the name Susan Whiting) and *Rain* (1987).

Age Book of the Year Awards, two in number, are presented annually, one for a work of imaginative writing, the other for a non-fiction work, which are of outstanding literary merit and express Australia's identity or character. In 1993 a poetry award in honour of Dinny O'Hearn was inaugurated; it went to John Tranter's *At the Florida*. The 1994 award was won by Dorothy Porter's *The Monkey's Mask*.

ALEXANDER, Alan (1941–), born Strabane, Northern Ireland, emigrated from Belfast to WA in 1965. With the assistance of two writing fellowships from the Literature Board and part-time teaching, Alexander has managed to support himself as a writer. He has published four books of verse: *In the Sun's Eye* (1977) and *Scarpdancer* (1982) reflect his response to new experiences and the beauty of the new land, the limestone area of WA's south coast and the wonderful shining granite of the Darling scarp. *Northline* (1987) celebrates, with photographs by Victor France, the inner-city area of Northbridge, an area rich in local history but now made equally rich by its colourful cosmopolitan ambience. The staid, rundown urban scene is now permeated with multicultural essences from Italy, Greece, Vietnam, Yugoslavia, Chile, Poland – as poems such as 'Zagreb Mick', 'Visitors', 'The Birth', 'Thelma Cutting Sandwiches' and 'Morning Till Night' affectionately indicate. Important in the evocative poems is the presence of one, she of the 'slim Norse head', who has much to do with the poet falling in love with Northbridge. *Principia Gondwana* (1992), the title's use of the ancient name of the great continent of which Australia was once considered a part, indicating the poet's linkage of past and present into a single universe of being, continues Alexander's skilful evocation of people and places in dramatically restrained and controlled verse. Figures from WA's history, both Aboriginal and White, inhabit a landscape that Alexander continues to muse on lovingly. 'Night of the Whales' was used as a theme poem by Rodney Waterman at the Contemporary Music Concert at the International Festival in Melbourne and at the Academy of Performing Arts in Perth. It was set to music by Glyn Marillier of Edith Cowan University.

ALLAN, J.A. (James Alexander) (1889–1956), born and educated in Melbourne, was a former editor of the *Victorian Historical Magazine* and heraldic adviser to the Royal Australian Navy. He published verse, *A Wineshop Madonna* (1911) and *Revolution* (1940); prose, *The Old Model School* (1934) and *Men and Manners in Australia* (1945); and a historical work, *The History of Camberwell* (1949).

ALLEN, L.H. (Leslie Holdsworth) (1879–1964) was born at Maryborough, Victoria, studied English and classics at the University of Sydney and completed a Ph.D. at the University of Leipzig in 1907. He held lecturing positions at the University of Sydney and Sydney Teachers' College before becoming professor of English at the Royal Military College, Duntroon, in 1918. From 1931 to 1951 he was sole lecturer in English and Latin at the Canberra University College, later the ANU. He became a member of the Commonwealth Book Censorship Advisory Committee in 1933 and was chairman of the Literature Censorship Board from 1937. His poetry, which reflects his classical interests, has a deft lyric touch. It consists of *Phaedra and Other Poems* (1921), *Araby and Other Poems* (1924) and *Patria* (1941). 'Patria', title poem of the last volume, is a series of nine sonnets which reflect on the future of Australia. Allen also published a book of children's poetry, *Billy-Bubbles* (1920), and a volume of prose sketches (with six poems), *Gods and Wood-things* (1913).

ANDERSON, Ethel (1883–1958), born Leamington, England, of Australian parents, was educated in Sydney before marrying a British officer serving with the Indian Army. After living for some years in India and England, she returned in 1924 to Australia, where her husband served on the staff of three State governors and the governor-general. Her published works include two volumes of poetry, *Squatter's Luck* (1942) and *Sunday at Yarralumla* (1947); two collections of essays, *Adventures in Appleshire* (1944) and *Timeless Garden* (1945); and three collections of short stories, *Indian Tales* (1948), *At Parramatta* (1956) and *The Little Ghosts* (1959). *The Best of Ethel Anderson*, edited by J.D. Pringle (1973), is a selection from her previous collections. Although she saw herself as primarily a poet, it is her prose work that is most distinctive. Bethia Foott's biography of her parents, Ethel and Austin Anderson, *Ethel and the Governor-General: A Biography of Ethel Anderson (1883–1958) and Brigadier General A.T. Anderson (1868–1949)*, was published in 1992.

ANDREONI, Giovanni (1935–   ), born Grossetto, Italy, left Italy in 1962, worked as a teacher in Tasmania (1962–63) and was at the University of WA (1964–68). He worked in NZ, 1968–73, returning to Australia to lecture at the University of New England. Before arriving in Australia, Andreoni had published a book of short stories, *Sedici Notti d'Insonnia (Sixteen Nights of Insomnia*, 1962). His later works include the semi-autobiographical novel, *Martin Pescatore (Martin Fisherman*, 1967). He has also written 'Abo Bianco', poems on the Australian outback, published in *Quaderni 4* (1971), and a book of short stories, *La Lingua degl'Italiani d'Australia e Alcuni Racconti (The Language of Italian-Australians and Some Stories*, 1978).

ANDREWS, J.A. (John Arthur) (1865–1903), born Bendigo, was educated in Melbourne and was a public servant for four years before his dismissal for insubordination in 1886. Soon after, he became active in the Melbourne Anarchists Club, and continued espousing the anarchist cause in pamphlets and public platforms after moving to NSW in 1891. Imprisoned twice in 1894–95, he edited *Anarchy* (1891–92) and published a magazine, *The Revolt* (1893–94), before returning to Victoria, although he was in Sydney again in 1897–99 reporting for the *Australian Worker* and the *Australian Workman*; he also wrote for *Melbourne Punch* and the *Bulletin* in the late

1880s, was briefly editor of the *Australian* (1888) and *Tocsin* (1902), and was a reporter for newspapers in Yea (1890) and Mudgee (1894). As 'Sebastian Bach' or under his own name, Andrews published three small volumes of verse, *Temple Mystic* (1888), *Teufelswelt* (1896) and *Poems of Freedom* (?1905); he may also have been the author of a fourth volume, *Apollyon*, suppressed during the 1890s.

'Andy's Gone With Cattle', a poem by Henry Lawson, laments the departure of a member of a selection family to go overlanding cattle. It was first published in October 1888 in the *Australian Town and Country Journal*, which also published the sequel, 'Andy's Return'. Some of the best-known lines of the poem are not Lawson's but are revisions by David McKee Wright when the poem was being prepared for publication in Lawson's *Selected Poems* (1918). The Andy of 'Andy's Gone With Cattle' (which is also in the repertoire of Australian folk-singers) is not the Andy of Lawson's poem, 'Middleton's Rouseabout', which traces the rise to wealth through thrift and hard work of a stolid rouseabout. J. Anthony King published an illustrated version of 'Andy's Gone With Cattle' in 1985.

Angry Penguins (1940–46), a quarterly journal of literary, artistic, musical and general cultural interest, was sponsored initially by the Adelaide University Arts Association but became an independent enterprise in its third number, published in Melbourne by Reed and Harris. Chiefly edited by Max Harris and John Reed, *Angry Penguins* was a self-consciously modernist magazine which coincided with a radical movement in Australian art and became a rallying point for artists and writers who had otherwise diverse interests. Rejecting all political creeds and influenced by the anarchist theories of Sir Herbert Read, *Angry Penguins* and its 1946 monthly supplement, *Angry Penguins Broadsheet*, attempted to present art as an organic whole, producing articles on cinema, jazz, the visual arts and literature. At the same time it attempted to link the Australian writer and artist to the European modernist movement, often publishing work by contemporary overseas writers such as Karl Shapiro and Dylan Thomas. Max Harris, who contributed a large range of material to the magazine, was particularly opposed to the nationalist socialism of such magazines as *Australian New Writing* and attacked what he saw as 'the tired and mediocre nationalism which passed for poetry, the pedestrian bush whackery which gave Australia a novel of unequalled verbal dullness'. Subject to inevitable 'excesses and absurdities', as Harris later admitted, and fatally attracted to any writing which presented itself as *avant garde*, *Angry Penguins* failed to survive the Ern Malley hoax. Alister Kershaw has written reminiscences of *Angry Penguins* and the hoax in *Hey Days* (1991) and the journal's history and impact are extensively discussed in Richard Haese's *Rebels and Precursors* (1981), and in Michael Heyward's *The Ern Malley Affair* (1993).

Anthologies. The earliest attempts to sample Australian writing in anthologies include Isaac Nathan's *The Southern Euphrosyne and Australian Miscellany* (1848), which contains 'original Anecdote, Poetry and Music'; *The Australian Souvenir for 1851* (1851), which contains stories, essays and poems; and W.H.H. Yarrington's *Prince Alfred's Wreath* (1868), which, with its selections from Henry Kendall, J. Sheridan Moore, W.M. Adams and others, is the first approximation to later verse anthologies. In 1869 William H. Williams introduced a form of anthology with his Christmas 'annuals' for holiday reading; his *Illustrated Australian Annuals* for 1869–70 and 1870–71 contain a medley of verse, short fiction and sketches, mostly by Australian writers. The 'annual' rapidly became a popular anthological device. One of the earliest examples of the anthology that comprises selections taken from a newspaper, magazine or journal is *Punch Staff Papers* (1872), a collection of short fiction, sketches and verse by members of the staff of *Sydney Punch*. The first significant anthology to combine selections *and* criticism was G.B. Barton's *Poets and Prose Writers of New South Wales* (1866).

The centenary of the colony in 1888 produced two busy anthologists, Douglas Sladen and Arthur Patchett Martin, who took advantage of the historic moment to promote Australian literature; their critical discrimination was, however, somewhat overruled by their enthusiasm and hampered by their lack of awareness of the new spirit of nationalism that was already affecting Australian writing. Sladen's first anthology, *Australian Ballads and Rhymes* (1888), was a selection of 'Poems inspired by Life and Scenery in Australia and New Zealand'. Sladen published a wider selection, *Australian Poets, 1788–1888* (1888). In all, he published the work of more than eighty poets; many were undeserving of recognition and were discarded by later anthologists. Sladen's sins were also of omission. Much of Adam Lindsay Gordon is missing, and the *Bulletin* writers are excluded. Martin had edited an earlier anthology, *An Easter Omelette in Prose and Verse* (1879).

Ignored by Sladen and Martin, the *Bulletin* proceeded to publish its own miscellanies; in 1890 J.F. Archibald in collaboration with F.J. Broomfield compiled *'A Golden Shanty': Australian Stories and Sketches in Prose and Verses by 'Bulletin' Writers*. Those represented include Henry Kendall, Victor Daley, Edward Dyson, A.B. Paterson, John Farrell and Henry Lawson; the fact that only Kendall appears in Sladen and Martin shows how lacking in literary discrimination the earlier anthologies were. A further *Bulletin* collection was *The Bulletin Reciter*, edited by A.G. Stephens in 1901; in 1920 Bertram Stevens selected and edited *The 'Bulletin' Book of Humorous Verse and Recitations*.

The first half of the twentieth century brought a continuous stream of anthologies of all kinds, some of which can now be seen as significant landmarks in Australian literary history. Bertram Stevens edited *An Anthology of Australian Verse* in 1906; from it came *The Golden Treasury of Australian Verse* (1909), the first collection that could be said to be truly reflective of Australian sentiment and attitude. Stevens produced other minor anthologies such as *Bush Ballads* (1908), *The Australian Birthday Book* (1908), *A Book of Australian Verse for Boys and Girls* (1915); and he collaborated with George Mackaness to produce *The Children's Treasury of Australian Verse* (1913) and *Selections from Australian Poets* (1913). The selections are characteristically Australian not only in content (Australian life, landscape and events) but also in their simple, direct and sometimes rugged style. Mackaness, an anthologist of other genres also, returned to verse anthologies twenty years later with *The Wide Brown Land* (1934), chosen by himself and his daughter Joan: perhaps the most famous of all Australian verse anthologies, it took its title from a phrase in Dorothea Mackellar's poem, 'My Country', and was often reprinted. Douglas Stewart continued the title with his 1971 anthology. A significant milestone was reached in verse anthologies in 1918 when Walter Murdoch edited the first *Oxford Book of Australasian Verse*; when the second edition was published in 1923 'Oxford' was omitted from the title. Murdoch's original selection did not please all critics but it was more wide ranging than most of those published earlier and less emphatic on Australian content than the 1913 anthology of Stevens and Mackaness. Murdoch's third edition (1945) was the subject of considerable criticism in *Southerly* (1946); the fourth edition, titled *A Book of Australian and New Zealand Verse* (1950), was edited jointly by Murdoch and Alan Mulgan; Judith Wright's *A Book of Australian Verse* (1956, second edition 1968), ultimately replaced the Murdoch Oxford anthologies. Another well-received verse anthology of the early twentieth century was Percival Serle's *An Australasian Anthology (Australian and New Zealand Poems)* (1927). Serle was assisted by 'Furnley Maurice' and R.H. Croll, both of whom were established critics; the combination produced a comprehensive and well-balanced selection and was accompanied by an account of the development of Australian and NZ poetry. The third edition of Serle's anthology (1946) added a short and rather unsatisfactory section on contemporary verse. Another significant anthologist of this period was J.J. Stable, professor of English at the University of Queensland, who compiled *The Bond of Poetry* in 1924. It combined English and Australian poems because Stable felt that poetry provided a bond that might keep nationalistic Australians linked to their British heritage. *The Bond of Poetry* remained a popular school text for many years, more so than Stable's later anthology, *The High Road of Australian Verse* (1929). One of the earliest movements towards the regional collection of verse was Stable's *A Book of Queensland Verse* (1924, with A.E.M. Kirwood), which was published in conjunction with the Brisbane centenary and illustrated the development of verse in Queensland. A verse anthology that stood deliberately apart from the nationalistic collections of this period was *Poetry in Australia 1923* (1923), edited by Jack Lindsay and Kenneth Slessor, with a preface by Norman Lindsay that decried nationalism in literature. Compelled to accept the 'accident' of geographical location and thus label its poetry 'Australian', the anthology is not representatively Australian in a general sense; its contributors were chosen largely to illustrate the Lindsay and *Vision* insistence on internationalism in literature and the importance of language in creative thought. Much of the selected poetry came from Hugh McCrae, Jack Lindsay and Kenneth Slessor, all of whom wrote at that time in accord with *Vision* attitudes. A notable specialised anthology of the period was Louis Lavater's *The Sonnet in Australasia* (1926), a collection of about 225 sonnets by more than 100 Australian poets. The occasional annual selection of the poetry of the period, e.g. *Australian Poetry Annual 1920–21* (1921), chosen from contributions to the magazine *Birth*, was the forerunner of the poetry magazines that proliferated after the middle of the century and of such annual selections of verse as *Australian Poetry*, published by Angus & Robertson and which ran 1941–73 (and revised later) with a different editor for each volume. Most of *Australian Poetry*'s editors were established poets/critics, e.g. Douglas Stewart, R.D. FitzGerald, Kenneth Slessor and Judith Wright, and the annual selections were, at least until the 1960s, conventional and predictable. Notable among the specialised verse anthologies of the first half of the century were those published by the Jindyworobaks. They ran 1938–53, included only poetry that satisfied the Jindyworobak criteria, and were edited by notable poets of the movement, e.g. Rex Ingamells, Flexmore Hudson, W. Hart-Smith, Ian Mudie and Roland Robinson.

After the Second World War poetry anthologies came in four main categories: general anthologies that gave a selection from colonial times to the present; those which attempted a periodic update of the contemporary scene prior to 1968; those which specifically illustrated the 'New Australian Poetry' which dated from 1968; and those which reflected sectional interests or illustrated particular types and periods of poetry. The general anthologies, largely a continuation of similar types published earlier in the century, include Judith Wright's *A Book of Australian Verse*, Geoffrey Dutton's *Australian Verse from 1805* (1976) and Rodney Hall's *The Collins Book of Australian Poetry* (1981). Most of those attempting an up-to-date view of poetry in the period up to 1968 convey their intention by using the word 'modern' in their titles; they include H.M. Green's *Modern Australian Poetry* (1946, rev. edn 1952); R.G. Howarth, Kenneth Slessor and John Thompson's *The Penguin Book of Australian Verse* (1958, titled *Modern Australian Verse* in 1961), which was replaced by Harry Heseltine's *The Penguin Book of Australian Verse* (1972); Douglas Stewart's *Modern Australian Verse* (1964), which is the second volume of the two-volume *Poetry in Australia*; Rodney Hall and Thomas Shapcott's *New Impulses in Australian Poetry* (1968), which concerns itself with the poetry of the 1960s but which appeared before the 'New Australian Poetry' had fully developed; David Campbell's *Modern Australian Poetry* (1970), which was also compiled before 1968 and which closes with the work of Geoffrey Lehmann, the only poet in the anthology who was born in the 1940s; Dennis Robinson's *Those Fabled Shores: Six Contemporary Australian Poets* (1972), which contains only the work of the mainstream poets, Slessor, Hope, Wright, James McAuley, Stewart and Fitz-Gerald; and Thomas Shapcott's *Contemporary American and Australian Poetry* (1976), which includes some post-1968 poetry but which continues to emphasise the older representatives of contemporary Australian poetry. The 'New Australian Poetry', which came after 1968, has been given almost blanket coverage, chiefly by the myriad poetry magazines that are a striking phenomenon of the modern literary scene, and to a lesser extent by more formal anthologies. The latter include Shapcott's *Australian Poetry Now* (1970), which is the companion to and extension of David Campbell's *Modern Australian Poetry* and which focuses on the poets who were on the verge of the new movement, e.g. Michael Dransfield, Robert Adamson, John Tranter and Roger McDonald; Robert Kenny and Colin Talbot's *Applestealers* (1974), a collection specifically stated to represent the 'renaissance in Australian poetry'; John Tranter's *The New Australian Poetry* (1979), which includes selections from twenty-four poets of 'Australian poetry's most exciting decade', e.g. Beaver, Dransfield, Adamson, Rae Desmond Jones, Nigel Roberts, Jennifer Maiden, Vicki Viidikas and John Forbes; Heseltine's *The Penguin Book of Modern Australian Verse* (1981), which includes both new and older writers, many born in the 1920s and 1930s; and two important attempts to assist the development of the then contemporary poetry, the Paperback Poets series of UQP which culminated in two paperback poetry anthologies (1974, 1981) and Angus & Robertson's Poets of the Month series. Robert Gray and Geoffrey Lehmann's *The Younger Australian Poets* (1983) brings the poetry scene up to date at that time, thereby relegating the 1968 revolution to history. The same two also produced *Australian Poetry in the Twentieth Century* (1992), a radically new overall approach to the poetry of the second Australian century.

Increasingly in recent years the anthology has been used as a device to espouse causes, highlight philosophies and attitudes, illustrate particular literary movements, types of writing and groups of writers, and draw attention to particular periods, places and regions. The feminist movement is represented by such collections as *Mother I'm Rooted* (1975), an anthology of Australian women poets edited by Kate Jennings; and *Hecate's Daughters* (1978), verse and prose edited by Carole Ferrier. The success of the feminist movement led to numerous further anthologies of women's writing, e.g. *The Penguin Book of Australian Women Poets* (1986), ed. Susan Hampton and Kate Llewellyn, and *The Oxford Book of Australian Women's Verse*, ed. Susan Lever (1995).

The experience of war had produced earlier anthologies such as C.E.W. Bean's *The Anzac Book* (1916) and Ian Mudie's *Poets at War* (1944). Modern variations on traditional war anthologies include the anti-war collection *We Took Their Orders and Are Dead* (1971), a protest against the Vietnam War compiled by Shirley Cass, Ros Cheney, David Malouf and Michael Wilding; and Geoff Page's *Shadows from Wire* (1983), which demonstrates, by juxtaposing modern reactions to the First World War with actual war photographs, the irony of the initial response to the war. The reaction to the experience of incarceration is collected in two volumes of poetry, *Poems from Prison* (1973), edited by Rodney Hall, and *Walled Gardens* (1978), poems from NSW prisons, published by the aptly named Ball & Chain Press.

Regionalism provides a constant impulse to anthologising and never so much as in the Bicentenary period: recent examples include *Wordhord: A Critical Selection of Contemporary Western Australian Poetry* (1989), ed. Dennis Haskell and Hilary Fraser, a collection of poetry written in the 1980s; and *Margins: A West Coast Collection of Poetry, 1829–1988* (1988), ed. William Grono. SA anthologies include *Dots Over Lines* (1981), *The Orange Tree* (1986), ed. K.F. Pearson and Christine Churches; and *The Inner Courtyard* (1990), ed. Anne Brewster and Jeff Guess, a collection of contemporary SA love poetry. Queensland was represented quite early in the century by Stable and Kirkwood's *A Book of Queensland Verse* (1924), then by the *Queensland Centenary Anthology* (1959), ed. R.S. Byrnes and Val Vallis, later by *Place and Perspective* (1983), ed. Barry O'Donohue, collecting the works of thirty Queensland poets, and *North of Capricorn: An Anthology of Verse* (1988), ed. Elizabeth Perkins and Robert Handicott. The Northern Territory's own collections include *Latitudes: New Writing from the North* (1986), ed. Susan Johnson and Mary Roberts; *North of the Ten Commandments* (1991), ed. David Headon, an anthology of various types of Territory writing. Tasmanian poetry was collected in *Effects of Light: The Poetry of Tasmania* (1986), ed. Vivian Smith and Margaret Scott, and poetry of the ACT in *The Poetry of Canberra* (1990), ed. Phillip Mackenzie. Gippsland is the base for *Shadow and Shine* (1988), ed. Patrick Morgan, and The Hunter Valley of NSW has various collections including Norman Talbot's *Hunter Valley Poets* (1973) and Ross Bennett's *This Place: Poetry of the Hunter Valley* (1980).

Typical of specific period anthologies has been the return to colonial writing in such collections as T. Inglis Moore's *From the Ballads to Brennan* (1964); Brian Elliott and Adrian Mitchell's *Bards in the Wilderness: Australian Colonial Poetry to 1920* (1970); G.A. Wilkes's *The Colonial Poets* (1974); *The Poet's Discovery: Nineteenth Century Australia in Verse* (1990), ed. R.D. Jordan and Peter Pierce; *The Penguin Book of Australian Ballads* (1993), ed. Philip Butterss and Elizabeth Webby; and *The Penguin Book of Nineteenth Century Australian Literature* (1993), ed. Michael Ackland.

A narrowing of the focus to inspect the most important decade of the nineteenth century – the Nineties – is made in Leon Cantrell's collection of writings from that decade, *The 1890s* (1977). A similar narrowing is seen in the somewhat frenetic efforts of anthologists to capture the character of contemporary literature, e.g. *Contemporary Australian Poetry* (1986), ed. Dimitris Tsaloumas; *The Tin Wash Dish* (1989), an anthology edited by John Tranter of the poetry entered in the ABC/ABA Bicentennial competition; *Contemporary Australian Poetry* (1990), ed. John Leonard; *The Australian Anthology of New Poets* (1989); *Picador New Writing* (1993), ed. Robert Dessaix and Helen Daniel; and *The Penguin Book of Modern Australian Poetry* (1991), ed. John Tranter and Philip Mead. Several anthologies continue to give an overall view, e.g. *Two Centuries of Australian Poetry* (1988), ed. Mark O'Connor; *The Heritage of Australian Poetry* (1984), ed. Geoffrey Dutton; *The New Oxford Book of Australian Verse* (1986, expanded 1991), ed. Les Murray, which extends from Aboriginal songs to modern verse; and *The Macmillan Anthology of Australian Literature* (1990), ed. Ken Goodwin and Alan Lawson, which, with its 629 pages, is about the largest, though undoubtedly not the last word, in complete anthologies.

Readily identifiable thematic groups of anthologies in recent decades include the book of erotic verse *Within the Hill* (1975), ed. Alan Gould and others; *The Oxford Book of Australian Love Poems* (1993), ed. Jennifer Strauss; the humorous collections *Comic Australian Verse* (1972), ed. Geoffrey Lehmann; *Robust, Ribald and Rude Verse in Australia* (1972), ed. Bill Wannan; *The Penguin Book of Australian Satirical Verse* (1986), ed. Philip Neilsen; *The Illustrated Treasury of Australian Humour* (1988), ed. Michael Sharkey; *The Flight of the Emu: Contemporary Light Verse* (1990), ed. Geoffrey Lehmann; and *The Oxford Book of Australian Light Verse* (1991), ed. R.F. Brissenden and Philip Grundy; the nationally oriented Wannan collections, *The Wearing of the Green* (1965) and *The Heather in the South* (1966); David Stewart's *Voyager Poems* (1960); and David Martin's book of left-wing verse, *New World, New Song* (1955).

Black Writing is contained in *Australian Aboriginal Literature: An Anthology* (1987), ed. Adam Shoemaker, *Inside Black Australia* (1988), ed. Kevin Gilbert, a collection of Aboriginal poetry, and *Paperbark: A Collection of Black Australian Writings* (1990), ed. Jack Davis et al. Les Murray collated the important and popular *Anthology of Australian Religious Poetry* (1986). This was followed by The *Oxford Book of Australian Religious Verse*, ed. Kevin Hart (1994). Symptomatic of the changes in public perception in recent times is the ready acceptance of gay and lesbian anthologies, e.g., *Edge City on Two Different Plans* (1983), ed. Margaret Bradstock, Gary Dunne et al., a collection of poems, songs and fiction; *The Exploding Frangipani* (1990), ed. Cathie Dunsford and Susan Hawthorne, featuring Australian and NZ lesbian writing; and *Australian Gay and Lesbian Writing* (1993), ed. Robert Dessaix.

Literary societies and groups have complied anthologies of the writings of their members: Wesley Milgate and Imogen Whyse produced the Poetry Society of Australia's first anthology in 1956; Nancy Keesing's *Transition* (1970) is a collection of the ASA; *Square Poets* (1971) groups the work of the Queensland FAW, as does *Breakaway* (1980) for the WA branch of the FAW, Barry Bannister's *Walk a Different Way* (1979) for the Darwin FAW and *Island Authors* (1971) for the Tasmanian Branch. *Tuesday Night Live* (1993), ed. Jeri Kroll and Barry Westburg, contains the work of eighty Friendly Street poets of SA. Selections from literary journals and newspapers have been gathered together in periodical collections, e.g. *Austro-verse* (1952) from *Austro-vert; An Overland Muster* (1965), selected by Stephen Murray-Smith from *Overland* 1954–64; *On Native Grounds* (1968), selected by C.B. Christesen and *The Temperament of Generations* (1990), by Jenny Lee, Gerald Murnane and Philip Mead from *Meanjin; The Vital Decade* (1968), chosen by Geoffrey Dutton and Max Harris from *Australian Letters; Poems from the Age 1967–79* (1979), edited by R.A. Simpson; and *Quadrant: Twenty-Five Years* (1982), selected by Peter Coleman, Lee Shrubb and Vivian Smith. Compatible groups of poets have been brought together in such volumes as Vincent Buckley's *Eight by Eight* (1963), Alexander Craig's *Twelve Poets 1950–1970* (1971), and Michael Dugan's *The Drunken Tram: Six Young Melbourne Poets* (1972). Poetry submitted to competitions is frequently collected; examples are those associated with the Mattara Spring Festival, the C.J. Dennis and the Harold Kesteven poetry competitions, and the Henry Lawson festivals at Grenfell, NSW.

The collections of folk-songs and ballads made from the beginning of the twentieth century formed a special kind of anthology. These began with A.B. Paterson's *Old Bush Songs*, published in 1905, which sold widely and went through several editions between 1905 and 1932. The 1950s was a decade of intense activity in collection and research, and was part of a general revival of interest in Australian folk-song which subsequently accommodated folklorists such as Ron Edwards, Bill and Alan Scott, Hugh Anderson, Wendy Lowenstein and John Meredith; scholars with university connections, including Russel Ward and Edgar Waters; and established writers such as John Manifold, Douglas Stewart and Nancy Keesing. Working sometimes in isolation and sometimes in partnership, they substantially enlarged the corpus of Australian folk-song by fieldwork among the surviving traditional singers and by research in the libraries.

In time, these research workers published collections or studies which reflected their individual emphases. Hugh Anderson's *The Story of Australian Folksongs* (1970), an expansion of his earlier *Colonial Ballads* (1955, 1962), and Ron Edwards's *The Big Book of Australian Folk Song* (1976), which incorporates material from successive editions of his *The Overlander Song Book* (first published in 1956) as well as from his *Black Bull Chapbooks* (1954–57), *Bandicoot Ballads* and other compilations, are examples of cumulative collections. Among other anthologies the most important are Stewart and Keesing's *Old Bush Songs* (1957), which takes the Paterson text as its basis, and *Australian Bush Ballads* (1955), both reprinted under their original and other titles; John Manifold's *The Penguin Australian Song Book* (1964); Bill Scott's *The Second Penguin Australian Song Book* (1976); and Russel Ward's *The Penguin Book of Australian Ballads* (1964). These anthologies usually have important introductions or notes on the groupings, origins, significance or transmission of Australian folk-songs. These subjects are also addressed in specialist studies (e.g. Anderson's study of Thatcher, *The Colonial Minstrel*, 1960); in Manifold's imaginative, speculative left-wing interpretation *Who Wrote the Ballads? Notes on Australian Folk Song* (1964), Anderson's *Farewell to Old England* (1964) and Thérèse Radic's *Songs of Australian Working Life* (1989); in more broadly based works, e.g. Ward's *The Australian Legend*, H.M. Green's *A History of Australian Literature* (1961) *The Oxford Companion to Australian Folklore* (1993), edited by Gwenda Beed Davey and Graham Seal, and several folklore compilations; in anthology-commentary combinations (e.g. Anderson's and Meredith's *Folk Songs of Australia and the Men and Women Who Sang Them*, 1967 reprinted in 1979 and a second volume in 1987 with assistance from Roger Covell and Patricia Brown); and in journals ranging from the literary-cultural (e.g. *Meanjin*) to the specialist folklore magazines (e.g. *Singabout, Gumsucker's Gazette, Australian Tradition; National Folk*) which were issued by the Sydney Bush Music Club, the Australian Folklore Society, the Folk Lore Society of Victoria and other emerging bush music and folklore societies.

Antipodean: An Illustrated Annual, The (1893–97) was edited by George Essex Evans and John Tighe Ryan, the third volume being edited by A.B. Paterson. In addition to poetry and short fiction by well-known contemporary writers (e.g. Paterson's 'The Geebung Polo Club' and Henry Lawson's 'The Bush Undertaker'), the annuals contained critical and descriptive articles.

Antipodes: A North American Journal of Australian Literature, established in 1987 with Robert Ross as editor is the official journal of AAALS, the American Association of Australian Literary Studies. Published twice a year, it is supported in part by the Literature Board of the Australia Council and the Information and Cultural Relations Branch of the Department of Foreign Affairs and Trade. Each issue contains a selection of previously unpublished poetry and fiction by Australian writers. Interviews with writers are also regularly published. *Antipodes* has an extensive book reviews section. Paul Kane is the poetry editor.

Applestealers (1974), selected and introduced by Robert Kenny and Colin Talbot, is a collection of what was termed the 'New Australian Poetry'. In the editors' prefaces the volume is said to represent 'what can be considered a renaissance in Australian poetry, which took place from about 1968'. In addition to the selection of poetry, *Applestealers* includes notes on the Poetry Workshops at La Mama; a statement on the origin and development of 'the new poetry in Australia' movement by Kris Hemensley; and a chronological check-list of the mini magazines of the period 1968–71, with brief notes on those poetry magazines extant in 1974.

ARDEN, George (?1820–54) arrived in Australia from England in 1838, settled in Melbourne, and at the age of 18 launched the weekly *Port Phillip Gazette*. He is credited with having written the first poem on Melbourne and having published (with Thomas Strode) in 1840, *Latest Information with Regard to Australia Felix*, the first book published in Melbourne.

ARGLES, Theodore Emile ('The Pilgrim', 'Harold Grey') (?1851–86), born London, was well known in Sydney, as both writer and bohemian, in the later 1870s and early 1880s. Under several pseudonyms (e.g. 'Harold Grey', 'A (The) Pilgrim', 'The Moocher') he wrote sensational and satiric prose and verse about low-life Sydney and other subjects. Among his other publications were *Sum Punkins* (1878), a series of poems and stories ostensibly read by the patients and staff of a Sydney asylum as they gather together over Christmas; the autobiographical *My Unnatural Life* (1878); *Scenes in Sydney by Day and Night* (?1878); and the verse satire *The Devil in Sydney* (1878), whose targets included several prominent journalists. Employed on the staff of the *Evening News*, Argles contributed spicy society gossip (some of which proved libellous), theatrical criticism and topical verse to the early *Bulletin*. His legendary escapades with Victor Daley included one in which they ran foul of the *Bulletin's* editor, W.H. Traill, after each appeared in turn in Traill's office to ask for money to pay for the other's funeral.

'Army of the Rear, The' is, like 'Faces in the Street', one of the early Henry Lawson poems which established his reputation as radical writer; it was first published in the *Bulletin* in 1888 as 'Song of the Outcasts' and under its better-known title in 1910. 'The Army of the Rear' is the legion of the poor and the outcasts of society, whom Lawson images marching towards revolution at the end of the poem.

Arna, the journal of the University of Sydney Arts Society, began in 1918 and appeared irregularly; it was incorporated into *New Literature Review* in 1975. Several subsequently well-known writers contributed to *Arna*, including A.D. Hope, Vincent Buckley, Bruce Beaver, Harold Stewart, James McAuley, Geoffrey Lehmann, Les Murray and Clive James.

Around the Boree Log and Other Verses (1921) by 'John O'Brien' is a book of ballad-like poems dealing mainly with the vicissitudes of Irish-Australian Catholic rural communities. The characteristics of good nature, obstinacy and religious faith traditionally associated with the Irish permeate such well-known and popular verses as 'The Old Bush School', 'Ten Little Steps and Stairs', 'Tangmalangaloo', 'At Casey's after Mass', and 'Said Hanrahan'.

ASTON, Tilly (1873–1947), born Carisbrook, Victoria, was blind from the age of 6 years. She became a teacher of the blind in Melbourne, was a founder of the library of the Victorian Association of Braille Writers (1894) and was, for many years, president of Victoria's Association for the Advancement of the Blind. She wrote several books of verse and prose, and an autobiography, *Memoirs of Tilly Aston* (1946).

ATKINSON, Rupert (1881–1961), born Bendigo, Victoria, and educated in Australia and England, was left comfortably off after his father's death and then led a leisurely life as a man of letters. A close friend of the poet Hugh McCrae, Atkinson published numerous volumes of lyric, narrative and philosophical verse, including *The Shrine of Desire* (1906), *Wayside Poets* (1913), *A Modern Magdalene* (1913, reprinted as *The Renegades* in 1921), and *A Flagon of Song* (1920), the last being a selection from previously published work together with some new poems. His series of twenty 'Melbourne Sonnets' gives some local flavour to his verse. Atkinson also wrote several plays including *A Nocturne* (1919) and *Each Man a Multitude* (1923).

'Atlas, The', a group of five poems by Kenneth Slessor, was published in *Cuckooz Contrey* (1932). The individual poems of the sequence, 'The King of Cuckooz', 'Post-Roads', 'Dutch Seacoast', 'Mermaids' and 'The Seafight', have no continuity or overall theme. Disconnected scraps from Slessor's omnivorous reading interests, they reveal his delight in the odd and exotic.

AUCHTERLONIE, Dorothy, see **GREEN, Dorothy**

'Australaise, The' was originally submitted by C.J. Dennis as an entry in a national song competition conducted by the *Bulletin* in 1908. Christened the 'Blanky Australaise' by the judge, because of the many blank spaces for the great Australian adjective 'bloody' to be inserted ('blessed' or 'blooming' were later suggested by Dennis for folk genteel), it won a prize of a guinea and was predicted to 'win its way to every heart in the back-blocks'. In 1913 an expanded version (from four to seven verses) was published in Dennis's *Backblock Ballads and Other Verses*. In 1915 it was reprinted as a leaflet for the Australian soldiers, to whom it was dedicated as a marching song. With a mixture of irony and sincerity typical of him, Dennis suggested that the song be sung to the tune of 'Onward Christian Soldiers'.

Australasia (1823), a poem by William Charles Wentworth, was an entry in the Chancellor's Gold Medal poetry competition at Cambridge in 1823 on the subject of Australasia. With his opening apostrophe, 'Land of my birth!', Wentworth made clear his special position in relation to the topic. The poem attempts to project a distinctively Australian viewpoint and, with its prophecy of future greatness, is one of the first outbursts in Australian literature of nationalistic pride. Although sometimes marred by the customary inflated rhetoric of the public poem of the day, *Australasia* has been praised for its well-planned structure and its vigorous, eloquent, if rugged, verse.

'Australia' (1), a sonnet by Bernard O'Dowd, is the introductory poem to the volume *Dawnward?* (1903). With its well-known opening line, 'Last sea-thing dredged by sailor Time from Space' and its questioning of the destiny of Australia, the sonnet is one of the best-known and most-anthologised of O'Dowd's works.

'Australia' (2), a poem written by A.D. Hope in 1939, was first published in 1943 and has frequently been anthologised. In a mood of cool appraisal, the poet dwells on the country's isolation, philistinism and cultural deprivation In the last two stanzas, however, he accepts this 'Australian desert of human mind' as home in the hope that 'Such savage and scarlet as no green hills dare/ Springs in that waste', and that 'still from the deserts the prophets come'. The last quotation provided Geoffrey Serle with the title of his historical study of Australian culture, *From Deserts the Prophets Come* (1973).

Australia Poetry series, begun in 1992 by Heinemann Australia with Jamie Grant as editor, published poets Alan Gould, Peter Kocan and Les Murray in 1992. Later volumes include work by Grant, Kate Jennings, Hal Colebatch, Robert Gray, Jan Owen and Kathleen Stewart.

'Australia to England', the poem by John Farrell to celebrate Queen Victoria's Diamond Jubilee, was published in the *Daily Telegraph* 22 June 1897, as 'Ave Imperatrix'. With slight alterations and under its new title the poem was reprinted in the same year as a booklet. Highly regarded at the time, the poem is a patriotic expression of hopes for Australia's future and an acknowledgment of the great achievements of the mother country.

Australian New Writing, anthologies of prose and verse, were issued annually from 1943 to 1946. Involved in editing the anthologies were Katharine Susannah Prichard, George Farwell, Bernard Smith and Ken Levis.

Australian Poetry was a series of annual anthologies of Australian poetry published by Angus & Robertson 1941–73. Distinguished writers and critics were invited to edit the anthologies, which contained the individual editor's choice of the outstanding Australian poetry published in the previous year. The series began with *Australian Poetry 1941*, edited by Douglas Stewart. Ensuing volumes were edited by: R.D. Fitz-Gerald (1942), H.M. Green (1943), R.G. Howarth (1944), Kenneth Slessor (1945), T. Inglis Moore (1946), Frederick T. Macartney (1947), Judith Wright (1948), Rosemary Dobson (1949–50), Kenneth Mackenzie (1951–52), Nan McDonald (1953), Ronald McCuaig (1954), James McAuley (1955), A.A. Phillips (1956), Hal Porter (1957), Vincent Buckley (1958), Nancy Keesing (1959), A.D. Hope (1960), Leonie Kramer (1961), Geoffrey Dutton (1962), G.A. Wilkes (1963), Randolph Stow (1964), John Thompson (1965), David Campbell (1966), Max Harris (1967), Dorothy Auchterlonie (1968), Vivian Smith (1969), Rodney Hall (1970), Chris Wallace-Crabbe (1971), R.F. Brissenden (1972), J.M. Couper (1973). A subsequent work *Australian Poetry* (1986) was edited by Vivian Smith. Penguin Australia began a later Australian Poetry series edited by Judith Rodriguez.

Australian Poetry Now (1970), an anthology of Australian poetry selected largely from the late 1960s, was edited with an explanatory preface by Thomas Shapcott. The anthology is chronologically arranged but since its purpose and emphasis are 'discovery', the older and/or better-known poets, such as Bruce Beaver, Bruce Dawe, Chris Wallace-Crabbe, Les Murray and Geoffrey Lehmann are given only token representation. The anthology is, in the main, representative of 'the New Australian Poetry' and gives a selection of poems that were (at the time of publication) experimental in form and theme.

'Backblocks Shearer, The' is an Australian folk-song in which a shearer, identified in the last verse as 'Widgigoweera Joe' (an alternative title for the song), first laments that he has never become a 'gun' shearer and then vows to improve his technique until he wins a shearing contest at a country show. The concluding lines of the song,

> Instead of Deeming, you will hear
> Of Widgigoweera Joe,

may date the composition of the song to around 1892, when the murderer, Frederick Deeming, was much in the news. An informant of Russel Ward has suggested that the song was written by a shearer named Bill Tulley at Howlong station in the Riverina.

BAILEY, Mary (1792–?), born Halstead, Essex, as Mary Walker, married an Anglican clergyman, William Bailey, in 1832 and followed him to Hobart in 1844 after he was convicted of an illegal financial transaction and transported. A poet with a keen interest in the classics, she had previously published religious and other poetry including *The Months and Other Poems* (2nd edn, 1833), *Reflections upon the Litany of the Church of England* (1833), and *Musae Sacrae: a Collection of Hymns and Sacred Poetry* (1835). In Hobart she regularly published verse and erudite translations in the *Colonial Times* between 1844 and 1850, and as 'Mary' or 'M.B.' contributed both verse and prose to the *Hobarton Guardian* in 1847 when her husband was its editor. Nothing is known of Mary Bailey's life after 1850, although in 1855 William Bailey left for Sydney, where he became involved in religious and other controversy, married again and died in 1879.

'Ballad of Bloodthirsty Bessie, The', a poem by Ronald McCuaig, was first published in the *Bulletin* (19 September 1951) and was later used as the title poem for McCuaig's *The Ballad of Bloodthirsty Bessie and Other Poems* (1961). Sometimes cited as an example of an especially macabre brand of humour, said to be Australian in character, McCuaig's poem tells of the stratagems used by a farmer near Sydney to keep himself in cheap labour and his amorous daughter, Bessie, in lovers. When the exhausted labourers ultimately try to leave, the farmer pushes them off a nearby cliff, at the bottom of which Bessie waits to finish them off with an axe. Seventeen farmhands end up in graves along the creek. A spying trooper is similarly dispatched and nine investigating soldiers are made drunk by the farmer, who pours rum on them and sets them alight. Bessie objects to this wholesale squandering of such valuable amatory material:

'Oh, father, I say it is cruel
Oh, father, I say it's unfair:
You're using my sweethearts as fuel
And doing me out of my share'.

She approaches her father menacingly, axe in hand. Thrusting sentimentality sternly behind him, he 'out with a pistol and shot her/ Through the heart for the first and last time'.

BALLANTYNE, Gina (1916–   ), born Adelaide, published several volumes of verse which gave expression to Jindyworobak sentiments, e.g. *Phantom* (1942), *Vision* (1942) and *Vagrant* (1943). She won the C.J. Dennis Memorial Prize in 1942 and edited the 1945 *Jindyworobak Anthology*.

'Banjo, The', see **PATERSON, A.B.**

'Banks of the Condamine, The', one of the few Australian folk-songs that take as their subject the relationship between men and women, begins with a shearer's announcement to his love that he is leaving to join 'the Sydney shearers/ On the banks of the Condamine' (River). He rejects his girl's request that she accompany him, on the grounds that the squatters have banned women from the shearing sheds and that her constitution would be too delicate. After rejecting her further request that he stay at home and take up a selection, the shearer departs with the promise that he'll return after the season is completed. The version of the folk-song included in some editions of A.B. Paterson's *Old Bush Songs* is entitled 'Banks of the Riverine'; there are other versions in which the departing bush worker is a horse-breaker or stockman rather than a shearer. 'The Banks of the Condamine' is an anonymous composition dating from the 1860s (after the passing of the Selection Acts) but clearly derives from 'The Banks of the Nile', an English broadside ballad of the earlier nineteenth century, in which the dialogue is between a girl and a soldier departing for the Egyptian front.

'Bannerman of the Dandenong', a popular and much-anthologised ballad by Alice Werner (1859–1935), is a sentimental tale of bush heroism and mateship. Bannerman and his mate are caught in a bushfire while on their way to the latter's wedding. Bannerman insists that his mate take Bannerman's faster horse. The mate escapes and Bannerman dies in the fire.

BANNING, Lex (1921–65), born Sydney, was, despite the disablement of cerebral palsy, a graduate of the University of Sydney and editor of *Arna*. He worked as a freelance journalist, writer for film and radio, librarian of the Mosman Spastic Centre (1954–62) and book reviewer for the *Sydney Morning Herald*. His first volume of poems, *Everyman His Own Hamlet* (1951), is a rueful indictment of the disillusioning experiences of life against which the only recourse is the poet's art. *The Instant's Clarity* (1952), as the title suggests, offers a momentary hope, but in *Apocalypse in Springtime* (1956) the mood of the title poem (which is perhaps Banning's best-known poem and which was read at his funeral) is again one of nihilism and despair. Highly regarded by fellow writers, and a considerable influence on the Sydney literati of the day, Banning is a poet of intellect and passion, neither of which is concealed by his characteristic sardonic mask. Both his published and unpublished verse have been revived by the 1987 *There Was a Crooked Man: The Poems of Lex Banning*, in which Richard Appleton supplies a biographical memoir and Alex Galloway an introduction to the poetry.

Bards in the Wilderness: Australian Colonial Poetry to 1920 (1970), edited (with an introduction) by Brian Elliott and Adrian Mitchell, is an extensive anthology that focuses on the growth of indigenous Australian poetry throughout the colonial period which, the editors suggest, has 'a kind of terminus' about 1920. The wide-ranging selection begins with Aboriginal poetry, extracts from English poets writing about the distant colony and anonymous early balladry, and includes not only the major colonial poets but also lesser-known figures.

BAYLDON, A.A. (Arthur Albert Dawson) (1865–1958), born Leeds, England, arrived in Brisbane in 1889 and contributed to the flood of bush balladry of the 1890s. A typical *Bulletin* poet, Bayldon reflected the ambivalent attitude of the day towards the outback and bush life; sometimes pessimistically depicting the hardships of that life, at other times caught up in the enthusiastic Arcadian vision of A.B. Paterson. His books of poetry include *Poems* (1897), *The Western Track and Other Verses* (1905), *The Eagles: Collected Poems* (1921), a further *Collected Poems* (1932), and *Apollo in Australia and Bush Verses* (1944). His only published work of fiction was *The Tragedy behind the Curtain and Other Stories* (1910); a novel and some various other works remain unpublished.

'BAYLEBRIDGE, William' (Charles William Blocksidge) (1883–1942), born Brisbane, adopted the name Baylebridge from about 1925. He lived in England 1908–19, publishing numerous limited editions of poetry and working in Intelligence during the First World War. He was assisted financially at this time by his mother's half-sister Grace Leven (Celia Grace Leven); in her memory he later established the annual Grace Leven Poetry Prize. He returned to Australia in 1919 but became an increasingly isolated figure in the Australian literary scene. Although critics such as H.M. Green and T. Inglis Moore have classed 'Baylebridge' as one of Australia's few philosophical and intellectual poets, others such as F.T. Macartney have seen him as a literary larcenist. He remains one of the more puzzling and enigmatic of Australian writers, the pages of his verse seldom turned by modern readers. In prefaces to several of his works he protested against the philistinism and cultural inertia of contemporary Australian society. His chief works (reprinted under the terms of his will in a memorial edition as *Salvage: Collected Works of William Baylebridge*, 1964) include *Love Redeemed* (1934), love sonnets; *This Vital Flesh* (1939), the application of his philosophy of vitalism to Australian nationalism; and *An Anzac Muster* (1921), short fiction centred on the Gallipoli campaign of 1915.

BAYNTON, Barbara (1857–1929), who claimed to have been born in 1862 after the elopement of her mother, Penelope Ewart, with an Indian army officer named Kilpatrick, may have been the daughter of a carpenter, John Lawrence, and his wife Elizabeth, and was born in Scone, NSW. Penne Hackforth-Jones (great granddaughter of Baynton) in *Barbara Baynton: Between Two Worlds* (1989) maintains that Baynton's father was named Kilpatrick but took the name John Lawrence and lived with Baynton's mother, Elizabeth Lawrence, after her arrival in Australia in 1840. Brought up on the Liverpool Plains, Barbara Baynton married a selector, Alexander Frater, in 1880, and bore him three children. In 1887 he ran off with his wife's niece; Barbara moved to Sydney, divorced him in 1890 and the next day married Thomas Baynton, a retired surgeon who moved in literary and academic circles. It was not until the 1890s that she began to write; her first story was published in the *Bulletin* in 1896. In 1902–3 she visited London, where *Bush Studies* (1902) was published, and after her husband's death in 1904 she alternated residence between Australia and England, becoming well known as a literary hostess and as a collector of antiques and furniture. In 1921 she married the fifth Lord Headley, a colourful engineer, sportsman and president of the Muslim Society; they separated soon after. As Lady Headley, Baynton continued to divide her time between Australia and England until her death.

Baynton's movement through society obviously led her to distort the facts of her early life and first marriage; yet this part of her past informs her fiction, which depicts the horrors of bush life and confirms Australia as the 'windblown, shimmering, shifting, awful waste,/ Fringed by a broken edge of green and grey' that she wrote about in the poem 'To My Country'. The malevolence of the bush is insisted upon throughout her work; so is the suffering of her female characters, who are consistently seen as the victims of predatory, brutal men. Baynton's output was small, but in both *Bush Studies* and her short novel *Human Toll* (1907) her grim realism, which is authenticated by the accumulation of detail and by the accuracy of the idiom her characters use, offers a powerful alternative to the romantic pictures of bush life. *Barbara Baynton* in the Portable Australian Authors series was edited by Sally Krimmer and Alan Lawson in 1980. She is one of the writers discussed by Thea Astley in *Three Australian Writers* (1979).

'Beach Burial', a poem by Kenneth Slessor first published in 1944, is set in the period when Australian soldiers were fighting in the Western Desert near El Alamein. The poem describes the hasty burial of seamen washed ashore from the naval battles of the Mediterranean. A fine poem, which reflects the futility of war, it expresses the bewildered pity of battle-hardened troops as they perform rough-and-ready but deeply tender last rites over the sodden, nameless corpses.

BEACH, Eric (1947–), born NZ, came to Australia in 1972 and has written plays, verse and short stories. Active in the Performance Poetry scene, his published works are *Saint Kilda Meets Hugo Ball* (1974), *In Occupied Territory* (1977), *A Photo of Some People in a Football Stadium* (1978), and *Hey Hey Brass Buttons* (1990).

BEAVER, Bruce (1928–) was born Manly, Sydney, where he spent much of his youth and where, after many nomadic years, he now lives. Beaver's childhood and adolescence, as revealed by his own frequent comments and in his autobiographical *As It Was* (1979), were unsettled and unhappy. He took refuge as a boy in the fantasy world of comics, radio serials and movies, and later became absorbed in books. From the age of 17 he had several periods of psychiatric treatment for manic-depressive psychosis. It was at that time that he said he came under the influence of poetry – Pound, Eliot, Yeats, Brennan, Lowell, Auden, Graves, Williams and Frank O'Hara. He lived and worked for a time on his uncle's farm on the south coast of NSW, spent six years as chainman for a surveyor in northern NSW and was at various times radio programme arranger, clerk and proofreader before settling on freelance journalism and writing as a career. He spent six months on Norfolk Island, a place he detested, in 1958 and lived in NZ from 1958 to 1962, an experience that he enjoyed.

Beaver published his first volume of poetry, *Under the Bridge*, in 1961. His later publications are *Seawall and Shoreline* (1964), *Open at Random* (1967), *Letters to Live Poets* (1969), *Lauds and Plaints: Poems, 1968–1972* (1974), *Odes and Days* (1975), *Death's Directives* (1978), *As It Was* (1979), *Selected Poems* (1979), *Headlands, Prose Sketches* (1986), *Charmed Lives* (1988), *New and Selected Poems 1960–1990* (1991) and *Anima and Other Poems* (1994). Beaver has also written novels, including *The Hot Spring* (1965) and *You Can't Come Back* (1966). Throughout his first three volumes of poetry, and with considerable success in individual poems such as 'Camp Shift', 'Seawall and Shoreline', 'Chainman's Diary' (winner of the 1964 *Poetry Magazine* Award), 'The Killers' and 'The Cranes of Auckland', Beaver pursues his search for an understanding of his disturbed life, maintaining a preoccupation with 'the celebration and lamentation of existence' that carries through into his first major collection, *Letters to Live Poets*. Written in 1966 under the spur of an illness that convinced Beaver he had only a couple of months of rationality left, *Letters to Live Poets* represents his attempt 'to make one clear readable statement before I stopped writing altogether'. In the form of the *livre composé*, the thirty-four separate poems piece together the jigsaw of existence and assess the worth of that existence. Influenced by Whitman's *Leaves of Grass* and

Brennan's *Poems 1913*, *Letters to Live Poets* ranges over the experiences of Beaver's childhood, his adolescence with its periodic bouts of mental illness, and his present middle age, attempting a 'spiritual, intellectual and emotional autobiography' set against the striking natural landscape and monotonous suburbia of seaside Manly. *Letters to Live Poets* won the Grace Leven Prize for Poetry, the Poetry Society of Australia Prize and the Captain Cook Bicentennial Prize for Poetry, all in 1970. *Lauds and Plaints*, by contrast with the hasty creation of *Letters to Live Poets*, was slowly (1967–72) and lovingly built. An extension of *Letters to Live Poets* ('the spirit of the body of *Letters*'), *Lauds and Plaints* turns from the poet's self-obsession to an awareness of others, for example the young man who kills himself jumping from a roof, the old Manly fisherman, Albert Fry, and Arthur Stace (Sydney's 'Mr Eternity'). The technical liberation that Beaver had celebrated in *Letters* ('My thoughts [once] ticked iambically in ten syllables') is complete in *Lauds and Plaints*, where visual and syntactical experimental forms (the shedding of punctuation and the unbridled rhetoric) complement the exultation that Beaver felt as a release from the pessimism of so much of *Letters to Live Poets*. The poems praise ('Lauds') those with largeness of spirit and blame ('Plaints') those lesser spirits, whose life vision never transcends the materialism of daily existence. *Odes and Days*, written by Beaver during a period spent at Grace Perry's Berrima house, comprises fifteen odes, eight addressed to himself or the house and seven addressed (as biographical sketches) to the composers Beethoven, Mahler and Delius and to the poets Holderlin, Brennan, Rilke and Hesse. The 'Days', which form a type of verse journal, are the forty-seven shorter poems of the second part of the book. Many of them, freed from Beaver's compulsive philosophising, record and rejoice in natural sights and sounds and contain some of his most attractive lyricism. *Death's Directives*, twenty poems in which Death variously suggests, reminds, advises or lays down directives to the poet about life, are the most relaxed of Beaver's poetry. The near genial tone and the absence of tension reflect, perhaps for the first time in the whole body of Beaver's poetry, an affirmation of life and a mental and emotional confidence. *As It Was*, the autobiographical prose poem which Beaver for a long time felt unable to write, confirms by the fact of its existence that affirmation and confidence. The *New and Selected Poems 1960–1990* selects from four decades of Beaver's poetry and emphasises again the considerable scale of his achievements. There are few poems from the early volumes but an impressive reminder of the most significant of his work from *Letters to Live Poets*, *Lauds and Plaints* and *Odes and Days*.

Headlands conveys in prose poems his sometimes sardonic but basically affectionate reactions to and reflections on the people he has known and the places he has been in Australia and NZ. *Charmed Lives* contains a verse biography of Rainer Maria Rilke, two sections of more personal poems, 'Silhouettes' and 'Solos' and a concluding section, 'Tiresias Sees'. In scope and power *Charmed Lives* is the equal of Beaver's *Odes and Days* and confirms his stature as one of Australia's most important poets. Beaver's 1994 volume, *Anima and Other Poems*, contains four sections ('Narrations', 'Night Watch', 'Revenants', and the title piece 'Anima'). The last-named recounts in fluent if at times undistinguished blank verse the tortuous process by which he and his wife Brenda ('my travelling companion of the soul') made a life together. 'A Nest of Nonnets' (nine-line stanzas) is a tribute to fellow poet Gwen Harwood, while 'Autumn Glory' offers sympathetic perceptions of Christopher Brennan. A rare mood of jauntiness pervades 'Genesis Rock', but on the whole this latest Beaver collection reinforces the sense of poetic solidity evident since *Letters to Live Poets*. An original and idiosyncratic writer, a fine exponent of the prose-poetry form and one of the earliest Australian poets to explore the possibilities of confessional poetry of the life studies genre, Beaver through his own work and in his role as adviser and contributing editor to *Poetry Australia* was an important influence in the 1970s rise of the 'New Australian Poetry'. He was awarded the Patrick White Literary Award in 1982, the Christopher Brennan

Award in 1983, both in recognition of the sustained distinction of his work, and was made AM in 1991 as a tribute to his contribution to Australian literature.

BEDFORD, Ruth (1882–1963), born Petersham, Sydney, published lyric verse, e.g. *Sydney at Sunset and Other Verses* (1911) and *The Learner and Other Verses* (1937); fiction (in collaboration with Dorothea Mackellar), e.g. *The Little Blue Devil* (1912) and *Two's Company* (1914); and children's verse, e.g. *Rosycheeks & Goldenhead* (1913) and *Hundreds and Thousands* (1934). She also wrote *Think of Stephen, A Family Chronicle* (1954), a delightful account of the family of Sir Alfred Stephen.

'Bell Birds', the much-anthologised Henry Kendall lyric poem, was first published in the *Sydney Morning Herald*, 25 November 1867. The poet hears, in imagination, the chiming notes of the bellbirds of his youth and re-creates in rich pictorial phrases the typical bellbird (and Kendall) landscape of 'channels of coolness', 'dim gorges' and 'cool wildernesses'. Like Wordsworth with his 'sensations sweet', Kendall is sustained by his recollections of natural beauty amid the ugliness of later years in the 'city and alleys'.

BENNETT, Stefanie (1945–   ), born Townsville, Queensland, followed a brief formal education by working as a factory hand, saleswoman, hairdresser, graphic artist, rock musician, reader/editor with various journals, and tutor at the Institute of Modern Languages, James Cook University. Among her publications are *Blackbirds of Superstition* (1973), *Madam Blackboots* (1974), *Five Poets* (1974), *Poems from the Paddy Wagon* (1975), *The Medium* (1976, prose and poetry), *Tongues and Pinnacles* (1976), *The Tenth Lady* (1977), *The Leaf, the Lion, the Lariat* (1992), and the novel *Stefan* (1978). With Joanne Burns and Ruth Fordham, Bennett contributed to the collection *Radio City 2 a.m.* (1976) and with R.G. Hay and Anne Lloyd to *Three North Queensland Poets* (1990).

BEVERIDGE, Judith (1956–   ), born London, came to Australia as a small child. She has worked as a teacher of creative writing and a library assistant. Her poetry has appeared in numerous periodicals and anthologies and in one collection, *The Domesticity of Giraffes* (1987). Rich in complex imagery, Beveridge's poetry is remarkable for its individual, sharply engraved perceptions and stylish language. *The Domesticity of Giraffes* won the Mary Gilmore Award and Premier's Awards from both Victoria and NSW.

Bibliographies of Australian Writers, a series published by the Libraries Board of SA, began in 1966 with Janette H. Finch's bibliographies of Patrick White and Hal Porter. Other authors covered in the series include A.D. Hope (1968), Judith Wright (1968), Randolph Stow (1968), Ian Mudie (1970), R.D. FitzGerald (1970) and C.J. Dennis (1979). After the series was discontinued the bibliographies were updated in *Index to Australian Book Reviews*.

Bibliography of Australian Poetry 1935–1955, compiled by Sue Murray, was published in 1992 by D.W. Thorpe in association with the National Centre for Australian Studies at Monash University.

'Bill the Bullock Driver', one of Henry Kendall's best-known and most-anthologised poems, published in the *Australian Town and Country Journal* in 1876, is an ironic portrait of one of the stock figures of Australian outback life and literature. While Kendall applauds the sturdy independence and easygoing nature of the teamster, he also subtly criticises his parochialism and insensitivity to the natural wonders that surround him.

BILLETER, Walter (1943–   ), born Sierre, Switzerland, came to Australia in 1966. He has written *Sediments of Seclusion* (poetry, 1973), *Dreamrobe Embroideries and*

Asparagus for Dinner (with John Jenkins, 1974), *Australian Novemberies* (prose, 1978) and *Radiotalk: 10 Pieces for Magnetic Tape* (1979). He has also published translations of German writers (e.g. Konrad Bayer and Paul Celan). In 1974 he co-founded with John Jenkins the magazine *etymspheres*, and in 1977 he co-edited with Kris Hemensley and Robert Kenny the anthology *3 Blind Mice*.

'Billy Barlow in Australia' is a folk-song which recounts the unfortunate experiences of an immigrant from London, who endures most of the hazards of colonial life in both town and bush, e.g. rapacious Sydney merchants who sell him poor stock, attacks by bushrangers and Aborigines when he moves up-country, and eventual arrest for debt. A typical example of new chum literature, 'Billy Barlow in Australia' was written by Benjamin Griffin and first performed by him as a concert piece in Maitland in 1843. In composing the song, Griffin provided an antipodean context for a character who had been the subject of an earlier series of British street ballads which were so popular that street singers impersonated Billy Barlow in selling their wares. The several sequels to 'Billy Barlow in Australia' are collected with it in Hugh Anderson's *Songs of Billy Barlow* (1956).

BINGHAM, Colin (1898–1986), born Townsville, Queensland, had a long and distinguished career as a journalist and administrator in the newspaper world; he was leader-writer on the *Sydney Morning Herald* 1949–57, associate editor 1957–60 and editor 1961–65. His publications include *Marcinelle and Other Verses* (1925), which includes Bingham's University of Queensland Prize poems (1920, 1923, 1924), A *Book of Verse* (1929), *Men and Affairs* (1967), *The Affairs of Women* (1969), *Decline of Innocence and Other Poems* (1970), *National Images and Other Poems* (1979) and *Wit and Wisdom: A Public Affairs Miscellany* (1982). His autobiography, *The Beckoning Horizon*, was published in 1983.

BINGHAM, Geoffrey (1919–), born Goulburn, NSW, was a POW in Changi during the Second World War and was ordained an Anglican priest in 1953. A regular contributor of short stories to Australian journals, Bingham has published several collections of short fiction including *To Command the Cats* (1980), *Angel Wings* (1981), *The Translation of Mr. Piffy* (1982), *The Concentration Camp* (1983), *Three Special Stories* (1983) and *Harps, Viols and Goodly Guitars* (1981), a collection of verse.

Birth: A Little Journal of Australian Poetry appeared, mostly monthly, 1916–22. A slight journal (usually only four pages), it began as the personal venture of William Mitchell, who edited the first few issues, and became the journal of the Melbourne Literary Club. Several well-known Australian poets featured in its pages and two small annuals (1920 and 1921) were published. Other editors of the magazine were, in succession, Gilbert Wallace, Bernard O'Dowd, Nettie Palmer, Frederick Macartney and Frank Wilmot; Louis Lavater was also involved in its production.

BIRTLES, Dora (1903–94), born Dora Toll at Newcastle, NSW, was educated at the University of Sydney. In 1923 Bert Birtles, Dora's future husband, then a non-degree evening student and subsequently the author of a book on Greek political history, was expelled from the university after one of his love poems, considered overly explicit by the Proctorial Board, was published in *Hermes*. Dora, who also had a poem on a related theme in the same issue, was rusticated for two years. Dora Birtles was a teacher before sailing in 1932 in the cutter *Gullmarn* from Newcastle to Singapore; living abroad for the next five years, she visited the Far East, Scandinavia, Russia and most European countries. She published travel books, short stories and poetry, but is best known as a writer for children. Her publications include *The Overlanders* (1946), the book of the Australian film made in that year.

'Black Bonnet', a poem by Henry Lawson, was first published in the *Lone Hand* in

1916; one of Lawson's most worked-over compositions, it was extensively revised after a detailed correspondence between Lawson and George Robertson in 1917 and revised again by David McKee Wright for inclusion in his edition of *Selected Poems of Henry Lawson* (1918). A tribute to Australian pioneer women (more specifically bush pioneers in the original version), 'Black Bonnet' pictures an old woman on her walk to church, her memories as she sits through the service, her talk with the local children after the service, and her return home where in dignity and contentment she resumes her domestic routine. Lawson's memories of his own grandmother Harriet Winn went into the writing of the poem (just as Robertson's recollection of 'my Mother' stimulated his involvement in the revisions), although he also revealed that his models at the time of composition were a great-aunt and a neighbour at Blues Point, North Sydney.

BLACK, George Mure (1854–1936), born Edinburgh, migrated to Australia about 1877 to work on a Gippsland station as a bookkeeper. He soon moved to NSW and by 1889 was sub-editor on the *Bulletin*. Active in the emerging labour movement of the 1890s, Black edited the *Australian Workman* 1891–92 and was a member of the NSW parliament 1891–98. He then resumed a journalistic career, editing the *Barrier Truth* (1898), the *Australian Worker* (1900–4) and the *National Advocate* (1908) before returning to the NSW Legislative Assembly 1910–17; during 1917–36 he was a member of the Legislative Council. One of the Labor Party's first historians, Black wrote *History of the NSW Labor Party* (1910), expanded 1926–29 into the seven-part *A History of the NSW Political Labor Party*. Among his other publications was *An Anzac Areopagus and Other Verses* (1923).

'Black Velvet Band, The', also known as 'The Girl With the Black Velvet Band' and 'The Black Ribbon Band', is a folk-song in which a convict recalls the circumstances of his transportation to Van Diemen's Land. As an apprentice in Dublin (Tralee and London in other versions of the song), he meets a young girl whose hair is tied with a black velvet band; she picks a gentleman's pocket but slips the proceeds into the apprentice's hand when the crime is discovered. 'The Black Velvet Band' is claimed as an Australian folk-song and was part of the repertoire of Blind Billy Huntingdon, but clearly derives from Ireland, where it is still sung in a longer version than that known in Australia. The brevity of the main Australian version is characteristic of the Irish-to-Australian process of transmission.

BLADEN, Peter (1922–   ), born Subiaco in Perth, WA, served in the RAN in the Second World War, and is a graduate of the University of WA and the University of Melbourne (MA). He published *The Old Ladies at Newington* (1953), a long poem which won first prize in the Commonwealth Jubilee literature competition in 1951. The poem gives a perceptive treatment of Australia's past and present as seen during the visit of a charitable group to the Newington state home for aged women in Sydney. It also develops the theme of human subjection to decay and death and thus a need for sympathy and understanding of those who are nearing that state. As 'L. Bladen' he published *Selected Poems* (1945); he has also written *Masque for a Modern Minstrel* (1962), *Island Trilogy* (1970) and *Adelaide Sonnets: A Biography of the City* (1975). In 1984 Bladen went to Turkey to live and has continued to write (although not publish) fiction, poetry and autobiographical works.

BLIGHT, John (1913–95), born Unley, SA, spent most of his life in Queensland. During the 1930s Depression he tramped the Queensland coast in search of work, settling in 1939 on an accountant's job in Bundaberg. After the war he became part-owner of a group of timber mills in the Gympie district but in 1968 he gave up those interests to return to Brisbane where, from 1973, he was a full-time writer. Blight's first poetry appeared in the *Bulletin* in 1939, his first collection, *The Old Pianist*, being published in 1945. His other volumes of poetry are *The Two Suns Met* (1954), *A Beachcomber's Diary* (1963), *My Beachcombing Days* (1968), *Hart: Poems* (1975), *Selected Poems 1939–1975* (1976), *Pageantry for a Lost Empire* (1978), *The New City Poems* (1980), *Holiday Sea Sonnets* (1985) and *Selected Poems 1939–1990* (1992). *A Beachcomber's Diary* won the Myer Award for the best Australian book of verse in 1964, the *Selected Poems* won a National Book Council Literary Award in 1976, and in the same year he gained the Patrick White Literary Award. He was awarded the Dame Mary Gilmore Medal in 1965, the Grace Leven Prize for poetry in 1977, and the Christopher Brennan Award in 1980.

   The Old Pianist sees Blight, in fellow poet Bruce Beaver's phrase, 'a reluctant lyrist', celebrating the 'mean, bounteous land' of Queensland, assessing both its landscape and its people. In *The Two Suns Met*, where he continues to explore his own Queensland and more general Australian experiences, Blight's innovations in punctuation and syntax, his staccato, idiomatic phrasing and ironic complexity, produce poetry which diverges considerably from the conventional poetry of the day. With the two 'Beachcomber' volumes (each of ninety sonnets) that explore everything marine 'from the periwinkle to the whale' and search for universal meanings in the everyday life of the sea, Blight established a reputation as Australia's leading poet of the sea. *Holiday Sea Sonnets* is his third book of sonnets about the sea. In the sardonic poem 'His Best Poems are About the Sea', in *Hart*, he rejects the inference that he is no other kind of poet. The best of the 'Beachcomber' sonnets include 'Death of a Whale', 'A Child's Essay about the Sea', 'The Beachcomber', 'Mud' and 'The Volutes'. Although not usually regarded as a confessional poet, Blight produced in his substantial volume *Hart* some individual and introspective poetry. Many of the brief poems are intensely personal statements, while others ('A Day', 'Racialism', 'Bricks') reflect on the total human condition. Other themes of the collection are urban life, especially the high-rise culture ('The New City Series'), women's beauty and the sexuality of old men. Similar themes persist in *Pageantry for a Lost Empire* where, in the title poem and in others such as 'Tenant at Number 9', the flight of time, the pathos of age and the disappointment of life itself are highlighted. Blight was regarded highly by fellow writers, as the Patrick White Literary Award of 1976 indicates. He was the holder of a Literature Board Emeritus Fellowship from 1984 and in 1987 was made AM for services to literature and education.

BLOOM, Norma (1924–   ), born Melbourne, has lived in England and NZ, but since 1960 has resided in Hobart. Widely represented in NZ and Australian literary journals and poetry anthologies, she has had two books of verse published: *The Larger View* (1972) and *When I See You* (1978).

'BLUEBUSH', see **BOURKE, J.P.**

BOAKE, Barcroft (1866–92) was born in Sydney, son of an immigrant Irish photographer. After an education better than was usual for the time, he decided to work in the bush, first (in 1886) as assistant to a surveyor in the Snowy River country, later as boundary-rider and drover. He believed bush life to be 'the only life worth living' and preferred droving to all other occupations, but he felt compelled by difficult family circumstances to return to Sydney in 1891. Taciturn and brooding by nature, and easily disposed to pessimism and depression, Boake failed to cope with the personal and financial difficulties facing him and his family. He disappeared on 2 May 1892 and his body, hanging by the neck from a stockwhip, was found eight days later in scrub at Middle Harbour, Sydney. His suicide recalled that of his poetic idol Adam Lindsay Gordon, twenty-two years earlier. Boake believed that there was 'a romance, though a grim one' in the story of outback life and that belief is well illustrated in his most notable poem, 'Where the Dead Men Lie', the title poem of his only book of poetry, published in 1897 by A.G. Stephens under the pseudonym 'Surcingle'. Boake's attacks on the absentee landlords and ruthless banking systems that exploited the hard-working, long-suffering bushmen were in line with the customary radical complaints of the time, but his obsession with the tragedy and despair associated with bush life set him apart from most contemporary bush balladists, whose stance was more light-hearted and ironic. The grimness of his vision, however, links him with Barbara Baynton and Henry Lawson. Clement Semmler's *Barcroft Boake: Poet of the Stockwhip* was published in 1965.

'BOAKE, Capel' (Doris Boake Kerr) (1895–1945), born Sydney, niece of the poet Barcroft Boake, published the novels *Painted Clay* (1917), *The Romany Mark* (1923), *The Dark Thread* (1936) and *The Twig Is Bent* (1946). Her poetry was published as *Selected Poems of Capel Boake* (1949), and she collaborated with Bernard Cronin in *Kangaroo Rhymes* (1922) under the pseudonym 'Stephen Gray'.

BOLTON, Ken (1949–   ), born Sydney, formerly editor of *Magic Sam* and currently *Otis Rush*, and involved in a small press venture, Little Esther Books, has written numerous books of poetry, both singly and in collaboration. His own works include *Four Poems* (1977), *Blonde & French* (1978), *Christ's Entry into Brussels: Or, Ode to the Three Stooges* (1978), *Two Sestinas* (1980), *Talking To You: Poems 1979–81* (1983), *Notes for Poems* (1984), *Blazing Shoes* (1984), *Two Poems (A Drawing of the Sky)* (1990) and *Sestina to the Centre of the Brain* (1991). With John Jenkins he has written *Airborne Dogs* (1988); *The Ferrara Poems* (1989), a hectic, mostly joyous account of a group of Australian (or Australian-minded) tourists having a riotous vacation in Italy; and *The Gutman Variations* (1992). Bolton's *Selected Poems 1975–1990* appeared in 1992, a summary to that point of his considerable poetic talents and achievements. Some poems are complemented by diary comments and observations that throw light on the creative process itself. He won the Wesley Michel Wright Poetry Prize in 1990.

Bookfellow, planned as early as 1895 by A.G. Stephens as a magazine in which the literary contents of the Red Page could be elaborated, appeared monthly, January–May 1899 under the auspices of the *Bulletin;* thereafter until 1906 it was incorporated in the Red Page. In 1907 Stephens, having left the *Bulletin*, briefly revived the *Bookfellow* as a separate weekly, but it lapsed when he became leader-writer for the *Evening Post* in Wellington, NZ. Back in Australia in 1909, he revived the *Bookfellow* (1911), which led a precarious monthly existence until 1925. In addition to being the leading, and sometimes the only, purely literary magazine of the period, the *Bookfellow* consistently encouraged the Australian book trade. In its pages was published a wide variety of Australian poetry, together with some of the best literary comment of the day. Under its imprint Stephens published volumes of verse by C.H. Souter, James Hebblethwaite, John Shaw Neilson and others.

BOOTE, H.E. (Henry Ernest) (1865–1949), born Liverpool, England, became apprenticed to a printer after leaving school at the age of 10, and emigrated to Australia in 1889. He soon became involved in the emerging labour movement and edited the *Bundaberg Guardian* (1894–96), the *Gympie Truth* (1896–1902) and the Brisbane *Worker* (1902–11). In 1911 he moved to Sydney to join the *Australian Worker*, which he edited 1914–43, exercising considerable influence in the labour movement. Active in artistic, music, library and literary circles, Boote wrote four volumes of verse, two works of fiction, two books of essays selected from his newspaper articles, and numerous political pamphlets.

BOSI, Pino (1933–   ), born Italy of an Italian father and an Austrian mother, arrived in Australia in 1951. He worked at a variety of occupations before taking a position with the paper *La Fiamma* in Sydney. He has continued to work for the Italo-Australian press, becoming editor of *Il Globo* and *Settegiorni* and founding and editing the magazine *Australia Ieri Oggi Domani*, published since 1984. He has also worked in radio and television and associated ethnic organisations both as a reporter and administrator. A Knight Commander of the Italian Republic, he has been made AM and has won several international awards for his writing. He has published extensively in both Italian and English, his English publications including *The Checkmate and Other Stories* (1973); the verse collections *I'll Say Good Morning* (1974) and *Thirteen Continents and a Rocket-Magi Lost* (1988); the biography *Blood Sweat and Guts* (1971); and the autobiography *Farewell Australia* (1972). His writing in Italian includes a novel, *Australia Cane* (1971).

BOSTOCK, Gerald (1942–), born Grafton, NSW, was a seasonal worker before joining the army and serving in Malaya and Borneo. After leaving the army he became interested in the history and welfare of his Aboriginal people. In 1972 he helped establish the Black Theatre in Sydney and has since been involved in various aspects of drama and film production. His important play 'Here Comes the Nigger' was performed in Sydney in 1976. He has also published poetry, *Black Man Coming* (1980). His poem 'Black Children' became a catchcry of the Aboriginal political movement.

'Botany Bay' is, along with 'Click Go the Shears' and 'The Wild Colonial Boy', one of the most popular Australian folk-songs. Several songs bearing the title 'Botany Bay' have survived; the best-known one (which begins 'Farewell to Old England for ever') is the lament of a male convict who has been transported to Botany Bay, although the warning embodied in the text is made less sombre by the jauntiness of the melody. The words in this version of 'Botany Bay' owe much to an early nineteenth-century English broadside about transportation, 'Farewell to Judges and Juries', but the song derives directly from a comic song in the burlesque drama *Little Jack Shepherd* which was performed in London in 1885 and in Melbourne a year later.

BOULT, Jenny (1951–), born England, came to Australia in 1966. Co-editor with Kate Veitch of *Pearls: Writing by South Australian Women* (1979–80), and *After the Rage* with Tess Brady (1983), she has published several volumes of verse: *The Hotel Anonymous* (1980), *Handbaggery* (1982), *The White Rose and the Bath* (1984) and *Flight 39* (1986), and a play, *Can't Help Dreaming* (1981). *The Hotel Anonymous* shared the Anne Elder Poetry Award for 1981.

BOURKE, John Philip ('Bluebush') (1860–1914), born Peel River diggings, NSW, was a schoolteacher who turned gold-digger and in 1894 went off to the WA diggings. Under the pseudonym 'Bluebush' he wrote ballads and lyric poems that were published in such WA newspapers as the Kalgoorlie *Sun* and the Perth *Sunday Times*. One of a group of popular versifiers writing in the west in the 1890s and at the turn of the century – others were E.G. Murphy ('Dryblower'), Julian Stuart ('Saladin') and Francis Ophel ('Prospect Good') – Bourke recorded, with vigour and realism, experiences in the outback and in the mines. His poems were collected into a volume, *Off the Bluebush: Verses for Australians, West and East*, edited by A.G. Stephens in 1915; Stephens had already, in a *Bulletin* review, 'The Manly Poetry of Western Australia' (1910), praised Bourke and his contemporaries for writing 'the most virile' poetry in Australia at the time.

Boys Who Stole the Funeral, The (1980) by Les Murray is subtitled 'a novel sequence' and has been variously described by Murray as 'a novel in poetry', 'a verse play' and 'a verse movie . . . because of its filmic construction'. Essentially it is a narrative in verse made up of 140 separate sonnets, some formal Petrarchan, others irregular in form and structure; some serious, even portentous in tone, others ironic, even tongue-in-cheek. The narrative tells how two young city men, Kevin Stace Forbutt, 'unemployed for speaking proudly under pressure', and former university student, Cameron Reeby, 'nicknamed Ratchet, for his prospects', steal the body of Kevin's great-uncle, Clarrie Dunn, from a city funeral parlour and take it by car for burial to the isolated farming community of Dark's Plain on the north coast of NSW where Clarrie was born. Throughout the drive north and later in 'Dunn's country', snatches of conversations and flashbacks reveal many facets of the characters' lives and attitudes: Cameron Reeby's violent altercation with feminists at the university and his later fracas with one of them, Noeline Kampff; Clarrie Dunn's nostalgia for his birthplace; the unbridgeable gap in attitudes and values between the Bush and City, exemplified by the contrast between Kevin and his father, Stacey Forbutt; Stacey's infidelity to Kevin's mother, which the son has discovered; Kevin's dissatisfaction with city life ('Sydney? It's a building site now') and his yearning for a meaningful life and occupation, 'not just employment'. After they arrive at the farm of Athol Dunn, Clarrie's nephew, the corpse is placed in the smokehouse ('he'll be on the turn to-night') then prepared ('rock salt and bagging needles and sheets') for the burial. Organisation of the funeral passes to the matter-of-fact ('It must not be let grow dramatic') postmistress Beryl Murchison, and the district, now accessory to the fact, seethes with a conspiratorial sense of community. As the funeral ceremony ends the police arrive and the two funeral-stealers escape into the bush. They hide out in a shack on the postmistress's farm and take a job driving a truck loaded with beef for illegal sale in Newcastle. Cameron Reeby is shot and killed by a policeman who stops their meat run and recognises them as the funeral-stealers. Kevin wanders into the bush and, dazed with shock and grief at his mate's death, falls into a coma. He is confronted by a vision of two figures from Aboriginal legend, Njimbin and Birroo-gun, the latter's name varying from the pure Aboriginal to the Irish-Australian 'Berrigan', illustrating the blend of both Black and White in early Australia. Kevin is put through a series of initiations and instructions and (in echoes of Aboriginal ritual) his soul is renewed by the 'crystal of Crystals'. He listens to 'the blood-history of the continent' and eats from the Common Dish carried by the spirit of Clarrie Dunn. Kevin is free to choose whether he eats or not from this dish but he is not free (nor is anyone) to merely taste in theory the 'work, agony, laughter' in it. It has to be 'body and soul'. As Kevin eats, his reaction deepens: 'It's – ordinary. It's – subtle. It is – serious.' He wakes from the coma with the vision's final injunction in his mind:

> 'Go back now, find your true work,
> Now you can be trusted with it.
> Go back. Keep faith with the battlers' food'.

Kevin, reborn after the vision, and again a part of the bush-inspired masculine world that is at the heart of Australia's nationalist democratic legend, makes his life with the rural 'battlers' of Dark's Plain on a part of Beryl Murchison's farm that was to have been Clarrie Dunn's. Cameron had been destroyed because he had never completely freed himself from the values of the city. *The Boys Who Stole the Funeral* is notable for its absorbing narrative, intricate symbolism, and innovatory technique. It expresses Murray's admiration for the mores and values of both legendary rural Australia and earlier Aboriginal culture.

BRADSHAW, Jack (1846–1937), born Dublin, arrived in Australia in 1860 and was a swagman and small-time confidence man in the outback before graduating to bank robbery. Arrested after a Quirindi robbery in 1880, he spent most of the next twenty years in prison. Released at the turn of the century, he became known as a topical balladeer, a Domain orator and a sensational chronicler of crime. Bradshaw's first publications were the autobiographical *The Quirindi Bank Robbery* (?1899) and *Twenty Years' Experience of Prison Life in . . . New South Wales* (?1899), but his best-known work was *The True History of the Australian Bushrangers* (?1924), in which he claimed personal acquaintance with Dan Morgan, Ned Kelly and others. A bitter opponent of the prison system, Bradshaw hawked his broadsheet poems and paperback books, which had several, sometimes combined, editions on the streets of Sydney and in the larger country towns of NSW.

BRADSTOCK, Margaret, born Melbourne, grew up in Bendigo, Mt Beauty and Cooma, and lectures in English at the University of New South Wales. She has published poetry and short stories in numerous periodicals, as well as a poetry collection, *Flight of Koalas* (1992). With Louise Wakeling and others she edited the collection *Edge City on Two Different Plans* (1983) and with Wakeling, *Words from the Same Heart* (1988). Wakeling and Bradstock have also published a joint collection of their poetry, *Small Rebellions* (1984).

BRADY, E.J. (Edwin James) (1869–1952), born Carcoar, NSW, was the son of an Irishman who came to Australia from America, where he had fought in the Civil War. Brady first worked as a shipping clerk on the Sydney wharves, thereby forming that strong link with ships and sailors that inspired his taste for sea shanties and ballads of the days of sail. Thereafter he followed, for brief periods, a variety of occupations in many places. As journalist, feature-writer, dramatic reporter and editor he was connected with the *Australian Workman*, the *Australian Worker*, the *Bull-Ant*, the *Arrow*, the *Native Companion* and the *Grip*. Brady settled finally on the Victorian east coast at Mallacoota (where Henry Lawson spent some time with him) and while living a simple outdoor life there continued to write, invent and plan prodigiously. Much of this can be gleaned from his entertaining autobiography 'Life's Highway', published in instalments in *Southerly* 1952–55. Brady's poetry, which first appeared in the *Bulletin* in 1891, was published in four main collections, *The Ways of Many Waters* (1899), *Bush-land Ballads* (1910), *Bells and Hobbles* (1911) and *Wardens of the Seas* (1933). It is as a writer of sea ballads that Brady has his particular niche in Australian literary history, but his literary talents were varied: he also wrote children's books, economic treatises, a biography, many short stories and a semi-fictional book on his father's adventures.

BRAND, Mona (1915–   ), born Sydney, worked during the Second World War as an industrial social-welfare worker. She was a research officer with the Department of Labour and National Service 1945–48, travelled and worked in Europe 1948–54 and lived in Hanoi 1956–57, where she assisted with the teaching of English. In 1958 she returned to Sydney. Her plays deal frequently with controversial political topics and reflect her dedication to socialism. Much of her early dramatic work gained a wider popularity overseas (especially in socialist countries) than in Australia. Her published writing includes three collections of poetry, *Wheel and Bobbin* (1938), *Silver Singing* (1940) and *Lass in Love* (1946); and *Daughters of Vietnam*, a collection of five novellas and five poems published in Vietnam in 1958. Brand has also written educational books for schools, and scripts for television and radio. She is married to the poet and writer Len Fox.

BRAY, J.J. (John Jefferson) (1912–95), born Adelaide and admitted to the Bar in 1933, had a distinguished career as chief justice of South Australia 1967–78. Steeped in classical learning, Bray was, nevertheless, a man of modern times. He wrote both of the classical and modern world, possessing the elegance and erudition of a scholar and the ironic wit and cool detachment of a perceptive observer of his own times. A member of Adelaide's Friendly Street since its beginnings in 1975, Bray dedicated his 1990 volume of poetry, *Seventy Seven*, 'To my colleagues, the Friendly Street Poets/ For comradeship, example and survival'. His published works include verse – *Poems* (1962), *Poems 1961–1971* (1972), *Poems 1972–1979* (1979), *The Bay of Salamis and Other*

Poems (1986), *Satura: Selected Poetry and Prose* (1988), *Seventy Seven* (1990), and *Tobacco: A Valedictory* (1990). He has also written a play, *Papinism* (1955), and *The Emperor's Doorkeeper* (1988), a collection of his speeches and addresses on academic occasions during his chancellorship. His poetry is usually a mix of contemporary verse and translations and adaptations from Greek mythology and other sources. *Seventy Seven*, for example (the title indicating his age at publication), has a section 'Recent Poems', a brief (five poems) section of European translations from French and German writers, and a lengthy section of adaptations from Greek writers (with some biographical notes) such as Archilochus, Alcaeus and Theognis. 'Recent Poems' reflects his characteristic personal tone: warmly humorous as in the two Ant pieces; acidic as in his retort to strident feminists ('In all public and social areas you are accepted as gender-free citizens,/ Behave as if you are'); impressively descriptive as in 'Winter Night'; and cleverly epigrammatic, as in his warning about rash promises ('Let all your awkward promises, . . . / Be metaphorical and imprecise'). They betoken the man as well as the poet.

Satura – Selected Poetry and Prose won the SA Festival Award for Literature in 1990; the Award now named in his honour is an attempt to recognise Bray's long and distinguished contribution to Australian culture. He was made Companion of the Order of Australia in 1979.

'Breaker, The', see **MORANT, Harry Harbord**

BREEN, B.A. (Barry Andrew) (1938–   ), born St Arnaud, Victoria, is a teacher in the Victorian Education Department. He has published two books of verse, *Behind My Eyes* (1968), *inter im* (1973, a tiny pamphlet); several anthologies for schools and a book of short stories, *Flop & Mick & John & Me* (1976). The quietly emphatic diction, easy informal style and sincerity, compassion, and sensitivity of Breen's poetry combine to make it appealing and accessible. *Behind My Eyes* includes numerous poems which reflect his teaching experiences e.g. 'To Let Her Think Shadows', 'The Gang-Gang Boy', 'Problem Children' and 'The Retard'. Others mirror the sadness that life brings, e.g. 'Widow', 'Point of Focus' and 'Requiescat'. Some, such as 'End of a Journey', portraying the Jews going to the gas chambers, and 'Oppenheimer', about the discovery of nuclear power and the results thereof, make effective narratives. The five comic sections 'Fragments of O'Flaherty' shared the *Poetry Magazine* Award for 1967.

BRENNAN, C.J. (Christopher John) (1870–1932), was born in Sydney, eldest son of Irish Catholic immigrants. He was educated at St Ignatius College (Riverview) and at the University of Sydney, where he studied classics and philosophy and graduated in 1892. In that year he won a travelling scholarship to the University of Berlin, where he intended to study philosophy. He was distracted from his original intention to obtain a doctorate by a love affair with Anna Werth (daughter of his German landlady), by the cultural life and institutions of Berlin and by the attraction of French symbolist writers, particularly Mallarmé. Returning to Sydney in 1894 Brennan gained a position in the Public Library and began to write poetry that differed markedly from the prevailing balladry and nationalist-radical verse of the day. He married Anna Werth in Sydney in 1897. During the next decade Brennan was disappointed many times in his efforts to secure an academic appointment at the University of Sydney. His jibes about the conservative reactions of some University senate members to the sexual nature of his poetry, his anti-British attitude in the Boer War controversy and his reputation for intemperate habits and behaviour led to his being passed over for numerous lecturing positions. In 1909 he was finally given a permanent lecturing position in modern literature and in 1920, in spite of a stormy career studded with many differences of opinion between himself and the University authorities, he was appointed associate professor in German and comparative literature. His contemporary and friend, John le Gay Brereton, then professor of English, underlined the brilliant scholarship and intellectual capacity of Brennan by indicating that he could have filled with distinction any of the University chairs in philosophy, classics, literature or languages. Some contemporary opinions stress Brennan's remarkable charisma and unpredictability as a teacher and his contribution to the intellectual life of the University. His domestic life, however, grew increasingly strained, especially after the addition to his household of his German mother-in-law, and after the birth of his children, of whom there were four by 1907. With the gradual failure of the marriage that had begun with such romantic expectations on his part, Brennan turned to Sydney café society where, e.g. in the Casuals Club and in the group known as 'les Compliqués', he became a notorious figure. His ebullience, wit and dominating personality made him a legend in the city's bohemian circles but to his wife and children he was often a ranting, drunken bully. In 1922 he formed a tender relationship with Violet Singer ('Vie'), a lively, fun-loving woman nearly twenty years his junior, with whom he lived until she was killed by a tram in 1925. The open scandal surrounding his affair with Violet Singer and the University's dissatisfaction with what they saw as his degenerate behaviour and irresponsible conduct led to his dismissal in June of that year. The alcoholism and poverty of his remaining years were occasionally alleviated by the attempts of friends and former students to rehabilitate him. In 1931 he was awarded a Commonwealth Literary Fund pension of £1 a week. Following a period of ill-health he gave up alcohol and returned before his death to his Catholic faith, which he had neglected since his early university days.

Brennan's first collection of verse was a booklet stereographed by himself (eight copies) entitled *XVIII Poems: Being the First Collection of Verse and Prose by Christopher Brennan* (1897). In the same year he also published *XXI Poems: (1893–1897) Towards the Source*. This booklet met a mixed critical reception: praise from friendly reviewers in *Freeman's Journal* and *Hermes* and from A.G. Stephens in the *Bulletin* Red Page, but contemptuous dismissal (e.g. 'musical, meaningless words to an accompaniment of equally futile and meretricious pessimism') from other critics. In 1903, with the help of John le Gay Brereton, he prepared several copies of a manuscript edition of poems written in response to the Boer War. Titled *XV Poems* it was not published until Harry F. Chaplin's 1953 edition *The Burden of Tyre: Fifteen Poems by C.J. Brennan*. Brennan was opposed to the Boer War and Australia's role in it; in common with many, he felt sympathy for the Boers and saw Britain ('Tyre') as an overbearing imperial power, prostituting herself to commerce. He denounced Christianity, which sanctioned the conquest and exploitation of the Boers, as the immoral, ideological support of the imperialist system. It was probably because of its stringent attack on Great Britain that the poems remained unpublished during Brennan's lifetime. Brennan's chief volume, titled *Poems* but usually referred to as *Poem (1913)*, was published in December 1914. It incorporates revisions of material published in both of the 1897 booklets and many earlier poems. It is made up of three major sections – 'Towards the Source', 1894–97; 'The Forest of Night', 1898–1902; 'The Wanderer', 1902, and two concluding segments, 'Pauca Mea' and 'Epilogues'. *Poems* (1913), although long a source of bewilderment to readers, has been largely interpreted and explained by the analysis and commentary of such writers as A.R. Chisholm and G.A. Wilkes. Wilkes was responsible for the interpretation of the poems as corresponding to Mallarmé's concept of the *livre composé* (i.e. the book of verse which, although made up of many separate individual pieces, is conceived and executed as a whole). With the publication in 1980 of Axel Clark's biography of Brennan, much of *Poems (1913)* can be seen to be biographically based. *Poems (1913)* has the overall theme of man's search for Eden, a paradisal state. The opening section, a mainly lyrical prelude, 'Towards the Source', has thirty individual poems that recall the courtship of Brennan and Anna

Werth in Berlin and reveal him as the impatient, expectant lover who is confident that the consummation of their love in marriage will achieve his Eden. Extravagantly expressed and highly embellished, these lyrical attempts (e.g. 'A Prelude', 'We Sat Entwined', 'Autumn', 'Deep Mists of Longing') to invest his love with an ethereal, paradisal quality are not highly regarded. In the second section 'The Forest of Night' (originally conceived as 'The Book of Lilith'), the search for Eden, apparently unsuccessful in the love affair of 'Towards the Source' (as the linking poem 'Luminary', written only four months after his marriage, clearly shows), is pursued into the deepest regions of the poet's inner self and into myth and legend where other searches for the paradisal state are recorded. The second cycle opens with the twelve-poem series 'The Twilight of Disquietude' and reveals the poet tormented by his 'vast and impotent' dreams. 'The Quest of Silence', which follows, explores the mythology and legendry of the past. At the centre of 'The Forest of Night' is the figure of Lilith, in Hebrew tradition 'Lady of Night', an ambivalent figure who is both the source of man's longing yet a source also of malignity which brings apprehension and horror. In Jewish legend Lilith is Adam's mate before Eve but is forsaken by Adam. Her revenge on Adam is to destroy his capacity for contentment in his new life and to instil in him a torturing vision of a lost paradise, which she represents, for which he is fated to yearn eternally but never attain. The essence of Lilith, a powerful concept containing within it Brennan's recognition of the dualistic view of man's divided nature, is conveyed in the thirteenth part with the lines beginning 'She is the night'. 'The Shadow of Lilith' section ends also in failure of the quest for the paradisal state. The concluding lines of 'The Wanderer' (the last of the major sections of *Poems (1913)*) sum up Brennan's life more aptly than any complex appraisal could do:

> I am the wanderer of many years
> Who cannot tell if ever he was king
> Or if ever kingdoms were.

'The Wanderer' abandons the quest for Eden through the Absolute and with an air of resolution turns to the Actual, the life-experience of the material world. 'Disabused of illusory hope' (Clark) he appears to accept that Eden, as he dreamed it, is unattainable. With that acceptance comes the calm of resignation.

> I feel a peace fall in the heart of the winds
> and a clear dusk settle, somewhere, far in me.

Such a peace never really settled on Brennan's life, but 'The Wanderer' does signal the poetic, if not the actual, end of his exhaustive search. Brennan's only other collection of poetry was *A Chant of Doom and Other Verses* (1918), the title poem, a violent denunciation of Germany's role in the First World War, having first been published in the *Lone Hand*, 1 August 1916. He wrote some love lyrics during the period he lived with Violet Singer. The tenderness and certainty of poems such as 'Midnight' and 'Because She Would Ask Me Why I Loved Her', indicate how important that relationship was to him. His critical works include 'German Romanticism: A Progressive Definition', which appeared in the *Modern Language Review of New South Wales* in January 1920; 'Studies in French Poetry', a planned series of sixteen articles for the *Bookfellow* in 1920, only six of which were completed; and 'Symbolism in Nineteenth Century Literature', a series of University Extension lectures, later published in *The Prose of Christopher Brennan* (1962), edited by A.R. Chisholm and J.J. Quinn. For a long time only dimly understood, yet reverenced the more because of that inaccessibility, Brennan is one of the first legendary figures in Australian literature. Unresponsive to, and seemingly uninfluenced by, the forces of nationalism and radicalism that dominated the contemporary Australian scene, he was a literary enigma standing apart from his own social and literary milieu, finding instead an intellectual affinity with European interest in philosophy and human psychology, and a literary affinity with the French symbolist writers. Although virtually unknown and unrecognised outside Australia, he is clearly part of the international mainstream of writing that gave rise to poets such as T.S. Eliot and William Butler Yeats. Axel Clark's 1980 study is a substantial Brennan biography; other important works on Brennan include A.R. Chisholm's *Christopher Brennan: The Man and His Poetry* (1946) and G.A. Wilkes's *New Perspectives on Brennan's Poetry* (1953). Terry Sturm edited *Christopher Brennan* (1984), in the Portable Australian Authors series, which draws on the whole range of Brennan's writing including his literary criticism and theory, his autobiographical writing and his letters. *Poems (1913)* was republished in 1992 (a facsimile edition in 1972 by Wilkes) with an introduction by poet Robert Adamson.

BRENNAN, Niall (1918–   ), born Melbourne and a freelance writer since 1942, has published numerous works on politics, moral philosophy and biography as well as several small volumes of verse. His two chief biographies are those of Archbishop Daniel Mannix (1964) and John Wren (1971). His other works include *The Ballad of a Government Man* (1944, a satire on public servants) and *Vice Versa: Verses and Poetry* (1975).

BRERETON, John le Gay (1) (1827–86), born Yorkshire, came to Australia in 1859 as a doctor and practised in Sydney. Father of John le Gay Brereton (2), he published the volumes of poetry, *The Travels of Prince Legion* (1857), *Poems* (1865), *The Goal of Time* (1883) and *Beyond* (1886).

BRERETON, John le Gay (2) (1871–1933), born Sydney, son of John le Gay Brereton (1), had a long association with the University of Sydney as student, librarian and, finally, professor of English literature. Well known for his charm and his interest in the writers who sought his advice (he was a close friend of Henry Lawson) he was an unusual academic for the time, never divorcing himself from the world of men outside the University. His charming though slight lyric poetry includes *The Song of Brotherhood* (1896), *Sea and Sky* (1908) and *Swags Up!* (1928). R.D. FitzGerald (Brereton's nephew) has an account of Brereton in *Of Places and Poetry* (1976); H.P. Heseltine wrote *John le Gay Brereton* (1965).

BRETT, Doris (1950–   ), born Melbourne, sister of Lily Brett and participant in the post-war Melbourne environment depicted in the latter's poetry and stories, is a clinical psychologist. Her first book of verse, *The Truth about Unicorns* (1984), won the Anne Elder Award and the Mary Gilmore Award. She has written a psychological novel, *Looking for Unicorns* (1992).

BRETT, Lily (1946–   ), born at the end of the Second World War in a displaced persons' camp in Germany, had Jewish parents who survived the Holocaust. She migrated with her parents to Australia in 1948 and spent her girlhood in Melbourne. Determined to understand more fully the horrors which, as a child, she had been only vaguely aware of in her parents' past, she went as a young woman to Poland to visit her parents' old home and Auschwitz itself. Of her childhood she wrote, 'I have walked through Melbourne as though it were Warsaw', and of her alter ego, Lola Bensky, in her stories 'Lola felt that she had been born with a backlog of sadness'. Brett has published two books of fiction, *Things Could be Worse* (1990) and *What God Wants* (1991), and five books of poetry, *The Auschwitz Poems* (1986), which won the Victorian Premier's Literary Award in 1987; *Poland and Other Poems* (1987), a group of fourteen poems from the 'Poland' section of that book having won the 1986 Mattara Poetry Prize; *After the War* (1990), *Unintended Consequences* (1992) and *In Her Strapless Dresses* (1994), the last three being less dominated by the Holocaust although its presence is never very far away. The best, the most poignant, of her poetry is linked to her mother's experiences in the ghetto and in Auschwitz. Brief poems, with even briefer lines (often of only a single word), distil the essence of the all-enveloping terror of those times:

> It was/ a frantic life
> nothing/ remained/ the same
> from/ minute/ to minute
> there/ was/ no peace
> there/ was/ no rest
> there/ was/ no rhythm
> there/ was/ no sense
> there/ was/ no life.

They depict the horrors of Auschwitz: the regular selections for the gas chambers, the nauseating sight of naked bodies covered with 'made to measure layers of sleek, shiny, white lice', the scorched flesh of those driven to suicide on the electrified fences, the methodical piling of bodies in the pits to ensure that they burned 'with a minimum of fuss and fuel', and then there is the final evidence, when one of the camps was liberated, of the destruction of a race of people: '38,000 pairs of men's shoes, 13,964 carpets, and 836,255 dresses.' The poems move back in time from Auschwitz to the innocent days before the war, then on to a new life in Australia, where the parents' anxieties about the past are carried over into their behaviour in the present – the fear of again being hungry ('the cupboards groaned/ the fridge shrieked') and the need for security ('four locks on the front door'). Lily Brett's visit to Poland (in *Poland and Other Poems*) conveys her hostility to a population that cared too much for its own security to bother about the Jews. She visits Lodz and the streets that still contain the buildings (some of which her great grandfather built) where her parents lived and from where they were 'emptied into the ghetto'. Ghetto tales about 'potato peel patties' and 'The Excrement Cart' are interwoven with more contemporary poems (in 'Kaddish for My Mother') describing in minute physical detail her mother's slow death from cancer. In *After the War* Jerusalem and Israel are the focus as are the scenes from a Jewish childhood in Melbourne. With a keen eye for detail, Brett conjures up a vivid picture of post-war Melbourne and its suburbs. *Unintended Consequences* also includes painful poems about the suffering of her parents and her own repressed anxieties as well as poems about her present life, including reflections on her life in New York (where she now resides).

Lily Brett's husband, David Rankin, a prominent Australian painter, has illustrated the books, movingly and poignantly in the case of the Holocaust poems.

BRIGGS, Ernest (1905–67), born Sydney, was a radio broadcaster in Brisbane, where he also wrote music and art reviews for the Brisbane *Courier Mail*. He published two volumes of meditative lyrics, *The Merciless Beauty* (1943) and *The Secret Listener* (1949). The 'merciless beauty' is that of the pure mind; the seven metaphysical-style poems of the volume emphasise the permanence of the mind of man in contrast with the transience of material things. The poems of a third volume, *The Timeless Flowers* (1952), are chiefly translations or derivations from the Chinese.

'Brighten's Sister-in-Law' is both a poem and a story by Henry Lawson in which the narrator's sick son is nursed through a fever by the sister-in-law of a shanty keeper, to whom the narrator has been guided by the vision of a woman he sees in the branches of a tree. When the poem was published in 1889 the narrator was a carrier and his son Harry a schoolboy with seven brothers and sisters; in the prose version, which forms part of the Joe Wilson sequence, the narrator is Joe and his son, Jim, is an only child of three years.

BRISSENDEN, R.F. (Robert Francis) (1928–91), born Wentworthville, Sydney, was educated at the universities of Sydney and Leeds. He joined the ANU (then the

Canberra University College) as a lecturer in English in 1953. He also held teaching and research positions at several Australian and overseas universities. At the time of his early retirement through ill health in 1985 he was reader in English at the ANU. He was a member of the Literature Board of the Australia Council 1977–78 and its chairman 1978–81. Associate editor of *Meanjin Quarterly* (1959–64) and first literary editor of the *Australian* (1964–65), Brissenden edited the anthologies *Southern Harvest* (1964, short stories) and *Australian Poetry 1972* (1972). He was elected a member of the Australian Academy of the Humanities in 1976 and was made AO in 1982 for his services to literature. In addition to critical work on English and Australian literature he published several books of poetry, *Winter Matins* (1971), *Elegies* (1974), *Building a Terrace* (1975), *The Whale in Darkness* (1980) and *Sacred Sites* (1990). He also wrote *Gough and Johnny Were Lovers: Songs and Light Verse Celebrating Wine, Friendship and Political Scandal* (1984) and was preparing *The Oxford Book of Australian Light Verse* (1991), in which he collaborated with Philip Grundy, at the time of his death. *Winter Matins* reveals Brissenden to be a romantic, even sensual, poet, strongly attracted to natural physical beauty, certainly of the sea (he loved the NSW South Coast) but also of bush landscapes. Most of his personal love poems in this early volume might more appropriately be called 'love-making' poems e.g. 'Another Place, Another Time', 'Winter Matins', 'Dream' and 'Isolde's Song'. His love also of the 'wet, salt sea-smell' runs throughout several poems. He is inspired by the sea partly through his own love of the classics:

> the same sea
> sang round the rocks
> On which Ulysses drove
> His battered wrecks
> And told his lies, while love
> Herself was born
> In the sea-foam

Ulysses's return home is also recorded in a twentieth-century version, an indication that modern and classical times both absorbed Brissenden's creative energies. He was equally at home in everyday culture as his poem 'Verandahs', which recalls the simpler, more agreeable aspects of traditional Australian country life, demonstrates. From *The Whale in Darkness*, 'Verandahs' takes its place with the popular poetry of Paterson, Lawson, Dorothea Mackellar, Kenneth Slessor, David Campbell and Judith Wright. Brissenden's final volume, *Sacred Sites*, sees him at his most skilful. In many ways his own epitaph, published shortly before he died, *Sacred Sites* recalls significant places and events in his life, e.g. his boyhood memories of a father who read Masefield to him and of the friends he made while at high school in Cowra. The series 'A Country Childhood' lingers lovingly over his own 'sacred sites' – 'The Pepper Tree', where he fed bread to the soldier bird, 'The Moreton Bay', where he first began to understand the magic of life revealed by the ripening body of his young girl playmate; 'The Fig Tree' where he sat viewing the world below him. Other 'sacred sites' were in the Greek Islands (the sonnet series 'Leros, 1982') and Aboriginal sacred sites ('Rock Climbers: Uluru, 1985' and 'South Coast Midden'). Brissenden's belief that both Black and White Australians now truly share the land is revealed in his poems. Intimations of mortality are ever present, and the rapidly deteriorating body and the restrictions it imposes are both bitterly resented and philosophically accepted. After his retirement Brissenden began to write crime fiction. *Poor Boy* (1987) and its sequel, *Wildcat* (1991).

The tributes that followed Bob Brissenden's death recognised that Australian literature had lost one of its best-liked and most human faces. In 1993 David Brooks, one-time student and long-time friend, edited, with an introduction, *Suddenly Evening: The Selected Poems of R. F. Brissenden*.

BROOKS, David (1953–), born Canberra, graduated from the ANU in 1974, before completing postgraduate studies at the University of Toronto, 1976–79. He has since taught in English departments at the University of WA, the ANU and the University of Sydney. While a student Brooks was involved in a small publishing venture, Open Door Press, and was North American editor for *New Poetry* 1976–80. In 1980 he edited *New South* (published in Canada), a small booklet of Australian poetry of the late 1970s which included R.F. Brissenden's 'Verandahs' as well as two of Brooks's own early poems. He also published *Five Poems* (1981) and *The Cold Front* (1983), the latter winning the Anne Elder Award for Poetry. Brooks's major impact as a writer came with his highly acclaimed short fiction, *The Book of Sei and Other Stories* (1985, republished in 1988 as *The Book of Sei*) and *Sheep and the Diva* (1990). Brooks has also published a book of essays, *The Necessary Jungle* (1990), which discusses 'poetry and poetics, advertising, the definition of literature, the perception and construction of gender, the ideas of pornography and excess', and provides, in 'The Blood of José Arcadio', a key to his own writing credo. He has edited *Suddenly Evening: The Selected Poems of R. F. Brissenden* (1993) and *Selected Poems by A.D. Hope* (1992).

BROOMFIELD, F.J. (Frederick John) (1860–1941), born Hampshire, England, was brought to Australia in 1868. For more than three decades from the 1880s he had wide experience as a journalist. As sub-editor on the *Bulletin*, Broomfield reputedly accepted Henry Lawson's first contribution and helped prepare the *Bulletin's* famous anthology, *A Golden Shanty* (1890). His creative work included several published songs and contributions to anthologies of prose and verse, but his major contributions to Australian literature were his encouragement of contemporaries like Lawson, John Farrell and Victor Daley, and his great assistance to Sir John Quick and later E. Morris Miller in the compilation of the pioneering bibliographical work, *Australian Literature From Its Beginnings to 1935* (1940). Broomfield was a flamboyant *Bulletin* bohemian and a central figure in the Dawn and Dusk Club and the Century Club, the latter a meeting place for artists, journalists, writers and others ('the best wits and the soundest brains in Sydney') from 1887 onwards.

BROPHY, Kevin (1949–), a teacher of developmental psychology and a tutor in the English Department of the University of Melbourne, is co-editor of the small literary magazine *Going Down Swinging*, a frequent reviewer of books and a well-known identity in literary circles in Melbourne. He is particularly interested in performance poetry and fiction. He has written three novels, *Getting Away With It* (1982), *Visions* (1989) and *The Hole through the Centre of the World* (1991). In his first book of verse, *Replies to the Questionnaire on Love* (1992), some poems deal with the personal – imponderables found in marriage, and parenthood – while others are concerned with social problems.

BROWN, Lyn (1918–), born Fairfield, NSW, graduated MA from the University of Sydney in 1940. Editor, librarian and language teacher, she has also published poetry: *Late Summer* (1970), *Jacaranda and Illawarra Flame* (1973) and *Going Home at Night* (1979).

BROWN, Pamela (1948–), born Seymour, Victoria, has held tutoring and lecturing positions in Newcastle and Sydney, was playwright-in-residence in 1989 at Performance Space, and works at the Badham Library, University of Sydney, and as a writer as well as a lecturer in film-making. She has published, over twenty years, numerous books of poetry, prose and drama. Her books include *Sureblock* (1972), *Cocabola's Funny Picture Book* (1973), *Automatic Sad* (1974), *Cafe Sport* (1979), *Correspondences* (1979), *Country & Eastern* (1980), *Small Blue View* (1982), *Selected Poems 1971–1982* (1984), *Keep it Quiet* (1987), *New and Selected Poems* (1990) and *This World, This Place* (1991). Her poems, often brief, enigmatic and epigrammatic, chart the terrain traversed by the newly freed woman of the 1960s, the search for identity and fulfilment that begins with gusto and optimism, wavers into doubt and misery and ends in resolution and wry self-acceptance. Brown's poems are 'a fever chart' (her friend, Kate Jennings's description) of a fearless, honest attempt to cope with and make sense of the often illusory freedom of the feminist decades. John Tranter's view that her *New and Selected Poems* 'have the flavour of Gertrude Stein sung to a blues guitar' catches the tough, brave poignancy of much of her writing.

BRUCE, Mary Grant (1878–1958) was born and educated at Sale in the Gippsland district of Victoria, and began writing as a young child. After thrice winning the essay competition of the Melbourne Shakespeare Society she settled into journalism in Melbourne. Employed on the staff of the *Age* to run, as 'Cinderella', the children's page of the *Leader*, she contributed short stories, articles on a wide variety of subjects, and serials not only to the *Age* and the *Leader* but also to *Woman's World, Woman* (both of which she temporarily edited), *Lone Hand, Pastoralist's Review, Table Talk* and other journals. In 1905–7 *A Little Bush Maid* was serialised in the *Leader*; published as a book in 1910, it inaugurated the Billabong series of children's books, which ran until 1942 and made Bruce one of the best-known Australian authors of her time. Sales of her work have been estimated at two million copies. Bruce went to England in 1913 and wrote for the *Daily Mail;* in 1914 she married her second cousin, George Bruce, who wrote two novels and many angling pieces. They spent most of the war in Ireland before returning to Victoria, where Mary resumed journalism in Melbourne and renewed contacts there with other women writers. In 1927 the Bruces settled in Ireland but following the accidental death of one of their two sons lived on the Continent and at Bexhill-on-Sea in Sussex until 1939, when they again settled in Victoria. In 1949 George Bruce died, and in 1954 Mary, visiting England for the centenary of her publisher, Ward, Lock & Company (whose 'stable' had also included her contemporary and competitor, Ethel Turner) moved once more to Bexhill, where her last years were spent.

In all, Mary Grant Bruce published thirty-seven children's novels 1910–42, usually at the rate of one a year; a book of Aboriginal legends, *The Stone Age of Burkamukk* (1922); a collection of radio talks, *The Power Within* (1940); and an enormous amount of journalism, short fiction and poetry, most of it uncollected. Alison Alexander's *Billabong's Author* (1979) is a biography.

BUCKLEY, Samuel ('Frank Blair') (1886–1950), born Strathpine, Queensland, served in the AIF in the First World War and taught in Queensland. His published poetry includes *They Shall Not Pass and Other Poems* (1943) and *'Neath Sunny Skies* (1944).

BUCKLEY, Vincent (1925–88) was born in Romsey, a small Victorian country town. Of Irish Catholic lineage (seven of his great-grandparents were Irish), he had a strong sense of identity with Irish culture, demonstrated by his long involvement in Australian Catholic intellectual life, his interest in Irish Republican politics and his love for Ireland itself, where he spent considerable time in his later years. In 1969 he founded the Committee for Civil Rights in Ireland. He was educated at a Jesuit college in Melbourne and at the universities of Melbourne and Cambridge. He was Lockie Fellow at the University of Melbourne 1958–60, and from 1967 held a Personal Chair in Poetry there. As poet, critic, academic and editor, Buckley was influential (especially in Melbourne) in the late 1950s and 1960s, when he was the central figure of a group of university poets and intellectuals with a distinctive philosophy of literature.

Buckley's volumes of poetry are *The World's Flesh* (1954), *Masters in Israel* (1961), *Arcady and Other Places* (1966), *Golden Builders* (1976), *The Pattern* (1979), *Late-Winter*

Child (1979), *Selected Poems* (1981) and *Last Poems* (1991). He also published the critical works *Essays in Poetry: Mainly Australian* (1957), *Poetry and Morality* (1959), *Henry Handel Richardson* (1961) and *Poetry and the Sacred* (1968). He edited *Australian Poetry 1958*, *The Campion Paintings, by Leonard French* (1962), *Eight by Eight* (1963), a poetry anthology, and *The Faber Book of Modern Australian Verse*, which appeared in 1991, after his death. From 1958 to 1964 he edited the magazine *Prospect*, and in 1961–63 he was poetry editor of the *Bulletin*, during which period (but not, according to Buckley, through his own editorial prejudices) the domination of the *Bulletin*'s pages by the then 'mainstream' poets was broken and a new set of poets came into prominence. Buckley's autobiographical *Cutting Green Hay* was published in 1983. Subtitled 'Friendships, movements and cultural conflicts in Australia's great decades' (Buckley refers to 1945–1965), it is both a social history and a personal statement. Buckley also published *Memory Ireland: Insights into the Contemporary Irish Condition* (1985), cultural analysis with an autobiographical flavour.

The poems of Buckley's first volume, *The World's Flesh*, the title referring to the body of Christ which sustains and nourishes the world, are essentially, if sometimes subtly and ambivalently so, poems of love – religious love, familial love and love of nature and of places. The complex ten-poem sequence 'Land of No Fathers' takes up, in its links with de Quiros, the voyager theme, relating it to Buckley's people, celebrating them and their pioneer endeavours. The second volume, *Masters in Israel*, taking its title from the Gospel of St John, contains better-known Buckley poems: 'Late Tutorial', 'Reading to My Sick Daughter' and 'Impromptu for Francis Webb' – all of which reflect largely on the poetic process – and 'In Time of the Hungarian Martyrdom' and 'Sinn Fein: 1957', which are Buckley's personal views of past and contemporary political and historical events. Buckley later judged the poetry of these first two volumes as glib, falsely spontaneous and couched in smooth, soft rhythms, 'not fit to express the things I was groping to express'. Other critics saw it as over-rhetorical, extrovert and too obviously didactic in stance. *Arcady and Other Places*, more moderate in tone and flexible in style, saw Buckley achieve some measure of the 'hardness in phrasing' that he desired so long as it was not inconsistent with the 'rhythmic impulse' that he believed to be the essence of poetry. The volume begins with the seven-part 'Stroke' (perhaps the earliest illustration of the influence on Buckley of the 'life studies' genre then popular in American poetry), which reveals, behind its terse language and often brutally frank description, the pathos of the final encounter between a father and son who had never in the course of their lives really 'learned to touch'. *Arcady and Other Places* has five other sections: poems with the familiar religious and family backgrounds; eight translations from Catullus; and 'Eleven Political Poems', satirical verses on the expediency of politics and certain of its practitioners. Ten years later Buckley published *Golden Builders*. Its opening sequence, 'Northern Circle', is a series of seven 'postcard' poems recording his experiences in Canada. They illustrate the other side of modern globetrotting, the boredom and loneliness that engulf the single traveller. 'Gunsynd', 'Jumps Jockey' and 'Kilmore Races' reflect Buckley's well-known fascination with the turf. 'Golden Builders', a 27-poem sequence set in Melbourne, examines the problems that modern city life poses for the human spirit. Despite the constant assault of the din, squalor and ugliness of the city, human resilience is seen to triumph. Buckley's innovations in the shape and spacing of the verses on the page, in the use of lower-case lettering and in the free-running speech rhythms, make *Golden Builders* his most technically adventurous work. *The Pattern* (1979) begins with a series of poems on Ireland which merge long-past historical events, such as the massacre at Smerwick in 1580 (Edmund Spenser and Sir Walter Raleigh were reputedly present), and more recent happenings (such as the internment of Patrick Shivers in the present 'trouble') with contemporary Irish life, with the vividly evoked Irish landscape and with the reflections of the visiting Irish-

Australian poet who seeks that part of himself that has its roots in Ireland. Ireland, 'the source country', flows imperceptibly into Australia, the Irish poems giving way to those with Australian settings – and the 'pattern' is demonstrated. While in Ireland writing these poems Buckley was awarded the 1977 Dublin Prize, a quinquennial award by the University of Melbourne for an outstanding contribution to art, music, literature or science. *Late-Winter Child* (1979) moves back to the personal world of man and wife, celebrating the birth to Buckley and his younger second wife of a daughter. *Late-Winter Child* reinforces the impression from his early poetry that Buckley, although sometimes accused of a certain academic detachment and lack of commitment, is a sensitive love poet. *Selected Poems* (1981) combine the poems of his first six volumes. *Last Poems* (1991), which won the Adelaide Festival of the Arts John Bray Award for Poetry, is a memorable work, setting the seal on Buckley's substantial achievements. Edited, with a foreword, by his wife Penelope, *Last Poems* reveals more about Buckley than all his earlier works and read together with *Cutting Green Hay*, provides a remarkable picture of the complete Buckley – poet, patriot, husband, father, intellectual and warm, volatile, compassionate individual. *Last Poems* has two parts, 'A Poetry Without Attitudes' and 'The Watch's Wheel – Pieces and Songs'. 'A Poetry Without Attitudes' contains many poems that Buckley intended for his next volume, which he proposed to call 'A General Order for the Night'. 'The Watch's Wheel' is more or less a 'workshop' collection of pieces, poems, songs, some complete, others in draft form. *Last Poems* has many childhood memories, poems about a present that has been shaped by his past, poems of love, poems about Ireland and poems of serenity in the face of approaching death. There is also still evident the typical biting criticism of a world where brutality, greed and injustice continue to flourish.

   Cutting Green Hay is an absorbing account of Buckley's own life, from boyhood in Romsey, through school and student days on to his years as poet and teacher. Interwoven with the autobiographical picture is a fascinating study of the culture and society of the time, including the Catholic university apostolate movement and other controversial social and political events. More than an autobiography, *Cutting Green Hay* is a chronicle of the 1950s and 1960s in Australia, and in Melbourne in particular.

   Buckley's published critical works began with *Essays in Poetry: Mainly Australian* (1957) which encompass individual poets (Kenneth Slessor, R.D. FitzGerald, A.D. Hope, Judith Wright and James McAuley), contemporary left-wing Australian poetry (especially John Manifold, John Thompson and Laurence Collinson), and the new generation of poets who were emerging in the *Bulletin*. By dismissing, or at least devaluating, such traditionally accepted influences as nationalism, radicalism and vitalism on the development of Australian literature, Buckley set up an alternative canon which, though controversial at the time, has proved to be significant and influential. The Vincent Buckley Poetry Prize, alternating between Australian and Irish poets, and instituted in Buckley's memory, was awarded for the first time in 1993. It was won by Lisa Gorton for a group of poems, 'Tidings'.

BUCKMASTER, Charles (1951–72), born Gruyere, Victoria, was closely involved in his brief life with the drug subculture of the 1960s and with the hostility of his generation towards the perceived materialism and sterility of Australian life. A strong supporter of the 'New Australian Poetry' movement, Buckmaster participated in the poetry workshops of La Mama and edited the small magazine *The Great Auk* which helped to disseminate the new poetry. He published two volumes of poetry, *Deep Blue and Green* (1970) and *The Lost Forest* (1971); before his suicide he is alleged to have burned many of his unpublished manuscripts. Buckmaster's poetry reflects both his enthusiasm for the traditional Australian Arcadia under threat and his repugnance at the shallow artificiality of some modern values. A collected edition, gathered from his surviving papers, was edited by Simon Macdonald in 1989. It reinforces the belief that in Buckmaster's early death Australia lost a potentially significant lyric talent. A small press, Wildgrass, inaugurated the Charles Buckmaster Poetry Prize in 1985.

'Buladelah – Taree Holiday Song Cycle, The', a long poem in thirteen sections by Les Murray, published in his volume of poetry *Ethnic Radio* (1977), won the C.J. Dennis Memorial poetry competition for 1976. The 'Holiday Song Cycle', claimed by Murray to be the first poem written by a White man in an Australian Aboriginal metre (derived essentially from music – clapsticks and didgeridoo – and dance), is based thematically and structurally on R.M. Berndt's translation of the Wonguri-Mandjikai song, 'The Moon-bone Song', from north-eastern Arnhem Land. Murray uses as his 'spirit country' the mid-north-coast countryside of NSW between Buladelah and Taree, renowned for its coastal strip of popular beaches and seaside resorts and its lush hinterland of dairy farms. To accord with the Aboriginal Moon-bone song, which illustrates harmony and total communication between all living creatures in an intimately known and coherent environment, Murray introduces into his north-coast world the annual migration of holiday-makers at Christmas time, many of whom are families returning to their ancestral places – the farms, rural villages and seaside towns from which they sprang a generation or so ago. There they recover or, in the case of the younger ones, discover, by communion with the bush, the mountains, the sea and by contact with their parents and grandparents, the origins of their being. The first section describes the pleasurable preparations in the country for the annual influx of visitors. In the second section the holiday-crammed Pacific Highway, which runs through the district, is described (ironically according to Murray but with inspired effect) as the 'great fiery but all-giving Rainbow Snake, writhing over the country and throwing out deadly little offshoots of excitement into the districts up back roads'. After their arrival in 'that country of the Holiday' the returnees rediscover many half-forgotten things, the poem's capitalising of seemingly commonplace things ('Wood Duck's Nest', 'Cattlecamp') bestowing on them a totemic significance. The cycle goes on to celebrate holiday activities and the animals, birds, topography, and events of the 'spirit country'. Murray's belief that place-names are an essential way for people to encapsulate the spirit of place and to link themselves with that spirit is manifested in the song-cycle's numerous place-names; some come from the Aboriginal ('Kiwarric', 'Bucca Wauka', 'Krambach'), others are associated with the White inhabitants and events of the district ('the place of Bingham's ghost', 'the place of the Plough Handles'). Murray sees the latter nomenclature as the White equivalent of the Aboriginal habit of naming from the spirit of place. The eleventh section describes the children establishing affinity with ancestral things: they bite into the old-fashioned summer fruits (china pear, quince and persimmon) of the abandoned 'fruit trees of the grandmothers' and absorb 'the taste of former lives, of sawdust and parlour song, the tang of manners'. In the final section the whole holiday experience is crystallised and evaluated; having gazed for a week or two 'at their year's worth of stars', the holiday-makers prepare to return to their ordinary concerns.

BULCOCK, Emily (1877–1969), born Tinana near Maryborough, Queensland, was an older sister of the novelist Vance Palmer. A schoolteacher and later a regular writer for Brisbane and southern newspapers, she was a life member of the Queensland Authors' and Artists' Association. She wrote several books of verse, *Jacaranda Blooms* (1923), *From Quenchless Springs* (1945) and *From Australia to Britain* (1961). Remembered particularly for her verses celebrating important national occasions, she remains somewhat underrated as a poet. At her best she displays a sensitive perception of life and nature, imaginative imagery and a firm control of poetic form and structure.

***Bulletin* Debate** began as a rather contrived argument in verse between Henry Lawson and A.B. Paterson and then widened into a full-scale controversy that involved numerous well-known writers, including John le Gay Brereton, Francis Kenna, Edward Dyson, A.G. Stephens, Henry Cargill ('The Dipso'), Joseph Furphy and James Brunton Stephens. At issue was the real nature of Australian life (at first in the outback, but ultimately in the whole country) and the responsibility of writers to interpret it truthfully. In literary terms it was the traditional argument between romance and realism. The debate began with Lawson's poem 'Borderland', later titled 'Up the Country', published in the *Bulletin* (9 July 1892). Lawson's outback was not a landscape of shining rivers and sunlit plains peopled by folk-heroes living happy, carefree lives. It was a callous land, inhabited by gaunt, haggard men and women, broken by the never-ending battle against natural disasters, voracious banking systems and unsympathetic absentee landlords. Paterson replied with 'In Defence of the Bush' (23 July 1892). He evaded Lawson's issue of literary honesty and dismissed his criticism with the jibe that Lawson had better stick to the city for he would 'never suit the bush'. Then followed (6 August 1892) Lawson's 'In Answer to 'Banjo' and Otherwise', later titled 'The City Bushman', and Paterson's 'Defence of the Bush' (1 October 1892), later titled 'An Answer to Various Bards'. Lawson's 'Poets of the Tomb' (8 October 1892) widened the discussion to include the role of literature in reforming the total Australian society and was followed (18 November 1893) by 'Some Popular Australian Mistakes', a list of romantic fallacies concluding with a rough handling of the mythical Australian outback folk-hero ('the real native outback bushman is narrow-minded, densely ignorant, invulnerably thick-headed'). Lawson's twenty-three facts and concluding summary are now recognised as an important early statement on Australian literary realism. Three years later Lawson began his crusade again. In the *Bulletin* (27 February 1897) he declared the 'bush bard' to be 'blinded to the Real', and in further articles, '"Pursuing Literature" in Australia', 'Crime in the Bush' and 'If I Could Paint', continued, often in the face of considerable hostility and in spite of personal attacks on his integrity, to insist on truth. The weakness of Lawson's attitude lay in his failure to recognise, or at least to admit, that literary nationalism, with its idealisation of the outback life, had helped to usher Australia out of colonialism and had made a significant contribution to the development of a national pride, a fact made evident by the huge sales of Paterson's *The Man from Snowy River and Other Verses*. What is obvious now, with the benefit of almost a century's hindsight, is that Lawson's insistence on realism instead of romance was, in the light of literary movements then in full force throughout the world, an inevitable step forward in Australian literature. What is equally clear is that his own stories of outback life settled the issue far more decisively than the doggerel verses of the 'Debate' and the angry outbursts in the *Bulletin* columns.

'Bullocky', a poem by Judith Wright, links the bullock-driver in his pioneer role of unlocking the land with Moses, leading his people into the promised land. In a dramatic switch to the present, the poem shows the long-dead bullocky and his teams continuing to nourish the land – 'the plough strikes bone beneath the grass'. The poem indicates that the continuing fruitfulness and progress of the country depend upon the past as much as the present; that Australia of the future will be shaped by its traditions and history. In recent times Judith Wright has forbidden the use of 'Bullocky' in anthologies because it has generally been considered to be a eulogy of the pioneers, many of whom (she felt) had despoiled the land and almost destroyed the Aboriginal people.

BURKE, Colleen (1943–   ), born Sydney of Irish Catholic background, graduated BA from the University of Sydney in 1974 and has worked variously as a clerk, research assistant, community worker and creative writing tutor. Active in poetry workshops, community writing groups and folk-music concerts, she was editor (1974–75) of the *Cornstalk Gazette*, magazine of the NSW Folk Federation, and was involved in establishing the Australian National Folk Trust 1974–75. She has published several books of verse, *Go Down Singing* (1974), *Hags, Rags & Scriptures* (1976, with two other women poets), *The Incurable Romantic* (1979), *She Moves Mountains* (1984) and *The Edge of It* (1992). A city girl – 'I was born and bred at Bondi under the smell of surging surf and sewage' – Burke writes of herself, her milieu ('asphalt days'), social justice, political outrages (e.g. the Irish question, nuclear testing) and the wonder of nature. Her simple, often vernacular, poems are saved from triteness by her capacity for fine images and skilled crafting. She has also written a biography of Marie Pitt, *Doherty's Corner* (1985).

BURNELL, F.S. (Frederick Spencer) (1880–?), born Sydney, was special correspondent for the *Sydney Morning Herald* with the New Guinea expedition in 1914 and compiled an illustrated account of that action, *How Australia Took German New Guinea* (1914), and an expanded version of the same, *Australia versus Germany: The Story of the Taking of German New Guinea* (1915). He also wrote several travel books and two volumes of verse, *Before Dawn and Other Poems* (1912) and *A Sallet of Songs* (1920).

BURNS, Joanne (1945–   ), born Sydney, is a teacher and has published several volumes of poetry, *Snatch* (1972), *Ratz* (1973), *Adrenalin Flicknife* (1976), *Radio City 2 a.m.* (1976, with Stephanie Bennett and Ruth Fordham), *On a Clear Day* (1992); three books of prose, *Correspondences* (1979, with Pamela Brown), *Ventriloquy* (1981) and *Blowing Bubbles in the 7th Lane* (1988). *On a Clear Day* (Burns would discard the capitals) is a collection of brief, anecdotal pieces of prose-poetry that examines with some acerbity the mores of modern middle-class existence and takes a somewhat cynical view of those who are enmeshed in that existence and the society that keeps them there. Nor does she spare herself in the process. Burns sees her poems (or her prose, since she sees no real distinction between the two) as performance pieces and they often have the characteristics – short, sharp lines and punchline conclusions – that performance requires. Her use of lower case and the prose form is, she maintains, a device to make poetry more humble, in accordance with her belief that the vernacular is best fitted to express complexities and ironies.

Bush Ballads and Galloping Rhymes (1870) is the second and more important of the collections of poetry of Adam Lindsay Gordon. Best-known poems are the opening verses, 'A Dedication'; narratives such as 'From the Wreck', 'How We Beat the Favourite' and 'The Romance of Britomarte'; the character sketch 'The Rhyme of Joyous Garde'; and Gordon's most significant poem, 'The Sick Stockrider'. The contents scarcely substantiate the impression given by the title of an overwhelming Australian flavour to this Gordon collection.

'Bush Christening, A', a poem by A.B. Paterson in the *Bulletin* 16 December 1893, and published in *The Man from Snowy River and Other Verses* (1895), is a rollicking account of how the traditional Irish preoccupations, whisky and religion, come together in the unique christening ceremony of the lad, Maginnis Magee. Probably taken by Paterson from the bush oral tradition where such tales thrive, the poem has been linked by Lucy Sussex to an anonymous story, 'Peggy's Christening', in the *Colonial Monthly*, April 1868, a quarter of a century before Paterson's poem. Paterson used the Irish Catholic community as the basis of many similar bush verses, e.g. 'Father Riley's Horse', 'Gilhooley's Estate' and 'Mulligan's Mare'.

Bush, The (1912), by Bernard O'Dowd, is one of the most important expressions of nationalist-radical sentiment in Australian literature. O'Dowd's most attractive poem, it forecasts future greatness for Australia once the ideals of radicalism are transplanted from the 'grottos of decrepitude' of the Old World into the eagerly waiting, green sanctuary of the Australian Bush.

BUTTROSE, Larry (1952–   ), born Adelaide, was a journalist with the ABC 1970–75 and has since been a freelance writer. In 1971 he founded *Dharma* with Stephen Measday; he was co-editor of *Real Poetry* 1977–78, and of *Number Three Friendly Street Poetry Reader* (1979). He has published two books of verse, *One Step Across the Rainbow* (1974) and *Random Leaves* (1976), and two more substantial collections, *The Leichhardt Heater Journey* (1982) and *Learning Italian* (1986), which illustrate his capacity to combine thematic depth and subtlety with colloquial idiom.

BYRNES, Robert Steel (1899–1979), born Goldsborough, Victoria, was educated at the University of Sydney and served with the AIF in the First World War before working as an administrator for the Presbyterian Church of Queensland. He was State and federal president of the Fellowship of Australian Writers and for twenty years a member of the Queensland Literature Board of Review. He was made MBE in 1964. Two collections of his poetry were published, *Endeavour and Other Poems* (1954) and *The Light of Setting Suns* (1980), and with Val Vallis he edited *The Queensland Centenary Anthology* (1959).

bystander, a biannual literary magazine emanating from the monthly Monday night readings in Lower Hawthorn Town Hall (Melbourne), began publication in 1993 with an editorial panel headed by John Irving who has been prominent for some years in writing workshops and community poetry readings. Contributors to the first issue included Kristin Henry, Alex Skovron, Mal Morgan, R.A. Simpson and Chris Wallace-Crabbe. There were interviews with poets Ken Smeaton and Kevin Hart.

[C]

CADDY, Caroline (1944–   ), born WA during the Second World War, went to the USA in infancy. There are echoes in her poetry of that phenomenon of the war years – American father and Australian mother. She returned to WA, still a schoolgirl, and has travelled through much of that State, living both in the northern and southern areas. She worked for some time in a travelling dental unit and now lives on a small farm on the south coast. She has published the poetry collections *Singing at Night* (1980), *Letters from the North* (1985), *Beach Plastic* (1989, winner of the 1990 WA Literary Week Award for poetry) and *Conquistadors* (1991, winner of the 1992 NBC Banjo Award for poetry). Caddy's poetry highlights the WA physical landscape, the title poem series, 'Letters from the North', for example, reflecting the demanding climate and topography of the northern iron ore country:

> Sometimes there is only heat, sometimes only wind.
> I have stopped expecting definite rivers or mountains.

Other poems deal with beach and seascapes and with the life found there, such as the pelicans:

> They preen
> practise sawing each other in half

Her poems also range widely over personal experience – childhood in America and the family characters that live in her memory, the voyage back to Australia, school in Australia where she was looked on as a Yank, love that is love, neither surrender nor submission. Her wit, humour, sense of the absurd, crisp and shrewd assessments of events and situations and sensitive, if austere, description all add up to a considerable poetic talent. The density and intensity of her language are accentuated by her favourite devices of fragmented lines and staccato phrases, often brought together in a final, elucidating image.

CALDWELL, Grant (1947–   ) graduated with a commerce degree from the University of Melbourne and taught, before travelling abroad. In 1975 he was imprisoned for six months in Tangiers for attempting to smuggle hashish. His impressions of that experience are contained in *Malabata* (1991), the title being the name of the prison. A writer since his release, he has published *The Screaming Frog that Ralph Ate* (1979), *The Bells of Mr Whippy* (1982), *The Nun Wore Sunglasses* (1984), *The Revolt of the Coats* (1988), and *The Life of a Pet Dog* (1992). Described as a 'post-modernist fabulist', Caldwell is frequently ironic, sympathising always with those who draw the shortest straws in the game of life, the battlers, the deprived, the perplexed, the lonely, the misfits. His simple, effective poetry often carries a sociological and political sting in its tail.

CALDWELL, Robert ('Andrew Cochrane') (1843–1909), born near Ardrossan, Scotland, came to Australia in 1849 and was a farmer and Methodist lay preacher. In 1884 he became a member of the SA House of Assembly. He published nine volumes of verse 1874–1908, including *A Vision of Toil* (1875), *The Australian Year* (1876), *In Our Great North-West* (1894), *The Pioneers* (1898) and *Adam Gowrie: Or, the Australian Farmer* (1903).

'Cambaroora Star, The', a poem by Henry Lawson about the rise and fall of a goldfields newspaper, was first published in the *Boomerang* in 1891. As the result of a reference in '"Pursuing Literature" in Australia', the *Cambaroora Star* has usually been identified as the *Boomerang* itself, which ceased publication four months later, but Lawson's 'A Fragment of Autobiography' specifies the *Republican* (1887–88), which he contributed to and nominally edited while it was under the management of his mother, Louisa Lawson.

CAMBRIDGE, Ada (1844–1926), born and raised in Norfolk, England, had published moral tales and verse which reflected her strong religious feelings by the time she married a young curate, George Frederick Cross, in 1870. Three weeks after their wedding the couple left for Victoria, where Cross served as an Anglican minister at Wangaratta, Yackandandah, Ballan, Coleraine, Sandhurst (Bendigo) and Beechworth, before moving to Williamstown in 1893. Two of their children died during this period and another son was to die in 1902 at the age of 24; *Thirty Years in Australia* (1903), Cambridge's first volume of autobiography, describes the vicissitudes of her experiences in rural Victoria as a clergyman's wife and her establishment of a writing career; a companion volume, *The Retrospect* (1912), deals mainly with her early years and her reactions to England during her first return visit in 1908. In 1912 she returned again to England after her husband's retirement, but following his death in 1917 moved back to Victoria.

By 1871 Cambridge was contributing short sketches and poems to the *Australasian* and the *Sydney Mail*, but her first significant work was the serial 'Up the Murray' in the *Australasian* (1875), a novel which initiated some of the themes she was to continue to pursue. For the next twenty years she contributed numerous serials mainly to the *Australasian*, but also to the *Sydney Mail* and the *Age*. Cambridge also contributed numerous short stories, poems and essays to the *Australasian, Sydney Mail, Australian Journal, Bulletin* and *Atlantic Monthly*. One collection of her short stories appeared in 1897, *At Midnight and Other Stories*, and she also published five collections of verse, *Hymns on the Litany* (1865), *Hymns on the Holy Communion* (1866), *The Manor House and Other Poems* (1875), *Unspoken Thoughts* (1887, republished in 1988, edited by Patricia Barton) and *The Hand in the Dark* (1913).

Her major novels include *A Marked Man*, (1890); *The Three Miss Kings*, (1891); *Not All in Vain*, (1892); *A Marriage Ceremony* , (1893); *Fidelis* (1895); *A Little Minx*, (1889); and *Materfamilias*, (1898). Two biographies have been published, *Rattling the Orthodoxies* (1991) by Margaret Bradstock and Louise Wakeling, and *Ada Cambridge* (1991) by Audrey Tate.

CAMPBELL, David (1915–79), born Ellerslie, the family property near Adelong in the Monaro district of NSW, was educated in Australia and at Cambridge, where his tutor was the well-known scholar E.M.W. Tillyard. In the Second World War he served with distinction as a pilot in the RAAF; after the war he lived on various properties in the Canberra area, dividing his time between a farming life and a career as a poet. In 1964 he became poetry editor of the *Australian*; he edited *Australian Poetry 1966* and *Modern Australian Poetry* (1970).

His first volume of poetry, *Speak with the Sun* (1949), is strongly Australian in tone. The poem 'Harry Pearce' forms a triptych with two other celebrated 'teamster' poems, Henry Kendall's 'Bill the Bullock Driver' and Judith Wright's 'Bullocky'. The first volume also contains his well-known war poem 'Men in Green'. *The Miracle of Mullion Hill* (1956), with 'The Speewah Picnics', 'The Westing Emu' and the title poem itself, shows Campbell's continued interest in balladry and the tall tale, but the meditative lyrist is evident in two of his best poems, 'Night Sowing' and 'Who Points the Swallow?' In *Poems* (1962) his characters and poetic landscapes are still Australian but have lost much of their parochial quality, taking on a universality that provides the basis for more mature, philosophical meditations. 'On Frosty Days', 'Winter Hills', 'Pallid Cuckoo' and 'Bindweed and Yellowtails', all from 'Cocky's Calendar', the twelve-poem sequence devoted to the countryman's life, are fresh and original nature lyrics with roots in the pastoral tradition. *The Branch of Dodona and Other Poems, 1969–1970* (1970) uses the Jason and Medea legend to offer a biting commentary on modern life and attitudes. *Devil's Rock and Other Poems, 1970–1972* (1974) begins with the biographical sequence *Starting from Central Station* (published separately in 1973), includes a tribute to Kenneth Slessor and contains 'Letters to a Friend', memories of pleasant activities shared with Douglas Stewart. The title poem, 'Devil's Rock and Other Carvings', is a series of brief, imaginative glimpses into the Aboriginal past. After the colloquial narrative and dramatic sequence entitled *Deaths and Pretty Cousins* (1975), came the collection *Words with a Black Orpington* (1978); its cameo nature lyrics, serio-comic travel verses, fragments from Sappho, and love poetry (whether the lusty 'Portrait of a Lady' or the tender 'Soundings') reveal Campbell adopting the free-ranging attitudes and experimental techniques characteristic of the poetry of the 1970s. In his final volume, *The Man in the Honeysuckle* (1979), he explores the relationship between physical science, Taoism and poetry.

Campbell published two volumes of short stories: *Evening under Lamplight* (1959) and *Flame and Shadow* (1976). With Rosemary Dobson and Natalie Staples he published *Moscow Trefoil* (1975) and *Seven Russian Poets* (1979), translations of Russian poetry; and with artist Keith Looby he produced *The History of Australia* (1976). Campbell received numerous awards in recognition of his poetry – the Henry Lawson Australian Arts Award in 1970, the Patrick White Literary Award in 1975, the NSW Premier's Prize in 1980 for *The Man in the Honeysuckle* and FAW's Christopher Brennan Award in 1980. *Poetry Australia* (December 1981), edited by Leonie Kramer, is a special David Campbell edition; it contains, in addition to numerous appreciations of one of Australia's most accomplished lyric poets, some unpublished poems and significant biographical material. *A Tribute to David Campbell* (1987), edited by Harry Heseltine, contains a series of papers given at a Campbell seminar at the Department of English, Royal Military College, Duntroon in 1985. Writers include Rosemary Dobson, Chris Wallace-Crabbe, Joy Hooton, R.F. Brissenden and Leonie Kramer. Campbell's *Collected Poems*, edited by Leonie Kramer, was published in 1989.

'Canticle, The', a poem in four parts by Francis Webb, was published in Webb's volume *Birthday* (1953). In notes to the poem Webb maintains that St Francis of Assisi had provided, in his *Canticle to the Sun* written at Assisi in the garden of the Minoresses of San Damiano shortly before his death, 'a great hymn of devotion, a rewarding personal document, and fine poetry'; excerpts from *Canticle to the Sun* are used in Webb's poem. Webb builds up the character of St Francis by observations from those in contact with him and by indicating the changes wrought in them through his influence. The first such observer is the leper, whose bitter sense of rejection by God and society is transformed to joy and peace through St Francis's loving embrace and cure of his putrefying body. St Francis's father (the cloth merchant, Pietro di Bernadone), the Jongleur, the Wolf of Gubbio, whom St Francis called 'brother', and the Knight and the Serf, are others regenerated through the saint's influence. The fourth part emphasises the veneration in which St Francis, the 'second Christ', is held by his devoted followers and concludes with a reference to the stigmata of Christ, which are said to have appeared on St Francis's body in the latter part of his life.

'Captain Dobbin', a poem by Kenneth Slessor in *Cuckooz Contrey* (1932), is based partly on a Captain Bayldon, retired sea captain and uncle of Slessor's first wife Noela, and owes some of its picturesque detail to Herman Melville's *Omoo*. The poem describes an eccentric old seaman, who has enshrined in his cottage by the harbour the treasures of his seafaring days. Slessor's colourful description of the exotic places and incidents that live in the old captain's memory and his contrast of those with the cold, alienating contemporary scene point to his own commitment to the romantic past. A fine piece of characterisation with the Slessor penchant for lavish and colourful imagery, 'Captain Dobbin' is one of his major poems.

Captain Quiros (1964), James McAuley's narrative poem describing the expeditions of the Portuguese explorer Pedro Fernandez de Quiros (1563–1614) in his search for the Great South Land, is an important contribution to the voyager theme in Australian literature. In 'The Inception of the Poem' the long-held fascination of the theme for McAuley is revealed:

> Then suddenly, unbidden, the theme returns
> That visited my youth; over the vast
> Pacific with white wake at their sterns,
> The ships of Quiros on their great concerns
> Ride in upon the present from the past!

The first part of the poem, 'Where Solomon was Wanting', records through the narrator, Belmonte, the voyage of Alvaro de Mendana in 1595 to Santa Cruz Island near the Solomon Islands with Quiros as navigator; the establishment of the abortive settlement at Graciosa Bay; the murder of the native chieftain Malope; and the forced withdrawal of the expedition. The second part, 'The Quest for the South Land', recounts Quiros's own expedition to establish the New Jerusalem in the South Seas. He comes to an island in the New Hebrides, which he names La Austrialia del Espiritu Santo (Southern Land of the Holy Spirit). A river to the west of the anchorage is named Jordan and a site is selected for a city to be called New Jerusalem. Quiros's great plan fails, not because of any defect on his part, but because no man can bring about the millennium – 'The New Jerusalem . . . shall never be Christ's bride save in eternity.' The third part, 'The Times of the Nations', presents Quiros's dying vision of the unveiling of the Great South Land (Australia) by the Dutch explorers and Bougainville and Cook; the formation of the initial colony 'under the shadow of harsh penal law'; and its growth to nationhood 'fortunate and free'. De Quiros is also the subject of a play, 'The Quest', by Louis Esson and of a television opera by Peter Sculthorpe in 1982.

CARBONI, Raffaello (1817–75) was born Urbino, Italy, spent a restless youth in which he studied at Urbino University, joined the Young Italy movement, was wounded in the rebellion of 1848–49, and was forced into exile in Germany and then London. He arrived on the Ballarat goldfields in 1853 and became a member of the miners' central committee supervising the events leading to the Eureka Stockade but was a spectator when the stockade was attacked, 3 December 1854. He was charged with treason for his role in the Eureka incident but was acquitted with the other participants. His account of the revolt, *The Eureka Stockade*, was published as by 'Carboni Raffaello' late in 1855 and was sold personally by Carboni at the site of Eureka on the first anniversary of the attack. Carboni left Australia in January 1856 after becoming a naturalised British subject and travelled widely for several years. He returned to Italy to participate in the Risorgimento, and in later years was a busy but unacknowledged dramatist and composer. Carboni's long allegorical poem 'Gilburnia', dealing with Eureka and the diggings, was discovered in 1980 by A.D. Pagiaro in Rome. Carboni and the Eureka Stockade are the subjects of John Romeril's play 'Carboni' (1980). He appears in other literature about Eureka, e.g. in Louis Esson's play *The Southern Cross* (1946) and in E.V. Timms's juvenile novel *The Red Mask* (1927). Desmond O'Grady wrote the biography *Raffaello! Raffaello!* (1986), which uncovered previously unknown facts.

CAREW, Elsie (1895–1971), born Auckland, NZ, had by her account a Cinderella-type existence as a child before setting out at 19 for an independent life in Australia. In her lonely and rather unusual life she spent long periods at the Salvation Army's Sydney People's Palace, where she died; she had a failed marriage, occasional bouts of travel including a trip to Moscow, and a penchant for writing esoteric verse and prose which she kept in tattered notebooks. Made known to Australian readers through the interest of Nancy Keesing, who wrote *Elsie Carew: Australian Primitive Poet* (1965), she still remains something of an enigma; her visionary experiences and dry perceptions on the follies of modern humanity are conveyed in direct and aphoristic verse. *The Passing Pageant: Poems and Prose by Elsie Carew* was published in 1970.

CARLETON, Caroline (?1820–74) migrated from England to Australia in 1839. She wrote 'The Song of Australia' (1858) and *South Australian Lyrics* (?1860), the latter the first recorded book of verse published by a woman in SA.

CARMICHAEL, Grace Jennings (1867–1904), born Ballarat, spent her childhood in the Gippsland area – there is a plaque to her memory in Orbost – and then trained as a nurse in Melbourne. She published prose sketches, *Hospital Children* (1891), and *Poems* (1895). After a tragic marriage she was left destitute in London, where she died in 1904. Her surviving three sons were rescued from the Northampton workhouse six years later and returned to Australia after some Australian writers called for funds to be raised on their behalf. Ian F. McLaren published *Grace Jennings Carmichael: from Croajingolong to London: with an Annotated Bibliography* (1986).

CASEY, Lady Maie (1892–1983), born Melbourne as Maie Ryan, was the wife of Baron Casey of Berwick. She published *An Australian Story 1837–1907* (1962), a history of four generations of her family in Australia; *Tides and Eddies* (1966), an account of her early married life; *Rare Encounters* (1980), reminiscences of several distinguished individuals; an account of Nellie Melba's life, *Melba Revisited* (1975); and two volumes of verse, *Verses* (1963) and *From the Night* (1976).

CASSIDY, Robert John ('Gilrooney') (1880–1948), born Coolac, NSW, worked in various bush occupations before joining the *Australian Worker,* then the *Barrier Truth* and the *Worker* again in 1912. Under the pseudonym 'Gilrooney' he published bush ballads, *The Land of the Starry Cross and Other Verses* (1911); a novel, *Chandler of Corralinga* (1912); and *The Gipsy Road and Other Fancies* (1919), a book of humorous prose sketches and verse.

CATALANO, Gary (1947–   ), born Brisbane and educated in Sydney, has been art critic for the *Age* since 1985 and has combined that career with writing several major books on Australian art and art criticism including *The Years of Hope: Australian Art and Criticism 1959–1968* (1981), *The Bandaged Image: A Study of Australian Artists' Books* (1983), and *An Intimate Australia: The Landscape and Recent Australian Art* (1985). His reputation as one of Australia's finest prose stylists gained from his critical writings has been confirmed in his purely literary works, including five books of poetry beginning with *Remembering the Rural Life* (1978), the title taken from a long personal poem dominating the volume. *Heaven of Rags: Forty Poems 1978–1981* (1982) sets most of its brief poems in normal verse lines but in section four uses the prose poem device of sentences and paragraphs, a technique which increasingly interested Catalano, *Fresh*

Linen (1988) being composed entirely of prose poems, some of which were repeated from _Heaven of Rags_. In his _Heaven of Rags_ Catalano would have 'all things aged, beaten and torn . . . stained with sweat and dirt and basking in the glory that only comes of use'. There are, in _Heaven of Rags_, some informal and witty travel poems, 'Postcards for Peter', and a group of poems that marvel at the intricate mechanisms and procedures of photography. _Slow Tennis_ (1984), _The Empire of Grass_ (1991), which won the Grace Leven Prize for Poetry in 1992, and _Selected Poems 1973–1992_ (1993) are his other poetry volumes. The 'Empire of Grass' is the Earth itself, the permanent Empire that remains greater than all the passing empires that man has endeavoured to place upon it. The presence of the artistic imagination is important in Catalano's poems, as is a nostalgia for the Australia depicted in Les Murray's 'weatherboard cathedral' and 'vernacular republic'. The occasionally sardonic and quizzical side of Catalano is seen in some grimy glimpses of the less pleasant side of cohabitation. Catalano often moves from depicting mundane (but useful) objects such as an old cup, or hat, or pair of boots to imaginative flights of fancy – from spoons to a flight of birds, from a row of decapitated toadstools to a vision of 'a group of refugees pausing at the edge of the abyss'. His imagery is often simple but striking, e.g. the writer regularly burning the contents of his waste-paper basket watches his 'old or abandoned thoughts perish once more'; or the vision of Hell as 'a landscape of torn and broken books' out of which each of us comes in turn to piece together an autobiography, a story that can only be known when, regretfully, complete and irreparable. The image that best encapsulates his writing is that contained in his own title, _Fresh Linen_. It is wholesome, elegant and attractive. Catalano has also published _The Woman Who Lives Here and Other Stories_ (1983), a book of five short stories and sixteen 'sketches'.

CATALDI, Lee (1942–   ), born Sydney of Italian and Australian parents, was educated at the Friends School, Hobart, and the University of Sydney. She later studied at Oxford University, lectured at Bristol University and became attracted to Marxism. From 1963 she worked as a teacher and linguist at Lajamanu School in the Northern Territory, producing books in the Warlpiri language and collecting and transcribing Warlpiri narratives. She has published two collections of poetry, _Introduction to a Marxist Lesbian Party_ (1978), winner of the Anne Elder Poetry Award, and _The Women Who Live on the Ground_ (1990). Other awards that Cataldi has won include the Northern Territory Red Earth Poetry Award and the Australian Human Rights Award. Cataldi writes a stripped-down, minimalist poetry, in which line variation is as important as vocabulary; wry, elliptical and often satirical when she writes of White culture and its inability to understand Aboriginal attitudes, she develops more sustained rhythms in those poems which deal directly with Black experience.

CATO, Nancy (1917–   ), born Adelaide, was a cadet journalist on the Adelaide _News_ 1936–41 and an art critic on the same newspaper 1957–58; since then she has been a freelance writer. Active in literary affairs, she edited the 1950 _Jindyworobak Anthology_, co-edited _Southern Festival_ (1960), and has been involved in the SA branch of the FAW (1956–64) and ASA (1963–64). Her most important work is her trilogy of historical novels set against the background of the Murray River, _All the Rivers Run_ (1958), _Time, Flow Softly_ (1959) and _But Still the Stream_ (1962). These were rewritten and combined into a single best-seller, _All the Rivers Run_ (1978) and screened as a TV series in 1983. The Murray River has a place also in her poems; 'Paddle Steamer', for example, emphasises the majesty of 'the endless river' in comparison with the humans who exploit it. Her two volumes of poetry, _The Darkened Window_ (1950) and _The Dancing Bough_ (1957), show her to be a lyrist with a capacity for serious, sometimes sombre, themes; _The Dancing Bough_, for example, is concerned with the twin forces that threaten existence – nuclear weapons and the more persistent enemy, Time. In 1984 she was made AM and received an honorary D.Litt. from the University of Queensland, and in 1988 was granted the Alice Award by the Society of Women Writers.

Celtic Twilight, see **DALEY, Victor**

CHANDLER, Alfred ('Spinifex') (1852–1941), born Geelong, was a journalist with the Hamilton *Spectator* and the *Register* in Adelaide, where he established *Quiz*, a satirical weekly, and published two books of verse, *A Bush Idyl* (1886) and *Songs of the Sunland* (1889). In 1894 he went to the goldfields of WA, where he played an important role in the rapidly developing newspaper scene; he edited the *Goldfield Courier*, the first newspaper in Coolgardie, the *Golden Age*, the *Coolgardie Miner* and the Perth *Sunday Times*, and was associated with the monthly magazine *Leeuwin*. With William Siebenhaar he published *Sentinel Sonnets* (1919), a book of war poetry; his other volume of verse is *'Beauty' and Other Poems: A Selective Anthology from the Author's Previous Books and Manuscripts* (1935).

CHOATE, Alec (1915–), born High Barnet, England, came to Australia at the age of 7. He served in the AIF 1940–45 in the Middle East and the Pacific, then spent thirty years (1945–75) as a surveyor in the Public Service. Choate, well disposed towards the Jindyworobak affinity with the land, had his early poetry published in that movement's anthologies immediately after the war. Co-editor of the WA anthology *Summerland* (1979), Choate has also written three books of verse, *Gifts upon the Water* (1978), *A Marking of Fire* (1986) and *Schoolgirls at Borobudur* (1990). He was awarded the Tom Collins Poetry Prize in 1976 and the Patricia Hackett Prize in 1989 for the outstanding poetry contribution to *Westerly* in the 1988 Bicentennial issue of that magazine. His third volume, written in retirement, is characteristic of all his poetry – good-natured, pleasantly sentimental and appreciative of the good things that life, nature, friendship, art and literature can offer. From *Schoolgirls at Borobudur*, the poem 'The Flute Girl' recalls his experiences of war in Syria, Libya, Egypt and Borneo, while the title poem records the poet's interaction with the two extremes – a group of schoolgirls and the classical wonder of Borobudur.

CHRISTESEN, C.B. (Clement Byrne) (1911–), born Townsville, was educated at the University of Queensland, then became a publicity officer for the Queensland government and later a journalist on the Brisbane *Courier* and the *Telegraph*. He worked briefly for the London *Times* and the *New York Times* before returning to Brisbane, where in 1940 he founded the literary magazine *Meanjin*, moving with it to Melbourne early in 1945. Christesen published four volumes of verse, *North Coast* (1943), *South Coast* (1944), *Dirge and Lyrics* (1945) and *Having Loved* (1979); edited the anthologies *Australian Heritage* (1949), *Coast to Coast 1953–54* (1955) and *On Native Grounds* (1967), a selection from *Meanjin*'s first twenty-five years; and edited *The Gallery on Eastern Hill* (1970). A selection of his own short fiction and poetry, *The Hand of Memory*, was published in 1970. In 1990 he published another book of stories, *The Troubled Eyes of Women*, which includes some earlier stories from *The Hand of Memory*. Although his lyrical verse and spare short stories have a modest reputation, Christesen is best known for his tireless promotion and encouragement of Australian writing, particularly as editor for thirty-four years of *Meanjin*, which he transformed from the little poetry magazine of 1940 into a major Australian cultural journal significant in the development of Australian literary criticism. Active also as broadcaster, writer of radio features and University Extension and CLF lecturer, he has been honoured by the gold medal of the Australian Literature Society (1965), the Britannica-Australia Award (1970), the first gold medal of the Foundation for Australian Literary Studies (1980), and an honorary D.Litt. from Monash University (1975). He was made OBE in 1962 and is an Emeritus Fellow of the Literature Board of the Australia Council. His work as editor is discussed in Lynne Strahan's *Just City and the Mirrors* (1984) and in Jenny Lee et al. (eds), *The Temperament of Generations* (1990).

Christopher Brennan Award, formerly known as the Robert Frost Prize, is given by FAW to a poet whose sustained work achieves distinction. Recipients of the award have included R.D. FitzGerald, Judith Wright, A.D. Hope, Douglas Stewart, Gwen Harwood, Rosemary Dobson, John Blight, Vincent Buckley, Bruce Beaver, Bruce Dawe, Les Murray, William Hart-Smith, Peter Porter, Harold Stewart, Roland Robinson, Chris Wallace-Crabbe, Elizabeth Riddell. It was also awarded posthumously to Francis Webb, James McAuley and David Campbell.

Christopher Columbus (1948) by William Hart-Smith is part of the voyager theme in Australian poetry. The sequence of forty-two poems begins in antiquity with its comfortable certainty that 'The world is flat/ And that's that' but moves rapidly to the late medieval world and 'the Brothers Columbus, Mapmakers of Lisbon'. The series encompasses Columbus's first voyage to the New World, his triumphant return to Spain, his second voyage and the discovery of the tragedy of the colony he left at La Navidad, the initial enchantment of the New World spoiled by the European taints of disease and greed, the founding of the city of Isabella, his final voyages and the decay of his great dream.

CHURCH, Hubert (1857–1932), born Hobart, Tasmania, spent lengthy periods in both England and NZ before settling in 1923 in Melbourne, where he was well known in literary circles. A poet of elegance and restraint, Church published *The West Wind* (1902), a *Bulletin* booklet republished in the anthology *A Southern Garland* (1904); *Poems* (1904); *Egmont* (1908); and *Poems* (1912), a selection from the earlier volumes with ten additional poems. He also wrote a novel, *Tonks: A New Zealand Yarn* (1916).

'Clancy of the Overflow', a poem by A.B. Paterson, was first published in the Christmas 1889 number of the *Bulletin* under the pseudonym 'The Banjo'. A great favourite with Australians, the poem established Clancy as one of Australia's best-known folk-heroes. The poem records the writer's distaste for city life as well as hymning the great outdoors; it pictures Clancy's carefree existence amid 'the vision splendid of the sunlit plains extended' and 'the everlasting stars'. A phrase from the poem, 'a thumbnail dipped in tar', has come to be used in modern times as a derogatory label for both the bush ballad genre and the unsophisticated, bucolic view of Australia which produced and encouraged it.

CLARK, Robert (1911–   ), born Darjeeling, India, came to Australia as a boy and was educated in Adelaide, where he practised as a solicitor. He is now retired and is a full-time writer. He won the 1956 *Sydney Morning Herald* prize for poetry for 'The Dogman' and has been widely represented in Australian anthologies. Co-editor of *Verse in Australia 1958–61* and *No. 8 Friendly Street Poetry Reader* (1984) he wrote the significant introduction on Max Harris in Harris's poems *A Window at Night* (1967). His own publications of verse are *The Dogman and Other Poems* (1962), *Segments of the Bowl* (1968), *Thrusting into Darkness* (1978) and *Walking to Bethongabel* (1986). A traditional poet concerned especially with language, most of his work is lyrical and meditative.

CLARK, Ross (1953–   ), born in the Darling Downs region of Queensland, has worked as a bookseller, teacher, editor and freelance writer. He has published verse in numerous periodicals and anthologies and in three collections, *Chameleon* (1982), *With Fires on Every Horizon* (1986), and *Still Waiting for the Thunder* (1992). Co-editor of *The Border Issue*, he is also editor and publisher of the SweetWater Poets series and has edited the collections *Lightning Lyrics* (1983, with Peter Burton and Audrey Heck) and

Turns of Phrase (1988, with Lawrie Ryan). Concerned with continuity and the problems of understanding the past, Clark's accessible, sometimes whimsical poetry is strongly evocative of Brisbane.

CLARKE, Donovan (1907–87), born Bristol, England, had a long career as schoolmaster and academic, poet and literary critic. Particularly interested in Australian colonial poetry, he wrote on the Henry Kendall–Charles Harpur relationship and edited a selection of Harpur's poetry in 1963. He also published two volumes of poetry, *Ritual Dance* (1940) and *Blue Prints* (1942).

CLAY, H.E. (Henry Ebenezer) (1844–96), born Cheshire, England, migrated in 1858 to WA, where he worked as a government clerk. His volume of verse *Two and Two: A Story of the Australian Forest, with Minor Poems of Colonial Interest* (1873) was the first separate publication of poetry in WA. His other works include *Westralian Poems* (1907), *Poems* (1910) and the proclamation song, *Rouse Thee Westralia* (1890). Although he wrote in a conventional English poetic style, Clay included such colonial ingredients as kangaroos, sheep, wild dogs, bushfires, and life on the diggings.

'Click Go the Shears', one of the best-known Australian folk-songs, was probably written in the early years of the twentieth century and derives from the English song 'Ring the Bell, Watchman'. It offers a picture of shearing life in the days of the blade shears, and each of its several verses focuses on a typical inhabitant of the shearing shed and his activities: the old shearer, the boss, the new chum, the boy supplying tar to seal a wound caused by the shears, the spree after the shearing season is over. The chorus,

> Click go the shears boys, click, click, click
> Wide is his blow and his hands move quick
> The ringer looks around and is beaten by a blow
> And curses the old snagger with the bare [blue]-bellied 'joe'.

refers to the sound of the shears, the shearing style of the ringer or fastest shearer, and his chagrin when his tally is bettered by a snagger, a shearer who works roughly. Robert Ingpen published a fine illustrated version of 'Click Go the Shears' in 1985.

CLOW, Robitt Jon (1876–1952), born Melbourne, was a minister of the Churches of Christ in Victoria, SA and Queensland in the early part of this century. He published two plays, fiction, *The Pillar of Salt: A Story of Station Life* (1903) and two collections of verse, *Vive la Australe* (1910) and *Australie . . . Three Poems* (1910).

COLEBATCH, Hal (1948–), born Perth, WA, the son of Sir Hal Colebatch (1872–1953), a prominent WA newspaper proprietor and politician, has been a lawyer, journalist and editor. He has published several volumes of poetry, *Spectators on the Shore* (1975), *In Breaking Waves* (1979), *Coastal Knot* (1980), *Outer Charting* (1985), *The Earthquake Lands* (1990), and *The Stonehenge Syndrome* (1993). He has also written fiction, *Souvenir* (1981), and radio drama. As the titles of his volumes of poetry suggest, Colebatch has an abiding interest in the sea and is a keen yachtsman and a maritime historian. One of his notable poems is 'Crowhurst', the story of the lone yachtsman Donald Crowhurst, lost at sea in a round-the-world yacht race. In Colebatch's poetry the sea is a potent force, one against which man has to summon all his dexterity and courage in order to survive, yet a source too of a code of honour that enriches those who spend much of their time in contact with it. A firm traditionalist, Colebatch has a strong regard for long-established poetic values – clarity, coherence, classical forms and formal verse structures. His poetry examines the age-old questions of human need and experience, weighing those against existing and often sterile philosophical and political practices. Something of his traditional outlook is apparent in his study *Return* *of the Heroes: The Lord of the Rings, Star Wars and Contemporary Culture* (1990), where he deplores the collapse of traditional Western values in the uneasy 1960s and 1970s and the subsequent rise of nihilism and the cult of the anti-hero.

COLLINSON, Laurence (1925–86), born Yorkshire, England, was brought to Australia in infancy and returned to England to live in 1964. He worked as a freelance writer for radio, newspapers and magazines; as a secondary teacher; and as actor, director and writer for Australian little theatres. He published four collections of verse, *Poet's Dozen* (1953), *The Moods of Love* (1957), *Who is Wheeling Grandma?* (1967) and *Hovering Narcissus* (1977) and a novel, *Cupid's Crescent* (1973). Of his numerous unpublished plays for stage, radio and television the best known in Australia is the stage play 'The Selda Trio', produced in Melbourne in 1961 and London in 1974. Collinson also contributed to the poetry collection *Eight by Eight* (1963) and was one of the editors of the magazine *Barjai*.

Although Collinson, a Marxist, was criticised on publication of *The Moods of Love* for his treatment of social and political issues, he was always more concerned with love and its disappointments, and with what he termed 'the self-destruction that pervades our personal and social lives', than with political themes. His interest in the formal aspects of poetry is especially reflected in his later verse, which is compressed and tightly structured. The same concern with love, the limitations of conventional morality and the 'admass' culture can be found in his plays.

Comic Australian Verse (1972, retitled *The Flight of the Emu: Contemporary Light Verse*, 1990), edited by Geoffrey Lehmann, begins with an anonymous epitaph on a headstone at St Matthew's cemetery, Windsor, NSW, and concludes with three poems by Bruce Dawe. Lehmann notes the importance of humorous verse as a literary form in the nineteenth century and its relative demise in modern times. The *Bulletin* is the chief source of his nineteenth-century selections; A.B. Paterson, W.T. Goodge and Joseph Tishler ('Bellerive') are his chief representatives from the early twentieth century; later poets represented are A.D. Hope, Douglas Stewart, Kenneth Slessor, Ronald McCuaig and Bruce Dawe.

Commonwealth Poetry Prize, an annual award, is administered jointly by the Commonwealth Institute and the National Book League. It is awarded for a first published book of poetry in English from a country other than the United Kingdom. Australian winners of the prize, first awarded in 1972, included Phillip Salom (1981), Peter Goldsworthy (1982) and Julian Croft (1985).

Concrete Poetry conceives of the poem as ideogram, as an instantly assimilable, visually ordered text in which the word stands both as physical spatial object and as a plurality of simultaneous meanings. Said to have originated with the publication of *Konstellationen* in 1953 by the Bolivian-born Swiss poet Eugen Gomringer, concrete poetry was evident in Australia in the 1960s but became more widespread in the 1970s with the growth of the little magazines. The all-concrete magazine *Born to Concrete* evolved in 1975 from *Fitzrete*, which was an all-concrete issue of *Fitzrot* (1975–77), which itself had developed as an outlet for concrete poetry under the leadership of 'ПО'. Other modernist magazines and journals, e.g. *Dharma*, *Magic Sam*, *New Poetry*, *The Saturday Club Book of Poetry*, *SCOPP* and *Your Friendly Fascist*, have published concrete poetry. The first issue of *Mixed Concrete Poetry* appeared in 1993.

Condolences of the Season (1971), the first selected volume of Bruce Dawe's poetry, was chosen by the author from the four earlier volumes, *No Fixed Address* (1962), *A Need of Similar Name* (1965), *An Eye for a Tooth* (1968) and *Beyond the Sub-divisions* (1969); it also contains nineteen new poems. An extraordinarily popular collection, *Condolences of the Season* was reprinted annually 1971–80, except in 1974. It contains many of Dawe's best-known poems: 'Public Library, Melbourne', 'Enter Without So Much as Knocking', 'Happiness Is the Art of Being Broken', 'Any Shorter and I'd Have Missed It Altogether', 'The Not-so-good Earth', 'Life-Cycle', 'A Victorian Hangman Tells His Love', 'Homecoming', 'Homo Suburbiensis' and 'Weapons Training'.

Contempa, a Melbourne illustrated magazine of poetry and prose, was published in two series. The first series of ten undated issues (1972–75) was edited by Phillip Edmonds and Robert Kenny. The second series (1978–   ) is also edited by Edmonds. Contempa Publications, also founded in 1972 by Kenny, Edmonds and Michael Dugan, has published works by contemporary writers such as Dugan, Colin Talbot, B.A. Breen, Walter Billeter, John Jenkins and Ken Taylor.

Convict Once (1871) is a long narrative poem by James Brunton Stephens. It has an intricate, melodramatic plot which revolves around a beautiful *femme fatale* – a 'convict once' but now a governess – who becomes romantically involved with several men but dies before disaster overtakes all concerned. Heavily ornate, and outmoded in its elevated literary tone, the poem at times conveys an impressive air of gravity and grace. Highly valued by contemporary critics, who regarded it as Stephens's most significant literary work, it has been largely ignored in recent years.

'Convict's Tour to Hell, A', a long witty poem in rhyming couplets, was written by 'Frank the Poet' probably in 1839 at Stroud, NSW. Modelled on the satires of Jonathan Swift, who attended school in Kilkenny (where MacNamara committed the offence which led to his transportation), 'A Convict's Tour to Hell' chronicles Frank's tour of the underworld, where he discovers that notorious penal administrators such as Captain Logan and Governor Darling are suffering the kind of hellish punishments that they inflicted on the convicts. At the end of the poem, just after Frank is admitted into Heaven, he awakens to find that he has been dreaming. There is evidence that 'A Convict's Tour to Hell', which is also known as 'The Convict's Dream' and 'Frank's Tour of Hell', was popular among the more incorrigible convicts.

CORENO, Mariano (1939–   ), born Frosinone, Italy, arrived in Australia in 1956. He has published five collections of poetry in Italian and has won several awards in Italy. In 1965 he began to write poetry in English, after encouragement by Judith Wright, and has published his poems in numerous anthologies and periodicals as well as in one collection, *Yellow Sun* (1980).

COUANI, Anna (1948–   ), born Sydney of Greek and Polish descent, was educated at the University of Sydney and teaches art and English at secondary level. Founder of the small-press publishing companies Magic Sam and Sea Cruise Books, she was a founding member of the Sydney women writers' group 'No Regrets'. She has published stories and prose poems in numerous periodicals and anthologies and in four collections, *Italy* (1977), *Were All Women Sex-Mad?* (1982), *The Train* (1983, published with Barbara Brooks's *Leaving Queensland*) and, with Peter Lyssiotis, *The Harbour Breathes* (1989), short-listed in the 1990 Victorian Premier's Literary Awards. She has also co-edited *Island in the Sun* 1 (1980), *Island in the Sun* 2 (1981), *Telling Ways: Australian Women's Experimental Writing* (1988) and *Angry Women* (1989). Preoccupied with what lies beneath the surface of everyday life, Couani's prose poems explore the disjunction between the apparent inconsequentiality of mundane happenings, images, gestures/expressions and their deep, hidden and even inexpressible personal consequences. Skilfully evoking the casual absorption of painful experience in external society, Couani exposes the disjunction between personal feeling and impersonality, between so-called rationality and impulse, recording sensations of alienation, dissociation, failures of relationship and general social malaise. Underlying all her work is a keen interest in the links between personal attitudes and public power structures, in the inexorable, insidious influence of politics on everyday living; as one of her narrators comments, people's behaviour can be explained 'in terms of power both attributed and actual, personal and public'.

COUNGEAU, Emily (1860–1936), born Essex, England, came to Australia in 1887. She published several books of verse, including *Stella Australis* (1914), *Rustling Leaves* (1920), *Palm Fronds* (1927) and *Fern Leaves* (1934). Her verse drama *Princess Mona* (1916) is a fantasy in which a pageant of Anzac is featured.

COUPER, J.M. (John Mill) (1914–   ), born Dundee, Scotland, came in 1951 to Australia, where he lectured in education and English at the universities of Queensland and NSW and Macquarie University. Couper has published several volumes of verse, *East of Living* (1967), *The Book of Bligh* (1969), *In From the Sea* (1974), *The Lee Shore* (1979) and *Canterbury Folk* (1984). *East of Living* has four sections: 'Cape Catastrophe', which tells of the drowning in the Great Australian Bight of the master and several of the crew of Matthew Flinders's ship the *Investigator*; a series of sonnets addressed to Mark Alexander Boyd (1563–1601), a Scottish poet with whom Couper, exiled in Australia, feels he shares experiences of love, life and nostalgia for home; 'Catterline', in which a born loser ultimately achieves self-respect and a resolution of his place in the scheme of things; and 'East of Living', which reflects Couper's own intellectual, cultural and spiritual estrangement in Australia and his attempt to come to terms with the situation. *Canterbury Folk*, continues Couper's predilection for both the sonnet form and for translations of the classics while again achieving his usual high quality of language and thought. *The Book of Bligh* is a contribution to the voyager theme in Australian writing, recounting the mutiny on the *Bounty* and the epic voyage of Bligh and his crew in a small boat to Timor. It also makes moral and psychological judgments on the Bligh story, contrasting the integrity and selfless sense of service displayed in those events with the hedonism of modern man. *In from the Sea* is more emphatically personal, with the values instilled in Couper's early life and upbringing in Scotland in obvious collision with the new Australian attitudes and environment.

Courland Penders, an old derelict family estate, is the setting for a sequence of poems by Michael Dransfield. The imaginary house, introduced in Dransfield's *Streets of the Long Voyage* (1970) in the poem 'Portrait of the Artist as an Old Man', is further described in 'Courland Penders: Going Home', 'Tapestry at Courland Penders', 'Library, Courland Penders', 'Birch Trees, Courland Penders' and 'Courland Penders: Reminiscences'. The obsession with vanished glory indicates the romantic strain in Dransfield.

CRAIG, Alexander (1923–   ), born Malvern, Victoria, studied at the universities of Melbourne and Iowa and served with the AIF in New Guinea, before teaching English at Macquarie University where he became director of literary craftsmanship. He has published three volumes of verse, *Far-Back Country* (1954), *The Living Sky* (1964) and *When No-One is Looking* (1977); and edited *Twelve Poets 1950–1970* (1971). Craig's poetry is included in numerous anthologies.

'Creek of the Four Graves, The', one of Australia's earliest narrative poems, was published by Charles Harpur in *The Bushrangers, A Play in Five Acts, and Other Poems* (1853). Its story of a group of settlers murdered by natives is presented with individuality and force. Set in the Hawkesbury district and the Blue Mountains, the poem combines a realistic narrative with effective description of the local Australian scene.

Creeve Roe (1947), a collection of Victor Daley's radical and satiric verse, was edited by Muir Holburn and Marjorie Pizer. The title (also Daley's pseudonym) is taken from the Red Branch Knights of Conchubar, one-time kings of Ulster. Most of the poems had been published earlier in the *Bulletin* and the *Tocsin*, a labour weekly which was edited in the 1890s by fellow radical Bernard O'Dowd. One of Daley's best-known satirical poems (mainly on A.G. Stephens) is 'Narcissus and Some Tadpoles', published in the *Bulletin*.

CROFT, Julian (1941–   ), born Newcastle, NSW, is associate professor of English and communication studies at the University of New England. Keenly interested in Australian literature, he helped in the establishment of the Association for the Study of Australian Literature (ASAL), whose journal *Notes & Furphies* he co-edited for many years. He has written a study of the Welsh poet T. Harri Jones who taught him as a student, and *The Life and Opinions of Tom Collins: A Study of the Works of Joseph Furphy* (1991). Croft has published the volumes of poetry, *Breakfasts in Shanghai* (1984, winner of the Asia-Pacific section of the Commonwealth Poetry Prize in 1985), which reviews 'the tugs and buffets of the years', savouring all life's experiences, even the seemingly commonplace; *Confessions of a Corinthian* (1991), in which poems of boyhood experiences give way to nostalgic recollections of the north coast and the tablelands of NSW and dismay at the mass migration of people to those areas, ruining their once-pristine beauty; and, with Michael Sharkey, *Loose Federation* (1979). As the title of *Confessions of a Corinthian* suggests, Croft is himself a classicist; critics have placed him in the company of such traditional Australian poets as Kenneth Slessor, R.D. FitzGerald (on whom he has written), A.D. Hope and David Campbell. His novel *Their Solitary Way* (1985) won a Best First Book Award in 1985.

CROGGON, Alison (1962–   ), born South Africa, came to Australia at the age of 7, was educated at Ballarat and worked as a cadet journalist on the Melbourne *Herald*. She has been a freelance journalist and a Melbourne theatre critic for the *Bulletin*. Her poetry, published in Australian and overseas journals, was performed at La Mama in 1988 as a theatrical presentation (*NOTES*). Her first collection of poems, *This is the Stone*, was published in 1991 (a shared volume with Fiona Perry's *Pharaohs Returning*). An intimately personal volume traversing a range of women's experience, *This is the Stone* is a sensitive, intelligent and deeply emotional collection. Its final series 'Quickening', with its sections 'Family Notes', 'Love Poems', 'Domestic Art' and 'Howl', is highly impressive.

CROLL, R.H. (Robert Henderson) (1869–1947), born Stawell, Victoria, combined a long career on the administrative staff of the Victorian Education Department with an unusually active participation in literary, artistic, bushwalking and educational organisations. One of Melbourne's best-known men of letters and a prolific contributor of verse and prose to Australian newspapers and journals, Croll published numerous works including *By-products: A Book of Verses* (1932), *The Open Road in Victoria* (1928), *Along the Track* (?1930), *Tom Roberts* (1935), *Wide Horizons: Wanderings in Central Australia* (1937) and *I Recall: Collections and Recollections* (1939). He edited *Collected Poems of John Shaw Neilson* (1934), *Smike to Bulldog* (1946, letters of Sir Arthur Streeton to Tom Roberts), and collaborated with Percival Serle and 'Furnley Maurice' to produce *An Australasian Anthology* (1927).

CROYSTON, John (1933–   ), born Enfield, Sydney, spent most of his career with the ABC as director, producer and editor. His own work includes *23 Poems* (1953, with Julian Woods); a verse drama, 'The Hills Shall Fly', and several plays.

CUMPSTON, Amy (1921–   ), born Melbourne, has been a writer for television and director of the International Theatre Forum. She has published poetry, *Human, My Race* (1955), *Borrow the Spring* (1961), *The Towers of Earth: Poems of the Blue Mountains*

(1969); and drama, *This Fatal Island* (1973) and *Woodrow Wilson* (1973). As Amy Mac-Grath she has published the verse collections *Australia My Home* (1991) and *Canberra, Home* (1992), and a fictionalised study of Kublai Khan, *Free From All Curses* (1983).

CUTHBERTSON, James Lister (1851–1910), born Glasgow, Scotland, came to Australia in 1875 and taught at Geelong Grammar School for most of the period 1875–96. His *Grammar School Verses* appeared in 1879 and his slim book of poetry, *Barwon Ballads*, in 1893; a memorial edition of his poems, *Barwon Ballads and School Verses*, edited by E.T. Williams, was published in 1912. His poem 'The Australian Sunrise' has been frequently anthologised. A dedicated school-master who helped to meld English school ways and methods to the Australian character and environment, Cuthbertson made a deep impression on the Geelong Grammar School where his memory is still revered.

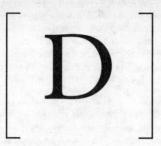

D'ARCY-IRVINE, Gerard Addington (1862–1932), born London, went with his family to NZ before moving to Goulburn, NSW, where his father conducted a school. He entered the Anglican ministry and was consecrated coadjutor bishop of Sydney in 1926. In 1899 he published his first verse collection, *Poems*, followed by *Additional Poems* in 1901 and a further collection, *Poems*, in 1903. In 1905 an illustrated edition of his work was produced and it was later reprinted and enlarged. His final volume, *Analects*, appeared in 1923. D'Arcy-Irvine preached at Henry Lawson's funeral.

DADSWELL, Mary (1943–) grew up in Sale, Victoria, and has lived and travelled in various countries in Europe and the USA. She graduated B.Litt. from the ANU, Canberra, where she now lives, and has worked as a nurse, teacher/librarian, proof-reader, jazz piano teacher and as the director of Canberra's first gallery for art photography. Her short stories and poems have appeared in newspapers, periodicals and anthologies and have won various awards including the FAW John Shaw Neilson Poetry Award, and have been published in one collection, *Circles of Faces* (1987).

DALEY, Victor ('Creeve Roe') (1858–1905), born County Meath, Ireland, came to Australia at the age of 20. For several years he roamed southern Australia as an itinerant journalist, but from 1882 began to establish himself as a popular lyric poet, contributing to *Punch*, *Freeman's Journal* and the *Bulletin*. In 1898 he published his first book of verse, *At Dawn and Dusk*; the Sydney literary coterie used the title for their bohemian Dawn and Dusk Club. With fellow poet Roderic Quinn he was part of the so-called 'Celtic Twilight', a small enclave of lyrical romanticism amid the intense nationalistic-radical writing and the noisy bush balladry that dominated the literary scene of the day. Although he, too, was a radical poet his chief poetic love was 'the shining shallows' of the lyric. After his early death from tuberculosis, several further volumes of his poetry were published – *Poems* (1908, a miniature edition), *Wine and Roses* (1911, ed. Bertram Stevens), *Creeve Roe* (1947), a selection of his radical verse edited by Muir Holburn and Marjorie Pizer, and *Victor Daley* (1963), edited by H.J. Oliver. A.G. Stephens wrote the biography *Victor Daley* (1905).

DALZIEL, Kathleen (1881–1969), born Kathleen Walker at Durban, South Africa, came to Australia at the age of 6 and lived in an isolated area of north-west Tasmania, where her parents were farmers. After her marriage she lived in Victoria and regularly contributed verse to the *Bulletin* after receiving encouragement from J.F. Archibald. Later she contributed to several American, English and Australian anthologies and periodicals, but continued to publish regularly in the *Bulletin*. Her verse appeared in one collection, *Known and Not Held* (1941).

DAVIES, Rowland (Lyttleton Archer) (1837–80), born Longford, Tasmania, the son of an archdeacon, studied engineering in England and pursued his profession in Tasmania, NZ and Victoria. He was also one of Australia's earliest poets although he preserved few of his manuscripts. Writing in the tradition of Wordsworth and the Victorian poets, he attempted with some success to express his affinity for the Australian landscape, though he failed to reach the same heights as Harpur and Kendall. A selection of his poetry was published in 1884, titled *Poems and Other Literary Remains*, edited with a biographical sketch by Charles Tomlinson.

DAVIS, Norma (1905–45), born Glenore, Tasmania, began her writing career by publishing verse in the *Woman's Mirror* under such pseudonyms as Norelda, Glenarvon, Malda, Malda Norris and Normalda as well as her own name. She also contributed to the *Bulletin, Meanjin, Poetry* and *Jindyworobak Anthology* and published two collections before her early death from cancer, *Earth Cry* (1943) and *I, the Thief* (1944). Davis's poetry, which reflects her passion for the Tasmanian bush and resembles that of Shaw Neilson in sensitivity and delicacy, won praise from such critics as Douglas Stewart, H.M. Green and E. Morris Miller.

DAWE, Bruce (1930–   ), born Geelong, Victoria, left high school at 16, a dissatisfied and uninterested student. A variety of briefly held jobs followed until he completed adult matriculation at night classes in 1953 and began a university course in 1954. Although he left the University of Melbourne after a year, that period had a significant influence on his developing literary interests. Of particular importance was his association with Philip Martin, whose continuing friendship and literary expertise have been acknowledged by Dawe as important in his own development as a poet. He was also associated with *MUM* (*Melbourne University Magazine*), *Compass* and *Farrago*, in the last of which he published the 'Joey Cassidy' stories. After a period as factory worker in Sydney and postman in Melbourne, he joined the RAAF. During his service (1959–68) he published two volumes of poetry, married a Toowoomba girl (Gloria) and completed his first degree (he now holds an MA and Ph.D.). In 1971 he became a teacher at Toowoomba's Downlands College, in 1972 a lecturer at the Darling Downs Institute of Advanced Education and was associate professor of literary studies at the University College of Southern Queensland at Toowoomba 1990–93. Dawe has written prolifically. His poetry volumes are *No Fixed Address* (1962); *A Need of Similar Name* (1965, the Myer Award for Poetry); *An Eye for a Tooth* (1968, the Sidney Myer Charity Trust Award for Poetry); *Beyond the Subdivisions* (1969); *Heat-Wave* (1970); *Condolences of the Season: Selected Poems* (1971); *Just a Dugong at Twilight: Mainly Light Verse* (1975); *Sometimes Gladness: Collected Poems 1954–1978* (the 1979 Grace Leven Prize for Poetry; second and third editions in 1983 and 1988); *Towards Sunrise: Poems 1979–1986* (1986) and *This Side of Silence* (1990). He has also written short fiction, *Over Here Harv! and Other Stories* (1983), which is a collection of the 'Joey Cassidy' and other stories; edited the poetry anthology *Dimensions* (1974) and selected and edited Old and New Testament parables, Rabbinic, Hindu, Buddhist and Islamic parables in *Speaking in Parables* (1987). Ken Goodwin collected Dawe's prose writings – essays, letters, radio broadcasts and interviews – as well as critical articles about him and his poetry in *Essays and Opinions* (1990). Goodwin also wrote *Adjacent Worlds: A Literary Life of Bruce Dawe* (1988). There are two recordings of Dawe reading from his own poetry, 1971 and 1983. Among his many awards are the Patrick White Award in 1980 and the FAW Christopher Brennan Award in 1983. He was made AO in 1992 for his contribution to Australian literature, especially poetry.

In a CLF lecture in 1964 Dawe regretted the lack of 'social awareness' in contemporary Australian poetry. His own poetry, by contrast, is one of unremitting social concern; it criticises governments, regimes, institutions and modes of life which oppress and deprive; its concern is for individuals, 'the lost people in our midst for whom no one speaks', and for modern man in general, 'homo suburbiensis', for whom happiness and meaning in life are mostly withheld. The early poems berate totalitarianism in 'Only the Beards are Different' and 'The Not-so-good Earth'; the church (Dawe was a convert to Roman Catholicism) in 'The Decay of Preaching'; and the self-centred insularity and nationalism of Australia in '"A" is for Asia' and 'Burial Ceremony. Hungary 1956–62'. Dawe's chief criticism, however, is for the oppressive force of modern life – 'one of the main things I would say ... about this awkward proposition known as Life, is that it can be a bit of a bastard.' Life's brevity and meaninglessness are at the heart of 'Enter Without So Much As Knocking' and 'Any Shorter and I'd Have Missed It Altogether'; its pettiness is illustrated in 'Two Ways of Considering the Fog', 'Beatitudes' and in the masterly evocation of Melbourne football mania, 'Life-Cycle'; its unrelenting pressure is exposed in 'Slow Coach' and 'Leasehold'; and its victims are categorised in 'No Fixed Address' (alcoholics), 'Happiness Is the Art of Being Broken' (the aged), 'Good Sport' (the ugly), 'Homecoming' (the casualties of war) and 'The Family Man' (the casualty of domesticity). The totality of human bondage, and Dawe's somewhat rueful recognition that it is a situation beyond mending, are illustrated in the closing words of 'Homo Suburbiensis'. Man's offering to the insatiability of life is all that he has to give: 'time, pain, love, hate, age, war, death, laughter, fever.'

The later poems show that, over three decades, Dawe has neither mellowed nor lost any of his crusading zeal. There are many simple, affectionate poems ('Katrina's Wedding' with its demonstration of a father's love) and compassionate poems where his sympathy is still for the unhappy individual who faces crises, great or small (the Kurdish rebel about to be shot, the mother whose daughter has been abducted, neighbours facing illness and death). The keynote to his later poetry can be found in the Epigraph to *This Side of Silence*, dedicated to 'those students around the world who have fought to free their countries from oppression', recalling Woodrow Wilson's axiom, 'the history of liberty is the history of resistance'. Many poems continue to illustrate the need to fight wherever liberty is at risk, and greed, corruption and the lust for power work against the common good, e.g. the students' struggle for democracy in Tiananmen Square; the world's battle against communism, strikingly triumphant with the fall of the Berlin Wall; the 'green' movement's fight to preserve the land; the need for vigilance against such political corruption as Queensland long experienced. His love of the land makes his own conservation poems both sensitive and appealing; nowhere is that better illustrated than in 'When First the Land Was Ours', where he links humanity and nature in the one great scheme of things:

> For we are part of the shimmering web
> that binds the vast and small,
> and what is done to a single strand
> has meaning to it all

Yet the bitter aftertaste left by contemporary crudities and excesses remains predominant, as the final poem of *This Side of Silence* reveals:

> As typical of these times I would include
> a dirty needle and rip-top can,
> pebbled glass from a windscreen, some spent cartridges,
> a singlet noose fresh from a prisoner's neck,
> a pamphlet proving
> pornography is love, a flash of tears
> from battered women (laced with children's blood) ...

And as a final parting shot at those who indifferently preside over such sordid disasters he cites

> a press release
> from the Bureau of Statistics showing
> things are getting better all the time.

Paradoxically Dawe's poetry is mostly neither sombre nor pessimistic. Humour, usually satirical, introduces a light tone, attractively mingling the serious and the droll. His early poems are invariably brief, succinct and pertinent, 'one-shot' poems that say only as much as they need to. Sometimes they end without the ultimate confrontation, but with a poetic shrug of the shoulders that, in characteristically Australian fashion, implies a laconic acceptance of things as they are. The later poems are less philosophic, much more trenchant, more damning and less humorously tolerant. The later Dawe sees more that is disturbing and, with the passing of time, fewer possibilities of improvement to humanity's overall condition. His articulate and readily understood response to situations and themes is expressed in speech cadences that combine the brashly colloquial of the spoken Australian language (and 'slanguage') with subtle and deftly placed lyricism. His success in blending these apparent incongruities of language is his most remarkable technical achievement. But his achievement as a poet goes far beyond mere technique. As David Headon comments on *This Side of Silence*:

> Bruce Dawe has thumbed his nose at contemporary literary fashion, preferring instead to write as a kind of contemporary prophet within the long and honoured tradition of poetry of commitment . . . His poetry simply and eloquently reinforces what's right in a world of confused moral distinctions and Post-Modernist torpidity.

DAWE, Carlton (1865–1935), born Adelaide, published three volumes of verse and two works of fiction before settling permanently in England from 1892. He then became a prolific writer of popular fiction (romance, mystery, crime) with more than seventy books published over forty years.

Dawnward? (1903), Bernard O'Dowd's first volume of poetry, speculates on the prospects of freedom, equality and fraternity in Australia and ponders the nation's future direction – 'To Failure's midnight sea or Dawnward?' The numerous inflammatory personified poems, e.g. 'Prosperity', 'Hate', 'Compromise' and 'Proletaria', heap abuse upon such enemies of society as 'Vested Rights', 'Mammon', 'Bacchantic Trade' and 'Lamias of Caste'. *Dawnward?* satisfied the radical tenets of O'Dowd's *Poetry Militant* but with its baffling maze of personification and allusion and its mesmerising 'fourteener' stanza it met a puzzled and unsympathetic reception from readers and literary critics of the day.

DAY, Sarah (1958–   ), born Lancashire, England, grew up in Hobart. She has been an English teacher and a teacher of English as a foreign language, both in Sydney and at the University of Tasmania. She has published three books of poetry: *A Hunger to be Less Serious* (1987), which won the Anne Elder Award for a first volume of poetry, *A Madder Dance* (1991) in the Australian Poetry series, and *Sarah Day* (1990) in The Pamphlet Poets series of the National Library of Australia.

DEAMER, Dulcie (1890–1972), born Christchurch, NZ, actor, freelance journalist, dramatist and writer of fiction, was a well-known figure in Sydney bohemian and literary society in the 1920s and 1930s. She published a book of short stories, *In the Beginning: Six Studies of the Stone Age and Other Stories* (1909). Her novels include *The Suttee of Safa: A Hindoo Romance* (1913), *Revelation* (1921), *The Street of the Gazelle* (1922), *The Devil's Saint* (1924) and *Holiday* (1940). Her two volumes of poetry are *Messalina* (1932), the first section, 'Nine Women', comprising portraits of classical or historically significant women; and *The Silver Branch* (1948), elaborately phrased verses.

'Dedication, A' is the opening poem of Adam Lindsay Gordon's final volume *Bush Ballads and Galloping Rhymes* (1870). The dedication was to English novelist G.J. Whyte-Melville, whose popular adventure novels appealed to Gordon. The chief interest in Gordon's lines is his reluctant admission that Australia, to which he had been exiled, had helped to inspire his verse. Despite his well-known but inaccurate claim that Australia is a land 'where bright blossoms are scentless/ And songless bright birds', Gordon makes, in the lines beginning 'In the Spring, when the wattle gold trembles', one of his rare acknowledgments of the land's natural beauty.

DEEBLE, R.J. (Russell John) (1944–   ), born Melbourne, has published several books of verse including *War Babies and Other Poems* (1965), *A Trip to Light Blue* (1968), *High on a Horse with Wax Wings* (1969), *You* (1970), *Just Before Eyelight* (1979), *A Poem That Wants to Be Painted* (1979) and *Aqualine and Other Poems* (1980).

DENNIS, C.J. (Clarence Michael James) (1876–1938), born Auburn, SA, spent much of his boyhood in the care of four maiden aunts. He worked briefly as a solicitor's clerk, was a journalist on the Adelaide weekly the *Critic*, filled in as barman at his father's hotel in Laura and then drifted off to become an odd-jobman about the mines of Broken Hill. Returning to Adelaide, he later became editor of the *Critic* and in 1906 commenced the short-lived satirical journal the *Gadfly*. In 1908 after a miserable period in Melbourne as a freelance journalist, he went with the artist Hal Waugh to Toolangi, an isolated timber settlement not far from Healesville north-east of Melbourne. At Toolangi, living in a tent and later in a timber-getter's hut, he worked hard at his writing, mainly, in his own words, 'to fend off the blues'. In 1913 he published through Cole's Book Arcade of Melbourne his first book of verse, *Backblock Ballads and Other Verses*, with a cover designed by the cartoonist David Low. The book was not successful so Dennis went off on a spree to Sydney, working there on the union journal the *Labour Call*, but was back in Melbourne early in 1915. From four verse stories of 'The Sentimental Bloke' in the *Backblock Ballads* he conceived the idea of a separate series, and late in 1915 *The Songs of a Sentimental Bloke* was published with an explanatory glossary 'for the thoroughly genteel'. Dennis's story of the young larrikin, Bill, who is enticed from his life with the 'push' to domestic bliss on a berry farm with his 'ideal bit o' skirt', Doreen, rapidly became popular, bringing fame and affluence to its creator. It sold more than 60 000 copies in Australia in less than eighteen months. A sequel dealing with the adventures of Ginger Mick, the Bloke's friend and 'best man', titled *The Moods of Ginger Mick*, was published in October 1916. In an inspired move Dennis had Ginger Mick answer the 'Call of the Stoush' and go off to 'the flamin' war' as so many young Australians had done. The book, and Mick, went straight to the hearts of the Australian soldiers serving overseas and the pocket editions of both *The Sentimental Bloke* and *Ginger Mick* were treasured possessions of many homesick diggers. In 1917, the year that Dennis married Olive Herron, he published the very different work *The Glugs of Gosh*, a satire on such pretentious community figures as lord mayors, councillors and petty government officials.

Dennis tried to repeat the Bloke and Ginger Mick formula with *Doreen* (1917), which looked at the lovers of *The Sentimental Bloke* in their married roles; and with *Digger Smith* (1918), the adventures of one of Mick's mates on Gallipoli who returned to Australia, not to the slums of Collingwood where he had been born but to the freshness and beauty of the Australian bush. But the public's love affair with the racy, vernacular verse was over. An attempt in 1924 to revive the passion with *Rose of Spadgers*, the saga of Ginger Mick's girl-friend of bygone days, also failed. Dennis's other works include the 'Australaise', a marching song (1908); the verse narrative *Jim of the Hills* (1919), a timber-getter's story told with only a smattering of exaggerated colloquialisms; a revised and enlarged *Backblock Ballads and Later Verses* (1918); *A Book for Kids* (1921), a whimsical mixture of verse and prose; and *The Singing Garden* (1935), prose and verse which reflect Dennis's long-sustained devotion to the landscape around Arden, his home at Toolangi. From 1922 until his death he held the highly unusual position of staff poet with the Melbourne *Herald*. His many contributions of prose and verse to the *Herald* include 'Epistles to Ab', a series of letters from a farmer to his son in the city; the 'Ben Bowyang' series; and the 'Miss Mix' series, snippets from the gossipy but deadly accurate pen of a country town seamstress.

After Dennis's death enthusiastic eulogies saluted him as Australia's national poet, one who had captured much of the essential Australian spirit. Prime Minister Joseph Lyons referred to him as the 'Robbie Burns of Australia'. Much of that adulation evaporated as the years passed and Dennis's ingenious verse came to be looked on as a literary curiosity, an idiosyncratic expression of the intense nationalism that gripped Australia from the 1890s until after the First World War. Some Australians found the Bloke and Ginger Mick nationally embarrassing and thus ignored them, while even well-disposed readers were puzzled by the extraordinary and exaggerated idiom and were doubtful about the authenticity of the central characters, larrikins with hearts of gold. The well-publicised Dennis centenary (1976), which was accompanied by a successful musical version of *The Sentimental Bloke* for television, and the later stage performances of John Derum, *More Than a Sentimental Bloke* (published in book form in 1990), have sparked a revival of interest in his work. Its ability to convey the quality of 'wit' in down-to-earth Australian humour makes it an integral part of this country's folk-literature. But there is more to it than that. Beneath its seemingly trite and banal surface there is, at times, a pathos, an appreciation of the foibles of human nature and a sophistication of thought that explores some of the complex issues of life. Henry Lawson, well qualified to judge talent and achievement in this area of literature, paid Dennis a significant tribute in the foreword to the first edition of *The Songs of a Sentimental Bloke*, when he echoed the Bloke's own words – 'I dips me lid.' Dennis was commemorated by the C.J. Dennis Award, an annual award (from 1976) provided by the Victorian government and administered by the Victorian branch of the FAW for a book about Australian natural history. Recently the C.J. Dennis Award has been for poetry and is one of the Victorian Premier's annual literary awards. A.H. Chisholm published the biography *The Making of a Sentimental Bloke* (1946); 'Margaret Herron' (Dennis's wife Olive), *Down the Years* (1953); I.F. MacLaren, *C.J. Dennis* (1961); and G.W. Hutton, *C.J. Dennis, the Sentimental Bloke* (1976). Barry Watts edited *The World of the Sentimental Bloke* (1976), which contains A.H. Chisholm's 'The Remarkable Career of C.J. Dennis' and articles by such associates of Dennis as David Low and R.H. Croll, together with excerpts from *The Sentimental Bloke* and *The Moods of Ginger Mick*. The first film of *The Sentimental Bloke* was the Raymond Longford 1919 production. A special screening of that film was given at the Cannes International Film Festival in 1987. Dennis wrote the screen play for F.W. Thring's 1932 film of *The Sentimental Bloke*.

DEPASQUALE, Paul (1938–   ), born Lockleys, Adelaide, of Italian parents, was a teacher 1959–70 and since 1974 has been a bookseller and publisher. He has published short stories, *In the Land of the Devil's Promise* (1962) and *Angelo* (1979); and verse, *The Will to Dream* (1968, with Janeen Samuel), *A Lonely, Venturesome Outgoing* (1969), *The Mad Priest Meditates* (1982), *The Dying Dago's Dance of Death* (1982), *The Mad Priest Foams with Rage* (1983), *The Dying Dago Dances Again* (1984) and *Love Songs for Vernon Knowles* (1985). His historical/critical publications include A *Critical History of South Australian Literature 1836–1930* (1978). Depasquale has also edited *Labor's Bard: the Broken Hill Poems of Tom Black* (1985) and *Selected Poems of Paul McGuire* (1980).

DERHAM, Enid (1882–1941), born Hawthorn, Melbourne, was educated at the universities of Melbourne and Oxford and held lecturing appointments in the department of English at Melbourne. A lyric poet, she published *The Mountain Road and Other Verses* (1912); a posthumous selection, *Poems* (1958), reveals her to be a poet of hitherto unsuspected emotional intensity.

DEVANEY, James (1890–1976), born Bendigo, Victoria, was educated in Sydney,

at St Joseph's College, where he entered the Marist Brothers juniorate in 1904. He
took his final vows in 1915. He was a teacher in several Australian States and NZ and a
tutor on outback stations before severe tuberculosis led to his departure from the order
in 1921 and sent him permanently to Queensland to full-time writing and journalism.
From 1924 to 1943 he published a weekly column of nature notes for the Brisbane
Courier-Mail under the pseudonym 'Fabian'. For years a leading literary figure in
Queensland, he was president of the Queensland Authors' and Artists' Association
(later the FAW) and gave CLF lectures on Australian literature in 1947.

Devaney's unpretentious, traditional lyric poetry, well regarded by contemporary
critics, began with the volume *Fabian* (1923), written during a period of ill health and
religious doubts. The chief poem, 'The Lost Love', reflects his mood of the time,
personal disquiet and a loss of delight in the natural world. *Earth Kindred* (1931) reveals
the delight regained, the disquiet gone. *Dark Road* (1938), a privately printed edition
of twenty-five copies which is now extremely rare, consists of six deeply personal
poems written in tribute to his wife, his nurse during his tubercular illness in Dia-
mantina hospital. From his later volumes, *Debutantes* (1939), *Where the Wind Goes*
(1939) and *Freight of Dreams* (1946), Devaney selected the bulk of the verses chosen for
his *Poems* (1950), a volume of wistful, pensive, melodious lyrics. Devaney also wrote
fiction, *The Currency Lass* (1927), *The Vanished Tribes* (1929) and *Washdirt* (1946). His
critical credo, *Poetry in Our Time* (1952), with its emphasis on the maintenance of
recognisable form and rhythm and the need for beauty and lucidity, was seen by some
as reactionary, but it embodied all that Devaney stood for. A friend and mentor of
John Shaw Neilson in his final years, Devaney wrote the biographical *Shaw Neilson*
(1944) and edited *Unpublished Poems of Shaw Neilson* (1947).

DIESENDORF, Margaret (1912–93), born and educated (MA, D.Phil.) in Vienna,
Austria, came to Australia in 1939. A gifted linguist, educationist, translator, editor
and creative writer, she played an active role in the Sydney literary scene for several
decades and later in Canberra; she was, for example, associate editor of *Poetry Australia*
in 1967–81 and during that time was also associate editor of the American magazine
Creative Moment. She received the Pacific Books Publishers 'Best Poems' Awards for
1972 and 1973 and the Borestone Mountain Poetry Award for 1974 and 1976. Widely
featured in anthologies and journals, she published *Light: Poems by Margaret Diesendorf*
(1981) and *Holding the Golden Apple* (1991), a collection of love poems, in which love
takes a myriad forms and is directed at many objects. Tributes to her are Gwen Harwood's 'Three Poems to Margaret Diesendorf', Grace Perry's 'Translation' and Philip
Grundy's 'To a Trilingual Poet'. She translated the work of Rilke into English, of
A.D. Hope into French, of Grace Perry into German as well as other works, e.g.
Rosemary Dobson's *Child with Cockatoo* into French.

DOBSON, Rosemary (1920–   ), born Sydney, joined the publishing firm Angus &
Robertson during the Second World War, working as editor and reader with Beatrice
Davis, Douglas Stewart and Nan McDonald. She has also been an art historian and
teacher. She has published numerous books of poetry: *In A Convex Mirror* (1944); *The
Ship of Ice* (1948); *Child with a Cockatoo* (1955); *Cock Crow* (1965); *Selected Poems* (1973, a
further edition in 1980); *Three Poems on Water Springs* (1973); *Greek Coins: A Sequence of
Poems* (1977); *Over the Frontier* (1978); *The Continuance of Poetry* (1981); *The Three Fates
and Other Poems* (1984); *Collected Poems* (1991) and *Untold Lives* (1992). Her poetry has
also been featured in the Australian Poets series (1963) and in the Australian National
Library's Pamphlet Poets series (1990). Her other publications include anthologies,
Songs for All Seasons: 100 Poems for Young People (1967); *Australian Voices, Poetry and
Prose of the 1970s* (1975) and *Sisters Poets I* (1979); *Moscow Trefoil* (1975, translations with
David Campbell and Natalie Staples of the Russian poets Anna Akhmatova and Osip
Mandelstam); *Seven Russian Poets* (1979, with David Campbell, versions or imitations

of poems from the Russian); *Summer Press* (1987), a novel for young adults; radio
scripts, essays and articles on various writers and artists and two critical works, *Focus on
Ray Crooke* (1971) and *A World of Difference: Australian Poetry and Painting in the 1940s*
(1973). A selection of her poems, *L'Enfant en Cacatoès*, translated by Louis Dautheuil
and Margaret Diesendorf, was published in 1967 in the series *Autour du Monde*.

The love of art, antiquity and mythology are in Dobson's poetry from the beginning. Endymion, Botticelli, Mars, Prometheus, Daphne, van Eyck, Brueghel, Icarus,
Raphael, Giotto, Calvi, Vermeer are but some of her early passing parade of artists and
mythical figures. In *Child with a Cockatoo* there is a group of fifteen 'Poems from
Paintings' (her favourite device is poems in series) and of them 'Paintings' emphasises
her conviction of the supremacy of Art over Time:

> Climate of stillness: though I hear
> No sound that falls on mortal ear
> Yet in the intricate, devised
> Hearing of sight these waves that break
> In thunder on a barren shore
> Will foam and crash for evermore
>
> .   .   .
>
> And you, grave Florentine, who turn
> And look at me with eyes that burn,
> I hear you asking – 'What is Time
> Since Art has conquered it? I speak
> Five hundred years ago. You hear.
> My words beat still upon your ear.'

Many of her poems – 'Still Life', 'Young Girl at a Window', 'Over the Hill', 'In a
Cafe', 'Painter of Antwerp' – are themselves word paintings, capturing moments of
existence frozen in time. Personal experiences – family ties, wife and motherhood –
take precedence in *Cock Crow*, with 'Child of Our Time', 'Out of Winter', 'Annun-
ciations', 'To Meet the Child' and 'To a Child', for example, being sensitive and
deeply poetic expressions of maternal love. 'Cock Crow', the title poem, portrays the
dilemma of divided loyalties – those owed to others and that owed to oneself. Self
appears, briefly, likely to prevail:

> And walking up and down the road
> Knew myself, separate and alone,
> Cut off from human cries, from pain
> And love that grows about the bone

It is only a momentary resolution. The daughter–mother 'love that grows about the
bone' has the final claim.

In the sequence 'The Devil and the Angel' Dobson displays a deft touch of whimsy
and fantasy with the Devil and an angel competing for the souls of those departing
from this life. There is a similar captivating jauntiness in 'The Sailor: May 1960',
which tells of a sailor, tired of the seafaring life, shouldering his oar and marching
inland, across the Great Divide, through many a 'one-horse town' and on across the
vast inland stock routes until finally he is asked 'What's that, mate, tied up on your
back?' There he stays, his journey ended. Ruefully the poet proposes making a similar
journey with a gun on her shoulder.

Several of Rosemary Dobson's smaller books of poetry have been published by her
husband Alec Bolton's Brindabella Press – Officina Brindabella – *Three Poems on
Water Springs, Greek Coins: A Sequence of Poems, The Continuance of Poetry* and *Untold
Lives. Greek Coins* comprises twenty four-line poems each of which sets out 'a visual
idea which could be contained within a circle – that is, within the coin-sized four line
stanza'. The poems, accompanied by her own line drawings, reflect her attachment to
Greek themes, love of antiquity and admiration for the wisdom and perception of the

Greek traveller Pausanias, who wrote a guide to Greece in the second century AD. *Over the Frontier* contains a section 'Poems from Pausanias', which includes the Greek Coins poems. *The Continuance of Poetry* (1981) contains another small series, twelve poems written after the death of fellow poet David Campbell. Simple, restrained poems, they recall pleasant times of friendship, returning often to the belief that those shared moments live still, in memory and in the continuing presence of Campbell's poetry. *The Continuance of Poetry* is contained also in *The Three Fates and Other Poems*, as is another poem of friendship, 'A Letter to Lydia', which moves beyond the personal to echo again Dobson's love of the classical past and the ancient lands, Greece and Crete. There is, in her later poetry, the occasional measured glance at approaching death and a sharper awareness of mortality but her joy and wonder at the treasure still to be gleaned from art, poetry, the loveliness of nature and the continuing miracle of life are undiminished. While there is life there is direction and purpose.

> Learn still; take, reject,
> Choose, use, create,
> Put past to present purpose. Make.

The *Collected Poems*, chosen from her earliest ('I have stood by the poet that I was') to her latest volumes, brings together about 200 poems written over half a century. They represent, as has been aptly said, 'a lifework of love and dedication to the craft of writing'. If that craftsmanship has often led to her classification as a poet's poet, the unassuming tone, lucid style and honest, direct presentation of her work make her also a reader's poet. Recognition of Rosemary Dobson's poetry has accumulated over many years. She won the *Sydney Morning Herald* Award for Poetry in 1948 for 'The Ship of Ice', the FAW Christopher Brennan Award in 1978, the Patrick White Award in 1984, the Grace Leven Poetry Prize in 1984 and shared the Victorian Premier's Literary Award in 1985, the last two with *The Three Fates*. She was made an honorary life member of the Association for the Study of Australian Literature and AO in 1987 for her outstanding contribution to Australian literature.

DOWNES, Marion Grace (?–1926), was the author of four novels, *Swayed by the Storm* (1911), *A Brave Bush Girl* (1912), *Flower o' the Bush* (1914) and *In the Track of the Sunset* (1919); and two volumes of poetry, *Wayside Songs for Women* (1921) and *Wayside Songs* (1927). Her verse, largely on religious themes and expressing the conventional attitudes of the period, was published in journals both in England and Australia and won an appreciative audience.

DRANSFIELD, Michael (1948–73), born Sydney, educated at Sydney Grammar School and, briefly, at the University of Sydney, worked intermittently on several newspapers and was for a time a government clerk. His short, restless adult life was spent largely in bohemian areas of Sydney (Balmain, Paddington, Darlinghurst), in the country at Cobargo and Candelo, NSW, or wandering over eastern Australia from Queensland to Tasmania. Failing to discover a meaningful role for himself in conventional society, Dransfield vainly sought an alternative in the drug culture. After a motor-cycle accident in April 1972 his health deteriorated and he died, aged 24. Dransfield published three volumes of poetry, *Streets of the Long Voyage* (1970), *The Inspector of Tides* (1972) and *Drug Poems* (1972). A further collection largely prepared by him, *Memoirs of a Velvet Urinal*, was published posthumously in 1975. About 600 other poems, collated and edited by Rodney Hall, were brought together in two volumes, *Voyage into Solitude* (1978, poems from the period 1969–71) and *The Second Month of Spring* (1980, poems from 1972). Dransfield's *Collected Poems* was also edited by Hall in 1987. First published in the late 1960s in the underground magazines that arose in criticism of the conservative nature of Australian poetry, Dransfield's talented verse soon became a regular feature of more established newspapers and journals. The consistent themes of his poetry include protest against the quality of contemporary Australian life, especially the monotony and regimentation of an urban existence; the drug culture and the addiction process; life's fragility; loneliness; the importance of human relationships; and the clash between an innate romantic spirit and the ugliness of contemporary life. *Streets of the Long Voyage*, his first and perhaps his most effective body of verse, won the University of Newcastle special Award for a work of literature by an Australian writer under 30. It contains the 'Courland Penders' group of poems; important drug poems such as 'Overdose', 'Fix' and 'Bum's Rush'; protest poems such as 'Lamentations' and 'That Which We Call a Rose'; and love poems such as 'Parthenogenesis', 'July with Her' and 'Dread Was'. Despite his view of himself as a radical figure, and some unconventional use of punctuation, typography and drug culture jargon, Dransfield's technique was only superficially *avant-garde*. In fact the influence of poets such as Tennyson and Swinburne is clearly seen in his work, both in structure and sensibility; his innovation was, in Geoff Page's words, his 'distinctly personal combination of certain traditional elements'. The best of his poetry combines lyrical beauty with a directness of expression and emotional honesty, as in 'That Which We Call a Rose' –

> 'I dremt of next week perhaps then we would eat
>   again sleep
> in a house again
> perhaps we would wake to find humanity where
>   at present
> freedom is obsolete and honour a heresy. Innocently
> I dremt that madness passes like a dream'.

Dransfield's later poetry is uneven in quality. Reluctant to revise his verse, he preferred to rely on his first inspiration, and is quoted as saying 'I operate on feelings, not thoughts'. Critics have also been irritated by his focus on stock counter-culture complaints; protest poems such as 'Endsong' and 'Prosperity' in *The Inspector of Tides* rail against pollution, commerce, urban ugliness and insensitive governments. In a slightly patronising fashion, Dransfield distanced himself from other, established 'Official Poets' who also voiced their dismay, but, he felt, merely in 'genteel iambics'. *Drug Poems*, which contains poems from earlier volumes, is both an insight into the process of addiction and an acknowledgment of the isolation and despair that face the addict. The final volume, *The Second Month of Spring*, consists mainly of poems written in the last few months of his life. They are angry and tragic expressions of his desperate attempts to survive the forces engulfing him. As a poet who expressed the anger and disillusionment of many of his generation, Dransfield's status as an anti-establishment cult figure was enhanced by his untimely death. His relatively small body of work, however, is sufficient to establish him as a gifted poet with an important place in the main-stream of Australian poetry. Livio Dobrez published *Parnassus Mad Ward: Michael Dransfield and the New Australian Poetry* (1990).

Drug Poems (1972), a collection by Michael Dransfield, gives an insight into the drug culture. Poems such as 'Bum's Rush', 'Fix', 'Overdose', 'Jam' and 'Getting Out' comment on many aspects of the drug experience – the isolation of the addict, the need for the 'fix', the terror of withdrawal and the difficulty of returning to normality.

DUGAN, Michael Gray (1947–   ), born Melbourne, has been involved with books and writing all his adult life. He was closely associated with the rise of the 'New Australian Poetry', produced the small magazine *Crosscurrents*, was involved in Contempa Publications with Robert Kenny and Phillip Edmonds, and edited *The Drunken Tram: Six Young Melbourne Poets* (1972). He has written and edited numerous children's books. Among his many publications are *Missing People* (1970), *Clouds* (1975), *Nonsense Places* (1976), *Dragon's Breath* (1978), *Dingo Boy* (1980), *Melissa's Ghost* (1986), *The Maltese Connection* (1988), *The Highjacked Bathtub* (1988) and *The Wombats' Party* (1990).

DUGGAN, Laurie (1949–), born South Melbourne, graduated from Monash University, lectured at Swinburne College (1976) and Canberra College of Advanced Education (1983) and was art critic for the *Times on Sunday* (1986–87). He went on the Australia Council and Department of Foreign Affairs reading tour of the USA in 1987 and spent a year (1990) at the Australian Centre of the University of Melbourne. He has written film scripts but his chief publications have been poetry: *East: Poems 1970–1974* (1976) which won the Anne Elder Poetry Award, the title poem 'East' having won the Poetry Society of Australia Award in 1971; *Under the Weather* (1978); *Adventures in Paradise* (1982); *The Great Divide* (1985); *The Ash Range* (1987); *The Epigrams of Martial* (1989, winner of the Wesley Michel Prize); *All Blues* (1989, a pamphlet of poems published in London) and *Blue Notes* (1990), which contains some of the poems from *All Blues*. *The Ash Range* won the 1988 Victorian Premier's Award; a historical anthology celebrating Gippsland, the home of Duggan's forebears, it gathers together in a poetry/prose schema many documents such as diaries, letters, maps, journal extracts, newspaper clippings and articles containing the history and legendry of Gippsland. *Blue Notes*, Duggan's latest poetry collection, contains four sections, 'All Blues', 'Trans-Europe Express', 'Dogs' and 'More Blues', all widely varied in form and theme. There are also translations of the Italian Futurist poets and a concluding nine-part poem, 'The Front', which deals in part with the art of making poetry or music in the face of 'prevailing imagery'. In earlier days Duggan was associated with the magazines *New Poetry*, *Surfers Paradise* and *Three Blind Mice*, and confesses that it was the Ern Malley poems which initiated him into the excitement of post-modernism. In 1994 he was appointed poetry editor of *Meanjin*.

DUKE, Jas. H. (James Hercot) (1939–92), born Ballarat, where his father was a teacher, became a laboratory assistant for the Department of Supply, then was a technical officer at the Melbourne and Metropolitan Board of Works. Such seemingly conservative occupations belied the real Jas. H. Duke, who left Australia in revolt against the Vietnam War (living in Brighton, England 1970–72) and, radically oriented through his Irish ancestry, kept up, on his return, a constant barrage of criticism in his writing against governments and governmental institutions, greedy and corrupt professionals and an uncaring society. A cult figure in the performance poetry milieu, Duke, beefy, bald and bearded, began, as he said, as 'a timid person with a stutter', but was converted by his anger and indignation into 'a bellowing bull, noted for my vehemence and intensity'. An ardent advocate of a change of direction for Australian poetry in the late 1960s poetry revolution, Duke published the best of his own poetry in *Poems of War and Peace* (1987), an impressive if esoteric work which, in mostly anecdotal verse, examines aspects of the Second World War and the shortcomings of contemporary society. It also contains a section of 'Concrete' poems, another of translations, and some extracts from *Destiny Wood*, a novel which Duke wrote in England but did not publish until 1978 in Australia. After his accidental death in 1992 a CD of Duke in performance poetry mode (claimed to be Australia's first poetry CD) was launched by fellow poet Alan Wearne, who balances one picture of Duke, as mad scientist and way-out poet, with his assessment as 'learned, committed and passionate'.

Dunciad Minor, a lengthy, mock-heroic satire in the eighteenth-century manner by A.D. Hope published in 1970, is based on an earlier, mainly unpublished work of 1950 titled 'Dunciad Minimus'. In 1950 when both Hope and A.A. Phillips took part in a series of radio broadcasts titled 'Standard Works I'd Like to Burn', Phillips's denunciation of Alexander Pope presented Hope with an ideal opportunity to write a modern *Dunciad*. Arthur Phillips, presented by Hope as descended from the infamous Ambrose Philips, is only nominally the butt of the satire, the main brunt of which is borne by modern literary criticism in general. Witty and lively and equipped with the required superstructure of footnotes, the poem is both an amusing *jeu d'esprit* and a serious criticism of academic pedantry.

DUNLOP, Eliza Hamilton (1796–1880), born County Armagh, Ireland, arrived in Australia in 1823 accompanied by four of her children and her second husband, David Dunlop, who was police magistrate and protector of the Aborigines at Wollombi and Macdonald River until 1847. A literary figure of considerable standing in her period, Eliza Dunlop had previously published poetry in Irish newspapers such as the *Dublin Penny Journal* and in Australia published lyrics in such newspapers as the *Australian*, the *Sydney Gazette*, the *Sydney Morning Herald*, the *Sydney Standard*, the *Atlas* and the *Maitland Mercury*; some were collected and titled 'The Vase', a manuscript which remains unpublished. Sympathetic to the plight of the Aborigines and interested in their culture, Dunlop was the first Australian poet to attempt transliterations of Aboriginal songs and poetry, and she carried out valuable research into Aboriginal languages. Her best-known poem is 'The Aboriginal Mother', a response to the Myall Creek massacre, which was first published in the *Australian* on 13 December 1838 and is one of several which were set to music by Isaac Nathan. It is reprinted in a selection of her poetry titled *The Aboriginal Mother and Other Poems* (1981).

DUNN, Max (1895–1963), born Dublin and educated in Scotland, France and America, came to Australia in 1924, having served in the First World War. An impressive intellectual with a somewhat obscure background, Dunn played numerous roles in the Melbourne scene in the years before and during the Second World War. He was a psychotherapist, a journalist with the *Argus*, *Smith's Weekly* and other papers and magazines, a publisher and a poet. His books of poetry include *Random Elements* (1943), *No Asterisks* (1944), *Time of Arrival* (1947), *Portrait of a Country* (1951), *The Journey of Diornos* (1953) and *The Mirror and the Rose* (1954). The poem 'The Journey of John Donne', which had appeared in *Time of Arrival*, was republished in 1952. A collection of his translations from the Chinese, *The City of Wide Streets by the Friendly River: Leaves of Jade: Poems from Dragon Land*, was also published in 1952. The best of his poetry is in *Portrait of a Country* and *The Mirror and the Rose*. The former, which reflects Dunn's views of the Australian environment, has been described as a kind of Australian *Waste Land*; the latter is a collection of eleven poems ('Reflections'), concerned with love, life and death, the rose and the mirror being the key symbols. His work is represented in the anthology *Eight by Eight* (1963). In 1955 Dunn became a Buddhist priest; he celebrated his ordination with the publication of the booklet *Into the Radiance*, which consisted of one short poem, one line of which was printed on each page of the booklet.

DUTTON, Geoffrey (1922–   ), was born at Kapunda, SA, where his great-granduncle founded that State's first stud sheep station in 1838. He was educated at the University of Adelaide before enlisting in the RAAF in 1941 as a flying instructor. During the 1940s Dutton was associated with the *Angry Penguins* group. Close friends included the poets Donald Kerr, Paul Pfeiffer, Max Harris and Alister Kershaw, and the painters Arthur Boyd and Sidney Nolan. The cover of his first book of poetry was designed by Sidney Nolan and he has continued to work closely with artists. He studied at Oxford 1946–49. After spending the early 1950s travelling extensively, he lectured in English at the University of Adelaide 1955–62. He was editor of Penguin Australia 1961–65 and in 1965 founded, with Brian Stonier, the paperback publishing firm Sun Books. He was joint founder and editor of the periodicals *Australian Letters* and *Australian Book Review*; was one of the editors of the annual poetry anthology *Verse in Australia* (1958–61); edited the *Australian Writers and Their Work* series 1962–66; and the *Bulletin*'s quarterly literary supplement 1980–85. Active in the Australian Council for the Arts 1968–70, and in other cultural organisations, he was made AO in 1976.

A versatile writer, Dutton has published nine collections of verse, *Night Flight and Sunrise* (1944), *Antipodes in Shoes* (1958), which was awarded the Grace Leven Prize, *Flowers and Fury* (1962), *Poems Soft and Loud* (1967), *Findings and Keepings* (1970), which is mainly a substantial collection from the preceding volumes, *New Poems to 1972* (1972), *A Body of Words* (1977), *Selective Affinities* (1985) and *New and Selected Poems* (1993); five novels, *The Mortal and the Marble* (1950), *Andy* (1968), *Tamara* (1970), *Queen Emma of the South Seas* (1976) and *Flying Low* (1992); a collection of short stories, *The Wedge-Tailed Eagle* (1980); two critical studies, *Patrick White* (1961) and *Walt Whitman* (1961); a full-length biography of Kenneth Slessor (1991); three substantial historical biographies, *Founder of a City* (1960), *The Hero as Murderer: The Life of Edward John Eyre* (1967) and *Australia's Last Explorer: Ernest Giles* (1970); several works of art appreciation, *The Paintings of S.T. Gill* (1962), *Russell Drysdale* (1964) and *White on Black* (1974, winner of the L.C. Weickhardt prize in 1978); two books of art and literary history, *The Innovators* (1986) and *Snow on the Saltbush* (1984); three travel books, *A Long Way South* (1953), *Africa in Black and White* (1956) and *States of the Union* (1958); three novels for children, *Seal Bay* (1966), *Tisi and the Yabby* (1965) and *Tisi and the Pageant* (1968); and a book of verse for young people, *On My Island* (1967). His work as an editor has been equally varied and includes the influential collection of critical essays *The Literature of Australia* (1964, 2nd edn 1976); two anthologies of verse, *Australian Poetry 1962* (1962) and *Australian Verse from 1805* (1975), and two of verse and prose, *Modern Australian Writing* (1966) and, with Max Harris, *The Vital Decade* (1968); two collections of essays on republicanism, *Australia and the Monarchy* (1966) and *Republican Australia?* (1977), and one on censorship in Australia (1970); a collection of photographs 1901–14 in the *Australia Since the Camera* series; an edition of Havelock Ellis's *Kanga Creek* (1989); a selection of Henry Lawson's writing, *The Picador Henry Lawson* (1991); and a selection of autobiographical accounts of rural childhoods, *Country Childhoods* (1992), as well as his complete autobiography, *Out in the Open* (1994). He has also written numerous uncollected critical essays, articles and reviews and published translations of the Russian poets Yevgeny Yevtushenko and Bella Akhmadulina. His less ambitious publications include several 'coffee-table' books of which the most significant are *A Taste of History* (1978) and *Patterns of Australia* (1980).

Dutton's early poetry, self-consciously modernist and experimental, has given way to an easy reflective lyricism marked by a strong visual element. He has written some topical and satiric poems but his most characteristic are those celebrating the joys of love, the beauties of the natural scene or the pleasures of friendship. Some of his best work is found in his more sustained autobiographical poems such as 'The Smallest Sprout' and 'Abandoned Airstrip, Northern Territory', where the tone is part-elegiac and part-humorous.

'Dying Stockman, The' is a lugubrious Australian folk-song which chronicles the last wishes of a stockman as he lies dying, his head supported by a saddle. His requests, communicated to his two mates, begin with the words of the chorus:

> Wrap me up with my stockwhip and blanket,
> And bury me deep down below,
> Where the dingoes and crows can't molest me,
> In the shade where the coolibahs grow.

The song was included as an anonymous composition in A.B. Paterson's pioneering collection *Old Bush Songs* (1905), but claims have been made for Horace Alfred Flower's authorship while he was a bank manager in Queensland in 1892. The song derives, from the English sentimental song 'The Tarpaulin Jacket'. The popularity of 'The Dying Stockman' is attested to by the many close parallels and parodies about dying shearers, bagmen, aviators, gunners, bargehands, fettlers and so on. Part of the reason for its popularity may well lie in its parallels with Adam Lindsay Gordon's earlier literary ballad 'The Sick Stockrider', although it is also one of the relatively few traditional Australian songs given currency in the twentieth century by hillbilly singers such as Tex Morton. More recently, Rolf Harris's popular song 'Tie Me Kangaroo Down, Sport', clearly belongs to the 'Dying Stockman' tradition, despite the unsentimental response to the last request of Harris's stockman:

> 'Tan me hide when I'm dead, Fred,
> Tan me hide when I'm dead;'
> So we tanned his hide when he died, Clyde,
> And that's it hangin' in the shed!

Ear in a Wheatfield, a poetry magazine edited by Kris Hemensley 1972–76, began as an extension of *Earth Ship*, a small literary journal that Hemensley had produced in England in 1970–72. It was succeeded by *The Merri Creek, or Nero* (1977–).

EDMONDS, Phillip (1949–), born Epping, Sydney, was educated in Melbourne, attending Monash University. Edmonds was deeply involved in the rise of the New Australian Poetry, editing the magazine *Contempa* and publishing contemporary poetry through Contempa Publications. Edmonds has taught creative writing and is a freelance journalist, writer and historian. He has published several books of short fiction – *Big Boys* (1978), *Everybody used to Know Each Other* (1987), *Locals* (1989) and *Don't Let Me Fall* (1991).

EDWARDS, Ron (1930–), born Geelong, Victoria, is an artist, writer and publisher who has been active for many years in the field of Australian folklore. In 1950 he founded the Galley Press, which became the Rams Skull Press in 1952. The Press specialises in books on Australian folklore and published the series *Bandicoot Ballads* (1951–55) and *Black Bull Chapbooks* (1954–57), illustrated by Edwards and including John Manifold and Hugh Anderson as authors. Edwards's major folk-song collections are *The Overlander Songbook* (1971) and *The Big Book of Australian Folk Song* (1976); his *200 Years of Australian Folk Song* (1988) is an index to some 2000 folk songs published in eighty-six sources. He has also written or compiled *The Australian Yarn* (1977), *Yarns and Ballads* (1981), *Australian Traditional Bush Crafts* (1975), *Skills of the Australian Bushman* (1979).

EE TIANG, Hong (1933–), born in Malacca of Chinese background, arrived in Australia in 1975 as a political exile and teaches at the WA College of Education. He became an Australian citizen in 1977. One of Malaysia's best-known poets, he has published three collections, *I of the Many Faces* (1960), *Lines Written in Hawaii* (1973) and *Myths for a Wilderness* (1976) and has contributed to anthologies in Australia. With Bruce Bennett and Ron Shepherd he edited the collection of essays, *The Writer's Sense of the Contemporary* (1982).

Eisenbart, Professor, an enigmatic creation of the poet Gwen Harwood, has been interpreted as a 'mask' through which the poet expresses certain anarchic or anti-Establishment views, and as a persona which allows her to reflect ironically on the human condition. Eight Professor Eisenbart poems form the second part of Gwen Harwood's *Poems* (1963). In 'Prize-Giving', the first poem in the series, Eisenbart, an ageing nuclear physicist, attends a girls' school speech night to present the prizes and is there bewitched by a girl pianist with titian hair who plays Mozart with extraordinary passion and skill. The remaining poems, in which she has become his mistress, demonstrate her maturity and wisdom compared with his erratic megalomania and his gradual acquisition, largely through her influence, of self-knowledge.

ELDER, Anne (1918–76), born Auckland, NZ, lived in Australia from the age of 3. As Anne MacKintosh she was a noted ballet-dancer with the Borovansky Ballet Company. She published her first book of poetry, *For the Record*, in 1972; a second volume, *Crazy Woman and Other Poems*, was published posthumously in 1976. *For the Record* contains some fine individual poems, especially those with deep personal associations for the poet, e.g. 'Midnight', which concerns her mother, and 'Journey to the North', with its immense joy in homecoming after an absence; and the sequence 'Four Elegies for the Death of Women'. A new selection of her work, *Small Clay Birds*, including some previously unpublished poems, was edited by Lynette Wilson in 1988. The Anne Elder Trust Fund Award for poetry is administered by the Victorian branch of FAW and is awarded annually to the best first book of poetry published. First awarded in 1977, it was won by Laurie Duggan for *East* and Graeme Curtis for *At Last No Reply*. The 1978 award went to Lee Cataldi for *Invitation to a Marxist Lesbian Party*; 1979 to Les Harrop for *The Hum of the Old Suit*; 1980 to Richard Lunn for *Pompeii Deep Fry*; 1981 to Jenny Boult for *The Hotel Anonymous* and Gig Ryan for *The Division of Anger*; 1982 to Kate Llewellyn for *Trader Kate and the Elephants* and Peter Goldsworthy for *Reading from Ecclesiastes*; 1983 to David Brooks for *The Cold Front*; 1984 to Doris Brett for *The Truth about Unicorns*; 1985 to Stephen Williams for *A Crowd of Voices*; 1986 to Jan Owen for *Boy with a Telescope*; 1987 to Sarah Day for *A Hunger to be Less Serious*; 1988 to Alex Skovron for *The Rearrangement*; 1989 to Mark Miller for *Conversing with Stones*; 1990 to Jean Kent for *Verandahs*; 1991 to Alison Croggon for *This is the Stone*, and 1992 to Nicolette Stasko for *Abundance*.

EMERSON, Ernest Sando ('Milky White') (1870–1919), whose father was a first cousin of the American poet Ralph Waldo Emerson, was born in Ballarat, Victoria, and became a journalist with the *Brisbane Courier* and a freelance writer and journalist. He published *A Shanty Entertainment* (1904, bush stories and poems) and *An Australian Bird Calendar* (1909, illustrated by Norman Lindsay).

ENGLAND, E.M. (Edith Mary) (1899–1979), born Townsville, Queensland, was a prolific contributor of verse and prose to a variety of Australian and overseas journals. Her publications include fiction, *The Sealed Temple* (1933), *Tornado and Other Stories* (1945), *Where the Turtles Dance* (1950), *House of Bondage* (1950) and *Road Going North* (1952, with Ray Albion); and verse, *The Happy Monarch and Other Verses* (1927) and *Queensland Days* (1944).

Ern Malley Hoax. The Autumn 1944 issue of *Angry Penguins* contained *The Darkening Ecliptic*, sixteen poems supposedly written by a recently deceased mechanic/insurance salesman named Ern Malley and sent to Max Harris, co-editor of *Angry Penguins*, by Ethel Malley, the sister of Ern Malley. On 25 June 1944 the Sydney *Sunday Sun* magazine section 'Fact' carried the news that the Ern Malley poems were a hoax, written by James McAuley and Harold Stewart. A statement by the co-authors in 'Fact' explained that their action stemmed from their anxiety over what they saw as 'the gradual decay of meaning and craftsmanship in poetry'. McAuley and Stewart believed that the avant-garde poetry of the day was 'insensible of absurdity and incapable of ordinary discrimination'. To put that belief to the test they compiled Ern Malley's 'life-work' in an afternoon with the aid of any books that lay within reach: the *Concise Oxford Dictionary*, a collection of Shakespeare's plays, a *Dictionary of Quotations*, Ripman's *Rhyming Dictionary* and an American report on the drainage of swamps where mosquitoes bred. In their words, 'We opened books at random, choosing a word or a phrase haphazardly. We made lists of these and wove them into nonsensical sentences. We misquoted and made false allusions.' The Ern Malley hoax was featured in the world press and a lively discussion ensued as to the literary merit of the concocted verses, which had been highly acclaimed by many literary experts of the day. The discussion was temporarily silenced by the action of the SA police in prosecuting Harris for the publication of 'indecent advertisements' in the form of some of the Ern Malley poems. A marathon trial followed and Harris was fined £5. More important than the hoax itself was the effect that it had on the development of Australian poetry. The vigorous and legitimate movement for modernism in Australian writing, espoused by many writers and critics in addition to the members of the Angry Penguins group, received a severe setback and the conservative element was undoubtedly strengthened. The Ern Malley controversy continued throughout the following two decades; Harris's views on it are given in the introduction to *Ern Malley's Poems* (1960), and in 'Angry Penguins and After', *Quadrant* (1963); James McAuley's attitude is given in 'The Ferment of the Forties' in *A Map of Australian Verse* (1975). Ian Kennedy Williams wrote *Malarky Dry* (1990), a fictional account of the hoax. *The Poems of Ern Malley* with commentaries by Max Harris and Joanna Murray-Smith was published in 1988, and the *Collected Poems of Ern Malley* with commentaries by Albert Tucker, Max Harris and Colin Wilson in 1993. *The Ern Malley Affair* by Michael Heyward, with an introduction by Robert Hughes, was also published in 1993.

Ern Malley's Journal, a journal of six numbers (1952–55) edited in Adelaide by Max Harris, John Reed and Barrett Reid, took its name from the 'poet' Ern Malley. Less extreme than the earlier *Angry Penguins*, *Ern Malley's Journal* reflected the editors' continuing interest in modernist literature and art.

'Essay on Memory', a long meditative poem by R.D. FitzGerald, was published in the *Sydney Morning Herald* 9 April 1938, having won the sesquicentenary prize for poetry. It was also published in FitzGerald's *Moonlight Acre* (1938) and later in *Forty Years' Poems* (1965). The intellectual content of the poem stems in part from the writings of the philosopher A.N. Whitehead. Rain images, FitzGerald's symbol for memory, dominate the poem, which was conceived while he was surveying the mountains of Veivatuloa in Fiji. Presenting memory as the total past – more than the past of an individual, or a people, or a nation, or a civilisation – the poem insists that it should activate the life of the present; the past influences the present and the present individual, for every individual is a composite of everyone and everything that has gone before him – 'we are the substance of their thought'. It also suggests (FitzGerald's abiding principle) that individual lives, perishable though they are, are made meaningful both in themselves and for the future by action. The themes of the poem, the continuing core of existence and meaning in the universe and the implications of this for individual lives, are solidly held in the logical structure of the poem and illuminated by effective, if complex, imagery.

ESSON, Louis (1879–1943), born Edinburgh, Scotland, was brought to Australia in childhood. He was brought up with his uncle, the painter Ford Paterson, and mixed with writers and artists in his youth. For most of his working life he was a freelance journalist, writing for such periodicals as the *Bulletin*, the *Socialist*, *Table Talk* and the *Lone Hand*, where he was able to give vent to his artistic-socialist ideals and iconoclastic wit. He travelled widely 1915–21 and became deeply impressed by the work of the Irish dramatists at the Abbey Theatre, Dublin, especially by his meetings and correspondence with W.B. Yeats. In 1921–22 Esson made a concerted effort to put Yeats's advice into action by collaborating with Vance Palmer and Stewart Macky in the formation of the Pioneer Players. His second wife was Dr Hilda Bull, who continued to promote his theatrical aims after his death and who was the financial mainstay of the family after Esson was afflicted with a nervous illness in the 1930s.

Esson's plays were published in several collections: *Three Short Plays*, which includes *The Woman Tamer*, *Dead Timber* and *The Sacred Place* (1911); *The Time is Not Yet Ripe* (1912); *Dead Timber and Other Plays*, which includes *The Drovers* (1920); *The Southern Cross and Other Plays*, which includes *The Southern Cross*, *Mother and Son* and *The Bride of Gospel Place* (1946, ed. Hilda Bull); and *The Woman Tamer* (1976). Esson also published two collections of poetry, *Bells and Bees* (1910) and *Red Gums* (1912), as well as numerous uncollected short stories. Often described as the first Australian playwright to achieve distinction for plays with Australian settings, Esson was in fact a naturally cosmopolitan, urbane and witty writer. He suppressed this gift in favour of nationalistic folk themes and poetic realism. The Victorian Premier's Literary Awards includes a Louis Esson Award for drama.

'Euabalong Ball, The' is an Australian folk-song which celebrates a dance at the bush hamlet of Euabalong on the Lachlan River in NSW. The humour of the song derives from the parallels drawn between the appearance and activities of the bucolic participants and the sheep and cattle with which they normally work; thus the shearers are 'stringy old wethers', the 'sheilas' are 'weaners' or 'two-tooths', and during the dancing

> There was bucking and gliding,
> pigrooting and sliding,
> When they varied the gait,
> there was couples colliding.

'The Euabalong Ball' was possibly adapted by A.L. Lloyd from an earlier song, 'The Wooyeo Ball', written by 'Vox Silvis' (?Rob Webster) and published in a history of Temora in 1888. The printed original reports a lively but not uproarious dance focused on the squatters and jackeroos rather than the pastoral workers.

'Eumerella Shore, The' is a well-known folk-song about the 'duffing' of cattle; there are a number of variant texts and titles including 'The Eumeralla Shore', 'The Numerella Shore' and 'The Neumerella Shore'. The references to free selection and Sir John Robertson make it clear that the 'Eumerella' district referred to is that in the NSW Monaro region, where there is a river known as the Numerella, and not the Eumerella River in south-eastern Victoria. It is less certain whether the song is the sarcastic lament of a squatter who feels his cattle will be stolen as a result of the Robertson Lands Acts or the boasts of a selector at the increased opportunities for 'duffing' as a result of the same Acts. 'Cockatoo Jack' is sometimes given as the author of the song, which was in print in the early 1860s.

EVANS, George Essex (1863–1909), born London, came to Australia in 1881. He tried farming then turned briefly to teaching, and later journalism as agricultural editor of the *Queenslander*. In 1888 he joined the public service, ultimately becoming district registrar at Toowoomba. His first volume of poetry, *The Repentance of Magdalene Despar*, was published in 1891. Two other volumes are *Loraine and Other Verses* (1898) and *The Secret Key and Other Verses* (1906). In 1901 he won £50 for his 'Ode for Commonwealth Day'. The *Collected Verse of George Essex Evans* was published as a memorial edition in 1928. His best-known individual poem, a great favourite in the first half of this century and frequently anthologised, is 'The Women of the West', a tribute to the women of the outback. His 'An Australian Symphony' is still considered highly as a patriotic poem, but in his other verse romantic themes predominate. More highly thought of in Queensland than elsewhere, Evans was undoubtedly a better poetic craftsman than many of his contemporaries among the bush balladists, but he failed to win the same popularity. His major narrative works, e.g. 'Magdalene Despar', although competent and enthusiastic, have lapsed into obscurity. In Too-woomba, where he worked and died, there is a monument to him and an annual George Essex Evans pilgrimage. Henry A. Tardent wrote *The Life and Poetry of George Essex Evans* (1913).

EWERS, J.K. (John Keith) (1904–78), born Subiaco, WA, was a schoolteacher in WA 1924–47, thereafter living by his writing. Foundation president of the WA branch of the FAW (1938–39), he was made a life member in 1967. Ewers published poetry, fiction, history and works of literary criticism and social analysis. His two books of verse were *Boy and Silver* (1929), the narrative of a boy and a kangaroo, and *I Came Naked* (1976), philosophical comments on life. Very much a favourite son of his home state and one of its first writers to gain Australia-wide recognition, Ewers is the subject of *The Ultimate Honesty: Recollections of John K. Ewers 1904–1978* (1982), published by the WA branch of the FAW and edited by Peter Bibby. His autobiography, *Long Enough for a Joke*, was published in 1983.

'Exequy, An' by Peter Porter from *The Cost of Seriousness* (1978), forms, with 'The Delegate', the crux of the volume. It displays his ability to blend artistic and deeply personal responses, the traditional and the contemporary. 'An Exequy' is modelled in metrics and theme on Bishop King's poem on the untimely death of his young wife, and explores with 'The Delegate' new avenues of the art of poetry. The title poem states that the 'cost of seriousness' is death, implying at once that it is his pursuit of poetry, his seriousness, which has robbed both him and his wife of her life, and moreover that his art is insufficiently alive to console the feelings aroused, feelings not only of loss but of guilt. In 'The Delegate' the wife's ghost is speaking to the poet; it seems she has been sent ahead and is reluctantly reporting and advising him on the afterlife. The images she uses are not comforting and disrupt his attempted consolings, leaving him with more shame and guilt and the 'punishment of remembrance'. In these poems, as in others in the volume, Porter's preoccupations with the landscape of the mind turns to the inability of art, particularly his, to offer any more than a public expression of feeling. The paradox is that in poetry which is so private in its source of feeling Porter is able, by earnestly questioning in language textured with artistic allusions, to convince the reader while he himself is left unconvinced.

JEFF DOYLE

'Eyre All Alone', a poem in fourteen parts by Francis Webb, was first published in its entirety in Webb's volume *Socrates* (1961), although parts of it (3, 10, 14) were published in the *Bulletin* in 1959. In Webb's *Collected Poems* (1969) 'Eyre All Alone' was printed as a separate section. The poem begins with the SA settler's 'dream of a stock-route' to WA. The explorer Edward John Eyre, who had failed in an alternative attempt to open up the north of SA, sets out to chart a stock-route to the west by way of the Great Australian Bight. The last stanza of the first part, beginning

> Walk, walk. From dubious footfall one
> At Fowler's Bay, the chosen must push on

which refers to the departure of Eyre, John Baxter, Wylie and two other Aborigines from Fowler's Bay to the distant goal of King George Sound, is repeated several times as a sonorous, almost biblical, refrain throughout the poem. The third part tells of Baxter's murder by the two Aborigines; the fifth part reflects Eyre's uncertainty about Wylie's loyalty; the eighth part dwells on the ever-present menace of the Aborigines who shadow them. In the tenth part, 'Banksia', virtually the climax to the sequence, Wylie sights the banksia tree in flower and their hazardous journey across the desert is almost over. Webb's use in this part of the dramatic technique of question and answer to further the narrative ('Wylie, what can you see?/ I see a flower') is particularly effective. Later at Thistle Cove they are given supplies and companionship by the

French whaler *Mississippi*, and the sequence ends with Wylie reunited with his tribes-men and Eyre about to make his dramatic entrance into Albany on King George Sound. In his notes to the poem Webb suggests that this journey, in which the hero's greatest discovery is not a stock-route but himself, might be symbolically interpreted: 'My insistence upon Eyre's aloneness is not an overlooking of Wylie, but comes from my seeing such a journey of discovery as suggestive of another which is common to us all.' The poem re-emphasises Webb's interest, reflected in the earlier 'A Drum for Ben Boyd' and 'Leichhardt in Theatre', not so much in the heroic events of Australia's past as in the characters of the men who shaped and were shaped by those events.

EYRE, Frank (1910–88), born Manchester, England, came to Australia in 1949. While in England he published *The Naiad and Other Poems* (1935), *Poems by Frank Eyre & Peter Lagger* (1936), *Selected Poems* (1941), *Loving in Truth* (1942) and *English Rivers and Canals* (1945), and also edited several anthologies including *The Quiet Spirit* (1946). After the war Eyre joined the editorial staff of OUP, became managing editor of Oxford children's book publishing and in 1952 published *Twentieth Century Children's Books*. As editorial manager of OUP in Australia from 1950 to 1975 he, advised by Grahame Johnston, made an important contribution to the study of Australian litera-ture by publishing a new series of *Australian Writers and their Work*, and books of Australian literary criticism. He also published important books by Australian writers at a time when other Australian publishers were rejecting them, e.g. *The Generations of Men, The Australian Legend*. With George Ferguson and others he helped to establish the Australian Book Publishers Association, of which he was president 1961–63. He was a member of the committee which was responsible for the *Commonwealth Style Manual*, and chairman of the one which produced the Victorian government's *Plain English*, and he was also a member of the final board of the CLF before its dissolution. His later publications include *Ian Clunies Ross* (1961), *British Children's Books in the Twentieth Century* (1971), *Scholarly Publishing 1976* (1977) and *Oxford in Australia* (1978).

'Face of the Waters, The', a long poem whose title comes from Genesis, 'And the spirit of God moved upon the face of the waters', was first published by R.D. Fitz-Gerald in the *Bulletin* (1944). FitzGerald explained that the poem, in free verse with occasional use of rhyme, was a 'pantheistic view of the universe modified by the recognition of a dualism somehow integral with it'. The poem is an expansion of the lines occurring in 'The Hidden Bole', 'the Nothing (contracted to some blackened point)/ Where wakes the dream, the brooding ultimate'. The poem attempts an account of Creation. The 'utter nothingness' of pre-existence is so inconceivable that a creator – God or some consciousness – is a necessity. But the creator so envisaged is given a duality that assists, and mockingly frustrates, the attempts of life to burst forth from the nothingness. The poem is also seen as a reworking, using terms and concepts of modern physics and metaphysics, of the myth of Creation, with the Nothing (or Chaos) transformed or even hatched (the 'egg' imagery of the poem) by the 'brooding Ultimate' (the spirit). The most puzzling and complex of FitzGerald's poetry, yet accepted as one of his most impressive works, 'The Face of the Waters' has been described by Judith Wright as 'a meditation on no less a subject than Creation, and on the impossibility of meditating on Creation'.

'Faces in the Street', one of the best-known protest poems of Henry Lawson, was first published in 1888 in the *Bulletin;* it was revised during the preparation of *Selected Poems of Henry Lawson* (1918). Written in a stirring rhythm from the perspective of a person whose 'window-sill is level with the faces in the street', the poem focuses on the flotsam and jetsam of the city who pass by from before dawn until after midnight. It concludes with the vision of a revolution which will do away with poverty and the other 'terrors of the street'.

FAHEY, Diane (1945–), born and educated in Melbourne, spent some years abroad before returning to SA in 1986. Her poetry has been widely published in journals, anthologies and newspapers and in the collections, *Voices from the Honeycomb* (1986), *Metamorphoses* (1988), *Turning the Hourglass* (1990), and *Mayflies in Amber* (1993). She has won several awards including the Caltex Bendigo Advertiser Manuscript Award for 1986, the Wesley Michel Wright Prize in 1987, the Mattara Poetry Prize in 1985 and the 1988 John Shaw Neilson Poetry Prize. With *Voices from the Honeycomb* Fahey established herself as an accomplished poet with an assured style. The lightly regular stanzas of this collection are perfectly attuned to their sustained lyric tone which often evokes the same sense of aesthetic completion and arrested emotion as still-life painting. Tranquillity is sometimes only at the poem's surface formal level, however, for Fahey gives full play to feelings, admitting emotions of fear, anxiety and grief. In 'Snapshots of a City', for instance, a traffic accident is described as 'someone's happiness/ vandalised by a hair's-breadth chance' and in Victoria Market derelicts sit and 'wait with faces open, wounded/ and wrinkled, like pierced hands'. In other poems natural scenes are the ostensible subject, but they are also invariably metaphors of emotion. The poems of *Metamorphoses* are feminist reworkings of classical myths; taking the Western patriarchal stories of Ovid, Euripides and others as a starting point, Fahey rewrites them from the point of view of women, showing how frequently they are the objects of the narratives' familiar violence. 'How often the myth of rape–/ the carrying off, the invasion–/ has been festooned with flowers,/ a sparkling atmosphere, a picnic lunch', muses the narrator of 'That Other Shore', which is a reimagining of the myth of Europa; Danae in the poem of that title experiences the rape of Zeus as 'Pennies from heaven', a 'celestial dew ... With immaculate conceptions/ there's so little to do –'. Accompanied by reproductions of celebrated paintings of mythical events and by explanatory notes, these poems are elegant, witty reconstructions whose irreverence often produces startling insights. *Turning the Hourglass*, constructed in five parts, charts a journey to freedom and self-discovery. In many of the poems the narrator discovers how to 'inherit [the] body more truly, move close to spirit whose home is body'. The meditative poems of *Mayflies in Amber* focus on creatures of the insect world, although they are often metaphors of human and metaphysical concerns. The easy grace and simple language of Fahey's limpid poems may give an initial impression of facility, but they are in fact intricately worked and well burnished.

FAIRBRIDGE, Wolfe (1918–50), born Cottesloe, WA, was a research officer with the CSIRO. He died from poliomyelitis at the age of 31; his poetry was posthumously collected as *Poems* (1953). Notable poems include 'Denial and Riposte', which won second prize in the *Sydney Morning Herald* competition in 1947; 'The Man Who Caught the Wind', an Aboriginal tale; and 'Consecration of the House', the poignant expression of the poet's quiet expectation of delight in a future that, tragically, was not to be.

FAIRFAX, James Griffyth (1886–1976), born Sydney into the *Sydney Morning Herald* Fairfax family, grew up in England and was largely an expatriate, visiting Australia only for brief periods. A poet of both lyric grace and intellectual subtlety, Fairfax published numerous volumes of verse including *The Gates of Sleep and Other Poems* (1906), *Poems* (1908), *The Troubled Pool and Other Poems* (1911), *The Horns of Taurus* (1914), *Side Slips: A Collection of Unposted Postscripts, Admissions and Asides* (1914), *The Temple of Janus: A Sonnet Sequence* (1917), *Mesopotamia: Sonnets and Lyrics at Home and Abroad, 1914–1919* (1919), *Carmina Rapta* (1919) and *The Fifth Element* (1937). Fairfax served in the First World War; four of his 'Mesopotamia' poems were included in *Valour and Vision: Poems of the War, 1914–18* (1920), ed. J.T. Trotter.

FALLAW, Lance (1876–1958), born Gateshead, England, joined the staff of the Rockhampton *Daily Record* in 1908 after a period as a newspaperman in South Africa. He was later editor of the *Charters Towers Telegraph, Cairns Post, Geelong Advertiser* and associate editor of the *Sydney Morning Herald*. He published a collection of verse, *Silverleaf and Oak* (1906), before he arrived in Queensland; later volumes of poetry were *The Ampler Sky* (1909), *Unending Ways* (1926) and *Hostage and Survival* (1939).

FARRELL, John (1851–1904), was born Buenos Aires, the son of Irish gold-rush immigrants who came to Australia in 1852 from South America. After a limited education he worked mainly as a brewer until he turned to journalism. A radical, he contributed frequently to the *Boomerang* and the *Worker* and enthusiastically shared William Lane's vision of an Australian Utopia. In the 1880s he contributed verse satires and narratives to numerous newspapers and journals, including the *Bulletin*, writing one of its earliest Australian stories, 'One Christmas Day' (1884); his first major book of verse, *How He Died*, was published in 1887. Farrell became involved with Henry George of the Single Tax movement, editing two of that movement's Australian journals, but worked mainly for the *Daily Telegraph*, briefly as editor but mostly as columnist, leader-writer and book-reviewer. Two of his minor verse successes were 'Australia to England', a poem written for Queen Victoria's Jubilee in 1897, widely esteemed and publicly praised by Kipling; and 'Hymn of the Commonwealth', sung by massed choirs at the Sydney Commonwealth celebrations. The main collection of his poetry, *My Sundowner and Other Poems*, published posthumously in 1904, was edited by Bertram Stevens. Although Farrell's was a minor poetic voice in the nationalistic radicalism of the 1890s, in his person and character he represented the best of that movement. Mary Gilmore's tribute that he most influenced her life and work is characteristic of contemporary sentiments about him.

FAUST, Clive (1932–   ), born Melbourne, graduated in philosophy from the University of Melbourne, lived in Japan for seven years and became a lecturer at Bendigo College of Advanced Education. Featured in the American magazine *Origin* (July 1978), he was included as a representative of the new wave of Australian poetry in John Tranter's anthology *The New Australian Poetry* (1979). Faust has published three books of verse, *Metamorphosed from the Adjacent Cold*, *Token and Trace* (both 1980), and *Leavetakings* (1986).

FAVENC, Ernest (1845–1908), born Surrey, England, came to Australia in 1864 and worked for fourteen years on stations in north Queensland. He led the 1877 expedition, financed by the *Queenslander*, for which he sometimes wrote under the pseudonym 'Dramingo', to investigate the feasibility of a railway linking Queensland to Darwin. His reputation as an explorer established, Favenc spent several years working for pastoral interests opening up the country along the south-western coast of the Gulf of Carpentaria and across into WA. He then joined the staff of the Sydney *Evening News* and began to turn his adventurous past as an explorer into a lucrative source of fiction and non-fiction. His short fiction includes *'The Last of Six': Tales of the Austral Tropics* (1893), *Tales of the Austral Tropics* (1894) and *My Only Murder and Other Tales* (1899). His novels are *The Secret of the Australian Desert* (1895), *Marooned on Australia* (1896) and *The Moccasins of Silence* (1896). Favenc's only volume of poetry, *Voices of the Desert* (1905), attempts to evoke something of the emptiness and silence of the inland. Cheryl Frost wrote *The Last Explorer: The Life and Work of Ernest Favenc* (1983).

FIELD, Barron (1786–1846), an unsuccessful legal practitioner in England, came to Sydney in 1817 as a judge of the Supreme Court of NSW. In 1819 George Howe, the government printer, published Field's *First Fruits of Australian Poetry*. The Colony's unfamiliar flora and fauna attracted him, but he disliked the uninviting terrain, the reversed seasons and the penal nature of the settlement. He saw it as a 'prose-dull land', a land without associations, and left it gladly in 1824. Back in England he edited *Geographical Memoirs on New South Wales* (1825), then went to Gibraltar as chief justice. Although Field's claim to be the first 'Austral Harmonist' is presumptuous, 'Botany Bay Flowers' and 'The Kangaroo', in spite of some ridiculing of the colonial scene, are among the first poems to evoke the Australian environment.

FINEY, George (1895–1987), born Auckland, NZ, sold his first drawings to local newspapers at the age of 14. In the First World War he served in France with the NZ forces both as infantry soldier and war artist, and studied briefly at art school in London before settling in Australia in 1919. His first cartoons were published in the *Bulletin*, but in 1921 he began a decade's association with *Smith's Weekly* and won a reputation as a superb caricaturist. His simple verse is included in *Poems* (1975) and *Book of Finey* (1976) as well as in his entertaining autobiography *The Mangle Wheel* (1981).

FINNIN, Mary (1906–   ), born Kildare near Geelong, Victoria, trained as an artist, held successful exhibitions of paintings, and has been an art teacher, critic and businesswoman. Her major literary interest has been poetry; her six volumes of verse include *A Beggar's Opera* (1938), *Look Down, Olympians* (1939), *Royal* (1941), *Alms for Oblivion* (1947), *The Shield of Place* (1957) and a collected volume, *Off Shears* (1958–1978) (1979). *The Shield of Place* (the title refers to her commitment to Victoria) includes the ballad 'The Ride of Richard Illidge', which commemorates an epic horse ride of 160 kilometres in a night to save a condemned prisoner from execution. Other poems with local Victorian flavour are 'Bacchus in the Marsh' and 'Rain in Glenrowan'.

First Boke of Fowle Ayres, The, a collection of unattributed scurrilous and bawdy verse by such poets as A.D. Hope, James McAuley, O.M. Somerville and Harold Stewart, was published in a limited edition in 1944. Epigrams from it and some verse by Somerville and Hope are included in *Comic Australian Verse* (1972), ed. Geoffrey Lehmann.

First Fruits of Australian Poetry (1819), by Barron Field, contains two poems, 'Botany Bay Flowers' and 'The Kangaroo'. On the title page, the lines 'I first adventure; follow me who list/ And be Australia's second harmonist' indicate Field's claim to be Australia's first poetic voice, and his book is, in fact, the first book of poems published in Australia. With 'Botany Bay Flowers' Field provides the first poetic description of wildflowers and native shrubs of the Sydney bush. 'The Kangaroo' depicts that animal as an antipodean oddity, an anomaly of the animal world yet typical of the equally strange Australian landscape. In spite of Field's amazement and amusement at colonial oddities of flora and fauna there is, in both poems, a sincere note of interest.

FISHER, Lala (1872–1929), born Rockhampton, Queensland, spent the years 1897–1901 in England where she published poetry, *A Twilight Teaching* (1898), and edited *By Creek and Gully* (1899), a mainly prose anthology of Australian writers then in England. Back in Australia she lived first in Charters Towers and wrote for various journals and newspapers, including *Steele Rudd's Magazine*. In 1909, in Sydney, she bought the *Theatre Magazine*, which she edited until 1918. Her later books of verse were *Grass Flowering* (1915) and *Earth Spiritual* (1918). A remarkably progressive and liberated woman for her time, Lala Fisher expressed in her poetry some of the sentiments that the restricting conventions of the day were prone to stifle.

FITZGERALD, R.D. (Robert David) (1902–87), nephew of John le Gay Brereton, was born at Hunters Hill, Sydney, where he lived for much of his life. He attended the University of Sydney in 1920–21 but abandoned a science course for surveying. Like many young writers of the early 1920s, FitzGerald came under the influence of Norman Lindsay, and participated, with Hugh McCrae, Kenneth Slessor and Jack Lindsay in the production of the journal *Vision*, in which several of his early poems were published. In 1931–36 he was mostly in Fiji, surveying the vague traditional boundaries of the tribal lands for the Native Lands Commission. In 1936–40 he was a private surveyor in Sydney, then municipal surveyor to the suburban councils of Manly and Ryde. Late in 1940 he joined the Commonwealth Department of the Interior, surveying sites for wartime aerodromes. He remained with the Department of the Interior after the war, ultimately becoming supervising surveyor of the NSW branch of the department before his retirement in 1965. In 1951 he was made OBE; in 1965 he shared the Britannica Australia Award; in 1974 he won the Robert Frost Medallion; in 1982 he was made AM and a life member of ASAL. In 1985 he was awarded an honorary D.Litt. from the University of Melbourne. He gave public lectures in Australian literature at the universities of Melbourne and Queensland in

1959 and 1961 respectively, published in 1963 as *The Elements of Poetry*, and in 1963 spent a semester as a visiting lecturer in poetry at the University of Texas. Best known a poet, FitzGerald was also a prolific reviewer of, and influential commentator on, modern Australian writing.

His first collection of verse, *The Greater Apollo: Seven Metaphysical Songs* (1927), consists of short meditative poems that reveal the predicament of man torn between the opposing attractions of the transcendent reality ('the Greater Apollo') and the material world. Although he recognises its transience, FitzGerald chooses the visible world with its obvious delights – 'It is enough that trees are trees/ That earth is earth and stone is stone.' His comment in the fourth part of 'The Greater Apollo', 'I look no more for gods among the lace-like ferns and twisted boughs', while further emphasising his decision in favour of the actual, might also be taken to indicate the end of his relationship with the exotic fantasies of the *Vision* group. *To Meet the Sun* (1929), a collection of thirty-three poems including 'The Greater Apollo' series, won recognition in England where it was awarded, before it was published in Australia, the Bronze Medal of the Festival of Arts and Letters sponsored by the Panton Arts club. *Moonlight Acre* (1938), which contains two groups of short poems, 'Moonlight Acre' (the phrase occurring in the poem 'Invasion') and 'Copernicus', and two long poems, 'The Hidden Bole' and 'Essay on Memory', won the Australian Literature Society's Gold Medal in 1938. It established FitzGerald, in the eyes of many, as the major Australian poet of the 1930s. 'The Hidden Bole', an intricately constructed elegy which contains a central aesthetic truth that transience is an inseparable part of beauty and uses as examples the banyan tree and the famous ballerina Pavlova, represents some of FitzGerald's most sensuous and lyrical writing. 'Essay on Memory', which won the Australia's 150th Anniversary Celebrations Council's sesquicentenary prize for poetry in 1938, insists, in the complex and knotty manner of FitzGerald's long speculative verse, on the vital influence of the past upon the present.

Heemskerck Shoals (1949) incorporates some shorter poems with the long dramatic monologue of that title, one of several works by FitzGerald with a Fijian background. The poem consists of the angry meditations of the Dutch seaman and explorer Abel Tasman, after the near disaster of his expedition on the reef which he named Heemskerck Shoals, near Nanuku Island, Fiji, in 1643. *Between Two Tides* (1952), drawn from *An Account of the Natives of the Tongan Islands* by J.M. Martin (1817), is a very long poem on which FitzGerald worked intermittently over many years. It was awarded the Grace Leven Prize for poetry in 1952. In five parts, the poem relates and discusses the life and exploits of Will Mariner, a young sailor on the privateer *Port au Prince*, which was attacked and burned by Tongan natives in 1806. Mariner survived the massacre of the crew and was adopted by the Tongan chief, Finau. The poem focuses on both Mariner and Finau, guiding the reader to an assessment of the two men and their achievements. Well constructed and impressively written, the poem urges 'the necessity for advance in action', for it is only by 'acts of resolution' that any man can fashion himself a recognisable identity. At the same time it recognises the fragility of individual human existence, which lasts only 'between two tides', the new, incoming tide washing away all traces of the individual's efforts and achievements. *This Night's Orbit* (1953) reprinted two of FitzGerald's most important poems, 'The Face of the Waters', which meditates on the Creation, and 'Fifth Day', an incident from the trial of Warren Hastings. 'The Wind at Your Door', a poem based on a convict-flogging incident which involved FitzGerald's ancestor Martin Mason, was published in the *Bulletin* (1958) and published separately in 1959. *South-most Twelve* (1962), incorporating the poems written after *This Night's Orbit*, includes the series 'Eleven Compositions: Roadside', and the well-known 'Bog and Candle', published in *Meanjin* (1960). 'The Wind at Your Door' and *South-most Twelve* won the Grace Leven Prize for poetry in 1959 and 1962 respectively. FitzGerald's Australian Poets selection and his American volume *Of Some Country*, published by the University of Texas, both appeared in 1963 and were followed in 1965 by *Forty Years' Poems*. It contains most of his later work and an opening section, 'Salvage', which reprints, with revisions, all the poems that FitzGerald wished to retain from the earliest period of his writing, 1922–30. The salvaged poems deal mainly with the alienation of the artist, e.g. 'Passed By', and romantic love, e.g. 'The Wall' and 'Black Woods'. After a considerable break he published *Product: Later Verses by Robert D. FitzGerald* (1977), its appearance a further proof of his lifetime principle of 'advance in action', of his Carlylean belief that 'Were it but the pitifullest infinitesimal fraction of a Product, produce it, in God's name!' Some of the poems express his protest at Australia's participation in the Vietnam War, others re-create early colonial times in Australia. In 'Just Once', his judgment of the present ('This age of shoddy') seems out of keeping with his normally optimistic view of life and humanity. *Of Places and Poetry*, a collection of FitzGerald's prose, appeared in 1976. He edited a volume of Mary Gilmore's verse in 1963 and the letters of Hugh McCrae in 1970.

FitzGerald was never a popular or fashionable poet. His use of poetry for the carriage of complex, philosophical ideas and for the examination of abstract, intellectual concepts made him less accessible than other contemporary poets. Meanwhile expert literary opinions of his work have varied widely and the prestige he enjoyed from the late 1930s to the 1960s has lately diminished. Some fellow poets and critics have judged his work, in spite of its integrity and painstaking conscientiousness, as ungainly, lacking in lyricism, grace and spontaneity. Opinions to the contrary are also widely held. He continues to be praised as a true and even great poet and has been judged, with Kenneth Slessor, as the major influence that compelled modern Australian poetry to address itself, in a professional manner, to a range of intellectual, philosophical and metaphysical themes that it had rarely attempted before. *R.D. FitzGerald* in the Portable Australian Authors series was published in 1987, edited by Julian Croft.

FITZGERALD, Ross (1944–   ), born Melbourne, educated at Melbourne High School, Monash University and the University of NSW (Ph.D. in political science), is a well-known historian (Griffith University, Queensland), political commentator, novelist and poet. Two of his novels, *Pushed from the Wings* (1986) and *Busy in the Fog* (1990), and a book of short stories, *All About Anthrax* (1987), record the misadventures of Grafton Everest, an academic at the fictional Bowen University of Queensland. He has also published a book of poems, *The Eyes of Angels* (1973, in The Saturday Centre Poets Series) and edited (with Ken Spillman) *The Greatest Game* (1988), an anthology of verse, short stories and humorous anecdotes about Australian rules football.

'Five Bells', the title poem of Kenneth Slessor's volume of poetry published in 1939 and acknowledged as his major work, is a meditation, compressed into memory's own time-scale as a ship's bell rings five bells in Sydney Harbour, on Slessor's drowned friend Joe Lynch. Able to recapture only disconnected, trivial scraps of the dead man's past existence and unsuccessful in his attempt to understand the significance of Joe Lynch's life, or to decide what purpose gave him life at all, the poet is forced to an admission of the futility of human existence. Although the emphasis is on the impermanence of all human relationships and thus the triumph of time (moved by 'little fidget wheels') over life, the affection expressed for the scruffy, unruly, unimportant Irishman gives the poem a tender and human character. Peter Fitzpatrick discusses the life and death of Joe Lynch in *Australian Literary Studies* (1988) and *The Sea Coast of Bohemia* (1992).

'Five Visions of Captain Cook', first published in *Trio* (1931) by Kenneth Slessor, builds the character of Captain James Cook from the reactions of those who sailed with him on his three major voyages. Based on Cook's journals and other contemporary writings, the poem is an important contribution to the voyager theme in Australian literature. The first section, focusing on the first *Endeavour* voyage of 1768–71, recounts Cook's historic decision to sail 'westabout' to Australia. The final section, the most attractive part of the poem, reviews the golden days with Cook through the nostalgic memories of retired sea captain Alexander Home. Full of memorable lines that attest to Slessor's delight in language, the poem is distinguished by its characterisation of Cook and Captain Home and demonstrates that men who change the face of the world inevitably change the lives of those who associate with them.

'**Flash Jack from Gundagai**' is an Australian folk-song in which a shearer, the self-proclaimed Flash Jack from Gundagai, sings of the shearing sheds and the practices he has experienced. Several times in the song Flash Jack pays tribute to 'Old Tom Patterson on the One Tree Plain'. Patterson was a pastoralist who took up Ulong station in the Riverina in 1871 and added to his holding until it measured more than 120 000 hectares and took in the whole of the One Tree Plain.

'**Flight of Wild Geese, A**', a highly regarded poem by Harold Stewart, published in his first volume of verse, *Phoenix Wings* (1948), depicts an imaginary incident concerning Wu Tao-tzu, the great Chinese artist who was commissioned by the Emperor Ming Huang of the T'ang Dynasty to paint a landscape roll. The poem's opening gloss indicates that Wu so enters into the spirit of the scene that he can walk about in the picture at will. One day he wanders over a distant mountain in the roll and is never seen again. During his wanderings Wu meets Chang Chih-ho, 'the Old Fisherman of the Waters and the Mists'. Their ensuing conversation is conducted with traditional Oriental decorum. Wu believes the old man to be evading life by his self-imposed exile; Chang responds that he 'fled not from the world but into it'. The conversation, charged with subtleties and innuendos that range deep into Oriental religious philosophies, is interrupted and illuminated by the sudden arrival and abrupt departure of a flight of geese.

FLOWER, Charles Augustus (?1856–1948), born Port Fairy, Victoria, worked as a jackeroo in Victoria before settling in Queensland, where he overlanded sheep and was employed as an accountant for a firm of railway contractors; he was later a pastoralist for many years in the Roma district of central Queensland. He is credited by some folklorists with the authorship of the overlanding song 'A Thousand Miles Away', which mentions the Roma railway, and 'The Broken-down Squatter', the lament of a pastoralist who has been forced by drought and high rents to give up his run. Similarly, Horace Alfred Flower, the elder brother of Charles (uncle in some less reliable accounts), is claimed as the author of another well-known Australian folk-song, 'The Dying Stockman'.

Folk-Song and Ballad see **Anthologies**

FOOTT, Mary Hannay (1846–1918), born Glasgow, Scotland, came to Australia in 1853. Educated at a private school in Melbourne, she trained as a teacher and taught 1862–68 before spending five years at the National Gallery School, where she studied under von Guérard and Buvelot. During these years she supported herself by contributing articles and poems to the Melbourne and Sydney *Punch*, the *Australasian*, the *Town and Country Journal* and the *Australasian Sketcher*. In 1874 she married Thomas Wade Foott and three years later accompanied him to south-west Queensland to take up land. After her husband's death in 1884 she went to Brisbane, where she opened a private school and contributed to the *Queenslander* and *Brisbane Courier;* she joined the staff of the *Queenslander* in 1887 and was editor of its women's page for about a decade, writing verse and stories, sometimes under the pseudonym 'La Quenouille'. She published two books of verse, *Where the Pelican Builds and Other Poems* (1885), expanded as *Morna Lee and Other Poems* (1890). Her best-known poem, frequently anthologised, is 'Where the Pelican Builds'; it records, from the viewpoint of the waiting women, the tragedy that so frequently struck the pioneer families – the loss of loved ones who were drawn by the lure of the land further out.

FORBES, 'Alexander' (William Anderson) (1839–79), born Banffshire, Scotland, was sent down from King's College, Aberdeen, for a youthful misdemeanour ('either snowballing or lampooning a professor') and came to Australia in 1862, wandering outback Queensland in a variety of menial jobs. His early Australian poems express resentment at his exile and disgust with the colonial environment. Gradually inured to the hardships of colonial life by alcohol, tobacco and the adoption of a rueful, ironic pose, Forbes, known widely as 'Alick the Poet', recovered from his nostalgia for Scotland and began to sing the praises of bush life. He published, as 'Alexander' Forbes, *Voices from the Bush* (1869); one of the earliest bush balladists, he expressed the humour and tragedy of the bush experience.

FORBES, John (1950–   ), born Melbourne, lived much of his early life in New Guinea, Malaya and Sydney. He graduated from the University of Sydney and has been a teacher of creative writing. He won the Poetry Society of Australia Award in 1972; the H.M. Butterley-F. Earle-Hooper *Southerly* Award for a young writer in 1976 for the poem 'Breakfast'; and was granted a travelling fellowship in 1975. He has co-edited the journal *Leatherjacket;* edits the magazine *Surfers Paradise;* and has published the volumes of poetry *Tropical Skiing* (1976), *On the Beach* (1977), *Stalin's Holidays* (1981), *The Stunned Mullet* (1988) and *New and Selected Poems* (1992), the last including many from the earlier selections and a section of sixteen new poems. Long regarded as a 'cerebral' poet with an outstanding passion for poetry, who conceals his meaning behind deceptive symbolism and subtle post-modernist devices, Forbes catches the essence of the contemporary world with wry accuracy. Although his canvas is small, his compressed lyrics have been compared to Helen Garner's fiction in terms of moral and artistic breadth; in Alan Wearne's words, 'Both the Forbes and Garner visions are generous, both have produced what may amount to guides on living in urban Australia, both chart how love both survives and helps you survive.' In *Ecstasy and Economics: American Essays for John Forbes* (1992), Meaghan Morris takes Forbes's poem 'Watching the Treasurer' as a starting-point for examining the cult of the economy and the effects of the mass media.

FORREST, Mabel (1872–1935), born near Yandilla, Queensland, was a versatile writer of short fiction, novels and verse. Her first book was the volume *Poems* (1893); *The Rose of Forgiveness and Other Stories* was published in 1904; another volume of verse, *Alpha Centauri*, followed in 1909 and a novel, *A Bachelor's Wife*, in 1914. Her other publications include a prose and verse collection, *The Green Harper* (1915); a book of verse, *Streets and Gardens* (1922); and a series of novels, *The Wild Moth* (1924), *Gaming Gods* (1926), *Hibiscus Heart* (1927), *Reaping Roses* (1928) and *White Witches* (1929). A collection of her poems submitted to journals in various countries was published as *Poems* in 1927. A freelance writer for more than thirty years, she was immensely popular in the 1920s.

FORSTER, William (1818–82), grandson of the explorer Gregory Blaxland, was born Madras, India, and in 1829 came to Australia. In 1840–67 he acquired land throughout northern NSW and Queensland, becoming one of the most successful squatters in the pastoral boom of the mid-nineteenth century. Elected to the NSW parliament when it was first constituted in 1856, Forster served almost continuously until his death and held many important offices, including that of premier briefly, 1859–60. A prolific writer of satirical, political and social essays and a sound literary critic with a wide awareness of the developing colonial literary scene, Forster contributed frequently to Robert Lowe's *Atlas* and Daniel Deniehy's *Southern Cross*. Two of his significant verse satires appeared in the *Atlas*, 'The Devil and the Governor', directed against Governor Sir George Gipps, and 'The Genius and the Ghost', an attack on the proposals for the renewal of transportation. Forster published other poetry and verse plays: *The Weirwolf* (1876), which included, in addition to the title work, sonnets on the Crimean War and other poems; *The Brothers* (1877); and *Midas* (1884).

FOULCHER, John (1952–), born Sydney, graduated with honours from the University of Sydney and has been a teacher in NSW and the ACT. Poetry editor in 1993 of the National Library's *Voices*, he has published several volumes of poetry, *Light Pressure* (1983), *Pictures from the War* (1987), *Paperweight* (1991) and *New and Selected Poems* (1993) and shared the National Library Poetry Award in 1988 with the poem 'Kosciusko in Summer', which is also included in *Paperweight* and *New and Selected Poems*. Simple, direct and convincing, Foulcher's poetry reflects common human experiences – joy in the present, regret for the errors and omissions of the past and faith, mixed with a dash of apprehension, for the future. Many of his poems deal with his family – a father who died when he was only a boy and whose death he did not (because of his age) know how to mourn; a mother whose long, slow dying came when he was a grown man and over whom he grieved fully; a wife and children in whom he delights but who arouse his anxiety as they face the daily struggles of life. *Pictures from the War* is about the war of life, its casualties weighed up against its rewards. Foulcher's range is wide. Biblically based poems such as 'Elegy for Lot's Wife', 'Moses at the Jordan' rub shoulders with historically based 'Botany Bay', 'First Fleet', 'Bora Ground', with the richness of the rural scene of 'Kosciusko in Summer', with the dramatic monologue of a woman blind from birth, who regains her sight ('First Sight'), and with the long 'Travel Sequence', and the partly tongue-in-cheek elegy for Don Bradman's final 'duck' which robbed him of a Test batting average of 100. A sensitive observer of both personal relationships and the wider human scene, Foulcher is building a strong reputation as a poet. His work has been set for several years for study in secondary schools.

Fourteen Men (1954), Dame Mary Gilmore's final volume of poems, was published when she was approaching her ninetieth year. The title poem recalls the massacre of the Chinese at Lambing Flat. The volume also contains the well-known poems 'Nationality' and 'The Pear Tree'.

FOX, Len (1905–), born Melbourne, was a teacher at Scotch College, Melbourne, 1928–32. In 1935 he became Victorian State secretary of the Movement against War and Fascism; in 1939 he went to Sydney where he worked on the Labor Party newspaper *Progress* (1940–45), and on the communist newspaper *Tribune* (1946–55). Fox and his wife, Mona Brand, lived in Hanoi 1956–57; on their return journey to Sydney in 1958 he joined the Miners' Federation paper *Common Cause* and was its editor 1965–70. A prolific writer of socio-political pamphlets, Fox has also published verse, short fiction and dramatic works. His verse, which includes *Chung of Vietnam* (1957, children's verse), *Gum Leaves and Bamboo* (1959), *Vietnam Neighbours* (1966), *Gum Leaves and People* (1967) and *Gum Leaves and Dreaming* (1978), clearly reflects his interest in the people of Vietnam and the Australian Aborigines. He also wrote *The Aboriginals* (1978), and edited *Depression Down Under* (1977), recollections of the 1930s in Australia. He was co-editor with Faith Bandler of *The Time Was Ripe* (1983), the history of the Aboriginal-Australian Fellowship, and collaborated with her in a children's novel, *Marani in Australia* (1980), based partly on her father's life. His recent writing includes a biography of his artist uncle, *E. Phillips Fox and his Family* (1985), and an edited history of the Fellowship of Australian Writers, *Dream at a Graveside* (1988).

'Frank the Poet', see MACNAMARA, Francis

'Freedom on the Wallaby', a poem by Henry Lawson, exists in two versions. The first, which has also become a well-known folk-song, is the poem as originally published in the Brisbane *Worker*, May 1891, when it contained a much-quoted reference to Eureka in the last verse:

> So we must fly a rebel flag
> As others did before us,
> And we must sing a rebel song
> And join in rebel chorus;
> We'll make the tyrants feel the sting
> O' those that they would throttle;
> They needn't say the fault is ours
> If blood should stain the wattle.

There were minor changes (e.g. 'bankers' replaced 'tyrants') when the poem was published in the Sydney *Worker* in 1894, and a major revision (including the deletion of the Eureka reference) for publication in *For Australia* (1913), which provides the text of the poem printed in most Lawson collections. Lawson's original poem was inspired by the 1891 shearing strikes in western Queensland; both the title and the last line have become familiar in the rhetoric of social protest, e.g. in Leslie Haylen's Eureka novel *Blood on the Wattle* (1948). The publication of the poem led to its being quoted in the Queensland parliament during a motion voting thanks to the strikebreakers, to which Lawson derisively replied in two further contributions to the Brisbane *Worker*, 'The Vote of Thanks Debate' and 'The Labour Agitator'.

Fremantle Arts Centre began in 1972 in the restored Fremantle Lunatic Asylum which had been built in the 1860s as an asylum for deranged convicts. Its founding director was Ian Templeman, now assistant director-general of cultural and educational services at the National Library of Australia. Soon after its opening the Centre established seasonal programmes in art and craft classes and in 1976 it established Arts Access which provided workshops for country people and incorporated a book-hire scheme for country and metropolitan book clubs. Creative writing figured prominently in the Centre's activities, supervised by Templeman, himself a poet, and employing recognised tutors, e.g. Elizabeth Jolley. Weekend writing seminars and conferences were held frequently. In 1975 the Centrepress was established; it ultimately became the Fremantle Arts Centre Press with both the Arts Centre and the Arts Centre Press under (until 1989) the direction of Ian Templeman, who now runs the Molonglo Press in Canberra. Since 1990 they have been separate organisations, housed and managed separately, June Moorhouse being the general manager of the Arts Centre and Clive Newman general manager of the press. The Arts Centre publishes *FAR*, a bi-monthly magazine which, among its other contents, includes new poetry and awards two annual prizes for poetry and short fiction, named the John Birch Awards to honour Birch's distinguished service as Fremantle City Librarian. The Centre conducts an annual winter season of local writers reading from their works and co-presents the Writers' Festival with the Festival of Perth every second year.

Fremantle Arts Centre Press has published, since 1976, more than 200 titles with a focus on high-quality literary works of prose and poetry, art, social history, autobiography, biography and children's literature. Among its most successful writers (usually West Australians) are Elizabeth Jolley, Nicholas Hasluck and Philip Salom, although virtually every West Australian author of merit has been published by the press. Its greatest successes have been *A Fortunate Life* by A.B. Facey and *My Place* by Sally Morgan. Strong on WA anthologies, it published in its first year, 1976, *Soundings* (poetry) and *New Country* (short stories) and for many years published a poetry magazine, *Patterns*, four times a year which grew out of the creative writing classes conducted by Ian Templeman and Elizabeth Jolley.

Friendly Street, a regular series of public poetry readings, began in Adelaide in November 1975, largely as a result of efforts by Ian Reid, Andrew Taylor and Richard Tipping. Although there is no such place in Adelaide, Friendly Street was the name chosen for the meetings because it indicated the friendly, welcoming atmosphere generated at the monthly (the first Tuesday night) gatherings at the Box Factory, Regent Street, Adelaide. Each year a *Friendly Street Poetry Reader*, selected from the work read at the monthly meetings, is published. There have been eighteen to 1995, the first edited by Richard Tipping in 1976. Other well-known editors have been Ian Reid, Andrew Taylor, Peter Goldsworthy, John Bray, Robert Clark, Graham Rowlands and Jeff Guess. In addition to the annual *Readers* many individual books of verse by Friendly Street regulars have been published, at first and for many years by the small collaborative press Friendly Street Poets, but more recently by Wakefield Press. Twenty-three individual collections have been published. The 1992 anthology, *Tuesday Night Live*, edited by Jerri Kroll and Barry Westburg, is a retrospective collection of about 160 poems by 80 poets, an indication of the variety of the Friendly Street performers. *Tuesday Night Live* also carries a valuable introduction detailing the history of Friendly Street.

FULLERTON, Mary Eliza ('E') (1868–1946), born in a bark hut in Glenmaggie, Victoria, became a devotee of literature and a strong campaigner on feminist issues. As 'Alpenstock', she wrote poetry and short fiction for newspapers and journals. She published poetry, *Moods and Melodies* (1908), *The Breaking Furrow* (1921) and *Bark House Days* (1921, published with additional material in 1931), her childhood reminiscences. Her friendship with Miles Franklin, continued by correspondence after Fullerton left Australia permanently for England in 1922, led to the eventual publication of her poetry in the 1940s under the pseudonym 'E'. The identity of 'E', the author of *Moles Do So Little With Their Privacy* (1942) and *The Wonder and the Apple* (1946), was one of the major literary talking-points of the time; adopted as a mark of reverence for her favourite authors, Emily Bronte and Emily Dickinson, and for her mother, it was revealed after her death.

GALLAGHER, Katherine (1935–   ), born Maldon, Victoria, worked as a laboratory assistant and secretary before graduating from the University of Melbourne in 1963. She taught in Melbourne high schools 1964–68 and in 1969 moved to Europe, living first in London and then in Paris (1971–79). Since 1979 she has lived in England. She has contributed widely to poetry anthologies and journals both in Australia and overseas and has published several volumes of verse, *The Eye's Circle* (1974, a second edition 1978), *Tributaries of the Love-Song* (1978), *Passengers to the City* (1985), *Fish-Rings on Water* (1989) and *Finding the Prince* (1993). Although resident overseas for more than twenty years, her connections with Australia remain strong. Many of her poems are delicate cameos of events and experiences significant to her. Sensitive, imaginative and at ease in either a colloquial or more formal style, Gallagher is especially impressive when she writes of those close to her or of the general human condition where loss, grief or sorrow are conveyed with eloquence and compassion. She won the Warana Poetry Prize in 1981.

GARDNER, Silvana (1942–   ), born Zadar, Dalmatia, subsequently Yugoslavia, has had numerous occupations – artist, domestic, nurse, interpreter – and has conducted and co-ordinated creative writing and art workshops. She graduated in fine arts and literature from the University of Queensland and her art work is represented in Australian and overseas galleries. She has published several books of poetry: *When Sunday Comes* (1982), *Hacedor* (1982), *With Open Eyes* (1983), *Children of the Dragon* (1985), *The Devil in Nature* (1987), *Ha Ha Hacedor* (1991) and *Cochineal Red* (1992, Pamphlet Poets series). Her best poems are the brief, enigmatic verses of the early volumes that recall her migrant childhood, including the ambience of the boarding house; her grandmother of the aristocratic profile and the black burial dress lovingly preserved 'for one last modesty'; searching in the sea for ambergris with her father; the name of their new street, 'Hope'; and the barely concealed contempt of her classmates for one of a different ethnic group. *With Open Eyes* describes and characterises a number of individuals: the lost soul, Marjorie; a fisherman and his son; the telegraph linesman; the 85-year-old 'Miss Regina'. It also contains poems written during a visit to America. *Children of the Dragon* was largely inspired by the children she met while conducting art, craft and literary workshops in schools, youth shelters and other places. The second part, 'of the Dragon', deals with the underprivileged youth at the Windsor Youth Emergency Shelter in Brisbane, where she was artist-in-residence for part of 1982. *The Devil in Nature* is more feminist in outlook, with a number of poems wryly and provocatively assessing male–female relationships.

Gargoyle Poets, see *Makar*

Gateway, The (1953), the third volume of poetry by Judith Wright, shows the poet moving away from the familiar world of the senses which characterises the earlier volumes, *The Moving Image* (1946) and *Woman to Man* (1949), to begin a quest for self-knowledge. The title poem speaks of 'the traveller' (the poet herself) passing through 'the gateway' to new perceptions. In addition to poems about other searchers for knowledge, e.g. 'The Journey' and 'The Cicadas', the volume contains poems such as 'Old House', 'Train Journey' and 'Eroded Hills', which reflect Wright's long-established interest in her ancestry and the New England environment.

GAY, William (1865–97), born Bridge of Weir, Scotland, emigrated to NZ in 1885 and then to Victoria in 1888 in a vain attempt to ward off tuberculosis. He taught briefly at Scotch College, Melbourne, and was a tutor on a Riverina station and later in Melbourne. He spent the last four years of his life in a Bendigo hospital but maintained his keen interest in writing poetry and helped foster literature in the Bendigo area. He published *Sonnets and Other Verses* (1894), *Sonnets* (1896) and *Christ on Olympus and Other Poems* (1896). A miniature edition of his poems was published posthumously in 1910; *The Complete Poetical Works of William Gay*, edited with a memoir by J. Glen Oliphant, appeared in 1911. His best-known individual poems are those which appeal for the establishment of the Australian Commonwealth, i.e. 'Australia 1894', 'Australian Federation' and 'Australia Infelix'. 'Christ on Olympus', a long poem in blank verse, shows the Olympian deities relinquishing their power to the greater God.

GEBHARDT, Peter has contributed poetry to several periodicals and has published two collections, *Killing the Old Fool* (1988) and *Secretary to Praise* (1992). Whether grounded in minute natural events as in 'Horizons' and 'The Rock' or in familiar historical ones, as in 'William John Wills Writes his Ending', Gebhardt's compressed lyrics explore life's paradoxes with irony and compassion.

GELLERT, Leon (1892–1977), born Walkerville, SA, was a schoolteacher before he was wounded at Gallipoli. In 1917 he published *Songs of a Campaign*, which won the University of Adelaide's Bundey prize for poetry and established Gellert as the soldier-poet of the day. In eloquent poems such as 'Through a Porthole', 'Patience', 'The Burial', 'The Diggers' and 'Attack at Dawn', Gellert recorded the dignity and courage of the soldier caught haplessly in the futility of war. In 1919 he published *The Isle of San*, a long allegorical poem divided into six dreams with a prologue and an epilogue and numerous songs and sonnets that are used as interludes between the dreams. In 1928 he included the connecting pieces of *The Isle of San* in a booklet, *Desperate Measures*, which is largely concerned with the vicissitudes of domesticity, Gellert having married in 1918. He taught in Sydney after the war before his friendship with Norman Lindsay, Sydney Ure Smith and Bert Stevens led him into journalism, initially with *Art in Australia*, then with *Home* and later as literary editor, columnist and book reviewer with the *Sydney Morning Herald* and the *Daily Telegraph*. His later publications included the satirical *These Beastly Australians* (1944), *Week after Week* (1953) and *Year after Year* (1956).

GERARD, Edwin Field ('Gerardy', 'Trooper Gerardy') (1891–1965), born Yunta, SA, worked on the WA goldfields and later served with the AIF at Gallipoli and in the campaigns in the desert. Under the pseudonyms 'Gerardy' and 'Trooper Gerardy', he contributed poems about the war to journals such as the *Bulletin* and published two volumes of poetry, *The Road to Palestine and Other Verses* (1918) and *Australian Light Horse Ballads and Rhymes* (1919). Sometimes dubbed 'the laureate of the Light Horsemen', Gerard produced in poems such as 'The Horse That Died for Me', 'El Maghara', 'South of Gaza' and 'Riding Song' his most vigorous and effective verse. After the war he was a journalist, then a farmer, and wrote prolifically for the

Bulletin in verses that reflected nostalgically on the vanished rural life of his youth.

GIBSON, G.H. (George Herbert) ('Ironbark') (1846–1921), born Plymouth, England, was a solicitor when he migrated to NZ in 1869 and thence in 1874 to Sydney, where in 1876 he joined the Department of Lands. His work as an inspector in that department took him to many outback stations, where he gained the knowledge of the bush that informs the light-hearted and lively ballads he published under the pseudonym 'Ironbark'. His books of verse are *Southerly Busters* (1878), *Ironbark Chips and Stockwhip Cracks* (1893) and *Ironbark Splinters from the Australian Bush* (1912), the last containing some of the poems from the earlier volumes.

GILBERT, Kevin (1933–93), born Condobolin, NSW, to an Irish father and part-Aboriginal mother, who both died when he was 7, was brought up in welfare homes and by relatives. After a limited education he worked through his teens as an itinerant labourer in towns of western NSW. Married at an early age, and with two children, Gilbert was found guilty in 1957 of the murder of his wife after a domestic argument and was sentenced to life imprisonment. In prison Gilbert, until then almost illiterate, became interested in art and literature. He soon showed a considerable talent for both lino cuts and painting, and his work from prison was exhibited in 1970 by the Australian Council for the Arts. In 1971, after fourteen years in prison, Gilbert was paroled. His play *The Cherry Pickers* (1988), a story of Aboriginal seasonal workers, written while he was in prison and staged in Sydney in 1971, earned Gilbert the distinction of being the first Aboriginal playwright to have a play performed in Australia. Gilbert rapidly became active in the wider Aboriginal cause, editing periodicals such as *Alchuringa* and *Black Australian News*, canvassing the federal government for a national inquiry into Aboriginal education, and working for the Centre for Continuing Research into Aboriginal Affairs at Monash University, Melbourne. In addition to *The Cherry Pickers* he published several volumes of poetry, *End of Dreamtime* (1971), *People Are Legends* (1978) and *The Blackside* (1990). His poetry is protest verse, displaying his anger against White society in 'End of Dreamtime', 'People Are Legends' 'Chained'; the indifferent treatment of the Aboriginal people in 'Trying to Save Joan Ella'; the degradation brought into their lives by the hopelessness of their common future in 'Goomee Jack'; the need for violence in order to gain basic land rights in 'Land Claims'; his own personal situation in 'Epitaph: Upon Expiration of the Aspirations of an Aborigine' and the tragedy of the part-Aborigine in 'Inhabitants of the Third World'. His contentious poem 'To My Cousin, Evonne Cawley' in the *Bulletin* (30 September 1980) attacked what he saw as her lack of involvement in Aboriginal problems. Gilbert's main political tract is the prose work *Because a White Man'll Never Do It* (1973). *Living Black* (1978), a collection of interviews conducted by Gilbert with Aborigines from all parts of Australia, won a National Book Council Award in 1978. In 1988 he published the anthology *Inside Black Australia*, which he described as 'the first collection of contemporary Aboriginal oral history from an Aboriginal viewpoint'. Awarded the Human Rights Award for literature in 1988, Gilbert returned it saying he could not accept it until Aborigines were granted human rights. In 1992 he was awarded one of the four-year fellowships to artists of high distinction granted by the federal government.

GILES, Barbara (1912–   ), born Manchester, England, came to Australia in 1923. She had to postpone her education for some years because of family circumstances but later spent some years teaching in Victoria. She was also involved in migrant education as a teacher and has written about migrants and their experiences in her poetry. She was co-ordinating editor of the magazine *Luna* for eight years and a founding member of Pariah Press Co-operative. A tutor of creative writing and a long-time reviewer for the ABC, Giles has published five books of poetry, all since her mid-sixties, *Eve Rejects Apple* (1978), *Earth and Solitude* (1985), *The Hag in the Mirror* (1989), *A Savage Coast* (1993) and, with Roy Fuller and Adrian Rumble, *Upright Downfall* (1983). *Earth and Solitude*, with its characteristic Giles eye for detail, is about the difficulty of the farming life. *The Hag in the Mirror* has many poems dealing with the mixed emotions of age, the passing of time and the approach of death but Giles, while willing to explore all the attitudes available to those confronting the later stages of life and even death, is positive and forceful in her reactions. Her intimate, simple, lyrical, witty, laconic and occasionally angry poetry carries much appeal. She won the FAW John Shaw Neilson Poetry Award in 1972. Giles had edited and co-edited several anthologies of verse for children and is well known for her children's novels.

GILLMORE, Terry (1945–) lives in rural Victoria and has contributed poetry to numerous periodicals and has published two collections, *Further, Poems 1966–1976* (1977) and *Surviving the Shadow* (1990).

GILMORE, Dame Mary (1864–1962) was born Mary Jean Cameron at Cotta Walla near Goulburn, NSW. After a bush childhood with sporadic formal schooling she completed her education by assisting in small schools in the Cootamundra, Wagga and Albury districts of NSW. In 1888–89 she taught in the mining town of Silverton, near Broken Hill, where close contact with the militant, working-class community aroused her lifelong interest in the labour movement. In 1890–95 she taught at Neutral Bay and Stanmore in Sydney and became involved in the developing radicalism of the day by supporting the maritime and shearers' strikes of the early 1890s. In those years her friendship with Henry Lawson began and she was influenced by three men, William Lane, John Farrell and A.G. Stephens, who, she said, 'shaped my mind and my life'. In 1896 she joined Lane's New Australia venture in Paraguay and in May 1897, at the Cosme settlement, married a Victorian shearer, William Alexander Gilmore. They returned to Australia in 1902 adopted an isolated farming existence in the Casterton district of western Victoria. In October 1903 her poetry was featured by A.G. Stephens in the Red Page of the *Bulletin*, and in 1908 she began to edit the Women's Page of the Sydney *Worker*, a task which occupied her until 1931. In 1910 her first volume of poetry, *Marri'd and Other Verses*, was published, and in 1912, when her husband joined his brother on the land in north Queensland, she and her son went back to Sydney. Her campaigns for the welfare of the young and old, sick and helpless, depressed and under-privileged, and her irate and constantly expressed disgust with privilege and corruption in high places filled the pages of the *Worker* and other newspapers for many years. In the two decades 1920–40, she published six volumes of poetry and three of prose. In 1937, in recognition of her literary achievement and her community and social activities, and as a tribute to her growing national status, she was made DBE, an honour which she cherished. During the tense months of 1942 after Singapore fell and the Japanese island-hopped towards Australia, her defiant and well-publicised poem 'No Foe Shall Gather Our Harvest' boosted public morale. In her remaining years, perched in her tiny flat in the heart of Sydney's bohemian Kings Cross, she continued her writing and encouragement of other writers, her social crusading, and gathering of the diminishing store of pioneer lore and legend. William Dobell's controversial portrait of her was unveiled for her ninety-second birthday in 1957. Her last years passed amid growing public acclaim; her death was mourned by a ceremonial state funeral through the streets of Sydney.

Mary Gilmore's earliest poems, *Marri'd and Other Verses*, are mainly spontaneous reactions, in a colloquial style, to the joys and sorrows of life's daily round; the short, lively lyrics are interspersed with occasional outbursts against injustice and inhumanity. *The Passionate Heart* (1918), with its emphasis on the desolation of war, is more mature verse. In *The Tilted Cart* (1925), *The Wild Swan* (1930) and *Under the Wilgas*

(1932), and in her prose anecdotes and reminiscences, *Old Days: Old Ways* (1934) and *More Recollections* (1935), her interest in re-creating pioneer times and her concern with the despoiling of the land and destruction of the Aboriginal tribes are paramount. *Battlefields* (1939) contains her most radical verse. 'The Baying Hounds' depicts the customary Gilmore stance, 'There was no hunted one/With whom I did not run', while 'Contest I Ask' affirms her lifelong belief, 'Better to wounded lie/ Than undeclared to die.' In the inscription to her final volume, *Fourteen Men* (1954), published when she was almost 90, she faces life's final encounter with the calm judgment that death is 'the last thing left to defeat'. Mary Gilmore's best poetry insists on love, courage and selflessness, and enshrines those values in some fine lyrics. Dymphna Cusack, T. Inglis Moore, Barrie Ovenden and Walter Stone compiled *Mary Gilmore: A Tribute* (1965); W.H. Wilde and T. Inglis Moore edited *Letters of Mary Gilmore* (1980) and Wilde wrote the biography *Courage a Grace: A Biography of Dame Mary Gilmore* (1988).

One-woman dramatic interpretations of the life and work of Mary Gilmore include Theatre ACT's production 'When Butter Was Sixpence a Pound' (Joan Murray, 1983), Melbourne Theatre Company's 'To Botany Bay on a Bondi Tram' (Beverley Dunn, 1984), and the Queensland Art Council's touring season of the same production in 1994. Mary Gilmore is one of the two Australian writers (A.B. Paterson is the other) featured on the 1993 ten-dollar note.

GLEESON, James (1915–   ), born Sydney, is on of Australia's best-known painters and art critics, frequently described as Australia's first surrealist. Art critic of the Sydney *Sun* newspaper 1949–76, he became director of the Sir William Dobell Art Foundation in 1971. He has been awarded the OAM and made AO and received an honorary D.Litt. from Macquarie University. Prominent in the debates on surrealism in the 1930s and 1940s, Gleeson contributed verse to such journals as *Angry Penguins*, *A Comment* and *Stream* and articles to *Art in Australia*. He also produced two groups of poem-drawings in 1938 and 1976, all using poetry written 1938–43 and creating dual written and visual images. His *Selected Poems*, drawn from the same group of poems, was published in 1993. His other publications include *William Dobell* (1964), *Masterpieces of Australian Painting* (1969), *Colonial Painters 1788–1880* (1971), *Impressionist Painters 1881–1930* (1971), and *Robert Klippel* (1983).

'Glen of the Whiteman's Grave, The', a narrative poem, was first published by Henry Kendall in an undated booklet (?1865); it was later published in *Leaves from Australian Forests* (1869) as 'The Glen of Arrawatta' and republished with minor variations as 'Orara' in 1881. The tale of a lone settler murdered by natives, Kendall's poem is similar in theme to the earlier Charles Harpur narrative 'The Creek of the Four Graves'.

GODDARD, Francis, see **MACNAMARA, Francis**

Going Down Swinging, an annual literary magazine begun in 1980 with Myron Lysenko as founding editor (later edited by Kevin Brophy and Lysenko) is an anthology of contemporary writing aimed especially at publishing the work of new, young or innovative writers. It is now (1995) edited by Lyn Broughton, Louise Craig and Carol Carter.

'Golden Builders', which takes its title from William Blake's 'Jerusalem', is a 27-poem sequence by Vincent Buckley forming the second half of *Golden Builders and Other Poems* (1976). The sequence emphasises the oppressive impact on the individual human consciousness of an urban environment, in this case the inner Melbourne suburbs where the University sits cheek by jowl with slums, high-rise flats, factories, hospitals and a cemetery. The oppression of noise 'piped up like muzak' from the eternal jack-hammers and ceaseless traffic is the constant accompaniment to the ugliness and sordidness of the city, the 'crouched brick houses', the garbage and rats, the graffiti, a woman seeking an abortion, a self-immolation, and doomed dogs howling in the cages of medical laboratories. Although the overwhelming impression of the poem is of an environment deeply depressing to the human spirit, the underlying theme, as indicated by the introductory reference to Blake and by the 'Practising Not Dying' sequences and other areas of the poem, is that the human spirit can find within itself the strength and resilience to survive.

GOLDSWORTHY, Peter (1951–), born Minlaton, SA, grew up in various SA towns and in Darwin. He graduated in medicine from the University of Adelaide in 1974 and has combined the practice of medicine with a busy writing career. He has published four books of short fiction, *Archipelagoes* (1982), *Zooing* (1986), *Bleak Rooms* (1988) and *Little Deaths* (1993); four books of poetry, *Readings from Ecclesiastes* (1982), *This Goes with This* (1988), *This Goes with That: Selected Poems 1970–1990* (1991) and *After the Ball* (1992); two novels, *Maestro* (1989, which has been filmed) and *Honk If You Are Jesus* (1992) as well as *Magpie* (1992), a somewhat madcap pastiche of a novel in collaboration with Brian Matthews. Successful in all three genres Goldsworthy won the 1982 Commonwealth Poetry Prize, the Anne Elder Award for Poetry and the SA Biennial Literary Award, all for *Readings from Ecclesiastes*, and the Bicentennial Grace Perry Award for Poetry for *This Goes with This*. Goldsworthy's poetry, with its laconic Australian idiom, is an attractively intelligent, rueful, sardonic assessment of contemporary life. His observation of people and situations is acute, the acerbity underlying much of what he has to say controlled and alleviated by wry wit and humour.

GOODFELLOW, Geoff (1949–), born Adelaide, grew up in a working-class environment, leaving school at 15 to begin almost twenty years of physical labour in a variety of jobs – on building sites, oil rigs, in trucks, and as a self-employed carpenter. Struck down by a severe back injury in 1982, he discovered poetry – in the form of A.B. Paterson – and from that time has followed a successful career as a performance poet and creative-writing teacher. He has taken poetry on to the streets, into clubs and pubs, prisons, schools, colleges and universities. He was a member (with fellow performance poets, Eric Beach and Jenny Boult) in 1984–85 of the SA 'New Mobile Poetry Workshop' and has conducted writing workshops in SA prisons and correctional institutions. He was made poet-in-residence in 1985 at Pembroke School, Yatala Labour Prison and SA rehabilitation and training centres. During 1988 he travelled through Canada, USA, Europe, Great Britain and China giving poetry readings and conducting writing workshops and seminars. He was awarded the Carclew Fellowship of SA in 1988 and in 1989 was appointed to the SA Youth Arts Board. In 1990 he was appointed by the Australia Council as poet-in-residence with CMEU, the Construction, Mining and Energy Union of SA, his role being to paint a poet's-eye view of the workings of a large trade union organisation. The somewhat grizzled and weatherbeaten portraits of Goodfellow on several of his books reflect their contents – tough, direct, no-nonsense but eloquent statements of personal experience. He has published three slim books of verse, *No Collars No Cuffs* (1986), *Bow Tie and Tails* (1989), *No Ticket No Start* (1990) and *Triggers: Turning Experiences into Poetry* (1992), a poetry workshop text for young readers which uses individual poems to demonstrate how poems are 'triggered' and finally written. *Triggers* also provides an insight into Goodfellow's own experiences.

No Collars No Cuffs deals first ('Locked In') with his childhood including an early education at the hands of the nuns, a hazardous experience given his rebellious spirit. Pubs and prisons provide the contexts of the next two sections ('Bending at the Bars', 'Bending Bars') and the book concludes with 'Locked Out', dealing with those (e.g. Aborigines, squatters, battered wives) whom life has treated badly. The most memorable poems in *Bow Tie and Tails* speak also for the distraught, disadvantaged and derelict: 'Poem for Annie' (his battered sister whose three husbands have 'all turned out mongrels'); 'Another City View' (street kids); 'An Old Bloke' (a schizophrenic); 'Epitaph for Robbie' (a young, and dead, drug addict); 'Stretched Out' (a victim of parental molestation now turned prostitute); 'Governor's Pleasure' (young men raped in prison). *No Ticket No Start* contains the poetic fruits of Goodfellow's residency with the CMEU. Mostly poetry of praise for the workers, the collection urges the need to keep fighting the bosses ('it's just another fight/ another bloody year'), the need to keep alive in all good working-class hearts the vision of the 'Light on the Hill'.

GOODGE, W.T. (William Thomas) (1862–1909), born London, went to sea as a steward but left his ship in Sydney in 1882 to go 'on the wallaby' for twelve years in outback NSW. In later life Goodge was a journalist. Goodge's comic journalism is part of the long line of notable Australian writing in that genre which includes the work of Lennie Lower, Alex Macdonald, Ross Campbell and Ron Saw. A popular *Bulletin* poet and assessed by Norman Lindsay as one of Australia's best writers of light verse, Goodge published *Hits! Skits! and Jingles!* (1899). His poems are filled with bush identities such as Temora Mat, Slippery Bill, Brandy Jack and the Melodious Bullocky, and with tall tales of the bush such as the story of Jock McPherson who rode the Oozlum Bird from the Centre to Sydney and back, and of Pat Ahearne who exhibited lobsters at outback shows as 'monster Sydney fleas'. Goodge's best-known poem is 'The Great Australian Adjective', which is also the title of a volume of his verse (1965).

GOONERATNE, Yasmine (1935–   ), born Sri Lanka, into the Dias Bandaranaike family, and educated at the universities of Ceylon and Cambridge, UK, came to Australia in 1972 and holds a personal chair in English at Macquarie University. Foundation director of the University's post-colonial literatures and language centre, she was made AO in 1990 and received the University's first earned D.Litt. in 1981. As well as numerous works of literary criticism and edited anthologies of Asian poetry and prose, Gooneratne has published a novel, *A Change of Skies* (1991); several volumes of poetry including *Celebrations and Departures: Selected Poems 1951–1991* (1991); and *Relative Merits* (1986) an account of her father's family.

GORDON, Adam Lindsay (1833–70) was born at Fayal in the Azores where his mother's father had a plantation. On his father's retirement from a commission with the Bengal cavalry he completed his education in England. After numerous youthful escapades Gordon was, in 1853, banished by his parents to SA, where he enlisted in the mounted police. Resigning from the constabulary after two years' service he drifted about SA dealing in horses and riding in steeplechases. With a sizable legacy from his parents' estate he purchased several properties, married, and lived in Dingley Dell, a small stone cottage still lovingly preserved near the seaside settlement of Port Mac-Donnell, not far from Mount Gambier. From those years come many stories of Gordon's daring feats of horsemanship, most notably the Blue Lake Leap. He had a brief and unspectacular parliamentary career in 1864–66, an abortive grazing venture in WA in 1866–67, and then conducted a livery stable in Ballarat in 1867–68. After a severe head injury in a riding accident, bankruptcy caused by a fire in the livery stable, and the death of his infant daughter, he left Ballarat for Melbourne. There he lived an unhappy and aimless existence, working spasmodically at his writing and suffering from depression, insomnia and pain from his numerous riding injuries. When an attempt failed to claim heirship to the ancestral Gordon lands in Scotland, he faced financial disaster. On 24 June 1870, the day following the publication of his poems,

Bush Ballads and Galloping Rhymes, he committed suicide on Brighton Beach, Melbourne.

Gordon's published works began with *The Feud* (1864), a ballad inspired by Noel Paton's engravings of scenes from the ballad 'The Dowie Dens o' Yarrow'. *Ashtaroth* (1867), his second publication, a long dramatic poem indebted to the Faust theme, has failed to arouse any critical enthusiasm. The two main volumes on which his poetic reputation rests are *Sea Spray and Smoke Drift* (1867) and *Bush Ballads and Galloping Rhymes*. In 1934 a bust of Gordon was unveiled in the Poets' Corner of Westminster Abbey, making him the only Australian poet to have been thus honoured. That mark of recognition reflects the adulation he attracted after his death and through the first decades of the twentieth century. His popularity sprang partly from the romantic aura of his life, his aristocratic background, his exile in the colony, his reckless riding exploits, and the pathos of his death. It sprang, too, from the gratitude of Australian nationalists for his poetry's acclaim of the outback way of life. His verses were loved and recited around camp-fires and in the homesteads and shearing sheds of the backblocks. Yet very little of Gordon's poetry reflects the fragrance of the wattle blossom, the blue of Australian skies, or the camaraderie of Australian mateship. Such Australian flavour is present only in 'The Sick Stockrider', 'A Dedication' and some parts of 'Ye Wearie Wayfarer'. Most of his poetry is modelled upon the conventional verse derived from his English education and background. Apart from the occasional narrative, notably 'The Rhyme of Joyous Garde', that poetry has little significance. The small Australian segment does, however, have undoubted historical importance, and 'The Sick Stockrider', in particular, is recognised as the poem which sketched in broad outline the territory which later balladists filled with profuse and picturesque detail; it thus pointed literature in a new definably 'Australian' direction. Poems to Gordon and his memory include Henry Kendall's 'The Late Mr A.L. Gordon: In Memoriam' and Will Ogilvie's 'Adam Lindsay Gordon'. Edith Humpris wrote *The Life of Adam Lindsay Gordon* (1934), C.F. MacRae, *Adam Lindsay Gordon* (1968), W.H. Wilde, the monograph *Adam Lindsay Gordon* (1972) and Geoffrey Hutton, *Adam Lindsay Gordon: The Man and the Myth* (1978). Ian F. McLaren compiled *Adam Lindsay Gordon: A Comprehensive Bibliography* (1986).

GORDON, J.W. (James William) ('Jim Grahame') (1874–1949), born Creswick, Victoria, was a mate of Henry Lawson and a possible model for Jack Mitchell, one of Lawson's most important fictional characters. Gordon wrote under the pseudonym 'Jim Grahame', a name reputedly given to him by Lawson. After 1903 he was a regular contributor of bush verse to the *Bulletin* and other journals, and published three volumes of verse: *Call of the Bush* (1940), *Home Leave and Departing* (1944) and *Under Wide Skies: Collected Verses* (1947).

GOULD, Alan (1949–), born London, his father a British Army officer and his mother, Valdergur, of Icelandic origin, came to Australia in 1966 after a childhood dominated by the frequent changes characteristic of a serviceman's family. As a student Gould was involved in the anti-Vietnam War protests and demonstrations; he graduated from the ANU with an arts degree and after a few brief casual occupations has settled to a life as a poet and novelist interspersed with occasional periods of teaching. He has lived mostly in Canberra and nearby Queanbeyan, was the founding editor of *Canberra Poetry* and the Open Door Press in Canberra, has been poetry reviewer for *Nation Review*, *Poetry Australia*, and other journals and newspapers, and is editor of the anthology, *Arteries in Stone* (1976). He has published numerous books of poetry, *Icelandic Solitaries* (1978); *Astral Sea* (1981, winner of NSW Premier's Poetry Award); *The Pausing of the Hours* (1984); *The Twofold Place* (1986); *Years Found in Likeness* (1988); *Formerlight* (1992, a *Selected* volume of the previous five books); and *Momentum* (1992).

Much of Gould's early poetry derives from his interest in Norse mythology and early ocean exploration. *Astral Sea* includes the sections, 'The Vinlanders', which owes much to Farley Mowat's reconstruction of Norse voyages in his book *Westocking* (1965), and 'The Songs of Ymir' which tells of the birth of the first man and woman and the first Frost giants. Ymir is killed and from his parts Heaven and Earth are made. *Astral Sea* also contains a series 'Marine Photographs', episodes of shipwrecks and near disasters at sea, mostly from the days of sail. The mesmerising focus of the sea is present also in *The Twofold Place* with its series 'A History of Shipping', which celebrates the feats of endurance and courage of the early seafarers – 'The Phoenician Helmsman', 'An Arab Merchant', 'The Norse Ship', 'Portuguese Carracks' and 'A Dutch Jacht'. *The Twofold Place* takes its title, however, from the imagination, that faculty that allows us to be wherever we wish, in the here and now or the there and then, and to see beyond the object to its deeper significance. Some autobiographical poems, 'Learning to Think', deal with Gould's boyhood of boarding schools, when he encountered two of his chief influences: the Ipswich River which ran alongside the school inspired thoughts of the vast oceans, and the school subject history, 'a constant B grade cinema', provided similarly expanded mental horizons. *Years Found in Likeness* brings another sea sequence, the extended voyager series 'The Great Circle', dealing with the life and explorations of Captain James Cook. Part of the poem was the libretto for a choral symphony commissioned for the 1988 Bicentenary. *Years Found in Likeness* also contains one of Gould's loveliest poems, 'Austral Bluebells in Molonglo Gorge'.

Momentum sees Gould in more experimental mode, using a striking array of poetic and verbal devices to explore emotional states. Intrigued by the archetypal Australian workman, Gould writes observantly and amusedly of the casual dexterity, laconic humour and good-natured contempt for those with more intellectual skills (including poets) characteristic of electricians, roof-tilers, tree-loppers, mechanics and the like. *Formerlight*, the *Selected* volume, which begins, appropriately, with a 'Homage' (from *Icelandic Solitaries*) to another lover of the sea, Joseph Conrad, gathers together an attractive, wide-ranging group of his best poems, establishing his claim to be one of Australia's finest contemporary poets.

Gould has also achieved similar distinction as a fiction-writer. His first novel, *The Man Who Stayed Below* (1984), won the James Cook University's Foundation for Australian Literary Studies Award in 1985. Gould's fictional *tour de force* is the novel *To the Burning City* (1991), which won the NBC Banjo Award for fiction.

Grace Leven Prize for Poetry, an annual award in memory of Grace Leven, who died in 1922, was established by her friend and admirer 'William Baylebridge'; she was his mother's half-sister. The award, first made in 1947 to Nan McDonald's *Pacific Sea*, is for the best volume of poetry published in the preceding twelve months by a writer either Australian-born and writing as an Australian, or naturalised in Australia and resident in Australia for not less than ten years. In 1948 the second award was made to Francis Webb's *A Drum for Ben Boyd*. The prize winners list reads like a roll-call of the greats of Australian poetry, e.g. Judith Wright, R.D. FitzGerald, A.D. Hope, James McAuley, Geoffrey Dutton, William Hart-Smith, Thomas Shapcott, Douglas Stewart, David Campbell, Rodney Hall, Gwen Harwood, John Blight, Vivian Smith, Peter Porter, Rosemary Dobson, Robert Gray, Chris Wallace-Crabbe, Rhyll McMaster, Elizabeth Riddell, John Tranter, Dorothy Hewett, Les Murray, Robert Adamson, Kevin Hart.

'GRAHAME, Jim', see **GORDON, J.W.**

GRANO, Paul (1894–1975), born Ararat, Victoria, graduated in law from the University of Melbourne but practised only briefly, working as an insurance salesman, advertising writer, commercial traveller and journalist. He went to Queensland in 1932 and worked in the Main Roads Commission until his retirement. Grano founded the Catholic Poetry Society in Brisbane in 1934 and the Catholic Readers' and Writers' Society in 1943. In 1946 he edited *Witness to the Stars*, an anthology of Catholic poetry of Australia and NZ. A Keatsian dedication to the ideals of truth and beauty, a wistful tone and skilful imagery are the hallmarks of his best verse. His volumes of poetry are *The Roads and Other Poems* (1934), *Quest* (1940), *Poet's Holiday* (1941), *Poems, New & Old* (1945) and *Selected Verse*, published posthumously in 1976.

GRANT, Jamie (James Beresford) (1949–), born Melbourne, graduated from La Trobe University. A brief career in advertising was followed by a decade as sales manager with Cambridge University Press. He is presently editor of Heinemann Australia's Poetry series. He has also been columnist and critic for the *Age Monthly Review* and a freelance journalist and editor. Well known as a critic of poetry, regarded by some as 'accurate and fearless' and by others as negative and destructive, Grant has, over the years, provoked considerable discussion. His own published works include *Turn Left at Any Time With Care* (a shared booklet with Graeme Kinross Smith in the Paperback Poets series, 1975), *The Refinery* (1985), *Skywriting* (1989) and *Mysteries* (1993). His love of cricket led to *The Longest Game* (1990, with Alec Buzo).

Demanding from the poets he reviews the highest standards of craftsmanship, Grant strives for similar excellence in his own work. Such excellence is hard won. Many of his poems become protracted chessboard battles with words, each phrase honed, shaped and positioned then followed by others even more worked upon in the search for the ultimate in description or analogy. Landscapes are especially important and his poems are frequently triggered by places and the impressions they leave or the reflections they arouse. Atmosphere and description are his forte, whether of natural scenes as in 'Snowfall over Water', 'Cold Weather', 'River Valley, House for Sale', 'Western District, Discovering Atlantis', or of people combined with places, 'Snow Holiday with Aunt', 'Grandfather's Clock', 'Sunlight at Montacute (Tasmania)', 'The Farmer's Widow, Home Again'. The intrusion of personalities into the poetry (an aunt with cancer, an autistic cousin in an asylum, the death of grandparents, echoes of marital disharmony) usually results in a gloomy reticence – 'ingrown pessimism', to modify slightly one of Grant's own phrases. 'Christopher Codrington' (one of several poems about Grant's unfortunate cousin) won the Northern Territory Government's Red Earth Poetry Award in 1988.

GRAY, Robert (1945–), born on the NSW north coast, grew up and was educated at Coffs Harbour, NSW. He left school to become a cadet journalist on a country newspaper but went to Sydney where he wrote for a magazine, was an advertising copywriter, a mail sorter and a bookshop assistant. With a growing literary reputation he became a reviewer of poetry with the *Sydney Morning Herald* and the ABC. He won the Marten Bequest Travelling Scholarship to the USA in 1981 and was a writer-in-residence in Japan. He supports himself almost wholly from his writing. His first volume of poetry, *Introspect, Retrospect* (1970), was followed by *Creekwater Journal* (1974), *Grass Script* (1979), *The Skylight* (1984), *Selected Poems 1963–1983* (1985), which won the NSW Premier's Award, the Adelaide Festival of the Arts Award and the Grace Leven Poetry Prize, all in 1986, *Piano* (1988), which was added to the original *Selected* to form an expanded *Selected* edition in 1990, and *Certain Things* (1993), which won the 1994 Victorian Premier's Literary Award. In 1990 he was the recipient of the Patrick White Award. He collaborated with Geoffrey Lehmann to produce the anthologies *Younger Australian Poets* (1983) and *Australian Poetry in the Twentieth Century* (1991), and, with Vivian Smith, *Sydney's Poems* (1992).

Applauded by fellow poets – 'the best eye in Australian poetry' (Les Murray) and 'as an imagist he is without a rival in the English-speaking world' (Kevin Hart) – Gray continues to receive increasing recognition. His constant poetic endeavour is to transform all that he sees and experiences in the freshest, most imaginative, yet realistic, verbal equivalents. Such poems as 'A Port of Europe', 'Very Early', 'The Swallows', 'Smoke', 'Under the Summer Leaves', 'Memories of the Coast', 'Journey: The North Coast' and 'A Country Town', are imagistic creations of rare quality. Yet the things described, as he confesses in 'Very Early' from *Piano*, have no need of poetic interpretation.

> 'If no-one saw all this, its existence would go on just
>   as well.
> And what is really here no words can tell'.

The north coast, where he grew up, is part of Gray's 'heart's blood' in much the same way as New England is Judith Wright's, Bunyah is Les Murray's. Many of the poems describing the area, 'Journey: The North Coast', 'Within the Traveller's Eye', 'North Coast Town', 'Memories of the Coast', 'Mr Nelson', capture the seedy, defeated, slothful inadequacy of people oppressed by the overpowering heat and humidity in contrast with the prolific, near tropical luxuriance of nature. Some of Gray's poems recall personal events – his boyhood visits to his grandmother, his recollections of his T.P.I. father's alcoholism and his mother's inadequacy in the face of that situation – but they lack any real sense of intimacy. It is almost as if the boy is emotionally dissociated from the personal strife around him. Gray's adult narrators convey something of the same impression. His eye for 'character', however, in 'Under the Summer Leaves' is unerring.

Adept at many verse forms and in both short and long poems, Gray is especially successful in the prose-poem genre. Remarkably accessible to the reader, his poetry denies the tenet of deconstruction that it is impossible to communicate what one means to others. 'Claritas', as Jamie Grant has said of him, is truly the essence of his work.

GREEN, Dorothy (Dorothy Auchterlonie) (1915–91), born County Durham, England, was educated there and at the University of Sydney. She worked as a broadcaster, journalist and news editor with the news service of the ABC 1942–49 and was co-principal of a well-known girls' school in Warwick, Queensland, 1955–60. She subsequently lectured in English at Monash University, at the ANU, at the Royal Military College, Duntroon, and at the Australian Defence Force Academy. In 1944 she married H.M. Green. Well known as an essayist and reviewer, she was a regular contributor to Australian literary magazines and published significant essays on Martin Boyd, E.L. Grant Watson, 'Henry Handel Richardson', Patrick White, C.J. Brennan, Christina Stead and Kylie Tennant. Her published works include a revised edition of her husband's *History* (1985); an extensively researched biography and critical study of 'Henry Handel Richardson', *Ulysses Bound* (1973), which won the James Cook University's Foundation for Australian Literary Studies Award and the Barbara Ramsden Award and appeared in a revised edition in 1986 titled *Henry Handel Richardson and her Fiction*; a collection of literary essays, *The Music of Love* (1984); three lectures delivered for the Foundation for Australian Literary Studies titled *The Writer, the Reader and the Critic in a Monoculture* (1986), which were reproduced in an expanded collection in 1991 titled *Writer Reader Critic*; and an edition of the writings of E.L. Grant Watson, *Descent of Spirit* (1990). With David Headon she edited *Imagining the Real: Australian Writing in the Nuclear Age* (1987). Her poetry, under the name Dorothy Auchterlonie, appeared regularly in literary magazines and in three collections, *Kaleidoscope* (1940), *The Dolphin* (1967) and *Something to Someone* (1983). She was awarded the OAM in 1984 and made AO in 1988; in 1987 she received an honorary doctorate from the University of New South Wales. Passionately concerned with the larger issues of culture, Dorothy Green approached literature from an interdisciplinary, nonconformist perspective. In her later years her uncompromising convictions on international and local political issues and on the moral responsibility of writers, readers and critics made her one of the most influential cultural figures. *Ulysses Bound* is her most substantial literary achievement, but her distinctive qualities as a critic, reflecting her wide-ranging interests and lightly worn but extensive scholarship, are most visible in her various essays and lectures.

GREEN, H.M. (Henry Mackenzie) (1881–1962), born Sydney, was educated in arts and law at the University of Sydney. After travelling in Europe for a year he returned to Sydney in 1907 and spent two years on the staff of the *Sydney Morning Herald*, followed by eleven years with the *Daily Telegraph*. He was librarian at the Fisher Library, University of Sydney, 1921–46. Green was married twice, on the second occasion to Dorothy Auchterlonie.

Green published two books of poetry, *The Happy Valley* (1925) and *The Book of Beauty* (1929), and edited *Australian Poetry 1943* (1944) and the influential collection *Modern Australian Poetry* (1946). But Green's most important work is his two-volume *A History of Australian Literature* (1961). A work of wide scope, thoroughness and painstaking scholarship, it is a mine of information, culled partly from Green's own unique knowledge of Australian writing, and is still the most significant literary history. The *History* was revised by his widow in 1985.

GREEN, James (1864–1948), born Newcastle-on-Tyne, England, was ordained a Methodist minister in 1893 and served as a chaplain with the Australian Bushmen's contingents in the Boer War and later with the Australian forces in the First World War. His publications include poetry, *The Story of the Australian Bushmen* (1903), *News from No Man's Land* (1917), *The Angels of Mons* (1921) and a collection of religious meditations, *From My Hospital Window* (1935). His fiction includes *The Selector* (1907) and *The Lost Echo* (1910).

GREEN, Judith, see **RODRIGUEZ, Judith**

GRIFFITHS, Bryn (1933–), born Swansea, Wales, was a seaman in the British merchant navy (1951–58) and a full-time writer (1962–76), before becoming cultural adviser and arts co-ordinator for industry with the Trades and Labour Council of WA; in 1989 he published *Wharfies: A Celebration of 100 years on the Fremantle Waterfront 1889–1989*. His interests lie in community arts, theatre, modern poetry and Celtic history; his books of poetry include *The Mask of Pity* (1966), *The Stones Remember* (1967), *Scars* (1969), *At the Airport* (1971), *The Survivors* (1971), *Beasthoods* (1972), *Starboard Green* (1973), *The Dark Convoys* (1974), *Love Poems* (1980), *The Shadow Beasts* (1981), and *Sea Poems* (1988). His radio plays, 'The Sailor' (1967) and 'The Dream of Arthur' (1968), were broadcast by the BBC.

GUESS, Jeff (1948–), born and educated in SA, is a high-school teacher, having graduated from Flinders University. Active in the Friendly Street writing community (he co-edited with Donna McSkimming the No. 12 *Friendly Street Reader* and with Yve Louis No. 18), he has published several small volumes of poetry: *Leaving Maps* (1984); *Four in the Afternoon* (1987); *Painting the Town – the Gawler Poems* (1988); *Replacing Fuses in the House of Cards* (1988), a *Poetry Australia* publication; *Rites of Arrival: Poems from the Museums of the History Trust of South Australia* (1990); *Out of Bounds* (1990); *Selected Sonnets* (1991) and *Early in the Cafe Boulevarde: The Adelaide Poems* (1991). With Anne Brewster he compiled *Inner Courtyard* (1990), an anthology of SA love poetry.

Guess's interest in history is evident in the poems inspired by the SA History Trust museums and by others such as 'The Map Maker' (Flinders and Kangaroo Island),

'Lambing Flat Massacre, 1861', 'Miners Cottages – Paxton Square'. His more personal poems such as 'Making Easter Cakes', 'Collecting Dickens' and 'Spring and Fall' are eloquent and attractive. 'Under Siege Now' won the Canning Literary Award in 1982 and 'The Bee Farm' won the Melbourne Poetry Society Award in 1986.

GURR, Robin (1934–   ), born Sydney, has published six small books of restrained, private poetry which is notable for intricate word-patterns and subtlety of language. They are *Song is a Mirror* (1963), *Music in the Grass* (1971), *A House of Cards* (1975), *Harvest of Birds* (1981), *Masques* (1986) and *The Tiger in the Head* (1987). She has also written books for children.

GYE, Hal ('James Hackston', 'Hacko') (1888–1967), born Ryde, Sydney, worked as a law clerk before pursuing three separate careers in Australian art and letters: as Hal Gye, illustrator of the original 1915 edition of C.J. Dennis's *The Songs of a Sentimental Bloke* with the now-famous winged cherubs and illustrator for Angus & Robertson and for the *Bulletin*, the *Melbourne Punch*, the Sydney *Daily Telegraph* and other papers; as short story writer 'James Hackston', who from 1936 wrote the 'Father' series of stories for the *Bulletin* and published two collections of short fiction, *Father Clears Out* (1966) and *The Hole in the Bedroom Floor* (1969); and as the *Bulletin* poet 'Hacko', whose pithy and often amusing verses appeared through the 1940s and 1950s on the 'Aboriginalities' page of the *Bulletin*. Elizabeth Lane's *Hal Gye: The Man and his Work* (1986) gives Gye's own account of his early years, further biographical data and selections from his art and writings.

[H]

HACKETT, Patricia (1908–63), daughter of Sir Winthrop Hackett, benefactor of the University of WA, graduated in law in London and practised in Adelaide. Her interest in drama led to her acquiring her own little theatre, the Torch, in Adelaide in 1934. In 1938 she published *These Little Things*, a volume of forty-one poems set in Adelaide and in the Solomon Islands where she lived on the island M'bangai, which she owned just before the outbreak of the Pacific War in 1941. The Patricia Hackett Prize was endowed in her memory in 1965 for the best original creative contribution published in *Westerly* each year.

HAENKE, Helen (1916–78) published two volumes of poetry, *The Good Company* (1977) and *Prophets and Honour* (1979), both characterised by wit, compassion, perceptive awareness of people and fine control of language. She also published a play, *The Bottom of a Birdcage* (1978).

HALES, A.A.G. (Alfred Arthur Greenwood) (1860–1936), nicknamed 'Smiler', was born Kent Town, SA, and wandered the outback working at a variety of jobs and contributing to country newspapers stories of his experiences, many of which were published in *The Wanderings of a Simple Child* (1890). He was a war correspondent in the Boer War, in which he was taken prisoner, a participant in the rebellion against the Turks in Macedonia in 1903, and a war correspondent in the Russo-Japanese war and the First World War. He then lived in England, where he continued to write a long line of adventure novels. He published a volume of poetry in the bush ballad tradition, *Poems and Ballads* (1909). His autobiographical works are *My Life of Adventure* (1918) and *Broken Trails* (1931).

HALEY, Martin (1905–80), born Brisbane, was a teacher in Queensland. He was, with Paul Grano, a foundation member of the Queensland Catholic Poetry Society and was president of the Catholic Readers' and Writers' Society. Haley published numerous books of verse and translations including *Poems and a Preface* (1936), *More Poems and Another Preface* (1938), *Translations (Mostly)* (1941), *Good Measure: A Century of Epigrams* (1950), *Middle Kingdom* (1952), *Asphodel and Wistaria* (1955, poems from Chinese and Greek), *Preciosa* (1962, poems from Spanish), *Beatrice, Being the Sonnets of Louis Labé 1525–66* (1963), *Lucretia and the Banks of the Anio* (1965), *The Central Splendour (Chung Hua): An Anthology from the Chinese* (1969), and *Trophies: Taken Mostly from the French of José Maria de Heredia* (1972).

HALL, Rodney (1935–   ), born Birmingham, England, came to Australia after the Second World War. He graduated from the University of Queensland in 1971 and has worked as a freelance script-writer for television and radio, as an actor, as film critic for the ABC, as a youth officer for the Australian Council for the Arts, and as a tutor and lecturer in music and creative writing. Poetry editor of the *Australian* 1967–78, he was poetry adviser to the publishers Angus & Robertson, 1972–75. He has travelled extensively in Europe, Asia and the USA, and for a long period has been actively involved in Aboriginal affairs. He was chairperson of the Australia Council 1990–93, and was made OAM.

A prolific writer, Hall contributed to *Four Poets* (1962) and has published the volumes of poetry *Penniless till Doomsday* (1962), *Forty Beads on a Hangman's Rope* (1963), *Eyewitness* (1967), *The Autobiography of a Gorgon* (1968), *The Law of Karma* (1968), *Heaven, In a Way* (1970), *Romulus and Remus* (1970), *A Soapbox Omnibus* (1973, winner of the Grace Leven Poetry Prize), *Selected Poems* (1975), *Black Bagatelles* (1978) and *The Most Beautiful World* (1981); the novels *The Ship on the Coin* (1972), *A Place Among People* (1975, a prizewinner in the Cook Bicentennial Celebrations Competition), *Just Relations* (1982, winner of the Miles Franklin Award); *Kisses of the Enemy* (1987), *Captivity Captive* (1988, winner of the Victorian Premier's Literary Award), *The Second Bridegroom* (1991) and *The Grisly Wife* (1993); and studies of the artist Andrew Sibley in 1968, and of the writer who has influenced him most, John Manifold, in 1978. He has also edited several significant collections of Australian verse: *New Impulses in Australian Poetry* (1968, with Thomas Shapcott), *Australian Poetry 1970* (1970), *Poems from Prison* (1973), and *The Collins Book of Australian Poetry* (1981); a collection of Australian poems and paintings, *Australians Aware* (1975); and three collections of Michael Dransfield's poetry, *Voyage into Solitude* (1978), *The Second Month of Spring* (1980) and *Michael Dransfield. Collected Poems* (1987). He has also written the text of the photographic collection, *Australia – Image of a Nation 1850–1950* (1983) and a meditative travelogue, *Journey Through Australia* (1988). Other awards won by Hall include the Barbara Ramsden Award (1982) and the Poetry Society Prize (1975).

Hall's poetry, ironically detached and frequently witty, is characterised by economy of form and diction, a wide range of tone and a familiarity with myth and legend. His concern with technical virtuosity, especially his use of free, flexible verse-forms and associated patterns of imagery, was evident from the first. Particularly striking is his development of the form he has termed a 'Progression', which consists of a series of short poems, sometimes as many as sixty, each of which is capable of standing alone, but which together form a tightly related unity resembling a single long poem.

Particularly well received in the USA, Hall's work has been translated into German, Swedish, Danish, French and Chinese.

HALLORAN, Henry (1811–93), born Cape Town, South Africa, son of L.H. Halloran, came to Sydney in 1822 and had a successful career in the public service. A well-known member of the Sydney literary society of the day and a frequent contributor to the *Month, Sydney Morning Herald* and *Sydney Gazette*, he also assisted young writers, e.g., Henry Kendall, for whom he obtained civil service employment. A minor poet himself, he published *Poems, Odes, Songs* (1887) and *A Few Love Rhymes of a Married Life* (1890); made translations from the Greek poems of Anacreon; and wrote numerous commemorative poems for the 1888 centenary.

HALLORAN, L.H. (Laurence Hynes) (1765–1831), born County Meath, Ireland, father of Henry Halloran, ruined a career as a chaplain and schoolmaster by indulgence in libellous verse and other acts. Indicted on a minor forging charge in 1818, he was transported for seven years. In 1819 he was given a ticket of leave by Governor Lachlan Macquarie, opened a private school in 1820, and in 1825 became principal of the Sydney Free Public Grammar School. His unpredictable behaviour, which led to constant litigation, finally deprived him of his schoolmastering career and he then published a journal, the *Gleaner* (1827), a voice for the emancipist cause. Governor Darling, in a kindly gesture, appointed him the Sydney coroner in 1828 but his last years were spent drawing up memorials for people with grievances – his own situation for much of his later life. His numerous publications prior to his transportation were minor poetry and drama. They included, under the pseudonym 'Philo-nauticus', *Odes, Poems and Translations* (1790) and *Newgate: Or, Desultory Sketches in a Prison* (?1819).

HAMMIAL, Philip (1937–), born Detroit, Michigan, USA, grew up in America and served with the US Navy. After a period travelling through Europe, Asia and Africa he settled in Sydney in 1972. He has published several small books of verse, *Footfalls & Notes* (1976), *Chemical Cart* (1977), *Mastication Poems* (1977), *Hear Me Eating* (1977), *More Bath, Less Water* (1978), *Swarm* (1979), *Squeeze* (1985), *Pell Mell* (1988), *Travel* (1989, published with Ania Walwicz's *Writing*) and *With One Skin Less* (1994).

HAMPTON, Susan (1949–), born Inverell, NSW, was formerly a teacher in English and creative writing and now lives on a farm in Majorca (Victoria). A poet, prose-writer and anthologist, she won the Dame Mary Gilmore Poetry Award in 1979 and has published two collections of poetry, *Costumes* (1981) and *White Dog Sonnets* (1987). The twenty-three sonnets of the *White Dog Sonnets* (there is also an accomplished longer poem, 'Stranded in Paradise') tell the story of a failing relationship and have been likened to a modern feminist version of the Astrophel and Stella series of Sir Philip Sidney. *Surly Girls* (1989), which won the 1990 Steele Rudd Award and comprises prose poems but includes stories, monologues and performance pieces, is an unusual collection which looks at contemporary women's experience. In all her writing there is warmth, sensitivity and wit. Hampton edited, with Kate Llewellyn, the significant collection *The Penguin Book of Australian Women Poets* (1985). She also co-scripted Ruby Langford Gibini's autobiography *Don't Take Your Love to Town* (1988) and published (with Sue Woolfe, 1984) *About Literature*. Her work is included in *Sisters Poets, 1* (1979, edited by Rosemary Dobson).

HANSCOMBE, Gillian (1945–), born Melbourne and now resident in Britain, has worked as a freelance journalist, teacher, lecturer, saleswoman and academic. Well known for her contribution to lesbian and feminist debates, she has published the collections, *Hecate's Charms* (1975), a verse and prose collection, which was later scored for string quartet and voices and performed in London, *Flesh and Paper* (1986), a verse sequence with Suniti Namjoshi, and *Sybil. The Glide of her Tongue* (1992), a verse sequence with explanatory sections by Suniti Namjoshi. She has also written several books of feminist literary criticism and polemic and the fictional *Between Friends* (1982).

HARFORD, Lesbia (1891–1927) was born Lesbia Keogh in Melbourne. From an early age she was subject to ill health but possessed a charismatic, eccentric and outspoken personality. After graduating in law and philosophy from the University of Melbourne in 1916, she worked as an art teacher, a confidential clerk in a business office and a freelance social researcher. This last role led her to work for some time in a clothing factory in order to understand women's working conditions. She was a prolific writer of lyrical poetry, some of which was collected after her death by Nettie Palmer and published as *The Poems of Lesbia Harford* (1941); apparently artless and even casual, her slender, remarkably frank lyrics focus on a variety of subjects from love to factory life. Her long-lost novel *The Invaluable Mystery*, probably written 1921–24, was published in 1987 with an introduction by Richard Nile and Robert Darby. A new edition of her poetry was published in 1985, introduced by Drusilla Modjeska. Darryl Emmerson's play *Earthly Paradise*, based on Lesbia Harford's life, was first performed by the Playbox Theatre Company in Melbourne in 1991 and published by Currency Press the same year.

HARPUR, Charles (1813–68), born Windsor of emancipist parents, was raised in the Hawkesbury River district; his later use of the pseudonym 'A Hawkesbury Lad' indicates his affection for that area. In young manhood his abrasive and radical personality led to erratic and unsatisfactory employment. His long courtship of Mary Doyle ('Rosa' of his love sonnets) culminated in their marriage in 1850. After a period as an unwilling sheep farmer in the Hunter Valley, Harpur in 1859 was appointed assistant gold commissioner at Araluen. In 1866 the goldfields position was retrenched; in 1867 his farm at Nerrigundah near Eurobodalla was ruined by floods, and his son Charles was killed in a shooting accident. These personal setbacks, combined with the lack of recognition of his literary efforts, made his final years bitter and frustrated.

Harpur's published works include *Thoughts: A Series of Sonnets* (1845), *The Bushrangers, A Play in Five Acts, and Other Poems* (1853), *The Tower of the Dream* (1865), and several smaller works: a broadsheet, *Songs of Australia, First Series* (1850); a pamphlet containing two poems, titled *A Poet's Home* (1862); and a four-page booklet, *A Rhyme* (1864). The first Harpur collected edition was the posthumous *Poems*, edited by H.M. Martin in 1883. Relied on for some years as the definitive edition of Harpur, it has now been largely discredited because of Martin's arbitrary handling of the text, excising whatever he felt was controversial or radical in Harpur and leaving him as little more than a descriptive nature poet. In 1948 *'Rosa': Love Sonnets to Mary Doyle* was published, edited by C.W. Salier; K.H. Gifford and D.F. Hall edited *Selected Poems of Charles Harpur* (1944), Elizabeth Perkins *The Poetical Works of Charles Harpur* (1984) and Michael Ackland *Charles Harpur, Selected Poetry and Prose* (1986). Elizabeth Perkins has also edited *Stalwart the Bushranger* and *Tragedy of Donohoe* (1987), the first and final versions of Harpur's 1853 play *The Bushrangers*.

In the early years of settlement, when colonial poetry was largely ignored or derided, Harpur's ambition was to be Australia's first authentic poetic voice. He believed that Australian poetry should be modelled upon traditional English verse before seeking its own individuality. Thus his own poetry relies heavily on traditional poetic techniques such as ornamental diction, wide use of personification and metaphor, solemnity of tone and ponderous movement, while attempting on some occasions at least to describe and interpret the colonial Australian scene. Such attempts include his nature poems, 'A Mid-Summer Noon in the Australian Forest', 'Dawn and Sunrise in the Snowy Mountains', 'The Bush Fire' and 'A Storm in the Mountains', which describe some of the typical though more dramatic components of the Australian landscape, and convey a sense of vast distance and wide horizons.

Ignored or badly mutilated in the 1883 collection were several substantial philosophical poems, *The Tower of the Dream*, 'The Witch of Hebron', 'Genius Lost', 'The World and the Soul' and 'The Temple of Infamy'. The long blank-verse dissertation 'The World and the Soul' combines the Darwinian theory of evolution with a highly unorthodox religious view of the universe and its purpose. The subject itself is so complicated and Harpur's treatment of it so unconventional that his editor, Martin, probably at a loss how to handle it, omitted it altogether. Only a few lyrics and choruses of the 2300 lines of 'Genius Lost', a series of poems on the death of Thomas Chatterton, appeared in the 1883 edition. 'Genius Lost', one of the most ambitious of colonial poetic efforts, demonstrates Harpur's grasp of technique and his intellectual capacity. 'The Witch of Hebron' was printed in the 1883 collection with about 400 lines, vital to the understanding of the poem, excised. The best-known Harpur narrative poem, 'The Creek of the Four Graves', the story of settlers murdered by Aborigines, was altered by Martin to highlight the descriptive rather than the narrative areas. The deficiencies of the 1883 collection resulted, for many years, in an undervaluing of Harpur's poetic achievements. Research and scholarship in recent times, however, have increased his reputation, and modern critical opinion sees him as the most substantial of the colonial poets.

In spite of his own unfulfilled dream to be acknowledged as 'the Muse of Australia', Harpur was an influential figure in the mid-century colony. Journals and newspapers such as the *Weekly Register*, the *People's Advocate*, the *Empire* and the *Sydney Morning Herald* carried his wide-ranging political, social and literary commentary, including outbursts against injustice and inequality, satirical tilts at squattocracy and snobbery, defence of the Aborigines, and literary articles and essays. With other currency lads such as Daniel Deniehy, Harpur attempted to direct the colony along the path of egalitarianism and democracy. J. Normington-Rawling published the biography *Charles Harpur, An Australian* (1962) and Judith Wright, a strong advocate of Harpur's talent, the monograph *Charles Harpur* (1963). Elizabeth Perkins's edition, the most complete to date, is accompanied by critical and bibliographical apparatus; Michael Ackland's brings together some of his best-known poetry and prose with correspondence and little-known material. Ackland and Perkins are collaborating in the proposed Academy Editions two-volume *Complete Poems* of Harpur.

HARRINGTON, Edward Phillip (1896–1966), born Colbinabbin near Shepparton, Victoria, served in the First World War in Palestine with the Australian Light Horse. Those experiences are recorded in his first book of verse, *Songs of War and Peace* (1920). He later wandered through the Victorian outback as rouseabout, drover and farmer, saturating himself in the atmosphere of the bush ('Oh the careless, droving, roving life is the finest life of all'). The last of the bush balladists, Harrington enshrines in his poetry such attitudes as mateship, egalitarianism and love of the bush. He lived for a time at Swan Hill in Victoria and later in Melbourne, where he was instrumental in founding the Bread and Cheese Club. His bush balladry is represented in his volumes *Boundary Bend and Other Ballads* (1936), *My Old Black Billy and Other Songs of the Australian Outback* (1940), *The Kerrigan Boys* (1944) and *The Swagless Swaggie and Other Ballads* (1957), which includes some verse from earlier books.

HARRIS, Max (1921–95), born Adelaide, grew up in Mount Gambier. He went from school in Adelaide to journalism to the University of Adelaide, where he obtained a degree in commerce. During the Second World War he worked as a government economist and published two volumes of verse and a novel. He also founded, owned and co-edited the literary and artistic journal *Angry Penguins*, which gave expression to the noisy revolutionary modernism in literature and the arts of a group of avant-garde young intellectuals known as the Angry Penguins. The failure of Harris and his co-editors to detect the deliberately concocted nonsense of the Ern Malley hoax and the publication of 'The Darkening Ecliptic' in the Autumn 1944 issue of *Angry Penguins* resulted in ridicule and prosecution for publishing indecent material. Harris's own career in literature, however, suffered little more than a minor setback from the Ern Malley affair. After the war he was involved in many successful literary projects, including the establishment of the Mary Martin bookshop chain (later sold to Macmillan), the creation and editing of *Ern Malley's Journal* (1952–55); the publication of *Ern Malley's Poems* (1961); the founding and editing, with Geoffrey Dutton, of *Australian Letters* (1957–68) and *Australian Book Review* (1961–74); the publication with Dutton of *The Vital Decade* (1968); the compilation, with Alison Forbes, of a pictorial history of Australia titled *The Land That Waited* (1967), based on his 1962 film script which won the AFI gold medal; a criticism of present-day Australian values, *Ockers: Essays on the Bad Old New Australia* (1974); a 1988 edition (subtitled the *Complete Poems*) with Joanna Murray-Smith of *The Poems of Ern Malley*.

As drama, art and literary critic, belletrist and, in his own description, 'socio-cultural diagnostician', Harris was for forty years one of Australia's most controversial figures. Some of the fruits of those years of acting as irritant of the political, social, literary and artistic establishment are preserved in *The Angry Eye* (1973), the aptly named collection of Harris's writing from the *Australian* and *Nation* (he was a columnist on the *Australian* for a record-breaking period). He also published *The Unknown Great Australian and Other Psycho-biographical Portraits* (1983), a collection of pen pictures of various Australian outsiders and eccentrics; *The Best of Max Harris: 21 Years of Browsing* (1987) which contains thirty-six of his contributions to the *Australian*; and a collection of articles on Australian English, *The Australian Way With Words* (1989). With Geoffrey Dutton he edited a collection of regional comments on a range of Australian politicians, *Sir Henry, Bjelke, Don Baby and Friends* (1971). He was made AO for his services to Australian literature.

Harris's creative writing began with *The Gift of Blood* (1940) and *Dramas from the Sky* (1942), two slight volumes of verse. The poems are love lyrics, responses to the local scene, and reflections on the Spanish Civil War. *The Coorong and Other Poems* (1955) is more noteworthy. Poems such as 'Incident at the Alice', 'Martin Buber in the Pub', 'Apollo Bay to Kingston', 'Allegory of Dante and the Apes' and 'On Throwing a Copy of the *New Statesman* into the Coorong' led readers and critics to hope that Harris would publish more frequently. But the next volume, *A Window at Night*, selected by Robert Clark, who wrote a valuable introduction discussing Harris as a poet, did not appear until 1967 and more than half the poems it contains had been published earlier. Harris had insisted in 'The Faded Years' in *Direction* (May 1952) that there was no room for 'posturing' in poetry and that poetry should establish a real relationship between the poet and the reader. The new poems attract the reader, often in quite different ways e.g. 'A Window at Night' with its intricate intimacy and 'The Death of Bert Sassenowsky' with its ironic narrative of Bert and his oxen disappearing into a volcanic hole in the Mount Gambier district. After another twelve years came the tiny volume *Poetic Gems* (1979), sarcastically titled and puzzlingly ambivalent. Many of the brief poems exhibit both an arrogant contempt for life and a strong fear of death, Harris treating life to the scornful 'Sirrah' which he claims to prefer that life directs at him, but the *enfant terrible* of the *Angry Penguin* days is still seen in such poems as 'I'm Shagging in the Wagon'. There are some 'gems' nevertheless, e.g. 'Love Poems for the Thompson Children'. Harris's early experimental novel *The Vegetative Eye* (1943) was not a success; he later published a section of another novel, provisionally titled 'Biography of a No-Hoper' in a 1960 anthology, *Southern Festival*.

HARRIS, Robert (1951–93), born Melbourne, was involved in the Vietnam War controversy, as were so many of his generation. He had a variety of occupations including labouring work and the teaching of creative writing. In the 1980s he was converted to Christianity and maintained passionate religious convictions until his death, surpassing but not replacing his passion for poetry which was, for a long period, his dominant interest. His first book of poems, *Localities*, was published in 1973 and was awarded the Harri Jones Memorial Prize for poetry in 1975. He also published *Translations from the Albatross* (1976), *The Abandoned* (1979), *The Cloud Passes Over* (1986) and *JANE, Interlinear & Other Poems* (1992), which won the C.J. Dennis Prize for poetry. A member of the editorial executive of *Overland*, Harris was also the journal's poetry editor for a period.

Harris's early poetry is idiosyncratic and difficult, saturated with abstraction and complex personal attitudes. Evidence of a religious conversion exists in the later books, many of the poems, e.g. 'Ray', 'The Call', 'The Eagle', 'The Prayer of the Blade', celebrating and confirming the significance of God in his life. Throughout his work there is compassion for the underprivileged, especially those 'untouchables' (the mentally and physically defective) who, under the guise of compassion, are 'battered' in playgrounds, offices, workshops and even in their own homes. The later poems, although still prone at times to esoteric thought and density of language, are more accessible to the general reader. *JANE, Interlinear & Other Poems* opens with a sequence, 'Seven Songs for Sydney', exploring the loss of HMAS *Sydney* to the German raider *Kormoran* in 1941. The unusual title of the book points to a sequence of thirty poems dealing with Lady Jane Grey, who lost her head on the block in 1554. In notes to the *JANE* poems Harris indicates that the structure used for most of them is mimetic of the interlinear Bible where the Hebrew text is presented with the English translation printed phrase for phrase directly below. The remaining three sections of the book are 'After the Process', 'Silver Buckle' and 'Recorder Music'. Throughout this last book, as in all of his poetry, there is abundant evidence of 'a profound intelligence at ease with its quest, sure-footed in its isolation', in the words of Fay Zwicky. The literary magazine *Ulitarra* awards an annual poetry prize in memory of Robert Harris.

HARRISON, Keith (1932–), born Melbourne, taught in Victoria and England before taking up an academic career in the USA. Represented in numerous Australian, English and American anthologies, Harrison has achieved a considerable international reputation as poet, editor, academic and critic. His poetry publications include *Points in a Journey* (1966); *Songs from the Drifting House* (1972), which won a British Arts Council award; *The Basho Poems* (1975), built around a central figure, Basho, whom Harrison describes as 'a kind of trickster figure . . . the kind of figure you see occurring in Red Indian mythology, who essentially upsets the expected order of things', and through whom Harrison deflates the ridiculous, stupid and pompous; *A Town and Country Suite* (1980); *The Sense of Falling* (1980) and *A Burning of Applewood* (1988), a combination of new and selected poems.

HARROP, Les (1948–), born Blackburn, England, and educated in England and Canada, taught in the USA before coming to Australia in 1977; he was poetry editor of *Overland* and later founding editor of *Helix*. Awarded the Greenwood Prize of the Poetry Society of Great Britain in 1976, the Stroud Festival Poetry Prize in 1977 and the Anne Elder Award in 1980, he has published, in Australia, *The Hum of the Old Suit* (1979), a volume of about eighty short poems, many of them in strong colloquial style about people and events from his past.

HARRY, J.S. (1939–), born Adelaide, has had a variety of occupations, publishing at infrequent intervals four small books of intense, sensitive and skilled verse. *The Deer Under the Skin* appeared in the UQP Paperback Poets series in 1971, *Hold, for a Little While, and Turn Gently* in 1979, *A Dandelion for Van Gogh* in 1985 and *The Life on Water and The Life Beneath* in 1995. Increasingly highly regarded for the originality, integrity and technical skill of her work, she was awarded the PEN International Lynne Phillips Poetry Prize in 1987. Meticulous in her fine-tuning (she admits to up to a hundred drafts of some poems), Harry is not interested in evolving a consistent line of technique, each poem being allowed to develop its own voice and method. Her poetry's obsession with language's multiple levels of meaning challenges the reader with its complexity.

HART, Kevin (1954–), born London, came to live in Brisbane at the age of 10. Keenly religious from his youth, his allegiance swung from Baptist to Anglican and in his twenties to Roman Catholicism. He graduated with honours in philosophy from the ANU and won a writing fellowship to Stanford University, California, 1977–78. He gained his Ph.D. from the University of Melbourne in 1986 and has been lecturer in philosophy and English there, senior lecturer in English at Deakin Univeristy and associate professor of English (critical theory) at Monash University. He has written extensively on literary theory and poetry, publishing *The Trespass of the Sign: Deconstruction, Theology and Philosophy* (1989), a radical rethinking of Derrida's writings. He has translated from the Italian the poetry of Giuseppe Ungaretti, *The Buried Harbour* (1990), and has written a full critical account of the poetry of A.D. Hope (1992) in the Australian Writers Series. He has also edited *The Oxford Book of Australian Religious Verse* (1994). His own books of verse are *The Departure* (1978), *The Lines of the Hand* (1981), *Your Shadow* (1984), *Peniel* (1990) and *New and Selected Poems* (1995), all of his poetry achieving critical recognition; among his awards are the FAW John Shaw Neilson Award 1976, the Mattara Poetry Award 1982, the Harri Jones Award 1983, the Wesley Michel Wright Award in 1984, the Victorian Premier's and NSW State Literary Awards in 1985 (for *Your Shadow*) and the Grace Leven Prize for Poetry in 1992 for *Peniel*. Religious feeling is evident in all his poetry, as is his preoccupation with ageing and death, symbolised by the frequent presence of clocks and references to time:

> Mirrors tell us that we must die
> but clocks announce they know just when

The first section of *The Departure* is entitled 'The Convert'. It recalls his boyhood habit of going to church while 'the family would lounge in bed till ten or so', he meanwhile stepping 'into a day of Grace'. 'The Old' (also from *The Departure*) is an exceptional poem on old age, but its emphasis finally is on the poet's own old age, a spectre that haunts him even in his prime of life.

> Someone old will be inside your flesh
> not long from now –
> I know the one who wants me,
> Sometimes I think I know his thoughts.
> He will know me very well.

There are similar sentiments, and presentiments, in 'The Lines of the Hand', title poem of Hart's second volume, 'Full Moon' and 'My Death', while 'To Christ Our Lord', 'The Yellow Christ' and 'To Our Lady' emphasise the fervour of this verse. *Peniel* marks a departure in technique from earlier volumes where Hart used variable stanza forms and a flexible line scheme, alternating from fluent iambics to equally fluent free verse. *Peniel* is structured into poems each of nine stanzas, each stanza of three pentameter lines. Each of the three sections of the book contains nine poems. Hart's skill with imagery recalls the 'conceit' of the metaphysical poets, while his intellectual subtlety and powerful imagination combine to produce poetry of the highest quality.

HART-SMITH, William (1911–90), born Tunbridge Wells, England, went to NZ as a boy and came to Australia in 1936. He worked in radio in Sydney before enlisting in the Australian Army in 1940. After the war he returned to NZ, where he was involved in adult education and advertising. He was back in Sydney in 1962 as an advertising manager, then radio technician, but went to Perth in 1970 and returned to NZ to live in 1978. He was president of the Poetry Society of Australia 1963–64 and taught creative writing at the WA University of Technology, now Curtin University. His poetry includes *Columbus Goes West* (1943), *Harvest* (1945), *The Unceasing Ground* (1946), *Christopher Columbus* (1948), *On the Level: Mostly Canterbury* (NZ) *Poems* (1950), *Poems of Discovery* (1959, which includes *Columbus Goes West* and *Christopher Columbus* and which won the Australian Literature Society Gold Medal), *The Talking Clothes* (1966, which shared the Grace Leven Prize for poetry), *Minipoems* (1974), brief verses based on Maori legends and proverbs, and evocations of the WA landscape, *Let Me Learn the Steps* (1977, with Mary Morris), subtitled 'Poems from a Psychiatric Ward' and the result of a briefly disturbed period in 1976. Soon after his arrival in Australia, Hart-Smith became involved with the growing Jindyworobak movement, largely because of his delight in the Australian spirit of place and his fascination with what he saw as the primitive animism of the Aborigines and the romantic mysticism of their legends. From 1940 his poems were regularly featured in the Jindyworobak anthologies and he edited the 1944 volume. Traces of Jindywor-

obak subjects and sentiment persist in his later poetry. Notable among his numerous
Jindyworobak verses were 'The Pleiades', a poem based on Aboriginal legend; 'Moon-
deen', a character-study of 'the oldest man of the river tribe'; and 'Nullarbor', his
account of a brief meeting with a young Aborigine in the desert and his consequent
conviction of his own white grotesqueness. Hart-Smith's poetic talents were too
considerable, however, to be limited to an expression of Jindyworobak philosophy.
His major poetic work is *Christopher Columbus*. With the incisive, delicately constructed, sometimes sombre, sometimes ironic, poems of personal observation, it
assured him a small but enthusiastic following among discerning readers, impressed
by the clarity, exactness and sensitivity of his observations and by his capacity for
communicating those observations in distinctive and often startling imagery. Hart-
Smith's *Selected Poems* were chosen and edited by Brian Dibble in 1985; *Hand to Hand,
A Garnering*, collected by Barbara Petrie in 1991 after Hart-Smith's death, contains
another 250 poems which the poet himself had chosen.

HARTIGAN, Patrick Joseph, see **'O'BRIEN, John'**

HARWOOD, Gwen (**'Francis Geyer', 'Walter Lehmann', 'Miriam Stone',
'T. F. Kline'**) (1920–) was born at Taringa, Queensland. Brought up and educated in
Brisbane, she developed strong interests in literature and philosophy as well as music,
later becoming organist at All Saints' Church in Brisbane. Her marriage in 1945 to
academic linguist William Harwood brought at the same time a reluctant move to
Tasmania and the discovery of her lifelong passion for the work of philosopher Ludwig Wittgenstein, which informs her entire opus. Apart from an early isolated poem
in *Meanjin* in 1944, her poems, stories, critical essays and reviews have appeared regularly in a wide range of Australian journals and elsewhere since the early 1960s. She
has written libretti for composers Larry Sitsky, James Penberthy, Don Kay and Ian
Cugley and other occasional words for music. In volume form, Harwood's poetry has
appeared in *Poems* (1963), *Poems: Volume Two* (1968), *Selected Poems* (1975), *In Plato's
Cave* (Broadsheet, 1977), *The Lion's Bride* (1981), *Journeys: Poems by Judith Wright,
Rosemary Dobson, Gwen Harwoood, Dorothy Hewett* (1982), *Bone Scan* (1988) and *Selected
Poems* (1990). *Blessed City: Letters to Thomas Riddell 1943*, finely edited by Alison Hoddinott, appeared in 1990. In one of her many interviews, Gwen Harwood has claimed
a 'deep inner necessity . . . to realise in words the moments that gave my life its
meaning'. Her work tells the story of her imaginative and intellectual life and its
continuing engagement with literature, music, philosophy, painting, with the beauties and cruel laws of the natural world and, as a binding dedicatory thread across its
voice through time, her conversation with many friends and, later, the ghosts of many
friends.

Many of the poems of her first volume tell of pain, direct physical pain as in 'The
Wound', 'In Hospital' and 'Ad Orientem', and the oblique pain of life's passing which
seems to bring no sense of fulfilment, either physically ('The Wine is Drunk') or
spiritually ('The Old Wife's Tale'). The self-scrutiny of the early poetry seems at its
most perturbed in 'Triste, Triste' and most confident in 'O Could One Write As One
Makes Love', a poem which suggests this poet's continuing delight in her own flair
for word-craft. Her early work creates two ironic figures, Professor Eisenbart, whose
eight poems constitute the second part of *Poems*, and Professor Kröte, soft-hearted
anti-hero whose drunken irritability is compensated by his keen eye for the charms of
life and keen ear for music, and who, unlike the scarifying Eisenbart, continues to
appear in Harwood's latest work.

The use of elaborate personae like Eisenbart and Kröte together with parody, varied
masks and pseudonyms, may suggest in this poet a considerable political animus as
much as playfulness. The Sydney *Bulletin*'s belated petulant response to its well-
deserved hoaxing by the publication in 1961 of two acrostic sonnets by 'Walter Leh-

mann' wholly vindicated Harwood's double point about editors' prejudice against women poets and farcical incompetence as poetry readers. The poems of the two tragi-comic figures Eisenbart and Kröte, the first an ageing nuclear physicist, the second a frustrated, alcoholic European musician set down in the unrelenting banality of mid-century Australian suburbia, form a running social satire laced with bone-dry truths about a bone-dry milieu. Their acid light moves across parlours, patios and beaches, mocking and deft. These poems show a sometimes intricate stanzaic development and tartly rhyme-clipped narrative pace which, in the case of Kröte, can yet indulge a self-ironising, lovable character. Kröte struggles hopelessly with a petty social world impervious to his sensitivities and ill-founded ambitions and can only cry 'Alas!' While Eisenbart's comic satire is bitterly explosive, Kröte's laughter in the suburbs is mellow, wry and attractive. By contrast, other later comic-satiric verse exploits a versatile, parodic balladry and a gift for black humour and the absurd which finally offers a brave, elegant stay against time and the 'sharpness of death' ('Night and Dreams').

Poetry is 'not a perfect game', and if it were we could 'not play' ('Thought is Surrounded by A Halo'). The point goes back to a universal sense of life itself, and to Eden, so the language 'game' of Harwood's poetry, exhilarating, playful, full of the warmth of good wine and fellowship, can play a deadly earnest. Her work pursues the imperfect game of poetry as part of a love and unquenchable desire for the knowable within a finally unknowable world. From the beginning, she writes of universal problems of existence: growth, ageing, death, and especially the limits of sense and expression. Within traditional metrical forms and subtle musical divisions, her verse achieves a fluid narrative and the sure colloquial tones of contemporaneity. It ranges from ironically structured comedy (the Kröte poems) to free-wheeling virtuoso pieces, abrasive, witty and satirical ('Meditations on Wyatt', 'Night Thoughts: Baby & Demon'), to brief philosophical lyrics, to measured movements of the tragic and deeply moving ('The Violets', 'Father and Child', 'Night Flight', 'Mother Who Gave Me Life'). And across this range there occurs an unusual capacity to blend opposing feelings: the painful with the funny, exhilaration with rue, black jokiness with the death's head, warmth and fun with nostalgia. As 'Mappings of the Plane' so complexly proposes, life as seen here is both exquisitely rhapsodic and sharp with the pain of memory and loss. Both the natural world and the phenomenal world present brilliant images of stability and renewal which turn again and again to violence, brutality or the great abiding swing of returning dark. This, most of all, is a poetry of memory and music and all that these compose; memory is joy and consolation but it is also change and loss.

Harwood's poetry is also a poetry of place, of the cool lights of Tasmania, of its estuarine landscapes, its birds, grasses, frosts, wide cool skies, of Tasmania's tragic history explored tentatively but pungently through a series of poems for the Aborigines which meet a necessary, expressive stop of bewilderment and awe: 'I ask them in no language to forgive/my dreadful freedom in the light of morning' ('After a Dream'). Also, in *The Lion's Bride*, of a part of this island's domestic life, its geese, sheep and cats who summon an eloquent goosegirl and, unabashed, can instruct her (and Wittgenstein) in essential philosophy.

So Kröte's rueful peregrinations record the comic side of Harwood's serious poetic habitation of a world that offers rich beauties in an order perennially treading the edge of chaos. The intolerable is funny, but it is also intolerable and asks eternal questions which have, in Harwood's lexicon, no answer. At the same time, wit, music and the epigrams of philosophy are joys in this verse as much as consolations, and the poetry throughout celebrates the richness of love, friendship, morning light, while it refuses to abandon the fun and mischief of the game of language. Beginning from her 'deep inner necessity ... to realise in words the moments that gave my life its meaning',

Harwood came to believe conversely and with Wittgenstein in the 'power of poetry to infuse experience with value'. The distinctive and impressive poetry which has emerged from these beliefs has led to an increasing critical and widespread popular attention. She was awarded the *Meanjin* Poetry Prize in 1958 and 1959, the Grace Leven Poetry Prize in 1975, the Robert Frost Award in 1977 and the Patrick White Literary Award in 1978. She received an honorary D.Litt. from the University of Tasmania in 1988 and two further honorary doctorates in 1994 from the University of Queensland and Latrobe University. Her late volume *Bone Scan* won the 1989 Victorian Premier's Literary Award and the J.J. Bray Award in 1990. Her book of letters, *Blessed City* (1990), won the *Age* Book of the Year Award in 1990.

Many critical essays have appeared on Harwood's poetry. Books include Elizabeth Lawson, *The Poetry of Gwen Harwood* (1991); Alison Hoddinott, *Gwen Harwood: The Real and the Imagined World* (1991); Jennifer Strauss, *Boundary Conditions: The Poetry of Gwen Harwood* (1992); and Stephanie Trigg, *Gwen Harwood* (1994, in Oxford's Australian Writers Series).

ELIZABETH LAWSON

HASKELL, Dennis (1948–   ), born Sydney, gained a Ph.D. from the University of Sydney, and is presently senior lecturer in English at the University of WA, where he also co-edits *Westerly*. Both poet and critic, Haskell has published two books of poetry, *Listening at Night* (1984) and *Abracadabra* (1993) and shared a small booklet, *A Touch of Ginger* (1992), with Fay Zwicky. He co-edited, with Hilary Fraser, the anthology of WA poetry of the 1980s, *Wordhord* (1989), compiled *The Sea Poems of Kenneth Slessor*, published in 1990 by Alec Bolton's (then) Officina Brindabella, and edited the UQP Australian Authors volume on Slessor in 1991.

An observant, fluent and accessible poet, Haskell comments perceptively and with occasional humour and disquiet on such everyday realities as relationships with parents, partners and friends and the ups and downs of domesticity. Alert also to the impact of new environments and milieux he has found much poetic material in the years he has spent in the West. Deeply inherent in his poetry, which is often self-searching, is an urge to 'value the ordinary', because in the seemingly commonplace lies perhaps the individual's best hope of personal satisfaction and fulfilment.

HASLUCK, Nicholas (1942–   ), born Canberra, son of Sir Paul and Dame Alexandra Hasluck, graduated in law from the University of WA in 1963 and Oxford in 1966. Following a brief period in Fleet Street as an editorial assistant he returned to Australia in 1967 and since 1968 has been a barrister in WA. He was deputy chairman of the Australia Council 1978–82 and was made AM.

An energetic writer, he has published more than a dozen books since 1976; three volumes of poetry, *Anchor* (1976), *On the Edge* (1981) and *Chinese Journey* (1985, with Christopher Koch); a book of short stories, *The Hat on the Letter 'O' and Other Stories* (1978); *Collage: Recollections and Images of the University of Western Australia* (1987, essays); and seven novels, *Quarantine* (1978), *The Blue Guitar* (1980, republished in 1989 and broadcast on radio 1991), *The Hand That Feeds You* (1982), *The Bellarmine Jug* (1984, winner of the *Age* Book of the Year Award), *Truant State* (1987), *The Country Without Music* (1990, joint winner of the WA Premier's Award for fiction) and *The Blosseville File* (1992).

HASLUCK, Sir Paul (1905–93) was born in Fremantle into a Salvation Army family. He graduated from the University of WA, where he taught history (1939–40, 1947–48). He served on the staff of the *West Australian* 1922–38, and in 1932 married Alexandra Darker. In 1941 he joined the Department of External Affairs and served on numerous missions to the UN. He was elected to the Australian parliament in 1949, serving as minister for Territories (1951–63), for Defence (1963–64) and for External

Affairs (1964–69). He was governor-general of Australia 1969–74. Hasluck published several collections of verse, *Into the Desert* (1939), *Collected Verse* (1969), *Dark Cottage* (1984), *Crude Impieties* (1991) and a 'discursive essay', *The Poet in Australia* (1975); two volumes of autobiography, *Mucking About* (1977) and *Diplomatic Witness* (1980); and two volumes in the official history of Australia in the Second World War, *The Government and the People 1939–41* (1952) and *1942–45* (1970). Robert Porter has written a political biography of Hasluck (1993).

'Hay and Hell and Booligal', a poem by A.B. Paterson, was published in *Rio Grande's Last Race and Other Verses* (1902). Hay and Booligal, two towns in the remote parts of south-western NSW, with their snakes and mosquitoes, heat and drought, 'sand, and dust, and stacks of flies', are rated in Paterson's poems on a par with Hell. The phrase, abbreviated to 'Hay, Hell and Booligal', denoting the unattractive nature of the isolated towns of the outback, has become a part of Australian idiom.

HAY, Robert Gordon (1933–), born Blair Athol, lectured in mathematics and computer science at the University College of Rockhampton before retirement. His poetry has been widely published in periodicals and anthologies and in a collection titled *Love and the Outer World* (1984). With Anne Lloyd and Stefanie Bennett he is a contributor to the collection *Three North Queensland Poets* (1990). Ranging from the elegiac to the wryly humorous, Hay mostly writes elegantly shaped lyrics which record significant moments of being or relationships with people and landscapes, although he occasionally turns to satiric dramatic monologues.

HAYWARD, Charles W. Andrée (1866–1950), born Herefordshire, England, was a lawyer in England and South Africa before his arrival in WA in 1894. He joined the *Geraldton Express*, contributing satire, sonnets, ballads and lyric verse; some of his poems, usually written under the pseudonym 'Viator', were published in 1897 as *Along the Road to Cue and Other Verses*. From 1922 until his death Hayward worked on the staff of the *Bulletin*, contributing copious light and topical verse under various pseudonyms, e.g. 'Thomas the Rhymer'.

Heart of Spring (1919), containing fifty-seven poems, was the first published collection of John Shaw Neilson. It met a mixed critical reception: A.G. Stephens in the book's preface called Neilson 'first of Australian poets'; Hubert Church described the poems as 'marvellous songs'; David McKee Wright in the *Bulletin* believed the poet to be 'a whispering person, not likely to be heard of again'.

HEBBLETHWAITE, James (1857–1921), born Preston, England, was a teacher in England before migrating to Tasmania in 1890 for health reasons and gaining a teaching position at the Friends' School, Hobart. He was later a minister of religion, initially with the Congregational Church, then the Church of England. A scholar and a graceful if limited lyric poet, Hebblethwaite published five books of poetry: *Verse* (1896); *A Rose of Regret* (1900); *Meadow and Bush* (1911); a collected edition, *The Poems of James Hebblethwaite* (1920); and *New Poems of James Hebblethwaite* (1921). His only novel, *Castlehill* (1895), is a romance associated with the convict period.

HEDLEY, Wilma (1927–), born Brisbane, has published two volumes of poetry, *Identity* (1968) and *Identity II* (1971). Although small in output, Hedley's compressed, spare poetry, which communicates a wide range of feeling from intense anger to bitterness to compassion, has attracted strongly favourable reviews.

HELLYER, Jill (1925–), born North Sydney, has been a consistent contributor of poetry to literary magazines such as *Westerly*, *Southerly*, *Meanjin* and *Overland* over many years. Instrumental in founding the Australian Society of Authors, she was its first executive secretary 1963–71 and was made a life member for her services. She has published verse, *The Exile* (1969) and *Song of the Humpback Whales* (1981); a novel, *Not Enough Savages* (1975); and edited a biographical work, *Fifty Years in Psychiatry: D. W. H. Arnott* (1980).

HEMENSLEY, Kris (1946–   ), writer, critic, editor, publisher, bookshop director, teacher, and passionate about all things literary, was born on the Isle of Wight, came to Australia in 1966 and quickly settled into the Melbourne literary scene, originally with the Melbourne New Theatre, then at La Mama, where in 1968–70 he helped to produce the poetry workshops that played a significant role in the rise of what has been termed the 'New Australian Poetry'. To publish that poetry Hemensley created the mini-magazine *Our Glass*. While in England in 1969–72 Hemensley edited the magazine *Earth Ship* (1970–72), and after his return to Australia continued his literary interests through poetry, prose and editorial activities. He edited a second series of *Earth Ship*, titled *The Ear in a Wheatfield* (1972–76), a third series, *The Merri Creek or Nero* (1981–84); in 1985 the selection *The Best of the Ear*, and other associated journals; became an advisory editor to *New Poetry* 1973–74; and was poetry editor of *Meanjin* 1976–78. His own publications of poetry, prose, drama and children's books have been prolific; they include *Two Poets* (1968, with Ken Taylor), *The Going* (1969), *Dreams* (1971), *No Word – No Worry* (1971), *The Soft Poems* (1971), *Mimi* (1973), *Rocky Mountains & Tired Indians* (1973), *Domestications* (1974), *Love's Voyages* (1974), *Here We Are* (1975), *The Rooms and Other Prose Pieces* (1975), *The Poem of the Clear Eye* (1975), *Sulking in the Seventies* (1975), *The Moths* (1978, prose/poetry), *Beginning Again* (1978, prose/poetry), *Down Under* (1978, a comic novel), *Games: An Exhibition 1970–72* (1978, prose), *The Miro Poems* (1979), *A Mile from Poetry* (1979), *Trace* (1984), *Christopher* (1987), and *The Site* (1987). One of Hemensley's many plays, 'Stephany', which was produced, as were several others, at La Mama, was made into a short film in 1972.

Hemensley's literary range is considerable: brief, enigmatic and personal poems such as those in *Domestications;* a long, complex examination of contemporary poetic attitudes in *The Poem of the Clear Eye*; the poetry-prose compositions, such as those in *Here We Are*, where fantasy and realism meet in a startling mix; his many works for radio and screen. An indefatigable Utopian and campaigner for world peace, an active and dedicated literary internationalist, and a regular commentator on Australian writing, Hemensley has long been a colourful and important figure in the Australian literary scene.

HENEY, Thomas William (1862–1928), born Sydney, father of the writer Helen Heney, spent a lifetime in journalism. He was editor of the *Sydney Morning Herald* (1903–18), the *Brisbane Telegraph* (1920–23), and the Sydney *Daily Telegraph* (1924–25). He published two novels with outback settings, *The Girl at Birrell's* (1896) and *A Station Courtship* (1899), and two collections of verse, *Fortunate Days* (1886), and *In Middle Harbour and Other Verse, Chiefly Australian* (1890).

HENRY, Kristin (1947–   ), born Chattanooga, Tennessee, USA, came to Australia with her parents when she was 17. During the 1980s she was active in the community movement and has been prominent in the performance poetry sphere. She has two published books of verse, *Slices of Wry* (1985) and *One Day She Catches Fire* (1992, in the Australian Poets series). Her poetry often deals with topical events, childhood experiences ('On Learning That Mothers Die') and feminist concerns such as the way that women's lives are all too frequently submerged by the demands of family and friends. She edited, with Joan Winter, *Valley Voices* (1985), an anthology of Diamond Valley (Victoria) writers.

HETHERINGTON, Paul (1958–   ), born Adelaide, has spent much of his life in WA but is now programme development officer of the National Library of Australia in Canberra. While in WA he was editor of the *Fremantle Arts Review* and now edits the monthly *National Library of Australia News* and the quarterly Library journal, *Voices*. He has published the collections *Mapping Wildwood Road* (1990) in the ANL Pamphlet Poets series, *Acts Themselves Trivial* (1991) and *The Dancing Scorpion* (1993). His delight in language and his meticulous craftsmanship create lyrical poetry, pleasantly ornamented with metaphor and imagery. His themes spring from the personal but often move out to embrace the more general and universal.

HEWETT Dorothy (1923–   ) was born and brought up in WA on her father's isolated wheat farm. Until the age of 12 she was educated by correspondence. At 19 her first poetry appeared in *Meanjin*, and by 22 she had won a drama competition and a national poetry competition. Her personal life at this time was turbulent: she failed her university course and attempted suicide. At 19 she joined the Communist Party. Marriage in 1944 to the lawyer and communist writer Lloyd Davies, and the birth of a son, provided a brief stability, but the marriage failed and Hewett left for Sydney in 1948. There she lived in the poorer areas and worked in a variety of factory jobs. For nine years she lived with Les Flood, boiler-maker and communist, by whom she had three sons. She became deeply involved in Party activities during the turbulent anti-communist period of the 1950s, but wrote little. In 1959 her novel *Bobbin Up*, based on her factory experiences, appeared and won immediate popularity. Her relationship with Flood having come to an end, she resumed her university studies in Perth in 1960 and married Merv Lilley, merchant seaman and communist, in the same year. In 1968, disillusioned by Soviet treatment of dissidents, she left the Communist Party. After some years of tutoring at the University of WA, she moved again to Sydney. *Wild Card* (1990), Hewett's acclaimed first volume of autobiography, describes her experiences to 1958. In 1975 Lloyd Davies began a series of libel actions against Hewett and other parties following the publication of a poem in *Rapunzel in Suburbia*; the actions, which stimulated much public debate, are justified by Davies in *In Defence of My Family* (1986).

Her poetry, a continued preoccupation, has appeared in the collections *What about the People!* (1961, with Merv Lilley), *Windmill Country* (1968), *Late Night Bulletin* (1969), *Rapunzel in Suburbia* (1975), *Greenhouse* (1979), *Journeys* (1982), *Alice in Wormland* (1987), *A Tremendous World in her Head* (1989), *Selected Poems* (1991) and *Peninsula* (1994). But she is also well known as a playwright. She has also written radio plays, numerous short stories and a second novel, *The Toucher* (1993), and edited a collection of WA literature, *Sandgropers* (1973). The first volume of her *Collected Plays* was published in 1992.

A romantic quest for the intrinsic but elusive self lies at the heart of Hewett's poetry and drama. It determines the emotional range and impact of her work, its vigour and frankness. Critics of her work also claim that her romantic commitment leads to structural weakness, thematic confusion and self-indulgence. Many of Hewett's dramatic themes, incidents and images are present in her poetry. Apart from some proletarian ballads, her verse is confessional and romantic in theme, wryly humorous, frankly bawdy, varied in tone and rich in imagery. Sexuality is her main subject, seen as both liberation and imprisonment, although increasingly she writes of the fear and attraction of death.

The most significant poems in *Peninsula* are those of the 'still-life ageing woman', who, burdened by 'the same old griefs', the legacy of a tormented and tumultuous life, searches for acceptance of the punishment life has exacted for her once being 'Careless young and passionately proud' and for 'having the courage to love'. While many poems reflect a new-found spirit of 'quiet forbearance' it is clear that there has been no submission. If Childe Roland could still to the dark tower come, all would be worth-while.

> one kiss would bring my lips alive
> one tear redeem my life.

The 'Upside-down Sonnets', a separate section of *Peninsula*, won the Mattara Poetry Prize and was first published in the 1991 Mattara anthology, *The Sea's White Edge*.

Hewett has won numerous awards for her work including the ABC Poetry Prize (1945 and 1965), the *Australian* Poetry Prize (1986), the Angus & Robertson Poetry Prize (1986), the Grace Leven Poetry Prize (1989), the Mattara Poetry Award (1991), the Victorian Premier's Award for non-fiction (1991), the NBC Turnbull Fox Phillips Poetry Prize (1994) and two Awgies (1972 and 1982). She has received several Literature Board writers' grants, is an emeritus fellow of the Literature Board of the Australia Council and has been made AO. Margaret Williams has written a study of her work, *Dorothy Hewett. The Feminine as Subversion* (1992).

'Hidden Bole, The', a complex philosophical poem by R.D. FitzGerald, was written in 1935 in Sydney while FitzGerald was convalescing from a severe operation. It was published in *Moonlight Acre* (1938). Highly valued by FitzGerald ('my chief claim to be a poet at all'), the poem reflects on the death of the ballerina Pavlova in 1931, moving from that event to a contemplation of the nature and essence of beauty and the relationship between beauty and time. The banyan tree, which puts out aerial roots to reinforce the original sapling, thus producing a maze of trunks, is taken as a natural example of continuous survival, that survival stemming from the original core, the 'hidden bole' itself. The individual blossoms of the tree, coming in profusion from the many trunks, have only a momentary existence and glory, but that glory (beauty) continues with the new blossoms that quickly replace the old. Beauty thus persists because, paradoxically, it is transient. Although the beauty of Pavlova's actual dance seems to die with her, it survives in the memory of those who witness it.

HIGGINS, Bertram (1901–74), born Malvern, Melbourne, went to Oxford in 1919 and remained in England until 1930 as a literary journalist and a reviewer for the *Times Literary Supplement*, the *Spectator*, the *New Statesman*, and the *Sunday Times*. After a brief period in Australia (1930–33), part of which time he worked on Cyril Pearl's short-lived magazine *Stream*, he returned to England, where he served in the RAF in the Second World War. In 1946 he returned to Australia. Higgins published *Mordecaius Overture* (1933), a complex work that saw him recognised by a small coterie as the intellectual and poetic equal of T.S. Eliot, but which remained only dimly understood. Mordecaius, a witness to both the crucifixion of Christ and the destruction of Pompeii, attempts to fit both events into a frame of reference which has some relevance to the confusion of his own life. Higgins's lack of other published works, deplored by his devotees, has been somewhat compensated for by the posthumous edition *The Haunted Rendezvous: Selected Poems* (1980), a selection made by Higgins, in collaboration with Robert King, in the year before his death. In addition to Higgins's best poems, *The Haunted Rendezvous* contains a selection of the sparse critical commentary available on Higgins, most of it written about the time *Mordecaius Overture* was published.

HIGHAM, Charles (1931–), born London, became a book-reviewer for the *Sydney Morning Herald* in 1956 and was literary editor of the *Bulletin* 1964–67 before moving to the USA. His first two volumes of poetry, *A Distant Star* (1951) and *Spring and Death* (1953), were published in England. His Australian publications are *The Earthbound and Other Poems* (1959), *Noonday Country* (1966), subtitled *Poems 1954–1965*, and *The Voyage to Brindisi, and Other Poems* (1970). He edited *Australian Writing Today* (1968), *They Came to Australia* (1961, with Alan Brissenden) and *Australians Abroad* (1967, with

Michael Wilding). He published a controversial biography of Errol Flynn in 1980, as well as several biographies of American stars.

HILL, Barry (1943–   ), born Melbourne, graduated from the University of Melbourne and has worked as a teacher, psychologist and journalist in Victoria and London. In 1972 he returned to Melbourne as founding editor of the education page of the *Age* but has been a full-time fiction writer since 1975. Hill has published two books of short fiction, *A Rim of Blue* (1978) and *Headlocks & Other Stories* (1983) and two novellas, *Near the Refinery* (1980), and *The Best Picture* (1988); a collection of poetry, *Raft* (1990), winner of the Anne Elder Poetry Award; and *Ghosting William Buckley* (1993), a meditation in verse on the adventures and experiences of escaped convict William Buckley which won the 1994 NSW State Liberary Award for poetry. *Ghosting William Buckley* has a remarkable range of poetic styles and rhythms, adapting well to the varied environments in which Buckley found himself – in the bush with the Aborigines, in Hobart and back in English society. Conceived in the myth cycle of hero banished into the wilderness and his ultimate return, *Ghosting William Buckley* is a complex work, brilliantly executed.

HILL, Fidelia S.T. (?1790–1854), born Pontefract, Yorkshire, published *Poems and Recollections of the Past* (1840), suggested as the first book of verse written by a woman to be published in Australia.

HILL, Samuel Prout (1812–61), born Devonshire, England, came to Australia in 1841. He alternated residence between NSW and Tasmania in various clerical occupations but made more of a reputation as a man of letters than of business. He published *Tarquin the Proud and Other Poems* (1843) and *Monody on the Death of Sir George Gipps* (1847). Hill was also a respected political writer with the Hobart *Mercury* in the late 1850s.

HOARE, Benjamin (1842–1932), born Buckinghamshire, England, arrived in Australia in 1856. After founding and editing the *Evening Times* and *Evening Star* in Geelong he joined the editorial staff of the Melbourne *Daily Telegraph* in 1886; he was leader-writer for the *Age* 1890–1914. Active in Catholic affairs, he helped found the *Catholic Magazine* in 1888. He published poetry including *The Maori* (1869) and *Figures of Fancy* (1869). His work reflects sincere if naive ideas and strong religious convictions.

HODGINS, Philip (1959–   ) grew up on a dairy farm near Shepparton, was educated at Geelong and later moved to Melbourne where he has worked in publishing. He was diagnosed as suffering from chronic myeloid leukaemia in 1983, a personal calamity which has affected both the content and volume of his poetry. He has published widely in anthologies and periodicals and has produced the collections *Blood and Bone* (1986), *Down the Lake with Half a Chook* (1988), *Animal Warmth* (1990), *Up On All Fours* (1993) and *Dispossessed* (1994). In 1986 he won the Wesley Michel Wright Prize, in 1987 the NSW Premier's Award, and in 1988 the Grace Perry Prize and the Prairie Schooner Readers Choice USA Award.

The poems of *Blood and Bone* are a frank confrontation with his own and others' mortality, moving from the metaphysical irony of 'The Passenger', which represents his leukaemia as a parasite draining nourishment from 'everything I eat. It gets the vitamins/ from every sorry beer I drink', and whose 'birth will bring me to a corpse', to the rural analogies of the crows of 'From County Down', which bring to mind life's grim, perennial realities and random cruelties. The poems of *Animal Warmth* and *Down the Lake with Half a Chook*, which draw on his childhood experience, mine with individual effects the same rich vein of Australian pastoral experience as Les Murray and David Campbell. Resurrecting the past is for Hodgins 'a detailed obsession', stimulated by childhood memories of the different tastes of milk straight from the cow, the shapes of gums, the antics of possums, the bar-room tricks of a mate, a paddock 'gridlocked' with hay bales or a confrontation with a goanna. Combining laconic language with striking visual imagery and assured control of phrase, rhythm and syntax, his best poems achieve a Horatian clarity and balance. *Down the Lake with Half a Chook* is divided into three sections, 'Hospital', which returns to his struggle with cancer, 'Boarding School', which focuses on specific childhood memories, and 'Country', which returns with the same Proustian nostalgia as *Animal Warmth* to the rural world. According to 'Sludge' re-creating the dairy-farming past is to be 'exhilarated by the mundane', an experience Hodgins transmits to the reader with tact, candour and freshness. As in his poems on the experience of incurable illness, toughness and humour are striking characteristics, achieved as much by confident control of the poetry's various metrical forms from free verse to more regular structures, as by controlled emotion.

Up On All Fours was praised by Peter Porter, who welcomed its extension of the Australian pastoral genre, with its 'tradition of yarning, balladry, legend and truculent attitudinising'. Divided into four parts, the work is notable for its heightened formal definition as for its renewed lyric impulse and characteristic lack of sentimentality. Much of the imagery is cool and memorable: 'the little kitchen spreading buttered light'; a farmer dipping his sheep like a gondolier; a dead snake becoming 'a line of common memory lying in the dust'. Poems such as 'Tail Paddock' and 'Driving through the Mallee' explore territory largely unfamiliar to his contemporaries, as in this stanza from 'The Rock Paddocks':

> They happen over centuries and stop
> when all they have to push against is air.
> So slow the paddocks are taken by surprise.
> And though it's time to strip this useless crop
> the man who owns the paddocks doesn't care.
> He knows there's more already on the rise.

Up On All Fours was quickly followed by *Dispossessed*, a novel in blank verse which investigates the tribulations of farming life and the psychology of eight survivors.

HOGUE, Oliver ('Trooper Bluegum') (1880–1919), born Sydney, was a journalist with the *Sydney Morning Herald* before enlisting as a trooper in the Sixth Light Horse regiment. He soon gained a commission and served at Gallipoli and in the desert campaigns; he survived the war only to die in the influenza epidemic in England in 1919. As 'Trooper Bluegum' he wrote articles for the *Sydney Morning Herald* which were collected in two books, both published in 1916, *Love Letters of an Anzac* and *Trooper Bluegum at the Dardanelles*. He also wrote *The Home-Sick Anzac and Other Verses* (1918) and a work of fiction, *The Cameliers* (1919).

HOLBURN, Muir (1920–60), born Sydney, was a journalist with the NSW public service 1947–59; he was president of the NSW branch of the FAW in 1948–50. Although well known as a poet, he did not publish a volume of poetry; with his wife, Marjorie Pizer, he edited *Creeve Roe* (1947).

HOLDSWORTH, Philip (1851–1902), born Sydney, was a public servant and member of the literary coterie of Sydney in the second half of the nineteenth century. He was editor of the *Illustrated Sydney News* in the 1880s, a contributor to the *Bulletin, Freeman's Journal* and *Athenaeum*, and a founding member of the Athenaeum Club. His only published work was *Station Hunting on the Warrego* (1885), the first poem a long account of a search by two pioneers for pastures for their flocks. He wrote a biographical note to *Poems of Henry Kendall* (1886), edited by Alexander Sutherland.

HOLT, Edgar (1904–88), born England, had a wide-ranging career as a journalist in

Brisbane, Sydney and Melbourne before becoming editor of *Smith's Weekly* 1947–50. He published poetry, *Lilacs out of the Dead Land* (1932) and a book of memoirs, *Politics is People* (1969).

'Homecoming', a poem by Bruce Dawe, published in *Beyond the Subdivisions* (1969), tells of the return to their homelands (both Australia and the USA are suggested) of the bodies of soldiers who died in the Vietnam War. With its deliberate air of casual inhumanity ('they're zipping them up in green plastic bags . . . they're rolling them out of the deep-freeze lockers'), the poem evokes the dehumanising effect and wastefulness of war. Its final line, 'they're bringing them home, now, too late, too early', hints at the bitterness and controversy that the Vietnam War engendered.

HOOTON, Harry (1908–61), born Hampstead, London, migrated to Australia in 1924. Unable to get employment, he wandered widely in Australia, finally settling in Sydney, where he worked for a time as a journalist and became connected with the libertarian group dominated by the philosopher John Anderson. An iconoclast who developed a philosophy, he called Anarcho-Technocracy, Power Over Things or the Dictatorship of Art, Hooton appears to have had more influence as a witty raconteur than as philosopher or poet, although he had become a minor cult figure in Sydney by the time of his death. He published three collections of poetry, *These Poets* (1941), *Things You See When You Haven't Got a Gun* (1943), which includes some prose, and *It Is Great To Be Alive* (1961); and with A.D. Hope, Garry Lyle and O.M. Somerville contributed to the booklets of verse, *No. 1, Number Two* and *Number Three* (1943–48). A film on Hooton's life was made by Arthur and Corinne Cantrill in 1972 and he appears as the poet Mulcahy in Hugh Atkinson's novel *Low Company* (1961). His *Collected Poems*, edited by Sasha Soldatow and including an account of his poetic theory and philosophy, was published in 1990.

HOPE, A.D. (Alec Derwent) (1907–), born Cooma, NSW, the son of a Presbyterian minister, spent most of his childhood in rural NSW and Tasmania. He graduated in 1928 from the University of Sydney, and took up a scholarship at Oxford the same year. Returning to a depressed Australia in 1931, he tried various occupations before becoming lecturer in education at Sydney Teachers' College in 1937, lecturer in English there 1938–44, moved to the University of Melbourne in 1945 and in 1951 was appointed to the chair of English at Canberra University College, later part of the ANU. He retired in 1968 to devote himself to poetry, but has continued to lecture and retains a close association with the University as emeritus professor.

Although Hope recognised his poetic vocation early, his work appeared only fugitively until 1955 when his first collection, *The Wandering Islands*, was published. His subsequent collections include *Poems* (1960), *A.D. Hope* (1963), *Collected Poems 1930–1965* (1966, republished in an expanded form 1972), *Selected Poems* (1973), *A Late Picking* (1975), *A Book of Answers* (1978), *The Drifting Continent* (1979), *Antechinus* (1981), *The Tragical History of Dr Faustus* (1982), *The Age of Reason* (1985), *Selected Poems*, selected by Ruth Morse (1986), *Orpheus* (1991), a volume in the Poets on Record series (1972), a lengthy mock-heroic poem, *Dunciad Minor* (1970), a play, *Ladies from the Sea* (1987), *Selected Poems*, selected by David Brooks (1992), and a collection of reminiscences, *Chance Encounters* (1992). A selection of his verse has been translated into Italian by G. Distefano, titled *Tre Volti Dell'Amore* (1983). A major figure in Australian critical work since the late 1940s, he has published several collections of essays: *The Cave and the Spring* (1965), *Native Companions* (1974), *The Pack of Autolycus* (1978) and *The New Cratylus* (1979); a study of Judith Wright (1975); a brief survey of Australian literature 1950–62 (1963); a scholarly, imaginative study of a sixteenth-century poem by William Dunbar, *A Midsummer Eve's Dream* (1970); and a variety of smaller monographs on aspects of literature. The international recognition that Hope's poetry has won is reflected in the diversity of his awards which include, among others, the Britannica-Australia Award (1965), the Arts Council Award for poetry (1965), the *Age* Book of the Year Award (1976), the Myer Award (1967), the Levinson Prize for poetry (Chicago, 1968), the Ingram Merrill Award, New York (1969), the Robert Frost Award (1976) and a special NSW State Literary Award (1989). He was made OBE in 1972 and AC in 1981. He has received an honorary D.Litt. from the ANU and the universities of Melbourne and New England as well as Monash University.

The distinctive note of Hope's poetry, authoritative, measured, rich in literary, biblical and mythological allusion and adhering to traditional rhythms and forms, led to his being classed at first as 'classic', 'academic' or 'intellectual'. The lack of any identifiable Australian experience, the satirical dismissal of much of modern life, the diversity of his interests and the emphasis on sexual experience bewildered most early readers. Many saw him as principally a satirist, opposed to the cowardice of techno-cratic man in preferring tame, vicarious, standardised experience. Certainly, rejection of conforming rituals which stifle life's resources of heroism and energy was, and is, a characteristic theme of Hope's verse. Poems such as 'Private Dick', 'The Brides', 'The House of God' and 'Conquistador' are hilarious treatments of the subject; others such as 'A Commination', 'Easter Hymn' and 'Toast for a Golden Age' are more bitter. But, as *The Wandering Islands* and the later collections reveal, satire is secondary in Hope's work and springs from his persistent concern with the nature of poetry and the serious, even sacred role that he accords it. As his fine poem 'William Butler Yeats' illustrates, he shares Yeats's romantic, heroic conception of the artist. In 'Invocation' he unequivocally describes the poet as one who 'alone' defends 'That darkness out of which our light is won' and celebrates the working of 'the spirit elect' in his own poetry; and in several other poems he has dealt explicitly with the elect role of the poet. Poetry's complementary communal role emerges in his perception of it as 'Cel-ebration', meaning not just 'admiration and delight' but 'an intellectual assent to the causes that make the natural world an order and a system, and an imaginative grasp of the necessity of its processes'. In essays and poems he has described the poet as one with the gift of night-time vision in a world where others see only by day, and as 'a man continually obsessed with a passion for a synoptic view', concerned always to present his subject, man in all aspects, 'under the aspect of eternity'. The poem 'Con-versation with Calliope' and the essay 'The Three Faces of Love' define his concep-tion of the poet's distinctive 'creative way of life', bringing 'new objects of desire into being'.

Hope also sees mythology as playing an indispensable part in this creative reinter-pretation; myths embody 'the great commonplaces' that define man's place in the universal order. Yet, as 'An Epistle from Holofernes' affirms, 'myths will not fit us ready made' and 'It is the meaning of the poet's trade/ To recreate the fables and revive/ In men the energies by which they live'. Frequently he refashions myth for his own purposes: 'Imperial Adam' and 'Paradise Saved' deal playfully with the Edenic myth; 'The End of a Journey' casts a new, bleak light on Ulysses' homecoming; 'The Return of Persephone' elicits sympathy for Dis; and in 'Coup de Grâce' even the story of Red Riding Hood is given an unexpected twist.

If Hope confidently sees the poet's task as sacred, he also presents it as hazardous, painful and even terrifying. In much of his verse regularity of form contrasts with strong emotional content, sensuality with intellectual detachment, but within some poems there is a struggle between opposites that is left unreconciled. Poems such as 'Flower Poem' and 'The Watcher', expressive of the terrors and pain of poetic vision, are balanced by others such as 'Pseudodoxia Epidemica' and 'As Well as They Can', which establish an emotional poise between suffering and achieved insight. Similarly, poems such as 'X-Ray Photograph', 'The Dinner' and 'Rawhead and Bloody Bones', testifying to the horrors of the mind's imaginings, are balanced by others such as

'Argolis', 'The Trophy' and 'On an Engraving by Casserius', which express a more harmonious acceptance of life's dualities. In his essays Hope has expressed his conviction of the poet's negative capability, and some of his finest poems are also his most impersonal: 'The Death of the Bird', 'Man Friday', 'Meditation on a Bone', 'Moschus Moschiferus' and 'On an Engraving by Casserius'. Other striking achievements include 'The Double Looking Glass', a complex, ornate, richly sensual poem, and the simpler 'Ode on the Death of Pius the Twelfth', which celebrates his mature, joyful intuition of a harmonious natural order.

The characteristic duality of his perceptions, both in terms of harmony and ambivalence, is particularly evident in his love poetry. Love is central to his work, and he has not only frequently drawn analogies between the transcending, creative experience of love and that of poetry but also expressed their interdependence. 'Chorale', 'The Gateway' and 'The Lamp and the Jar' are his most explicit celebrations of this dependence. Others such as 'Pygmalion', 'The Coasts of Cerigo', 'Fafnir', 'The Damnation of Byron' and 'The Dinner' are more ambivalent expressions of the conflicting pull of delight and revulsion, surrender and freedom.

Most of Hope's discursive critical work reflects his preoccupations as a poet. Witty, original and incisive, his essays in *The Cave and The Spring, The New Cratylus* and *The Pack of Autolycus* develop his ideas on the nature and forms of poetry, including an energetic defence of rhyme and poetic modes that have fallen into disuse. Regarding poetry as a damaged 'ecology' of forms, he particularly laments the passing of that 'middle form of poetry' successfully resurrected in much of his own verse. As a trenchant, individual, witty reviewer and unrelenting enemy of the second-rate, he has had a strong influence on Australian critical standards and has often been notoriously and valuably unsettling. *Native Companions* reprints some of his essays and reviews written over four decades. Hope's poetry is the subject of numerous critical essays and of monographs by Leonie Kramer (1979) and Kevin Hart (1992). A bibliography, compiled by Joy Hooton, was published in 1979.

HOPEGOOD, Peter (1891–1967), born Essex, England, came to Australia in 1924 after serving in the First World War. He worked as a hand on a pearling lugger in Broome and a jackeroo on north-west cattle stations; he then became a journalist and freelance writer. A man-of-action turned mystic, Hopegood became obsessed with myth, attempting to indicate in his verse and in several essays that there are correspondences between the myths of diverse races. In the title poem of his first book of verse, *Austral Pan and Other Verses* (1932), the subject is the eternal, ubiquitous spirit of Pan, known to 'Ovid's ancient rustic clan' in rural Italy 2000 years ago and equally present in the Australian bush today – 'his steps outback with glee are bent/ He sniffs the saltbush with content.' Hopegood's echo of the vitalism of the time, and his link with the contemporary vision of poets such as Hugh McCrae, Kenneth Slessor and the Lindsays are evident. His second book of verse, *Thirteen from Oahu* (1940), sees him chiefly in the role of myth-interpreter. Oahu is the Hawaiian Place of the Setting Forth for Hawaiki, the Isles of the Blessed. Regeneration is the central theme and the poems are accompanied by copious explanatory notes, which are often more effective and interesting than the poems they illustrate. His chief poetic work, *Circus at World's End* (1947), is prefaced by an essay which sets out his poetic/philosophic theory; at the heart of all the myths of the diverse races of the world and of all literature and psychoanalytic theory there is a single underlying concept of earth consciousness, the union of earth and man. Hopegood said that his poems in *Circus at World's End* were 'written in emulation of the skill of the myth-makers' and especially the makers of the traditional ballads. That Hopegood can write effectively in the medieval ballad style is illustrated in 'Swastika Stepmother', which echoes the Scottish 'Lord Randal' but is translated from the German traditional ballad 'Die Stiefmutter'. By adding the word 'swastika' to the title, Hopegood allows the poem to become a reflection on the contemporary German people. *Snake's-eye View of a Serial Story* (1964), Hopegood's first collection for seventeen years, sees him still using myth, from Australian ballad to Maori legend and Scots pibroch. The simplest and least pretentious of his verse, however, is the most effective. Acknowledged by his contemporaries as a significant poet, Hopegood has been roundly attacked for the obscurity of his major poetry; friend and fellow poet R.D. FitzGerald believed that he sacrificed his artistic integrity to his mystical preoccupations. Hopegood published the autobiographical *Peter Lecky by Himself* in 1935, 'Lecky' being the pseudonym he adopted in an earlier literary competition.

HORNE, R.H. (Richard Henry) (1802–84), who in 1867 substituted 'Hengist' for his second name, was born Edmonton, in London, and became ambitious for a poetic career after reading Shelley's *Queen Mab.* He became a literary celebrity through his successful editorship of the *Monthly Repository*, and the triumph of his epic poem *Orion* (1843), which ran to six printings in its first year, causing him to be later dubbed 'Orion' Horne. In 1852 he came to Australia, partly to escape a dramatic decline in his personal situation, partly to restore his fortunes on the Australian goldfields. He held and lost minor administrative positions on the Victorian diggings, failed to win election to the Victorian parliament, was briefly and unsuccessfully a commissioner for Melbourne's sewerage and water supply, and drifted, often unemployed, until 1863, when he was made warden of the Blue Mountain goldfield near Trentham in Victoria. There he returned to serious writing. In 1864 *Prometheus the Fire-Bringer*, a lyrical drama, was published and in 1866 he wrote, for the Intercolonial Exhibition of Australasia, *The South Sea Sisters, A Lyric Masque*, which contains his poetic version of an Aboriginal corroboree. Restored to literary prestige and influence, he was an important member of the Melbourne literary circle, centred on the Yorick Club. He returned to England in 1869, continuing to write profusely but unprofitably. Horne's Australian writings, except for his prose work *Australian Facts and Prospects* (1859), were of little significance in themselves, but the presence in the colony of such an established literary figure did much to bolster the respectability of the literary profession in the hitherto sceptical colonial mind and acted as a stimulus to such rising literary talents as Henry Kendall, Adam Lindsay Gordon and Marcus Clarke. Biographical works include Cyril Pearl's *Always Morning: The Life of Richard Henry 'Orion' Horne* (1960) and Anne Blainey's *The Farthing Poet* (1968). Barry Oakley's play *The Ship's Whistle* (1979) focuses on Horne.

'How He Died', the title poem of John Farrell's (1887) volume of bush ballads, is a sentimental tale of the station boozer, Nabbage, who gives his life to save his 'little mate', the squatter's boy, Freddie. It was published first in the *Bulletin*, 1883.

'How M'Dougall Topped the Score', the title poem of T.E. Spencer's 1906 collection of verse, is the story of the historic cricket match between Piper's Flat and Molongo. When challenged by Molongo to a single-innings match, the loser to pay for a slap-up lunch at McGinnis's pub, Piper's Flat can only muster ten players. They reluctantly recruit the old Scotsman, M'Dougall, from nearby Cooper's Creek, to make up the number. Molongo are dismissed for 66 and when Piper's Flat in reply are 9 wickets down for 17, M'Dougall marches to the crease. He hits the first ball gently back towards the bowler and in response to his command, 'Fetch It', his aptly named old sheepdog, Pincher, seizes the ball and makes off, with the whole Molongo team in wrathful but vain pursuit ('brain the mongrel with a bat'). M'Dougall, meanwhile, begins his initially swift but eventually ponderous and painful but successful pursuit of the 50 runs needed for victory:

> Then Pincher dropped the ball, and, as instinctively he knew
> Discretion was the wiser plan, he disappeared from view
> And as Molongo's beaten men exhausted lay around
> We raised M'Dougall shoulder high, and bore him from the ground.

Both sides then repair to McGinnis's to celebrate with 'whisky-punch' the historic occasion when 'M'Dougall topped the score'. Spencer's poem celebrates the bushman's talents for devising ingenious but essentially harmless methods of besting a rival; it takes its place alongside A.B. Paterson's accounts of the stratagems of drovers to outwit squatters and of racehorse owners and jockeys to outwit bookmakers.

HOWARTH, R.G. (Robert Guy) (1906–74), born Tenterfield, NSW, graduated from the universities of Sydney and Oxford before being appointed to the English Department at the University of Sydney in 1933. In 1955–71 he was professor of English literature at the University of Cape Town, South Africa. Widely acknowledged by contemporaries as one of Australia's finest literary scholars and regarded as an inspiring and encouraging teacher by a generation of literature students at Sydney, Howarth early in his academic career produced several important works on English literature. He was foundation editor (1939–56) of *Southerly*. An enthusiastic advocate of Australian literature, he edited Hugh McCrae's *Forests of Pan* (1944) and *The Best Poems of Hugh McCrae* (1961), and collaborated with John Thompson and Kenneth Slessor in *The Penguin Book of Australian Verse* (1958). Howarth's poetry, which has not received sufficient recognition, appeared in the collections *Spright and Geist* (1944), a series of epigrammatic love poems, *Involuntaries* (1948) and *Nardoo and Pituri* (1959).

HUDSON, Flexmore (1913–88), born Charters Towers, Queensland, graduated from the University of Adelaide and was a teacher, freelance writer and seaman in the Australian coastal trade. His published poetry includes *Ashes and Sparkle* (1937), *In the Wind's Teeth* (1940), *With the First Soft Rain* (1943), *Indelible Voices* (1943), *As Iron Hills* (1944), and *Pools of the Cinnabar Range* (1959). He edited *Poetry*, a quarterly, 1941–47, and the 1943 *Jindyworobak Anthology*; contributed numerous short stories to various periodicals and anthologies; and wrote a book of aesthetics, *The Child Discovers Poetry* (1941). His stories were collected by Adam Dutkiewicz, who edited them as *Tales from Corytella* (1987).

Involved in the Jindyworobak movement almost from its beginning, Hudson was strongly committed to the unique Australian spirit of place. Unlike Rex Ingamells, the Jindyworobak founder, however, Hudson wished to interpret the Australian environment, first in his own individual way, then in more universal terms. He was not willing to visualise the Australian landscape specifically through a pattern of Aboriginal legend ('a good many of us find the Alcheringa myth unpalatable and unprofitable'). His love for the Australian countryside, embracing everything from the harshness of the Mallee environment, which produced his much-anthologised 'Drought', to the softer beauty of a Murray River sunrise, gives his landscape lyrics warmth and sincerity. Less effective are his Jindyworobakish radical and political homilies, which are prominent in *Indelible Voices* and which mar the effect of individual poems such as 'To a Boy on His Eleventh Birthday'.

HUGHES, E.F. (Edward Francis) (1814–79), born Kidderminster, England, and who sometimes wrote under the pseudonym 'Frederick Gundase Shaw', published (in Australia) drama, *Bernard: A Drama of the Year 1848* (1859) and poetry, *Portland Bay: A Poem* (1864), *Efforts to be Heard* (1872), *The Millennium: An Epic Poem* (1873), a ten-book work which encompasses the whole scope of biblical history, and *Lays for Thoughtful Workers* (1875). Hughes had earlier (1846) published in London *The Benighted Trav-*

eller: A Tale and Other Poems. He established the Portland *Chronicle*, which he edited from its inception in 1855.

HUMPHRIES, Barry (1934–   ), born Melbourne, was educated at the University of Melbourne, where he appeared in revues. After leaving university he toured Victoria in *Twelfth Night* with Ray Lawler and others, entertaining the company with a party turn in which he impersonated a suburban housewife. Lawler suggested that Humphries incorporate the act into the Melbourne Union Theatre's Christmas revue, and thus in December 1955 Edna Everage made her stage debut in Melbourne. Humphries moved to Sydney, where he established himself as a revue artist with the Phillip Street Theatre. In 1959 he went to England, but before leaving released *Wild Life in Suburbia*, two records of the monologues of Edna and Sandy Stone, the latter a 'decent humdrum little old man' whose character Humphries first created on stage in 1958. Through Edna and Sandy, he satirised the philistinism, emptiness, materialism and pretension of the Australian suburban middle class.

In England Humphries worked as a theatre and television actor, and in 1962 toured Australia in 'A Nice Night's Entertainment', the first of the one-man shows for which he has become famous. Barry (Bazza) McKenzie, is a character in a comic strip written by Humphries and drawn by Nicholas Garland which was published for over a decade in the English satirical magazine *Private Eye.* The strip, which focuses on the innocent Bazza's search for sexual satisfaction and his gargantuan capacity for alcohol, cleverly exploits mutual English-Australian prejudices, with the Poms characteristically portrayed as unwashed and avaricious and the Ockers, like Bazza, as unsophisticated vulgarians.

By the end of the 1960s Humphries's reputation was firmly established in Australia and abroad; in the next decade that reputation was consolidated, particularly in England, with a further series of one-man shows. Characters which Humphries created later include Lance Boyle, a wheeler-dealing union official, and Sir Les Patterson, Australia's cultural ambassador at the Court of St James whose view of the 'Yartz', a common Humphries target, is presented in *Les Patterson's Australia* (1978) and his *The Traveller's Tool* (1985). Despite these later creations, Humphries has been increasingly identified with Edna Everage, who has evolved from the pretentious, self-opinionated suburban housewife of 1955 into an outrageous international superstar. A 'gladdi-maniac', made DBE by Gough Whitlam in the second McKenzie film in 1974, eight years before Humphries's own award of AO, she assails her television and stage audiences in two hemispheres, dispenses advice in the *Australian Women's Weekly* and is the 'author' of *Dame Edna's Coffee Table Book* (1976) and *Dame Edna's Bedside Companion* (1982) as well as an autobiography, *My Gorgeous Life* (1989). Under his own name, Humphries has compiled a controversial anthology, *Bizarre* (1965); *The Barry Humphries Book of Innocent Austral Verse* (1968), a collection of 'bad' verse which includes poems of Barcroft Boake, E.J. Brady and Louise Mack as well as more thoroughly primitive poets; *Barry Humphries' Treasury of Australian Kitsch* (1980); the important retrospective *A Nice Night's Entertainment: Sketches and Monologues 1956– 1981* (1981); and *Neglected Poems and Other Creatures* (1991), which includes his own and his characters' verse.

Much admired by other writers who have drawn on suburban idioms, Humphries has been identified as 'Australia's only true Augustan' and his material described as 'Joyce Grenfell rewritten by Jonathan Swift'. On stage he has been part-satirist, part-caricaturist, and part-music-hall entertainer, sometimes in league with, sometimes antagonistic to, his audience. Some of his phrases, notably the alliterative euphemisms for urination which characterise the speech of Barry McKenzie, have become part of the Australian lexicon. For much of his career Humphries has attacked, with an ambivalent mixture of cruelty and affection, the pretension, self-centredness, prejudices and vulgarity of his imaginary Australian characters, 'accurately based on real people who have never lived'. The cruellest portraits have led to criticisms that Humphries is misanthropic and reactionary, presenting his overseas audiences with an Australia that is dated and even distorted. John Lahr's study of Humphries's personality and comic style, *Dame Edna and the Rise of Western Civilization* (1991) and Peter Coleman's *The Real Barry Humphries* (1990) give valuable insights into the sources of his dramatic creativity, but the most revealing study of the roots of his iconoclasm has been provided by Humphries himself in his autobiography, *More Please* (1992). A self-conscious portrait of his elusive self, *More Please* intensively recalls the oppressive dullness of his Melbourne childhood and the even more oppressive years at Melbourne Grammar School where he preserved his individuality by conducting guerilla-type subversion of the School Spirit.

Hunter Valley Poets first emerged as an identifiable literary group with the publishing by Norman Talbot of *XI Hunter Valley Poets + VII* (1966) and the anthology *Hunter Valley Poets* (1973), which presents not only the work of established and lesser-known writers of the region but also a sampling of poetry from schoolchildren. *IV Hunter Valley Poets* (1975) was a first collection from each of four poets of the region, T.H. Naisby, Maureen Bonomini, Denis King and Ross Bennett. T.H. Naisby, more than a poet of a particular place, has also published *The Fabulous Dross* (1979), a second and more expanded collection of verse. Ross Bennett, in addition to publishing another work, *River* (1980), a long poem set mainly in the Upper Allyn, a rainforest area near the Barrington Tops, edited *This Place: Poetry of the Hunter Valley* (1980), an anthology of the prose and poetry of thirty-three writers. Bennett's anthology was accompanied by *The Companion to This Place: Studies in Hunter Valley Poetry and Glossary of Poetic Terms* (1980), which was intended for the valley's secondary school students. *V Hunter Valley Poets* (1978) presents another five first collections, those of Jean Talbot, Christopher Pollnitz, David McQualter, Jess Dyce and Tim McGee. Jean Talbot has also edited *Huntress: Women Poets of the Hunter Valley* (1981) and Norman Talbot and Zeny Giles have edited *Contrast and Relief: Short Stories of the Hunter Valley* (1981). *Riverrun*, a little magazine produced by Keith Russell and Brian Musgrove, published some of the more experimental of the Hunter Valley poets. Ken Stone published *Hunter* (1980), a collection of poems which expresses his affection for the landscape and people of the region.

HUTCHINSON, Garrie (1949–   ), born Melbourne, was involved with the La Mama writers' workshops and is a freelance journalist and writer who was speechwriter for the former Australian prime minister, R.J. Hawke. His published poetry includes *Dart Objects: Poured Concrete, 1967–71* (1971), *Nothing Unsayable Said Right: 50 Poems, 1968–72* (1974) and *Terror Australis: Poems* (1975). He has also written numerous works on sport, including *The Barracker's Bible* (1983, with Jack Hibberd), and *Great Australian Football Stories* (1989, formerly *Great Australian Book of Football Stories*). Co-founder of Hoopla Theatre (later Playbox) in 1976 and the Melbourne Writers' Theatre in 1981, he has written for stage, television and film.

'Imperial Adam', a poem by A.D. Hope was first published in 1951. A fresh, sensuous look at the Edenic myth, the poem describes Adam's discovery of Eve, 'Man's counterpart/ In tender parody', their joyous love-making and Eve's subsequent travail in childbirth, aided by the 'first gentle midwives of mankind', the 'gravid elephant', the 'calving hind', the 'she-ape big with young' and the 'teeming lioness'. The poem's final comment on the birth of 'the first murderer' and other possible ambivalences are the subject of influential essays by James McAuley, Vincent Buckley and S.L. Goldberg, to which Hope has replied in his essay 'The Practical Critic', in *The Cave and the Spring* (1965).

In the Days When the World Was Wide, Henry Lawson's first major book of verse, was published in 1896; dedicated to J.F. Archibald, it carried on the title page a sketch by Frank Mahony of Lawson 'humping his bluey'. *In the Days When the World Was Wide* contains many of the best Lawson poems, including famous bush verses such as 'The Roaring Days', 'The Free-Selector's Daughter', 'Andy's Gone with Cattle' and 'Middleton's Rouseabout'; several important poems of political and social protest, including 'Faces in the Street', 'The *Cambaroora Star*' and 'The Star of Australasia'; and the best of Lawson's contributions to the *Bulletin* debate. *In the Days When the World Was Wide* went into a revised edition in 1900, when new poems such as 'Past Carin'' were added.

INGAMELLS, Rex (1913–55), poet and founder of the Jindyworobak movement, was born at Ororoo, a small town in outback SA. Educated at the University of Adelaide, he was a high-school teacher, freelance journalist, then a representative of a Melbourne publishing firm. His first book of verse, *Gumtops* (1935), carried a foreword by L.F. Giblin stressing the need for Australian poets to give 'their firsthand, direct reaction to nature and man as they find them in Australia'. This directive, P.R. Stephensen's *The Foundations of Culture in Australia* (1936) and Ingamells's irritation with G.H. Cowling's article on Australian literature in the *Age*, 16 February 1935, led to his own prose manifesto, *Conditional Culture* (1938), and the formation of the Jindyworobak movement in 1938. In 1941 Ingamells joined the Australia First movement, whose political aims were to some extent complementary to the literary ambitions of the Jindyworobaks. Ingamells's own political attitudes and his thwarted hopes for a massive takeover of the literary scene by the Jindyworobaks are summed up in his poem 'The Gangrened People', published in *At a Boundary* (1941). In 1951 he was appointed a judge of the Commonwealth Jubilee literary competition and he lectured in Australian literature at the Melbourne Technical College.

Ingamells's publications of poetry include *Gumtops* (1935), *Forgotten People* (1936), *Sun-Freedom* (1938), *Memory of Hills* (1940), *At a Boundary* (1941), *Content Are the Quiet Ranges* (1943), and *The Great South Land* (1945), which won the Grace Leven Prize for poetry. He wrote a novel, *Of Us Now Living* (1952). He was general editor of the *Jindyworobak Anthologies*, published annually 1938–53, compiled *The Jindyworobak Review 1938–1948* (1948) and edited an anthology for schools, *New Song in an Old Land: Australian Verse* (1943). Although Ingamells's own poetic talent was inadequate for the task of carrying the Jindyworobaks to the eminence he desired for them, he was a competent craftsman with a capacity for graceful imagery and picturesque description. These qualities are particularly evident in poems such as 'Forlorn Beauty', 'Sun-Freedom' and 'Memory of Hills', which are filled also with sensitivity to the spirit of place, and in 'The Forgotten People' and 'Uluru', where his emotional affinity with the Aboriginal people lifts the verse above the ordinary.

'IRONBARK', see **GIBSON, G.H.**

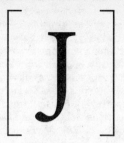

JAMES, Clive (1939–), born and educated in Sydney, was literary editor of *Honi Soit* and wrote for university magazines such as *Arna*. He worked briefly for the *Sydney Morning Herald* before settling in England in 1962. After completing a second degree at the University of Cambridge, he became a freelance literary journalist and critic and has written for the *New Statesman, Encounter*, the *Listener*, the *Times Literary Supplement* and other publications in England and the USA; in 1972–82 he was the highly respected television critic for the *Observer*, and has an international reputation as a television broadcaster, interviewer and performer, appearing regularly on BBC television. He was made AM in 1992. James's eclectic interests range from high culture to mass entertainment and embrace literature, television, films and popular music. Apart from several mock-heroic epics, e.g. *Peregrine Prykke's Pilgrimage through the London Literary World* (1976) and rock lyrics, he has published books of reviews and literary criticism, such as *The Metropolitan Critic* (1974), *At the Pillars of Hercules* (1979), *From the Land of Shadows* (1982), *Snakecharmers in Texas* (1988) and *The Dreaming Swimmer* (1992); several selections of his television journalism; selections of his verse including *Fan-mail: Seven Verse Letters* (1977), *Other Passports* (1986) and *Poem of the Year* (1983); the autobiographies *Unreliable Memoirs* (1980), a hilarious account of his experiences growing up in and leaving Australia; *Falling Towards England* (1985), the story of his experiences in London in the 1960s; and *May Week Was in June* (1990), which closes in 1968 as his career at Cambridge comes to an end; and three novels, *Brilliant Creatures* (1983), *The Remake* (1987), and *Brrm! Brrm!* (1991). James describes himself as preoccupied with the obvious: 'my field is the self-evident.' Nevertheless he takes pride in casting a fresh light on the prosaic, including himself with self-deprecating wit in that category. Verbal dexterity, a pungent wit and extraordinary metaphoric inventiveness are surface characteristics of his exuberant writing but behind the facade of frivolity he is often both erudite and serious. Notwithstanding his reputation as an expatriate metropolitan critic, his style and humour have been recognised as quintessentially Australian and have led him to be described, not necessarily unkindly, as 'the highbrow coming on as Chips Rafferty'.

JANAVICIUS, Jurgis (1926–), born Lithuania, arrived in Australia in 1948. His poetry has appeared in anthologies and periodicals and in two collections, *Journey to the Moon* (1971) and *Umph* (1972). The poems of *Journey to the Moon* are spare, witty lyrics, dealing for the most part with the experience of immigration; the comic verse of *Umph*, accompanied by drawings, records the experiences of a lump of live jelly of undefined size which 'observes the outside world through its slightly protruding aperture'. Janavicius is also a cartoonist whose work has been published in *Aspect* and *Outrider*.

JENKINS, John (1949–), born Melbourne, writer and journalist, was associated with the rise of the 'New Australian Poetry' and the small magazines which accompanied it. He edited the brief-lived *A and Aardvark* in 1970, and was co-editor, with Walter Billeter, of *etymspheres: The Journal of the Paper Castle* in 1974–75 and, with Rudi Krausmann, of *Aspect* in 1976–77. He has also been involved with Billeter in Paper Castle Publications, publishing with him *Dreamrobe Embroideries & Asparagus for Dinner* (1974); with Robert Kenny in Rigmarole Publications; and with Michael Dugan in *The Outback Reader* (1975). Associate editor of *Helix* (1981–82), he was also editor of the small Brunswick Hills Press 1984–88. His own poetry includes *Zone of the White Wolf and Other Landscapes* (1974), *Blindspot* (1977), *The Inland Sea* (1985), *Chromatic Cargoes* (1986), *The Wild White Sea* (1991) and *Days Like Air* (1992). With Ken Bolton he published *Airborne Dogs* (1988), *The Ferrara Poems* (1989) and *The Gutman Variations* (1992), and edited with Antonia Bruns *Soft Lounges* (1984). He has also written for screen and radio. His first non-fiction book, *22 Contemporary Australian Composers*, appeared in 1988.

JENKINS, Wendy (1952–), born Perth, has published poetry in periodicals and in one collection, *Out of Water into Light* (1979). She also edited with B.R. Coffey a collection of WA writing, *Portrait* (1986) and, with Amanda Curtin, Alfredo Strano's *Luck Without Joy: A Portrayal of a Migrant* (1986).

JENNINGS, Kate (1948–), born near Temora, NSW, was raised near Griffith. At Sydney University in the late 1960s and early 1970s she was active in left-wing politics and feminism and edited the well-known collection of contemporary women's verse *Mother I'm Rooted* (1975). Her own verse has appeared in two widely separated collections, *Come to Me My Melancholy Baby* (1975) and *Cats, Dogs & Pitchforks* (1993). The 1975 collection confronts the difficulties of surviving the pain, disappointments and loneliness of life as a feminist poet enclosed in an a 1970s environment of brittle relationships and ephemeral experience; the verse of the 1993 collection is equally passionate and direct but is both more finely honed and more generous in range and tone, achieving what Jennings has described as the 'fast disappearing' art of 'Saying simple things well or complicated things simply'. In 1979 Jennings left for New York, where she works as a writer and editor. Her subsequent publications, selections of essays, *Save Me, Joe Louis* (1988) and *Bad Manners* (1993) and a collection of short stories, *Women Falling Down in the Street* (1990), reveal a marked shift from her earlier radicalism.

JEPHCOTT, Sydney (1864–1951), born Nariong, Upper Murray, Victoria, lived most of his life in the Mount Kosciusko area, whose beauty and grandeur he claimed influenced his literary imagination. He published two books of poetry, *The Secrets of the South* (1892) and *Penetralia* (1912), which contained some verses from the earlier volume. The short, meditative lyrics are frequently solemn and stately in tone; 'Thredbo River', for example, conveys well the atmosphere of the snow country.

'Jim Jones at Botany Bay', one of the best early Australian folk-songs, is the bitter lament of an English convict who has been transported for poaching and who at the end of the song vows defiantly that he will join Jack Donohoe's bushranging gang and take revenge on the 'tyrants' who have ill-treated him at Botany Bay. The reference to Donohoe suggests that the ballad was written around 1830, although it was not collected until 1907, when it was published as a 'typical song of the convict days' in Charles MacAlister's *Old Pioneering Days in the Sunny South* (1907). Usually sung to the tune, 'Irish Mollie, Oh!', 'Jim Jones at Botany Bay' has features which link it with the English street ballad tradition; it is one of the few treason songs, reputedly banned by the authorities, to have survived from the penal days.

Jindyworobak Movement, the most extreme expression of the revival of national-ism in Australia in the 1930s, arose partly as a reaction against contemporary colonialist attitudes and partly as a counter to the international influences that had made steady inroads into Australia's isolation throughout the 1920s. It came into being in 1938 when Rex Ingamells founded the Jindyworobak club in Adelaide, published *Conditional Culture*, a prose manifesto explaining the aims and methods of the move-ment, and produced the first *Jindyworobak Anthology* of poetry. The anthologies were continued annually until 1953, and in 1948 a historical account of the movement, *Jindyworobak Review* (1938–48), was compiled by Ingamells. *The Jindyworobaks* (1979), edited by Brian Elliott in the Portable Australian Authors series, is a comprehensive historical and critical account of the movement. Many writers were associated, with varying degrees of commitment, with the Jindyworobaks. In addition to Ingamells those most closely involved, although briefly in some cases, included Ian Tilbrook, Flexmore Hudson, Max Harris, Ian Mudie, Colin Thiele, David Rowbotham, John Blight, William Hart-Smith, Victor Kennedy, Paul Grano, Roland Robinson, Gina Ballantyne, Nancy Cato, Judith Wright, Gwen Harwood and Geoffrey Dutton. Considerable as the early Jindyworobak body of literary talent was, it contained no outstanding Australian poet. By the mid-1950s the movement had lost much of its impetus but has not even now disappeared entirely: Elliott sees evidence of a Jindy-worobak continuation in the work of Xavier Herbert, Les Murray and Peter Porter.

The word 'Jindyworobak' was adapted by Ingamells from 'Jindy-worabak', a term used in the glossary of James Devaney's *The Vanished Tribes* (1929) with the meaning 'to annex, to join'. Ingamells chose the word as the name for the movement because it was 'aboriginal', 'outlandish', i.e. likely to arrest attention, and 'symbolic', i.e. direc-ting Australian writers to what should be their distinctive material. Major stimuli to the creation of the movement were P.R. Stephensen's *The Foundations of Culture in Australia* (1936), an aggressively nationalistic demand for a distinctive Australian cul-ture based largely on the spirit of place, and D.H. Lawrence's sensitive reaction to the bush in his novel *Kangaroo* (1923). Ingamells's first exposition of Jindyworobak phil-osophy came with *On Environmental Values*, an address delivered in 1937, later expanded into *Conditional Culture*. He applied the term 'Jindyworobak' to 'those individuals who are endeavouring to free Australian art from whatever alien influ-ences trammel it, that is, to bring it into proper contact with its material'. Ingamells insisted that the national culture depended on a clear recognition of 'environment values' and an understanding of Australian history and traditions, primaeval, colonial and modern. Australian writers were urged to express their distinctive environment, not in conventional terms suited to other countries but in language indicating its own primal essence. Ingamells concluded *Conditional Culture* with the celebrated and much-ridiculed linking of the Jindyworobak philosophy with Aboriginal culture. He believed that 'the laws, the customs, and the art of the Australian Aboriginals went to make a culture which was closely bound in every way with their environment'. The inference was that the Jindyworobak culture could best develop by assimilating the spirit of Aboriginal culture and by identifying with it. From Aboriginal art and song modern Australian culture could learn the necessary techniques and from Aboriginal legend ('sublimated through our thought') would come the required 'pristine outlook on life'. The Jindyworobaks, or some of them, came to see a fitting symbol in the Aboriginal 'Dreamtime' (more properly 'Alchera' or 'Alcheringa') the myth of the 'first time', the time of creation itself, the root of all Aboriginal lore. They felt that the order and spiritual wholeness implanted in Aboriginal life through the concept of Alcheringa could be taken as a symbol or image which might provide a key for a larger Australian 'Dreamtime'. Contrary to popular opinion, they had no intention of ped-dling Aboriginal culture for its own sake. It seemed to them to offer a suitable example of environmental values in action. Misconception of their emphasis on Aboriginal culture, exacerbated by the infrequent but much-publicised Jindyworobak habit of using Aboriginal words in poetry, led to misrepresentation, even ridicule of the movement as a whole. R.H. Morrison's coining of the term 'Jindyworobakwardness' reflected the reaction of many people to the idea of basing modern literary culture on an Aboriginal one. In that the movement was symptomatic of a deeply felt need to perceive and express a sense of national identity, it met with some encouragement and support. In that it attempted to force Australia's literary development into narrow nationalistic channels it failed, both because it was too idiosyncratic and backward-looking and because it was parochial and isolationist. In the final outcome it was simply swept aside by the inevitable movement of Australia after the Second World War into the wider international arena, where the simplicity, perhaps naivety, of the Jindyworobak dream appeared to have no real relevance.

JOHNSON, J.C.F. (Joseph Colin Francis) (1848–1904), born Adelaide, and widely known as 'Alphabetical' Johnson, became experienced and knowledgeable in mining operations, on which he wrote the successful handbooks *Practical Mining* (1889) and *Getting Gold* (1897). A journalist with the SA *Register*, subsequently proprietor and editor of *Adelaide Punch*, and Minister for Education in SA and the NT 1887–89, he contributed bush verse to the *Savage Club Annual* and the *Observer Miscellany*, and published several collections of fiction and verse that caught, with considerable affection, the atmosphere of bush and mining life and mirrored typical characters from those environments. His published works were *On the Wallaby: Or, Tales from the Men's Hut* (1872), *Christmas on Carringa* (1873), *Over the Island* (1873) and *An Austral Christmas* (1888).

JOHNSTON, Martin, (1947–90), born Sydney, the son of George Johnston and Charmian Clift, worked as a cadet reporter, a freelance book reviewer, and as a subtitler and sub-editor for SBS television. Brought up partly in Greece, he returned there to live for some years and also travelled widely in Europe. He published the collections of poetry *Shadowmass* (1971), *The Sea-Cucumber* (1978), and *The Typewriter Considered as a Bee-trap* (1984); a novel, *Cicada Gambit* (1984); and a series of translations of modern Greek poetry, *Ithaka* (1973). A selection of his poetry and prose, edited by John Tranter, was published in 1993 and includes some poems not published in book form before, essays, book reviews, excerpts from interviews and family photographs. The selection allows for a more complete view of Johnston than was previously available, underlining his wide-ranging interests, scholarly background and political commitment. Tranter's introduction also throws light on his early death from alcoholism, suggesting that the cultural shifts he experienced in childhood and the consequent sense of rootlessness, coupled with his parents' style of living and subsequent family tragedies were major contributions. Cerebral, occasionally inaccessible and responsive to literary traditions different from those recognised by other Australian poets of his generation, Johnston found it difficult to reach a wide audience. Martin Duwell has suggested that reading his poetry sometimes draws on skills similar to those required for reading chess, a game which was one of Johnston's obsessions; Christopher Pollnitz, who ranks the title poem of *The Sea-Cucumber* as 'one of the handful of major Australian poems this decade', sees particular creative strengths in his tangential position. Tranter's poem 'Cicada Gambit' describes Johnston as 'Exiled by circumstance and inclination/ from the land and language of his childhood' and as declining to Darlinghurst, where he exchanged 'the dialect/ of Callimachus and Cavafy for the meat-pie-eaters'/ drab vernacular'. 'Without Preamble: Martin Johnston 1947–1990' in Kate Jennings's collection of verse *Cats, Dogs & Pitchforks* (1993) reflects on his achievements and early death.

JONES, Evan (1931–   ), born Preston, Victoria, was educated at the University of Melbourne and Stanford University in the USA. Jones taught history and English at the University of Melbourne and the ANU. He has published four volumes of poetry, *Inside the Whale* (1960), *Understandings* (1967), *Recognitions* (1978) and *Left at the Post* (1984). He edited, with Geoffrey Little, *The Poems of Kenneth Mackenzie* (1972) and wrote the monograph *Kenneth Mackenzie* (1969). In the 1950s Jones was one of a group of writers at the University of Melbourne which included Vincent Buckley and Chris Wallace-Crabbe. His early poetry is seen as being in a 'rigidly imitation Classical manner'; his later poetry, although more modern in both technique and language, retains its emphasis on traditional values. Strongly personal in tone, Jones's poetry subjects life, himself and human relationships to a close and mildly sardonic scrutiny.

JONES, Jill (1951–   ) lives in Sydney and has had a variety of occupations, e.g. second-hand bookseller, editor of legal books, policy analyst in the NSW public service. *The Mask and the Jagged Star* (1992) won the Mary Gilmore prize for a first book of poetry; her second collection, *Flagging Down Time*, was published in 1993. Although she has, especially in the latter book, diversified both in range and tone, she has come to be regarded as a poet of Sydney – 'my city', 'my hollow city'. The grimy urbanscape is exemplified in bottle shops crammed with Johnny Walker, Fosters and 2.2, in bars where 'human animals' engage endlessly in 'the pacing, the pissing, the prowl', on streets where queues of greedy/needy individuals constantly extract 'money from the wall'. The menace of the city is ever present – the anxious woman hurrying home from late night buses, the young hooligans gathering in threatening packs on darkened suburban streets. The obverse is also present – the little rituals of suburban life, such as Saturday morning shopping, the comfort of familiar rooms, the sense (as in 'a ceremony for ground') that no matter how spiritually desolate the urban terrain may seem, a part of it 'is green and brown, smells and sings like home'. Several poems (e.g. 'the administration of winter') carry echoes of T.S. Eliot's 'unreal city'. Jill Jones seeks to combine 'intelligence and passion', aims at being 'serious but not earnest'. She has made an auspicious start.

JONES, John Joseph (1930–   ), born London, migrated to Australia in 1948 and has been a teacher of English in WA. Singer, musician, poet, theatre director and playwright, Jones is a well-known WA identity. As a folk-singer he compered and sang at the first Winthrop folk festival for the ABC. From his 1964 recitals at the Adelaide Festival of Arts sprang his five records of ballads, *Five Australian Ballads, Songs and Ballads of Australia*, *Songs of John Shaw Neilson*, *Australian Songs and Ballads* and *Ballads of Durack and Sorensen*. He has also published an opera, *My New-Found Country* (1963), *Love* (1983, sonnets and paintings) and *A Day at Hiroshima, Parkerville and Other Poems* (1983).

JONES, Rae Desmond (1941–   ), born Broken Hill, graduated in 1976 from the University of Sydney. He has worked at various occupations and as a teacher. Jones has published four books of verse, *Orpheus with a Tuba* (1973), *The Mad Vibe* (1975), *Shakti* (1977), and *The Palace of Art* (1981). He also published a novel, *The Lemon Tree* (1990), the short-story collection *Walking the Line* (1979), and one side of the poetry record *Two Voluminous Gentlemen* (1977). He was the founding editor of the modern poetry journal *Your Friendly Fascist*. Jones's early poetry, personal in tone, modernistic in language and theme, and violent in attitude, reflected his own individual 'mad vibe', a term that he adopted to indicate the anti-social, self-destructive characteristic present in most people but dominant in some. His later poetry focuses more on the external world.

JONES, T. Harri (1921–65), born Llanafan, Wales, served in the Royal Navy during the Second World War and graduated from the University of Wales in 1947. In 1951–59 he taught English at the naval dockyard in Portsmouth before his appointment as lecturer in English at Newcastle University College. He published three books of poems: *The Enemy in the Heart* (1957), *Songs of a Mad Prince* (1960) and *The Beast at the Door* (1963). An active and popular member of the Newcastle community who did much to foster poetry in the Hunter River district, Harri Jones died by drowning 29 January 1965. A posthumous volume, *The Colour of Cockcrowing*, was published in 1966, and *The Collected Poems of T. Harri Jones*, bringing together all four volumes and some uncollected poems, was edited by Julian Croft and Don Dale-Jones in 1977.

In Jones's unpublished poem 'Thinking to Write an Ode' are the lines 'Thinking to write an ode, I thought of my country' and 'Thinking to write an ode, I thought of love!'. Wales and love are the constant subjects of his mostly elegiac poetry. The poems written in Australia about his sense of exile from his country are mainly collected in the second section, 'Hiraeth', of *The Beast at the Door*; typical of them is 'The Welshman in Exile Speaks'. The progress of love is recorded almost chronologically in his published verse; the early sensuous enjoyment and the 'impatient debonair' love of 'The Bridegroom' give way to a bewilderment about the loss of personal identity in love, to a state of disillusionment and hostility, and finally, in the 'Eros' poems of *The Beast at the Door*, to a resigned acceptance of disappointment and futility. A deeply personal poet, Jones had scarcely time to achieve the potential that his verse seemed to promise. His long poem, 'Cotton Mather Remembers the Trial of Elizabeth How: Salem, Massachusetts, 30th June 1692', reconstructs the thoughts of the Calvinist preacher and judge as he writes of the Salem witch trials; it is notable for its evocation of character and its subtly ambivalent exploration of the nature of good and evil. Julian Croft's study, *T.H. Jones* (1976), has a brief biography and a sensitive and detailed commentary on the poet's work; Croft had been a student of Jones. The poet is commemorated in the Harri Jones Memorial Prize for poetry.

JOSE, A.W. (Arthur Wilberforce) (1863–1934), who has been described as 'one of the best Australians ever born and educated in England', was born in Gloucestershire, England, and at 19 emigrated to Australia for his health. In 1885–99, after experience in the bush, he worked mainly as a teacher and university extension lecturer; after a five-year interlude spent in South Africa, India and England, he returned to Australia as correspondent for the London *Times* (1904–15). Jose's first publication was *Sun and Cloud on River and Sea* (1888), an early Angus & Robertson collection of verse written under the pseudonym 'Ishmael Dare'; later he made substantial contributions to Australian writing as a historian, editor, essayist. His *A Short History of Australasia* (1899), expanded as *History of Australasia*, went through fifteen editions by 1929. He was editor-in-chief of the first edition of the *Australian Encyclopaedia* (1925–26). Jose's most significant work, however, was *The Romantic Nineties* (1933), which played an influential part in the development of the legend of the Nineties. A publisher's reader for many years, he edited major collections of Henry Lawson and A.B. Paterson.

JURGENSEN, Manfred (1940–), born Flensburg, then in Denmark now in West Germany, came to Australia in 1961 after living in Germany, Switzerland and the USA. He was educated at the universities of Melbourne and Zurich and now holds a personal chair in German literature at the University of Queensland, which awarded him the degree of D.Litt. in 1991. Interested in the study of comparative literature and bilingualism in poetry, Jurgensen has written more than thirty books, including studies of Goethe, Grass and Bernhard. His poetry collections in English are *Signs & Voices* (1973), *A Kind of Dying* (1977), *A Winter's Journey* (1979), which records details of a return visit to Flensburg, *South Africa Transit* (1979), *The Skin Trade* (1983), *Waiting for Cancer* (1985), *Selected Poems 1972–1986*, edited by Dimitris Tsaloumas

(1987), *My Operas Can't Swim* (1989), *Continental Flicks and Other Passions* (1989), *The Partiality of Harbours* (1989) and *Shadows of Utopia* (1994), which traces Australia's history in 15 cantos. Founding editor of the multicultural magazine *Outrider*, he has also edited a celebration of *Outrider*'s first decade, *Queensland: Words and All* (1993). Jurgensen's writing in German includes the poetry collections *Stationen* (1968), *aufenthalte* (1969), *innere sicherheit* (1979) and *Erste Gegenwart* (1988).

JURY, C.R. (Charles Rischbieth) (1893–1958), born Glenelg, SA, was educated at Oxford, served with the British Army in the First World War and became a lecturer in English at the University of Adelaide in 1933. In 1946–49 he was professor of English at the University; the chair was later named in his honour. A considerable contemporary influence on the SA literary scene, he held strictly classical and traditional concepts of poetry. Represented in *Lamps and Vine Leaves* (1919), he also published *Spring is Coming and Other Poems* (1906), *Perseus and Erythia and Other Poems* (1912), *Love and the Virgins* (1929, expanded in 1958), *Galahad, Selenemia, and Poems* (1939), *Icarius* (1955, a Greek drama), *The Sun in Servitude and Other Plays* (1961) and *Well Measur'd Song* (1968); the last is an essay on prosody, in particular on his own use of quantitative and quasi-quantitative verse, edited by Barbara Wall and D.C. Muecke. Wall and Muecke also edited *The Dweller on Delos* (1993) at the instigation of the Friends of C.R. Jury to mark the centenary of his birth.

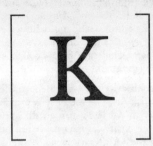

KALAMARAS, Vasso (1932–), born Athens, Greece, of Roumelian and Cretan descent, was educated in Athens in a cultural milieu dominated by music, ballet, theatre and literature. In her late teens she married Leonidas Kalamaras, whose father had migrated to WA in 1924. In 1951 she and Leonidas joined his father in tobacco farming at Manjimup, WA. She returned with the family for a year to Greece in 1960–61, publishing there a collection of poems, *Stalagmaties (Droplets)* (1959) and *Other Earth. Greek-Australian Stories* (1961). After the collapse of the tobacco market led the family to seek employment in Perth, Kalamaras began teaching Greek classes to adult Australians at the Claremont College of the Arts and from 1973 has taught modern Greek at the Perth Technical College. Her impressions of the immigrant experience and its hardships inform all her writing. Although bilingual, Vasso Kalamaras writes mainly in Greek and uses translators (Reg Durack, June Kingdon, Con Castan, David Hutchison) to assist her in presenting her work in English. Those English translations include *Other Earth* (1977, four stories), *Twenty Two Poems* (1977), *Landscape and Soul. Greek Australian Poems* (1980), *Bitterness* (1983, five stories), *The Bread Trap* (1986) and *The Same Light* (poetry and short fiction 1989). The winner of several literary prizes in Greece and Australia, Kalamaras is widely represented in Australian anthologies. An account of her life and work is given in Con Castan's *Conflicts of Love* (1986).

KAN, Diana (1934–), born and educated in Melbourne, studied at the Art Institute of RMIT and began publishing poetry in the 1970s. A series of poems, 'The Hill of the Cross', was included as a special feature in *On the Move*, published by the joint Board of Religious Education of Australia and NZ. Her own published books are *Happy Families and Other Poems* (1973) and *The Bird-man* (1984). She was joint winner of the Patricia Hackett Prize for Poetry in 1983.

KAVANAGH, Paul (1941–), born Sydney, graduated from the University of Sydney and gained his Ph.D. at the University of Newcastle, where he presently teaches English. He has published two volumes of poetry, *Wild Honey* (1974) and *The Summerhouse* (1978). Closely involved with the Mattara Spring Poetry Festivals, he has edited several of their anthologies, *The Members of the Orchestra* (1981), *Instructions for Honey Ants* (1983), *Poem of Thanksgiving* (1985), *Properties of the Poet* (1987), *Hunter Kids' Book* (1988), *Pictures from an Exhibition* (1989) and *The Sea's White Edge* (1991). In 1988 he collaborated with Allan Chawner in two exhibitions of poetry and photographs, *Soundings* (1988). He edited (with Peter Kuch) *Conversations: Interviews with Australian Writers* (1991).

KEESING, Nancy (1923–93), born Sydney, graduated from the University of Sydney and was a social worker at the Royal Alexandra Hospital for Children 1947–51.

She was also a freelance writer and active in numerous literary organisations, e.g. the English Association (committee member 1940–73); ASA, whose journal, the *Australian Author*, she edited 1971–74; the Literature Board (member, 1973–74 and chairperson 1974–77); and the National Book Council. She edited, with Douglas Stewart, the important anthologies *Australian Bush Ballads* (1955), *Old Bush Songs* (1957) and *The Pacific Book of Bush Ballads* (1967); and compiled *Gold Fever* (1967), *Transition* (1970, an ASA anthology), *The Kelly Gang* (1975), *The White Chrysanthemum* (1977), *Henry Lawson: Favourite Verse* (1978), *Shalom* (1978, Australian Jewish short stories, reprinted 1988 with five additional stories), *Lily on the Dustbin: Slang of Australian Women and Families* (1982) and *Just Look Out the Window* (1985). She also wrote children's novels, *By Gravel and Gum* (1963) and *The Golden Dream* (1974); two books of memoirs, *Garden Island People* (1975) and *Riding the Elephant* (1988); a biographical work, *John Lang and 'The Forger's Wife'* (1979); and collections of poetry, *Imminent Summer* (1951), *Three Men and Sydney* (1955), *Showground Sketchbook* (1968) and *Hails and Farewells* (1977). She was made AM for her services to literature.

KEFALÁ, Antigone (1935–   ), born Braila, Romania, of Greek parents, has lived in Romania, Greece, NZ and Australia. She graduated from Victoria University, Wellington, in 1960, has worked as a librarian, as an arts administrator and as a teacher of English as a second language, and is a prominent commentator on Australian multicultural writing. She has published four books of poetry, *The Alien* (1973), *Thirsty Weather* (1978), *European Notebook* (1988) and *Absence: New and Selected Poems* (1992); and three short novels, *The First Journey* and *The Boarding House*, under the title *The First Journey* (1975), and *The Island* (1984). Migration is an important theme in Kefalá's work but it is largely a starting-point for exploring larger themes of estrangement, from others, from self and from 'reality'. Her novels, which concentrate more on inward development than external action, are clearly the work of a poet, sensitive to the aura of words and images. In all three, the central narrator is engaged in a search for stability and meaning in which language figures as a seductive but unreliable agent. The same mood of un-belonging characterises her poems; austere and unrelenting in their confrontation of loneliness and death, they combine strength with delicacy, flexibility with precision.

KELEN, Christopher (1958–   ), born Sydney, the son of Stephen Kelen and the brother of S.K. Kelen, is resident in Japan, where he teaches English. He has published verse in numerous anthologies and periodicals and in the collection *The Naming of the Harbour & the Trees* (1992). He has also published a novel, *Punk's Travels* (1980). In 1988 Kelen won first prize in the Australian Bicentennial/ABC poetry competition. *The Naming of the Harbour & the Trees* contains travel poems, political pieces, drug poems and numerous other inventives, all couched in the typically innovative and intellectually sharp Kelen fashion.

KELEN, Stephen K. (1956–   ), born Sydney, the son of Stephen Kelen and brother of Chistopher Kelen, studied philosophy and literature at Sydney University and has worked as a Commonwealth government public servant and as a teacher of creative writing. His poetry has appeared in numerous periodicals, in several anthologies and in the collections *The Gods Ash Their Cigarettes* (1978), *To the Heart of the World's Electricity* (1980), *Zen Maniacs* (1980), *Atomic Ballet* (1990), and *Dingo Sky* (1993). He has also edited the collection *(The) Final Taxi Review* (1981). In 1973 Kelen won the *Poetry Australia* prize for writers under 18. Contemporary issues and concerns mingle with the small incidents of daily life in Kelen's witty, often lightly ironic verse; reflecting his various travels and wide reading and frequently sharply suggestive, it also reflects a relish of what is paradoxical and quirky and a detached, almost anthropological interest in contemporary idioms and icons. Described as 'rarely self-conscious', Kelen in fact occasionally satirises the pretensions of poetry while expressing his delight in it, suggesting in 'The Boy With the Sun in his Pocket', for instance, that it may be necessary to 'accept the sky has its own significance/ & is not waiting for your interpretation/ or metaphor' if one is to find 'the perfect cliche'.

KELLAWAY, Frank (1922–   ), born London of Australian parents, graduated from the University of Melbourne in 1948 and worked as a librarian and as a lecturer at the Preston Institute of Technology in Melbourne. His volumes of poetry are *Beanstalk* (1973) and *Mare's Nest* (1978). He has also written fiction, *A Straight Furrow* (1960), *The Quest for Golden Dan* (1962) and *Golden Dan* (1976), and verse libretti for the music of George Dreyfus in operas performed in Australia and abroad. He won first prize in the inaugural National Poetry Competition in 1986.

KENDALL, Henry (1839–82), born near Milton on the NSW south coast, spent his impressionable boyhood in the coastal districts of Illawarra in the south and the Clarence River in the north. Their cool moist rainforests, deep-shadowed gullies and lush pastures became the centrepieces of Kendall's best-known poetry, the landscape lyrics such as 'Bell Birds', 'September in Australia', 'Araluen' and 'Narrara Creek'. After a difficult childhood with loving but impractical parents, and a stint of two years at sea in a whaler, Kendall settled into the literary coterie of Sydney, making his mark with poems in Sydney journals and newspapers from 1859 onwards. His first volume, *Poems and Songs*, was published in 1862 with the assistance of J. Sheridan Moore. Although generously received by local and some English critics, the volume failed to sell its first edition of 500 copies. Beset by debts and personal problems, including a growing dependence on both literary patronage and alcohol, Kendall sought a new life in Melbourne after his marriage in 1868; his second volume, *Leaves from Australian Forests*, was published there in 1869. The failure of the Melbourne venture, which led to increasing poverty, alcoholism and the death of his daughter Araluen, brought his return to Sydney in 1870, where the rapid disintegration of his personal and literary life continued. This painful period, described by him as 'The Shadow of 1872', brought alienation from his wife and periods of treatment for addiction in the Gladesville asylum. He was restored to health and sanity, and cured of alcoholism, by the extraordinary kindness of the Fagan family, timber merchants of Gosford and Sydney, who for two years, 1873–75, supervised his rehabilitation in their home near Gosford. In 1876 Kendall was reunited with his wife and family when he began a new life at the Fagan timber mill at Camden Haven on the north coast of NSW. His return to writing was signalled by his winning the *Sydney Morning Herald's* International Exhibition poetry competition in 1879 and by the publication of his final volume, *Songs from the Mountains*, in 1880. In 1881 he was appointed inspector of forests by Sir Henry Parkes, the long-time patron whom Kendall offended many times but never more deeply than with his satire 'The Gagging Bill' in 1879. Kendall's health deteriorated under the strain of the travelling and work associated with his new position; he died in Sydney of phthisis when only 43.

Kendall's literary reputation, extraordinarily high in his own lifetime and immediately after his death but never at the same peak in this century, still rests chiefly on his lyric poetry. 'Bell Birds', 'September in Australia' and 'The Song of the Cattle Hunters', with their elaborate word pictures, extravagant melody and haunting melancholy, endeared themselves to succeeding generations of Australian readers and established Kendall as a favourite schoolroom poet. Some modern critical opinion, while not denying the importance of these popular lyrics, has drawn attention to the many-sided nature of Kendall's poetic talent, ignored when the nationalistic fervour of the 1890s and the early decades of this century dismissed his work as derivative. Kendall's neglected narrative poems, whether with an Australian setting such as 'The Glen of Arrawatta' or 'A Death in the Bush', or with biblical backgrounds such a

'King Saul at Gilboa' and 'Manasseh', or based on the Homeric legends of Ulysses such as 'The Voyage of Telegonus', now attract attention because of their significant themes and their controlled narrative skill. Kendall's affectionate though tart commentaries on the colonial outback types, e.g. 'Bill the Bullock Driver' and 'Jim the Splitter' are now seen to have anticipated Henry Lawson and A.B. Paterson's portraits of similar bush characters. In the role of literary hatchetman, as in the satires 'The Gagging Bill' and 'The Song of Ninian Melville' and to a lesser extent 'The Bronze Trumpet', he reveals a vindictiveness that does not surprise those who know the correspondence of his early manhood. His love poetry, especially 'Rose Lorraine' and 'At Nightfall', which tell of his lost love for Rose Bennett, and the poignant 'Araluen' and 'On a Street', which reflect his guilt over the broken years 1869–72, are powerful statements of the problems of his troubled life. His patriotic verse, such as 'The Far Future', which attempts to create new loyalties and new hopes; his public poems, written for important occasions such as the 1879 International Exhibition in Sydney; his memorial verses for Charles Harpur, James Lionel Michael and Adam Lindsay Gordon; and his attempt in the fragmentary 'The Australian Shepherd' to begin the first Australian rural epic, all support the claim that Kendall was the most substantial poet of the colonial period. T.T. Reed compiled the definitive edition of Kendall, *The Poetical Works of Henry Kendall* (1966) and wrote *Henry Kendall: A Critical Appreciation* (1960). W.H. Wilde published the biographical and critical account *Henry Kendall* (1976). Ian F. McLaren compiled *Henry Kendall: A Comprehensive Bibliography* (1987) and Russell McDougall edited *Henry Kendall: The Muse of Australia* (1992), which includes excerpts from Kendall's work and essays about his life and work by various authors.

KENNA, Francis (1865–1932), born Maryborough, Queensland, worked in a post office, was a teacher, member of the Queensland parliament and a newspaperman. He was editor of the Queensland *Worker*, the *Clarion*, the Brisbane *Sun* and the Charters Towers *Telegraph*, and owned and edited the Bangalow *Herald* and the *Logan and Albert Bulletin*, now the *Gold Coast Bulletin*. A regular *Bulletin* poet, Kenna often used the pseudonym 'K'; he contributed to the *Bulletin* debate in the 1890s, siding with Henry Lawson and satirising A.B. Paterson with his parody 'Banjo of the Overflow'. Kenna published two volumes of verse, *Songs of a Season* (1895) and *Phases* (1915), which range from the easy vernacular of the bush ballad to elegiac poetry of considerable intensity. A devoted Labor Party man, Kenna shared the sentiments of poets such as Lawson and Barcroft Boake, fulminating against the 'Lords of the Money' and their oppression of the working class.

KENNEDY, Victor (1895–1952), born Eaglehawk, Victoria, spent a lifetime in journalism and freelance writing in WA, Queensland and Victoria. A Jindyworobak in outlook, he wrote *Flaunted Banners* (1941), an essay in defence of the Jindyworobak movement, and edited the Jindyworobak anthology of verse for 1942. His poetry includes *The Unknown Anzac and Other Poems* (1917), *Farthest North and Other Verses* (1928), *Light of Earth* (1938) and *Cyclone: Selected Poems* (1949). With Nettie Palmer he wrote the biographical and critical work *Bernard O'Dowd* (1954).

KENNY, Robert (1950–   ), born Melbourne, was co-founder and co-editor until 1974 of *Contempa* magazine and publications. In 1974 he founded the Rigmarole of the Hours series of publications. He co-edited with Colin Talbot the verse anthology *Applestealers* (1974) and with Kris Hemensley and Walter Billeter, *3 Blind Mice* (1977). Writer, editor and graphic designer, he has published several books of verse, *Dead Oceans Poems* (1975), 'Poem' (1975), *Dark Lyrics* (1987) and *Fear* (1991). His prose includes fiction, *A Book of Detection* (1978), *Etcetera* (1978) and *The Last Adventures of Christian Doom* (1982).

KENT, Jean (1951–   ), born Chinchilla, near Brisbane, spent her early formative years (as her poetry shows) in subtropical Queensland. She completed an arts degree in psychology in 1971 and has worked mainly as a counsellor with TAFE in NSW. She has contributed poetry and short fiction to literary journals and anthologies and has won numerous prizes, e.g. the 1988 and 1989 Henry Kendall competitions, the Patricia Hackett Award in 1982 and 1990, the National Library Award 1988, the Mary Gilmore Award and the Anne Elder Award, both in 1990, for her first collection, *Verandahs* (1990) and the FAW John Shaw Neilson Award in 1992 for her second collection, *Practising Breathing* (1991).

Jean Kent returns many times in her poetry to the innocent days of childhood, *Verandahs*, for example, opening with nostalgic memories of her parents' and grandparents' homes in southern Queensland, of the country school 'hardly bigger than a kitchen' which she attended, of hours spent high in the branches of a Moreton Bay fig tree trying to see over the range to the city and ocean, of her invalid father (to whom the book is dedicated) 'communing with nature' on his beloved verandah every afternoon, of their country neighbours given to few words and long silences, and of Christmases with 'cousins cousins cousins aunts and uncles, mothers fathers'. Poems of more mature experiences, focusing on her work as a counsellor, subsequent homes and different places, are less animated, finding harmony only in flowers, gardens, poetry and thoughts of childhood. Although 'After Reading Poetry in My Lunchbreak' appears to question whether poetry has any relevance for ordinary life, in other poems the implied answer is affirmative, while the minutiae of day-to-day living (e.g. her small gem 'To the Ironing Board') provide the impetus for much of their whimsical creativity. *Practising Breathing* is more ambitious than *Verandahs*, including longer, more sombre poems, e.g. the long sequence of the title poem about a young man's suicide and the 'Poems after the Death of a Young Child'.

KERBY, Corinne, a radio broadcaster, television compère and civil rights activist, published two collections of poetry, *Mainly Affirmative* (1968) and *The Living Thing* (1971). Celebrations of marital and family love, the lyrics of *Mainly Affirmative* are more accessible than those of *The Living Thing*, although their certainties are already ringed round with a sense of transience and mortality. Even more sparing of language and crafted with delicacy, the poems of Kerby's second collection share the metrical assurance, clear images and condensed thought of *Mainly Affirmative*; in this collection, however, the surface control contrasts with a turbulent, almost despairing struggle for existential meaning.

KERR, D.B. (Donald Bevis) (1920–42), killed in air operations in New Guinea in the Second World War, was a poet whose talent was recognised by critics such as Max Harris and Geoffrey Dutton. A founder of the *Angry Penguins* journal and a leading figure in the avant-garde poetry movement of the early 1940s, Kerr is represented by the small posthumous collection, *Death Be Not Proud* (1943).

KERSHAW, Alister (1921–1995), born Melbourne, was a member of the city's artistic counter-culture of the 1930s and 1940s, contributing to such magazines as *Comment* and *Angry Penguins*. He left Australia in 1947 and was secretary for some years to the British writer Richard Aldington, but has lived in France for much of his life. During the 1960s he was the ABC's Paris correspondent and has published some of his talks in *A Word from Paris* (1991). His other publications include five books of poetry, *The Lonely Verge* (1943), *Excellent Stranger* (1944), *Defeat by Time Past* (1947) *Accent & Hazard* (1951) and *Collected Poems* (1992).

Kiley's Run, from the poem 'On Kiley's Run' by A.B. Paterson published in *The Man from Snowy River and Other Verses* (1895), is usually identified with the station Narambla, where Paterson was born and spent many happy boyhood times. In its opening verses the poem presents an attractive glimpse, in the usual Paterson manner, of the carefree existence and camaraderie of bush life. But with droughts and unpaid overdrafts, Kiley's Run is eventually lost and passes through the bank to an absentee landlord in England. As Chandos Park Estate, it becomes merely an investment. Paterson had in 1888 written a pamphlet, 'Australia for Australians', urging land reform; 'On Kiley's Run' is a further attack on the evils of the land grant system, made more personal by its echoes of a situation that had occurred in the poet's own family years earlier.

KINSELLA, John (1963–   ), born Perth, has studied at the University of WA and travelled extensively in Europe, the Middle East and Asia. Editor of the poetry magazine *Salt*, he has published his own poetry in numerous periodicals and anthologies and in the collections *Night Parrots* (1989), *The Book of Two Faces* (1989), *Eschatologies* (1991) and *Full Fathom Five* (1993); *SYZYGY*, an experimental poem, was published separately in 1993. Kinsella also contributed, with Anthony Lawrence, to the volume *Ultramarine* (1991) and edited an anthology of verse from the magazine *Salt*, *The Bird Catcher's Song* (1992). Often responsive to paintings or to the WA landscape, whose light, heat and dryness are prominent features, Kinsella's poetry is both intense and freshly lyrical. Myth-making is also a characteristic, *Night Parrots* including sequences on Lasseter and Nebuchadnezzar and *Eschatologies* an extended version of the Lilith myth.

KNORR, Hilde (1920–   ), born in the Warragul–Moe district of Victoria, studied music in Melbourne before marrying the Bavarian-born sculptor Hans Knorr. She began writing in 1958, contributing articles and short stories to newspapers and magazines, and has published three novels, *Shoemaker's Children* (1975), *The Mystic Lake* (1976), *Group with Lady* (1978); two collections of short stories, *Fire Won't Burn Stick* (1972), and *A Private Viewing* (1982); a volume of poetry, *From an Australian Homestead* (1980); and an account of her and Hans Knorr's earlier lives and their experiences after marriage, *Journey With a Stranger* (1986).

KNOWLES, Lee (Lee Jean Johnson) (1941–   ), born WA, is a dance teacher who performs Middle Eastern dances and was previously a writer with the WA Education Department. Living on an ocean-going yacht in Fremantle Boat Harbour she writes poetry which features the Fremantle, Swan River, Indian Ocean milieux. Her three books of poetry are *Cool Summer* (1977), *Dial Marina* (1986) and *Sirocco Days* (1993). She has won several awards, including the Tom Collins Poetry Prize (1980), Mazzucchelli's Love Poem Competition (1986) and the WA Week Award in 1987 for *Dial Marina*.

KNOWLES, Marion Miller (1865–1949), born Wood's Point, Victoria, was a teacher in Victorian schools in the 1880s and 1890s; between 1899 and 1927 she conducted a women's column and children's page in the Melbourne *Advocate*. She was a prolific writer of simple poetry and fiction dealing with experiences of Australian bush life, often filtered through devout Roman Catholic attitudes. Her poetry includes *Songs from the Hills* (1898), *Fronds from the Blacks' Spur* (1911), *Roses on the Window Sill* (1913), *Songs from the Land of the Wattle* (1916), *Love, Luck and Lavender* (1919) and *Ferns and Fancies* (1923). Her *Selected Poems* was published in 1935. Her fiction includes *Country Tales and Sketches* (1896), *Barbara Halliday* (1896, partly autobiographical), *Shamrock and Wattle Bloom* (1900), *The Little Doctor* (1919), *Meg of Minadong* (1926) and *Pretty Nan Hartigan* (1928). She is featured in J.R. Stevens's *Adam Lindsay Gordon and Other Australian Writers* (1937).

KNOWLES, Vernon (1899–1968), born Adelaide, worked on the Adelaide *Register* then went to England to continue a journalistic and writing career; he remained an expatriate but the influence of his Australian boyhood frequently surfaces in his work. His works of fiction include *Bypaths* (1921), which combines prose and verse. His poetry includes *Songs and Preludes* (1917), *Poems* (1925), *The Ripening Years* (1927) and *Love is My Enemy* (1947). He also wrote a verse play, *Prince Jonathan* (1935) and a critical work, *The Experience of Poetry* (1935). Paul Depasquale has published an appreciation, *The Life and Work of Vernon Knowles* (1979).

KNOX, James (?1810–65) arrived in Hobart from England about 1832. An indefatigable contributor to journals and newspapers, he published *Poetic Trifles* (1838), a small book of simple immigrant lyrics which he claimed as the first book of poetry published in Tasmania.

KOCAN, Peter (1947–), born Newcastle, NSW, spent much of his boyhood in Melbourne, later returning to NSW where, at 19, he was sentenced to life imprisonment for the attempted murder of the then leader of the Australian Labor Party, Arthur Calwell. He spent the next ten years either in gaol or in Morissett Mental Hospital. In that period he became engrossed in poetry, publishing a small booklet, *The Other Side of the Fence* (1975), dealing largely with the experience of being in an institution. In 1980 he published a second book of poems, *Armistice*, followed by two semi-fictional works, *The Treatment* (1980) and *The Cure* (1983, published in one volume in the USA in 1985), based on his incarceration. Since his release, with considerable assistance from the Literature Board of the Australia Council, Kocan has maintained himself as a full-time writer. By 1985 he had published a third book of poetry, *Freedom to Breathe*, the title poem adapted from Solzhenitsyn's prose poem indicating that Kocan now felt his 'lost faith' finally returning. Many poems of *Freedom to Breathe*, however, ('Retards Out Walking', 'Post Mortem' and 'Morissett Winter') imply the persistence of past traumas. Other poems show him attempting to breathe that freedom by visiting legendary literary places abroad – Culloden, Cambridge, Glastonbury – although even these create a sense of the 'loner' seeking the spiritual fulfilment that continues to prove elusive. In *Standing With Friends* (1992) Kocan appears finally to have achieved his freedom. The times, as he sees them, are sadly out of order, but compassion, faith and affection may yet set things right. The simple, modest, finely crafted poems are themselves filled with compassion for the sufferers in a world characterised by, at best, insensitivity and, at worst, brutality and viciousness. The victims are many and varied – the savagely murdered Anita Cobby, the suburban family suffering from the Recession, the three unmourned, innocent policemen murdered by the Kelly gang at Stringybark Creek, a puppy chained up and growled at by its inhumane owner, a little girl killed and her unrepentant, uncomprehending killer. Keenly interested in amateur theatricals as writer, actor and producer, Kocan has written several plays, some of which have been performed. He won the 1982 Mattara Poetry Prize for 'From the Private Poems of Governor Caulfield' and the 1983 NSW Premier's Literary Award for *The Cure*.

KOMNINOS (Komninos Constantine Zervos) (1950–), born Richmond, Melbourne, of Greek parents, has an honours degree in science but since 1985 has devoted much of his life and energy to furthering performance poetry in Australia. His published works include *The Komninos Manifesto* (1985), *The Second Komninos Manifesto* (1986), *The Last Komninos Manifesto* (1987), *Wordsports* (1989), *High Street Kew East* (1990), *Komninos: The Poet and His Poetry* (1991), *On the Way to the Fridge for a Snack* (1991), *The Baby Rap* (1992), *The Venus of Marrickville* (1993) and *Komninos by the Kupful* (1994). His performances have taken place in schools, libraries, prisons, factories, pubs, clubs, on street corners and in writers' trains.

Komninos's poems tell of life as it is lived in everyday places – the work place, the pub, suburban homes, city streets – and reflect the situations people face in the family, with friends, enemies and fellows. The poems are usually humorous or sad, often satirical and dramatic, mostly boisterous and lively. His instructions to a rock and roll audience on how to appreciate poetry reveal the attitude of the performance poet to audience participation.

> If you feel like sleeping, sleep
> or chatting at the back of the crowd
> if you feel like snoring, snore
> but please don't snore too loud
> – if you feel like laughing, laugh
>   if you feel like shouting, shout
>   if you feel like clapping, clap
>   that's what poetry's all about.

Reactions to such performance have been mixed. Komninos's own comments indicate the difficulties facing the performance poet: 'most think you're a poof – they all think you're a bludger.' To offset audience scepticism the performance poet has to work harder than his more traditional counterpart, the published poet:

> you have to make your words electric
> to sizzle with energy and still be euphoric
> to dabble and dribble in dialectic metaphoric
> without too much boring didactic rhetoric
> to spell out the truth and still have aesthetic
> to bend words and change words 'til they're brightly
>   neonic
> to capture the sounds at speeds supersonic

The performance poet's goal, finally, is

> to free the words from their traditional prisons
> of books and libraries and academic institutions,
> to undress them, expose them to the whole
>   population . . .
> to take the words off the page, give them wings,
> and let them fly to new destinations.

Komninos's most effective poems include 'childhood in richmond' which gives glimpses of the sadness of a young boy growing up in a household where economic and social pressures were intense; 'bustalk', which catches the speech cadences and rhythms of women gossiping on a bus; 'it's great to be mates with a koori', which is riotously rollicking and full of easy rhythm; 'i hate cars', which effectively displays the verbal power of performance poetry.

The traditional poet's attitude to performance poetry like Komninos's is ambivalent. Geoff Page, for example, sees value in the attempts of performance poets to win back some of poetry's earlier entertainment function which has been largely surrendered to television, but he warns that in the process they risk underestimating the true depth of their art as poets. The rapid growth of performance poetry has led, however, to increased sales of books of poetry and to greater public awareness of poetry as entertainment. In 1993 Komninos won the $20 000 Ros Bower Memorial Award for outstanding achievement in Community Arts.

KRAUSMANN, Rudi (1933–   ), born Mauerkirchen, Austria, came to Australia in 1958 but returned to Europe for three extended periods before settling in Sydney in 1966. He has worked as a journalist in Salzburg, as a language teacher in Sydney and Melbourne, and is now a freelance writer and editor. In 1975 he founded *Aspect: Art and Literature*, a magazine which attempted to bring the visual and literary arts together and ran until 1989. He also edited the collection *Recent German Poetry* (1977) and with Michael Wilding a collection of Australian short stories in German, *Air Mail From Down Under* (1990). His own published works include the prose collection *From*

Another Shore (1975), and three volumes of poetry, *The Water Lily and Other Poems* (1977), *Paradox* (1980, illustrated by Brett Whitely) and *Flowers of Emptiness* (1982).

KROLL, Jeri (1946–   ), born New York, USA, where she gained a Ph.D. from Columbia University, came to Australia in 1978 and has taught at Adelaide and Flinders universities. She has published four collections of poetry, *Death as Mr Right* (1982), winner of second prize in the Anne Elder Award of 1982, *Indian Movies* (1984), *Monster Love* (1990) and *House Arrest* (1993), and a collection of short stories, *The Electrolux Man* (1987). With Robert Clark she edited the eighth number of *Friendly Street Poetry Reader* and, with Barry Westburg, *Tuesday Night Live: Fifteen Years of Friendly Street* (1993). Her poetry and short stories have appeared in numerous periodicals and anthologies. Economy of expression and striking metaphors are characteristic of both Kroll's poetry and short fiction. The poems of her first two collections move between Australia, New York and India, exploring the personalities of places and the difficulties, ambivalences, pleasures and pains of relationships. Sharply observant and coolly witty in their response to the variety and pressures of contemporary existence, they explode female and male stereotypes. Motherhood is the subject of *Monster Love*, but an ambivalent, unsentimental motherhood which represents frankly the frustrating, exhausting experience of caring for a small child and rereads the personal and cultural past from the new/old perspective of maternity. Set partly in America and partly in Australia and projected via a series of narrative perspectives, the stories of *The Electrolux Man* range from the bizarre to the mundane, detailing the tensions, contradictions, griefs and absurdities of contemporary experience. In 1981 Kroll won the *Artlook* National Poetry contest.

Kröte, Professor, a creation of the poet Gwen Harwood, is a European musician who finds himself alienated in a materialistic Australian environment, where he must keep body and soul together by teaching music and giving performances. Most of the Kröte poems were published in Gwen Harwood's second collection *Poems: Volume Two* (1968), but her continued interest in him is indicated by his reappearance in several of the 'New Poems' of her *Selected Poems* (1975) and in 'A Music Lesson', 'A Scattering of Ashes' and 'The Silver Swan' of *The Lion's Bride* (1981). Sympathetically portrayed by her ('I should think I like Kröte'), the professor of music, with his vagaries of behaviour and unfulfilled dreams and expectations, is in constant conflict with, but never defeated by, the unsympathetic and stuffily conventional society which surrounds him.

LAKE, David (1929–), born India, spent his childhood in Calcutta. A graduate of the University of Cambridge, he taught in English schools until 1959 and at tertiary level in Vietnam, Thailand and India 1959–67; in 1967 he joined the University of Queensland. He has contributed verse to such periodicals as *Westerly*, *Southerly* and *Makar* and has published one collection, *Hornpipes & Funerals* (1973), and a satiric poem, *The Portnoyad*, first published in 1970.

La Mama Poetica is the name given to a series of regular poetry readings which began at La Mama in February 1985, presented by Mal Morgan and John Irving. In 1989 Morgan edited an anthology collected from the readings at La Mama Poetica in the four years since it had been established.

LAMBERT, Elisabeth (1918–), born England, went to Jamaica as a teenager before coming to Australia. She worked as a journalist and feature-writer in Sydney as well as a court reporter and theatre critic. She contributed verse in the 1940s to such periodicals as *Meanjin*, *Southerly* and *Angry Penguins*, and edited with Harry Roskolenko the September 1944 issue of the American magazine, *Voices*, which was devoted to Australian poetry. She also published three collections of verse, *Insurgence* (1939), *The Map* (1940) and *Poems* (1943), and a novel, *The Sleeping House Party* (1951). She went to New York to live in 1951.

LANG, John Dunmore (1799–1878), born Greenock, Scotland, arrived in Sydney in 1823 as the city's first Presbyterian minister. For the next fifty years he was an energetic and controversial figure in the colony's religious and political scene. He established the Scots Church and the Australian College in Sydney; was a member of the Legislative Council; was dismissed from his ministry by the Australian synod but retained his own congregation based on the Scots Church; and campaigned assiduously for the abolition of transportation, Protestant immigration, the separation of Victoria and Queensland from NSW, a system of national education, republicanism and federation. On the statue erected to his memory in Wynyard Park (close by the Scots Church) are the words 'Patriot and Statesman'. Lang wrote numerous historical, political and religious books and pamphlets, lectured widely, addressed countless meetings, and wrote public letters on every possible topic of colonial interest. James Bonwick, indefatigable researcher, dubbed him 'The Father of Australian Literature'. His several volumes of poetry are consolidated in *Poems: Sacred and Secular* (1872), which is chiefly religious in tone but contains some satire, humour, and translations from Greek and German. The most substantial biography is Don Baker's *Days of Wrath: A Life of John Dunmore Lang* (1985).

LANG, Mary (1914–), born Sydney, grew up in the Monaro district and in Sydney, completing her education in London where her first book of poems, *The Strange*

Battalion, was published in 1933. In 1936 she published a second collection, *Tom Groggin*, which was well received, but she is now best known for *Home Was Here* (1987), a history of her Irish ancestors.

LANGFORD, Gary (1947–), born NZ, moved to Sydney in 1974. A versatile writer, he has contributed to numerous NZ and Australian anthologies and periodicals, and has written for television, stage, radio and film. He has published seven volumes of poetry, *The Family* (1973), *Four Ships* (1982), *The Pest Exterminator's Shakespeare* (1984), *Bushido* (1987), *Strange City* (1988), *Love at the Traffic Lights* (1990) and *Jesus the Galilee Hitch-Hiker* (1991). He won the Vera Bladen Poetry Award in 1970.

LANSDOWN, Andrew (1954–), born Pingelly, WA, and a graduate of Murdoch University, has worked as an education officer in various WA prisons. He has published six books of poetry, *Homecoming* (1979), *Counterpoise* (1982), *Windfalls* (1984), *Waking & Always* (1987), *The Grasshopper Heart* (1991) and *Between Glances* (1993); a collection of short stories, *The Bowgada Birds* (1986); and an analysis of homosexual activism, *Blatant and Proud* (1984). An imagist in the tradition of Wallace Stevens, Lansdown's short poems have been praised for their precise observation and keen insights; inventive both metrically and in terms of imagery, his poems are also frequently characterised by a religious, celebratory sense of a Maker immanent in natural and human worlds. *Between Glances* won the 1994 SA Festival Award for Poetry.

'Last of His Tribe, The', a widely anthologised poem by Henry Kendall, was first published in the *Sydney Morning Herald*, 1864. In it Kendall captures the attractive nature of Aboriginal life and sentimentally mourns its passing.

LAVATER, Louis (1867–1953), born Melbourne of a Swiss father who came to Victoria during the 1851 gold rush, was educated at Wesley College and began a medical course at the University of Melbourne which he soon abandoned for music. Subsequently prominent in Melbourne's musical circles, he was at various times president of the Association of Music Teachers of Victoria, music critic for several Melbourne newspapers, frequent adjudicator of musical competitions and founder of the Guild of Australian Composers. Also a well-known literary figure, he contributed verse and short stories to numerous anthologies and to such journals as the *Lone Hand* and the *Bulletin*, and edited the little magazine *Verse* (1929–33). He also published three collections of verse, *Blue Days and Grey Days* (1915), *A Lover's Ephemeris* (1917) and *This Green Mortality* (1922); and edited a popular anthology, *The Sonnet in Australasia* (1926), revised in a second edition edited by Frederick Macartney (1956). Among his musical compositions were *Swagman's Treasure: Five Camp-fire Ditties* (1937).

LAWRENCE, Anthony (1957–), born Tamworth, NSW, left school at 16 and became a jackeroo in the Riverina. He later travelled overseas for three years. The next seven years he spent in Wagga Wagga, NSW, trying to become a teacher. While there he and David Gilbey organised a successful association for Wagga Wagga writers. He taught for a time, then went to the north coast of WA, where he wrote and worked as a fisherman. A literary fellowship enabled him to remain at Geraldton, indulging his two passions, writing and fishing. His travel experiences are reflected in such poems as 'Sandstorm', 'Negere Desert', 'Bethlehem', 'Island Meditation', 'Heraklion' and 'Incident at Heraklion'. 'The Flight Sonnets', from his first book, *Dreaming in Stone* (1989), describe the swifts and barn owls of Northumbria. From his time on the land came 'The Art of Killing', 'Shooters' and 'Cro-Kill'. They highlight the casual savagery that is a part of the daily life on the land. The killing process in Lawrence's poems lacks the saving grace of a natural and essential rural order that characterises similar actions in, for example, Les Murray's poem 'Blood'. 'Blood Oath', the major sequence of Lawrence's second book *Three Days Out of Tidal Town* (1991), describes a real-life incident in which two young jackeroos meet their deaths fleeing from their vicious, crazed boss in the desert. 'Blood Oath' was runner-up in the Grace Perry Memorial Award in 1988. Numerous other poems from the WA period deal with fishing, but Lawrence's chief obsession is poetry: 'wherever I turn, poetry astounds me with its quiet visitations . . . my poetry my love'. His third book of poetry, *The Darkwood Aquarium* (1993), deals in part with his own childhood and adolescence while focusing also on other young passionate and stormy characters. One of the book's four sections, 'Howling in Tandem', pays homage to, but at the same time shows Lawrence freeing himself from, the influence of those who played a part in his becoming a poet. In the coastal section he believes he has achieved the type of poetry he is most comfortable with – narrative with a strong lyrical vein. He has also written *A Book of Dying Sayings* (1991).

LAWSON, Henry (1867–1922) was born on the goldfields at Grenfell, NSW, the eldest son of Niels Hertzberg Larsen (Peter Lawson, 1832–88), a Norwegian ex-sailor, and his wife, Louisa; his surname was registered as Lawson, which became the family one. Peter and Louisa had been living near Mudgee at New Pipeclay, later called Eurunderee, and returned there soon after Lawson's birth. They moved to the Gulgong goldfields in 1871, but settled back at New Pipeclay on a selection in 1873. In 1883 they separated, Louisa moving to Sydney to become active in publishing and the women's movement.

Henry's early life was difficult: the family was poor, the tensions between his parents have some parallels in the short stories, and from the age of 9 he was afflicted by deafness. He attended several schools at Eurunderee and Mudgee and then worked with his father on building contracts until 1883, when he joined Louisa. Over the next few years he was based in Sydney, worked mainly as a coach-painter and, influenced by his mother's radical friends, became interested in the republican movement. In 1887 his first published prose piece appeared in the *Republican*, of which he became nominal publisher, and his first poem, 'A Song of the Republic', in the *Bulletin*. The *Bulletin* also published his first short story, 'His Father's Mate', several days before his father's death on New Year's Eve 1888. In 1890 he left Sydney to find work in Albany, WA, where he wrote for the *Albany Observer*. He returned in September 1890 before accepting early in 1891 an offer of employment on the radical Brisbane newspaper the *Boomerang*, to write a digest of news from the provincial press. After six months he was retrenched and returned to Sydney, then in the grip of the depression of the Nineties. To this point Lawson had established himself primarily as a writer of verse: some of his enduring poems of bush life, e.g. 'The Teams', 'Andy's Gone With Cattle', 'The Roaring Days', date from before 1892; so do the major poems of social and political protest, e.g. 'The Watch on the Kerb', 'Faces in the Street', 'Freedom on the Wallaby', 'The Army of the Rear', which made him the obvious model for Arty, the People's Poet, in William Lane's *The Workingman's Paradise* (1892). But from the time of his return to Sydney after working with the *Boomerang*, his talent as a writer of short stories began to emerge as he drew more and more on his own observation to supplement his past experiences and the experiences of his family. In 1892, despite the diversion of the *Bulletin* debate, which he conducted with A.B. Paterson about the right way to represent bush life, he wrote the Arvie Aspinall series, his first major fiction sequence, and a series of bush stories including 'A Day on a Selection', 'The Drover's Wife' and 'The Bush Undertaker'. Later that year, unable to find regular work, he was funded by J.F. Archibald and went on a celebrated trip to Bourke, where he worked as a house-painter for some months before tramping with his swag to Hungerford and back in the midst of a fierce drought. The experience, his first of the real outback, was crucial for Lawson in several ways: it confirmed the horrors of bush life; it not only provided him with the immediate copy for such stories as 'Hungerford' and 'The Union Buries Its Dead', but also by its intensity enslaved his imagination to the point where his fiction subsequently became repetitive.

At the end of 1894 his first collection, *Short Stories in Prose and Verse*, was published. It was a poor production, but nevertheless confirmed his growing reputation, which was consolidated by the appearance in 1896 of the first two volumes in a long publishing partnership between Lawson and Angus & Robertson: *While the Billy Boils*, generally considered as his best prose collection, and *In the Days When the World Was Wide*, a collection of verse. By now he had met Bertha Bredt. Soon after their marriage in 1896 the Lawsons went to WA then continued their itinerant life by travelling in 1897 to NZ, where they taught at a Maori school at Mangamaunu, near Kaikoura. Although he eventually became frustrated by the isolation of Mangamaunu, Lawson wrote steadily and was relatively free of his dependence on alcohol, which had become apparent a decade before. His drinking problem surfaced again on their return to Sydney in 1898, especially during his membership of the bohemian Dawn and Dusk Club, but he managed to complete contracts with Angus & Robertson, which resulted in the publication in 1900 of two more collections of prose and a collection of verse, *Verses Popular and Humorous*. Like many of his books they consisted largely of material first published in Australian periodicals and subsequently revised. An essay, '"Pursuing Literature"' in Australia', published in the *Bulletin* in 1899, shows his dissatisfaction at this time with Australia and his wish for wider recognition for his work. In 1900 Lawson left with his wife and two children for England, assisted in the endeavour by the governor of NSW, Earl Beauchamp, the bibliophile David Scott Mitchell, and the publisher George Robertson. In England he wrote some of his finest stories and published *The Country I Come From* (1901), a selection of his previous work; *Joe Wilson and His Mates* (1901); and *Children of the Bush* (1902), which contains the material subsequently published as *Send Round the Hat* (1907) and *The Romance of the Swag* (1907). By 1902 the climate, poverty, illness and perhaps other unexplained reasons caused the Lawsons to leave England, the marriage failing. Thereafter, with the exception of a few weeks immediately following their return to Sydney, Lawson lived apart from Bertha and the children, with increasing bitterness on both sides.

Lawson's best work was now behind him, and the remaining twenty years of his life were years of spasmodic literary output in which he produced more verse than prose, and of steady personal disintegration. He was in and out of prison, particularly 1905–10, for drunkenness and arrears of maintenance, spent some time in mental and 'convalescent' hospitals and became a familiar sight on the streets of Sydney, a dishevelled, cadging drunk. That he survived so long was the result of the devotion of friends, old literary colleagues such as J. le Gay Brereton and E.J. Brady but in particular George Robertson, who assisted him financially, and Mrs Isabel Byers, a woman twenty years his senior who regularly provided care and lodging for him after 1904. There were political friends as well, including T.D. Mutch and W.A. Holman, which led to his being granted a sinecure in 1916 to live in Leeton, a prohibition area, in order to write material advertising the Murrumbidgee Irrigation Area. The interest of parliamentarians in him was also in evidence in 1920–22, when he was awarded a CLF pension and negotiations were conducted between the federal and NSW governments over a supplement to the pension.

The ostensible reason for Lawson's deterioration was his collapse into alcoholism and mental illness, although several commentators, viewing his dependence on alcohol more as a symptom than as a cause, have suggested other sources for his decline: the failure of his marriage; the death of his close friend Hannah Thornburn just before his return from London; and, perhaps more significantly for his reputation as a prose-writer, an artistic crisis in the same period deriving from a failure of creativity, which led to his eventual increasing reliance on melodrama, contrivance and romance, features of some of his very first stories. That Lawson had little new to say explains the return to the past which is characteristic of his later prose.

Lawson's decline after 1902 did not mean, however, that he lost his appeal for the Australian public. In part this was because his verse, in such volumes as *When I Was King* (1905), *The Skyline Riders* (1910), *For Australia* (1913), *My Army, O, My Army* (1915) and *Song of the Dardanelles* (1916), continued to strike a popular chord. Some of his best-known poems, e.g. 'One-Hundred-and-Three' and 'Black Bonnet', date from this period; he was particularly prolific during the First World War, when his poetic affirmation of the imperial link was such as to see him later accused of jingoism and apostasy of his socialism and republicanism of the 1880s. A second reason for his continuing appeal was the publishing programme of George Robertson, who repub-lished Lawson's earlier prose and verse, often in series bearing such titles as *While the Billy Boils*, as well as arranging for the first collection of poetry, *Selected Poems of Henry Lawson* (1918). Also involved in the preparation of *Selected Poems* was David McKee Wright, who edited Lawson extensively while working on the much-criticised *Poetical Works of Henry Lawson* (1925). Notwithstanding the scholarly edition of Colin Roderick, *Poetical Works of Henry Lawson* has been the most popular collection of Lawson's verse and has remained in print under various titles.

In 1921 Lawson suffered a cerebral haemorrhage, from which he recovered suffi-ciently to be still writing reminiscences of his visit to London when he died at Abbotsford on 2 September 1922. The extent of the Lawson legend in his lifetime can be measured by the fact that he was the first Australian writer granted a state funeral. Since his death he has remained Australian literature's most famous son, commem-orated by a statue in the Sydney Domain, sculpted by George Lambert using Lawson's children as models, and by memorials elsewhere, as well as by his appearance on the Australian ten-dollar note when decimal currency was introduced in 1966. He has been the subject of one-man shows by Leonard Teale and Robin Ramsay, and of numerous plays, films, stories, readings and television series. In Melbourne there is a Henry Lawson Literary and Memorial Society, which publishes the *Lawsonian* and conducts an annual gathering at the 'Lawson Tree' at Footscray. In Sydney, apart from the Domain statue, there is a Henry Lawson Bookshop and a Henry Lawson Literary Society, and the FAW conducted for some years annual pilgrimages to his grave at Waverley cemetery and to the Domain statue. Sydney University undergraduates compete annually for the Henry Lawson Prize for Poetry. The Lawson publishing industry has not remained confined to reprints deriving from the earlier Angus & Robertson collections. The same publishers issued *The Stories of Henry Lawson*, edited by Cecil Mann in 1964, which was trenchantly criticised. Not until the appearance in 1972 of *Henry Lawson: Short Stories and Sketches 1888–1922* and *Henry Lawson: Auto-biographical and Other Writings 1887–1922*, the first two of Colin Roderick's three-volume edition of Lawson's prose, was a reliable text established. Roderick had earlier edited several Lawson selections: in 1967–69 he edited the three-volume *Henry Law-son: Collected Verse*, which provided an authoritative text of the poetry, and sub-sequently *Henry Lawson: Letters 1890–1922* (1970), the anthology *Henry Lawson Criticism 1894–1971* (1972) and *Henry Lawson: the Master Story Teller: Prose Writings* (1984–85). Important biographical studies, some of them anecdotal, include his daughter Bertha Lawson and J. le Gay Brereton's collection of tributes, *Henry Lawson by His Mates* (1931); his wife Bertha's *My Henry Lawson* (1943); Denton Prout's *Henry Lawson: The Grey Dreamer* (1963); W.H. Pearson's *Henry Lawson Among Maoris* (1968); the controversial *In Search of Henry Lawson* (1978) by Manning Clark; Colin Roder-ick's *The Real Henry Lawson* (1982) and Xavier Pons's *Out of Eden: Henry Lawson's Life and Works* (1984), a psychoanalytical study of Lawson's life and works which attempts to explain Lawson's failures rather than his successes. The most substantial biography is Colin Roderick's *Henry Lawson: A Life* (1991), the culmination of a lifetime of research and writing. Some of the most interesting commentary on Lawson's life has appeared in significant critical studies, among them A.A. Phillips's *The Australian Tradition* (1958) and *Henry Lawson* (1970), Stephen Murray-Smith's monograph, *Henry Lawson* (1975), and Brian Matthews's *The Receding Wave* (1972). In 1989 Chris Kempster published *The Songs of Henry Lawson*; Lawson's poems set to music in the 1980s and 1990s have featured in the ABC National radio programme 'On the Wall-aby', in Frank Hardy's play 'Faces in the Street' and the Dick Diamond revival *Reedy River*.

In general there have been two schools of Lawson criticism: a popular one which has seen many of Lawson's short stories as artless yarns and regards him as the poet of the people, a folk-writer whose galloping rhythms and facility for rhyme articulate the voice and attitudes of Australians; and a professional one, which sees mainly historical interest now in the poetry and finds enduring virtues in the prose. Despite the continuing appeal of the stirring calls for social change in 'Faces in the Street' or 'Freedom on the Wallaby', the lyricism of 'Andy's Gone With Cattle' or 'Black Bonnet', the sardonic sharpness of 'The Uncultured Rhymer to his Cultured Critics' or 'The Captain of the Push', and the robust balladry of 'The Roaring Days', only Roderick among recent critical writers has argued for more than a handful of Lawson's poems. Far more attention, particularly among literary critics, has been focused on the quality of the prose. The peak of Lawson's achievement is now usually seen to be in *While the Billy Boils* and *Joe Wilson and His Mates*. In stories like these Lawson's fundamentally pessimistic fictional bush world is memorably and dramatically realised. Lawson did more than write the Australia of the 1890s: at his best he has few superiors anywhere in the field of the short story.

LAWSON, Louisa (1848–1920), the mother of Henry Lawson but an important figure in her own right in the history of Australian radicalism, feminism and publishing, was born near Mudgee, NSW, the daughter of Henry Albury and his wife Harriet Wynn. In 1866 Louisa married Niels Hertzberg (Peter) Larsen, a Norwegian ex-sailor some years her senior; they moved soon after to the Grenfell goldfields – where Henry, the first of their five children, was born – before returning to New Pipeclay, near Mudgee, where they were based until 1883, apart from a stint at Gulgong. The marriage had its periods of tension, with Larsen usually characterised as gentle with his children but somewhat stolid, and Louisa as strong-willed, temperamental and increasingly frustrated with the poverty of selection life. Her radicalism and sensitivity could find no outlet at New Pipeclay and in 1883 she moved to Sydney, where she was quickly in contact with leading figures in the spiritualist, republican and women's movements. By 1885 her house was a meeting-place for reformists, and in 1887 she took over the radical monthly the *Republican*. The following year she founded the *Dawn*, the first Australian feminist journal, and the Dawn Club; active also in the women's suffrage movement, she established the Association of Women in 1889, merging her activities with those of Rose Scott and the Womanhood Suffrage League in 1891. In 1894 Louisa brought out Henry's first collection, *Short Stories in Prose and Verse*; it was poorly produced and contributed to the estrangement between mother and son. Louisa's own published work includes a novel, *Dert and Do* (189?), and a book of poems, *The Lonely Crossing* (1905). Brian Matthews wrote the controversial award-winning biography *Louisa* (1987).

LAWSON, Will (1876–1957), born Durham, England, was brought to Australia as a child and educated in Brisbane. In the 1890s his family moved to Wellington, NZ, where Lawson worked as a clerk for an insurance company. In 1912, after contributing some verse to the *Bulletin*, he came to Sydney where he joined the staff of the *Evening News* and later worked as a freelance writer for newspapers and magazines, including the *Bulletin* and *Smith's Weekly*. A familiar figure in Sydney's bohemian circles, he was friendly with such writers and artists as Roderic Quinn, Edward and Will Dyson, Percy Lindsay, Randolph Bedford and Livingston Hopkins. Enthusiastic about Australia's sailing and coaching past, especially the coaching days, Lawson wrote numerous ballads, publishing six collections, *The Red West Road* (1903), *Between the Lights* (1906), *Stokin' and Other Verses* (1908), *The Three Kings* (1914), *Bush Verses* (1943) and *Bill the Whaler* (1944). He also drew on the same sort of material for several novels, including *The Laughing Buccaneer* (1935), *When Cobb and Co. Was King* (1936), *Old Man Murray* (1937), *In Ben Boyd's Day* (1939), *Red Morgan Rides* (1940), *Bound for Callao* (1942), *Black Diamonds* (1945), *The Lady of the Heather* (1945), *Forbidden Gold* (1945), *Paddle-Wheels Away* (1947), *Galloping Wheels* (1947) and *Moira of Green Hills* (1950). He also edited an anthology, *Australian Bush Songs and Ballads* (1944). Although not related to Henry Lawson he was a friend of Bertha Lawson and collaborated in her reminiscences of her husband, *My Henry Lawson* (1943).

'Lazy Harry's' is perhaps the best-known Australian folk-song to chronicle the notorious 'lambing down' of shearers by shanty-keepers. In the song two shearers travel through the Riverina towards Sydney but go on a spree at Lazy Harry's shanty on the road to Gundagai and are relieved of their shearing cheques. The rueful tone of 'Lazy Harry's' is repeated in other Australian folk-songs about bush workers in shanties.

LEA, Shelton (1946–   ), born Melbourne, left school at the age of 12 and spent periods in gaol as a young man, including eighteen months in Goulburn Gaol at the age of 18. While there he wrote love poems for detainees, payment being in tobacco. Part-performance poet (he declares he will read poems wherever he can find an audience), part-critic of contemporary Australian life and attitudes, he is 'by birth and nature urban', with inner-city areas his natural habitat. His comfortable milieu is the city pubs – 'great brewing palaces of beer' – and city life, with its violence, crime, drugs, alcoholism, gutter and park derelicts ('in defence of drunks', 'coming down – delirium tremens'). Shelton Lea also writes of love in his more tranquil verse ('having watched you', 'love poem', 'i dream of the soft slide of light'). His complaint about the sterility of modern Australian life and politics is evident in 'i'm here today for a whinge' and 'occupied' – where he accuses, in Jindyworobakish accents:

> we are occupied by our own greed . . .
> we are making of this place a desert,
> a land of rutted soil
> of ruined earth, leached of its true wealth,
> its dreamtime,
> rather than living in harmony, as once the koories did,
> treating this land as a kindred soul

Many of Lea's poems are slanted towards performance, carrying within such verses as 'The Dip's Dilemma' and 'Picnic Day at the Drouin Races', echoes both of C.J. Dennis and an early Bruce Dawe. Commenting on the modern proliferation of easy-going, slang-type verse (including much of his own) Lea says that the times themselves prohibit traditional-type verse, ('well-ordered thoughts well shaped and moulded into a perfectly metrical form'). There are too many distractions in modern society – television, the media and 'the accostation of cars and trucks/ the imperterbable [sic] rumble of suburbs and/cities'. Lea has published several books of verse, *Corners in Cans* (1969), *Chrysalis* (1972), *The Paradise Poems* (1973), *Chockablock with Dawn* (1975), *Palantine Madonna* (1978), *Poems from a Peach Melba Hat* (1985), *I am Nebuchadnezzar* (1991) and a *Poets on Record* (1976, tape recording with text).

LEAKEY, Caroline Woolmer ('Oliné Keese') (1827–81), born and educated in

Exeter, England, returned there after spending five years (1848–53) in Tasmania with her sister. Her life was dominated by ill health and a strong Christian faith. The former limited her schooling, made her an invalid for most of her time in Australia, caused her return to England and severely restricted her activities after 1871; the latter led her, when able, to become involved in a variety of charitable works and to write for the Religious Tract Society and the *Girls' Own Paper*. Religion and the problems of sickness and death are major themes in her collection of poems *Lyra Australis*, published under her own name in 1854, and important ingredients also of *The Broad Arrow*, a novel about the convict system.

Leaves from Australian Forests, the second volume of verse published by Henry Kendall in 1869, contains the well-known lyrics 'Bell Birds' and 'September in Australia'; the important narratives 'The Glen of Arrawatta' and 'King Saul at Gilboa'; the love poem 'Rose Lorraine'; and memorial poems to Charles Harpur, James Lionel Michael and Adam Lindsay Gordon.

LEE, Gerard (1951–   ), born Melbourne, grew up in Melbourne and Brisbane, and graduated from the University of Queensland in 1974. He has worked as a teacher, clerk, journalist and house-painter and has contributed verse and short stories to a range of periodicals. Lee has published a collection of prose poems, *Manual for a Garden Mechanic* (1976); a collection of short stories, *Pieces for a Glass Piano* (1978); two novels, *True Love and How to Get It* (1981), *Troppo Man* (1990); and *Eating Dog* (1993), a selection of his experiences from two decades of wandering. He has written several screenplays including *Sweetie*, co-authored with Jane Campion and winner of the 1989 AFI Award for best screenplay.

LEE, Joyce (1913–   ), born Murtoa, Victoria, has been a pharmacist with the Richmond Community Health Centre, a lecturer in poetry writing at Victoria College, Toorak, and has been involved with Pariah Press. She has published verse, 'Poems from the Wimmera' in *Sisters Poets 1* (1979), *Abruptly from the Flatlands* (1984) and *Plain Dreaming* (1991). Her reminiscences about her childhood in the Wimmera in the 1920s, featured in her books, are the best of Joyce Lee's writing. They indicate, as has traditionally been the case, that the landscape and environment are among the strongest inspirers of poetry. Joyce Lee won the Grenfell Henry Lawson Festival of the Arts Award in 1978 and the MacGregor Prize for Poetry, 1982.

LEHMANN, Geoffrey (1940–   ), born Sydney, graduated with degrees in arts and law from the University of Sydney, where he also studied German literature and was associated with fellow poet Les Murray co-editing the magazines *Arna* and *Hermes*. Lehmann practised as a solicitor and lectured in law at the University of NSW. He is now a partner in a major international accounting firm in Sydney. His published verse consists of *The Ilex Tree* (1965, a shared volume with Les Murray), *A Voyage of Lions and Other Poems* (1968), *Conversation with a Rider* (1972), *From an Australian Country Sequence* (1973), *Extracts from Ross' Poems* (1976), *Ross' Poems* (1978), *Nero's Poems* (1982), *Children's Games* (1990), and *Spring Forest* (1992; a 1994 edition by Faber & Faber, published in England, includes one additional poem, 'Prickly moses'). His *Selected Poems* was published in 1976. Lehmann has also written a novel, *A Spring Day in Autumn* (1974); edited the anthologies *Comic Australian Verse* (1972, retitled *The Flight of the Emu, Contemporary Light Verse*, 1990), *The Younger Australian Poets* (1983, with Robert Gray), and *Australian Poetry in the Twentieth Century* (1991, also with Gray); and published a book of art criticism, *Australian Primitive Painters* (1977).

In *The Ilex Tree* Lehmann's predilection for family poetry is shown in the four 'Pieces for My Father' and the long seven-part poem 'For William Rainer, My Grandfather'. *A Voyage of Lions and Other Poems* is dominated by the much-admired historical series 'Monologues for Marcus Furius Camillus, Governor of Africa', and

other shorter poems with an ancient Roman setting. As a background to the observations and meditations of the ageing Camillus there is a passing parade of Roman
decadence – victory marches, lavish banquets, slave girls, gladiators, ornate villas, lush
vineyards and olive groves. The monologues, which are also included as the opening
section of Lehmann's later *Selected Poems*, convey well the fatal combination of opu-
lence and ennui that marks a civilisation near collapse. The highlights of the series are
the dolphin and lion poems. The capture and transhipping of the African lions to the
Colosseum ('A Voyage of Lions') are taken up by the following poem, 'Colosseum',
and in a later volume, 'Colosseum at a Distance'. The lion sequence pinpoints the
ultimate barbarity of Roman civilisation, the charnel-house of the Colosseum where
the burial pits were 'So foul that workmen digging two thousand years later/
Sickened by the smell will lay down their spades'. *Conversation with a Rider* combines
poems on historical personages such as Pope Alexander VI and Cellini with those on
family and friends. The sequence of eleven poems, which recalls experiences from the
life of Lehmann's father, lovingly and good-humouredly charts the close relationship
between the two. The 'Roses' sequence, with its patterning of natural beauty and
grace against man's destructiveness, is more complex, both technically and thematically, than Lehmann's usual lucid, undemonstrative compositions.

Ross' Poems, Lehmann's most popular and impressive work, is a long poem seg-
mented into seventy-five separate pieces. Taking as persona Lehmann's then father-
in-law, Ross McInerney, the poem describes his experiences as a farmer in central-
western NSW. Partly memoirs, partly anecdotes and partly reflections, the poems
build up a composite of close-knit family life in a typically Australian rural community. *Ross' Poems* form part of the Australian 'vernacular republic' of Lehmann's
fellow poet Les Murray, and are an important illustration of the modern resurgence of
interest in the bush and its people. In *Nero's Poems* Lehmann returns to the ancient
world which had intrigued him in *A Voyage of Lions*. He resumes the successful dramatic monologue of the Camillus poems to explore the enigma of Nero and to
examine and even account for that ruler's bizarre character and conduct. The poems
are accompanied by Lehmann's introductory comments on Nero. *Spring Forest* incorporates much of the original *Ross' Poems*, revised and expanded with thirty new poems
added. Essentially a single poem and accompanied by photographs, *Spring Forest* is
based on the life and stories of Ross and Olive McInerney as was *Ross' Poems*. *Children's
Games*, a quiet, restrained, meditative collection deals initially with the problems
associated with a marriage breakdown, its impact on the participants and the children.
The latter part of the book includes an unusual series of cryptic sonnets.

'Leichhardt in Theatre', a poem by Francis Webb, was published as 'Leichhardt
Pantomime' in the *Bulletin*, 1947. In 1952 it was published with other poems in a
revised form with a new title, 'Leichhardt in Theatre', in a volume of that name. The
opening section of the original poem, 'Introduction in a Waxworks', was replaced by
a segment titled 'Advertisement', and the 'Epilogue' of the original poem was omitted. The poem's central figure is the explorer Ludwig Leichhardt. The poem opens
with a vision of the earlier explorer Charles Sturt who, thwarted in his several
attempts to establish the existence of an inland sea, left an 'Impasse at the Centre'. The
solving of that 'Impasse' provided much of the lure for Leichhardt. Webb's portrait of
Leichhardt begins by emphasising the visionary side of his nature ('This is a land
where man becomes a myth'), then, by introducing a clown and by the use of a type of
music-hall doggerel, he pictures Leichhardt as a buffoon who does not know 'north
from south' but who is clever at 'playing with windmills in the Never Never'.
Glimpses of Leichhardt's expeditions follow: the first triumphant journey of fifteen
months and 5000 kilometres to the Gulf of Carpentaria, marred only by the death of
botanist John Gilbert; and the second journey, a farcical failure led by the equally

farcical figure of Leichhardt. In the interval between the second and third expeditions Leichhardt is forced to confront the painful realisation of the conflicting duality of his nature. The third expedition, although only briefly exposed in the poem, sees purpose and significance restored. The outcome is seen as uncertain, but that is unimportant – the venture is everything ('Where they will go, how perish – this is nothing'). In its use of psychological analysis and self-analysis for characterisation rather than the simple observer technique employed in 'A Drum for Ben Boyd', 'Leichhardt in Theatre' is more skilful and subtle than the earlier Webb poem. It builds up a fascinating and deeply unified vision of the enigmatic and contradictory character of the Prussian explorer. Douglas Stewart included 'Leichhardt in Theatre' in his anthology *Voyager Poems*, in 1960.

LETTERS, F.J.H. (Francis Joseph Henry) (1897–1964), born Queensland, graduated from the University of Sydney in 1918 and practised as a barrister 1927–37 before joining the foundation staff of the New England University College in 1938 to lecture in classics and English. He published several works of academic criticism on classical and European literature; a collection of general essays, *In a Shaft of Sunlight* (1948); and three volumes of poetry, *Darkness and Light* (1934), *The Great Attainder* (1943) and *Aurora Australis* (1963). A collection of essays on classic literature, *For Service to Classical Studies*, was published in 1966 in his honour. He was awarded an honorary D.Litt. by the National University of Ireland in 1956.

LEVY, Julia Ethel, who frequently used the pseudonym 'Juliet', published several lightweight and conventional one-act plays, novels and volumes of poetry in the 1920s. Her novels include *A Soul of Sincerity* (1923), *God's Good Woman* (1926), *Devotion* (1927) and *The Snob and the Lady* (1929); her collections of verse are *Songs of Solace* (1922) and *Signposts on Life's Highway* (1926).

'Life-Cycle', one of Bruce Dawe's best-known poems, was published in his volume *An Eye for a Tooth* (1968). Both a satire on, and a celebration of, the Victorian obsession with Australian rules football, the poem presents the ingredients of the Saturday afternoon football ritual – the wearing of the club colours and the shouting of club nicknames ('Tigers', 'Demons', 'Saints'); the barracking chant ('Carn . . . carn'); the abuse of umpires ('ooohh you bludger'); and the football spectator's fare ('hot pies and potato-crisps'). Like some mass opiate, Aussie rules adds meaning to otherwise meaningless lives. Old-timers by boundary fences 'dream of resurgent lions and centaur-figures from the past' and visualise present salvation 'in the six-foot recruit from Eaglehawk'. With his parody of the threnody 'For the Fallen', Dawe catches, in serio-comic fashion, the analogy between the football game and life itself.

> They will not grow old as those from more
> northern States grow old,
> for them it will always be three-quarter time
> with the scores level and the wind advantage
> in the final term.

LILLEY, Merv (1919–   ), born Rockhampton, left school early, served in the army 1941–44, and has worked as drover, cane-cutter, seaman and wharf labourer. He has contributed verse and songs to numerous periodicals and is represented in several well-known anthologies. He collaborated with Dorothy Hewett, whom he married in 1960, in a volume of verse with a socialist theme, *What About the People?* (1962), has published an independent collection, *Cautious Birds* (1973), and a collection of stories, reminiscences, poems and bush cookery ideas titled *Git Away Back! A Knockabout Life* (1983).

LINDSAY, Jack (1900–90), son of Norman Lindsay, was born Melbourne and brought up in Brisbane. He graduated from the University of Queensland in 1921. Although hardly aware of his father during his childhood after his parents separated, he came strongly under Norman's influence from 1919 and in 1921–26 was a part of the lively cultural life of Sydney that he described in *The Roaring Twenties* (1960). Profoundly impressed by his father's ideas, especially as expressed in *Creative Effort* (1920), he was the major force behind the establishment of the journal *Vision*. He also edited with Kenneth Slessor and Frank Johnson the anthology *Poetry in Australia 1923* (1923). His first book of verse, *Fauns and Ladies* (1923), was illustrated by Norman Lindsay's woodcuts. In 1926 he left for England with the object of establishing himself as a poet and disseminating the Lindsay aesthetic via the Fanfrolico Press, which he founded and ran with Jack Kirtley and P.R. Stephensen. The same motives prompted his establishment of the journal the *London Aphrodite* (1928–29). By 1930 Lindsay's contact with a wider culture and international political issues had counteracted the influence of his father's ideas and by 1936 he had moved from Nietzscheanism to Marxism, a commitment that persisted. His importance to the Soviet cause was recognised in 1968 when he was awarded the Soviet Badge of Honour, but he remained a philosophical adherent rather than a political activist. During the war he worked as a private in the signals corps and then in the War Office as script-writer for army drama groups. He subsequently supported himself by his prodigious writing. Poet, dramatist, editor, historian, translator, classical scholar, biographer, novelist and critic, he had a formidable international reputation, especially in the last five fields. Author of over 150 books, he also contributed to many of the better-known journals in Australia and England. Although he never returned to Australia, he retained a lively interest in its culture and frequently contributed to Australian literary debates. His autobiographical trilogy, *Life Rarely Tells* (1958), *The Roaring Twenties* (1960) and *Fanfrolico and After* (1962), is particularly valuable as socio-cultural history. Paul Gillen has edited a compendium of his writing, *Jack Lindsay. Faithful to the Earth* (1993). In 1968 his services to Australian literature were recognised by a D.Litt. from the University of Queensland. In 1980 he was elected a life member of the Association for the Study of Australian Literature; in 1981 he was made AM. *Culture and History: Essays Presented to Jack Lindsay*, edited by Bernard Smith, was published in 1984. Lindsay was the model for the character Willie Weaver in Aldous Huxley's novel *Point Counter Point*.

LINTERMANS, Tony (1948–   ), born on a farm in Victoria, has worked as a teacher, speechwriter and editor. He has written for radio and television and has published poetry and short stories in numerous periodicals and anthologies. In 1986 he won the Northern Territory Red Earth Poetry Award, in 1987 the John Shaw Neilson Poetry Award, the Grenfell Henry Lawson Award, the Harold Kesteven Poetry Prize and the Poetry Day Prize. He has published two collections of poetry, *Inside the Circle* (1979) and *The Shed Manifesto* (1989). Lintermans's spare, arresting poems frequently centre on aspects of rural landscapes as starting-points for striking metaphoric insights illuminating and transforming the mundane. His landscapes, sometimes explicitly dependent on the perceiving eye, are vigorously and idiosyncratically alive: in poems which celebrate the mysterious energy of nature ('Nothing moves except mystery, the splendour/ of not knowing what makes this place ache/ beauty'), a creek 'meanders towards oblivion', 'Brown grass dithers on the ridge', or from the top of Mount Hotham 'valleys peel off like pages in a prayer book/ viciously crumpled'. Other poems express the poignant pain of loneliness or lost love, or wittily evoke the wry experience of achieving middle age. One of his best known, 'The Shed Manifesto', reminiscent of Murray's 'Wearing Shorts', and dwelling with loving detail on sheds and their place in male culture, is characteristic in combining imaginative breadth and concentration on the concrete: 'whatever his car, career, position, a man's shed/ is coagulation, unburdened essence of himself. It is also the shed itself.' Lintermans's short stories, often focusing on urban life, resemble his poems in range, wit and assurance.

'LISLE, Mary' (1897–1973), born in the Riverina, NSW, lived and farmed at Coonamble after her marriage to D.M. Cornish in 1925. She contributed verse to such periodicals as *Country Life*, the *Bulletin*, *Poetry*, *Southerly, Prism* and *Vision*; and published two collections, *The Secret Fire* (1947) and *The Inlander* (1968).

LITCHFIELD, Jessie (1883–1956), born Sydney as Jessie Phillips, was a pupil of Mary Gilmore. In 1908 she married a tin-miner, Valentine Litchfield, and travelled with him in many parts of the Northern Territory until 1917, meanwhile raising seven children. Her reminiscences of ten years of wandering, *Far-North Memories*, were published in 1930. She also contributed poems and short stories to the *Bulletin*, *Age* and *Woman's Mirror*, and was editor of the *Northern Territory Times* in Darwin 1930–42 until the family was evacuated after enemy bombing. She returned to Darwin in 1946 to work as a librarian and in 1951 unsuccessfully contested the Territory's federal seat in parliament as an independent candidate. The Jessie Litchfield Award, established in her will and administered by the Melbourne Bread and Cheese Club, is presented annually to a new and unknown writer. Her biography, which also includes several of her poems, *Jessie Litchfield – Grand Old Lady of the Territory* (1982), was written by her granddaughter, Janet Dickinson.

LITTLE, William (1839–1916), born Cumberland, England, arrived in the Colony in 1851. He was mayor of Ballarat in the 1890s. He published two works of fiction, *The Trinity of Man* (1896) and *Visit to Topos* (1897), and numerous booklets of verse including *Reveries* (1896), *A Dream of Paradise* (1904) and *Sonnets by Lambda* (1908).

LITTLEJOHN, Agnes, a regular contributor of short stories and verse to the *Sydney Mail* and the *Sydney Morning Herald* from before the First World War until the 1930s, published several works of fiction and collections of verse 1907–39. Described in reviews of the time as graceful, charming, spontaneous and fluent, her work has now more historical than literary value, reflecting in its willed floweriness very conventional, imported notions of beauty. Her fiction includes *The Daughter of a Soldier* (1907), *A Lapse of Memory* (1909), *Mirage of the Desert* (1910), *The Breath of India* (1914), *The Silver Road* (1915), *Star Dust and Sea Spray* (1918), *Rainbow Dreams* (1919), *The Sleeping Sea-Nymph* (1921), *The Lost Emerald* (1924) and *The Pipes o' Pan* (1939). Her verse was published under the following titles: *Verses* (1914), *Poems* (1915), *Patriotic Poems* (1915), *War Poems* (1916), *Lyrics and Lyrical Prose* (1927), *Lyrics and Mystic Sketches* (1928), *The Lady of the Doves* (1929), *The Guardian of the Gate* (1933), *The Unforgotten Watch* (1935), *Drowsy Hours* (1936) and *Lighthouse Keepers* (1938).

LLEWELLYN, Kate (1940–   ), born Tumby Bay, SA, has worked as a registered nurse and joint owner/director of an art gallery and now lives at Leura in the Blue Mountains region of NSW, where she writes full-time. The mother of three children, she became a writer after first undertaking university study in 1970. She has contributed verse and prose to numerous periodicals and anthologies, including *Sisters Poets 1* (1979), and has published five books of poetry, *Trader Kate and the Elephants* (1982, joint winner of the Anne Elder Award for poetry), *Luxury* (1985), *Honey* (1988), *Figs* (1990), *Selected Poems* (1992) and *Crosshatched* (1994); and the prose works *The Waterlily* (1987), *Dear You* (1988), *The Mountain* (1989) and *Angels & Dark Madonnas* (1991). With Susan Hampton she edited the anthology, *The Penguin Book of Australian Women Poets* (1986). Llewellyn's verse has a distinctive direct voice that is rueful, sensual and witty, whether interpreting familiar classical myths from a contemporary, feminist perspective or reflecting on the minutiae of everyday existence. Unafraid of the physical aspects of life and often frankly earthy about female sexuality, her verse celebrates the arrival and departure of love, childbirth and childhood, the familiarity become strangeness of parent–child relationships, foreign cities, gardening and simple natural phenonema which suggest the complexities of human experience. In her most recent poetry, *Crosshatched* (1994), famous women – Cleopatra, Joan of Arc, Dido and others – tell in everyday tones of events that have become legendary. As always, however, it is the personal voice that most strongly affects the reader. The emotional calm that time has brought is welcome but not all-satisfying. The spirit still needs extending.

> If we stand and stare
> and don't set out
> from shore
> we will be safe
> but never reach the island.

LLOYD, A.L. (Albert Lancaster) (1908–   ), born London, was the son of folk-singers who had died by the time he came to Australia in the middle 1920s. Over the next eight or nine years Lloyd worked mainly in the bush in NSW, learning a number of folk-songs and ballads in the years before the revival of interest in Australian folk-music after the Second World War. From 1950 Lloyd worked as a freelance folklorist and ethnomusicologist, paying a return visit to Australia in 1970 to lecture and per-form. His major interest and writing was in British and European music, but he made a number of albums of Australian folk songs, including *The Banks of the Condamine* (1957) and *Across the Western Plains* (1958), and helped establish songs like 'Flash Jack from Gundagai', 'The Euabalong Ball' and 'The Lime-Juice Tub' within the canon of Australian folk-song and ballad.

LONG, Richard (1873–1948), born England, was brought to Australia at the age of 5 and settled at Sandringham, Melbourne. A ship's carpenter and joiner, he was a member of the Socialist Party of Victoria, the Free Religious Fellowship and the Australian Peace Alliance and was familiar with such prominent individuals as John Cain, Adela Pankhurst, Marie Pitt, Bernard O'Dowd and Frederick Sinclaire. From 1911 he began contributing verse and articles to the *Socialist* and later verse to *Fellowship* and *Birth*, some of which was reprinted in his one collection, *Verses* (1917), with a foreword by Sinclaire.

LONGBOTTOM, Audrey, born Coramba, a small north-coast town near Coffs Harbour, NSW, began to write poetry and prose after attending the University of Wollongong as a mature-age student. She has published three groups of poems, *Relatives and Reliques* (1979), *Replay* (in *Trillium*, 1983) and *The Solitary Islands* (1986), which contains most of the poems from *Replay*. *Relatives and Reliques* has five sections, 'Under Mount Keira', '10 Mins from Shops', 'Traveller's Tales', 'Conditioned Response' and 'Relatives and Reliques'. It contains, as does *The Solitary Islands*, poems of personal experience, reflections on and reminiscences about life and people. There is a nostalgic, occasionally acerbic and regretful tone in poems such as 'Reflections', 'You Can See how the Town's Come On', 'After Taste' and 'Character Piece'. In general, however, her treatment of people, the past and the contemporary scene, is benign, such criticism being tempered by gentle humour and quiet understanding. She won the Grenfell Henry Lawson Award for verse in 1981.

LORIMER, Philip Durham (1843–97), born Madras, India, was a Scotsman who migrated to Sydney in 1861, worked mainly as an overlander in Queensland in the 1860s, and in the 1870s became a swagman poet known to many as 'Old Phil the Poet'. He spent much of his time wandering in outback NSW and Victoria, repaying the hospitality of diggers, bush workers, station owners and newspaper editors with extempore verse. His *Songs and Verses* (1901), mainly descriptive and lyrical verse, contains an appreciation by E.A. Petherick and incorporates material published in two earlier selections.

'Love's Coming', a brief lyric poem by John Shaw Neilson, was published in the Sydney *Sun* in 1911. It was later set to music by Dr W.G. Whitaker of the London College of Music. Acknowledged as one of Neilson's most attractive lyrics, there is a perfect harmony between the poem's simple but artistic form and its delicate imagery.

LOYAU, George Étienne (1835–98), born London, arrived in Sydney in 1853 and spent seven years travelling extensively in Australia and working at a range of occupations from gold-digger to private tutor. From the 1860s to the 1880s he had extensive experience in journalism and as a newspaper editor in Queensland, NSW, Victoria and SA, editing the *Maryborough Chronicle* (1861–62), the Gawler *Bunyip* (1878–79) and the *Illustrated Adelaide News* (1880–81). He also published three volumes of verse, *The Australian Seasons* (1871), *Australian Wild Flowers* (1871) and *Colonial Lyrics* (1872); an autobiographical account titled *The Personal Adventures of George E. Loyau* (1883); and two collections of biographical studies, *The Representative Men of South Australia* (1883) and *Notable South Australians* (1885). Founder and editor of the short-lived Adelaide magazine, the *Australian Family Herald* (1877), he also edited *The South Australian Annual: Australian Tales by Well Known Writers* (1877). Hugh Anderson wrote the biography, *George Loyau: the Man Who Wrote Bush Ballads* (1991). It incorporates two rare songbooks, *The Queenslanders' New Colonial Camp Fire Song Book* (c.1865) and *The Sydney Songster* (c.1869), with lyrics and musical scores, both songbooks written by Loyau.

LUNN, Richard (1950–   ), born Sydney, has worked as a teacher in Australia and England and lectured in creative writing at the Macarthur Institute of Higher Education. His publications include *Pompeii Deep Fry* (1980), which won the Anne Elder Award for poetry, and two books of short stories, *The Divine Right of Dogs* (1982) and *The Taxidermist's Dance* (1990).

LYLE, Garry, a Melbourne poet, founder and publisher of the untitled booklets of verse *Number One*, *Number Two* and *Number Three* (1943–48), contributed verse to such periodicals as *Bohemia* and *Venture*, and published one collection, *Eighteen Poems* (1940). His verse is also represented in the anthology *Dawnfire* (1941), ed. John Cremin.

LYNCH, Arthur Alfred (1861–1934), born near Ballarat of an Irish father who had taken part in the Eureka rebellion and of a Scottish mother, graduated from the University of Melbourne in 1886, and also trained as a civil engineer. He later studied science, physiology, psychology and electrical engineering in Europe, qualified as a doctor in London, worked for a time as a journalist and in 1892 tried unsuccessfully to enter the House of Commons as a Parnellite candidate. He served with the Boers during the Boer War. In 1901 he was elected to the House of Commons as Nationalist candidate for Galway but was imprisoned and tried for treason in 1902. Convicted in 1903, he was sentenced to life imprisonment but was released on licence a year later after Theodore Roosevelt interceded with Edward VII, and subsequently won a free pardon. A prominent Irish member of parliament until 1918, he was active in British interests during the First World War. The author of nearly thirty books on a range of subjects including science, psychology, ethics and the Irish problem, Lynch also published an autobiography, *My Life Story* (1924); five volumes of verse, some of which shows a satirical wit, *A Koran of Love* (1894), *Our Poets!* (1894), *Religio Athletae* (1895), *Prince Azreel* (1911) and *Sonnets of the Banner and the Star* (1914); and two works of fiction, *Poppy Meadows* (1915) and *O'Rourke the Great* (1921). A man of wide-ranging interests and talents, Lynch in his combination of affection for Australia and fierce love of Ireland is an extreme representative of a common political phenomenon in Australia before 1918.

MACARTNEY, F.T. (Frederick Thomas) (1887–1980), born and educated in Melbourne, left school at 12 and followed a variety of occupations including stints as a clerk, a bookkeeper on a Riverina station, a shorthand reporter, a freelance journalist and a Victorian government employee, until his appointment in 1921 to the Northern Territory public service. Macartney returned to Melbourne in 1933 and, apart from 1942–47 when he was employed as a public servant and 1948–54 when most of his energies were devoted to the revision of E. Morris Miller's bibliography *Australian Literature* (1940), he worked as a freelance broadcaster, reviewer and lecturer.

Active in Melbourne literary circles from his early twenties, Macartney helped to found the Melbourne Literary Club in 1916 and was editor of its journal, *Birth*, in 1920; he was prominent in the Australian Literature Society, PEN and the FAW. Although he contributed short stories to periodicals and anthologies and illustrated some of his books with linocuts, his main creative activity was as a writer of cool and crafted verse which ranges from the densely philosophical to the lightly satiric. His major volumes were *Preferences* (1941) and *Selected Poems* (1961), which both include material from earlier volumes, e.g. *Dewed Petals* (1912), *Earthen Vessels* (1913), *Commercium* (1917), *In War-Time* (1918), *Poems* (1920), *Something for Tokens* (1922), *A Sweep of Lute-Strings* (1929), *Hard Light* (1933), *Ode of Our Times* (1944), *Gaily the Troubadour* (1946) and *Tripod for Homeward Incense* (1947). His other work includes *A Historical Outline of Australian Literature* (1957); *Australian Literary Essays* (1957); an autobiography, *Proof Against Failure* (1967); a biography, *Furnley Maurice (Frank Wilmot)* (1955); a revision of Louis Lavater's 1926 anthology, *The Sonnet in Australasia* (1956); and the 1947 number of *Australian Poetry* (1948).

McAULEY, James (1917–76), born Lakemba, NSW, was educated at the University of Sydney where he gained his MA in 1940 with the thesis 'Symbolism: An Essay in Poetics', a topic which foreshadows the classical stance he later adopted in his poetry. Although he was regarded by some as an arch-conservative in later life, McAuley's university days were filled with the usual dalliances with atheism, anarchism, radicalism and idealism. Drafted for military service in 1942, he was appointed to the Australian Army Directorate of Research and Civil Affairs under A.A. Conlon, where he helped to train the personnel of the Australian New Guinea Administration Unit (ANGAU), whose post-war task was to re-establish civil administration in the island. Thereafter New Guinea was a major factor in McAuley's life. In 1946–60 he was a member of the instructional staff of the Australian School of Pacific Administration in Sydney. He visited New Guinea frequently, becoming deeply interested in the problems facing its primitive society and fascinated by its exotic landscape. His writings on New Guinea, published throughout the 1940s and 1950s in the journal *South Pacific*, won him an international reputation among scholars of Oceania. In 1956 he became editor of the literary and current affairs journal *Quadrant*; in 1961 he was appointed reader in poetry at the University of Tasmania, Hobart, then professor of English, occupying the chair until his death. McAuley was instrumental in establishing *Australian Literary Studies*, and was president of the Australian Association for the Teaching of English 1970–75. In 1972 he won the Britannica-Australia Award; in 1975 he was made AM.

McAuley's first collection of verse was *Under Aldebaran* (1946). In 1947–49 he wrote 'Prometheus', 'The Death of Chiron', 'The Ascent of Heracles' and 'The Tomb of Heracles', the four poems which make up his important work 'The Hero and the Hydra', first published together in his second volume, *A Vision of Ceremony* (1956). Using the Greek tales based on the Prometheus legend, McAuley comments adversely on modern civilisation and affirms traditional moral and spiritual values. His *Selected Poems* appeared in 1963. The epic narrative *Captain Quiros* was published in 1964. *Surprises of the Sun* (1969), a series of mainly autobiographical lyrics, disappointed critics who felt that after *Captain Quiros* McAuley would continue to write public poetry with substantial themes. Two of the poems, 'In the Huon Valley' and 'St. John's Park, New Town', reflect McAuley's reaction to his new Tasmanian environment, a reaction more fully explored in the posthumous collection *A World of Its Own* (1977), where his handwritten poems in praise of the Tasmanian east-coast area near Coles Bay are combined with paintings and drawings by Patricia Giles. *Collected Poems 1936–1970* appeared in 1971, and in the year he died *Music Late at Night: Poems 1970–1973* and *Time Given: Poems 1970–1974* were published; both titles reflect his awareness of approaching death. McAuley's chief prose works are *The End of Modernity* (1959), essays on modern literature, art and culture in general, *The Personal Element in Australian Poetry* (1970), and *The Grammar of the Real* (1975), essays and literary criticism. *A Map of Australian Verse: The Twentieth Century* (1975) combines samples of the work of Australian poets with critical commentary, biographical and bibliographical information.

One of the so-called 'University' poets of the 1950s, McAuley was considered a classicist because of his belief, expressed in 'The Magian Heresy' (*Quadrant*, September 1957), that in the 'high world of Virgil and Chaucer and Dante and Shakespeare . . . the true proportions of things are recognized' and because of his stance, taken in 'An Art of Poetry' (*A Vision of Ceremony*), that 'only the simplest forms can hold/ A vast complexity'. McAuley eschewed 'individual, arbitrary/ And self-expressive art', demanding (and providing in his own writing) traditional control and order, grace and precision. Such attitudes explain his impatience with what he saw as the self-indulgent, 'immense deviation' of the avant-garde verse of the 1940s and the resultant Ern Malley hoax. Those opposed to his viewpoint saw his stance as arch-conservative and his attitudes as reactionary. To some of his admirers the graceful autobiographical lyrics of his later volumes represent his most pleasant poetry, but they do little to enhance the reputation and prestige he gained from the more substantial earlier works, *Under Aldebaran*, *A Vision of Ceremony* and *Captain Quiros*. His final years, however, brought an increasing recognition of his stature as critic and intellectual, although his reputation as a poet, has, since his death, suffered a decline. Peter Coleman wrote *The Heart of James McAuley: Life and Work of the Australian Poet* (1980); Leonie Kramer edited *James McAuley* (1988), which includes a personal commentary and a selection of McAuley's poetry and essays; and Lyn McCredden wrote *James McAuley* (1992) in Oxford's Australian Writers series. The James McAuley Lecture is delivered annually at the University of Tasmania in his honour. An account of McAuley's involvement in the Ern Malley hoax is contained in Michael Heyward's *The Ern Malley Affair* (1993).

McCAULEY, Shane (1954–), born Surrey, England, has lived mostly in WA, although he completed his postgraduate education in Sydney before working for the WA Department of TAFE. His poetry and short stories have appeared frequently in anthologies and periodicals and he has published three collections of poetry, *The Chinese Feast* (1984), *Deep-Sea Diver* (1987) and *The Butterfly Man* (1991). With Julie Lewis he edited the anthology *Breakaway* (1980). In 1976 he won the Tom Collins Short Story Prize and in 1988 the UTA/*Poetry Australia* Bicentennial Poetry Prize; in 1983 he was co-winner of the Tom Collins Poetry Prize. McCauley's poetry, ranging from philosophical contemplation to dramatic monologue to love lyric, reflects his wide interests and reading. Particularly striking is his interest in history, which includes Australia's history. The latter has inspired some poems on military themes such as 'The Landing', which captures the impotence of men locked into a situation they cannot escape in 'the scrub' of war and the absurdity of their transient emotional reactions to the crisis, and 'Dardanelles Spring', which compares the ancient peace of the Gallipoli Peninsula where no men had walked for a thousand years with the dead men now littering the landscape, 'hands raised/ In the supplication rigor brings,/ Ignored but for insect interrogation'. Other poems spring from the cultures of ancient Greece, China and Japan, such as 'An Old Samurai Arranges Flowers' which opens his third collection and which contrasts the aesthetic delicacy and control of Japanese culture with its historical violence. For the old man the ascetic way of life in painful old age is a matter of pride, a challenge to a purer stoicism: 'My chest is as thin as these immaculate/ Paper walls, but in my small way/ a harmony can be re-instated', while the inoffensive carnations he is arranging, 'easier to preserve than human lives', suggest the grim reality of war: 'Swift as the shock of the sword/ Releasing exploding chrysanthemums/ Hidden in the neck, the sprawl/ Of depleted bodies, war's spattered banners'. Similarly, the characteristically elegant, humorous title poem of his third collection garners Eastern wisdom in a quest for balance and the sort of maturity which recognises the need to 'be a little gnarled' to 'Love what is imperfect' in the self. But some of his most attractive poems spring from personal inward experience, such as 'Visitor', a brief poignant lyric on lost love. Technically assured and sustained by coherent imagery and subtle internal rhymes, McCauley's poetry is formally sophisticated and well matured if in some poems the emotional intensity strikes the reader only at second or third reading.

McCRAE, George Gordon (1833–1927), born Leith, Scotland, son of Andrew Murison McCrae and Georgiana Huntly McCrae and father of the poet Hugh McCrae, came to Australia in 1841. The family settled in 1843 at Arthur's Seat on the Mornington Peninsula, an area described in his mother's journal and in his *Recollections of Melbourne & Port Phillip Bay in the Early Forties* (1987, originally published in the *Victorian Historical Magazine* 1911–12). McCrae entered the civil service in Melbourne in 1854, ultimately rising to the post of deputy registrar-general. Artistic in temperament, he became an important member of the Melbourne cultural and literary scene, being one of the founders of the Yorick Club and an associate of such literary figures as Marcus Clarke, Henry Kendall, Adam Lindsay Gordon and R.H. Horne. Two of McCrae's poems, *Mamba ('The Bright-Eyed'): An Aboriginal Reminiscence* and *The Story of Balladeadro* (both 1867), are among the earliest Australian poems on Aboriginal themes. They found favour with contemporaries such as Henry Kendall, who judged McCrae 'the highest poet in Australia' whose voice was for 'scholars and thinkers only', but they soon came to be considered too romanticised and unrealistic in their treatment of the Aborigine. *The Man in the Iron Mask* (1873), a long poem in blank verse, was enlivened, like all McCrae's work, by some graceful passages, but its story of the imprisonment of a mysterious royal Frenchman held little attraction for Australian readers. A further collection, *The Fleet and Convoy and Other Verses*, was published in 1915, and his only novel, *John Rous*, in 1918.

McCRAE, Hugh (1876–1958), born Melbourne, son of George Gordon McCrae and grandson of Georgiana Huntly McCrae, was initially articled to a Melbourne architect but, influenced by the Norman Lindsay set that included Randolph Bedford, Lionel Lindsay, Edward and Will Dyson, sought a living by freelance writing and illustration. In 1904 he moved to Sydney where he became involved with J.F. Archibald, A.G. Stephens and Frank Fox. In 1914 he went to the USA, where he attempted to earn a living as an artist and actor, but suffered extreme financial hardship. Back in Australia, he played Adam Lindsay Gordon in an Australian film released in 1916, performed in Shakespearean productions and was employed as a decoder in the wartime Censor's Office in Melbourne. In 1922 he returned to Sydney and continued to live there apart from a few years at Camden. Co-editor of the *New Triad* (1927–28), he also wrote poetry, prose, drama and letters, gave radio talks and public lectures, wrote for newspapers and compiled and edited personal and family memoirs. In 1953 he was made OBE.

McCrae's first collection of poetry is *Satyrs and Sunlight* (1909), illustrated by Norman Lindsay; the title was also given to a 1928 collection of his poetry. McCrae's other volumes of poetry include *Colombine* (1920); *Idyllia* (1922) which contains a short extract from the work McCrae hoped would be his masterpiece, the verse drama 'Joan of Arc', a further extract being included in the 1928 *Satyrs and Sunlight*; *The Mimshi Maiden* (1938); *Poems* (1939), a selected volume; *Forests of Pan* (1944), containing a number of earlier poems which were not reprinted in *Poems* (1939); and *Voice of the Forest* (1945). R.G. Howarth, who edited *Forests of Pan* and arranged and introduced *Voice of the Forest*, also edited *The Best Poems of Hugh McCrae* (1961), which includes the whole of the incomplete 'Joan of Arc'. A selection of his poems made by Douglas Stewart was published in the Australian Poets series in 1966. McCrae wrote a musical fantasy, *The Ship of Heaven* (1951), which was produced in 1933; a prose work, *The Du Poissey Anecdotes* (1922); and a prose collection, *Story-Book Only* (1948), which includes the *Du Poissey* pieces and his reminiscences of his father and his times, *My Father and My Father's Friends*, first published in 1935. He edited *Georgiana's Journal* (1934), the diaries of his grandmother. McCrae also wrote an endless stream of letters to friends and acquaintances, each beautifully handwritten letter illustrated with figures and scenes and often accompanied by a verse composed for the occasion. A selection of his letters was edited by R.D. FitzGerald in 1970. A Hugh McCrae number of *Southerly* appeared in 1956.

McCrae's poetry has consistently attracted a small band of devotees: fellow Rabelaisian Kenneth Slessor, who believed that *Satyrs and Sunlight* (1909) ushered modern Australian poetry into being; Mary Gilmore, who was delighted by McCrae's verbal artistry and regarded him as Australia's finest poet; literary historian H.M. Green, who saw him as 'a prince of lyrists' with 'as near an approach to pure beauty as can be made by means of the purely physical'; and Judith Wright, who found in him 'a poet to love and admire and be proud of'. With the gradual disappearance of the generation who knew McCrae personally, much of that ardour has evaporated. Recent judgments tend, in the main, to reject the whimsy, the exotica and the seductive carnival of colour and sound that characterise his verse, finding instead incoherence of thought and lack of control over imagery and syntax; in effect, little more than imaginative chaos. He remains, however, of importance in Australian literary history, both because he anticipated the *Vision* school and because he offered, with other lyrists, an alternative to the balladry that had dominated Australian poetry in the preceding generation.

McCUAIG, Ronald (1908–93), born Newcastle, NSW, began writing for radio in 1927 and was employed by *Wireless Weekly* 1928–38. During the Second World War he worked for the ABC and for *Smith's Weekly*. He was a special writer and occasional literary critic for the *Sydney Morning Herald* 1945–46, and *Smith's Weekly* 1947. In 1949 he joined the editorial staff of the *Bulletin* where as 'Swilliam', he wrote much topical verse and numerous literary and theatre reviews. He also became fiction editor of the *Bulletin*. McCuaig's poetry publications include *Vaudeville* (1938), *The Wanton Goldfish* (1941) and the cumulative collections, *Quod Ronald McCuaig* (1946) and *The Ballad of Bloodthirsty Bessie and Other Poems* (1961, which was a 'collected' based on the earlier three). He also wrote *Tales out of Bed* (1944, essays and short stories) and *Australia and the Arts* (1972). He edited the 1954 edition of *Australian Poetry*. With his shrewd, and sometimes crude, satirical observations of life, his talent for dry and witty cynicism, and his delicately humorous love lyrics, McCuaig seemed likely to occupy an important place in the post-war poetry scene; however, the success of 'The Ballad of Bloodthirsty Bessie', a rollicking fantasy which combines greed, lust, religious mania and superbly portrayed indifference to human life, was followed by virtual poetic silence. The best of McCuaig's serious work is in *Vaudeville*. Among his best-known poems are 'The Commercial Traveller's Wife', 'Au Tombeau de mon Père', 'Music in the Air', 'The Passionate Clerk to his Love' and 'Bessie'. His *Selected Poems*, published in 1992 with an introduction by Peter Kirkpatrick, confirms that McCuaig was a highly original avant-garde poet, who was both satirical comedian and serious artist. In 1992, not long before his death, McCuaig was presented with a NSW State Special Award for his outstanding contribution to Australian literature.

McDONALD, Andrew (1942–   ), born England, came to Australia in 1971 and has worked as a lecturer in English and in television. He has published poetry in anthologies, periodicals and newspapers and in two collections, *Absence in Strange Countries* (1976) and *The One True History* (1984). In 1979 he won the Ian Mudie Award. Rich in literary allusion and sometimes addressing jokes or puns to an implied academic reader, McDonald's first collection is in the tradition of Hardy, Gunn and Larkin, although his second is more decidedly Australian; varied in range from the macabre to the elegiac, and reflecting among other matters his travels, his responses to the country of his birth and to Australia, the difficulties of creative work, the challenge of language, and family relationships, his verse is equally varied in metrical structure.

McDONALD, Nan (1921–74), born Eastwood, Sydney, was educated at the University of Sydney. As publishing editor for Angus & Robertson she made a considerable contribution to the publication of Australian literature in the decades following the Second World War. She edited the annual anthology *Australian Poetry* in 1953. Her own volumes of poetry are *Pacific Sea* (1947), which won the inaugural Grace Leven Prize for poetry, *The Lonely Fire* (1954) and *The Lighthouse and Other Poems* (1959). Her *Selected Poems* was published in 1969. *Pacific Sea* captures in smooth, attractive verse the beauty of the Sydney bushlands, the grandeur of the Hawkesbury district and the pleasant seascapes of the NSW south coast. In philosophic poems such as 'The Ship' and 'The Tollgate Islands' she probes the future, wondering 'what dark fee, what cruel payment' life may exact from her. *The Lonely Fire*, more powerful and at times quite sombre, uses a series of masks, like the old tramp in the title poem, to lay bare the human condition. 'The Lighthouse' is a long dramatic study of a lighthouse-keeper who spends three days of terror fighting to regain his self-control after discovering the dead body of his companion.

McDONALD, Roger (1941–   ), the son of local historian Lorna McDonald, was born at Young, NSW, educated at Temora and Bourke before attending Scots College, Sydney and the University of Sydney. He was a high-school teacher and a radio and television producer with the ABC in Brisbane and Hobart before becoming, in 1969, a professional editor with UQP, which published his two volumes of poetry,

Citizens of Mist (1968) and *Airship* (1975). In his seven years with the press McDonald was involved with the Paperback Poets series which both reflected and stimulated the 'New Australian Poetry'; his selection from the first series was published in 1974 as *The First Paperback Poets Anthology*. In 1976 he moved to Canberra to work on *1915* , a novel about the Gallipoli experience. Published in 1979, *1915* proved an outstanding success, winning the *Age* Book of the Year Award and the SA government's Biennial Literature Award; Peter Yeldham adapted it into a seven-part television series which was shown in 1982. In 1981 he was awarded the Canada-Australia Literary Prize. His subsequent work includes the novels *Slipstream* (1982), *Rough Wallaby* (1989) and *Water Man* (1993); the semi-autobiographical *Shearers' Motel* (1992), winner of the Banjo Award for non-fiction in 1993; the fictionalised biography *Melba* (1988), and the script of the television mini-series of the same title (1988); the television script *John Simpson* (1988) and a novel, *Flynn* (1992), based on the 1992 screenplay of the life of Errol Flynn by Frank Howson and Alister Webb.

In the intensely political world of Australian poetry since the 1960s McDonald has been much admired for his editorial activities, which helped significantly to establish or consolidate the reputation of a number of (mainly younger) Australian poets. His own poetry occupies a corner of Les Murray's 'Vernacular Republic' and is distinguished by a selection of detail and by metaphoric observations which give freshness and resonance to his metaphysical exploration of experience. His fiction also reflects his intention to 'write out of the Australian character and in the Australian accent': in practice this has often meant the exploration of the Australian character within a historical framework, as in *Citizens of Mist* which includes poems on Adam Lindsay Gordon and other historical subjects.

McGRATH, Raymond Herbert (1903–77), born Sydney, studied arts and architecture at the University of Sydney, where he was art director of *Hermes*. He also studied painting under Julian Ashton and won a reputation as a woodcut artist. Well known in literary circles, he contributed short stories to *Art in Australia* and other journals and anthologies, and published a collection of verse, illustrated, bound and printed by himself on J.T. Kirtley's private press, *The Seven Songs of Meadow Lane* (1924). At the age of 23 he won the Wentworth Travelling Scholarship to London, and later settled in Dublin; he became one of the leading architects of the modern movement. He is one of the poets recalled by J. le Gay Brereton in his reminiscences of Sydney's literary life in *Knocking Round* (1930).

McKAY, Hugh (1877–?), born Melbourne, studied medicine in a desultory way at Melbourne University in the 1890s while leading a bohemian existence and becoming familiar with such literary figures as E.J. Brady, Louis Esson and Spencer Brodney. He eventually became a registered chemist after a period spent as a freelance writer. A member of the T.M.J. (the Too Much Jesus Society), McKay developed an interest in the speculative possibilities of science and a personal aesthetic based partly on Nietzschean ideas, publishing a series of articles and short stories in the *Lone Hand* 1908–10, similar to the genre which H.G. Wells popularised. Regarded as a genius by some of his contemporaries and noted for his satirical wit, he published light verse in the *Bulletin*, which consistently rejected his serious poetry. From 1915 to 1921 he ran a pharmacy in North Perth but then returned to Sydney, where he reverted to bohemianism in the company of the sons of Norman Lindsay and the *Vision* group of writers. Some of his poetry was included in the *Vision* anthology *Poetry in Australia: 1923*, but his only individual collection is *In the Changing Crystal* (1909). He later became the science writer for *Smith's Weekly* and a journalist on the staff of the *Daily Telegraph*, abandoning serious literature and becoming more reclusive. Memorable more for his distinctive personality, recalled by several of his friends in their autobiographies, than for his achievements, McKay has been described as a significant figure in the pre-1914 cultural scene.

MACKAY, James Alexander Kenneth (1859–1935), born Wallendbeen, NSW, was a member of the NSW Legislative Council and vice-president of the Executive Council 1899–1900, and a distinguished military officer, rising to the rank of major-general. In 1897 he raised the 1st Australian Horse, a volunteer cavalry regiment recruited from NSW country districts and commanded the NSW Imperial Bush-men's Contingent in South Africa 1900–1. Chairman of a royal commission on the administration of Papua 1906–7, his personal account, *Across Papua*, was published in 1909. He was director-general of the Australian Army reserve during the First World War. He frequently contributed articles and verse to Australian newspapers and, as Kenneth Mackay, published two novels, *Out Back* (1893) and *The Yellow Wave: A Romance of the Asiatic Invasion of Australia* (1895), and three collections of verse, *Stirrup Jingles from the Bush and the Turf* (1887), *A Bush Idyl* (1888) and *Songs of a Sunlit Land* (1908).

MACKELLAR, Dorothea (1885–1968) was born in Sydney into a well-established and wealthy family, and was educated privately and at the University of Sydney, acquiring a facility for languages which proved useful during her wide-ranging travel in Australia and overseas. At 19 she wrote a poem (the second verse of which is probably the best-known stanza in Australian poetry) which was published in 1908 in the London *Spectator* as 'Core of My Heart'. When revised and published in her first book, *The Closed Door* (1911), it carried the title 'My Country', and has become familiar to generations of Australian schoolchildren. Mackellar published three further volumes of poetry, *The Witch-Maid* (1914), *Dreamharbour* (1923) and *Fancy Dress* (1926), which confirm her delight in nature as well as her facility at verse translations, but for many Australians she remains the author of one famous poem. With a sculpture of her on horseback in the centre of the town, Gunnedah in NSW claims Dorothea Mackellar for its own. Her family owned a substantial property in the district, which she often visited. Its typical Australian scenery is said by some to have provided the inspiration for 'My Country'. Before prolonged ill health forced her largely to abandon writing in the middle 1920s she also wrote three novels, *The Little Blue Devil* (1912), *Outlaws' Luck* (1913), and *Two's Company* (1914), the first and last in collaboration with Ruth Bedford. Made OBE in 1968, she was for some years active in and patron of the English Association. A collection of her poetry was published in 1971 as *The Poems of Dorothea Mackellar* and *My Country and other Poems* in 1982. *I Love a Sunburnt Country: The Diaries of Dorothea Mackellar* was edited by Jyoti Brunsdon in 1990 and Adrienne Howley, who nursed her for the last decades of her life, has written a biography, *My Heart, My Country: The Story of Dorothea Mackellar* (1989).

McKELLAR, J.A.R. (John Alexander Ross) (1904–32), born Dulwich Hill, Sydney, left school at 15 to work in a bank. At a time when he was regarded as a poet of some potential, encouraged by such writers as Kenneth Slessor, Hugh McCrae and H.M. Green, and was also establishing a reputation as an athlete, McKellar died suddenly of pneumonia. He contributed poetry to the *New Triad* and published one collection in his lifetime, *Twenty-Six* (1931), selected by Kenneth Slessor. Some of his poems have appeared in anthologies but it was not until 1946 that his *Collected Poems* was published, edited by J.W. Gibbes; *Southerly* published a commemorative issue in 1944. A keen classical student, McKellar expressed his admiration for Greek literature in his choice of subject and style.

MACKENZIE, Kenneth ('Seaforth') (1913–55), born Perth, was educated at Guildford Grammar School, Muresk Agricultural College and the University of WA. His periods of education were all incomplete: at 16 he ran away from school and never returned. He left university without taking a degree. After moving to Sydney in 1934 at the suggestion of Norman Lindsay, he tried journalism, but his dislike of routine, combined with an increasing dependence on alcohol, made him an unreliable employee. He married Kathleen Bartlett, an art teacher, in 1934 and they had two children. In 1942 he was drafted into the army and served as a corporal attached to a compound of Italian prisoners at the POW camp at Cowra. A mass breakout of Japanese prisoners there in 1944 was used by Mackenzie as the subject of his novel *Dead Men Rising*. After some time in an army hospital in 1945, he attempted to rejoin the civilian work-force but his handicaps persisted and the family was eventually forced to separate. During his last few years Mackenzie lived on a very small property at Kurrajong owned by his wife, while she supported their children in Sydney by teaching sculpture. In 1955, during a visit to a friend at Goulburn, he drowned in a creek.

His novels, all first published under the pseudonym 'Seaforth' Mackenzie, include *The Young Desire It*, which won the Australian Literature Society's Gold Medal, *Chosen People* (1938), *Dead Men Rising* (1951) and *The Refuge* (1954). Two collections of poetry under the name Kenneth Mackenzie were published in his lifetime and two posthumously. They include *Our Earth* (1937, illustrated by Norman Lindsay), *The Moonlit Doorway* (1944), *Selected Poems* (1961, ed. Douglas Stewart) and *The Poems of Kenneth Mackenzie* (1972, ed. Evan Jones and Geoffrey Little).

Mackenzie's early poetry, with its penchant for romantic melodrama and vitalist themes, shows the influence of Norman Lindsay and Hugh McCrae. His second collection is marked by an unusually frank exploration of sexual relationships. Later he began to write a more austere poetry which turns on the themes of pain, isolation, time, family relationships and death and which achieves, at its best, a controlled tranquillity and compassion. Among his finest pieces are those he wrote about his experiences in hospital, published for the first time in full in the 1972 collection. Evan Jones wrote the critical study *Kenneth Mackenzie* (1969).

McKNIGHT, Roger (1925–), born Jamestown, SA, served in the AIF in the Second World War and has subsequently worked as a dairy farmer and woodworker. He has published poetry in anthologies and periodicals and in two volumes, *You Can Hear Grass Grow* (1970) and *The Grass-Trees* (1988). Relying mainly on the rural landscape, he draws analogies between natural features and phenomena and human emotions and experiences, often in a mood of whimsy or fantasy.

McLEOD, Alan Lindsay (1928–), born Sydney, was educated at the University of Sydney, where he edited the magazines *Vesperis* and *Descant*, and has taught for many years in the USA. The author of numerous articles on Australian literature and of three collections of poetry, *The Change of Light* (1953), *Beyond the Cresting Surf* (1959) and *Chautauqua Canticles* (1962), he has also edited, with Richard Preston, *The Lincoln Anthology 1951* (1951), a selection of writing by young Australians, and the essay collections *The Commonwealth Pen* (1961) and *The Pattern of Australian Culture* (1963). McLeod has also edited *Australia Speaks* (1969), a selection of speeches, and an account of Walt Whitman's reputation in Australia and NZ (1964).

McLEOD, Marjorie (1893–?) was born in Dimboola, Victoria. Founder of the Swan Hill National Theatre, of which she was director and producer for many years, she worked as a teacher of speech and as an actor and writer for ABC radio before moving to Swan Hill in 1946. Two of her plays were published in anthologies, *Travail* in *Eight Plays by Australians* (1934) and *Moonshine* in *Five Plays by Australians* (1936), and she also published *Within These Walls* (1948), a four-act historical play first produced in Melbourne in 1936, and *Four Period Plays* (1958). She also published a poetry collection, *Verses from Swan Hill* (1946), which includes a verse drama, 'The Enchanted Tryst'.

McMASTER, Rhyll (1947–), born Brisbane, has published four books of poetry, *The Brineshrimp* (1972), for which she was awarded the Harri Jones Memorial Prize; *Washing the Money* (1986), which shared the Victorian Premier's Literary Award (the C.J. Dennis Award) for Poetry in 1985 and won the Grace Leven Poetry Prize for 1986; *On My Empty Feet* (1993) and *Flying the Coop: New and Selected Poems 1972–1994* (1995). In all her books she recalls scenes and events from childhood – 'freeze frames' as she aptly describes them. Poems such as 'Crab Meat', 'Underneath the House', 'Profiles of My Father', 'Washing the Money' and 'Eeling' describe specific moments of a seemingly placid and secure childhood in clear and unpretentious language. More sophisticated imagery enhances poems on other subjects and themes. 'Vertebrae' and 'Light' are more complex poetic constructions, combining close observation of external details with a compelling sense of strangeness and mystery. The central poem of *On My Empty Feet*, 'My mother and I become victims of a stroke', a powerful study of a stifled life, unites with others evoking alienation, fragmentation and displacement. Rhyll McMaster has also written short fiction and been a reviewer of fiction for the *Sydney Morning Herald* and in 1994 was poetry editor for the *Canberra Times*.

MACNAMARA, Francis (1811–?), a convict who was probably the writer best known as 'Frank the Poet' and also as Francis Goddard, was born in Ireland and transported to NSW in 1832. His original offence was stealing but he may, in addition, have been a political agitator. Certainly he was a recalcitrant during his first decade in Australia: he absconded several times, suffered numerous floggings and other punishments, and served extended terms as a member of a chain gang. In 1839, while employed as a shepherd with the Australian Agricultural Company, he composed 'A Convict's Tour to Hell', an anti-authoritarian satire which passed into oral tradition. In 1842 MacNamara was sent to Port Arthur, where his conduct improved to the point that he was given a ticket of leave in 1847 and his freedom in 1849. Known as a composer of cheeky, extempore verse, he reputedly farewelled the audience which had come to see him off at Launceston with the verse, which exists in several versions:

> Land of Lags and Kangaroo,
> Of 'possum and the scarce Emu,
> The farmer's pride but the prisoner's Hell
> Land of Buggers [Bums] Fare-thee-well!

MacNamara's movements after leaving Tasmania are largely unknown, although John Meredith and Rex Whalan in *Frank the Poet: The Life and Works of Francis Mac-Namara* (1979), who first linked 'Frank the Poet' with the Francis MacNamara transported in 1832, suggest he may have been 'the Poet', a balladeer living in a Melbourne doss-house whom Marcus Clarke wrote about in 1868. Among the other poems associated with 'Frank the Poet', who appears as a character in Michael Boddy's play 'Cash' (1972), are a ballad about Bold Jack Donohoe (which may have been the source of the later 'Wild Colonial Boy' song about Jack Doolan), and the convict laments 'Labouring with the Hoe', which shows the influence of Robert Burns, and 'The Convict's Arrival', known also as 'Moreton Bay'.

McNICOLL, David (1914–), born Geelong, Victoria, and one of Australia's best-known journalists, began his career as a cadet on the staff of the *Sydney Morning Herald*. A war correspondent during the Second World War, he covered the campaigns in the Middle East and the invasion of Normandy. He was special correspondent 1945–54 for the Sydney *Daily Telegraph* to which he contributed the front-page column 'Town Talk', and was editor-in-chief of Sir Frank Packer's newspaper empire 1953–72. He has published two volumes of verse, *Air Mail Palestine* (1943) and *The Round Dozen* (1947); and a volume of memoirs, *Luck's a Fortune* (1979).

MAGOFFIN, Richard (1937–), known as 'The Boredrain Balladist', is a writer of bush verse, songs and yarns and is well known in outback Queensland for his recitations. He is the author of the often-reprinted *We Bushies* (1968), *Chops and Gravy* (1972), *Fair Dinkum Matilda* (1973), which is an important contribution to Waltzing Matilda literature, *Down Another Track* (1982) and *Waltzing Matilda: Song of Australia* (1983). *'How Would You Be?'* (1984) is a selection of verse from earlier publications.

MAIDEN, Jennifer (1949–), born Penrith, NSW, left school at 13 and spent several years working at casual jobs before returning to study, graduating BA from Macquarie University at the age of 24. Since then she has been a professional writer, has tutored in creative writing, conducted writing workshops and seminars in the western suburbs of Sydney and been poet-in-residence at the ANU and the University of Western Sydney. She has published numerous books of poetry: *Tactics* (1974), *The Problem of Evil* (1975), *The Occupying Forces* (1975), *Mortal Details* (1977, poems and two short stories), *Birthstones* (1978), *The Border Loss* (1979), *For the Left Hand* (1981), *The Trust* (1988), *Selected Poems* (1990), *Bastille Day* (1990), *The Winter Baby* (1990) and *Acoustic Shadow* (1993). She has won several poetry prizes, including the English Association Prize, the Harri Jones Memorial Prize, the Grenfell Henry Lawson Festival of Arts Award, the NSW Premier's Prize (the Kenneth Slessor Award) and the Victorian Premier's Award (the C.J. Dennis Award), the last two for *The Winter Baby*. She has also written two novels, *The Terms* (1982) and *Play with Knives* (1990).

Jennifer Maiden's first volume, *Tactics*, brought a new and distinctive poetic voice – complex, intense, private, and urgent in its effort to distil thoughts and emotions into language that seemed barely expansive enough to contain them. It proved to be the first glimpse of what one critic (Martin Duwell) called 'Maidenland', a terrain that demanded skill and patience if the reader was to negotiate a way successfully but one that offered considerable rewards if the effort were made. Her second volume, *The Problem of Evil*, is set totally in 'Maidenland'. The long title section appears to be based on a military encounter in which two female partisans are captured by a male invading force. One is killed, the other tortured but ultimately rescued as the withdrawing invaders poison the land they are leaving. The rescued partisan is unable to warn her fellows about the land – 'I harsh on wordless phlegm to warn/ those keepers from their soil.' The reader is kept well enough in touch with what is happening if agile enough to make the leap from one informative rock to another across the stream of the narrative. The other sections of the book are 'Mobiles', 'The Sponge', and 'A Solstice Miscellany', all concerning shadowy incidents occurring in 'Maidenland'. The challenging complexity of the whole volume stems from subtleties of thought and theme cleverly couched in even more subtly manipulated language. *The Occupying Forces* is a series of poems integrated by the usual experiences and preoccupations of life, while *Birthstones* is structurally based on introductory poems related to each month's precious or semi-precious stones. *The Border Loss* and *For the Left Hand*, the latter a special issue of *Poetry Australia*, present the usual problems for the reader of unravelling sufficient clues to trace the patterns of thought developed by means of a highly original structure of language and image. *The Trust*, however, is more accessible. *Bastille Day*, a brief volume in the NLA Pamphlet Poet Series, takes its title from the poet's wedding day, 14 July 1984.

The *Selected Poems*, which carries a tribute from A.D. Hope on its cover ('great originality of line and image'), contains selections from all the earlier volumes and a group of new poems, 'Fin de Siécle' (1988–89), highlighted by the poignant 'Tiananmen Square'. *The Winter Baby* explores an entirely new landscape, peopled now with recognisable figures. The shadowy, anonymous personae of 'Maidenland' have given way to real flesh and blood – 'the winter baby' herself, Katharine Margot Toohey; the poets Doug Stewart and Bob FitzGerald, who like to sit with backs against a wall; Donna, who has done the Assertiveness Course at the Tech.; and an MP caught off-guard in a morning interview. 'Maidenland', valid and justifiable as it undoubtedly once seemed to its creator, has faded and the poet is content to accept the change:

> Poems about poems don't seem
> as abstract as once they did.

In *Acoustic Shadow*, the tone is assured, the commentary confident, the effect crisp, lucid, controlled. An acute observer of the contemporary scene, Maiden links local politicians (Joan Kirner, Janet Powell, Cleary of Wills) with those larger on the world stage (Nelson Mandela, George Bush, Saddam Hussein), blends local radical feminists with overseas terrorists (the Locherbie disaster) and allows bulls at the Sydney Show to share the spotlight with the travelling Guggenheim Exhibition. There are many family-oriented poems. Perhaps the most entertaining poem is the long 'Guarding the Cenotaph'; a high-school cadet stands guard in the black hours before dawn against the possible incursions of the 'Rape-in-War' protestors. He ultimately confronts a lone protestor, a young university girl who wants to spray four lines of Elizabeth Riddell's 'The Soldier in the Park' on the Memorial. He convinces her to settle for a single phrase from Kenneth Slessor and they depart to the beach to celebrate their own encounter.

Makar, a magazine of new writing published by Makar Press, ran 1960–80, edited successively by Graham Rowlands, Martin Duwell and Rodney Wissler. It began as the quarterly magazine of the English Society of the University of Queensland, its title using the Middle Scots form of the word 'maker', meaning poet. In 1972 one of the quarterly editions was replaced by three small books of verse which inaugurated the Gargoyle Poets series, the name deriving from the University of Queensland's gargoyles, four of which had been depicted on *Makar*'s covers. With Martin Duwell as general editor, the Gargoyle Poets series included works by Graham Rowlands, Alan Wearne, Richard Packer, Peter Annand, Antigone Kefala, Rae Desmond Jones, Kris Hemensley, Graeme Curtis, John Griffin, Stephanie Bennett, Eric Beach, Carol Novack, John Tranter, Shelton Lea, Philip Neilsen and Jennifer Maiden. *Makar* also conducted a series of interviews with significant contemporary writers; some of those interviews (and others unpublished in the journal) were incorporated into *A Possible Contemporary Poetry* (1982) edited by Duwell.

MALOUF, David (1934–   ), born Brisbane of Lebanese and English parents, was educated at the University of Queensland. He lived in Europe 1959–68, and worked for a time as a relief teacher in London before taking up a permanent teaching position at Birkenhead. He taught English at the University of Sydney 1968–77, but now devotes himself to full-time writing, living partly in Australia and partly in southern Tuscany. Well known as a poet, Malouf has published the volumes of verse *Bicycle and Other Poems* (1970), published in New York with the title *The Year of the Foxes and Other Poems* (1979), *Neighbours in a Thicket* (1974), *Poems 1975–76* (1976), *Wild Lemons* (1980), *First Things Last* (1980), *Selected Poems* (1981), *Selected Poems* (1991) and *David Malouf: Poems 1959–89* (1992). He has also written the novels *Johnno* (1975), *An Imaginary Life* (1978), *Harland's Half-Acre* (1984), *The Great World* (1990) and *Remembering Babylon* (1993); four novellas, *Child's Play*, which was first published in 1981 with *Fly Away Peter* (titled here *The Bread of Time to Come*) and republished in 1982 with two other novellas, *The Prowler* and *Eustace* (the retitled *Fly Away Peter* was also published separately in 1982); a group of autobiographical essays, *12 Edmonstone Street*

(1985); a play, *Blood Relations* (1988); and a collection of short stories, *Antipodes* (1985). Malouf also contributed verse to the collection *Four Poets* (1962) and has edited an anthology of Australian verse, *Gesture of a Hand* (1975) and, with others, *We Took Their Orders and Are Dead* (1975). He contributed to the collection *New Currents in Australian Writing* (1978) and is the author of the libretto of Richard Meale's opera *Voss*, which is based on Patrick White's novel, and of *Baa Baa Black Sheep: A Jungle Tale* (1993), the libretto for an opera with music by Michael Berkeley. *David Malouf* (1990), edited by James Tulip in the UQP Australian Authors series includes *Johnno*, short stories, poems, essays and an interview.

An exceptionally diverse writer, Malouf is concerned with certain fundamental, consistent and unifying themes: the relationships between past and present, continuity and change, animal and human, and the role of language as a mediator of experience. Drawn by the force of his own early experience, and regional in his preoccupations in that much of his poetry and fiction re-creates his childhood in Brisbane, Malouf is nevertheless thoroughly European in his interests and attitudes. The linked essays of *12 Edmonstone Street* form one of Malouf's most revealing and subtle studies of the relation between place and self. Analytical rather than nostalgic, the collection explores ways of seeing and knowing and the roles played by architecture, landscape, region and cultural grouping.

Malouf's verse, distinguished by arresting images and an urbane, dispassionate tone, shows the same delight in concrete detail and the same interest in the immediacy and tenacity of the past as his prose fiction. Language is once again celebrated as bridging past and present, change and permanence, the perceiving 'eye' and the material object, the individual life and the totality of things. Describing the poet in 'A Poet Among Others' as one 'holding/to the is-ness of things', Malouf has sometimes been compared to Wallace Stevens although his work resists categories. If European and American roots are revealed as powerful creative forces, childhood experience and the distinctive cultural and historical inheritances that make up his exotic Australia are equally powerful.

Malouf has won numerous awards, including the 1974 Grace Leven Prize, the 1974 Foundation for Australian Literary Studies Award, and the Australian Literature Society's Gold Medal in 1974 for *Neighbours in a Thicket*; the NSW Premier's Literary Award in 1979 for *An Imaginary Life*; the *Age* Book of the Year Award for 1982 for *Fly Away Peter*; and the Australian Literature Society's (now ASAL's) Gold Medal in 1983 for *Child's Play* and *Fly Away Peter*. *The Great World* won the 1991 Miles Franklin Award, the Adelaide Festival Award and two international awards, the 1991 Commonwealth Prize for fiction and the Prix Femina Étranger in France for the best foreign novel. *Antipodes* won the Vance Palmer Prize for fiction in the Victorian Premier's 1985 Literary Awards. *Remembering Babylon* won the NSW Premier's Prize for fiction in 1993. In 1988 Malouf was awarded the inaugural Pascall Prize (the richest literary prize in Australia) for excellence in creative writing. Malouf was made AO in 1987. His work is the subject of studies by Philip Neilsen (1990), Karin Hansson (1991) and Ivor Indyk (1993).

'Man from Ironbark, The', one of A.B. Paterson's most humorous ballads, was published in the *Bulletin* (December 1892). A city barber, who pretends to cut the throat of the man from Ironbark, gets more than he bargains for when the bushman, holding his throat to 'save his vital spark', wrecks the barber's shop. In Ironbark the oft-told story reinforces traditional bush suspicion of the city and leads to a pronounced fashion in beards.

'Man from Snowy River, The', first published in the *Bulletin* (April 1890), is the title poem of A.B. Paterson's first collection *The Man from Snowy River and Other Verses* (1895), the most successful volume of poetry ever published in Australia. Other well-known Paterson poems in the collection include 'Clancy of the Overflow', 'The Man from Ironbark', 'A Bush Christening' and 'The Travelling Post Office'. Paterson's story of the Snowy River poem's origin is that it was not based on a specific event but was written to describe the cleaning up of wild horses in his district. Wanting to create a character who could ride better than anybody else he 'naturally' chose a man from the Snowy mounted on a typical horse of the district, a half-thoroughbred mountain pony. Various names have been suggested in an attempt to identify the original Man from Snowy River; they include Jim Troy, Jack Riley, whose grave in the Corryong cemetery has a tablet naming him as Paterson's character, Owen Cummins, Jim Spencer, Jack Clarke and Lachie Cochrane. Probably Australia's most famous poem, 'The Man from Snowy River' tells of a hectic chase after the valuable colt from 'Old Regret' who had broken out of his station yard and joined the wild bush horses. A select band of horsemen gather at the homestead to take part in the chase; among them is 'a stripling on a small and weedy beast' who is at first excluded but is finally allowed to join the hunt because Clancy of the Overflow indicates that he and his horse come from the Snowy River country, a sure sign of courage and skill. The wild horses flee to the shelter of the mountains and when the pursuing riders fail to turn them before they reach the summit of the first mountain, the colt's owner angrily stops the chase, declaring 'We may bid the mob good day/ No man can hold them down the other side'. The Man from Snowy River has other ideas. At breakneck speed he gallops his horse down the steep mountain side, runs the mob relentlessly until 'cowed and beaten' they are brought back single-handedly by him to the station. Around the hills of Kosciusko the ride becomes a legend; with its combination of courage, daredevilry and horsemanship, qualities much prized in rural Australia from pioneer times, the ride has also become part of Australian legend. A highly successful Australian film was shown in 1982. A series of paintings inspired by the film, which illustrate the poem line by line, was done by Robert Lovett in 1984.

MANIFOLD, J.S. (John Streeter) (1915–85) was born in Melbourne into one of the oldest and richest rural families of western Victoria. After an education at the University of Cambridge, where he was a friend of the poet David Campbell, he joined the Communist Party and was later employed as editor-translator by a German publishing firm in the Rhineland. During the Second World War he was in the British army intelligence corps. By 1949, when he returned with his English wife to Australia, he was recognised in England and the USA as a rising literary star. His Communist Party allegiance caused family difficulties, so Manifold left Victoria to live in Brisbane. He became occupied with freelance writing, the composition and teaching of music, the collection and recording of bush songs and ballads and the establishment of the Realist Writers group. Manifold's early books of poetry are *Verses 1930–1933* (1933), *The Death of Ned Kelly and Other Ballads* (1941), *Trident* (1944, with David Martin and Hubert Nicholson) and *Selected Verse* (1946). After his return to Australia he produced *Nightmares and Sunhorses* (1961) and *Op. 8: Poems 1961–69* (1971). His *Collected Verse* was published simultaneously in 1978 with Rodney Hall's *J.S. Manifold: An Introduction to the Man and His Work*; his volume *On My Selection* (1983) includes his old favourites and a number of new poems. His interest in bush ballads and songs led to *Bandicoot Ballads* (1953), broadside forms of Australian folksongs which were set to music and sung at the weekly music nights at Manifold's house in Wynnum, Brisbane; *The Violin, the Banjo & the Bones: An Essay on the Instruments of Bush Music* (1957); *The Queensland Centenary Pocket Songbook* (1959), of which he was chief editor; and the popular, much-reprinted *The Penguin Australian Song Book* (1964), which includes musical scores and notes on provenance. In 1964 he published *Who Wrote the Ballads? Notes on Australian Folksong*, an important book on the origins of Australian folk-song and balladry. Manifold was an important but neglected poet. His preference was for the lyric, especially in the style of the seventeenth century; for satire, often aggressive and violent; for lively, swaggering verse set, with touches of a Byronic romanticism, in an Australian Arcadia; and for war poetry. His elegy 'The Tomb of Lt. John Learmonth A.I.F.' is perhaps his best and best-known poem.

MANN, Leonard (1895–1981), born Toorak, Melbourne, worked as a clerk in the public service before serving in France in the First World War. After the war he graduated in law from the University of Melbourne and in the 1930s was secretary of the Victorian Employers' Federation. In that period he published *Flesh in Armour* (1932) and two other works of fiction, *Human Drift* (1935) and *A Murder in Sydney* (1937), as well as his first book of verse, *The Plumed Voice* (1938). In the 1940s and 1950s he was a senior public servant; after his retirement he farmed at Macclesfield in the Dandenong Ranges. In 1960 he moved to Olinda, also in the Dandenongs, and later to Inverloch in South Gippsland, locales which allowed him the privacy to write. His other volumes of poetry are *Poems from the Mask* (1941), *The Delectable Mountains* (1944) and *Elegiac and Other Poems* (1957). Less regarded as a poet than a novelist, Mann exhibits much the same attitudes in all his writing: criticism of a world order which sanctions the barbarity of war and the social and economic strictures that depress the lives of ordinary people, yet a sense of optimism about the innate worth of life itself. Rugged, prosy and careless as it sometimes is, his poetry is often strikingly effective.

MANNING, Emily (1845–90), the daughter of Sir William Manning, a prominent lawyer and politician, was born and educated in Sydney. After a period in England, when she began her career in journalism by contributing to such periodicals as C.F. Yonge's *Monthly Packet of Evening Readings*, she returned to Sydney in the early 1870s to become one of the first women to contribute regularly to Australian newspapers and journals. Marriage to Henry Heron and the subsequent birth of six children made no interruption to her prolific writing. Either anonymously or as 'Australie', she contributed to the *Sydney Morning Herald* and the *Australian Town and Country Journal* and was briefly on the staff of the *Illustrated Sydney News* and the *Sydney Mail*. She wrote on art and literature as well as on the public questions of the day but was best known as a poet; her book *The Balance of Pain and Other Poems* was published in 1877. A well-known member of Sydney society, she is featured in Ruth Bedford's *Think of Stephen* (1954) and was linked romantically with David Scott Mitchell.

MANNING, Frederic (1882–1935), born Sydney, son of Sir William Manning, four times lord mayor of that city, had a limited formal education, being taught mainly by private tutors because he suffered from bronchial asthma. He went to England for eighteen months at the age of 16, with Arthur Galton, former private secretary to Sir Robert Duff, governor of NSW. He returned to Australia with his parents but after three years was back in England and lived with Galton in Lincolnshire. Through Galton, who acted as mentor, educator and friend, Manning became devoted to a scholastic, recluse-like existence, steeping himself in literature and the classics. Before the First World War Manning published *The Vigil of Brunhild* (1907, poetry), *Scenes and Portraits* (1909, prose) and *Poems* (1910), and was a reviewer for the *Spectator*. At the outset of the war Manning took the unexpected step of joining the King's Shropshire Light Infantry Regiment as a private. He served on the Somme front in August 1916 and on the Ancre front in November. During 1917 he was a subaltern in Ireland, where the British Army had been sent to quell disturbances. Personality clashes with his fellow officers, a dislike of the pretensions of the officer class and continuing poor health led to his resigning his commission in 1918. Manning's post-war life was uneventful. He returned to an isolated existence, with study and writing his twin pursuits. He published *Eidola* (poetry) in 1917 and wrote the *Life of Sir William White* (1923), White being the designer of the first dreadnought. In 1929 *The Middle Parts of Fortune: Somme & Ancre 1916* was published anonymously, an expurgated edition appearing in 1930 as *Her Privates We* by 'Private 19022' by which name and form it was known until the original was published in 1977. Manning died of pneumonia in 1935, virtually unknown in Australia and largely neglected by critics in England after the initial surge of excitement about his novel. *The Middle Parts of Fortune* is now internationally acknowledged as one of the most comprehensive and authentic documents of the First World War. Jonathan Marwil wrote the biography *Frederic Manning: An Unfinished Life* (1988) and Verna Coleman *The Last Exquisite: A Portrait of Frederic Manning* (1990).

MANSELL, Chris (1953–   ) graduated with an economics degree from the University of Sydney. She founded *Compass*, a poetry and prose magazine, and was its editor 1978–87. A participant in the NSW Poets in Schools programme 1983–84 and lecturer in writing at the universities of Wollongong and Western Sydney, she has published several brief books of poetry, *Delta* (1978), *Heart, Head & Stone* (1982), *Redshift/Blueshift* (1988) and *Shining Like a Jinx* (1991, winner of the 1988 USA Amelia Chapbook Award). A passionate believer in the complexity of language, Mansell looks upon ambiguity and experimentation with structure as essential poetic activities. Deeply interested in the techniques of poetry, she rejects the conservatism and conformity of the past but acknowledges the vital criteria of reader accessibility – that all writing must ultimately communicate.

MARSHALL, Rocky (1924–   ), born Adelaide, left school at 14 and worked as a rural and industrial labourer, serving in the RAAF in the Second World War. It was not until his late fifties that he began writing. He travels the outback gathering tales of bush characters for his stories and his narrative poetry. At folk gatherings he is well known for his recitations and his playing of the harmonica. He has had numerous writer-in-residence stints at SA schools. His verse includes *Front Bar Politicians* (1984) and *Down the Track* (1985). He has won the Kapunda Bush Verse Award, 1984, 1986, the SA Folk Federation Song Writing Award, 1984 and the Laura Literary Award, 1989.

MARSHALL-HALL, G.W.L. (George William Louis) (1862–1915) was born in London, where he studied at the Royal College of Music. In 1888 he was appointed conductor of the choral and orchestral societies of the London Organ School, and in 1891 Ormond professor of music at the University of Melbourne. A charismatic but impetuous and volatile personality, he was frequently involved in acrimonious debates with music critics in Melbourne's newspapers. He also became well known as a conductor and in 1892 founded the Marshall-Hall Orchestra, recognised by visiting musicians as equal to European first-rank orchestras. In 1895 he established, with W.A. Laver, the University's Conservatorium of Music. In 1897 he published two booklets of verse, *Hymn to Sydney* and *A Book of Canticles*, neither of which attained a circulation of fifty copies, but which succeeded in offending large numbers of citizens by their alleged eroticism. His next collection, *Hymns, Ancient and Modern* (1898), aroused ill-founded claims of irreverence and lasciviousness, and prompted the University council to dismiss him, an action which sparked an intense controversy. He subsequently established a private conservatorium in East Melbourne, the Marshall-Hall Conservatorium. In 1914 he was again appointed to the Ormond Chair but died shortly afterwards. He also published two historical tragedies, *Aristodemus* (1900) and *Bianca Capello* (1906); another collection of verse, *To Irene* (1896); and wrote both music and libretti for three operas. At his death, Sir Herbert Brookes published a part-prose, part-verse elegy in his memory, *At the Graveside*. Thérèse Radic published *G.W.L. Marshall-Hall: Portrait of a Lost Crusader* (1982), an introduction to the Marshall-Hall collection of the Grainger Museum, which includes a brief biography of Marshall-Hall.

MARSHALL-STONEKING, Billy (1947–   ), born and raised in the USA, came to Australia in the early 1970s to teach, first at Lake Koorat High School. He spent some time at Yandamincka in the NT, then moved to Papunya in Central Australia. He had a long association with the Pintupi people of Central Australia making several significant documentary films (he also went to film school in Sydney) including *Desert Stories* (1984) and *Nosepeg's Movie* (1988). Poet, playwright, screenwriter, he wrote *Lasseter: The Making of a Legend* (1985), a substantial work on Harold Bell Lasseter of the Lost Reef fame, and was co-writer of the ABC TV series *Stringer* (1988). Active in performance poetry, he won the Bill Harney, 1988 Poetry Prize for his poem, 'Seasons of Fire'. His book *Singing the Snake*, consisting of poems from the Western Desert 1979–1988, was published in 1990 and a play, *Sixteen Words for Water*, dealing with Ezra Pound, in 1991. His 'auto-fictography' *Taking America out of the Boy* was published in 1993.

MARTIN, A.P. (Arthur Patchett) (1851–1902), born Kent, England, was brought to Australia in 1852. A member of the Victorian public service, he took an active role in Melbourne's literary life and was editor of the *Melbourne Review* from its inception in 1876 until he left for London in 1882 to work as a journalist. Martin edited three anthologies which included contributions from prominent Australian writers, *An Easter Omelette* (1879), *Oak-bough and Wattle-blossom* (1888) and *Over the Sea* (1891); wrote one of the earliest surveys of Australian literature, *The Beginnings of an Australian Literature* (1898); the historical accounts *Australia and the Empire* (1889) and *True Stories from Australasian History* (1893), and a biography of Robert Lowe (1893). A composer of conventional, romantic verse, he contributed to various anthologies such as *Hash* (1877), *The 'Vagabond' Annual* (1877) and *Under the Gum Tree* (1890); and published three collections, *Lays of Today* (1878), *Fernshawe* (1882) and *The Withered Jester* (1895). *Fernshawe*, which includes some prose sketches, reprints material from the *Melbourne Review* and other journals, e.g. 'Two Australian Poets' (on Adam Lindsay Gordon and J.B. Stephens). He also wrote a book of verse and fiction, *Sweet Girl Graduate* (1876). His wife was Harriette Anne Martin.

MARTIN, C.E.M. (Catherine Edith Macauley) (1847–1937), born on the Isle of Skye, was the daughter of Samuel Nicholson Mackay, a crofter, and Janet Mackay. In 1855 the family arrived in Adelaide and moved to Naracoorte, presumably to help work pastoral properties belonging to other Highland families. The death of Samuel in about 1856 was a major blow. Little is known of Catherine Martin's education, but she appears to have gained a knowledge of French and German. By the early 1870s she was living in Mount Gambier, where she ran a school with her sister Mary. From at least 1868 she published poetry and verse translations in the Mount Gambier and Adelaide newspapers and in 1874, under the initials M.C., her first book, *The Explorers and Other Poems*. After moving shortly afterwards to Adelaide, where she became friendly with Catherine Spence, she published what appears to be her first novel, *The Moated Grange*, in 1877. In the same year she took a position as a clerk in the Education Department but lost it in 1885, possibly as a result of discrimination. She married Frederick Martin in 1882 and lived for a time at the Alma gold-mine near Waukaringa where Frederick was the accountant. This experience provided her with material for her novel, *The Silent Sea* (1892). Her best known novel, *An Australian Girl*, had been published anonymously in 1890. Between 1890–1904 and 1904–7 the Martins travelled extensively in Europe. After Frederick Martin died in 1909 Catherine made several more trips abroad and continued to take a lively interest in literature, social issues and international relations. Her last novel, *The Incredible Journey* (1923), was published under her own name. Extremely reticent, Martin left little in the way of biographical or bibliographical records. Her work, popular with her contemporaries, was subsequently neglected, although two of her novels, *An Australian Girl* and *The Incredible Journey*, were republished in 1987. Her verse collection includes a long narrative poem, 'The Explorers', on the Burke and Wills story, which includes an idyllic vision of the Australian future, as well as some ballads and lyrics and translations from Herder, Goethe, Schiller and other European poets.

MARTIN, David (1915–   ) was born Ludwig Detsinyi into a Jewish family in Hungary and subsequently changed his name by deed poll. He was brought up in Germany, a country for which he has ambivalent feelings and which he left at 17. After some time in Holland, where he worked on the reclamation of the Zuider Zee, and a year in Palestine, where he lived on a kibbutz, he served as a first-aid orderly in the International Brigade in Spain 1937–38. In 1938 he settled in London, where he worked for the *Daily Express* and later for the European service of the BBC. He married Richenda Powell, a schoolteacher and writer, in 1941. He was literary editor of *Reynolds News* 1945–47, and foreign correspondent in India for the *Daily Express* 1948–49. In 1949 he visited Australia, was impressed by the peaceful, extrovert life, and decided to stay. For many years a member of the Communist Party, Martin left it in 1956 but retains his left-wing sympathies.

Although German is his native language, Martin began writing verse in English in the 1940s and had established a reputation as a poet, short-story writer, novelist and playwright before his arrival in Australia. He has published eight collections of verse, *Battlefields and Girls* (1942), *Trident* (1944, with Hubert Nicholson and John Manifold), *From Life* (1953), *Rob the Robber* (1954, under the pseudonym 'Spinifex'), *Poems of David Martin 1938–1958* (1958), *Spiegel the Cat* (1961), *The Gift* (1966) and *The Idealist* (1968). His verse has also appeared in numerous anthologies including *Eight by Eight* (1963) and *Modern Australian Writing* (1966). He has written six novels, *Tiger Bay* (1946), *The Stones of Bombay* (1949), *The Young Wife* (1962), *The Hero of Too* (1965, published in New York as *The Hero of the Town*), *The King Between* (1966, published in New York as *The Littlest Neutral*) and *Where a Man Belongs* (1969); two collections of short stories, *The Shoes Men Walk In* (1946) and *Foreigners* (1981); two autobiographical narratives, *Fox On My Door* (1987) and *My Strange Friend* (1991); numerous books for children; and a collection of verse for children, *I Rhyme My Time* (1980). In *Armed Neutrality for Australia* (1984) he has projected a radically different Australian defence policy. As well as numerous essays and reviews, he has edited two collections of verse, *Rhyme and Reason* (1944) and *New World, New Song* (1955); written a travel book, *On the Road to Sydney* (1970); and provided the text for a collection of photographs on migrant life in Australia, *I'll Take Australia* (1978). He was made AO in 1988 and in 1991 won the Patrick White Award.

Martin's verse has moved from simple and stirring revolutionary themes that address 'all who love life and peace above war and death' *(From Life)* to the more personal, lyrical and complex. His predilection for humorous satire emerges in some shorter poems and in *The Idealist*, a narrative about a Reverend Eric Green who chooses to live literally as a Christian. His comic versatility is seen at its best in *Spiegel the Cat*, a narrative poem based on a tale by the nineteenth-century Swiss writer Gottfried Keller.

MARTIN, Philip (1931–   ), born Richmond, Melbourne, graduated from the University of Melbourne in 1958 and has taught at Monash University, Melbourne. Critic, translator and script-writer for radio and television, Martin is probably best known as a poet. His volumes of poetry include *Voice Unaccompanied* (1970), *A Bone*

Flute (1974), *From Sweden: Translations and Poems* (1979), *A Flag for the Wind* (1982) and *New and Selected Poems* (1988). Martin was an important influence on Bruce Dawe in the 1950s.

MAS, Joan (1926–74), born Sydney as Joan Morgan, was a freelance writer for the ABC and was for a time editor of *Poetry Magazine*. She contributed verse to numerous Australian anthologies and periodicals as well as to overseas journals, and published two collections *Isis in Search* (1966) and *The Fear and the Flowering* (1975).

MATHEW, Ray (1929–   ), born Sydney, was a NSW schoolteacher (1949–51), a freelance journalist (1951–52), a member of the CSIRO (1952–54) and a tutor and lecturer with the University of Sydney (1955–60). In 1961 he left Australia, has subsequently lived in London, Italy and New York and now lives permanently in the USA where he is a freelance writer and art critic. One of Australia's most enterprising playwrights of the 1950s, Mathew wrote a series of experimental dramas which anticipate a number of themes and modes used by writers of the late 1960s renaissance. His published plays include *We Find the Bunyip* in *Khaki, Bush and Bigotry* (1968), *The Bones of My Toe* in *Australian One-Act Plays, Book One* (1962), and *A Spring Song* (1961). It was his misfortune to be writing ahead of his time and he is now often classed with Peter Kenna and Jack McKinney as one of the 'lonely playwrights'. Mathew also published three volumes of verse which demonstrate his unusual verbal techniques and ability to create a well-defined regional identity: *With Cypress Pine* (1951), *Song and Dance* (1956) and *South of the Equator* (1961). His other publications include a novel, *The Joys of Possession* (1967), which is partly autobiographical and draws on his talent as social comedian, and studies of Miles Franklin (1955) and Charles Blackman (1965).

Mattara Spring Festival Poetry Prize, sponsored by the Hunter District Water Board and the University of Newcastle and under the administration of the Department of English of the University, has been awarded annually since 1981 and has come to be recognised as one of the more important annual verse prizes. In 1981 the prize was shared by Les Murray and Kevin Hart; in 1982 it was won by Peter Kocan for 'From the Private Poems of Governor Caulfield'; in 1983 by Craig Powell for 'Five Pieces for a Homecoming'; in 1984 by John A. Scott for 'St Clair'; in 1985 by Diane Fahey for 'Poem of Thanksgiving'; in 1986 by Lily Brett for 'Poland'. Later winners have included Kristophe Saknussenm, John Bennett, Gabrielle Davieu, Tracy Ryan and Dorothy Hewett. Selected entries for the prize have been incorporated into anthologies: *The Members of the Orchestra and Other Poems* (1981), edited by Paul Kavanagh; *Lines from the Horizon and Other Poems* (1982), edited by Christopher Pollnitz; *Instructions for Honey Ants and Other Poems* (1983), edited by Paul Kavanagh; *Neither Nuked nor Crucified and other Poems* (1984), edited by Pollnitz; *Poem of Thanksgiving and other Poems* (1985), edited by Kavanagh; *An Inflection of Silence* (1986), edited by Pollnitz; *Properties of the Poet* (1987); *Pictures from an Exhibition* (1989); and *The Sea's White Edge* (1991), the last three edited by Kavanagh. In 1991 a new sponsor, Butterfly Books, the publishing house established by Ross Blackwood, lent its support to Mattara.

MATTHEWS, Harley (1889–1968), born Harry Matthews, at St Leonards, Sydney, served in the First World War at Gallipoli and in Egypt and France. Although he was qualified as a solicitor and had experience as a journalist, he became a vigneron at Moorebank near Sydney in 1922; his vineyard was a popular gathering-place for writers in the 1930s. Suspected of being a member of the Australia First movement, Matthews was imprisoned for six months in 1942; cleared by the royal commission into the movement in 1945, he was awarded £700 compensation. He spent the remainder of his life on a small farm at Ingleburn on the outskirts of Sydney.

Matthews published several books of verse, the first two of which (1912, 1916) had the same title, *Under the Open Sky*, but contained mostly different poems. To *Trio* (1931), which he shared with Kenneth Slessor and Colin Simpson, he contributed the Gallipoli narrative poem 'Two Brothers'. One of his best early poems, *The Breaking of the Drought*, was published as a separate pamphlet in 1940. *Vintage* (1938), a group of four war poems and four lyrics, also contained 'Two Brothers'. His best book of mostly lyrical verse, *Patriot's Progress* (1965), reflects Matthews's independent spirit, love of the rural scene and scorn for convention and materialism. His two books of short stories are *Saints and Soldiers* (1918) and *Wet Canteen* (1939). He also edited an anthology of short stories, *Pillar to Post* (1944).

'MAURICE, Furnley' (Frank Wilmot) (1881–1942), born Collingwood, Melbourne, published most of his work under the pseudonym 'Furnley Maurice', a combination of the names of two of his favourite Melbourne haunts, Ferntree Gully and Beaumaris. Inclined to nationalism and radicalism by his background, 'Furnley Maurice' published his first verses in Bernard O'Dowd's radical journal *Tocsin*. He worked for thirty-five years, from errand boy to manager, in Cole's Book Arcade in Melbourne, was active in the Melbourne Literary Club which sponsored the magazine *Birth*, printed on his own treadle press, was a member of Louis Esson's Pioneer Players, became the successful manager of Melbourne University Press, helped to establish the Victorian branch of the FAW, was on the advisory board of the CLF and presented the fund's inaugural lectures on Australian literature at the University of Melbourne. 'Maurice's' early poetry, *Some Verses* (1903) and *Some More Verses* (1904), are home-made booklets produced on an old hand printing press which also produced his small and short-lived monthly magazine the *Microbe*. After *Unconditioned Songs* (1913) came some of 'Maurice's' most significant work, the poetry which contains his reaction to the First World War. In the poem 'To God: From the Warring Nations' and in the volume *Eyes of Vigilance* (1920) he expresses his disgust at the glamorising of war, at the pressures on young men to enlist and at the criminality of war itself. His radical-nationalist views are evident in his condemnation of Australia for departing from the nationalist dream of moulding her separate destiny to follow the European pattern of ancient hatreds between nations. During the war he also wrote, for his two small sons, some excellent children's verse, *The Bay and Padie Book* (1917). *Arrows of Longing* (1921) with its preface by Bernard O'Dowd, also reflects 'Maurice's' deep concern, with the memory of war still fresh, for the future of Australia and of the human race in general. 'Maurice' was fundamentally a townsman but he loved the bushland of the Dandenong Ranges, as his poem 'The Gully' (1925), which has been equated with Bernard O'Dowd's 'The Bush', indicates. 'Maurice's' most significant literary achievement is *Melbourne Odes* (1934). In the preface to the odes 'Maurice' expounds the principles of modern European and American poetry and stresses the need for new methods, techniques and objectives for Australian poetry. In the *Odes* 'Maurice' seeks to employ the best features of the modern movement in verse; the work is thus experimental and educational and its impact on the development of modern Australian verse, though long and perhaps still underestimated, is undoubted. Vance Palmer wrote *Frank Wilmot (Furnley Maurice)* (1942); Hugh Anderson, *Frank Wilmot (Furnley Maurice): A Bibliography and a Criticism* (1955); and F.T. Macartney, *Furnley Maurice (Frank Wilmot)* (1955). The impact of his life is also discussed in David Walker's *Dream and Disillusion* (1976), and he is one of *The Three Radicals* in W.H. Wilde's monograph of that title (1969).

MEAD, Philip (1953–), born Brisbane, and educated in Australia, England and the USA, has contributed poetry to numerous anthologies and periodicals, published the collections, *Songs from Another Country* (1975), *Be Faithful Go* (1980), *The Spring-Mire* (1982) and *This River is in the South* (1984). Poetry editor for *Meanjin* until 1994, he has taught creative writing at the University of Melbourne as Lockie fellow, and has been associated with poetry-publishing since 1972. With John Tranter he edited *The Penguin Book of Modern Australian Poetry* (1991), and with Gerald Murnane and Jenny Lee, *The Temperament of Generations: Fifty Years of Writing in Meanjin* (1990). With Alan Gould, David Brooks and Mark O'Connor, Mead was one of the founders of the journal *Canberra Poetry*. The natural landscape is often the grounding for Mead's meditative poetry, although he is concerned mostly with inward experience, the consciousness of mutability, the curious paradoxes of memory, the contradictory power and impotence of words, or the promise of meaning offered by the natural scene and doubts about its validity, as in 'Looking Towards the Major Mitchell Plateau'. In this poem the landscape offers new access to the 'inner city of the heart, overlaid by now/ with crumbled brick and dust and written words/ but still chequered with the weathers/ of the four-fold year'; but turning away from it, 'the rain at our backs/ like a coat', it is more difficult 'to know how we will live . . . What is the order of our lives? What continues to sing/ in its blessing?' Other poems take paintings, memories of a Queensland childhood, or Australian myths and historical figures as lyrical starting-points.

Meanjin, a journal known as *Meanjin Papers* (1940–47), *Meanjin* (1947–60, 1977–) and *Meanjin Quarterly* (1961–76), began in Brisbane in December 1940 with an eight-page edition of eight poems, two each by the editor, C.B. Christesen, James Picot, Brian Vrepont and Paul Grano. Bi-monthly in 1940–42, *Meanjin* has been quarterly since 1943. It takes its name from the Aboriginal words *migan* (spike) and *chagun* (earth, place, land), the composite word 'meanjin' (*mianjin*), referring to the site where Brisbane was first established. In 1945 *Meanjin* moved with Christesen to Melbourne, where the University of Melbourne gave it the home it has occupied to the present time. The constant battle for financial viability has seen *Meanjin* partly supported from Christesen's own resources then assisted by grants-in-aid from the Lockie Bequest, University of Melbourne (since 1949), from the CLF and the Literature Board, and the Ministry for the Arts, Victoria. *Meanjin* certainly owed its survival to its long-standing (1940–74) editor Clem Christesen. He was succeeded by Jim Davidson (1974–82), who changed the appearance of the magazine, introduced new features such as the regular interviews with contemporary writers, but retained much of the traditional *Meanjin* political stance and interests. In 1982 Judith Brett became editor. Perceiving *Meanjin*'s role as offering 'a broad review of ideas with a strong contemporary focus', she encouraged articles on general cultural matters as well as literary. In 1987 Jenny Lee became *Meanjin*'s fourth editor and continued the journal's traditional role as an organ of socio-political and literary comment as well as creative writing. Christina Thompson became editor in 1994. Opinions of *Meanjin*'s political leanings have ranged from a 'fellow-travelling publication' (the description of James McAuley, editor of *Meanjin*'s right-wing rival *Quadrant*) to Christesen's own phrase, 'democratic left of centre', which more accurately describes its liberal humanist stance. Other judgments have obviously differed. Financial support was withheld in 1948–49, and during the 1950s political and intellectual opposition to the *Meanjin* stance became widespread. The number and intensity of its polemical articles increased in the late 1960s with the Vietnam War, and Christesen, on his retirement in 1973, is reputed to have indicated (in a letter to Jim Cairns) his satisfaction that he did 'not allow *Meanjin* to become a right-wing *Quadrant* type of magazine'. Although *Meanjin* has regularly published or focused on overseas writing, its major literary importance has been in its publication of Australian poetry and short fiction and its establishment of a body of seminal criticism on a wide range of Australian writers. *On Native Grounds* (1968), edited by Christesen, and *Sideways from the Page* (1983), a selection of Davidson's interviews with writers, are both volumes which reprint material first published in *Meanjin*. The Meanjin Press, also associated with the journal, published several volumes in the 1940s, e.g. Judith Wright's *The Moving Image* (1948). Lynne Strahan's *Just City and the Mirrors: Meanjin Quarterly and the Intellectual Front, 1940–65*, a history of *Meanjin* and the literary life of that first quarter-century of the journal's existence, was published in 1984. In 1990 *Meanjin's* fiftieth anniversary was celebrated with the publication of *The Temperament of Generations: Fifty Years of Meanjin*, an anthology of essays, poetry, fiction and correspondence from the journal's archives, edited by Jenny Lee, Philip Mead and Gerald Murnane.

Melbourne Odes (1934) are among the most important poems of 'Furnley Maurice'. The opening ode, 'Melbourne and Memory', won the Melbourne centenary poetry competition. Other odes in the volume deal with places and events familiar in the life of the city: the Victoria Markets, the annual agricultural show and orchestral concerts in the Melbourne Town Hall. Together they represent the first attempt by an Australian poet to depict life in the modern city. 'Upon a Row of Old Boots and Shoes in a Pawnbroker's Window', with its grim account of the plight of the unemployed of the 1930s Depression and its macabre description of the ghostly march of the boot-pawners, is a powerful radical commentary on the economic misery and injustice of the time.

MEREDITH, Louisa Anne (1812–95), born Louisa Anne Twamley at Birmingham, England, married her cousin Charles Meredith in 1839 and went with him to NSW, where he had pastoral interests. In 1840 they moved to Tasmania, where Charles was a successful member of parliament 1860–79. An energetic, talented and strongly independent woman, Louisa wrote and illustrated several autobiographical books which are vividly descriptive of colonial life and society and native flora and fauna, including *Notes and Sketches of New South Wales* (1844), *My Home in Tasmania* (1852) and *Over the Straits; A Visit to Victoria* (1861). She also published numerous illustrated books of poetry, e.g. *Some of My Bush Friends in Tasmania* (1860), *Our Island Home* (1879) and *Bush Friends in Tasmania, Native Flowers, Fruits and Insects* (1891); poetry for children, e.g. *Waratah Rhymes for Young Australia* (1891); and several novels including *Phoebe's Mother* (1869), *Tasmanian Friends and Foes, Feathered, Furred, and Finned: A Family Chronicle of Country Life* (1880), which is of most relevance to Australia and includes coloured plates from her own drawings, and *Nellie* (1882). It has been said of her that she was 'a poet in feeling, an artist by instinct, a naturalist by force of circumstances, a keen botanist, and an ardent lover of landscape scenery'. She won numerous medals and prizes for her paintings at exhibitions in England, Australia and India and after the death of Charles Meredith was awarded a small pension by the Tasmanian government. She may well have been the first person granted a government pension in Australia for services to science, literature and the arts. Vivienne Rae Ellis's biography *Louisa Anne Meredith: A Tigress in Exile* (1979) gives a vivid impression of this resourceful and talented woman.

MICHAEL, James Lionel (1824–68), born London, was educated in languages and the arts and entered the legal profession in England. He came to Australia in the gold-rush period but preferred the more comfortable existence of the Sydney legal world to a stint on the goldfields. He became a member of the Sydney literary coterie of the day, contributing verse, essays and literary criticism to the *Month*, edited by James Sheridan Moore, and the *Southern Cross*, edited by D.H. Deniehy. He extended patronage to the fledgeling poet Henry Kendall, allowing him access to his ample library and employing him as a clerk. Near bankruptcy, Michael went to Grafton in 1861 to open a legal practice but died there by drowning. He published a collection of lyric poems, *Songs Without Music* (1857) and a semi-autobiographical narrative poem, *John Cumberland* (1860). His poetry is pleasantly smooth and graceful but devoid of originality or significant theme. Kendall wrote two poems in tribute to Michael after his death, 'James Lionel Michael' and 'Lines to J.L. Michael'. Sheridan Moore published *The Life and Genius of James Lionel Michael* (1868). Geoff Page wrote a series of short poems reflecting on Michael's life and character and pondering on the puzzle of his death; titled 'From the Life and Death of James Lionel Michael', the poems were published in *Instructions for Honey Ants*, the 1983 Mattara Spring Festival anthology. Ian McLaren has published *James Lionel Michael: a Comprehensive Bibliography* (1989).

MICKLE, Alan (1883–1969), born Melbourne, lived mostly as a full-time writer, although he developed an interest in painting late in life. His publications include eight collections of philosophical essays; several volumes of reminiscences; two novels, *The Pilgrimage of Peer* (1938) and *The Execution of Newcome Bowles* (1948); a book of sporting reminiscences, *After the Ball* (1959); and six collections of poetry, of which only the juvenile verse has continued to receive attention, *The Poor Poet and the Beautiful Lady* (1931), *Pemmican Pete and Other Verses* (1934), *The Great City* (1935), *The Loony Cove* (1940), *Mine Own Land* (1944) and *The Ballad of Flatfoot Fred* (1944).

'Midsummer Noon in the Australian Forest, A', published in the *Empire*, 1858, is Charles Harpur's best-known and most-anthologised descriptive poem. Although often praised for its creation of the hushed somnolent atmosphere of the summer noonday in the Australian bush, the poem lacks Australian definition.

MILLETT, John (1921–   ) served as a RAAF air gunner in Britain during the Second World War, and subsequently practised as a lawyer in Sydney and on the Gold Coast. He has contributed poetry to numerous Australian and international periodicals and has published several collections, *Calendar Adam* (1971), *The Silences* (1973), *Love Tree of the Coomera* (1975), *West of the Cunderang* (1977), *Tail Arse Charlie* in *Poetry Australia* (1982) and as a chapbook in the USA in 1983, *Come Down Cunderang* (1985) and *The Nine Lives of Big Meg O'Shannessy* (1990). He has also written a play with Grace Perry, *Last Bride at Longsleep* (1981), and an eight-part verse novella, *Blue Dynamite* (1987), also published as a chapbook in the USA in 1987 and adapted for stage in 1988. Another publication, *Voyeur from Australia*, was published in the USA in 1988. An elusive and strikingly individual poet, Millett has a strong sense of place and a fascination with language, which he uses with zest and dexterity. His gift for sharp imagery and his pronounced, self-conscious use of a persona add power and colour to such spiritually autobiographical sequences as *Calendar Adam* and *Love Tree of the Coomera*. *Tail Arse Charlie*, his simplest work, which was broadcast on radio in a dramatised version in 1981–82, is a powerful anti-war sequence, bolstered by photographs and records from the Australian War Memorial. Partly based on his memories of the air war, it is also evocative of the experience of all the 'old-young men' involved in the Battle of Britain. Millett was for a long period associated with *Poetry Australia*.

Modern Australian Poetry, 1920–70: A Guide to Information Sources (1979), by Herbert C. Jaffa, is a bibliographical guide covering Australian poetry from Kenneth Slessor to the new Australian poets of the late 1960s and early 1970s. Sections annotating bibliographies, bibliographic guides, background reference material, critical studies and anthologies precede author check-lists which cover the author's work and an annotated selection of bibliographical and critical material. The author sections are organised within the categories of major poets (Slessor, R.D. FitzGerald, A.D. Hope, Douglas Stewart, Judith Wright, James McAuley), important and established poets (e.g. David Campbell, Francis Webb, Les Murray), Jindyworobak poets, Angry Penguins poets, expatriate poets, other poets of the 1940s-1960s, and younger poets.

MOLL, E.G. (Ernest George) (1900–   ), born Murtoa, Victoria, was educated at schools in NSW. In 1920 he left for the USA and studied at Lawrence College, Wisconsin, and Harvard University. From 1928 to 1966 he was professor of English at the University of Oregon. Moll's verse, which is represented in numerous Australian anthologies, has appeared in several collections, including *Sedge Fire* (1927), *Native Moments* (1931), *Campus Sonnets* (1934), *Blue Interval* (1935), *Cut from Mulga* (1940), *Brief Waters* (1945), *Beware the Cuckoo* (1947), *The Waterhole* (1948), *The Lifted Spear* (1953), *Poems 1940–1955* (1957), *The Rainbow Serpent* (1962), *Briseis* (1965), *The Road to Cactus-land* (1971) and *The View From a Ninetieth Birthday* (1992). He has also written a critical study, *The Appreciation of Poetry* (1933); and *Below These Hills: The Story of a Riverina Farm* (1957), an account of his family's farm. Strongly indebted to his rural Australian experience, Moll has often been classed as a regionalist, although his work is by no means restricted to Australian subjects.

MOLONEY, Patrick (1843–1904), born Melbourne, graduated in medicine from the University of Melbourne in 1867. One of the editors of the *Australian Medical Journal* and a contributor to the *Melbourne Punch*, he wrote verse for the *Australasian* as well as a series of papers headed 'Under the Greenwood Tree'. He was a member of the Yorick Club and is recalled in Hugh McCrae's *My Father and My Father's Friends* (1935) and in *Yorick Club Reminiscences* (1911). His verse also appeared in several contemporary anthologies and his sonnet sequence, *Sonnets: Ad Innuptam*, originally published in the *Australasian* under his pseudonym 'Australis', in *An Easter Omelette* (1879), edited by A. Patchett Martin.

MOODIE HEDDLE, Enid (1904–   ), born Elsternwick, Victoria, was educated at the University of Melbourne and taught in Australia and England 1927–34. In 1935–46 she was educational adviser in Australia to Longmans Green and to William Collins and in 1947–60 educational manager for Longmans in Australia. The author or editor of more than thirty books, Enid Moodie Heddle wrote two books of verse, *Solitude* (1937) and *Sagitta Says* (1943); and *Boy on a Horse* (1957, with H.J. Samuel), the story of Adam Lindsay Gordon. She published *Australian Literature Now* (1949) and *How Australian Literature Grew* (1962) but is best known as editor of the Boomerang Books series. Moodie Heddle edited the Australian editions of *The Poet's Way* (1942, 1943, 1944), *Discovering Poetry* (1956, 1957) and *A Galaxy of Poems Old and New* (1962).

MOORE, Tom Inglis (1901–79), born Camden, NSW, was educated at the universities of Sydney and Oxford and taught in the USA and at the University of the Philippines (1928–31). In 1934–40 he was on the staff of the *Sydney Morning Herald* as reviewer and leader-writer. After service in the Second World War he joined the Canberra University College, later the ANU, where he remained until his retirement in 1966. He was a long-serving member of the CLF advisory board and active in the FAW, the ASA and the English Association. His creative writing includes a novel, *The Half Way Sun: A Tale of the Philippine Islands* (1935); a radio play in verse, *We're Going Through* (1945), and three books of verse, *Adagio in Blue* (1938), *Emu Parade: Poems from Camp* (1941) and *Bayonet and Grass* (1957). As an editor he published *Best Australian One-Act Plays* (1937, with William Moore); *Australia Writes: An Anthology* (1953); *Henry Kendall* (1957); *Poetry in Australia* (1964, in collaboration with Douglas Stewart); and *Letters of Mary Gilmore* (1980, in collaboration with W.H. Wilde). His critical writing includes *Modern American Poetry* (1935), *Six Australian Poets* (1942), *The Misfortunes of Henry Handel Richardson* (1957), *Mary Gilmore: A Tribute* (1965, with others), and *Social Patterns in Australian Literature* (1971).

Moore's poetry, largely of love and war, appeals because of its attractive imagery, its spontaneity of feeling, whether of joy in loving or anger at the plight of a war-torn world, and its sprinkling of Australian symbols to explain and illustrate universal attitudes. His valuable contribution as a pioneer teacher of Australian literature and as one of its earliest scholarly critics was recognised when he was made OBE in 1958.

MORAN, Rod (1952–), born Victoria, lived for part of his boyhood in WA. After graduating BA Dip. Ed. from the University of Melbourne he became a teacher and later a lecturer in curriculum and communications at the Hawthorn Institute of Education. He returned to WA in 1986 and is a full-time writer and freelance journalist. Moran has published three books of poetry, *High Rise Sniper* (1981, the first of the Artlook Australian Poets series), *Against the Era* (1988) and *Listening to the Train Passing* (1994). Moran believes that the human condition is the valid subject 'of every possible form of poetry'. Where that human condition is under threat, as in the Vietnam War, in world-wide terrorism, in political and social corruption, in nuclear experimentation, Moran's poetry is quick in its defence. In his own personal observation of the human condition wherever he meets it – in country pubs and towns, in his travels on the road, in the bleakness of a city winter, among a group of 'Carlton poets' or friends – literary intellectuals – his perceptive eye (coupled with rich and inventive language) provides many memorable cameos: 'Farms with eyes the colour of dust'; 'The pied cormorant is a clucking priest'; 'Leather-clad, an ambush of crows/Inspects a broken carcass'. A poet of wide-ranging interests, and essentially optimistic by nature, Moran writes of the war histories of the men in his family, of his delight in nature, friends and family, of the typical WA obsession with water. Perhaps his strongest and best poem is 'What Waits Behind the Shadow', an affirmation of the essential 'thisness' of things, that what *is* is real, 'The object and its full silence', 'the core design/faithful to its purpose', 'the ancient promise of beauty/the chemistry of all ineffable hope'. A skilled 'performance' poet and an energetic publicist for poetry, Moran was the poetry editor in 1995 for the National Library's magazine, *Voices*.

MORANT, Harry Harbord (?Edwin Henry Murrant) (?1864–1902), whose death by firing-squad at Pretoria, South Africa, 27 February 1902 provoked one of the most prolonged controversies in Australian military history, was a minor balladist of the 1890s. His origins are somewhat uncertain. By his own account he was born at Bideford, Devon, in 1865, son of Admiral Sir Digby Morant. Subsequent research (*In Search of Breaker Morant, Balladist, and Bushveldt Carbineer* by Margaret Carnegie and Frank Shields, 1979) strongly suggests that he was Edwin Henry Murrant, born at Bridgwater, Somerset, 9 December 1864, son of Edwin Murrant and his wife Catherine, née Riely; that he sailed for Australia from Plymouth 1 April 1883; that he landed in Townsville in northern Queensland in June 1883; that he took a job with a travelling rodeo and ended up in Charters Towers where, on 13 March 1884 he married a Daisy May O'Dwyer who was later to become the well-known Australian identity Daisy Bates. The marriage supposedly lasted a few brief weeks, Morant, by which name he was known in April 1884 according to Charters Towers court records, taking off on a nomadic life of droving and horse-breaking. His skill and daring as a horse-breaker and rider led to his nickname 'The Breaker'. He developed a widespread reputation for riotous and unpredictable behaviour, but his horsemanship, swagger, poetry, and cheerful nature generally won him more friends than enemies. He enlisted in the SA Mounted Rifles to get to the Boer War and ultimately joined the Bushveldt Carbineers, dubbed 'the Buccaneers', a cavalry regiment especially formed to combat the Boer commandos. After the death and mutilation of his close friend Captain Hunt at the hands of the Boers, Morant was court-martialled with several others for the murder of some Boer prisoners and a German missionary, and executed with another Australian, P.J. Handcock. Morant and his associates, although almost certainly guilty of the charges against them, came to be regarded by many as pawns in the game of war and politics sacrificed by Kitchener to appease the German government or expended in an effort to secure a cease-fire in the war.

Although Morant's literary talent was meagre, the bizarre circumstances of his life and death have added piquancy to the public image of him as a poet. His first verses, 'A Night Thought', signed by 'The Breaker', were published in the *Bulletin* in 1891. During the next ten years he wrote about sixty poems for the *Bulletin* with occasional contributions to the Sydney *World News* and the *Windsor and Richmond Gazette*. Best known of his verses are 'Since the Country Carried Sheep', 'West by North Again', 'Who's Riding Old Harlequin Now?', 'Stewed' and 'Beyond His Jurisdiction'; 'Butchered to Make a Dutchman's Holiday', written in Pretoria Gaol on the eve of his execution, was featured on the *Bulletin* Red Page 19 April 1902. *The Poetry of 'Breaker' Morant: from the Bulletin 1891–1903* was published in 1980 with a foreword by David McNicoll. Although Morant did not publish a volume of verse, selections of his work are included in some of the books that have been written about him. He was one of the multitude of 'back-block bards' of the 1890s; his verse is lively, breezy, and entertaining, and conveys in an ebullient, rough-and-ready fashion both the flavour of outback life and the laconically humorous, devil-may-care attitude of the Australian bushman of legend. A notable Australian film, *Breaker Morant*, focusing on the events in South Africa, was released in 1980. Paintings by Pro Hart illustrated a Breaker Morant series which was compiled by Dawn Ross and published in 1981. Kit Denton, who wrote *The Breaker* (1973), a fictionalised account of Morant's exploits, has reversed his attitude to his subject in *Closed File* (1983), where Morant is assessed as a vicious, amoral type. Other works on Morant include F.M. Cutlack's *Breaker Morant* (1962), Frank Fox's *Bushman and Buccaneer, Harry Morant* (1902) and George R. Witton's *Scapegoats of the Empire* (1907), Witton being one of the Bushveldt Carbineers who was imprisoned with Morant and later released from an English prison.

MORGAN, Mal (1936–   ), of Polish-Jewish extraction, was born in England and came to Australia at the age of 12. Now a pharmacist at Melbourne Royal Children's Hospital, he was one of the 'underground' poets of the late 1960s 'New Poetry' revolution in Australia, attending poetry readings at La Mama run by Kris Hemensley and Michael Dugan in 1969 and involved with the small poetry magazine explosion – *Crosscurrents, Our Glass, Great Auk, Flagstones, Free Poetry, Parachute, Mindscape* – of those years. Seldom included in the early 'New Australian Poetry' anthologies, Morgan has in recent years become a well-known 'performance' poet; he convened La Mama Poetica poetry readings 1985–91 and edited the anthology *La Mama Poetica* (1989), has directed the Montsalvat National Poetry Festivals, and organises regular readings, frequently performing his own work. *Walking the Dogs* (1994), edited by Mal Morgan, is an anthology of poets from the Pariah Press co-operative. His publications include *Poemstones* (1976), *Statues Don't Bleed* (1984), *A Handshake with the Moon* (1987) and *Once Father and God* (1992). His poetry communicates a concern for humanity, anger at such evils as racism and delight in satirising pretentiousness and hypocrisy. For Morgan, love is the greatest worker for good. Most of his poems are brief, pointed and questioning, self-consciously Jewish in their irony and wry wisdom.

MORRIS, Myra (1893–1966), born Boort, Victoria, was brought up in the Mallee district. A freelance writer, she published verse, short stories and articles in newspapers and magazines. Her collections of verse include *England and Other Verses* (1918) and *White Magic* (1929). She also published a collection of short stories, *The Township* (1947); two novels, *The Wind on the Water* (1938) and *Dark Tumult* (1939); and edited the selected poems of 'Capel Boake' (1949). Morris's simple, rhythmic, ballad-style verses, which exuberantly reflect her love of the outdoor life, found a ready acceptance in the 1920s and 1930s.

MORRISON, R.H. (Robert Hay) (1915–   ), born South Yarra, Melbourne, the brother of Alistair Ardoch Morrison, studied modern languages at the University of Melbourne and was employed by the army as an Italian translator during the Second World War. He worked for the ABC, mostly as a radio and television State news editor, before resigning in 1968 to pursue his interests as a poet, verse translator and literary reviewer. He has published the volumes of poetry *Lyric Images* (1954), *Opus 4* (1971), *Leaf-fall* (1974), *In the Ear of Dusk* (1977), *The Secret Greenness and Other Poems* (1978), *For the Weeks of the Year* (1981), *Poems for an Exhibition* (1985) and *Poems From My Eight Lives* (1989). His other publications include translations of Mandelstam's poetry (1990) and of Pushkin's (1951) and the more general translations *Australia's Russian Poets* (1971), *Australia's Ukrainian Poets* (1973), *Australia's Italian Poets* (1976), *One Hundred Russian Poems* (1979), *Ancient Chinese Odes* (1979) and *Sonnets from the Spanish* (1980). He has also compiled a collection of verse by South Australian poets, *A Book of South Australian Verse* (1957).

MORTON, Frank (1869–1923), born England, came to Australia at the age of 16. He spent some years in Singapore and India, where he worked as a journalist, and returned to Australia in 1894. He contributed to the *Bulletin*, the *Brisbane Courier* and the Hobart *Mercury*, before moving to NZ, where he worked for the *Otago Daily Times* and, as editor, for the monthly magazine the *Triad*. While in NZ he published a collection of verse, *Laughter and Tears: Verses of a Journalist* (1908) and two novels, *The Angel of the Earthquake* (1909) and *The Yacht of Dreams* (1911). Back in Sydney by 1914, he contributed to the *Bulletin*, the *Lone Hand*, *Native Companion*, *Bookfellow* and other journals, and became the main contributor to the Australian edition of the *Triad* 1915–23. Gregarious and broad-minded, he was a familiar host to Sydney's bohemia in the 1920s. He also published the subsequent poetry collections *Verses for Marjorie* (1916), *The Secret Spring* (1919) and *Man and the Devil: A Book of Shame and Pity* (1922).

MOSES, Jack (1860–1945), born Sydney, spent most of his working life as a commercial traveller in wine, and became known on the agricultural show circuit of NSW and other States both as a salesman and as a reciter of Australian ballads; *The Bulletin Book of Humorous Verses and Recitations* (1920) was dedicated to him as a 'good Australian' who was 'for many years a *Bulletin* reciter in the bush'. One of his favourite authors was Henry Lawson, who in the poem *Joseph's Dreams* (1923) refers to Moses in stating 'my best friend was a Yid'; Moses recalled their friendship in *Henry Lawson by His Mates* (1931). A long-time contributor to the *Bulletin*, the *Sydney Mail*, *Smith's Weekly* and other journals, Moses wrote *Beyond the City Gates* (1923), a volume of sketches and poems in which he celebrates bush life as the 'matrix of our Australian nation', and *Nine Miles from Gundagai* (1938), a volume of verse; the title piece is the well-known poem about the dog on the tucker box at Gundagai. After his retirement Moses settled again in Sydney, where he was an affectionately regarded street character who distributed postcards of his poems.

Moving Image, The (1946), the first volume of poetry by Judith Wright, takes its title from Plato's 'Time is a moving image of eternity'. The title poem is a philosophical meditation on the metaphysical role of the poet as interpreter of the processes of change wrought by time. The volume includes poems celebrating her affection for New England, e.g. 'South of My Days' and others which present figures and themes from Australia's past, e.g. 'Bullocky', 'Bora Ring' and 'Remittance Man'.

MUDIE, Ian (1911–76), born Hawthorn, SA, was a freelance writer who also worked as a publisher's editor and lecturer in creative writing. Active in literary affairs, he was federal president of the FAW. In 1978 the SA FAW instituted the annual Ian Mudie Award for poetry with an Australian theme.

A prolific poet, Mudie published numerous volumes of verse, including *Corroboree* to the Sun (1940), This Is Australia (1941), The Australian Dream (1943), Their Seven Stars Unseen (1943), Poems (1945), Poems 1924–1944 (1945), The Blue Crane (1959), The North-Bound Rider (1963), winner of the Grace Leven Prize for poetry, Look, The Kingfisher (1970) and Selected Poems 1934–1974 (1976), which contains about forty uncollected poems written while he was in his early sixties. He also edited numerous works and anthologies, including Poets at War: An Anthology of Verse by Australian Servicemen (1944) and the Jindyworobak Anthology (1946); and wrote several histories.

A member of the Australia First movement and attracted to Rex Ingamells's Jindyworobak movement through his patriotism, affinity with the landscape, and concern and respect for the Aborigines and their lore, Mudie was a strident champion of the 'good old days' of pioneer Australia. Aggressively conservationist, much of his early poetry tells of a once lovely land 'turned to barrenness, made dead by the lust of men', and of once proud tribesmen, dispossessed so that their lands, 'cut up and divided by Torrens title', could be given to the White man for his 'five-roomed coffins'. 'This Land' and 'This is Australia' are representative of Mudie, the ardent nationalist, the Jindyworobak proselytiser. Sensitive also to the paradox of 'a harsh land . . . that scorches its flowers of spring', Mudie sought to employ a poetic language that captured the spirit and character of the land and the people who survived there. He settled in the main for spare, laconic and often colloquial style. At its best that style produced poetic flashes, at its worst it was prosaic and slangy. His most popular successes were the colloquial 'They'll Tell You About Me', 'Hey Blue, It's Raining', and 'I Wouldn't Be Lord Mayor'. Mudie's poetry is, however, not confined to Jindyworobak and nationalist preoccupations. The North Bound Rider, the prize-winning collection of 1963, has numerous reflections on city and suburban life. Personal lyrics are plentiful in The Blue Crane, Look, The Kingfisher and Selected Poems 1934–1974. Popular for his camaraderie, yarns and good nature, Mudie embodied much of the best and most characteristic features of the traditional bush ethos.

MUDROOROO (Colin Johnson) (1939–   ), born Narogin, WA, was raised in a Roman Catholic orphanage and had minor brushes with the law as a young man before leaving for Melbourne, where he worked for a period in the Victorian public service. Active in Aboriginal cultural affairs, he is a member of the Aboriginal Arts Unit committee of the Australia Council and was a co-founder with Jack Davis of the Aboriginal Writers, Oral Literature and Dramatists Association. He has also helped to initiate courses in Aboriginal literature at several Australian universities. After travelling widely in Australia and spending seven years in India where he lived for some time as a Buddhist monk, he settled in Bungawalbyn in northern NSW, to write full-time. A prolific writer of poetry and prose, his publications include the novels Wild Cat Falling (1965), the first novel to be published by an Aboriginal writer, Long Live Sandawara (1979), Doctor Wooreddy's Prescription for Enduring the Ending of the World (1983), Master of the Ghost Dreaming (1991), Wildcat Screaming (1992) and The Kwinkan (1993); the verse collections The Song Circle of Jacky (1986), Dalwurra (1988) and The Garden of Gethsemane (1991); a study of modern Aboriginal literature, Writing from the Fringe (1990); and an autobiographical narrative, Doin Wildcat (1988). Mudrooroo is also one of the editors of the first comprehensive anthology of Aboriginal writing, Paperbark (1988), and has written several plays including 'Big Sunday' (1987) and 'Mutjinggaba' (1989). Mudrooroo has won several awards including the Jessie Litchfield Award in 1965, the Patricia Weickhardt Award in 1980 and the WA Literary Award for poetry in 1989.

Mudrooroo's poetry, often markedly satirical of White society, combines innovative treatment of the poetic traditions of his culture with a wide range of other poetic traditions, both Eastern and Western.

Mulga Bill, the central figure in A.B. Paterson's poem 'Mulga Bill's Bicycle' published in *Rio Grande's Last Race and Other Verses* (1902), is one of Paterson's well-known comic folk-characters. Concerned to keep abreast of progress, Bill turned away 'the good old horse that served him many days' and 'caught the cycling craze'. After a brief but spectacular encounter with the 'two-wheeled outlaw', Bill ended up, with the cycle, in Dead Man's Creek. There he left it, the lesson learned: 'a horse's back is good enough, henceforth for Mulga Bill.' Mulga Bill takes his name from his habitat, the mulga, which in colloquial speech denotes the remote bush or outback. Will Ogilvie's poem 'The Mulga Mail', demonstrates how news travels through the outback via the bush telegraph.

MURDOCH, Nina (1890–1976), born Melbourne, worked first as a schoolteacher. A contributor of verse to the *Bulletin*, she won a prize for a sonnet on Canberra and subsequently published two collections, *Songs of the Open Air* (1915) and *More Songs of the Open Air* (1922). In 1914 she joined the staff of the Sydney *Sun* and transferred to the Melbourne *Sun* in 1922. Retrenched from the *Herald* in 1930, she began working in radio broadcasting, managing Children's Corner on 3LO from the inception of the ABC, and founding the children's programme 'The Argonauts', which she ran until 1934, when she moved to Adelaide. She also published three novelettes; a biographical account of Sir John Longstaff, *Portrait in Youth* (1948); and four books which reflected her keen interest in travel.

MURPHY, Edwin Greenslade (1866–1939) was born in Victoria but joined in the great gold rush to Coolgardie in WA in 1893. From prospecting he turned to journalism and the writing of topical verses, becoming, as 'Dryblower', one of the best-known and most colourful identities of the West. For forty years he wrote a column of jingles, 'Verse and Worse', for the Perth *Sunday Times.* Two collections of his verses were published, *Jarrahland Jingles* (1908) and *Dryblower's Verses 1894–1926* (1926). He also published a novel, *Sweet Boronia: A Story of Coolgardie* (1904). Unpretentious in style, his poems are humorous and full of affection for the ordinary toilers of the world; his pseudonym 'Dryblower' was the name given to the rudimentary apparatus used by miners in the waterless West to separate the gold from dirt and gravel. Murphy's personality and career are described in Arthur L. Bennett's *Dryblower Murphy. His Life and Times* (1982).

MURPHY, Peter (1945–   ), born Melbourne, works as a teacher and has published four collections of verse, *Escape Victim and Other Poems* (1974), *Seen & Unseen* (1975), *Glass Doors and Other Poems* (1977) and *Lies* (1983); and two collections of short stories, *Black Light* (1979) and *The Moving Shadow Problem* (1986).

MURRAY, Les (Leslie Allan) (1938–   ), born Nabiac in the Manning River district of the lower north coast of NSW, spent his childhood and adolescence on his grandfather's dairy farm in the nearby Bunyah district. His Murray forebears had arrived on the Manning in the 1840s and he has always been proud of both his Gaelic and pioneer Australian ancestry. A placid but solitary rural childhood ended when he was 12 with the death of his mother, an event recalled in his 'Three Poems in Memory of My Mother, Miriam Murray née Arnall'. In 1957 he began an arts degree at the University of Sydney. After four years of pursuing his own interests – usually in the Fisher Library or in the company of kindred literary spirits such as Geoffrey Lehmann and Bob Ellis – he left without a degree but with something of a reputation as a wit and an intellectual and with an attraction to Roman Catholicism, which faith he later officially embraced. In 1962 he married Budapest-born Valerie Morelli. During 1963–67 he was a translator of foreign scholarly and technical material at the ANU. In 1965, after the collaborative volume *The Ilex Tree* (with Lehmann) won the Grace Leven Prize for poetry, Murray attended the British Commonwealth Arts Festival Poetry

Conference at Cardiff. In 1967 he resigned his ANU position and lived with his wife and two children for more than a year in England and Europe. He was briefly (1970) a public servant in Canberra but returned to Sydney (Chatswood) determined to make a career as a full-time writer. Aided, over the years, by numerous Literature Board grants, several editorial positions, income from book reviews, articles and essays in newspapers and journals, and royalties and prizes from about twenty books of poetry and prose, he could be said to have adequately achieved that aim. From 1973 to 1979 he was editor of Grace Perry's *Poetry Australia*, holding the fort as long as he could against the inroads of the so-called New Poetry, of 'literary modernism', that surfaced in Australia in those years. One of his complaints about post-modernism was that it removed poetry from widespread, popular readership, leaving it the domain of a small intellectual clique. From 1976 to 1991 he was poetry editor of Angus & Robertson and in 1990 became literary editor of *Quadrant*. By 1978 his literary stature was such that he became writer-in-residence at the University of New England (the first of several such literary tenancies to be held by him) and he began to be invited to overseas literary festivals and conferences. By the 1980s he was widely recognised as one of Australia's leading contemporary poets and literary personalities. His poetry has won numerous awards, among them the Grace Leven Prize on three occasions – *The Ilex Tree* in 1965, *The Boys Who Stole the Funeral* in 1980 and *Dog Fox Field* in 1991; the Captain Cook Bicentenary Literary Competition Prize for 'Seven Points for an Imperilled Star' included in *Poems Against Economics* (1972); the C.J. Dennis Memorial Prize for *The Vernacular Republic* (1976); the National Book Council Award for *Lunch and Counterlunch* (1975); the Canada-Australia Literary Award, the FAW Christopher Brennan Award, the NSW Premier's Award for Poetry and the Australian Literature Society's Gold Medal, all in 1984 and all for *The People's Otherworld*; the 1993 C.J. Dennis Award in the Victorian Premier's Literary Awards, the NBC Banjo Award for poetry in 1993, and the 1993 NSW Premier's Literary Award, all for *Translations from the Natural World*. Two of his volumes, *The Daylight Moon* (1987) and *Dog Fox Field* (1990) became the annual choices of the UK Poetry Society. In 1989 he was awarded an Australian Creative Arts Fellowship; in 1991 he was the subject of an ABC television programme in the True Stories series; he has been made AO and has received an honorary D.Litt. from the University of New England.

Notwithstanding his success in the literary world both in Australia and overseas and his high public profile, Murray never wavered in his resolve to return to the privacy of Bunyah to live. In 1975 he was able to buy back part of the lost family farm and returned there for brief recuperative periods whenever possible. In late 1985, after an exhausting lecture and reading tour of Canada, North America and Europe, he returned with his family permanently to Bunyah – 'I had been twenty-nine years away', he lamented in 'The Idyll Wheel'. Long labelled by the tabloids 'The Bard of Bunyah', he had finally taken up his favourite poet-in-residence position. The return did not, however, indicate an indolent, bucolic retirement. Two anthologies of verse compiled and edited, four further volumes of poetry written and two books of essays published since his return attest to his continuing contribution to Australian writing.

Murray's volumes of poetry are *The Ilex Tree* (1965, with Lehmann), *The Weatherboard Cathedral* (1969), *Poems Against Economics* (1972), *Lunch & Counterlunch* (1974), *The Vernacular Republic* (1976, a Selected Poems volume which has been regularly updated, e.g. 1983, 1984, 1986, 1988), *Ethnic Radio* (1977), *The Boys Who Stole the Funeral* (1980), *The People's Otherworld* (1983), *The Daylight Moon* (1987), *Dog Fox Field* (1990) and *Translations from the Natural World* (1992). In 1991 a *Collected Poems* was published; a selection from his previous volumes (except *Dog Fox Field*) rather than a full *Collected* edition, it won the 1992 FAW Barbara Ramsden Award. He has collected the best of his book reviews, articles and essays in four prose volumes, *The Peasant*

Mandarin (1978), *Persistence in Folly* (1984), *Blocks and Tackles* (1990) and *The Paperbark Tree* (1992). He edited *The Australian Year* (photographs by Peter Solness) in 1985; subtitled *The Chronicle of Our Seasons and Celebrations*, it is a well-informed, lyrical and loving evocation of Australia. Murray's two anthologies are *The New Oxford Book of Australian Verse* (1986) and the *Anthology of Australian Religious Poetry* (1986). *The New Oxford Book of Australian Verse* (critically well received) is a somewhat eccentric collection with no more than three poems from any one writer, no accompanying notes about poets or poems, no long-standing favourite A.B. Paterson characters, a sprinkling of religious poems and numerous (thirty-one) translations of Aboriginal songs and song-cycles. It is also a typical Murray selection in that more than half the book illustrates the Murray reverence for the land and the landscape and the Murray belief in the Bush and Bush values. The bulk of the poems in the religious anthology come from the post-Second World War period. Unorthodox, in that the term 'religious' in the title is sometimes loosely interpreted, the anthology has proved popular with readers, necessitating a second edition within five years of publication. It incorporates the work of many of Australia's best poets – James McAuley, A.D. Hope, Judith Wright, Rosemary Dobson, Bruce Dawe, Francis Webb, Roland Robinson, Kevin Hart and Murray himself – twenty-three of his own pieces. Murray's account of the compiling of the anthology was given in the 1986 Aquinas Lecture, later reproduced in *Blocks and Tackles*.

There is a richness and diversity in Les Murray's poetry which quickly disposes of the simplistic labelling of 'disguised autobiography' that some critics have occasionally sought to apply to it. Murray himself does not accept that his 'various books constitute chapters of the one work' but there is, nevertheless, an obvious unity and wholeness in much of his writing. At the core of that unity is his consistent commitment to the ideals and values of what he sees as the real Australia, that is, the Australia centred – as the nationalistic 1890s version has it – on its rural heartland, the Bush. For Murray that rural-centred Australia (his 'vernacular republic'), although superficially modified by modern times and technologies, exists today essentially the same as it was in earlier times. The continuing themes of much of his poetry are those inherent in that traditional nationalistic identity – respect, even reverence, for the pioneers; the importance of the land and its shaping influence on the Australian character; admiration for that special Australian character, down-to-earth, laconic ('we are a colloquial nation') and based on such Bush-bred qualities as egalitarianism, practicality, straightforwardness and independence; special respect for that Australian character in action in wartime ('the country soldiers'); and a brook-no-argument preference for the rural life over the sterile and corrupting urban environment. Such themes appear early in his published poems, e.g. in 'Noonday Axeman' from *The Ilex Tree* and 'Evening Alone at Bunyah' from *The Weatherboard Cathedral*. 'Noonday Axeman' reveres the toil and endurance of the pioneer Murrays:

> A hundred years of clearing, splitting, sawing,
> a hundred years of timbermen, ringbarkers, fencers
> and women in kitchens, stoking loud iron stoves
> year in, year out, and singing old songs to their children.

From those pioneers, and others like them, have come, for Australia, 'the rough foundation of legends'. Wielding his own noonday axe where his 'great-great-grandfather . . . with his first sons' had done the same, he acknowledges the claim that the land and the past have on him. Distracted as he would certainly be down the years by 'the talk and dazzle of cities' he knew that 'the city will never quite hold me. I will be always coming back here . . .' In 'Evening Alone at Bunyah' the finality of 'This country is my mind. I lift my face and count my hills' indicates the only course open to Murray when those distractions have ultimately been put aside. The final return to

Bunyah took longer than he would have anticipated and the poems themselves trace the continuing saga of loss and recovery – 'The Away-bound Train', where he dreams of his 'left-behind hills' on one of his half-reluctant journeys back 'to the twentieth century'; 'Blood', where his 'smart city life' has made him momentarily squeamish about the slaughter of the pig, until his cousin's mild reproof reminds him of the natural rural order that requires such acts; 'SMLE', where, on another brief visit to Bunyah, he goes out shooting, a country action that when done 'rightly according to its nature' is one of the rare valid uses to which a rifle is put; 'The Bulahdelah-Taree Holiday Song Cycle', where he and his family, and other city families like them, crowd back briefly to the country for the Christmas holidays to recover their origins, 'walking out, looking all around, relearning that country'; 'Cowyard Gates', where the old house he lived in as a boy has finally been pulled down, an event which he partly blames on his own repeated desertions of it; 'Laconics: The Forty Acres', where having at last bought back 'our beautiful deep land', he can plan in detail for the ultimate return. And when the recovery has been effected there are poems to tell of that – 'Extract from a Verse Letter to Dennis Haskell', where what has been regained ('the milk and honey I came home for') are 'Trees, space, waterbirds – things of that ilk/ plus people of my own kind'. The distractions of 'this metropolitan century' are at last rejected with the ultimatum that the years away finally brought: 'get out of Yuppie City or go mad'.

'Aspects of Language and War on the Gloucester Road' has him safely returned, nostalgically recalling events from his own and Bunyah's past. In 'The Idyll Wheel' he describes, in a baker's dozen poems (there are two Aprils), the month-by-month cycle of the first year back. A labour of love, 'The Idyll Wheel', which appeared in a limited edition in 1989, in parts in *Dog Fox Field* and *in toto* in the 1991 *Collected*, is rich in verbal imagery. Heart, mind and eye banquet on Keatsian colours – 'purple, foam-white, skims of leek and sherry, tawny, bronze and citrine, rosy-blue' – and on the beauty of Spring:

> Burning days ... die out over west mountains/ erased with azure

> Emerald kingparrots, crimson-breasted, whirr/ and plane out of open feed sheds

> Poddy calves wobbling in their newborn mushroom colours

> Bees and pollen drift/ through greening orchards.

The preference for rural life and values exhibited in the above poems is private and personal. That same preference was aired in a more universal, public and hence more controversial, manner in Murray's essay 'On Sitting Back and Thinking about Porter's Boeotia', published in 1978 in Elkin's *Australian Poems in Perspective* and later included in *The Peasant Mandarin*. Porter's judgment of Australia, in 'On First Looking into Chapman's Hesiod', was that it was Boeotian in character and attitude and likely to remain so, Boeotian equating to primitive, unpolished, uncultured and over-traditional. 'Australians', he said, 'are Boeotians', and he described the Boeotian poet Hesiod in terms clearly applicable to Murray:

> Like a Taree small-holder splitting logs
> And philosophising on his dangling billies

Chris Wallace-Crabbe later saw Murray somewhat similarly – 'Oscar Wilde in mole-skins' – though Murray, indeed, has a marked preference for shorts and 'Wellies'. In his thoughts on Porter's poem Murray dated the fundamental tension that has long existed between the two models of civilisation – the rural and the urban – from the rivalry that sprang up between the newly established Athens of the sixth century BC and the older, rural Boeotia. Urban-minded Athens grew scornful of traditional, pastoral Boeotia, whose people and ways it held to be boorish and old-fashioned and whose art and culture it saw as unsophisticated and unexciting. Porter envisaged 'a new land' of the future where the individual would be valued for his intellect and culture but Australia was unlikely to become that new land, being too limited by its Boeotian past and present. Murray, however, saw merit in Australia's Boeotian-ness – it was the only true distinctiveness that Australia possessed ('our distinctiveness is still firmly anchored in the bush'). Australia, he felt, could become Porter's 'new land', but only if it retained the Boeotian quality that came with its beginnings, only if it refused to allow that rural character to be swamped by an imported, imposed Athenian culture. Among the distinctive Boeotian figures are the Aborigines – 'their culture is a Boeotian source of immeasurable value to us all'. There is 'wisdom in Australia's Boeotian-ness' and the idea of our 'deliberately remaining Boeotia is full of exciting possibilities'

> It would be something indeed, to break with Western culture by not taking, even now, the characteristic second step into alienation, into élitism and the relegation of all places except one or two urban centres to the sterile status of provincial no-man's-land largely deprived of any art or any creative self-confidence. This is what is at stake.

In each of his volumes Murray has produced memorable poems. *Poems Against Economics* (1972) is a composite of three sequences, 'Seven Points for an Imperilled Star', which won the Captain Cook Bicentenary literary competition in 1970, 'Juggernaut's Little Scrapbook' and 'Walking to the Cattle Place'. The 'Imperilled Star' sequence includes 'Toward the Imminent Days', an epithalamium for his friends Geoff Lehmann and Sally McInerney. 'Walking to the Cattle Place', a complex meditation sequence of sixteen 'cow' poems (few poets have found poetry in dairy cows) is given some framework but little explanation by Murray's comment, 'I set out to follow a cow and I found a whole world, a spacious, town-despising grassland where Celt and Zulu and Verdic Aryan were one in their concerns.' The most substantial poem in *Ethnic Radio* is 'The Bulahdelah-Taree Holiday Song Cycle', a group of thirteen poems (songs) in the style and metre of R.M. Berndt's translation of 'The Moon-bone Song' from the Wonguri linguistic group of the Aboriginal Mandjigai (Manjikai) tribe of north-eastern Arnhem Land. A remarkable fusing of ancient Aboriginal and modern White Australian urban and rural cultures (for example, the Pacific Highway in holiday time is described in terms of the all-giving Rainbow Snake), the 'Holiday Song Cycle' is an imaginative poetic statement of the Jindyworobak dream that White Australians should have the same affinity with the environment as the Aborigines had, and is also another emphatic illustration of the loss suffered when children grow up and desert their rural origins for urban life.

The Boys Who Stole the Funeral, a sequence of 140 sonnets, is a novel-in-verse. Two young men, Kevin Forbutt and Cameron Reeby, steal the body of a First World War veteran, Clarrie Dunn (Kevin's great-uncle), from a Sydney funeral parlour and carry it by car to the old man's native place, an isolated spot named Dark's Plain on the NSW north coast. In carrying out the old man's wish to be buried at Dark's Plain, Kevin manages also to escape from the unrewarding urban environment into a more satisfying rural existence.

The People's Otherworld (the title a joking reference once made by him to Australia), in which Murray allowed an exuberance of language that matched his customary rich visual imagination, so dazzled the critics and literary judges that it won virtually every poetry prize in 1984. Several poems both admire and question the impact of modern technology, especially where it is dramatically changing the once familiar face of the urban landscape. Commenting on the book he remarked, 'The old idea that Murray only writes about rural stuff is an exaggeration'. In spite of that protest about a critical view that has really never been widely held, 'the governing pastoral vision with all its ambivalence toward technology', in the words of Lawrence Bourke, remains firmly in place in these poems. 'The Sydney Highrise Variations' (first published in the *Bulletin*, 1980) contains five poems. The first, 'Fuel Stoppage on Gladesville road bridge in the year 1980', sets the scene. Compelled by a car breakdown to wait 'atop a great building of the double century' (the bridge), Murray has the opportunity to take in the 'View of Sydney, Australia, from Gladesville road bridge'.

In 'The Flight from Manhattan' he attributes the modern Sydney city skyline to the New York skyscraper influence. The remaining pieces, 'The C19–20' and 'The Recession of the Jones', link the technology that produces such vast urban structures to the cargo cult of consumerism that consumes the lives of so many in contemporary times. 'Variations' certainly reflects Murray's awestruck wonder at the miracles of modern technology, but the ultimate message of the poems is regret that, in the onward march of technological genius, the old, familiar, accessible and fondly remembered Sydney that he knew has been all but obliterated. 'Machine Portraits with Pendant Spaceman', which shared the 1981 Mattara Poetry Festival Prize, is a spectacular set of ten Spenserian stanzas divided by a single sonnet (the 'Pendant Spaceman'). This is a free-wheeling, exuberant set of verses, crammed with poetic devices and sparkling with witty verbal flourishes. The machines portrayed – e.g. a bulldozer, combine seeder, satellite dish, space shuttle, crane, geophone and river ferry – demonstrate the mechanical ingenuity that Murray clearly admires but carry with them a somewhat intimidating mystique that raises the question whether they indeed are the slaves or the masters. The poems of *The Daylight Moon*, wide-ranging as ever, include a number of narratives (tall tales of the bush) based on local oral history – e.g. 'The Megaethon: 1850, 1906–29', the story of the steam engine ordained by its owner to be walked from Sydney to the Hunter Valley; 'Physiognomy on the Savage Manning River', starring the tempestuous Isabella Mary Kelly; and 'Federation Style on the Northern Rivers' in which the astute storekeeper, J. Cornwell, to save his impecunious rural customers, outwits the city auditor. Prominent in *The Daylight Moon* also are poems dealing with the return to Bunyah, e.g., 'Extract from a Verse Letter to Dennis Haskell' and 'Aspects of Language and War on the Gloucester Road'. Murray's stated aims for *Dog Fox Field* – to recover, or learn, the art of brevity and to use rhyme freely – were born of his long-held desire to make poetry accessible to a wider reading public. Poems such as 'The Up-to-date Scarecrow', 'Midnight Lake', 'The Ballad of the Barbed Wire Ocean', 'Spotted Native Cat', 'The Tin Wash Dish' and 'Low Down Sandcastle Blues', while admittedly brief and mostly rhyming, are, at best, semi-doggerel. Defending this marked change in technique Murray indicated (in *Blocks and Tackles*) his admiration for similar nineteenth-century verse – 'news-paper' verse and the populist poetry of the *Bulletin* school – which was, he said, 'a colloquial middle-voice poetry' that caught 'a great deal of ordinary human experi-ence' and shared it 'in an unfussed way with a broad range of people'. Until *Dog Fox Field* Murray, a truly modern bushman, had made no attempt to actually locate himself or his poetry in the Boeotian world of the Bush, no matter how strongly he and his poetry had urged the worth of that world. Some critics have seen little merit in his attempt to restore and revalue the colloquial poetry that was characteristic of it. *Dog Fox Field*, in spite of some exceptional poems – 'The Transposition of Clermont', 'The Emerald Dove', 'Hastings River Cruise' and 'Spring' – sometimes gives the impression of a poet momentarily out of sorts with himself, his muse and even the world about him. *Translations from the Natural World* indicates, having been published by Heinemann in the Australian Poetry series, that Murray's break with Angus & Robertson is complete. A multi-award winner, it also sees him return to his full capacity for brilliantly conceived and executed poetry. The book takes its title from the second section (of three) subtitled 'Presence'. Each of the forty poems in 'Presence' takes a particular natural object and attempts to 'translate' the essential presence of that object into poetry, and to link such individual presences to the one all-encompassing presence of the natural (which includes the human) world.

The Peasant Mandarin gathers together a first selection of Murray's prose, the book reviews, articles and essays that he had written from 1972 to 1977. *Persistence in Folly* (1984), a further prose collection, includes the major essay 'The Human Hair Thread', in which he pays tribute to the Aborigines and to the Jindyworobak movement, acknowledging aspects of both as the sources of his own view of the Australian psyche. *Blocks and Tackles* brought together his articles and essays from 1982 to 1990. 'Poems and Poesies' and 'Poemes and the Mystery of Embodiment', complex examinations of the inner workings of poetry and an essay on the timber-working history of the lower north coast, are notable pieces. *The Paperbark Tree*, published in England, contains thirty-eight prose pieces, all of which have appeared in other publications.

Lawrence Bourke's *A Vivid Steady State* (1992) is the first of an undoubted stream of major critical works on Murray destined to appear in the future.

My Army, O, My Army! and Other Songs, the book of poems which briefly re-established Henry Lawson as a leading verse commentator on public events, was published in 1915; the following year the contents of the volume were reassembled and published as *Song of the Dardanelles*. The poems in *My Army, O, My Army!*, which were mostly written in 1914–15 and first published in the *Bulletin*, reflect Lawson's reaction to the outbreak of the First World War. His early enthusiasm for the war as good for national character is apparent in *My Army, O, My Army!*; so also is the imperial fervour which stands in contrast to his socialist republicanism of the 1880s. The title poem, however, in which the army referred to is the same army of the poor as in 'The Army of the Rear', is remarkably prophetic of the Russian Revolution.

'My Country', a poem by Dorothea Mackellar, was first published as 'Core of My Heart' in the London *Spectator* 5 September 1908, but was published in the *Sydney Mail* 21 October 1908 as 'My Country', the title which has acquired fame in Australian literature. A recitation and anthology favourite, 'My Country' is a poem of six eight-line stanzas which contrasts a love of the English landscape,

> The love of field and coppice,
> Of green and shaded lanes,

with the poet's love of Australia represented, for example, in its famous second stanza:

> I love a sunburnt country
> A land of sweeping plains,
> Of ragged mountain ranges,
> Of droughts and flooding rains.
> I love her far horizons,
> I love her jewel-sea
> Her beauty and her terror
> The wide brown land for me!

Most versions of the poem print 'rugged' in the third line, although Mackellar is recorded as having intended 'ragged'. Similarly, there are several versions of the poem's origins: by one account it was written in response to the 'anti-Australianism . . . of many Australians we knew', by another it was inspired by the breaking of the drought on the Mackellar property of Torryburn, near Maitland in NSW. The popularity of 'My Country' is evidenced in the way some of its phrases have been appropriated. Despite the preference for 'a sunburnt country' in her most famous poem, Mackellar was attracted in other moods to other landscapes. For example, in 'Merry England' (*Dreamharbour*, 1923) she writes that

England wrapped me in her cloak
Silvery-grey, silvery-gold,
Silvery-grey and gold and green,
Whose touch can heal the sorest stroke –
Mother and Priestess, Nurse and Queen.

NANKIVELL, Joice (?–1988), born Queensland and brought up partly in Gippsland, published a collection of sketches of bush and city life, *The Solitary Pedestrian* (1918); and an account of life in Moscow from 1923 to the death of Lenin, *The Fourteen Thumbs of St Peter* (1926). Her *Collected Poems* appeared in 1980. With her husband, Frederick Loch, she also published an account of a visit to Ireland 1920–21, *Ireland in Travail* (1922); and of life in Eastern Poland after the First World War, *The River of a Hundred Ways* (1924). The Lochs settled in Greece 1923–29, combining work for refugees with writing, worked for Polish refugees in Bulgaria and Romania 1939–44, and returned to Greece after the war. Their experiences are described in Joice Nankivell's autobiography *A Fringe of Blue* (1968), which she published under her married name.

NAPIER, Sydney Elliott (1870–1940), born Sydney, trained as a solicitor. He served with the AIF during the First World War and returned in 1919 to Australia, where he worked as a legal officer and freelance journalist; in 1925 he joined the *Sydney Morning Herald*. Subsequently assistant editor of the *Sydney Mail* and leader-writer of the *Sydney Morning Herald*, he compiled, with P.S. Allen, *A Century of Journalism: The Sydney Morning Herald and Its Record of Australian Life 1831–1931* (1931). He contributed prose and verse to numerous English and Australian journals and newspapers, and published a collection of essays, *The Magic Carpet* (1932); a collection of biographical sketches, *Great Lovers* (1934); and two collections of verse, *Potted Biographies* (1930) and *Underneath the Bough* (1937). He also wrote a history of the Sydney Repertory Theatre Society (1923); a series of travel accounts, *On The Barrier Reef* (1928), *Walks Abroad* (1929), *Men and Cities* (1938) and *This Roundabout* (1938); and edited *The Book of the Anzac Memorial* (1934).

'Nationality' is a brief poem published in *Fourteen Men* (1954) in which Mary Gilmore, while conceding the need for internationalism, acknowledges the pre-eminent claims of race and blood:

> All men at God's round table sit
> And all men must be fed;
> But this loaf in my hand,
> This loaf is my son's bread.

NAYMAN, Michele (1956–   ), born London and educated in Johannesburg and Melbourne, has had a varied career. She holds a degree in town planning from Melbourne and a master's degree in journalism from Columbia University, New York. She has worked as a journalist and a marketing executive in Australia, Asia and Europe. Now a freelance writer, she has published a book of poetry, *What You Love*

You Are (1977) and two books of fiction, *Faces You Can't Find Again* (1980) and *Somewhere Else* (1989).

NEILSEN, Philip (1949–   ), born Brisbane, was educated at the University of Queensland, where he gained a Ph.D. He has taught at several Queensland universities, specialising in literature and cultural studies. He has published some short stories, but his main interest has been verse, which he has contributed to various periodicals, newspapers and anthologies, including *Poet's Choice*. He has published three collections of verse, *Faces of a Sitting Man* (1975), *The Art of Lying* (1979) and *Life Movies* (1981). Flexible and accessible, Neilsen's verse frequently mingles an easy wit and a sinister surrealism with unpredictable effects. Several, such as 'Veronica Lake', 'The Poet Imagines Himself an SS Officer', 'Superman in Our Town', 'Son of Dracula' and 'The Bushranger Comes Home', take a fresh, humorously disturbing look at familiar myths and cultural heroes. With Barry O'Donohue he published *We'll All Go Together* (1984) and he edited *The Penguin Book of Australian Satirical Verse* (1986), which was republished in a revised version in 1993 as *The Sting in the Wattle: Australian Satirical Verse*. He has also written *Imagined Lives: A Study of David Malouf* (1990). Neilsen has edited the literary magazine *Imago*, and is chairman of Warana Writers' Week, the Brisbane literary festival.

NEILSON, John (1844–1922), the father of John Shaw Neilson, was born in Scotland and came to Australia at the age of 9. Proficient at a variety of bush trades, he worked at shearing, sheep-herding and road-making, married in 1871 and settled at Penola. In 1881 he took up land at Minimay in the south-west of Victoria, but was severely handicapped by lack of capital and in 1889 moved to Nhill, where he was forced to rely on road-making for a living. Another move in 1895 to Sea Lake in the central Mallee proved disastrous and again he had to turn to manual work. At the turn of the century he took up land at Eureka, where he lived by wheat-growing. The father of nine children, he was married twice. Although he was entirely self-educated, he acquired a reputation as a bush poet, contributing verse from his early thirties to the Mt Gambier newspapers and the *Adelaide Punch*, and later to the *Australasian* and other journals, and winning two prizes (in 1893 and 1897). Much of his verse has been lost but three volumes have been published, *Poem for Recitation: Love's Summer in the Snow* (1893), *The Men of the Fifties* (1938) and *The Song of the Shearer* (1960). His life is described in James Devaney's *Shaw Neilson* (1944); in *John Shaw Neilson* (1972) by Hugh Anderson and L.J. Blake; and in *The Autobiography of John Shaw Neilson* (1978).

NEILSON, John Shaw (1872–1942), born Penola, SA, was the eldest son of Scottish-born parents, John Neilson and Margaret McKinnon. Beset by debts the Neilson family moved in 1881 to a selection at Minimay in the Wimmera region of western Victoria. Poor as the country was, it proved rich in associations and experiences for the young poet. He revelled in the limitless space of the inland and was fascinated by the bird and animal life. Recollections of life at Minimay are seen in his poem 'The Poor, Poor Country', where his own attitude is made clear – 'in that poor country no pauper was I.' Neilson's formal education lasted only two and a half years, including a final year at Minimay when he was 13. In 1889 the family moved north to Dow Well, near the new township of Nhill. By 1895 they had taken up blocks in the Mallee country, where life continued to be difficult and unproductive. The clearing of the scrub, the severe climate, the terrible dust storms, the rabbit plagues, the drought years 1895–1903, and the long despairing wait for a cash crop all made for an existence of poverty and misery. In 1896 Neilson's poem 'Polly and Dad and the Spring Cart' was published in the *Bulletin*, thus beginning a relationship with A.G. Stephens, his literary

adviser, editor and financial mentor, that spanned almost forty years. Stephens's influence on Neilson's literary career was not wholly beneficial and his editorial liberties
with the poetry were excessive, but without his guidance and promotion the inex-
perienced bush poet would have made little or no impact. Neilson's eye trouble began
in 1905 and his resultant inability over the years to read anything but large print was a
great hindrance to his writing. Until 1928 Neilson was an itinerant labourer, clearing
land, navvying in quarries, on roads and railways, fencing, potato-digging, fruit-
picking – work that seemed incompatible with the delicate poetry he produced. In
1901, J.F. Archibald of the *Bulletin* published 'Sheedy was Dying' and asked for more.
In 1905 Stephens bought three poems (for £1), including 'The Land Where I Was
Born'. The *Bookfellow* (1907) published 'Old Granny Sullivan' with a full-page illustration by Dagmar Ross. In 1909 twenty-eight of Neilson's poems were published in
Randolph Bedford's *Clarion*. 'Love's Coming' was published in the Sydney *Sun* in
1911, and in October 1912, Stephens used it and 'You and Yellow Air' to illustrate an
article on him. The first proposed volume of his poetry, *Green Days and Cherries*,
remained unpublished except for three proof copies. His first published volume, *Heart
of Spring* (1919), was followed in 1923 by *Ballad and Lyrical Poems* and by *New Poems* in
1927. In 1928 a position was secured for him as messenger with the Country Roads
Board in Melbourne. This supposedly congenial position with a guaranteed weekly
wage was expected to lead to increased writing, but the city environment lowered his
poetic impulse. His *Collected Poems*, edited by R.H. Croll, was published in 1934 and
Beauty Imposes in 1938. In 1941, his health failing, he went to Queensland to visit James
Devaney, who had replaced Stephens as his friend and adviser, and he died soon after
in Melbourne of heart trouble. After his death Devaney edited *Unpublished Poems*
(1947); in 1970 *Witnesses of Spring: Unpublished Poems* was edited by Judith Wright, Val
Vallis and Ruth Harrison; in 1981 *Green Days and Cherries* finally appeared, edited by
Hugh Anderson and L.J. Blake.

Most of the Australian poetry written in the 1890s and the first two decades of this
century is now less regarded than when it was written, but the best work of Neilson,
who felt that 'five shillings seems a good deal for people to pay for my verses', has so
grown in esteem that he is now claimed by some to be pre-eminent among Australian
lyrists. The incongruity between the grace, delicacy and subtlety of his poetry and his
hard life and rough background have also made him Australia's chief literary enigma,
but those who knew him well have never subscribed to the popular theory that he was
merely a literary fluke. Victor Kennedy found him remarkably well informed and
intellectually aware, 'steeped in the current philosophies – rationalism, evolution, the
labour movement and Australian poets and poetry'. The immediate impression his
poetry gives, with its spareness, brevity and uncomplicated structure, is that of simplicity, even naivety. Some of it *is* naive, even trivial and banal. But in his finest work
the combination of disturbing mysticism and haunting language, well exemplified in
the enigmatic 'The Orange Tree', shows him to be a sensitive and unusually gifted
poet. The John Shaw Neilson Society was formed in 1987 in Footscray and the Victorian branch of the FAW annually honours his memory with the John Shaw Neilson
Award for poetry. *The Autobiography of John Shaw Neilson* was published in 1978 with
an introduction by Nancy Keesing. Hugh Anderson compiled *Shaw Neilson: An
Annotated Bibliography and Checklist, 1893–1964* (rev. edn 1964). Cliff Hanna wrote
The Folly of Spring: A Study of John Shaw Neilson's Poetry (1990) and edited *John Shaw
Neilson* (1991), a collection of poems, letters, memoirs and autobiographical fragments. Darryl Emmerson has written a play based on his life, 'The Pathfinder', first
performed at the Spoleto Festival, Melbourne, in 1986.

NELSON, Jeremy Lockhart (1933–   ), born Sydney, grew up in the Hunter
Valley and was educated at the University of Sydney. Now retired from Sydney

Grammar School, he has lived in India, Greece and England. He has published two books of verse, *City of Man* (1983) and *Diagrams of Paradise* (1989).

New Australian Poetry was the vague and somewhat grandiloquent title bestowed by its proponents on the wave of poetry, mainly from young poets of the so-called 'Generation of '68', which found expression in poetry readings and in the small and often briefly lived magazines which sprang into existence in the late 1960s and 1970s. Although the practitioners of the new poetry held various, and sometimes opposing, views on its character, attitude, and limits, they felt a common antagonism to the mainstream of Australian poetry as represented by the work, for example, of A.D. Hope, R.D. FitzGerald, Judith Wright and James McAuley, who had dominated Australian poetry for the previous quarter of a century. The new poets judged the established poetry to be, in its form and content, traditional and conservative to the point of atrophy. The new poetry movement took much of its inspiration from contemporary American poetry as represented in, for example, Donald Allen's *The New American Poetry* (1960) and Donald Hall's *Contemporary American Poetry* (1962), both of which were having an impact in Australia in the mid-1960s. The movement sought to have contemporary Australian poetry reflect a similar modernity of attitude and technique. The genesis of the movement is difficult to be exact about but the obvious originating forces were, in Melbourne, the poetry readings held at Monash University 1967–69, and the poetry workshops 1968–69 at the La Mama Theatre and other venues; and, in Sydney, the 1964 birth of Grace Perry's *Poetry Australia*, the annual Balmain poetry and prose competitions, the poetry readings run by Robert Adamson, and the 1971 rise of the journal *New Poetry* from the ashes of *Poetry Magazine*. The movement's growth was spurred by the rise of a myriad of little magazines that carried the poetry and the message. Magazines such as *Our Glass, Mok, Crosscurrents, The Great Auk* and *Free Poetry* flourished briefly and disappeared but were replaced by others almost immediately, some, such as *Parachute Poems* and *Flagstones*, being equally short-lived, others, such as *The Saturday Club Book of Poetry* and *Contempa*, proving more durable. Such magazines, and the rapid development of printing technology, allowed the new poets easy access to the publication both of their individual poems and small inexpensive volumes of their work, access which had previously been available only to poets with an established reputation. These publication opportunities were augmented in the 1970s by the emergence of such printing houses as South Head Press, Outback Press, Wild and Woolley and Rigmarole of the Hours; by the increased activity of UQP, which catered for the new poetry in its Paperback Poets series and anthologies; and by the traditional publisher, Angus & Robertson, which introduced an innovatory Poets of the Month series. In addition to the dissatisfaction with existing poetry and the impact of contemporary international writing, other causes of the rise of the new poetry are said to have been the influence of the 1950s decade in which the new poets grew up; the ready availability of tertiary education to their generation; the influence of the new rock music; the impact of drugs; the sense of outrage that accompanied the Vietnam War and Australia's participation in it; conscription; the belief in poetry as part of the weaponry in the struggle for wider freedom; and the impact of such poets as Francis Webb and Bruce Beaver. Although many poets who published during the period were involved in the movement to some degree, the more important figures were Beaver, Thomas Shapcott, Rodney Hall, Robert Adamson, John Tranter, Kris Hemensley, Michael Dugan, Bruce Dawe, Les Murray, Michael Dransfield, Charles Buckmaster, Ken Taylor, Robert Kenny, Garrie Hutchinson, Walter Billeter, Vicki Viidikas, Mal Morgan, Paul Smith, Alan Wearne and John A. Scott. Many of these worked independently of the literary cliques that developed and many were not in agreement with each other or even with the theory of a 'New Australian Poetry'. The new poetry is represented in the anthologies *Australian Poetry*

Now (1970) and *Contemporary American & Australian Poetry* (1976), both edited by Shapcott; *Applestealers* (1974), edited by Kenny and Colin Talbot; *The New Australian Poetry* (1979), edited by Tranter; and *The Younger Australian Poets* (1983), edited by Robert Gray and Geoffrey Lehmann. *New Impulses in Australian Poetry* (1968), edited by Hall and Shapcott, is not properly descriptive or illustrative of the movement, although it indicates the changes that were then emerging.

That the 'New Australian Poetry' would inevitably be supplanted by a similar movement, and that the 'Generation of '68' had become the anti-establishment establishment, to be replaced by a further anti-establishment force, was foreshadowed by the October 1977 special issue of *Australian Literary Studies*, titled 'New Writing in Australia'. The new poetry was subjected to considerable criticism in Richard Packer's 'Against the Epigones', *Quadrant* (1975) and Mark O'Connor's 'The Graying of the Underground', *Overland* (1979). The explosion of poetry in the decade 1970–80, and the resultant confusion over standards, is well exemplified in Thomas Shapcott's article 'Australian Poetry 1970–1980: Some Statistical Observations', *Australian Literary Studies* (1983). The extent to which the then contemporary American poets had an influence on the New Australian Poetry is investigated in *The American Model: Influence and Independence in Australian Poetry* (1983), edited by Joan Kirkby. Many of the standard-bearers of the New Australian Poetry movement of the 1960s and 1970s have become recognised leaders in the poetic scene of the 1990s.

New Impulses in Australian Poetry (1968), an anthology of Australian poetry of the 1960s, was edited, with an introduction, by Rodney Hall and Thomas W. Shapcott. The keynote of these 'new impulses' was 'a suspicion of idealism, and an inbred awareness of the consequences of totalitarian beliefs'. Authoritarianism in religion and politics was eschewed, as was the concept of national and international aggression. Major established poets such as Kenneth Slessor, Judith Wright and A.D. Hope are not represented because the editors felt that their poetry of the decade added little to their already defined stances. Their contemporaries, however, Gwen Harwood and Francis Webb, are given considerable space because they are important influences on younger poets.

New Poetry was the magazine of the Poetry Society of Australia. It replaced *Poetry Magazine* in 1971, which had replaced *Prism* in 1961, as a result of a dispute among the Society's members over the amount of non-Australian writing that the magazine should contain. Edited initially by Robert Adamson and Carl Harrison-Ford and later mostly by Adamson alone, *New Poetry* was published bi-monthly, quarterly and sometimes irregularly until 1982. One of Australia's major poetry magazines, *New Poetry* played an important role in the rise of the 'New Australian Poetry' during the 1970s and, by publishing contemporary American poetry in particular, kept Australian poets and readers abreast of modern developments in poetic form and content. It published an extensive range of contemporary poetry from well-known Australian and overseas poets, as well as lesser-known writers and previously unpublished writers. It also contained critical articles, reviews, notes and comments.

NICHOLSON, John Henry (1838–1923), born England, was a close friend of Ludwig Leichhardt and came to Australia in 1854. He tried various occupations, including prospector, theatre manager, bird-collector and schoolteacher, finally settling in Queensland. In his later years he suffered periodic bouts of mental illness. He wrote verse, plays and prose sketches, acquired a temporary and local reputation for his patriotic song 'Rouse Australians!' in the late 1880s, but is now best known for his moral and religious allegory *The Adventures of Halek* (1882) and its sequel *Almoni* (1904). Nicholson also published two volumes of humorous prose sketches, *The Mysterious Cooks* (1867) and *My Little Book* (1873); a volume of prose and verse, *The Opal*

Fever (1878); two collections of verse, *Hubert and Other Poems* (1879) and *A Book of Verses* (1916).

NISBET, Hume (1849–1923), a Scottish artist who was an associate of John Ruskin, taught art at Edinburgh and exhibited at the Royal Scottish Academy, visited Australia 1865–72, 1886 and 1895. On his first visit he travelled extensively in eastern Australia and tried acting in Melbourne. He published more than forty books of fiction, plays, verse, works on art and painting and accounts of his travels. His verse, some of which is Australian in context, was published in several collections, *Memories of the Months* (1889), *The Matador and Other Recitative Pieces* (1893), and *Hathor and Other Poems* (1905).

NISSEN, Rosemary (1939–   ), previously the proprietor-manager of Abalone Press, has taught creative writing, been a librarian and is an alternative health practitioner. She has published two books of verse, *Universe Cat* (1985) and *Small Poems of April* (1991), as well as co-editing several publications, e.g. *Directory of Australian Poets 1980* (1980), *The Great White Hunter Meets Darkest Africa* (1986), *Surprise Witness* (1988) and *Yarra Valley Writers* (1990).

'No Foe Shall Gather Our Harvest', a stirring poem written by Mary Gilmore in 1940, proved a remarkable morale booster in the tense days of the Japanese threat to Australia in 1942. The poem, with its refrain 'No foe shall gather our harvest/ Or sit on our stockyard rail' was at the time considered as a possible battle hymn, even national anthem.

NOONUCCAL, Oodgeroo (1920–93), of the Noonuccal tribe of Stradbroke Island off the Queensland coast near Brisbane, was the first of the modern Aboriginal protest writers. Known for most of her life as Kath Walker, she returned to her tribal name in 1988 in opposition to the Bicentenary celebrations. She was educated only to primary school level, then at 13 worked in domestic service in Brisbane. At 16 she wanted to be a nurse but was rejected because she was an Aborigine. By 1961, when she was State secretary of the Federal Council for the Advancement of Aboriginals and Torres Strait Islanders, she was deeply involved in the Aboriginal activist movement. She campaigned strenuously and successfully for the 1967 abolition of Section 52 of the Australian Constitution which discriminated against Aborigines. In the 1970s she served as chairperson of the National Tribal Council, the Aboriginal Arts Board, the Aboriginal Housing Committee and the Queensland Aboriginal Advancement League. In her life and through her writings she constantly sought to generate cultural self-pride by emphasising the value of her people's way of life. This crusade often led her to criticise White Australian attitudes and to demand basic Aboriginal rights. She was made MBE but returned the honour in 1988 in protest at the federal government's failure to legislate nationally for Aboriginal land rights. She was awarded honorary doctorates by Macquarie University and Griffith University. Her first volume of poetry, *We Are Going* (1964), is not, as its title might imply, an indication of her resignation to the loss of Aboriginal identity. She meant it, in her own words, 'as a warning to the white people: we can go out of existence, or with proper help we could also go on and live in this world in peace and harmony . . . the Aboriginal will not go out of existence; the whites will'. Her second volume, *The Dawn Is at Hand* (1966), won the 1967 Jessie Litchfield Award. *My People: A Kath Walker Collection* (1970) reprinted the poems of the two earlier collections, together with some new poems, short stories, essays and speeches. *Stradbroke Dreamtime* (1972) is a collection of thirteen whimsical stories of her childhood and fourteen traditional stories from Aboriginal folklore or new ones in traditional form. She also published children's books, including *The Rainbow Serpent* (1988). As Oodgeroo Noonuccal she provided stories and verse for the illustrated volumes *Australian Legends and Landscapes* (1990) and *Australia's Unwritten History* (1992).

Her best-known poems, 'We Are Going', 'Gooboora, the Silent Pool' and 'Last of His Tribe' express nostalgia for the lost Aboriginal past, while anger at White intolerance and cruelty is expressed in poems such as 'Dark Unmarried Mothers', 'Acacia Ridge' and 'God's One Mistake'; a sense of fairness, nevertheless, compels her to admit, in 'Civilization' and 'Integration – Yes!', that some benefits have flowed to the Aboriginal people from contact with White culture. 'Aboriginal Charter of Rights' is a straightforward declaration of the basic rights of her people, while 'Tribal Justice' and 'The Food Gatherers' idealise the Aboriginal existence of primitive times. 'I Am Proud' is an angry assertion of pride in her Black identity, conforming with her description of her poetry as 'sloganistic, civil rightish, plain and simple'. Oodgeroo also won the FAW Patricia Weickhardt Award in 1977 and the Mary Gilmore Award. In 1977 she won the Black Makers Award in San Francisco for her performance in the film *Shadow Sister*. Ulli Beier has written *Quandamooka. The Art of Kath Walker* (1985), which includes biographical information and some of Oodgeroo's art work. Kathie Cochrane wrote the biography *Oodgeroo* (1994).

'O'BRIEN, John' (Patrick Joseph Hartigan) (1878–1952), born Yass, was ordained a Roman Catholic priest in 1903. In 1910, after a curacy of seven years at Albury, he was appointed inspector of Catholic schools in the Goulburn diocese. He administered the last rites (prematurely) in 1911 to Jack Riley of Brigenbrong, who had some claims to having been A.B. Paterson's 'The Man from Snowy River'. He was priest-in-charge at Berrigan in 1916 and parish priest at Narrandera 1917–44. He published two volumes of verse under the pseudonym 'John O'Brien', *Around the Boree Log and Other Verses* (1921) and *The Parish of St Mel's* (1954), the latter a tribute to his Narrandera parish. A selection of his poems, illustrated by the paintings of Patrick Carroll, was published in 1978 as *Around the Boree Log*. He also wrote *On Darlinghurst Hill* (1952), *The Men of '38 and other Pioneer Priests* (1975). The 'John O'Brien' poetry is simple, homely balladry centred on the Irish-Australian, Catholic, rural communities. Its great successes are 'Said Hanrahan', 'The Old Bush School', 'At Casey's, After Mass' and 'Tangmalangaloo'. The *Around the Boree Log* poems were made popular by the recitations of John Byrne ('The Joker'); they were made into a film in 1925; twenty of them were set to music by Dom. S. Moreno of New Norcia, WA, in 1933. 'O'Brien's' nephew Frank Mecham published the biography *'John O'Brien' and the Boree Log* in 1981.

O'CONNOR, Mark (1945–   ), born Melbourne, the son of a judge, graduated in English and classics (after abandoning engineering) from the University of Melbourne, then taught briefly but has spent most of the time since as a full-time writer, especially of poetry. While resident in Canberra in the early 1970s, he was editor of *Canberra Poetry* 1973–75, and won the *Poetry Australia* Biennial International Prize with his first published poetry in 1973, winning the same award in 1975.

A travelling scholarship, the Marten Bequest Travelling Scholarship, allowed him to spend several years in Europe, chiefly in Italy. He returned to Australia in 1980 and was attached to James Cook University in Townsville in 1982, which was also a return to the Barrier Reef, the inspiration of his first book of poetry, *Reef Poems* (1976). In 1984 he was writer-in-residence for the NSW National Parks; a knowledgeable amateur biologist, he has had a lifelong concern for the Australian environment and its protection. A series of Literature Board Fellowships and numerous prizes for his work have enabled him to continue his writing. In 1987–88 he was the Thomas Ramsay Science and Humanities Scholar at the Museum of Victoria, and he has been writer-in-residence in several academic institutions, notably at East China University; in 1993 he won the substantial ACT Literary Award, after which he took up a residency at the University of Oregon. In 1995 he became poetry editor of the *Canberra Times*. Among the numerous minor poetry and short fiction awards that O'Connor has won are the Shell *Artlook* Prize (1979), the Commonwealth Short Story Prize (1979), the

London *Times* Kenneth Allsop Memorial Prize (1980), the FAW John Shaw Neilson Poetry Award (1981), the Tom Collins Poetry Prize (1983), the Charles Thatcher Prize (1985) and the Grace Perry Prize (1988). His chief publications have been poetry: *Reef Poems* (1976); *The Eating Tree* (1980, a collection of poems based on his European experiences); *The Fiesta of Men* (1983); *Poetry in Pictures: The Great Barrier Reef* (1986, a republication of *Reef Poems* in conjunction with photographer Neville Coleman); *Selected Poems* (1986); *Poetry of the Mountains* (1988, the subject being the Blue Mountains of NSW, photographs by Ian Brown); *The Ship Trans-Time* (1989, inspired by the Museum of Victoria's collections); *The Great Forest* (1989) and *Fire-Stick Farming: Selected Poems 1972–90* (1990). O'Connor has also edited the anthology *Two Centuries of Australian Poetry* (1988 revised and updated edition 1995).

Section One, 'Coelenterate Islands', from *Reef Poems* highlights the teeming life of that North Queensland paradise, the birds (herons, gannets, sea-eagles, terns and cormorants) holding pride of place. The threat of man's pollution ('On a rusted drum of poison') spoils an otherwise perfect scenario. *The Fiesta of Men* captures incidents and atmospheres of O'Connor's wanderings through Greece, Italy, Yugoslavia, Norway, England's Lake District ('Wordsworth's House at Rydal') and North Queensland where, in 'Planting the Dunk Botanic Gardens', he tells of his own almost frenzied attempt to establish a huge tropical garden on E.J. Banfield's paradise island. 'Riding a Hired Lambretta', from *The Fiesta of Men*, won the 1981 John Shaw Neilson Poetry Award. O'Connor's first *Selected Poems* adopts the unusual practice of segmenting the poems by years rather than by the books in which they were published. The years range from 1972 to 1984, with only 1981 missing. *Poetry of the Mountains* is saturated with the natural beauty of the Blue Mountains of NSW, the verbal brilliance of the poems complemented by some striking photographs. 'Fire-Stick Farming' from the Blue Mountains poetry provides the title for O'Connor's second *Selected* volume. A remarkably fine collection, *Fire-Stick Farming* reinforces the impression that O'Connor's poetry draws strongly on the external natural scene, and the diversity of flora, fauna and landscapes. Interwoven with those externals, however, are frequent, sensitive insights into the nature of existence itself. A poet who has won a popular following, O'Connor has also won a reputation as one of Australia's major contemporary nature poets.

O'DOHERTY, Eva (1830–1910), born Ireland as Mary Eva Kelly, was an early contributor of nationalistic ballads and poems to Charles Gavan Duffy's magazine *Nation*, earning for herself the name 'Eva of the *Nation*'. She became engaged to Kevin Izod O'Doherty, a medical practitioner and political activist, who was sentenced to transportation in 1848. After O'Doherty was set free in 1854, the two married, lived for a time in Paris and Dublin and finally settled in Brisbane, where O'Doherty practised medicine and had some success as a politician. In 1886 they returned to Ireland, where O'Doherty joined the Irish National Party and was briefly a member of the House of Commons, before returning to Queensland. Eva O'Doherty published two collections of verse, *Poems* (1877) and *Poems* (1880). Popular as O'Doherty's verse was in her lifetime both in Ireland and Queensland, her predictable themes, images and rhymes are now only of historical interest. Ross and Heather Patrick have written *Exiles Undaunted: the Irish Rebels Kevin and Eva O'Doherty* (1989).

O'DONOHUE, Barry (1947–   ), born Innisfail, Queensland, was conscripted into the Australian Army in 1967 and spent a year on active service in Vietnam. He now lives in Brisbane and is writing, in prose and poetry, of his Vietnam experiences. He has been involved in several magazines in an editorial capacity, e.g. *Image*, *The Border Issue*, *Arts National* and *LiNQ* and has also edited *Queensland Youth Festival Young Writers 1979* (1980) and a collection of contemporary Queensland poetry, *Place and Perspective* (1984). He has published short stories, articles, literary reviews and poetry widely in Australia. His poetry has also appeared in France, Canada and the USA. His verse has been published in several collections, *From the Edge of the World* (1979), *Addiction to False Landscapes* (1981), *Latitudes South* (1983), *View from a First Floor Window* (1983) and, with Philip Neilsen, *We'll All Go Together* (1984).

O'DOWD, Bernard (1866–1953), born Beaufort, Victoria, the son of Ulster immigrants, grew up in Ballarat, strongly compelled by his Irish background and the events of the recent Eureka Stockade to radical socialism. He had both arts and law degrees before he was 30, a considerable achievement for those times. After periods of teaching, O'Dowd moved to Melbourne, entered the State public service by way of the crown solicitor's office, and ultimately became chief parliamentary draftsman in 1931. He married Eva Fryer in 1889 but later left her for the socialist poet Marie Pitt, with whom he lived from 1919. O'Dowd's strong radical tendencies found full expression in Melbourne at the turn of the century. He was a member of the Progressive Lyceum, edited its manual, the *Lyceum Tutor*, until his views became too vehement even for that coterie of radicals, and attended Charles Strong's Australian Church, which was renowned for its radical sermons and debates and its emphasis on intellectual freedom. His first writings of note appeared in the *Bulletin* and in the *Tocsin*, a journal which he produced and edited. His *Tocsin* column 'The Forge', under the pseudonym 'Gavah the Blacksmith', consistently attacked the Establishment and the injustices of the contemporary social system. His belief, which he shared with Walt Whitman, that the poet's true socialist role was to further the best interests of mankind was contained in his 1909 address *Poetry Militant*. His first volume of poetry, *Dawnward?* (1903), indicated by its question mark O'Dowd's uncertainty about Australia's future direction. The sonnet 'Australia' is the volume's best-known poem. *The Silent Land* (1906) speculates about a mystic world which exists beyond the physical world, influencing and being influenced by it. *Dominions of the Boundary* (1907) examines the nature and purpose of the deities such as Hermes, Vulcan and Bacchus and attempts to bestow contemporary significance on them. *The Seven Deadly Sins* (1909), a series of sonnets on those sins, contains some unusually fine imagery. *The Bush*, O'Dowd's most substantial and worthwhile poem, envisages a future in which Australia occupies a place of glory similar to that occupied by Greece and Rome in antiquity. O'Dowd's last major composition was *Alma Venus* (1921), a remarkable but largely ignored poetic exploration of the mystery of sex. From 1921 until his death in 1953 O'Dowd maintained an almost complete poetic silence. Apart from radical verse like *Dawnward?* and *The Bush*, in which he assumed the role of standard-bearer of the nationalist radical movement, O'Dowd's poetry made little impact. His concern with 'Poetry Militant' made his verse too obviously didactic for general taste and his predilection for classical allusions made it largely incomprehensible to the ordinary reader. But he attempted to make a meaningful examination of Australian life and not simply describe, as the balladists had done, its more picturesque aspects. He also wrote a book of essays, *Fantasies* (1942). Victor Kennedy and Nettie Palmer wrote *Bernard O'Dowd* (1954) and Hugh Anderson, *Bernard O'Dowd* (1968).

OGILVIE, Will (William Henry) (1869–1963), born near Kelso, Scotland, arrived in Australia at the age of 20, drawn to the colony by his love of horses and adventure, and by his admiration for the poet Adam Lindsay Gordon, whose tragic story had captured his imagination. He spent twelve years in a nomadic existence on far-flung stations like Belalie on the Warrego and Maroupe in SA, droving, mustering, breaking in horses and capturing, in hastily scribbled, buoyant, romantic verses, the many experiences of outback life. A prolific contributor to the *Bulletin* and popular also with readers of the *Australasian* and the Mount Gambier *Border Watch*, he published his popular and best-known volume of verse, *Fair Girls and Gray Horses* (1898), before his return to Scotland in 1901. The poems, a mixture of ballads and lyrics, celebrated 'all

Fair Girls' and 'all Gray Horses', for Ogilvie believed that 'Golden and Gray are the loves to hold'. The classic droving poem 'From the Gulf', with its nostalgic refrain 'Store Cattle from Nelanjie', the sentimental, horsebreaker poem 'The Riding of the Rebel', and the poem that celebrated the courage and endurance of the teamsters, 'How the Fire Queen crossed the Swamp', are examples of Australian balladry at its best. But it is in lyrics such as 'A Telltale Tryst' and 'The Bush, My Lover', where the loveliness of fair girls blends with the shimmering Australian moonlight, that Ogilvie's singular contribution to the verse of the period lies. In the mostly pragmatic and masculine world of bush verse, his was virtually the only, and certainly the best, romantic voice. His later volumes of Australian content, *Hearts of Gold* (1903), *The Australian* (1916) and *Saddle for a Throne* (1952), compiled by Thelma E. Williams and published by R.M. Williams, were all published in Australia, although Ogilvie did not return to this country. In Scotland Ogilvie continued to write verse and was acclaimed for his Border poetry by such luminaries as Hugh MacDiarmid, but died in relative obscurity. He wrote an account of his Australian adventures in *My Life in the Open* (1908).

O'HARA, J.B. (John Bernard) (1862–1927), born Bendigo, was educated at the University of Melbourne, where he achieved distinction, and became a lecturer in mathematics and physics at Ormond College in 1886. In 1889 he established a girls' school, South Melbourne College, of which he was headmaster until 1917. Katharine Susannah Prichard and Elsie Cole were two of his pupils and protégées. A respected poet in his lifetime, he won a prize in a competition connected with the Melbourne Exhibition of 1880, although his bland, meditative verse, reminiscent of the late Victorians, has now dated. He published nine collections of verse, mostly short lyrics, although his second volume, *Songs of the South Second Series: The Wild White Man and Other Poems* (1895), includes a narrative poem relating the adventures of William Buckley. His other volumes are *Songs of the South* (1891), *Lyrics of Nature* (1899), *A Book of Sonnets* (1902), *Odes and Lyrics* (1906), *Calypso and Other Poems* (1912), *The Poems of John Bernard O'Hara* (1918), *At Eventide* (1922) and *Sonnets and Rondels* (1925).

'Old Bark Hut, The' is an anonymous Australian folk-song which exists in several versions; the best-known one introduces the singer as Bob the Swagman, who chronicles the misfortunes he experiences while living on rations in an old bark hut, poorly furnished and open to the elements. The song was one of the most popular of Australian folk-songs in the nineteenth century. Its jaunty melody, simple four-line stanza, and chorus which repeats the last line of each verse, permit the kind of extension which gave rise to the legend that a party of shearers once started singing the song as their train pulled out of Bourke, and finished it as the train arrived at Central Station in Sydney.

Old Bush Songs Composed and Sung in the Bushranging, Digging and Overlanding Days, The was compiled and edited by A.B. Paterson in 1905. The first major collection of Australian folk-songs, it rescued from oblivion many old ballads and songs which had existed precariously as songs or recitations around the camp-fires and in the shearing sheds of the outback. The first edition contained about fifty songs; by 1926 the fifth edition contained more than seventy, some with choruses, many with footnotes and identification of the tunes to which they were sung. Among the well-known inclusions were 'The Wild Colonial Boy', 'The Eumerella Shore', 'The Stringy Bark Cockatoo', 'The Dying Stockman', 'The Old Bark Hut' and the Paddy Malone songs.

'Old Granny Sullivan', a sentimental poem by John Shaw Neilson, was published in the *Bookfellow* in 1907; A.G. Stephens published it again in 1916 as a leaflet and it was also used in school publications. Based, according to Neilson, on an old lady who lived in Penola when he was a boy, the poem recounts the typically sad story of a woman in early colonial times.

O'LEARY, P.I. (Patrick Ignatius) (1888–1944), born Adelaide, was an organiser for the SA labour movement in his early years. He later worked as a journalist for newspapers in Broken Hill, Adelaide and Melbourne. Editor of *Design*, he was also editor in Melbourne of the *Advocate* 1920–44, dominating the literary page and contributing poetry, political comment and leading articles. Connected with the Pioneer Players, he was also a member of the Bread and Cheese club. Pseudonyms he used included 'M', 'Historicus', 'Francis Davitt' and 'P.I.O.L.'. Some of his essays, which include several studies of Australian writers, were published in 1954, edited by Joseph O'Dwyer and titled *Bard in Bondage*. Although O'Leary tends to be prolix and even declamatory when his Irish nationalism is aroused, as in 'The Heroes of Easter Week', his judgments are often sound. He also edited an anthology, which includes verse by Roderic Quinn, E.J. Brady, John Shaw Neilson, Edward Harrington and others, *The Bread and Cheese Book* (1939), and published a volume of his own verse, *Romance and Other Verses* (1921).

'On First Looking Into Chapman's Hesiod', by Peter Porter, published in his verse collection, *Living in a Calm Country* (1975) is central to the understanding of Porter's relationship with Australia. The vehicle of the poem is the purchase at a village fête of a copy of Chapman's *Hesiod* and Porter's recognition of the similarity of the attitudes of Boeotian poetry to Australian life; both are robust and innocent, essentially physical and direct in their emotions. Porter identifies his own preference as the European 'Athenian' culture of 'precept and the Pleiades'. The evocation of Australia is sharp in visual and aural detail but the irony is tender and amused rather than scabrous, as in his earlier satires on human folly; his admiration for Australian modes is also made clear. In view of Porter's self-avowed lack of simple and direct response, the poem's tone even suggests partial envy of such Australian modes. His exile from Australia is explained as a feeling of homelessness, a seeking for the 'permanently upright city' which is not London but the 'new land', the world of ideas which dominates his poetry, especially the later volumes *The Cost of Seriousness* (1978) and *English Subtitles* (1981). In an interview with Bruce Bennett (*Westerly*, 1982) Porter spoke of the 'new land' as the republic of the imagination 'where everyone is as gifted as the great men of the past and where you are made welcome as a confrère'. His preference is personal, imposing no clear-cut advocacy of the exiled over the native, more a resignation to the difference between his attitude and the Australian. See also Murray, Les.

JEFF DOYLE

'Orange Tree, The', one of John Shaw Neilson's best-known poems, was inspired by the beauty of the orange groves at Merbein near Mildura in the Murray River irrigation area, where Neilson was fruit-picking in 1917. The poem was completed in 1919 and published in his *Ballad and Lyrical Poems* (1923). Neilson's comments, 'I was struck with the very beautiful light there is in May . . . the dark green of the orange trees and beautiful sunlight give them enchantment hard to describe', explain the genesis of the poem. He partly attributes the mysticism of the poem to his reaction to a print of Botticelli's *Spring*. In the poem the young girl's instinctive response to the beautiful light that glows within the orange tree has sometimes been interpreted as youth's innate understanding of the natural beauty of life, an understanding that requires none of the hapless and complex explanations offered by the experience of age.

O'REILLY, Bernard (1903–75), born Hartley, NSW, was a member of a pioneering family which opened up the McPherson Ranges on the border of NSW and

Queensland. He became a national hero in 1937 when he single-handedly searched for and discovered a crashed plane on the Lamington Plateau and rescued the two survivors. He served in New Guinea and Borneo during the war, and subsequently ran a well-known tourist lodge in the Lamington National Park. He published a popular account of the exploits of his family and a record of the 1937 rescue, *Green Mountains* (1940), two collections of memories, *Cullenbenbong* (1944) and *Over the Hills* (1963); and a collection of verse, *Songs from the Hills* (1971). A television documentary of his life was made in 1975.

O'REILLY, Dowell (1865–1923), born Sydney, was elected to the NSW parliament in 1894. He later taught at his old school, Sydney Grammar, and then became a public servant in Sydney. In 1914 his first wife died and in 1917 he married his cousin, Marie Miles. The correspondence of their courtship, *Dowell O'Reilly From His Letters* (1927), edited by his wife, reveals much of his personality and character. The contemporary and friend of Henry Lawson, John le Gay Brereton, and Mary Gilmore, O'Reilly was active in the Sydney literary scene. Because he was such a rigorous critic of his own writing, O'Reilly's output was small but impressive. His verse includes *Australian Poems* (1884) and *A Pedlar's Pack* (1888), both published under the pseudonym 'D'. His fiction includes the novel *Tears and Triumph* (1913) and *Five Corners* (1920), short stories of excellent quality. *The Prose and Verse of Dowell O'Reilly* (1924) is a composite selection of his work. Eleanor Dark the novelist was his daughter.

O'REILLY, John Boyle (1844–90), born Drogheda, Ireland, was a printer and reporter in Ireland and England before becoming a Fenian. In 1863 he enlisted as a trooper in the British Army for the express purpose of winning his fellow soldiers to the cause but was arrested in 1866. After stints in prisons at Millbank, Portsmouth and Dartmoor, O'Reilly was transported to WA in 1868 on the *Hougoumont*, the last convict ship to be sent to the Australian colonies; he helped edit the *Wild Goose*, a journal produced on board the ship. In 1869 he staged an extraordinary escape to America, where he became prominent in Boston as editor of the *Pilot* and as a publicist and lecturer on Irish affairs. In 1875 he was part of the daring plan organised by the Clan na Gael to rescue six Irish prisoners from Fremantle gaol. The plan was successfully carried out in 1876 and is celebrated in the Australian folk-song 'The Catalpa'. O'Reilly's sudden death in 1890, from an accidental overdose of chloral, stunned the Irish community in Boston, where a memorial to him was erected as well as in his native Drogheda. The heroic dimension of his life is captured in J.J. Roche's hagiographic *Life of John Boyle O'Reilly* (1891), a work which incorporates his poems and speeches; in W.G. Schofield's anecdotal *Seek for a Hero: The Story of John Boyle O'Reilly* (1956) and in Paul Buddee's children's book *The Escape of John O'Reilly* (1973). He was the model for Morres Blake in Rosa Praed's novel *Outlaw and Lawmaker* (1893). Like other transported political prisoners, including George Loveless, Thomas Muir and John Mitchel, O'Reilly had a relatively brief sojourn in Australia and has a larger reputation overseas. In Ireland he is remembered as a folk-hero, his poetry is included in standard anthologies of Irish political verse, and he himself edited an anthology, *The Poetry and Song of Ireland* (1887); in the USA he is remembered additionally as a fine sportsman who composed the important sporting treatise *Ethics of Boxing and Manly Sport* (1888). He wrote several volumes of verse, including *Songs from the Southern Seas* (1873), *Songs, Legends and Ballads* (1878), *The Statues in the Block* (1881), and *In Bohemia* (1886); in each there are poems relating to Australia, notably several verse narratives. His major contribution to Australian literature, however, was *Moondyne*, generally recognised as the first WA novel and significant in convict literature.

OSBORNE, Charles (1927–   ), born Brisbane, studied music in Brisbane and Melbourne and worked in literary and musical journalism and as an actor before leaving Australia in 1953. He earned a living in England by freelance writing and occasional acting before becoming assistant editor of *London Magazine* 1958–66; he joined the Arts Council of Great Britain in 1966 and was its literature director 1971–86. He has published several books on literature and music, including a substantial biography in 1980 of W.H. Auden, with whom he was friendly from the 1960s. His books which have relevance to Australia include a biography of Ned Kelly (1970), and another of the Australian actor Max Oldaker (1989), a collection of poems, illustrated by Sidney Nolan, *Swansong* (1968), and an autobiography, *Giving It Away: Memoirs of an Uncivil Servant* (1986), which includes a chapter on his Australian years.

Our Glass, a Melbourne magazine associated with the rise of the 'New Australian Poetry', was edited by Kris Hemensley. It contains a selection of the poetry from the La Mama poetry workshops and was published 1968–69.

Overland, one of Australia's major contemporary literary magazines, began publication in Melbourne in 1954. It originally incorporated the *Realist Writer*, a left-wing journal which had begun publication under editor Bill Wannan in 1952 but severed its connection with the Realist Writers groups after the Hungarian uprisings of 1956. The original role of *Overland* was, in Ian Turner's words, 'to develop a radical tradition, including within that the Marxist tradition; to encourage a working-class audience and working-class writers . . . and to take part in polemics against the Right'. *Overland's* successful struggle to survive the factional difficulties and lack of government patronage in its early years was largely due to the energy and devotion of its original and long-standing editor, Stephen Murray-Smith, and Ian Turner. Others involved in its continued existence have been John McLaren, Barrett Reid, Nancy Keesing, Leonie Sandercock, Ken Gott, Gwen Harwood and Martin Duwell. *Overland* gives expression to a diversity of literary and social attitudes and opinions but its overall tone and spirit reflect its motto, 'Temper democratic, bias Australian', derived from Joseph Furphy's description of *Such is Life* (1903). *An Overland Muster* (1965), an anthology of writing from the pages of *Overland* between 1954 and 1964, was edited by Murray-Smith. Barrett Reid took over as editor in 1988 after Murray-Smith's death. He was followed in 1993 by John McLaren.

OWEN, Jan (1940–   ), born Adelaide, has worked as a librarian and as a teacher of creative writing. She has published poetry in numerous periodicals and anthologies and in four collections, *Boy With a Telescope* (1986), *Fingerprints on Light* (1990), *Blackberry Season* (1993) and *Night Rainbows* (1994). In 1981 she won the Ian Mudie Award, in 1984 the Jessie Litchfield Prize, and in 1985 the Grenfell Henry Lawson Award; her first collection also won the Mary Gilmore Prize and the Anne Elder Award. A poet with a keen eye for detail, who is also sensitive to nuance, Owen concentrates on significant moments of experience, or significant natural scenes which express a human meaning. 'Pear Tree', for instance, begins with a moonlit vision of the tree and radiates outwards into an intense, highly compressed reflection on time, loss and change; 'Poppies' and 'Red Carnations' are even more subtle expressions of the insidious, delicate quality of natural transience which implicitly includes human experience; 'Orthodera ministralis' is an elegantly witty statement on the praying mantis and the human associations of the contradiction expressed in his predatory/pious behaviour. Other poems reflect on family relationships, celebrate joyful memories or express the poignancy of loss and the resilience of grief. The poems of *Fingerprints on Light* are particularly wide-ranging, garnering topics from diverse cultures, periods and places, although they show the same sensitivity to minutiae and the links between physical and human nature. In *Night Rainbows* she is at her most whimsical. The 'Parts of Speech' series is quirky and amusing. 'Impersonations' are parodies of fellow poets

John Tranter, Andrew Taylor, Kate Llewellyn (a poet similar to herself), John Forbes, John A. Scott and Jennifer Maiden. 'The Marriage' is a sensitive account of how Mary and Joseph come to be real lovers after the birth of Jesus. Part of *Night Rainbows* was awarded the 1991 Wesley Michel Wright Poetry Prize.

Oxford History of Australian Literature, The edited by Leonie Kramer, was published in 1981. The history comprises an introduction by Kramer, surveys of fiction (by Adrian Mitchell), drama (by Terry Sturm) and poetry (by Vivian Smith) and includes a descriptive bibliography (by Joy Hooton).

Oxford Literary Guide to Australia, The published in 1987 under the general editorship of Peter Pierce and researched by many contributors throughout Australia, was sponsored by Mobil Australia and OUP in collaboration with ASAL. The Literary Guide provides an extensive coverage of the links and associations of many places with Australian writers and books. Grouped according to State or Territory, and in alphabetical order, the entries give writers' places of birth, domicile and death and the association between actual places and their counterparts in Australian literature. An index of authors provides biographical details and links authors with places named in the text. A second edition was published in 1993.

PAGE, Geoff (1940–), born Grafton, attended The Armidale School before going on to the University of New England. His family's connection with the Clarence River district dates back to the middle of the nineteenth century; the river's influence on him and his family is summed up in the admission,

> The Clarence that I know has flowed
> through every second of my life.

It has flowed, too, through much of his poetry, giving it the same essential spirit of place that Bunyah gave to Les Murray, New England to Judith Wright and Gippsland to Eve Langley. Page went to Canberra to teach in 1964 and has remained there. He was, for some years, in charge of the English Department of Narrabundah College and has been writer-in-residence at several educational institutions as well as a member of academic groups visiting and lecturing in Europe, America and China.

Page's beginning as a writer was modest; he shared a volume of UQP's Paperback Poets series in 1971 with Phillip Roberts. In the following seven years he published two more books of poetry, *Smalltown Memorials* (1975) and *Collecting the Weather* (1978). The years 1980–92 were extraordinarily prolific, however. In that time he published seven books of his own poetry, *Cassandra Paddocks* (1980), *Clairvoyant in Autumn* (1983), *Collected Lives* (1986), *Smiling in English, Smoking in French* (1987), *Footwork* (1988), *Selected Poems* (1991), *Gravel Corners* (1992) and *Human Interest* (1994). He also edited *Shadows from Wire: Poems and Photographs of Australians in the Great War* (1983), *Century of Clouds: Selected Poems of Guillaume Apollinaire* (translations – with Wendy Coutts, 1985) and *On the Move: Australian Poets in Europe* (1992). He has also written two novels, *Benton's Conviction* (1985), the story of David Benton, and *Winter Vision* (1989). Page also published *Invisible Histories* (1989), a selection of his well-crafted, lucid and unpretentious prose with poems from earlier books.

Page's poetry was influenced from the beginning by American writers such as William Carlos Williams, especially Williams's plain use of language, evocation of strong physical and spiritual realities and expression of a distinctive personality. Much the same virtues are present in Page's own poetry. The physical reality is his ancestry and its relationship with the Clarence River country, and his immediate family – father and mother, son – and then his extended family of grandparents, cousins and other relatives. The spiritual reality is the inevitability of old age and death and the ultimate nothingness. The physical reality of his family and farming background gives a remarkable warmth to his poetry and runs through all his books, e.g. grandmother and grandson together in 'Detail', and memories of his father in 'Departure and Return', both from *Cassandra Paddocks*, as well as the striking hymn of praise ('Grit') for his mother and other pioneer women. *Collected Lives* is the story of the whole family; each of the six sections recounts the life of one member of the Page family, the poet's own life being represented in it ('1940–   '). When that life is complete, it is his wish, expressed in 'Codicil' from *Gravel Corners*, that his ashes be consigned in 'a long descending curve' to the waters of the Clarence. *Gravel Corners*, which ends with two poems about his father (to whom the book is dedicated), 'The Proverb' and 'My Father in His Silver Frame', brings Page's celebration of his family to a fitting conclusion. The spiritual reality in Page's poetry, his concern with transience and death, is perhaps responsible for the melancholy note which has frequently been said to mark his work. Page is not, however, a sombre poet; he has a remarkably ironic eye but makes only the gentlest of mischief with it. War, with its cost of so many innocent lives and the brutal massacre of Aborigines in the early stages of settlement are also topics that he returns to frequently in his writing. While age and death greatly occupy him there is solace in the comfort that the aged – husband and wife – can bring to each other in their final years. From 'Love at the End' comes the thought,

> Fingers linked, we float towards that last
> stopped moment when one will hand the other through
>
> alone
> to disbelief . . . and silence.

The title poem of *Human Interest* is a four-part series based on several macabre incidents demonstrating the fragility of the human psyche. 'Kokoda Corrective' is a timely rebuke to those who continue to ignore Aboriginal history, 'The Clarence of Copmanhurst' is surely one of our finest 'river' poems; in it, as in all significant poetry, man and nature are one.

The proof of Page's considerable appeal as a poet is his presence in so many contemporary anthologies. Among his most popular poems are 'Grit', 'Bondi Afternoon 1915', 'Inscription at Villers-Bretonneux', 'Cassandra Paddocks', 'Detail', 'Roots and Branches' and 'Country Nun'. His sequence 'Five Australian Maps' (published later in *Gravel Corners*) won the Queensland Premier's Poetry Prize in 1990.

PAGE, Tony (1952–   ), born Melbourne, travelled in Europe and Asia after graduation and has worked as a teacher and as a film and theatre critic. He has contributed verse to numerous periodicals and to the anthology *La Mama Poetica* (1989). He has published two collections, *They're Knocking at My Door* (1986) and *Satellite Link* (1992).

PALMER, Aileen (1915–88), daughter of Vance and Nettie Palmer and sister of Helen Palmer, was born in London and educated at the University of Melbourne. She served with the British medical unit and medical service of the International Brigade in Spain 1936–38 and with the London Auxiliary Ambulance Service, 1939–43. She contributed verse to such journals as *Overland, Meanjin, Southerly, Vietnam Advances* and *Realist Writer* and published two collections, *World Without Strangers?* (1964) and *Dear Life* (1957), under the pseudonym 'Caliban'. Judith Keene has written a poignant account of her life and ultimate mental breakdown in *Crossing Boundaries: Feminisms and the Critique of Knowledges* (1988), ed. Barbara Caine et al.

PALMER, Nettie (1885–1964) was born Janet Gertrude Higgins at Bendigo, Victoria. She graduated from the University of Melbourne in 1909 and in 1910 left for Europe to study languages, first in London, then in Marburg and Paris. She returned to Australia in 1911, completed her MA degree at the University of Melbourne in 1912 and left again for London in 1914 to marry Vance Palmer. Their marriage was to be a remarkable literary partnership, of great importance to Australia's cultural life. Although Nettie Palmer's life centred mainly on her husband and her two daughters, Aileen and Helen, she made an independent contribution and there were important distinctions between her work and her husband's. At a personal level she seems to have been at least as influential as Vance Palmer and in particular her relationship with 'Henry Handel Richardson' was important. Her prolific literary journalism, especially during the 1920s and 1930s, when Vance Palmer was concentrating on creative work and when Australian publishing and literary debate were at a low ebb, was of inestimable significance. She moved easily in international literary circles and in 1935 she attended the Writers' Congress in Paris. There she made contact with the Australian writer Christina Stead and with many international writers, including André Gide, Paul Elvard, André Malraux and E.M. Forster. Only a few of her penetrating impressions there are recorded in her published journal extracts *Fourteen Years* (1948), although others survive in manuscript form. Nettie Palmer was also in the forefront of the Palmers' practical work for refugees and immigrants, especially during the Spanish Civil War. In addition, she frequently worked closely with Vance Palmer in research for his novels and in particular on the 1937 abridgement of Joseph Furphy's *Such is Life*. Like her husband, she was a familiar broadcaster on ABC radio in the 1940s and 1950s and on several occasions lectured in Australian literature for the CLF. After her husband's death in 1959 she continued to write, concentrating on her projected autobiography, but rapid deterioration of her health prevented its completion.

Her published work consists of two volumes of poetry, *The South Wind* (1914) and *Shadowy Paths* (1915); a critical appreciation, *Modern Australian Literature 1900–1923* (1924); a collection of essays, *Talking It Over* (1932); a memoir of her uncle, Henry Bournes Higgins (1931); *Fourteen Years: Extracts from a Private Journal, 1925–1939* (1948); a study of 'Henry Handel Richardson' (1950) and, with Victor Kennedy, one of Bernard O'Dowd (1954); and *The Dandenongs* (1952). In 1977 Vivian Smith edited a selection of her and Vance Palmer's letters, 1915–63, and in 1988 an edition of *Fourteen Years* with selected poetry, articles, reviews and essays. In 1959 when *Meanjin* published an issue in tribute to the Palmers, some attempts were made to assess her contribution, but Drusilla Modjeska, who has written extensively on her difficulties and achievements in *Exiles at Home* (1981), and Vivian Smith in his study *Vance and Nettie Palmer* (1975) and in other essays and introductions have done the most to establish her reputation.

Nettie Palmer's creativity found its fullest scope in her prose work; her poems, mainly simple lyrics, are now interesting mainly as period pieces. The Victorian Premier's Awards includes a Nettie Palmer Award for non-fiction.

PALMER, Vance (1885–1959) was born at Bundaberg, Queensland, the youngest in a family of eight. His father was a schoolmaster with diverse literary interests and his childhood was spent in a succession of Queensland country towns. He rejected the idea of a university education, spent some time as a private secretary, and in 1905 left for London, where he stayed for two years earning his living as a 'Grub Street hack'. He returned to Australia by way of Finland, Russia and Japan, tried salesmanship and schoolteaching, and spent some time as tutor, bookkeeper and drover in north-west Queensland. Five of his early novels and many of his short stories reflect these experiences. In 1910 he revisited London, this time making contact with several British writers, most importantly with A.R. Orage, the editor of the *New Age*, who encouraged his writing and influenced his social philosophy. He returned briefly to Australia in 1912, travelling through USA and Mexico, which was at that time in revolution. In 1914 he married Janet Higgins in London. Before their return to Australia in September 1915, Palmer had begun his literary career with collections of poetry, *The Forerunners* (1915), and short stories, *The World of Men* (1915), and with numerous articles for the *New Age*, the *Manchester Guardian Fortnightly*, and the *British Review*. His return to Australia at the height of imperialist fervour generated by the

war quickened his commitment to his own culture and his concern for the development and preservation of its distinctive identity. A vigorous opponent of conscription,
he nevertheless enlisted in the AIF in 1918 and was sent overseas, but was too late to see
action. For the next decade, spent at Emerald, Palmer was actively engaged in the
cause of Australian literary nationalism as an essayist and reviewer and as a leading
member of the Pioneer Players. This period also saw the publication of another collection of poetry, *The Camp* (1920), a collection of plays, *The Black Horse and Other
Plays* (1924), and five novels: *The Shantykeeper's Daughter* (1920), *The Boss of Killara*
(1922), *The Enchanted Island* (1923), *The Outpost* (1924) and *Cronulla* (1924). In 1925 the
Palmers left for Caloundra, a small fishing port in Queensland. Freelance literary
journalism, largely undertaken by Nettie Palmer, provided a living, while Vance
Palmer worked on a group of novels: *The Man Hamilton* (1928), *Men are Human* (1930),
The Passage (1930), *Daybreak* (1932) and *The Swayne Family* (1934). In order to educate
their daughters, the family returned to Melbourne from 1929 to 1932, spent some time
at Green Island, Queensland, in 1932 and then at Kalorama, Victoria, 1932–35, before
revisiting Europe in 1935–36, where they witnessed the beginning of the Spanish
Civil War. Apart from another visit to Europe in 1955 and winter holidays in Queensland, Palmer lived in Melbourne for the rest of his life. By the 1940s his reputation as
Australia's pre-eminent cultural figure was well established, reinforced by his regular
talks and reviews for the ABC. He served on the CLF, 1942–53. His other publications
are the novels *Legend for Sanderson* (1937), *Cyclone* (1947) and the trilogy *Golconda*
(1948), *Seedtime* (1957) and *The Big Fellow* (1959); the collections of short stories *Separate Lives* (1931), *Sea and Spinifex* (1934), *Let the Birds Fly* (1955) and the reprinted
selection *The Rainbow-Bird and Other Stories* (1957); the plays *Ancestors*, in *Best Australian One-Act Plays* (1937), and *Hail Tomorrow* (1947); and the essays and studies
National Portraits (1940), *A.G. Stephens: His Life and Work* (1941), *Frank Wilmot (Furnley Maurice)* (1942), *Louis Esson and the Australian Theatre* (1948) and *The Legend of the
Nineties* (1954). He was instrumental in both the reissue of Joseph Furphy's *Such is Life*
in 1917 and the abridged edition (1937); and compiled a collection of bush ballads, *Old
Australian Bush Ballads* (1951). *Intimate Portraits* (1969), ed. H.P. Heseltine, is a selection of his essays and talks, and a selection of his and Nettie Palmer's letters, edited by
Vivian Smith, was published in 1977. In 1959, when *Meanjin* published a special issue
in tribute to Vance and Nettie Palmer, many of the writers for whom Palmer had been
an important influence expressed their appreciation. His preoccupations and achievements are explored in Harry Heseltine's *Vance Palmer* (1970), Vivian Smith's *Vance
Palmer* (1971) and *Vance and Nettie Palmer* (1975) and David Walker's *Dream and Disillusion* (1976).

The pervading theme of all Palmer's work is his firm belief in an 'Australia of the
spirit' and in literature as its influential and lasting expression. For Palmer, Australian
literature was, or should be, an integral part of the fabric of national life, an expression
of its inner spirit and values, its distinctive 'undertones'. As he asserted in an early
essay, writers 'must be at one with the purposes and aspirations of the people and their
hearts must beat in unison with them'. A profound admirer of Henry Lawson, Barbara
Baynton, Bernard O'Dowd and Joseph Furphy, he saw the 1890s as the period in
which their national identity was first revealed to Australians, primarily through the
work of the *Bulletin* writers. He perceived this revealed national consciousness as
robust, masculine, close to nature and physical work, democratic, taciturn, sardonic,
frugal, unsentimental and communal; he rapidly saw the communal concept as a
threatened ideal, subject to erosion by the materialism of the expanding cities. These
values inform his own work. His verse, characterised by simple forms and generalised
emotions, clearly fails as a means of giving rein to his keenest concerns, although 'The
Farmer Remembers the Somme' is one of Australia's most effective war poems.
Palmer's wide-ranging literary journalism displays tact, discrimination and practical,

intuitive evaluations rather than critical theories or strikingly original perceptions. His series of books on key national figures written between 1940 and 1954, and especially his seminal *The Legend of the Nineties*, reflect his preoccupation with the inner life of Australia and his concern to preserve its distinctive democratic quality. The Victorian Premier's Awards include a Vance Palmer Award for fiction.

Pamphlet Poets is a set of beautifully produced pamphlets in individual paper wallets emanating from the National Library of Australia, each containing eight poems by a single writer. The series began in 1990, the first series comprising John Bray's *Tobacco: A Valedictory and Other Poems*, Sarah Day's *Sarah Day*, Rosemary Dobson's *Seeing is Believing*, Paul Hetherington's *Mapping Wildwood Road*, Jennifer Maiden's *Bastille Day* and Tom Shapcott's *In the Beginning*. Series 2 in 1992 comprised Silvana Gardner's *Cochineal Red*, Peter Goldsworthy's *After the Ball*, Gwen Harwood's *Night Thoughts*, Judith Rodriguez's *The Cold*, Philip Salom's *Tremors* and John Tranter's *Days in the Capital*. Another Pamphlet Poets series is that published by Metro Arts, Brisbane. The first series included the work of Queensland poets Gary Maller, Anna Cameron, Maria Fresta and Eluned Lloyd.

Paperback Poets, a series initiated by UQP in 1970, presented a wide range of contemporary Australian poetry. The first series of eighteen books, mostly edited by Roger McDonald, was published 1970–73, and comprised David Malouf's *Bicycle and Other Poems* (1970), Michael Dransfield's *Streets of the Long Voyage* (1970), Rodney Hall's *Heaven, in a Way* (1970), Andrew Taylor's *The Cool Change* (1970), Geoff Page and Philip Roberts's *Two Poets: The Question and Single Eye* (1971), J.S. Harry's *The Deer under the Skin* (1971), R.A. Simpson's *Diver* (1972), Dransfield's *The Inspector of Tides* (1972), Rhyll McMaster's *The Brineshrimp* (1972), Richard Tipping's *Soft Riots* (1972), Thomas Shapcott's *Begin with Walking* (1972), Leon Slade's *Slade's Anatomy of the Horse* (1972), David Lake's *Hornpipes & Funerals* (1973), Judith Rodriguez's *Nu-Plastik Fanfare Red and Other Poems* (1973), Andrew Taylor's *Ice Fishing* (1973), Rodney Hall's *A Soapbox Omnibus* (1973), Manfred Jurgensen's *Signs and Voices* (1973), and Vicki Viidikas's *Condition Red* (1973). *The First Paperback Poets Anthology*, edited by McDonald, was published in 1974.

The second series of nineteen books was published 1974–81 and comprised Jennifer Maiden's *Tactics* (1974), Paul Kavanagh's *Wild Honey* (1974), Robert Gray's *Creekwater Journal* (1974), McDonald's *Airship* (1975), Page's *Smalltown Memorials* (1975), Graeme Kinross Smith and Jamie Grant's *Turn Left at Any Time with Care* (1975), Robin Thurston's *Believed Dangerous* (1975), Peter Skrzynecki's *Immigrant Chronicle* (1975), Tipping's *Domestic Hardcore* (1975), Roberts's *Will's Dream* (1975), Peter Kocan's *The Other Side of the Fence* (1975), Simpson's *Poems from Murrumbeena* (1976), Andrew McDonald's *Absence in Strange Countries* (1976), Alan Wearne's *New Devil, New Parish* (1976), Martin Johnston's *The Sea-Cucumber* (1978), Alan Gould's *Icelandic Solitaries* (1978), Kevin Hart's *The Departure* (1978), Gary Catalano's *Remembering the Rural Life* (1978), and Susan Whiting's *Between Breaths* (1981). *Consolidation: The Second Paperback Poets Anthology* comprising selected poems from the second series, edited by Thomas Shapcott, was published in 1981.

PARADISSIS, Aristides (George) (1923–   ), born China of Greek parents, arrived in Australia in 1949. After gaining a Licence en Droit from the Universite l'Aurore, Shanghai, he completed further studies at the universities of London and Melbourne and at La Trobe University. He has taught at secondary and tertiary level in China, Egypt and Australia and was lecturer and senior lecturer in French, Spanish and European literature at La Trobe University 1967–85. He has contributed poems in English to anthologies and periodicals and has published three collections, *A Tree at* *the Gate* (1971), *The City of the Tree* (1981) and *The Bing Book of Verse. Poems in Memory of Bing Crosby* (1983).

PARKES, Sir Henry (1815–96), born Warwickshire, England, grew up in Birmingham, where he received only a meagre education. Unsuccessful business ventures as a young man led to his departure from England in 1839, a situation which he deplored in some verses, 'A Poet's Farewell'. In Australia he tried a variety of jobs before turning to politics, supporting the causes of liberalism and anti-transportation. He was assisted financially, in 1850, to become an editor of the newspaper the *Empire*, an important voice in the developing democracy of the day. He was elected to the Legislative Council in 1854 and the first Legislative Assembly in 1856. Years of political and commercial crises followed, his fortunes in both arenas fluctuating wildly, but Parkes, a natural survivor, became premier in 1872, a position he was to hold on five subsequent occasions. Often called the 'Father of Federation', Parkes played a key role in the Federation conventions of 1890–91. An important figure also in the colonial literary milieu, he was a friend of Charles Harpur and the long-suffering patron of Henry Kendall. His own publications include the volumes of verse *Stolen Moments* (1842), *Murmurs of the Stream* (1857), *Studies in Rhyme* (1870), *The Beauteous Terrorist and Other Poems* (1885), *Fragmentary Thoughts* (1889) and *Sonnets and Other Verse* (1895). His chief prose work is the autobiographical *Fifty Years in the Making of Australian History* (1892). The outstanding account of his life and work is A.W. Martin's *Henry Parkes* (1980).

'PARTRIGE, Sydney' (Kate Margaret Stone) (1871–1953) was the wife of Hal Stone (1872–1956), whose private Wayside Press produced numerous publications by Australian writers and who edited the magazines the *Red Ant, Ye Kangaroo* and *Ye Wayside Goose*. She published two collections of verse, *The Lie and Other Lines* (1913) and *The One Life and Other Verses* (1936); two novels, *Rocky Section* (1907) and *The Mystery of Wall's Hill* (1921, with Cecil Raworth); and a collection of short stories reprinted from the *Bulletin*, the *Australasian* and other magazines, *Life's Wallaby* (1908).

Passionate Heart, The (1918), a volume of poems by Mary Gilmore, was dedicated to 'The Fellowing Men', the soldiers of the First World War. Poems such as 'The Measure', 'The Satin of the Bee', 'Corn' and 'Gallipoli' tell of the loss and heartache of war as seen through a woman's eyes and reflect the general disenchantment with war that followed the Allied victory in 1918. Other poems, such as 'Life-Song', 'Life at Autumn' and the title poem, carry the typical Mary Gilmore affirmation of life.

'Past Carin'', a poem by Henry Lawson which records the lament of a bush woman whom hardship and tragedy have made 'past carin'', was published in 1899. It subsequently became the title of the second part of '"Water them Geraniums"', a story in the Joe Wilson sequence, which chronicles the spiritual disintegration and death of the bush woman Mrs Spicer.

PATERSON, A.B. (Andrew Barton) (1864–1941), widely known as 'Banjo' Paterson from the pseudonym 'The Banjo', which he adopted for his early contributions to the *Bulletin*, was born at Narambla Station, near Orange, NSW. Growing up in the bush on Illalong Station near Yass, NSW, he had an early acquaintance with identities such as drovers, teamsters and even bushrangers, with occasions such as picnic race meetings, and with relationships such as the animosity between squatters and drovers. Those early experiences provided him with a fund of incidents, characters and scenes, which his later writings turned into legend. After early schooling in the small town of Binalong he completed his education in Sydney, then entered a lawyer's office as clerk, and was ultimately admitted as a solicitor. A literary celebrity after the rapturous reception of *The Man from Snowy River and Other Verses* in 1895, the handsome, well-bred, athletic Paterson rapidly became the toast of the country; he is portrayed as such in Nigel Krauth's novel *Matilda, My Darling* (1983). His later life was full of glamour and adventure. He went crocodile-hunting and buffalo-shooting in the Northern Territory, dived for pearls with the Japanese at Broome, was a war correspondent in the Boer War, and travelled to China to cover the Boxer Rebellion. Back in Australia he was successively editor of the Sydney *Evening News* and the *Australian Town and Country Journal*. In the First World War he was initially a war correspondent but, dissatisfied with his inability to get to the front in France, returned to Australia and enlisted in the Remount Service which provided horses for the Australian cavalry in the Middle East. After the war he returned to journalism, edited the *Sydney Sportsman*, continued to indulge his love for all sports, especially the turf, and wrote further verse and fiction as well as scripts for radio. He had lived periodically in the country on the property Coodravale on the upper Murrumbidgee, fulfilling the dream he had expressed years earlier in 'A Mountain Station', but from 1919 he lived in Sydney.

Paterson's books of verse are *The Man from Snowy River and Other Verses* (1895), *Rio Grande's Last Race and Other Verses* (1902) and *Saltbush Bill J.P. and Other Verses* (1917). A *Collected Verse* was published in 1923. His fiction comprised two novels, *An Outback Marriage* (1906) and *The Shearer's Colt* (1936); and short stories, *Three Elephant Power and Other Stories* (1917). Reminiscences of his travels and adventures were brought together in the semi-autobiographical *Happy Dispatches* (1934). He also compiled the seminal anthology *Old Bush Songs* (1905). Paterson left several unpublished works, including 'Racehorses and Racing' and 'Illalong Children', both of which were published in 1983, *Singer of the Bush* (writings 1885–1900) and *Song of the Pen* (writings 1901–41). Published by Lansdowne Press as *The Complete Works of Banjo Paterson*, it remains a best-seller. A recent selection by Richard Hall reprints some of Paterson's journalism, *Banjo Paterson. His Poetry and Prose* (1993).

Paterson is the chief folk-poet of Australia. 'Waltzing Matilda', Australia's national song, and 'The Man from Snowy River', Australia's national narrative poem, substantiate that claim. Add such folk-figures as 'Clancy of the Overflow', 'Saltbush Bill', 'The Man from Ironbark' and 'Mulga Bill', set them 'On Kiley's Run', at 'Conroy's Gap', along 'The Road to Gundagai' or 'By the Grey Gulf Water', have them sing 'A Bushman's Song', dream 'A Dream of the Melbourne Cup', swap old yarns of 'Father Riley's Horse' and 'The Geebung Polo Club', or ruefully recount 'How the Favourite Beat Us', and the outlines of the map of Australian folklore are broadly drawn. That mythical map's outlines coincide with actual geographical boundaries. It begins in the western plains of NSW, takes in the Murrumbidgee and the Monaro, heads north to the Queensland Downs and the Northern Territory, encompassing the whole limitless outback. It is 'the land of lots o' time', signposted with fabled names, the Overflow, the Castlereagh, the Snowy, Dandaloo, Gundaroo, Come-by-Chance, Hogan's Gap, Hay and Hell and Booligal. It is Australian Arcadia, created by all the bush balladists and in his more optimistic moods even contributed to by Henry Lawson himself, but it is indisputably Paterson country. Whether Australian Arcadia ever existed in the way Paterson pictured it is problematical, but the general Australian populace has long been beguiled by his vision. The first edition of *The Man from Snowy River* sold out in the week of publication; it went through four editions in six months and still outsells any other volume of Australian poetry ever published. The Arcadian view was strongly challenged in the *Bulletin* debate with Lawson in 1892–93, but Paterson did not, in his own opinion, ignore those aspects of the outback which coloured Lawson's attitude – the minor irritants like dust, heat and flies, or the darker calamities like droughts, floods, despair and tragedy. His Arcadians simply accepted their lot, good or bad, with cheerful, laconic patience.

Paterson is the supreme balladist of the horse. In bushman fashion he viewed the horse as an animal trained for and useful in specific tasks and he admired it for its excellence in those tasks, one of which is racing. Racing involves feats of speed, courage and endurance and there is plenty of human drama associated with it. 'Rio Grande's Last Race', 'Father Riley's Horse', 'The Old Timer's Steeplechase', 'Mulligan's Mare' and 'In the Droving Days' are notable Paterson stories of the horse, but 'The Man from Snowy River' is the undisputed classic of that genre. Paterson belongs also to the stream of nationalist-radical writers that the 1890s nurtured. In 'A Bushman's Song' he is the radical, putting the case for the ordinary drover and shearer against the squatter and the absentee landlord, while 'Song of Federation', 'Song of the Future' and 'Old Australian Ways' express nationalist sentiments.

Paterson is commemorated in the Banjo Paterson Award made biennially by the Orange Festival of Arts Committee for one-act plays and poetry and the National Book Council's annual awards which, since 1988, have been known as the Banjo Awards. The major biographical and critical study for many years was Clement Semmler's popular *The Banjo of the Bush: The Work, Life and Times of A.B. Paterson* (1966). Semmler has also edited, with an introduction, *The World of 'Banjo' Paterson* (1967) and the beautifully illustrated *The Collected Verse of A.B. Paterson* (1992) and has written *A.B. Paterson* (1967) in the Great Australian series, *A.B. Paterson* (1965) in OUP's Australian Writers and Their Work series and *A.B. 'Banjo' Paterson* (1992) in UQP's Australian Authors series. Colin Roderick in the recent (1992) biography *Banjo Paterson: Poet by Accident* combines his own lengthy experience of the bush poet genre with wider-ranging research into much primary Paterson material.

Patrick White Literary Award is an annual award established by Patrick White in 1973 with the proceeds of the Nobel Prize for Literature which he won that year. It is awarded to an older Australian writer whose work, in the opinion of the administrators of the fund, has not received the critical acclaim or the financial rewards it deserves. Several poets have won the award: David Campbell (1975), John Blight (1976), Gwen Harwood (1978), Randolph Stow (1979), Bruce Dawe (1980), Bruce Beaver (1982), Rosemary Dobson (1984), William Hart-Smith (1987), Robert Gray (1990), David Martin (1991), Amy Witting (1993) and Dimitris Tsaloumas (1994).

PATTERSON, Henry (1867– ?), born Scotland, came to Australia in 1878 and acquired ownership of several country newspapers in Victoria. A prolific, conventional and flowery poet who specialised in elevated, patriotic themes, Patterson published nine volumes of verse. They are *The Litany of Liberty* (1918), *Song of the Anzacs* (1918), *Sunrise Hymns and The Litany of Liberty* (1919), *Morning Songs* (1922), *More Morning Songs* (1924), *Joan of Domremy* (1925), *The King's Chamberlain* (1939), *Armageddon* (1940) and *Kingdom Come* (1944). Both *The King's Chamberlain* and *Armageddon* were published under the pseudonym 'Bartimaeus'.

PEARCE, Harry Hastings (1897–1984), born Creswick, Victoria, worked as a gold-miner and farm labourer and lived in NZ for fourteen years before settling in Melbourne. A professed atheist and rationalist, he published several pamphlets in support of his views. A member of the Melbourne Bread and Cheese Club, treasurer and secretary of the Australian Poetry Lovers' Society from 1948 until its demise in 1973, and editor of its little magazine, the *Poetry Lover*, 1955–73, he was also active in the Henry Lawson Memorial and Literary Society and in the Folklore Society of Victoria. He published two collections of poetry, *The Song of Nature* (1948) and *Dreams and Arrows* (1969); a narrative poem, *Thomas Kennedy's March from Creswick's Creek* (1954), written to commemorate the centenary of Eureka; and a detailed argument concerning the origins of 'Waltzing Matilda' (1971).

PELL Olive (1903–), born Kalgoorlie, has worked as a secretary and librarian. She has written numerous radio features, short stories, plays for radio and television, and has published three collections of poetry, *Gold to Win* (1964), *I'd Rather Be a Fig!* (1976) and *Patient Reaction* (1991).

PERRY, Fiona (1958–), born Brisbane, now lives in Townsville where she conducts a drama studio and is the artistic director of a youth theatre company. She has published *Pharaohs Returning* (1991), in the Penguin Australian Poetry series (a short volume with Alison Croggon's *This is the Stone*). The title poem is in a group of 'Five Sonnets for Egypt', based upon Lord Carnarvon's discovery of the tomb of Tutankhamen. The 'Pharaoh Returning' would find, says Perry, 'desecration after desecration . . . nothing to worship'. Egypt and the past are strong elements in Perry's work, which also includes poems about Maria Theresa, Empress of Austria, Marie Tagliani, the first ballerina to dance on the tips of her toes, and the more contemporary subject of Sylvia Plath's suicide. The personal is also present in her poetry e.g., 'Nursery Song', 'Mango Season', 'Acknowledgment' and 'Committed'.

PERRY, Grace (1927–87), born Melbourne, was educated in Queensland and Sydney, then graduated in medicine from the University of Sydney in 1951. She combined family life with a career as a paediatrician and an extremely energetic involvement in contemporary literary affairs as poet, editor, publisher, founder member of the ASA and convenor/organiser of numerous Sydney poetry workshops and writing schools. At Berrima, where she lived in her last years, she ran a 2000-acre property and maintained an interest in stud breeding. She was editor of *Poetry Magazine*, 1961–64; in 1964 she inaugurated *Poetry Australia*, which she edited until her death. She founded South Head Press in 1964. Her own published poetry began with teenage volumes, *Staring at the Stars* (1942) and *I Live a Life of Dreams* (1943). Her first mature volume, *Red Scarf* (1963), is in two sections: 'Where the Wind Moves', love poems in which natural scenery, usually seascapes, is used to reflect personal emotions; and 'Red Scarf', striking poems born out of her experiences as a doctor, which express the horror and fascination of disease and death. *Frozen Section* (1967), notable also for its considerable medical sequence, reflects the problem that is nearly always present in Grace Perry's writing, the accommodation of the clinical detachment of the physician with the sensitive involvement of the poet. *Two Houses* (1969) contains the sequence 'Notes on a Journey', small intense landscape images of the picturesque Warrumbungles and western NSW, and poems of contemporary events such as President Lyndon B. Johnson's Australian visit. *Black Swans at Berrima* (1972), an ambitious sequence of more than a hundred individual lyric pieces, begins with the building of the historic magistrate's house at Berrima, describes a journey from Sydney to Berrima, and explores the passing of time and the approach of age and death. Following *Berrima Winter* (1974), Perry published *Journal of a Surgeon's Wife and Other Poems* (1976), the title poem a long verse diary of the experiences of an immigrant doctor's wife in early colonial Australia. The poem captures the sense of exile that so oppressed the early settlers. Another book of poetry, *Snow in Summer* (1980), was followed in 1981 by a play, with John Millett, *Last Bride at Longsleep*. *Poetry Australia* No. 119 (1989) consists of poetry by Perry with German translations by Margaret Diesendorf. In 1985 Perry won the NSW Premier's Special Award for services to literature, and in 1986 was made AM.

PETSINIS, Tom (1953–), born Macedonia, Greece, came to Australia in 1959, grew up in Fitzroy, Melbourne, and studied mathematics at the University of Melbourne. He teaches at the Victoria University of Technology. He has published a novel, *Raising the Shadow* (1992), and a book of poetry, *The Blossom Vendor* (1992), which re-creates scenes, events and characters from Petsinis's original homeland and other European countries. The poems are set in such places as Thassos, Salonika,

Florence, Rome, Alexandria and are peopled by an assortment of literary, mythical, historical and colourful characters. Among the last-named are the 'The Blossom Vendor', 'The Book Vendor' and 'The Lottery Vendor' – all three from Salonika. Direct and economical, the poems convey with imaginative precision the essence of place and character.

'Phil the Poet', see **LORIMER, Philip Durham**

PHILP, J.A. (James Alexander) (1861–1935), born Stirling, Scotland, was a journalist in Queensland and sub-editor of the *Bulletin*, to which he also contributed short stories. He published two collections of verse, *Jingles That Jangle* (1918) and *Songs of the Australian Fascisti* (1923). His short stories, several of which are set in NZ, where he was educated, were collected in 1916, titled *Some Bulletin Stories*.

PICOT, James (1906–44), born England, came to Australia in 1923 and graduated from the University of Queensland. In 1941 he enlisted in the AIF and died as a POW on the Burma–Thailand railway. He was one of the four contributors of verse to the first issue of *Meanjin*, which published a selection of letters, personal recollections and critical appreciations of his work in 1954. His extant poems were collected after his death, titled *With a Hawk's Quill* (1953). Influenced by such poets as Robert Browning, T.S. Eliot and Gerard Manley Hopkins, Picot was a brilliant linguist, who had a promising career in prospect as poet and critic.

'ΠΟ' (1951–   ), born Greece, has been resident in Australia since infancy. A draftsperson in the Victorian public service, he is well known out of working hours as an anarchist and a reader and writer of concrete verse. Regarded initially as a bizarre figure by some, ΠΟ has proved extremely durable, writing and promoting poetry for more than two decades, especially that concerned with and emanating from Melbourne's large immigrant population. A member of a number of collective presses, he has edited such underground poetry magazines as *Fitzrot, Born to Concrete, Free, Free Too, Free Read, i's and e's* and *9.2.5*, and is a familiar contributor to such magazines as *Ploughman, Contempa, Magic Sam, Luna* and *Your Friendly Fascist.* An enthusiastic supporter of poetry readings in schools, prisons, universities, at political demonstrations and on radio, ΠΟ has played a leading role in the upsurge of performance poetry. He has contributed verse to several anthologies and published numerous collections including *Fitzroy Brothel* (1974), *Poems by Pi O* (1974), *Shade* (1974, with Stephanie Bennett), *Emotions in Concrete* (1975), *Street Singe* (1976), *Pi O Revisited* (1976), *Humble Pi* (1977), *Panash* (1978), *The Fuck Poems* (1982) and *Re: The National Neurosis: Ockers* (1983). *The Fitzroy Poems* (1989) is a selection of his poetry, much of it in a Greek-Australian dialect. He edited *Off the Record*, a collection of works by about fifty Australian poets working in pubs, cafés, clubs and on the streets, and *Missing Form: Concrete, Visual and Experimental Poems* (1981).

Pipes were anonymous scurrilous verses, which were occasionally circulated in NSW during the early years of settlement and which lampooned those in authority from the governor down. The name may derive from the verb 'to pipe', meaning to observe and victimise an individual, or from the habit of folding the lampoon in the shape of a pipe. The first pipes, directed against Governor King, were written in 1803 and others to suffer from the lampoons were Samuel Marsden and Lieutenant-Colonel George Molle. W.C. Wentworth is known to be author of some pipes and other alleged authors are Michael Massey Robinson and some officers of the NSW Corps.

PITT, Marie (1869–1948) was born at Doherty's Corner, a small mining town in Gippsland as Marie McKeown and received little schooling owing to her family's extreme poverty. After she married William Pitt, a Tasmanian farmer, later a goldminer, in 1893, she lived in mining and farming areas of Tasmania, moving to

Bairnsdale in 1905 and subsequently to Melbourne after her husband contracted miners' phthisis. Pitt died in 1912 and Marie supported her three children by writing for newspapers and clerical work. A familiar figure in feminist and socialist circles, a member of the Victorian Socialist Party, and, with Frederick Sinclaire, editor for a time of the *Socialist*, she wrote several ballads which have an underlying note of social protest. Friendly with such writers as Vance and Nettie Palmer, Mary Gilmore and Louis Esson, she was particularly influenced by Bernard O'Dowd, with whom she lived from 1920. Her verse, which first began to appear in the *Bulletin* in 1900, and subsequently appeared in the *Clarion*, *Birth* and the *Socialist*, was published in four collections, *The Horses of the Hills* (1911), *Bairnsdale and Other Poems* (1922), *The Poems of Marie E. J. Pitt* (1925) and *Selected Poems* (1944). Pitt's best-known work is contained in her studies of landscape, her most radical verse being omitted from the 1944 selection. In 1944 she won the ABC's national song lyric competition with 'Ave Australia'. Colleen Burke has written a biography of Pitt, *Doherty's Corner* (1985), which includes a selection of her poetry and prose.

PIZER, Marjorie (1920–), born Melbourne and educated at the University of Melbourne, lives in Sydney where she works as a psychotherapist. She has published several collections of poetry, *Thou and I* (1967), *To Life* (1969), *Tides Flow* (1972), *Seasons of Love* (1975), *Full Summer* (1977), *Gifts and Remembrances* (1979), *To You, the Living* (1981), *The Sixtieth Spring* (1982), *Selected Poems 1963–1983* (1984), *Equinox: Poems* (1987), *Fire in the Heart* (1990) and *Journeys* (1992), and with Anne Spencer Parry, *Below the Surface* (1982). She has also edited an anthology of poetry, *Freedom on the Wallaby* (1953); a selection of stories and poems by Henry Lawson, *The Men Who Made Australia* (1957); and with her husband, Muir Holburn, a collection of verse by Victor Daley, *Creeve Roe* (1947). Pizer and Holburn were founders of the Pinchgut Press in 1947, which published *Creeve Roe* and *Freedom on the Wallaby* and which was revived in 1975 to publish Pizer's poetry and Anne Spencer Parry's series of fantasy novels. With Drusilla Modjeska she edited *The Poems of Lesbia Harford* (1985). Pizer's poems celebrate the simple things and everyday compensations of life in the face of death, war and transience.

Poems and Songs, Henry Kendall's first volume of verse, was published in 1862. Many of these early Kendall poems attempt, however imperfectly, to reflect the spirit and character of Australian life and to picture the beauty of the Australian coastal landscape. Kendall the sentimental young romantic is also evident in them. Well-known poems include 'The Muse of Australia', 'Wild Kangaroo', 'The Curlew Song' and 'Morning in the Bush'.

Poetry: A Quarterly of Australian and New Zealand Verse, founded and edited by Flexmore Hudson, was published in Adelaide, 1941–47. Uncommitted to any particular ideology, the magazine published a mixture of notable and negligible talents; it changed its subtitle in 1946 to the *Australian International Quarterly of Verse* to reflect the subsequent inclusion of British, Irish and American poets. Contributors included Judith Wright, 'Brian Vrepont', Gina Ballantyne, Rex Ingamells and A.D. Hope.

Poetry Australia, a quarterly poetry magazine founded, managed and edited by Grace Perry, was first published in 1964 when Perry led a movement away from the Poetry Society of Australia and its journal *Poetry Magazine*, later *New Poetry*. Both *Poetry Australia* and the publishing house South Head Press were the result of Perry's resolve to produce a fine poetry magazine devoid of factions, fostering Australian talent but also one which was truly international. *Poetry Australia*, aided by editorial advice and assistance from poets such as Bruce Beaver and Les Murray (joint editor Nos 66–73), and from critics and academics such as Ronald Dunlop, James Tulip, Clement Semmler and Leonie Kramer, has published both new and established Australian writers, as well as modern overseas poetry. It has also published special issues of NZ, Canadian, Italian, Japanese, Dutch and Flemish, American, Gaelic, French, Austrian, Swedish and Papua New Guinean poetry; commemorative issues on Francis Webb and David Campbell; Young Poets issues; regional poetry of the various Australian States and special issues devoted to individual poets. Based in Sydney, *Poetry Australia* has also played a leading part in poetry readings and workshops, in literary seminars, and in visits by overseas writers of distinction. An account of the *raison d'être* of *Poetry Australia* and its history is given by Les Murray in 'Inside *Poetry Australia*', *Quadrant* (1983). *Poetry Australia – Twenty One Years* (1985), a collection of about thirty-five poems mostly by well-established Australian poets, celebrates twenty-one years of publication. The prize awarded in connection with that twenty-first milestone went to Keith Russell's 'The Trains South'. In its later years Grace Perry and John Millett were responsible for publication with assistance from guest editors for the special issues. It has been edited since 1988 by John Millett. Its achievements were recognised in 1985 by the NSW Premier's Special Literary Award.

Poetry Magazine, see **Poetry Society of Australia**

Poetry Militant is the name given to the poetic credo expressed by Bernard O'Dowd in a presidential address to the Australian Literature Society in 1909. The poet is to be 'the ferment who alters for the better, the ordered, natural, inert sequence of things'; his role is to accelerate the process of intellectual and moral evolution. Poetry Militant stresses the need for the poet to concern himself with worthy themes, e.g. politics, religion, sex, science, social reform, and with simple forms. It eschews 'Poetry Triumphant', the poetry of beauty and ornamentation, until the proper social order has been achieved.

Poetry Monash, emanating from the English Department of Monash University began in July 1977 under the editorship of Dennis Davison. Initially published twice yearly and later thrice yearly, it contained poems from writers and students associated with Monash. In 1987 Davison, having edited it about twenty times, became its business manager and Lynette Wilson succeeded him as editor.

Poetry Society of Australia was founded in Sydney in 1954 to encourage the study of poetry and to establish an active fellowship with a love of poetry as a common bond. In addition to performances by members of the Society (Shelley's *The Cenci* was produced in its first year), lectures and poetry competitions, the Society commenced publication in July 1954 of a journal, *Prism*. *Prism* was superseded in 1961 by *Poetry Magazine*, a bi-monthly publication edited, until 1964, by Grace Perry, assisted by Roland Robinson and others. *Poetry Magazine* ran until 1970 when a dispute over the question of how much space should be devoted to American and English writers saw its disappearance and replacement by *New Poetry* in February 1971.

Poet's Choice, see **ROBERTS, Philip**

Poets of the Month was a series of slim booklets of verse published monthly by Angus & Robertson, each booklet featuring the work of a single poet. The booklets were consolidated in several series, 1976–80.

Poets on Record, a series of recordings of well-known Australian poets reading from their own works, was published by UQP and edited by Thomas Shapcott. The series ran 1970–75.

POLITZER, Ludwig, editor of the *Centenary Journal 1934–35* (1935) and the author of two volumes of verse, *Autumn Leaves* (1934) and *In Introspective Mood* (1944), compiled several useful bibliographies of French, German and Dutch writing on the subject of Australia (1952, 1953).

PORTER, Dorothy Featherstone (1954–   ), born Sydney, was educated at the University of Sydney and has taught creative writing at the University of Technology, Sydney. Her poetry has appeared in numerous periodicals and anthologies and in six collections, *Little Hoodlum* (1975), *Bison* (1979), *The Night Parrot* (1984), *Driving Too Fast* (1989), *Akhenaten* (1992) and *The Monkey's Mask* (1994). She has also written a novel for young adults, *Rookwood* (1991). Sensuous and sharply witty, Porter's finely honed lyrics are charged with an immediate rhythmic energy and strikingly original imagery. The *Bison* collection draws on Porter's interest in music, painting, sculpture, and the figures of myth and legend. The poems of *The Night Parrot* circle around the description of the rare bird in the *Reader's Digest Complete Book of Australian Birds* ('Some naturalists believe it to be extinct, but there is evidence to suggest that a few individuals may survive in the spinifex country of the interior') to create an original companion or occasional adversary and spokescreature of the libido. *Driving Too Fast* moves from objective presentations of Carmen and Don Jose, Truganini, the Antarctic explorers Oates and Wilson, and British twins who chose to speak to no one but each other and are now incarcerated separately in a psychiatric hospital, to personal erotic poems of electric intensity: 'Our love stabs so deep/ I'm amazed the cuts/ can't fountain a power/ to fight death/ to the death.' Akhenaten, king of Egypt from 1378 BC to 1362 BC, is the subject of the collection of that title, which imagines the extraordinary/ordinary experiences of a man who attempted to eradicate all the old gods and replace them with one, Aten, the sun. The volume includes his perception of Nefertiti, his cousin and wife, who loves, despairs and hates. *The Monkey's Mask*, clever, satirical and written in verse, is a tongue-in-cheek crime thriller at the centre of which is a lesbian love affair. It won the *Age* Book of the Year Award for poetry in 1994.

PORTER, Hal (1911–84), the eldest of six children, was born in Melbourne, and educated mainly at Bairnsdale in Gippsland, where his family moved when he was 6. He began writing early and had a number of short stories and poems published in school magazines. After leaving school he worked briefly as a cub reporter on the *Bairnsdale Advertiser* but then turned to schoolteaching, living in Williamstown 1927–37. In 1929 the death of his mother, who is lovingly recalled in the first volume of his autobiography, *The Watcher on the Cast-Iron Balcony* (1963), was a severe blow. Although he was writing steadily in the 1930s and 1940s, he published little. He married in 1939 and in the same year suffered a severe traffic accident which kept him in hospital for twelve months and prevented him, to his regret, from taking part in the Second World War. Divorced in 1943, he never remarried. He spent the rest of the war in Adelaide, where he taught at private schools, and resumed his writing. After the war Porter had numerous occupations, including cook, actor, hotel manager, hospital orderly, theatrical producer, schoolteacher and librarian. He was attached as a teacher to the Occupation Forces in Japan 1949–50, an experience which proved seminal; his last appointment was as a librarian at Bairnsdale and Shepparton, 1953–61, after which he became a full-time writer. By that time he had published two novels and a collection of poetry, but his reputation was not firmly established until the mid-1960s. He won most major literary awards in Australia, some of them more than once. In 1967 he received, with Randolph Stow, the Britannica-Australia Award; in 1982 he was made AM. An intimately revealing biography by Mary Lord was published in 1993.

A prolific and versatile writer, Porter published three novels, *A Handful of Pennies* (1958), *The Tilted Cross* (1961) and *The Right Thing* (1971); three collections of poetry, *The Hexagon* (1956), *Elijah's Ravens* (1968) and *In an Australian Country Graveyard* (1974), which includes his own drawings; seven collections of short fiction, *Short Stories* (1942), *A Bachelor's Children* (1962), *The Cats of Venice* (1965), *Mr. Butterfry and*

Other Tales of New Japan (1970), *Selected Stories* (1971), *Fredo Fuss Love Life* (1974) and *The Clairvoyant Goat* (1981); three autobiographical works, *The Watcher on the Cast-Iron Balcony* (1963), *The Paper Chase* (1966) and *The Extra* (1975); and three plays, *The Tower* in *Three Australian Plays* (1963), *The Professor* (1966) and *Eden House* (1969). He also wrote an account of modern Japanese life and culture, *The Actors* (1968), and a history of his home town, *Bairnsdale: Portrait of an Australian Country Town* (1977); and a book of theatrical biography, *Stars of Australian Stage and Screen* (1965). In addition, he edited two collections of short stories, *Coast to Coast* (1962) and *It Could Be You* (1972), and one of poetry, *Australian Poetry* (1957). *Hal Porter* (1980), edited by Mary Lord, is an extensive selection of his writing.

Porter is best known for his three autobiographies, especially *The Watcher on the Cast-Iron Balcony*. A work of sustained imaginative power, it is a remarkably vivid re-creation of childhood and youthful experience that fully extends Porter's ability to present the past as an immediate, almost tangible, present. Particularly striking are his acute awareness of the effects of time and the unique phenomenon of memory, and his frank, retrospective self-analysis; the latter is made more compelling by the constant impression of an older narrator who, from his experienced perspective, watches the child who is also a watcher, an analyst both of the inner self and of the external changes in his widening world. *The Watcher* takes Porter to the age of 18 and the death of his mother; *The Paper Chase* covers the period between 1929 and 1949. *The Extra*, which takes Porter to the 1970s, takes its title from one of his poems and emphasises his stance as observer rather than as participant. Concerned more with events and people than with the self, this volume contains numerous portraits of Australian writers.

Porter's verse is both less abundant and less original than his prose work. Framed in traditional forms, his poems dwell in a brief way on many of the same general themes as his fiction: the passage of time, the fact of death, the anguish of disillusionment and the paradoxes of personality.

PORTER, Peter (1929–   ), born Brisbane, educated as a boarder at Church of England Grammar School and then Toowoomba Grammar school, worked in 1947–48 as a cadet journalist for the *Courier-Mail*. After a short time in business in 1951, and always disquieted about Australia, he left for England where, apart from a brief period in 1954, he remained until 1974, when he returned at the invitation of the Adelaide Festival for a longer stay. In England he developed connections with many other young poets, notably with the writers known as The Group. Since 1974 he has visited Australia much more frequently, but he still makes his home in central London. He has worked as a bookseller, journalist, clerk and advertising copywriter. Since 1968 he has lived as a full-time freelance writer, apart from producing poetry, providing contributions and reviews for journals such as *New Statesman*, *London Magazine*, the *Observer*, *Times Literary Supplement*, *Encounter*, and the *New Review*, and from the late 1980s *Scripsi*, *Overland* and *Westerly*. He has broadcast regularly for the BBC, has been a judge for numerous literary prizes, and has had appointments as writer-in-residence in universities and academies in the UK and Australia. Porter is the author of fourteen major volumes of verse, as well as a collected and a selected volume, a number of smaller volumes of verse and libretti, four volumes of illustrations and poems made in collaboration with Arthur Boyd, and a number of unpublished radio scripts broadcast by the BBC. He is now widely considered as one of the finest poets writing in English of the late twentieth century; he has been awarded a number of honorary D.Litts, the Duff Cooper Memorial Prize (1983), The Whitbread Prize for Poetry (1988), and the Gold Medal of the Australian Literature Society (1990).

His early poetry, *Once Bitten, Twice Bitten* (1961), *Poems Ancient and Modern* (1964) and A. Alvarez's selection for *Penguin Modern Poets 2* (1962) displays an ironic wit tinged with melancholy, formal structural control, wide variety of subject matter, skilful use of aphorisms, and the strong influence of several earlier writers, chiefly Auden. Such poems as 'Story from a Time of Disturbance' and 'An Anthropologist's Confession' with their acute verbal play and lurid, even scabrous, details, highlight a variety of social follies with an Auden-like control and pleasure in detailed satire. 'Your Attention Please', 'Soliloquy at Potsdam' and 'The Frankenstein Report' among other early works reveal the influence of Browning's monologues. In this early verse too is the first fruit of his experiences of being an outsider in the English scene. In 'Beast and Beauty' and 'Made in Heaven' the persona of the self-deprecating outsider scathingly attacking English folly comes close at times to self-pity and envy. This edgy tonality marks much of Porter's early and middle works and may have contributed to the difficulty of empathy which some early and partly critical reviews express. It may also have contributed to the paradoxical situation that for some critics, in particular Australians, Porter's verse was too English, while for others it was not English enough. As such his early work was mostly neglected in his homeland, and treated with respectful if somewhat 'outsider' interest in the UK. Already notable in the early volumes, all of Porter's verse is full of dense cultural allusions, a focus which only widens as his knowledge of Europe is enhanced by time and modified by an increasing though often diffidently amused awareness of modern popular culture, mostly from the USA.

In some early work the affirmation of human capacity afforded by art, its ability to balance modern life's artlessness, in poems such as 'John Marston Advises Anger' or 'Homage to Gaetano Donizetti', is countered by nagging doubts about the fictional deferral of real experience (a theme of great centrality in later volumes) in 'What a Lying Lot the Writers Are'. At one level the sheer enjoyment of ideas, irony and paradox pervades Porter's early poetry, buoying it and demonstrating art's ability to make palatable the essential difficulty and hopelessness of life; at another it is the very art itself, the language which distances the poet from the experience. None of this is handled in straightforward language. Porter's intellect is reflected in his verse, difficult, dense but highly rewarding.

In this early verse the ambivalent adoption of European civilisation counters an uneasy, often mistrustful, atttitude to Australia. Porter had expressed (*Times Literary Supplement*, 1971) his self-exile in part as his own version of the cringe, as an aversion to Australian bluntness and physicality, and to its lack of sophistication in response to complexity in life and art; this attitude is reflected in such poems as 'Sydney Cove, 1788' from *Poems Ancient and Modern* and 'The Recipe' from his third volume, *A Porter Folio* (1969). Other poems, which recall a bitter-sweet boyhood in Brisbane and Queensland, 'A Christmas Recalled' and 'Two Merits of Sunshine', are melancholy rather than antagonistic. Others take up family history, presenting it as a means of discussing traditions of Australian culture. Notable here is 'Forefathers' View of Failure' from *Once Bitten*, which delves into a tradition of country town poems taken up with greater scope by Les Murray and Geoff Page.

Two small volumes, *Words without Music* (1968) and *Solemn Adultery at Breakfast Creek: An Australian Ballad* (1968), the latter a collaboration with musician Michael Jessett, were followed by *A Porter Folio* (1969) and *The Last of England* (1970), which consolidated his reputation as a difficult but valuable poet. These volumes continue his use of witty personae ('The Return of Inspector Christopher Smart', 'A Consumer's Report'), widen the range of formal experiments ('The Sanitized Sonnets', 'The Widow's Story') and develop a more personal voice which, though still involved with complex analysis of art confronting experience, often laments the poet's inability to feel except through the mediation of art.

Two volumes of translations, *Epigrams by Martial* (1971), and *After Martial* (1972), cover a wide range of topics together with an increasing confidence and maturity;

both are evident in one of his finest volumes, *Preaching to the Converted* (1972). 'La Déploration sur la Mort D'Igor Stravinsky', 'Fossil Gathering', 'May 1945', and several other poems continue the exploration of aesthetic immortality opposing physical death, each poem twisting the focus of enquiry as Porter's discrimination of all gradations of meaning becomes a moral pursuit, a way of living in and through the world of ideas.

A small collection, *A Share of the Market* (1973), and two collaborations with Arthur Boyd, *Jonah* (1973) and *The Lady and the Unicorn* (1975), precede his seventh major volume, *Living in a Calm Country* (1975); all confirm the growing trend of urbane complexity in his work. Not regarded as one of his finest books, *Living in a Calm Country* contains, nonetheless, a number of significant poems, two of which have become central to understanding Porter's evolution. The theme of increasing age, as it is linked to both an increased understanding of life and art, and as it points to mortality and loss, has always featured in Porter's verse. In 'The Story of My Conversion' he laments the condition of the poet/intellectual, having been converted by inclination and age to the seriousness and difficulty of the life of ideas. Moving into the realm of the over-forties, which he dubs 'the new land of disappointment', Porter looked forward even in his own forties towards death as the only certainty, and to the failure of a life of the mind to learn, to accept, simplicity. Another poem of major importance, 'On First Looking into Chapman's *Hesiod*', refracts that situation through Porter's differences with Australia, at once the lost land of simplicity, and a satirised Boeotian land of inadequacy.

Another small volume, *Les Très Riches Heures* (1978), preceded the next and, of the middle work, the best single volume of his verse, *The Cost of Seriousness* (1978). This volume was universally praised by critics for its display of a new maturity, especially in its approach to the darker and tragic sides of love, an area which Porter's perceived detachment and earlier (claimed) lack of experience had denied him. That ironic lack of experience was just one of the profoundly handled subjects in the volume, the central poems of which find a tragic expression for the untimely death of the poet's first wife in 1974. In *The Cost of Seriousness* the sufficiency of art's, of language's, consolation in the face of deeply felt grief is subjected to rigorous inspection; it is often found to be unable to 'alter human circumstances or alleviate human distress'. In two of the finest poems in an outstanding volume, 'An Exequy' and 'The Delegate', refuge in art is found wanting as the poet seems the more isolated by its making. Paradoxically, this stance seemed to provide a moving consolation for many of the reviewers. It is probably still his best-known volume. From this volume on the relation of Porter's biography to his art was almost totally fused, and from it the readership detected even greater depths of emotion allied to the perception of a melancholic intellect; Porter's verbal skills, meanwhile, were rapidly gaining him recognition as one of the finest poets in the language.

With the next volume, *English Subtitles* (1981), Porter took up the theme of loss and artistic inadequacy, with 'Alcestis and the Poet' and 'Good Ghost, Gaunt Ghost', while the theme of ageing reappeared in a number of outstanding pieces: 'The Werther Level', 'What I Have Written I Have Written', 'The Unfortunate Isles', and 'At Lake Massaciuccoli'. In this volume seriousness as a mode of living is re-examined and found to provide at least the most effective means of sustaining life in the face of a world of superficial values. Against the specious life of late twentieth-century culture Porter poses the value of serious art and the moral value of a satirical eye and ear of the poet always ready to point at folly, as he does in the significant final poem of the volume, 'Landscape with Orpheus'.

In 1983 his *Collected Poems* was awarded the Duff Cooper Memorial Prize and he returned to Australia as writer-in-residence for the University of Melbourne. The *Collected* revived interest in the early satirical and formally innovative Porter and reinforced the general perception of him as more than a mere skilled aphorist. The next volume, *Fast Forward* (1984), whose title indicates Porter's increasing focus on the ironies of modern popular culture, demonstrates a refreshing new series of Porter voices, reflecting the effects of new influences, including Ashbery, Stevens and a few other trans-Atlantic poets as well as Gray and Murray among many Australians. Another of the Porter-Boyd collaborative volumes, *Narcissus* (1984) also came out in 1984.

Nineteen eighty-seven saw another residency, this time at the University of WA, and the volume *The Automatic Oracle*, which was awarded the Whitbread Prize for Poetry in 1988 and received highly favourable reviews. Porter was now widely known in Australia, and in parallel his verse contained a larger proportion of material rehabilitating his childhood in newer and often nostalgic lights. But the linguistic agility and philosophic eye were as vigorous as ever. His satirical eye was more definitely turning to popular culture and the political state of Thatcherite Britain and its parallels in Reagan's USA. In this volume these matters are controlled by the metaphor of the title. The title poem 'The Automatic Oracle' sees the oracle as both the language of the poet and his task as a priestly messenger warning of the ills of political expediency. As always Porter's emphasis in this volume falls on his need to preserve the values and responsibilities inherent in words.

These themes are evident also in the next two volumes, *Possible Worlds* (1989) and *The Chair of Babel* (1992). In 1988 he produced *Mars*, another collaboration with Boyd, and in between the solo volumes published *A Porter Selected* (1989). Nineteen eighty-nine was Porter's sixtieth year and his interest in age and ageing provided a series of occasions to muse on the value of verse in the face of mortality, history and memory, in poems such as 'The Child at Sixty' from *Babel* and 'Night Watch' and 'They Come Back More' from *Possible Worlds*. Many of the poems in the first volume present a harder-edged dystopian view of England than earlier views. 'An Ingrate's England' and the last poem of the volume, 'The New Mandeville', are typical if significant examples and present almost Swiftian images of the old world. In this and his next volume, *The Chair of Babel*, Porter reassesses the differences between the real and the mental geographies of his perceptions of the old world and of Australia as two among many 'possible worlds'. The melancholic certainty lodged in the earlier verse in the old world seems less secure in these later volumes, while the assertion that art is the best weapon available is strongly held and argued, as it has been from the middle work of the late 1970s and early 1980s. To that end Porter is fascinated by, but resistant to, the linguistic jargon of academic, or political power which he aphorises as 'cultspeak' in 'The Chair of Babel'. Against this the poet may be reduced to the seemingly lowly task of explication, as in 'The Village Explainer' or 'His Body to Blaise Pascal'; or of becoming the 'Cassandra of the market-place', as Porter styles one of his 'babbling' voices, although these become the callings of essential salvation, the means of surviving the specious life of the next century.

Millennial Fables (1994), in the Oxford Poets series, comes recommended by the Poetry Book Society of UK, a testament to Porter's standing. The opening poems, 'Forty Years On' and the ironically titled 'Littoral Truth', confront again Porter's decision to quit Australia for England. Seen more as a Lotus Land than Boeotia, Australia was rejected in favour of 'this working hemisphere'. Unlike England, Australia offered no ties of consanguinity, and it seemed destined to remain, in Porter's view, merely an empty shore on which men could do nothing more than mark their physical presence. 'Connect Only' and 'Covent Garden in the Sixties' continue Porter's rueful self-audit of past relationships while the continuing battle of emotions and intellect against the seeming futility of existence waxes and wanes - prospects of intuition and understanding in 'Not the Thing Itself but Ideas about It' and 'Happiness' counterbalanced by the despondency of 'Nil by Mouth', 'Estates and Sunshine' and 'Into the Garden with the Wrong Secateurs'. Other Porter battlegrounds revisited include the contrast between rational thought and dogma; a momentary victory for the words of truth, which will ultimately 'testify/ beyond their written shape'. The final lines of 'Trinacrian Aetna's Flames Ascend Not Higher' reveal in superb poetry Porter's vision of what might be possible if man and woman (certainly not 'Clive and Olive') were to become worthy of the souls they have been given. The second section of *Millennial Fables* (the impressive long final poem, 'Death's Door' is notable) are dedicated to Robert Browning. Many of the poems of this section are crammed with allusions born of Porter's extraordinary erudition and spiced with wit, irony and paradox that would overwhelm all but the most expert and initiated of readers. Never far away, however, is that most overwhelming of all questions, how to

> Cut through the blackened and immensurate
>   Mystery of Life
> To the consummation of death. . .

Nineteen ninety also saw the award of the Gold Medal of the Australian Literature Society and a number of other markers of recognition of his high status within his own country. By the end of the 1980s many articles and chapters had begun to pay him the attention he deserved. *Peter Porter: A Bibliography 1954–1986* (1990), compiled by John R. Kaiser, was followed by the critical biography by Bruce Bennett, *Spirit in Exile: Peter Porter and His Poetry* (1991) and the shorter critical analysis by Peter Steele, *Peter Porter* (1992) in the Australian Writers Series.

JEFF DOYLE

POUSSARD, Wendy (1943–   ), born Melbourne, has worked in many Third World countries. Director of the International Women's Development Agency, a community-based organisation which works with international women's groups, and previously a staff member of the Asian Bureau of Australia and editor of the *Asian Bureau Newsletter*, she has published several books dealing with life in the Third World and the experiences of Asian refugees, including *Today is a Real Day* (1981). Her verse, which reflects her commitment to the peace movement and familiarity with Asian poetry and politics, has appeared in numerous periodicals and anthologies and in two collections, *Outbreak of Peace. Poems and Notes from Pine Gap* (1984) and *Ground Truth* (1987).

POWELL, Craig (1940–   ), born Wollongong, graduated in medicine from the University of Sydney in 1964, later specialising in psychiatry. In 1972 he left Australia to spend ten years in Canada, where he trained in psychoanalysis. Returning to Australia permanently in 1982, he won the 1983 Mattara Spring Festival Poetry Prize for 'Five Pieces for a Homecoming'. In private practice in Sydney as a psychoanalyst, he also teaches at the NSW Institute of Psychiatry. A contributing editor of *Phoenix Review*, he edited *New Canadian Poetry* as no. 105 of *Poetry Australia*, 1986.

Widely represented in anthologies, journals and newspapers, Powell has published seven books of poetry, *A Different Kind of Breathing* (1966), *I Learn by Going* (1968), *A Country without Exiles* (1972), *Selected Poems* (1978), *Rehearsal for Dancers* (1978, published in Canada), *A Face in Your Hands* (1984, *Poetry Australia* no. 97), *The Ocean Remembers It Is Visible: Poems 1966–1989* (1989, in the *Quarterly Review of Literature*, Princeton, New Jersey) and *Minga Street: New and Selected Poems* (1993). Powell's prize-winning 'Five Pieces for a Homecoming' is included in *A Face in Your Hands*, and three of the 'Pieces' are also in *Minga Street*. The latter includes poems from most of the earlier volumes, with a group of new poems.

'Bringing the Hay in on Mike's Farm' (the third of 'Five Pieces') captures the essential quality of Powell, especially his combination of realism and mysticism. The bales of hay are like poetry itself, 'dark at the very centre'. The precise but imaginative observer is evident in his description of the Australian male, 'the men you work with bandy scabrous insults/ they are embarrassed by liking each other'. 'The Milk Run' (the fourth of 'Five Pieces') captures the madcap joy of youthful exploits such as riding on the milkman's and baker's cart, while reflecting ruefully on time's capacity to mar that young innocence with later tragedies. Many of Powell's poems reflect on events of his life ('The Horse Gang', 'Boomerang', 'The Snapshot Never Taken', 'Obituary', 'The International') and the people closest to him ('Death Poems for My Father', 'Katie at Twenty-One'). His association with fellow poets is manifest in his dedications – *A Face in Your Hands* to David Brooks, 'Spring Thaw' to Francis Webb ('I Loved Your Friendship'), 'The Child Explains' to Brooks and a poem titled 'For Bruce Beaver in Sydney'. Powell structures his poetry tightly and forcefully, preferring the broken-line schema, which often leads to staccato and emphatic effect. An early poem, 'Tree and River Bank', which concerns two of his family, the dead grandfather of 81 and the dead son of three weeks, won the Henry Lawson Festival Award in 1969. He also won the *Poetry Magazine* Award in 1964. He is a leading figure in the literature and psychiatry seminars held for a decade in Canberra at the Australian Defence Force Academy and latterly in Sydney.

POWELL, S.W. (Sydney Walter) (1878–1952), born England and educated partly in South Africa, served in the Boer War before coming to Australia in 1904. He joined the army and was drafted to Thursday Island, where he began writing for the *Bulletin* under the pseudonym 'Wyben'. He left Australia in 1908, spent some time in NZ and Tahiti but returned in time to enlist in the AIF. A participant in the landing at Gallipoli, he was wounded and invalided back to Sydney in 1916. His war poem 'Gallipoli' was awarded first prize in the John Masefield competition, 1932, and included in his collection, *One-Way Street and Other Poems* (1934). Powell subsequently traded in the Paumotu Archipelago before joining the Commonwealth public service; in 1925 he returned to England. Powell wrote seventeen romances and novels between 1920 and 1937.

POWER, Helen (1870–1957) was born at Campbell Town, Tasmania, the granddaughter of a surveyor-general of Tasmania. A distinguished member of Hobart's literary community, she contributed verse to the *Bulletin*, the *Australasian* and numerous poetry magazines, especially during the years 1912–32. Her work, which is represented in several anthologies, appeared in two collections, *Poems* (1934) and *A Lute with Three Strings* (1964), introduced by Clive Sansom. Conventional and simple, Power's lyrics dwell on such themes as death, love, growing old, the loss of friends and the persistence of the past in the present.

PRICHARD, Katharine Susannah (1883–1969), born Levuka, Fiji, was the daughter of Tom Prichard, editor of the *Fiji Times*. Her childhood, re-created in her children's book *The Wild Oats of Han* (1928), was spent initially in Tasmania, and then in Melbourne. On matriculating from South Melbourne College, where she came under the influence of poet and teacher J.B. O'Hara, she spent two years as a governess at Yarram in South Gippsland and then at Turella sheep station in the far west of NSW. Returning to Melbourne to teach, she attended night lectures in English literature under the auspices of Walter Murdoch.

In 1908 Prichard made her first trip to London as a freelance journalist for the Melbourne *Herald* and on her return accepted a position with the newspaper as social editor of the women's page for two years. In 1912 she again left for England to pursue her career as a writer. Her first novel, *The Pioneers* (1915), was made into an Australian film in 1916 (and remade in 1926). It has much in common, in terms of contrived plot and characterisation, with its successor, *Windlestraws* (1916).

In 1916 Prichard returned to Australia. She married Hugo Throssell (VC recipient) in 1919, went to live in WA and immersed herself in both politics and writing; the first, some critics say, to the detriment of the second. In 1920 she became a founding member of the Communist Party of Australia and served for a period on its central committee. She wrote some simple political pamphlets such as *The New Order* (1919), and later a book, *The Real Russia* (1934), which reported on her experiences and observations as a traveller in the Soviet Union the previous year. She was elected, in 1935, federal president of the Australian Writers' League (an organisation she had helped to establish the previous year) and three years later became a founding member of the WA branch of the FAW which later nominated her for a Nobel Prize.

Her initial attempt to embody political concepts in her novels came with the publication in 1921 of *Black Opal. Coonardoo*, which shared the 1928 *Bulletin* novel prize and was praised as the first realistic and detailed portrayal of an Aborigine, and *Working Bullocks* are regarded as the basis for Katharine Susannah Prichard's literary reputation.

Numerous short stories of uneven quality have been collected and published in *Kiss on the Lips* (1932), *Potch and Colour* (1944), *N'Goola* (1959), *On Strenuous Wings* (1965) and *Happiness* (1967). Prichard published two volumes of poetry, *Clovelly Verses* (1913) and *The Earth Lover* (1932).

Two critical books on her writing are Jack Beasley's *The Rage for Life: The Work of Katharine Susannah Prichard* (1964), reworked and extended as *A Gallop of Fire* (1993), and Henrietta Drake-Brockman's monograph *Katharine Susannah Prichard* (1967), while information on her life is to be found in her autobiography *Child of the Hurricane* (1963) and a biography by her son Ric Throssell, *Wild Weeds and Wind Flowers* (1975).

SANDRA BURCHILL

Prism, the journal of the Poetry Society of Australia, appeared in July 1954, edited by Peter Daventry, and was thereafter published, usually monthly, until it was succeeded in 1961 by *Poetry Magazine*. *The Poetry Society of Australia: First Anthology* (1956), edited by Wesley Milgate and Imogen Whyse in 1957, was a selection of verse from the pages of *Prism*.

PRITCHARD, Selwyn (Selwyn Pritchard Hughes) (1933–   ), born England and educated at Oxford University, lives in Tasmania, where he is a secondary school teacher. He has contributed verse to numerous periodicals in Australia, NZ, North America and UK and has published the collections *Homage to Colonel Rainborough* (1984), *Being Determined* (1990), *Stirring Stuff* (1991) and *Quack Quack Floreat* (1991).

PURNELL, Kathryn, born Vancouver, Canada, was educated there and later at the University of Melbourne. She married an Australian and has lived in various parts of the world. She has been a creative writing tutor and an active member of literary organisations such as the Society of Women Writers, and an editor in the *Luna* collective. Her published works include poetry, *Pandora* (1979), *Safari* (1979), *Trillium* (1983, with Audrey Longbottom and Susan McGowan), *Otway Country* (1984) and *Magic Perhaps* (1987). She has edited several anthologies, including *A Spin of Pink Heath* (1980), *A Spin of Gold Wattle* (1982) for the Society of Woman Writers, and *Herb Spin* (1984). Her strongly compassionate and sensitive poetry has won numerous awards, e.g. the Victorian Premier's Literary Award 1966, the Society of Women Writers' Award 1972, the International Poetry Society's UK Prize 1979 and the Charles Meeking Poetry Prize for Women 1979.

QUINN, Patrick (1862–1926), born Sydney, was the brother of Roderic Quinn and father of Marjorie Quinn (1889–1972), who wrote poems and short stories. He was a member of the NSW parliament 1898–1904, was deputy commissioner of trade for NSW in San Francisco for six years, returned to Australia in 1917 and subsequently worked on the staff of the Sydney *Daily Telegraph*. He published verse and fiction in the *Bulletin*; a detective novel, *The Jewelled Belt* (1896); and a collection of short stories, *The Australian Storyteller for an Idle Afternoon* (n.d.). After his death some of his poems were collected and edited by Marjorie Quinn, titled *Selected Poems* (1970).

QUINN, Roderic (1867–1949) was born in Sydney of Irish parents who had come to Australia about 1853. He was educated in Sydney with his lifelong friends E.J. Brady and C.J. Brennan, studied law briefly, was a country schoolteacher, then returned to Sydney as a freelance journalist. His chief publications are the romantic novel *Mostyn Stayne* (1897) and three books of verse, *The Hidden Tide* (1899), *The Circling Hearths* (1901) and *Poems* (1920), his major volume. He also wrote short stories for the *Bulletin*. From the mid-1890s to the mid-1920s Quinn made a modest living from his poetry, which was greatly admired by his contemporaries. Although linked with Victor Daley as poets of the so-called Celtic Twilight, Quinn lacked Daley's easy, lyric artistry. He often attempted more, however, for in addition to capturing the spirit and atmosphere of the Australian outdoors he sought a hidden meaning beneath the externals of life and nature.

RANKIN, Jennifer (1941–79), born Sydney as Jennifer Haynes, graduated from the University of Sydney and worked both in England and Australia in the social sciences and education. Married first to John Roberts, and then to the painter David Rankin, she also lived for a period with Frank Moorhouse, who dedicated *Futility and Other Animals* to her. Her poetry, which was published widely in magazines in Australia, England and the USA, appeared in four collections, *Ritual Shift* (1976), *Earth Hold* (1978), illustrated by John Olsen, *The Mud Hut* (1979, published in Canada) and the posthumous *Collected Poems* (1990), edited by Judith Rodriguez. Rankin's intense, compressed poetry often deals with repressed childhood experiences and relationships, the loss of a father, mental and physical illness, adult love and experiences of vulnerability.

RAYMOND, Vicki (Vicki Kathleen Irwin) (1949–   ), born Daylesford, Victoria, lived as a child in Adelaide, later settling in Tasmania, where she gained a BA; in 1981 she moved to London. Her first book of poems, *Holiday Girls and Other Poems* (1985) won the British Airways Commonwealth Poetry Prize for a best first volume. She was one of four poets to represent Australia at Struga Poetry Evenings in Yugoslavia. Her second volume of poems, *Small Arm Practice*, was published in 1989. Witty, ironic but sensitive to those who deserve sensitivity, she has a discerning eye for foibles and vanities. The title poem, 'Holiday Girls' (in both volumes) is a perceptive view of the British holiday mania as well as a poignant account of the tragedy of those unlucky girls. Her *Selected Poems* was published in 1993.

Red Page, the major literary section of the *Bulletin* 1896–1961, was so named because it appeared on the inside of the journal's distinctive red cover. The Red Page was the innovation of A.G. Stephens, who developed it from 'Books of the Day' and 'The *Bulletin* Book Exchange', the lists of new literature with occasional editorial comment that replaced advertisements in the *Bulletin* 1894–96. Stephens, satirised as the Red Page Rhadamanthus in Victor Daley's poem 'Narcissus and Some Tadpoles' (1899), was editor of the Red Page until 1906 and was succeeded by A.H. Adams, Bertram Stevens, David McKee Wright, Cecil Mann and most importantly Douglas Stewart (1940–61). A selection of Stephens's Red Page criticism was published as *The Red Pagan* (1902); some of Stewart's criticism is included in *The Flesh and the Spirit* (1948) and *The Broad Stream* (1975).

Reedy River, a musical play based on Australian folk-songs gathered by the actor John Gray, with a script by Dick Diamond, was first produced by the Melbourne New Theatre in 1953, when it attracted large audiences; published in 1970, the play has since been regularly revived. The rather sketchy plot concerns a group of shearers who in spite of the failure of the strikes of the 1890s continue to oppose the use of scab labour. The play's real attractiveness lies in its combination of folk-songs and ballads sung to the accompaniment of a bush band. The title song comes from Henry Lawson's poem 'Reedy River'; other well-known pieces include 'Click Go the Shears', 'The Eumerella Shore', 'Flash Jack from Gundagai' and 'The Old Black Billy', most of which carry nostalgic echoes of the nationalist and radical sentiments of the 1890s and continue to appeal to urban audiences.

REITER, David P. (1947–   ), editor of the literary magazine *Redoubt* 1988–90, has published poetry in many Australian, North American and European periodicals and in three collections, *The Snow In Us* (1989), which largely reflects his experience of Canada, *Changing House* (1991), winner of the 1989 Queensland Premier's Poetry Award, and *The Cave After Saltwater Tide* (1994), which stems from his experiences in Australia and Thailand as well as Canada. 'The River Under Kwai Bridge' is an effective and impressive series.

RIDDELL, Alan (1927–77), born Townsville, Queensland, was educated in Scotland and lived in Greece, Spain and France, as well as Australia, where he worked as a journalist for the *Age, Daily Telegraph* and *Sydney Morning Herald*. Founder of the Scottish poetry review *Lines*, which he edited 1952–55 and 1962–67, he contributed verse to Australian and overseas journals and anthologies and published four collections, *Beneath the Summer* (1952), *Majorcan Interlude* (1960), *The Stopped Landscape* (1968) and *Eclipse* (1972). Editor of the Scottish section of *Young Commonwealth Poets '65* (1965), he also edited the anthology *Typewriter Art* (1975). In 1956 Riddell won the Heinemann Lyric Prize and a Scottish Arts Council Prize in 1968. Originally a traditional poet, he became interested in concrete and visual poetry in the 1960s.

RIDDELL, Elizabeth (1910–   ), born Napier, NZ, settled in Australia in 1928, when she was hired by Ezra Norton to work on the Sydney *Truth*. In due course she established a reputation as one of Australia's most distinguished journalists, winning a Walkley Award for a series of articles on the brewing industry. From 1935 to 1939 she lived mainly in England, where she worked briefly for the *Daily Express*. Sent to New York at the outbreak of war to open the bureau of the *Daily Mirror*, she was transferred to London and Europe, where she saw some action behind the lines and witnessed the German defeat and withdrawal. She later worked for *Smith's Weekly* and the *Daily Telegraph*, and was a special writer with the *Australian* and News Limited Group, before becoming a freelance book-reviewer and feature-writer. In 1935 she married another journalist, 'Blue' Greatorex, who died in 1964. She has published seven collections of poetry, *The Untrammelled* (1940), *Poems* (1948), *Forbears* (1961), *Occasions of Birds* (1987), *From the Midnight Courtyard* (1989), *Selected Poems* (1992) and *The Difficult Island* (1994), from the newly established Molonglo Press. She has won the Grace Leven Prize, the Christopher Brennan Award in 1991 and the NSW State inaugural Book of the Year Award for *Selected Poems* in 1992; she was awarded the Gold Medal of the Australian Literature Society in 1993 and a Creative Fellowship from the Literature Board of the Australia Council.

Riddell's poetry, controlled, spare, frequently witty and lightly lyrical, concrete and sensuous, has been compared to that of Judith Wright and Kenneth Slessor, although the sparsity of her writing and the period of silence from 1961 to 1987 resulted in a relative critical neglect. Death has been a recurring theme in her verse from *The Untrammelled*, but the overall effect is nevertheless of gaiety and colour. Surety of expression characterises all her collections, but her later poetry is more sardonic and analytical; as Riddell herself has commented in an interview in *Tall Poppies* (1984): 'I've nothing to lose. I'm trying to write totally what I mean. When I was younger I was very addicted to the beautiful phrase. Now I'm ruthless with it.'

Rigmarole of the Hours, based in Melbourne, was a small press which operated 1974–79, publishing seventeen titles of new writings in Australia. Initially it was a magazine, *Rigmarole of the Hours*, which intended to publish books as special issues; after the first number in August 1974, edited by Robert Kenny, the magazine disappeared and the press began publishing books by writers such as Katherine Gallagher, Walter Billeter, Kris Hemensley, Robert Kenny, Laurie Duggan and Jennifer Maiden. Rigmarole of the Hours stopped publishing in 1980 but resumed in 1982 as Rigmarole Books when John Jenkins joined Kenny. It then published works by Anna Couani, Philip Jenkins, Ken Bolton, Anna Walwicz and Gerard Lee, but closed again at the end of 1986.

'Rio Grande's Last Race', one of A.B. Paterson's favourite ballads, is the title poem of his second collection of verse, *Rio Grande's Last Race and Other Verses* (1902). The poem's theme, a jockey's premonition of death, is unusual in Paterson, who prefers to applaud the deeds of racehorses and riders or to depict the humour and irony associated with the turf. Jack Macpherson's dream of his last fatal ride on Rio Grande is a traditional rather than a bush ballad. The language, which matches the sombre theme, is lifted above the usual colloquial style of the bush poem and the narrative moves with impressive urgency towards its fatal climax.

'Roaring Days, The' is a phrase referring nostalgically to the gold rushes. Its best-known literary use is in Henry Lawson's poem 'The Roaring Days', written from Lawson's boyhood memories of Gulgong and Pipeclay. The poem was first published in the *Bulletin* in 1889.

ROBERTS, Barney (1920–), born Flowerdale, Tasmania, where he lives on a farm, was a POW in the Second World War. He has published two books of verse, *The Phantom Boy* (1976) and *Stones in the Cephissus* (1979); a novel, *The Penalty of Adam* (1980); an autobiography of childhood, *Where's Morning Gone?* (1987), an account of his years in Europe as a prisoner of war, *A Kind of Cattle* (1985); and a collection of short stories, *Tales I Carry with Me* (1988).

ROBERTS, Bev (Beverley Dale) (1939–) has made an important contribution to the Australian literary scene in her various roles as assistant editor of *Meanjin*, as Victorian literature field officer and as co-ordinator of the Victorian Writers' Centre. Her own books of poetry are *The Transvestite Next Door* (1986), *Here Come the Pumpkins* (1991) and *The Exorcism Trip* (1991). A subtly humorous and modest poet, Bev Roberts writes with sensitivity and quiet charm about both the good and bad of life. Where there has been pain or injustice there is little rancour in their recollection, while the myriad irritations and irritators of daily life are quenched with wit and imagination. People, places, the past, mortality and the pleasure of poetry itself are the regular themes of her writing.

ROBERTS, Nigel (1941–), born Wellington, NZ, has lived in Australia since 1965 and teaches art. One of the significant identities of the poetry revolution in Australia in the late 1960s–1970s, Roberts was a leading member of the Balmain Poetry Group 1970–76 and was associated with the magazines *Free Poetry*, *Package Deal* and *Living Daylights*. Roberts has published only two volumes of poetry, *In Casablanca for the Waters* (1977) and *Steps for Astaire* (1983), but is a prominent figure in the Australian poetry scene. He is represented in such 'New Poetry' anthologies as John Tranter's *The New Australian Poetry* (1979) and Gray and Lehmann's *The Younger Australian Poets* (1983). A witty and ironic poet, Roberts writes with lively, biting relevance about the modern scene and is innovative with verse forms and techniques. Informal in language, experimental with the shape of the poem on the page, and iconoclastic in his ribald derision of sacred cows, either in life or poetry, Roberts is one of the more strikingly individualistic of contemporary writers.

ROBERTS, Philip (1938–   ), born Canada, studied at the universities of Acadia (Canada), Oxford and Sydney, and has worked as a sub-editor for Reuters news agency in London, and as a public relations consultant. In 1967–79 he taught English at the University of Sydney and since 1980 he has been a writer, now resident in Canada. Founding editor of Island Press, Sydney, 1970–79, he was poetry editor of the *Sydney Morning Herald* 1970–74, and editor of the annual anthologies, *Poet's Choice*. He began writing poetry at Oxford, where he was encouraged by Robert Graves, and has published six collections, *Just Passing Through* (1969), *Single Eye* in *Two Poets* (1971, with Geoff Page), *Crux* (1973), *Will's Dream* (1975), *Selected Poems* (1978) and *Letters Home* (1990). Cosmopolitan, sophisticated, condensed and polished, Roberts's poetry has a musical finesse that reflects his talents as a pianist. *Will's Dream*, his most ambitious and extended work, is a sequence of poems which deftly builds up an original interior world and which features four characters, one of whom is Will, the dreamer of the sequence. The poems of *Selected Poems* and the earlier collections are taut, witty, deceptively laconic comments on a multiplicity of subjects, some of them literary. Island Press, in addition to publishing *Poet's Choice*, has produced works by Kevin Gilbert, Martin Johnston, Robert Adamson, Phillip Hammial, Andrew Taylor, Ken Bolton, J.S. Harry and many others. Roberts has also written *How Poetry Works* (1986) and *Plain English: A User's Guide* (1987).

ROBINSON, Michael Massey (1744–1826), lawyer turned blackmailer, arrived in NSW as a convict in 1798. His legal experience gained him appointment as secretary to the deputy judge-advocate of the Colony. Corrupt use of his office and the charge of 'promoting discords', probably by the writing of lampooning verses known as pipes, saw him in 1805 at Norfolk Island. Pardoned in 1811, he advanced to principal clerk in the police office before he died. Under Governor Lachlan Macquarie, Robinson composed odes to celebrate the birthdays of George III and Queen Charlotte 1810–21. With one exception they were published in the *Sydney Gazette* and read by Robinson at the annual birthday ceremonies at Government House. In 1818 and 1819 he was repaid 'for his services as Poet Laureate' by a grant of two cows from the government herd, probably the first royalties to a poet in Australia. The odes, in the stilted flowery language of the public-poem genre, lavished praise not only on the royal couple but also on their subjects, who were energetically evangelising the new southern land to the British way of life. The odes blatantly flattered Macquarie also, for the governor, accepting Oliver Goldsmith's opinion that a bold peasantry was its country's pride, favoured the development of peasant farming and a cottage economy, and Robinson depicted the settlement in the romanticised manner of Macquarie's hopes for it. On Macquarie's resignation Robinson lost his poetic 'office' but vented some of his spleen on Governor Sir Thomas Brisbane by celebrating in several ballads the virtues of Macquarie over his successor. Twenty-seven of Robinson's poems, including twenty royal birthday odes, were published by George Mackaness in his monograph *Odes of Michael Massey Robinson* (1946). He appears as a character in Eris O'Brien's play *The Hostage* (1928). Robinson's role in Macquarie's vision of a neo-classical culture in NSW is examined by Robert Dixon in *The Course of Empire* (1986).

ROBINSON, Roland (1912–92), born County Clare, Ireland, was brought to Australia when 9 years old. After a brief schooling he began work as a rouseabout on a sheep station near Coonamble, NSW, and subsequently worked as a boundary-rider, railway fettler, fencer, dam-builder, factory-worker, ballet-dancer, gardener and golf-course groundsman. He was a book reviewer and ballet and literary critic for the

Sydney Morning Herald, editor of *Poetry Magazine* 1965–69, and president of the Poetry Association of Australia. During the Second World War he worked in the Northern Territory, an experience which provided contact with tribal Aboriginal life to add to his existing familiarity with detribalised Aborigines from his youthful wanderings in the bush and his later experiences in the 1950s when, with the assistance of CLF grants, he gathered stories from the Aborigines of NSW. Strongly attracted to the Australian landscape and spirit of place long before the Jindyworobak movement and before he met its founder, Rex Ingamells, in 1944, Robinson came to be accepted as the best and most dedicated of the Jindyworobak poets, but he is not as stereotyped as the Jindyworobak label would imply. His published verse began with *Beyond the Grass-tree Spears* (1944), twenty-one brief poems, the first of which indicates, in its opening lines, Robinson's poetic stance:

> I made my verses of places where I made my fires;
> of the dark trees standing against the blue-green night
> with the first stars coming; of the bare plains where a
> bird broke into running song, and of the wind-cold scrub
> where the bent trees sing to themselves, and of the night
> black about me, the fire dying out, and the ashes left.

Later volumes include *Language of the Sand* (1949), *Tumult of the Swans* (1953), and *Deep Well* (1962), which incorporated selections from the earlier volumes and added new poems exploring his pantheistic vision of the land and its primal inhabitants, the Aborigines, and in other verses examining the 'deep well' of his own self. *Grendel* (1967) has, in addition to its Aboriginal legends, a section on the impact of White settlement that tends, especially in a poem such as 'The Pioneers', to suggest the ultimate meaninglessness of all human endeavour. *Altjeringa and Other Aboriginal Poems* (1970) is a collection of Robinson's earlier, but revised, Aboriginal poems. The first part of the volume contains translations of poems that he had gathered from the Aborigines themselves; the second part has his own poetry on Aboriginal themes. *Selected Poems* (1971), a surprisingly small collection, is made up of poems mostly in accord with the Jindyworobak movement. His eighth volume of poetry, *The Hooded Lamp*, was published in 1976; a second *Selected Poems* (1983) was edited by A.J. Bennett and Michael Sharkey and a third in 1989, edited by Robert Gray. Robinson's prose collections, which include his own and Aboriginal work, indicate, by their titles, his deep interest in Aboriginal lore and narrative. They include *Legend & Dreaming* (1952), *The Feathered Serpent* (1956), *Black-feller, White-feller* (1958), *The Man Who Sold His Dreaming* (1965), *Aboriginal Myths and Legends* (1966), *The Australian Aboriginal in Colour* (1968) and *The Nearest the White Man Gets* (1989). The last is a book of Aboriginal narratives and poems from NSW with an introductory essay by Norman Talbot. He published three autobiographical volumes, *The Drift of Things* (1973, NBC Award winner), *The Shift of Sands* (1976), and *A Letter to Joan* (1978). Robinson was awarded the OAM, received the Patrick White Award in 1988, the FAW Christopher Brennan Award in 1989 and in 1991 a D.Litt. from the University of Newcastle. He was also an emeritus fellow of the Australia Council.

RODRIGUEZ, Judith (1936–   ), born Perth as Judith Green and brought up in Brisbane, was educated at the universities of Queensland and Cambridge. She has taught literature and/or conducted professional writing courses in many parts of the world – England, the West Indies, America, several Australian universities and institutes of higher education – and has been active also as poet, anthologist, editor, reviewer and writer-in-residence. She taught at La Trobe University, Melbourne, 1969–85, later at the Macarthur Insitute, Sydney, and since 1989 has been lecturing in professional writing at the Victoria College, Melbourne. She has had writing residencies at Ormond College, the University of Melbourne, Royal Melbourne Institute of Technology and Rollins College, Florida. From 1979 to 1982 she was poetry editor of *Meanjin* and has edited the Penguin Australian Poetry Series since 1989. She has also edited *Mrs Noah and The Minoan Queen* (1983, Australian women poets); *Swedish Poets in Translation* (1985, with Thomas Shapcott); a selection of poems from twenty years of the *Australian* (1985, with Andrew Taylor); and a collection of Australian poems (1946–88) in Italian (1988). She has collected the poems of Jennifer Rankin (1990), written (with Vicki Pauli) the art text, *Noela Hjorth* (1984), compiled a poetry-writing course (1976), and edited the Foundations of Professional Writing Series 1988–89. Her own poetry includes *Nu-Plastik Fanfare Red* (1973), *Water Life* (1976), *Shadow on Glass* (1978), *Mudcrab at Gambaro's* (1980), *Witch Heart* (1982), *Floridian Poems* (1986), *New and Selected Poems: The House by Water* (1988) and *The Cold* (1992). In 1962 she shared (with *A Question of Ignorance*) the volume *Four Poets*; the other poets were David Malouf, Rodney Hall and Donald Maynard.

Judith Rodriguez's early poems (*Nu Plastik Red*, *Water Life*, *Shadow in Glass*) often deal with personal, family and domestic experiences, but they also range out to cover women's experience more broadly. With *Mudcrab at Gambaro's* a new emotional experience provides an exultation that is palpable, the word 'mudcrab' itself coming to stand for excitement, joy, fulfilment, the ingredients of a new situation. *Witch Heart* (1982) brings the obverse side, the aftermath of divorce and the sense of dislocation that follows such a personal upheaval ('Leaving', 'Leaving the Trees', 'Travelling'). Always vigorously responsive to experience, she specifies 'clarity' and 'energy' as desirable qualities in any writing. Such qualities are abundantly evident in her own poetry, as is a reliance on the expressiveness of direct and forthright language, enhanced frequently by intricate verbal sound-patterning and effective imagery. In 1974 she began making linocuts and woodcuts for book decorations, some of which are included in *Water Life*, *Shadow on Glass* and *New and Selected Poems*. She won the inaugural SA Biennial Prize for Literature in 1978 for *Water Life*, the International PEN/Peter Stuyvesant Prize for Poetry and the Shell/Artlook Prize for *Mudcrab at Gambaro's*.

ROLLS, Eric C. (1923–), born Grenfell, NSW, has farmed near Narrabri. His poems have appeared in four collections, *Sheaf Tosser* (1967), *The Green Mosaic* (1977), *Miss Strawberry Verses* (1978) and *Selected Poems* (1990). A versatile, exuberant poet with a gift for satire, wry irony and the macabre as well as for the simple nature lyric, Rolls focuses mainly on his farming and family experiences in *Sheaf Tosser* and on his memories of New Guinea in *The Green Mosaic*. Both collections demonstrate his keen interest in animals and the processes of nature. *Miss Strawberry Verses* is a collection of humorous poems for children. Rolls has also written an account of the importation into Australia and subsequent proliferation of the rabbit and other pests, *They All Ran Wild* (1969). Revised for children and titled *Running Wild* (1973), it also won the John Franklin Award. Rolls's other writings are *The River* (1974), an autobiographical essay, *Doorways: A Year of the Cumberdeen Diaries* (1989), *Sojourners: the Epic Story of China's Centuries-Old Relationship with Australia* (1992), *A Million Wild Acres* (1981), *Celebration of the Senses* (1984), a partly autobiographical work, and *From Forest to Sea: Australia's Changing Environment* (1993). He has also edited *An Anthology of Australian Fishing* (1991). In 1992 Rolls was made AM.

ROSE, Peter (1955–) spent his boyhood in Wangaratta, and graduated from Monash University. He worked as a medical bookseller before joining OUP, Australia, where he is publisher of general and reference works. Rose has published two books of poetry, *The House of Vitriol* (1990) and *The Catullan Rag* (1993). His poem 'Vantage' was awarded the St Kilda Centenary Poetry Prize in 1990; 'The Catullan Rag' won the Queensland Premier's Poetry Prize in 1991 and 'Dog Days' won the same prize in 1992. Rose won the Harri Jones Award in 1991.

A late first book (Rose was thirty-five when it was published), *The House of Vitriol* reflects Rose's major cultural interests – literature, music and the classics. It is marked by a somewhat sardonic, self-deprecatory tone that appears resigned to the limits life is likely to impose. 'Pathology', 'These Questions I would Ask', 'Imagining the Inappropriate', 'Darlinghurst Poem' and 'Three Fingers of Gin' are quietly pessimistic evaluations of personal and social situations. Self-revelation is not, however, Rose's aim; the reader is mostly kept at arm's length by a persistent ironic mask, complex language and obscure references and allusions. His frequent use of rare and archaic words and inventive analogies has led to accusations of poetry that is mostly 'gesture and flourish' (John Foulcher). Some of that 'flourish' (e.g. 'the sadness of ancients/ craning for trams', 'rousing and ringing/ as a coital cry') is, however, spectacular and effective. Links with T.S. Eliot have been suggested; the title poem, 'The House of Vitriol', has echoes of 'The Wasteland' and 'Ash Wednesday', and there are Prufrockian touches in other poems.

The Catullan Rag has two sections, the first of St Kilda scenes, concerts, the crowded loneliness of city life, and personal frustrations. In many of them, 'Confetti', 'Miseracordia', 'Sacrifice', 'Notionalism', associations are in Rose's own words 'becoming quite wild and uncontrolled'. Occasionally the mask slips, as in 'Dog Days', perhaps Rose's most effective poem. It tells of a walk through the park with his affable old dog, who takes frequent 'aromatic detours'. The walk eases the tensions built up by a literary festival he has just left. Frustrated with his present way of life, he thinks back to a more carefree past in 'some convivial harbour' where there is 'wine and fish and company'. That past is, however, neither available nor, if it were, would it now be satisfying. In spite of himself he seeks more order, certainty and even discipline.

> I long in my own way
> for the faint impress of the collar,
> the slow bruise of the familiar,
> the sharp tug on the gnostic leash.

The prize-winning 'Vantage' voices a moment of accord with life around him springing from a loving and satisfying relationship.

'The Catullan Rag', fourteen pieces imitating the Roman poet Catullus, but in contemporary tone and mode, make up the second section of the book. Brilliantly targeted are Lesbia, a NASAL (read ASAL) conference, and the poet Suffenus (read any number of ASAL literary 'personalities'). Inaccessible to some, Rose is, nevertheless, making a significant impact on the contemporary literary scene, representing in Peter Porter's judgment, 'an enterprising new voice [in] Australian poetry'.

ROSKOLENKO, Harry (1907–80), born New York, was self-educated and worked at numerous occupations including sailor, law clerk, factory-hand and patent-researcher before joining the US Army in 1942. Posted to the Pacific area, he made numerous visits to Australia in the 1940s, became friendly with poets of the *Angry Penguins* group, and contributed to Australian magazines. Two volumes of his poetry were published in Australia, *A Second Summary* (1944) and *Notes from a Journey* (1947), illustrated by Sidney Nolan. When he returned to America in 1945 he acted as the *Angry Penguins* representative, acquiring contributions from such writers as Kenneth Rexroth and Harold Rosenberg and contributing a 'Letter from America'. With Max Harris he also edited the tenth issue of *Angry Penguins Broadsheet* and, with Elisabeth Lambert, edited an Australian issue of the American poetry magazine *Voices* (1944). Roskolenko subsequently travelled widely and was a familiar contributor to such magazines as *New York Times Book Review*, *New Republic* and *Partisan Review*. He published novels, travel books, autobiographies and several collections of poetry, some of which reflect his experience in Australia. In 1969 he visited Australia again and in 1970 published another collection of poetry in Melbourne, *American Civiliz-ation*, illustrated by several well-known Australian artists.

Ross' Poems (1978), a collection of seventy-five poems by Geoffrey Lehmann, is illustrated by old photographs of some of the personalities and places mentioned and by etchings of rural scenes done by Sally McInerney, 'Sally' of the poems. *Ross' Poems* traces the establishment by Ross and Olive McInerney, Lehmann's then parents-in-law, of the property Spring Forest near Cowra in the Lachlan Valley of central-western NSW in the period just after the Second World War. Interspersed with incidents and events in the development of Spring Forest are Ross's memories of his own rural childhood. The poems present an analytical ('my laboratory is the dust where I stand') account of country life and a catalogue of country characters, includ-ing the bagman Mr Long, who, walking all day on the western plains, sustains himself 'with a line of trees on the horizon'; Ross's father who at 87 still rides a horse; his Auntie Bridge who at 80 still plants trees; and the parsimonious neighbour who sends his horses to the knackery when their working lives are over. The poems also carry Ross's country-wise reflections on such features of modern life as 'lurid newspaper headlines' that contain 'all the trash of our world'; the constant exposure to violence, the built-in obsolescence of modern machines, and the insidious attraction that the city ('the son and daughter stealer') holds for young people. The undemonstrative Lehmann style adapts easily to the flat, laconic tones of the countryman narrator, but a judicious use of reverie frequently elevates the poems from an ordinary to a highly imaginative plane. Some of the poems were published in 1976 in the Poets of the Month series, as *Extracts from Ross' Poems*. Lehmann's *Spring Forest* (1992) is an expanded and revised edition of *Ross' Poems*.

ROWBOTHAM, David (1924–   ), born Toowoomba, Queensland, served in the RAAF in the Pacific in the Second World War and subsequently studied at the uni-versities of Queensland and Sydney, where he won prizes for his poetry. He has worked as a journalist, broadcaster and academic; from 1969–79 he was literary and theatre critic for the *Courier-Mail* and from 1980–87 its literary editor. A prominent Australian poet since the 1940s and a regular contributor to the *Bulletin* when Douglas Stewart was editor of the Red Page, Rowbotham has published nine collections of poetry, *Ploughman and Poet* (1954), *Inland* (1958), *All the Room* (1964), *Bungalow and Hurricane* (1967), *The Makers of the Ark* (1970), *The Pen of Feathers* (1971), *Selected Poems* (1975), *Maydays* (1980) and *New and Selected Poems 1945–1993* (1994), which includes selections from all earlier volumes and a group of new poems titled 'Honey Licked From a Thorn'; a novel, *The Man in the Jungle* (1964); and a selection of short stories, *Town and City* (1956). He has also edited an anthology of verse and prose, *Queensland Writing* (1957). Among other awards Rowbotham won the Grace Leven Prize for Poetry in 1964 and second prize in the Cook Bicentenary literary competition. He was made AM, and, in 1988, emeritus fellow of Australian Literature by the Australia Council.

Originally perceived as primarily a poet of the Queensland landscape, preoccupied with transience and the pattern of life in rural Australia, Rowbotham has moved in his later work towards a more idiosyncratic vision that resists categorisation. Writing in a bare, physically precise and metrically conservative style, he often explores funda-mental philosophical problems through reflection on homely objects and ostensibly ordinary themes. He is convinced, however, that poetry should deal with larger issues than 'pots and pans'. Poetry, he believes, is part of the process of 'finding wisdom out of pain and struggle'. 'Silhouette', from his latest volume is, he said, his 'shot at [his] epitaph'. Included by critics and fellow writers, e.g. David Malouf, as among those who have been involved in a radical redefinition of Australian poetry, Rowbotham has also gained international attention. His *Selected Poems* and *Maydays* have been particularly praised, e.g. in the USA, for their skilful conjunction of personal, national and universal themes. J. Strugnell has written the monograph *Focus on David Rowbotham* (1969).

ROWE, Richard ('Peter Possum') (1828–79), born Doncaster, England, came to Australia in 1853 and worked first as a tutor before being befriended by literary patron N.D. Stenhouse and becoming part of the Sydney 1850s literary *coterie* that included Frank Fowler, J. Sheridan Moore, Henry Kendall, Henry Halloran and Daniel Deniehy. A regular contributor to the *Month*, the Sydney *Punch*, *Freeman's Journal* and the *Sydney Morning Herald*, Rowe published a collection of his essays and verse as *Peter Possum's Portfolio* (1858), one of the first such colonial collections; he returned to England in 1858. Among his best works are *Episodes in an Obscure Life* (1871) and *Friends and Acquaintances* (1871), part of his writings about the London poor. Rowe is described in Ann-Mari Jordens's *The Stenhouse Circle* (1979).

ROWLAND, John Russell (1925–   ), born Armidale, NSW, joined the Department of Foreign Affairs in 1944 and served in London, Washington, Saigon, Malaysia, Paris, Moscow and other East European countries. He was ambassador in Moscow 1965–68, and in Paris 1979–82, and is an Officer of the Order of Australia (AO). He has published five collections of poetry, *The Feast of Ancestors* (1965), *Snow and Other Poems* (1971), *Times and Places* (1975), *The Clock Inside* (1979) and *Sixty* (1989). Rowland writes an elegant, controlled poetry, which often deals with the Australian landscape, re-creates the atmosphere of other countries or celebrates the daily realities of family life. One of his best-known poems, 'Canberra in April', evokes the social and physical landscape of the national capital of the 1950s and 1960s. He has also edited translations of poems by Andrei Voznesensky, *The Sculptor of Candles* (1985).

ROWLANDS, Graham (1947–   ), born Brisbane, was educated at the University of Queensland and Flinders University, SA, where he gained a Ph.D. He has been an academic, freelance journalist, educational editor and reviewer and presently lectures in Australian politics and crime prevention planning at Adelaide College of TAFE. He was one of the chief organisers of the Friendly Street poetry group in Adelaide and, for many years, poetry editor of *Overland*. He also edited *Dots over Lines* (1980), an anthology of then recent SA poetry and, with Pauline Wardleworth, *No 9 Friendly Street Poetry Reader* (1985). His own books of poetry include *Stares and Statues* (1972, the first of the Gargoyle Poets series), *Replacing Mirrors* (1975), *Poems Political* (1976), *Adam Scolds* (1976, with Grahame Pitt and Lyndon Walker), *Dial-a-Poem* (1982), *On the Menu* (1988) and *Selected Poems* (1992).

RYAN, Gig (Elizabeth) (1956–   ), born England, worked on the feminist journal *Luna* 1975–78, and has published four books of poems: *The Division of Anger* (1980), which shared the Anne Elder Poetry Award, *Manners of an Astronaut* (1984), *The Last Interior* (1986) and *Excavation* (1990). An extremely original and distinctive voice, Ryan melds her poems from disparate, cryptic fragments and fractured syntax, forming striking images from the unlikely, ugly clutter of contemporary urban life. Her difficult, intense and pain-filled poetry, which unsentimentally and often poignantly reflects a hostile world, combines the personal and the political, implicitly illustrating their complicity. Intimate relationships, sexual desire, the flight of love, the pursuit of power, events on the world stage and the perverse human tendency to inflict hurt on self and others intermingle in poems which speak directly and with uncompromising urgency. Spare, technically taut, sharply witty, her poems often probe the experiences common to those who have chosen the ghetto life of the inner city. *Excavation* is subtitled 'arguments and monologues', a fitting description of many of her poems which are interior monologues, characterised by hard-edged feelings which range from anger to a fatalistic acceptance of loss to a wry humour. But Ryan is also a lyrist with an outstanding linguistic ability to create aesthetically exciting moments from what is emotionally painful. In her simply titled 'Poem', for instance, what might in other hands have become a long drawn out lament for lost love is turned into an intensely compressed and moving expression of the perennial contrast between the uncaring serenity of the external world and inner anguish:

> The day is beautiful
> He doesn't love me
> Pieces of me fly in formation
> Across the sky's blue lung

If Ryan's vision is a dark one, her expression of it is intrinsically stimulating, especially to other writers.

RYAN, Tracy (1964–), born Perth, has worked as a librarian and tutor. Her first volume, *Killing Delilah*, was published by Fremantle Arts Centre Press in 1994. The poem sequence 'Streams in the Desert', about a religious vocation eventually abandoned, shared, in an expanded form, the 1987 Mattara Poetry Prize. Many of the poems are thoughtful, intelligent but ultimately passionate accounts of love and marriage. 'Four Poems', all dealing with the act of love, 'In the First Place', 'Contraband', 'At Night, After' and 'Old Love', are uncompromising in their examination of the impact of love on the feminine psyche. Many of the poems also carry autobiographical echoes, e.g. 'Morningswood', 'Wise & Foolish Virgin', 'Tea for Two'.

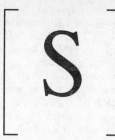

'**Said Hanrahan**', one of the most popular and frequently anthologised of the poems of 'John O'Brien', was published in *Around the Boree Log and Other Verses* (1921). The poem catches to perfection the legendary pessimism of the farmer, who sees prospects of ruin in every variation of weather. The lugubrious lament of the poem, 'We'll all be rooned', has passed into Australian folklore.

SALOM, Philip (1950–   ), born in the Brunswick Junction farming district of WA, trained to be a scientist but later completed a degree in English and turned to writing as a career. From 1983 to 1989 he wrote poetry while tutoring in creative writing at Curtin University, WA, and held several writer-in-residences. Particularly active in the WA literary scene, he has been a judge of numerous WA literary awards and a member of several literary committees. In 1987 he was an Australian representative and guest writer at the Struga International Poetry Readings in Yugoslavia. He has also organised DISK READINGS, Perth's major venue for regular literary readings.

Salom has published (to 1993) six books of poetry – *The Silent Piano* (1980), which won the 1981 Commonwealth Poetry Prize; *The Projectionist* (1983), winner of the 1984 WA Literary Award for Poetry; *Sky Poems* (1987), which repeated his success in the Commonwealth Poetry competition (the only writer to have won the award twice) and which also won the 1988 WA Literary Award for Poetry; *Barbecue of the Primitives* (1989), another WA Literary Award winner; *Tremors* (1992) in the NLA Pamphlet Poets Series; and *Feeding the Ghost* (1993). *Sky Poems*, in particular, reflects the influence on Salom of the hill country (the Darling Range) near Perth, where he has lived for some time. The sky itself is prominent in some of that poetry. Salom is much more than a landscape poet, however; his work traverses a broad range of subjects, many of which stem from mundane experience but are then transformed by his fine craftsmanship and intellectual agility into rich and provocative poetry. A poet already formed, as the success of his first book which dealt mainly with his family and historical figures indicates, Salom has expanded energetically into more conceptually sophisticated and stimulating writing with each successive volume. He forges, in the words of the critic, 'the best aspects of the Symbolist and Surrealist traditions' into a highly distinctive and distinguished body of poetry, much of which illustrates his own assertions that 'the mind is the biggest city of all' and that the poet's true role is 'to know the times, to question the times into intensity'. Among his notable poems are 'Poets and Allegories', 'Properties of the Poet', the clever and amusing 'The Sex of Autostrada Driving', 'Barbecue of the Primitives' and the three pieces on the Swedish tenor Jussi Björling.

Salom published his first novel, *Playback*, in 1991. It emulated the success of his poetry, winning the WA Premier's Award for Fiction in 1992.

239

Saltbush Bill, one of A.B. Paterson's best-known characters, appeared in five poems, 'Saltbush Bill' (in *The Man from Snowy River and Other Verses*, 1895), 'Saltbush Bill's Second Fight' and 'Saltbush Bill's Gamecock' (both in *Rio Grande's Last Race and Other Verses*, 1902), and 'Saltbush Bill, J.P.'. and 'Saltbush Bill on the Patriarchs' (both in *Saltbush Bill, J.P. and Other Verses*, 1917). As a drover in charge of travelling sheep, Saltbush Bill sparks fear and anger in the hearts of squatters like Stingy Smith, on to whose best runs his sheep always manage to stray. When his natural cunning occasionally fails him, his determination usually wins the day. In the character of Saltbush Bill, Paterson incorporates many of the qualities he considered essential for survival in the rough and tumble of outback life: determination, ingenuity, a wry sense of humour and a talent for sharp practices.

'Sam Holt', an Australian folk-song in which a bushman sardonically recalls the seamy past of a former mate, Sam Holt, who has finally succeeded as a digger and returned to a gentleman's life in England, was originally a poem, 'A Ballad of Queensland', written by G.H. Gibson and published in the *Bulletin* 26 March 1881. A parody on the English popular song of the 1840s, 'Ben Bolt', 'Sam Holt' passed into oral currency and was included as an anonymous composition in A.B. Paterson's *Old Bush Songs* (1905). The opening lines of 'Sam Holt',

> Oh! don't you remember Black Alice, Sam Holt –
> Black Alice, so dusky and dark,
> The Warrego gin, with the straw through her nose,
> And teeth like a Moreton Bay shark

are quoted with minor variations in Xavier Herbert's *Capricornia* (1938) and illustrate the racist attitudes of much of Australian folk-song and ballad. Earlier parodies of 'Ben Bolt' were written by the goldfields entertainer Charles Thatcher.

SANDES, John (1863–1938), born Cork, Ireland, and educated at Oxford, migrated to Australia in 1885 and for fifteen years from 1887 worked for the *Argus* as music and drama critic. One of the first contributors to the 'Oriel' column of the newspaper, he also used the pseudonym independently. In 1903 Sandes joined the Sydney *Daily Telegraph* and attended the London peace conference in 1919 as that newspaper's representative. From 1925 to 1938 he edited *Harbour*, a monthly shipping magazine. Sandes's topical, patriotic poetry found a ready audience, especially his 'With Death's Prophetic Ear', a poem on the Boer War which was published in numerous contemporary anthologies. He published five collections of verse, *Rhymes of the Times* (1898), *Ballads of Battle* (1900), *The House of Empire* (1909), *Landing in the Dawn* (1916) and *The Escort* (1925); three adventure novels; and, under the pseudonym 'Don Delaney', a group of novels mainly with bushranging themes.

'Sandy Maranoa, The' is a rollicking Australian folk-song which celebrates the life of the overlanders moving cattle to and from the Maranoa pastoral district in central-southern Queensland, through which runs the Maranoa River, named by Sir Thomas Mitchell in 1846. 'The Sandy Maranoa' was included in A.B. Paterson's *Old Bush Songs* (1905) as an anonymous composition, 'The Maranoa Drovers', but claims have been made that it was composed at the end of the nineteenth century by a young Queensland stockman, A.W. Davis.

SANSOM, Clive (1910–81) lived in London until 1950, when he migrated to Tasmania. A speech educationalist, he was the author of several collections of verse or verse plays on religious and historical themes, *In the Midst of Death* (1940), *The Unfailing Spring* (1943), *The World Turned Upside Down* (1948), *The Witnesses and Other Poems* (1956), *The Cathedral* (1958), *Dorset Village* (1962), *Return to Magic* (1969), *Francis of Assisi* (1981); and a novel, *Passion Play* (1951). His *Selected Poems*, chosen by Ruth

Sansom, were published in 1990 and four of his verse plays, titled *Four Verse Dramas*, in 1991. His poem 'The Witnesses', one of the prize-winning entries of the Festival of Britain competition, was also published in *Poems 1951* (1951) and separately in 1971. In addition, Sansom compiled anthologies of poetry for adults, including *The English Heart* (1945) and *The World of Poetry* (1959), as well as numerous anthologies of verse and plays for children. *Clive Sansom by Forty Friends*, edited by Ruth Sansom, was published in 1990.

SANT, Andrew (1950–   ) was born and lived on the outskirts of London until he came to Australia with his family in 1962. He graduated in arts from La Trobe University, lives in Tasmania and has been a part-time teacher, editor and writer. He was joint editor of *Island Magazine* 1979–89, co-editing with Michael Denholm the anthology *First Rights: A Decade of Island Magazine* (1989). He has produced for radio, *First Hearing: New Verse by Australian Poets* (1982, 1990) and *Antarctica: The Imagined Continent* (1986); has been a member of the Literature Board of the Australia Council; and has edited *Toads: Australian Writers: Other Work, Other Lives* (1992), in which twelve Australian authors describe the problems of being a writer. Sant's four books of verse (to 1993) are *Lives* (1980), a small book of twenty-one poems, *The Caught Sky* (1982), *The Flower Industry* (1985) and *Brushing the Dark* (1989).

Sant's strength as a poet lies in his capacity for keen and sensitive observation and in his ability to capture nuances of character and scene. The title poem of *Lives*, for example, catches to perfection the emigrant Dutch farmer Henk Ramek, who 'drinks regularly to celebrate the good life' here in Australia, and his wife, who, stoically milking the cows, greets his stumbling return home from the pub with 'you olt buggar'. Two other poems involving these two are 'A Small Holding' and 'Milking Three Cows at Nightfall'. Other notable Sant poems are the three-poem series 'Rural Episodes', 'Literacy Lessons' (the vicissitudes of teaching English to unemployed youths), 'A Mount Wellington Sequence', 'Old Woman in Apple Country', 'The Beekeeper's Directory', 'Kelp Harvesters (King Island)' and the popular 'Homage to the Canal People', where those who ply the canals, 'cloth caps pulled down against complacency', view with mildly contemptuous indifference the passing parade of towns and villages.

SARIBAN, Michael (1939–   ), born Berlin, of Russian parents, arrived in Australia in 1948. He began a career in librarianship at the National Library but moved to Brisbane in 1966. He has published two collections of verse, *At the Institute for Total Recall* (1984) and *A Formula for Glass* (1987).

Saturday Club Book of Poetry, The, a Sydney magazine, was edited by Patricia Laird. First published in 1972 as an issue dedicated to Kenneth Slessor, it was replaced in 1977 by *Scopp*, a magazine that included prose as well as poetry, also edited by Laird. *Scopp* ceased publication in 1980.

Satyrs and Sunlight: Silvarum Libri, the first volume of poems by Hugh McCrae, was published in Sydney in 1909. The first part of the title, *Satyrs and Sunlight*, was also used for McCrae's 1928 collected verse. The seventy-nine poems, mainly short lyrics, were highly regarded by the bohemian literary set of the day, of which Norman Lindsay was the centre. Poems such as 'I Blow My Pipes', 'The Satyr's Lass', 'Bacchanalia', 'Fantasy' and 'Muse-Haunted', filled with fauns and nymphs, dryads, centaurs, Bacchanals and the god Pan, all whirling and cavorting in an exultant, sensuous vitality, were a startling contrast to the homespun balladry of the previous two decades.

Scarp, published initially by the Department of English at the University of Wollongong, began life as *First Draught* in September 1980, three issues of that title being edited by a collective which included James Wieland. The title *Scarp* began with Autumn 1982; *Scarp* is published twice yearly and is now under the aegis of the School of Creative Arts, with a strong graphic art as well as literary content. In conjunction with Five Islands Press, *Scarp* publishes the work of new poets, e.g. in 1994 that of Peter Boyle, James Bradley, Paul Cliff, Peta Spear, Beth Spencer and Adrian Wiggins.

Scopp, see **Saturday Club Book of Poetry, The**

SCOTT, John A. (1948–   ), born Sussex, England, graduated from Monash University, Melbourne and spent some years writing for television and radio (e.g. the Aunty Jack Show and the Gary McDonald Show) before lecturing in media studies and professional writing at the Canberra College of Advanced Education (later University of Canberra). He then joined the Creative Arts Department of the University of Wollongong.

Although Scott was a leading figure in the lively poetry scene at Monash in the 1960s, winning the University's Writing Awards in 1966–67, and contributed to the burgeoning poetic revolution of the period, winning the Poetry Society of Australia Award in 1970, it was with the long narrative poem, 'St Clair', that he established himself as a leading contemporary poet. 'St Clair' won the 1984 Mattara Poetry Prize, appearing in the 1984 Mattara anthology *Neither Nuked nor Crucified*, and was published in 1986 with two other lengthy works by Scott, titled *St Clair: Three Narratives*. The other two were 'Preface', which won the 1985 Wesley Michel Wright Award from the University of Melbourne, and 'Run in the Stocking'. A revised edition of the 'Three Narratives' was published in 1990 with an introduction by Christopher Pollnitz who had published 'St Clair' initially in the Mattara anthology. Pollnitz demonstrates that much of the 'Three Narratives' has been present in Scott's work for a number of years; that 'St Clair', for example, is St Clair Convalescent in *The Barbarous Sideshow* of 1976; that Carl Brouwer, the chief figure of 'Preface', is contained to some extent in the character Gus, in *From the Flooded City* of 1981, and that Brouwer, Finchley Watson and Julia feature in *The Quarrel with Ourselves* and *Confession* of 1984, while other poems from those books have echoes of the self-investigations of Dover Anderson/Terry Rutherford in 'Run in the Stocking'. The degree of interconnectedness between Scott's poems, both in the repetition of poems from one volume to another and in the extension and expansion of parts of poems from one volume to another, has been readily admitted by the poet, who sees such repetitions, expansions and reworkings as a writer's natural attempt to attain the ultimate goal of a 'finished' work.

The first of the 'Three Narratives', 'Preface', a series of prose poems, has the narrator, Finchley Watson, committed to examining a series of letters written by Carl Brouwer to his former lover, Julia. The letters cover more than eighteen months, from March 1982, during which Carl leaves Sydney to begin an obsessive search (leading to his death) for A––, the original, quintessential female. Full of sexual obsessions, the letters show Carl drifting towards ultimate mental disintegration. The second narrative, 'St Clair', whose nineteen sections are all in verse, is set in an English psychiatric institution run by the government to 'condition' (by either rehabilitation or destruction) its political dissidents. Both those treated (e.g. the academic, Sheehan) and those administering the treatment (e.g. the psychologist, Warren) are shown to be victims of the barbarity that masquerades as modern (especially politically motivated) psychiatry. The third narrative, 'Run in the Stocking', is a psychological mystery-thriller, set in a totalitarian Australia of the twenty-first century. Whether academic Terry Rutherford, who had become an outspoken opponent of the government, did murder his lover Anne Morris and then commit suicide, or whether Dover Andersson, refashioned in a contrived hospital operation, is actually Rutherford, now removed from society by deleting his old identity and being given a new, less harmful one, is the central question. All three narratives – a combination of varied techniques that require considerable mental agility in the reader – extend the boundaries of contemporary Australian poetry. Not all critics are enthused by such techniques; 'tricky formlessness' that leads to the 'removal of narrative coherence' and a slavish adherence 'to post-structuralist insistence on the writer's automatism' is how the narratives are seen by fellow poet Fay Zwicky. Scott's shorter poems are well exemplified in *Singles*, where the reader attunes with ease to the sensitivity and dexterity of such stylish works as 'My Favourite Things', 'The Chicago Blues Style', 'The Park', 'The Passing, at Boho' and 'Breath'. Notable poems from other volumes include 'The Celebration' (*From the Flooded City*), 'The Apology' (*Translations*) and the translations of the French poet Emmanuel Holquard (*Translations*).

Scott's first novel, *Blair* (1988), lampoons the academic world, as numerous others have before him, peopling it with inept, bumbling, ridiculous figures. *What I have Written* (1993), a novella, won the 1994 Victorian Premier's Literary Award.

John A. Scott's published poetry includes *The Barbarous Sideshow* (1975), *From the Flooded City* (1981), *Smoking* (1983), *The Quarrel with Ourselves*, and *Confession* (1984, two volumes in one), *St Clair: Three Narratives* (1986, revised version 1990), *Singles: Shorter Works 1981–1986* (1989), *Translations* (1990) and *Selected Poems* (1995). *St Clair: Three Narratives* shared the 1986 Victorian Premier's Literary Award.

SCOTT, Margaret (1934–   ), born Bristol, England, graduated MA from Cambridge and Ph.D. from the University of Tasmania. She came to Australia in 1959 and taught at the University of Tasmania from 1966 to 1989, her chief academic interests being seventeenth-century drama and modern Australian poetry. She has written several books of poetry, *Tricks of Memory* (1980), *Visited* (1983) and *The Black Swans* (1988). Her first novel was *The Baby-Farmer* (1990). With Vivian Smith she edited the anthology *Effects of Light: The Poetry of Tasmania* (1985). She won the Borestone Mountain Poetry Award in 1974 and 1976.

Scripsi, primarily a literary magazine supported by the Literature Board and by the Victorian Ministry of the Arts, began in 1981, taking its name from Pontius Pilate's assertion 'Quod scripsi, scripsi' ('What I have written, I have written'). *Scripsi* offered a wide variety of contemporary Australian and international fiction, poetry and literary criticism as well as art criticism. Some of its issues included whole books of poetry, e.g. Laurie Duggan's *The Epigrams of Martial* in 1990. Among its editors were Peter Craven, Michael Heyward and Andrew Rutherford. Publication ceased in 1994.

Sea Spray and Smoke Drift (1867) is the first collection of poems by Adam Lindsay Gordon. The main poem of the collection is 'Ye Wearie Wayfarer'. There are several ballads, e.g. 'The Roll of the Kettledrum', and some melancholy personal poems in which Gordon regrets his youthful follies and wasted opportunities. 'Hippodromania', a poem in five parts, is an indication of the importance of horses and horse-racing both to Gordon and to Australia.

Sentimental Bloke, see *Songs of a Sentimental Bloke, The*

'September in Australia', a well-known Henry Kendall lyric poem, was published in *Leaves from Australian Forests* in 1869. The poem celebrates, in a riot of alliterative musical phrases, the coming of the Australian spring.

Shabbytown Calendar (1975), by Thomas Shapcott, with cover design and illustrations based on the paintings of Charles Blackman, is a series of twelve sequences of poems, one for each month of the year. 'Shabbytown' is Ipswich, the Queensland city where Shapcott spent much of his early life. The poems reflect, with gentle irony for the most part but sometimes with acerbity, the barrenness of provincial life. Symbols of that barrenness range from events such as church socials, engagement parties and service club activities, to local identities such as retired schoolmasters, salesmen and shopkeepers. Victims of it include Tommy Jennings who commits suicide and the anonymous housewife who every day buys groceries, lingerie, books and magazines – 'something that might alter the world'. Shapcott also reflects on Shabbytown's influence on his own personality and character and sees the dramatic tropical climate as a factor in the eccentricity of the inhabitants' behaviour. The series contains brief memorial poems to Francis Webb and Michael Dransfield.

SHAPCOTT, Thomas (1935–   ), born and educated at Ipswich, Queensland, left school at 15 and worked as a clerk in his father's accountancy business. He completed an accountancy degree in 1961 and was a public accountant until 1978. He graduated in arts from the University of Queensland in 1967. In 1973–76 he was a member of the Literature Board and its director 1983–90, and is currently (1995) executive director of the National Book Council. As critic, editor and anthologist, Shapcott was an influential supporter of the 'New Australian Poetry' that sprang up in the late 1960s. In addition to being one of the most interesting of present-day poets he continues to be a major reviewer of and authority on contemporary Australian poetry.

Shapcott's publications include the poetry collections *Time on Fire* (1961), which was awarded the Grace Leven Prize; *Sonnets 1960–1963* (1964); *The Mankind Thing* (1964); *A Taste of Salt Water* (1967), which won both the Sir Thomas White Memorial Prize and the Myer Award for poetry; *Inwards to the Sun* (1969), which also won the Myer Award for poetry; *Fingers at Air* (1969); a group of poems for opera, *The Seven Deadly Sins* (1970); *Begin with Walking* (1972); *Shabbytown Calendar* (1975); *Selected Poems* (1978, rev. edn 1989); *Turning Full Circle* (1979), *Welcome* (1983), *Travel Dice* (1987) and *In the Beginning* (1990). He has also published novels, *Flood Children* (1981), *The Birthday Gift* (1982), a book of 'prose inventions', *Stump & Grape & Bopple-Nut* (1981), *White Stag of Exile* (1984), *Hotel Bellevue* (1986), *The Search for Galina* (1989) and *Mona's Gift* (1993); a collection of essays, articles, speeches, reviews and autobiographical reflections titled *Biting the Bullet: A Literary Memoir* (1990); two collections of short stories, *Limestone and Lemon Wine* (1988) and *What You Own* (1991); several books for young readers; and a history of the Literature Board (1988). He has also written two studies of the artist Charles Blackman, *Focus on Charles Blackman* (1967) and *The Art of Charles Blackman* (1990). He edited the anthologies *New Impulses in Australian Poetry* (1968, with Rodney Hall), *Australian Poetry Now* (1970), *Contemporary American and Australian Poetry* (1976) and *Consolidation: The Second Paperback Poets Anthology* (1982). Other distinctions Shapcott has won include the Canada-Australia Literary Award (1978) and the Struga Golden Wreath International Poetry Award (1989). In 1989 he was awarded an honorary D.Litt. by Macquarie University and made AO the same year. He is married to the poet Judith Rodriguez.

Shapcott's verse reflects his interest in experimental poetic techniques, although his early poetry, as seen in *Time on Fire* and *The Mankind Thing*, is conventional in both form and theme. It is also largely autobiographical, reflecting the country boy's distaste for the garish city environment; the wakening of young love; courtship; marriage, parenthood; and a preoccupation with transience. The fourteen-part 'Two and a Half Acres', the story of the poet, his wife and child settling on their small property, is typical of this intimate, lyrical early verse. With *A Taste of Salt Water* and *Inwards to the Sun*, self-understanding ('Self's the unique toy that I grapple with') and the ultimate understanding of human nature, especially in the light of transience, become his abiding concerns and are illuminated by a wide use of mythology, history, religious and social commentary. In these volumes Shapcott's interest in innovatory techniques is illustrated, e.g. in the blank opening page of *Inwards to the Sun* ('This

Blank Page . . . is where I begin to exist'), and in the experimental settings of 'Night Songs' and 'Ceremony for Cedar'. That interest is given free rein in his book of experimental verse, *Fingers at Air*. Substantial Shapcott poems of this period are 'The City of Acknowledgement', a fourteen-part ironic treatment of the life of Christ; the sonnet sequences 'Suite of Sonnets' and 'Minotaur'; and the historically based 'Portrait of Captain Logan'. Shapcott's best-known and most widely acclaimed work is *Shabbytown Calendar*; 'Shabbytown' is the poet's home town of Ipswich, its 'calendar' ranging over a year from the 'mango weather' of January to the thunderstorms and Christmas bells of the following December. The course of life in the provincial town is conveyed with precision and irony. Shapcott's volume of *Selected Poems* is structured in four chronological sections from 1956 to 1976; his volume *Turning Full Circle* comprises eight sections of prose poems; *Welcome* contains a selection of his most important work since the *Selected Poems* and indicates a new poetic direction consolidated in his subsequent collections and the revised *Selected Poems*.

SHARKEY, Michael (1946–   ), born Canterbury, NSW, has had a varied and colourful career, graduating BA from the University of Sydney and Ph.D. from the University of Auckland. A volatile and voluble poet who is keen on performance poetry (he was a member of La Mama Poetica), Sharkey writes with colloquial directness and élan. Deeply sympathetic towards the 'battler' and 'toiler', he is antagonistic and even contemptuous towards those, such as run-of-the-mill politicians, who display a lack of humanity. While fully aware of formal literary tradition, his own verse is often experimental to the point of formal anarchy. His many publications include *Woodcuts* (1978), *Loose Federation* (with Julian Croft, 1979), *Barbarians* (1981), *Robert Solay's Dreaming* (1983), *The Way It Is: Selected Poems* (1984) and *Alive in Difficult Times: Poems 1985–1991* (1991). He has also edited the *Illustrated Treasury of Australian Humour* (1988) and is writing a biography of David McKee Wright. With A.J. Bennett he edited *Selected Poems (1944–1982)* (1983) of Roland Robinson, and with A.J. Bennett and Winifred Belmont, the verse anthology *No Standing* (1980).

SHAW, Winifred (1905–   ), born Maitland, NSW, married R.M. Taplin and was interned in Singapore's Changi prison camp during the Second World War. She subsequently lived in England. While still in her teens she published three collections of lyrical ballads which show a striking technical control, *The Aspen Tree* (1920), *The Yellow Cloak* (1922) and *Babylon* (1924).

'Shearer's Dream, The', one of the poems of Henry Lawson which was subsequently set to music and became an Australian folk-song, was written in 1901. It tells the story of a shearer who, until he wakes up and finds that he has been dreaming, imagines himself in a shed with electric fans and mahogany pens, shearing sheep that have been washed before they are shorn, and served drinks every hour by female rouseabouts who also attend to the other 'needs' of the shearers. The poem first appeared in print in a story, also titled 'The Shearer's Dream', which was included in *Children of the Bush* (1902). Mitchell and Lawson, camped for the night, listen to the song coming from an adjoining camp, although the singer is silenced before he reveals that he 'woke with my head in the blazin' sun to find ' 'twas a shearer's dream'; this ending, however, was revealed when the poem was published in *When I Was King* (1905). A similar Australian folk-song is 'The Drover's Dream', in which the drover dreams that the bush fauna put on a concert for him until he is rudely awakened by his boss, demanding to know where the sheep have gone.

'Sheedy Was Dying', a poem by John Shaw Neilson, published in the *Bulletin* 1901 Christmas number, records the lonely death that usually comes to drifters in the outback.

'Ship of Ice, The', a long, dramatic poem by Rosemary Dobson, won the *Sydney Morning Herald* prize for poetry in 1946 and was published in three parts in that newspaper in 1947. The ship of ice is the English schooner *Jenny*, which lay locked in the Antarctic ice from 1823 to 1860 until discovered by a whaling vessel. 'Snap-frozen' as it were in an instant of time, the bodies of the crew had been perfectly preserved, caught for thirty-seven years in their frozen postures until released by discovery into conventional death. The poem's seven individual voices (the captain, his wife, and five of the crew) comment on the event in the light of their own personalities and philosophies.

'Sick Stockrider, The', a popular and well-known poem of Adam Lindsay Gordon, was written in 1869 and published in *Bush Ballads and Galloping Rhymes* (1870). The ballad of the dying stockman, with its creed of mateship, its laconic acceptance in true bush style of whatever life and death may offer, led Marcus Clarke to assert that in Gordon's work lay the beginnings of a national school of Australian poetry. 'The Sick Stockrider' is accepted as the progenitor of the Australian literary ballad but differs markedly in tone and language from the later bush ballads of the *Bulletin* school.

'Silkworms, The', a poem by Douglas Stewart, was published in *Quadrant* (1957). Generally regarded as one of Stewart's finest lyric poems, 'The Silkworms' belongs, according to its author, to 'a sequence of suburban satires' inspired by his residence in a Sydney northern suburb, St Ives. The poem's opening phrase, 'All their lives in a box!', represents not only the silkworms but also their human counterparts, the sub-urb-dwellers. The human situation in which freedom of action and choice is limited by environment-conditioned attitudes is linked to the inertness of the silkworm's existence consequent upon generations of confinement and restriction. The poem's deliberate but restrained gravity, its measured but unemphatic tone and quiet, relaxed movement accentuate the tragic frustration of the situation it represents.

SIMMONS, Samuel Rowe (1871–1952) was a Melbourne printer who established two small private presses, the Argonaut Press and the Simmons Press, which published his own verse and criticism and other works, e.g. the poems of the English writer Christopher Smart. Of Simmons's six books, the most important was *Sonnets and Other Verses* (1925), published under the pseudonym 'Oswald Gray'.

SIMPSON, R.A. (Ronald Albert) (1929–), born Melbourne, studied at the Royal Melbourne Institute of Technology and taught in schools in England and Australia before his appointment in 1968 to the Chisholm Institute of Technology where he is senior lecturer in art. Poetry editor of the *Bulletin* 1963–65, he has been poetry editor of the *Age* since 1969. His poetry has appeared in numerous collections, *The Walk along the Beach* (1960), *This Real Pompeii* (1964), *After the Assassination and Other Poems* (1968), *Diver* (1972), *Poems from Murrumbeena* (1976), *The Forbidden City* (1979), *Selected Poems* (1981), *Words for a Journey: Poems 1970–1985* (1986) and *Dancing Table – Poems and Drawings 1986–1991* (1992). He has also edited *Poems from the Age 1967–79* (1979).

One of a group of Melbourne poets that came to prominence in the late 1950s and included Vincent Buckley, Evan Jones and Chris Wallace-Crabbe, Simpson has written, over thirty years, a consistently urbane, understated and cerebral poetry that is more international than Australian in style. His collections include some light satires and verse on political subjects, but his preoccupations are the texture of ordinary life, the difficulties and joys of communication, both in art and with people, and the tensions between the desire for permanence and the reality of change, between aspiration and actuality. Complex but intelligible, spare and rigorous in thought and expression, often ironic and provocative, Simpson's verse has an analytical sensitivity that is sometimes uncompromisingly directed at the self. In his later work he achieves a relaxed, flexible and deceptively artless style. Throughout much of his work there is a faintly elegiac tone, but the sadness is phlegmatic rather than acute. That tone is struck in the words of 'Making', the final poem of *Dancing Table*.

> I dislike
> every poem
> I've ever written
> but I'm stuck with them.
>
> But even now
> I'm fashioning another
> stitching patches together.

Long overdue recognition of his achievement came with the 1992 Victorian FAW Christopher Brennan Award.

'Singapore', a poem by Mary Gilmore, was published in the *Australian Women's Weekly* in March 1942, soon after the fall of Singapore to the Japanese forces in the Second World War. Much weakened because of wartime censorship from its original scathing indictment of corruption and ineptitude, the poem echoed the widespread belief that Australian troops in Malaya, and possibly the ultimate safety of this country, had been needlessly sacrificed to other Allied interests.

SKOVRON, Alex (1948–), born Poland, spent a year in Israel before coming to Australia in 1958. Educated at Sydney University (MA), he has worked in Sydney and Melbourne as an editor. He has published two highly regarded volumes of poetry, *The Rearrangement* (1988), which won both the FAW Anne Elder Award for Poetry and the Mary Gilmore Award, and *Sleeve Notes* (1992). A highly intelligent and sophisticated poet, Skovron can be intellectual, abstract and formal and at other times pragmatic and plain-speaking. His range is wide and versatile: in language – from the polished and erudite to the simple, even colloquial; in form – from the complex, intricate and formal to blank and free verse; in theme – from the past, the future, history, philosophy, music, the shape of reality, the complexity of the human situation to the ordinary and mundane. His notable poems include the narratives from *The Rearrangement*, e.g. 'Lines from the Horizon', 'Fugue' (which won the 1983 Wesley Michel Wright prize), and the title poem itself, a sixteen-sonnet sequence recording an old man's obsession with order in his library, a ritual that both sustains and diminishes him. Music is one of the chief themes of *Sleeve Notes*, the title poem in twelve parts being inspired by Mozart's life and music and 'Elgar Revisits Worcestershire, 1984' in which the composer's ghost angrily comments on modern man's inability to truly know 'my music's dark communion'. The personal reminiscences, 'The Waterline Poems' and the reflective 'Life' are also impressive. Making few concessions to attract a wide and popular audience ('I want the reader to make a journey with each poem'), Skovron has met with considerable acclaim from fellow poets.

SKRZYNECKI, Peter (1945–), born Germany of Polish-Ukrainian descent, came to Australia in 1949 and grew up mainly in Sydney. He has worked as a teacher. His poetry has appeared in several collections, *There, Behind the Lids* (1970), *Headwaters* (1972), *Immigrant Chronicle* (1975), *The Aviary: Poems 1975–1977* (1978), *The Polish Immigrant* (1982), *Night Swim* (1989) and *Easter Sunday* (1993). He has also written a novel, *The Beloved Mountain* (1988) and two collections of short stories, *The Wild Dogs* (1987) and *Rock 'n' Roll Heroes* (1992), and edited an anthology of writing from Australians of non-English-speaking backgrounds, *Joseph's Coat* (1985). He won the Grace Leven Prize in 1972.

Immigrant experience in a new land is the dominant theme of Skrzynecki's gently lyrical and accessible poetry. In the earlier collections the dominant experience of loss is most closely associated with the father's irretrievable loss of home and the son's equally irretrievable separation from experience of that particular home. In the later collections a more personal, contemporary sense of loss, associated with separation from wife and children and with the emotional impact of a serious heart attack, makes itself felt. Technically assured and controlled, Skrzynecki's poetry is also remarkable for delicacy of observation and sensitivity to landscape, expressed in direct, precise and unaffected language. The same sense or premonition of loss and cherishing of memory expressed in his poetry colour his short stories.

SLADE, Leon (1931–   ), born Melbourne, has published three collections of verse, *Wilderness* (1970), *Slade's Anatomy of the Horse* (1972), and *Bloodstock Breeding* (1979). Often humorous or satirical, Slade uses colloquial diction and imagery to express his urban, contemporary themes.

SLESSOR, Kenneth (1901–71) was born in Orange, NSW, of German-Scottish ancestry. His father, Robert Schloesser, was a mining engineer, but came from a distinguished family of musicians, and was something of a polymath himself. Margaret, his wife, presumably shared some of her husband's intellectual interests as she was a schoolmistress at the time that they met. Both her parents came from the Hebrides. Her father ran a store in Orange and became mayor of that municipality. Perhaps the most influential aspects of this diverse inheritance for Kenneth were his father's intensely serious philosophical musings and his mother's strong Presbyterianism. That the family name was anglicised in 1914 to avoid unpleasantness consequent upon their Germanic connections may also have left a mark on the young Slessor. Certainly his first poems published in the *Bulletin* while he was still at school are anxious to convey an appropriate patriotism; they celebrate the 'derring-do' of the Anzacs, and Slessor remained devoted to the myth of the Australian soldier for the rest of his life.

Despite his early effusions in a popularist mode, the young Slessor soon developed his serious work in a different, more aristocratic direction, while maintaining an involvement with popular writing through his burgeoning career as a journalist. Slessor worked for the Sydney *Sun* from 1920 to 1925, and then briefly for the *Melbourne Punch* and Melbourne *Herald*. In 1927 he returned to Sydney and joined *Smith's Weekly*, with which he stayed until 1939 and the outbreak of the Second World War. The 1920s and 1930s were the years of his productivity as a poet. He published his first volume, *Thief of the Moon*, in 1924 and this was followed by *Earth-Visitors* (1926), *Trio*, with Harley Matthews and Colin Simpson (1931), *Cuckooz Contrey* (1932), *Darlinghurst Nights and Morning Glories* (1932) and *Five Bells* (1939). A selection of his work, published under the title *One Hundred Poems* in 1944, was reprinted with an additional two poems in 1957. Since then this selection of Slessor's poems has often been reprinted. Another volume of light verse (*Darlinghurst Nights* was the first) edited by Julian Croft entitled *Backless Betty from Bondi* was published in 1983. A selection of Slessor's literary essays and other prose writings, *Bread and Wine*, appeared in 1970.

The poems in Slessor's first two volumes pursue the great themes of the Romantic-Symbolist tradition, turning obsessively upon the conflicts between art and nature, beauty and time. A fear of death, that most difficult of subjects for the Romantic imagination to confront, lurks behind many of the utterances. Here too is manifest the powerful influence of Norman Lindsay. Slessor met the Lindsays in the early 1920s and collaborated with Norman and Jack in the production of a short-lived periodical, *Vision*, which gained a certain notoriety for what many considered to be its salacious content. The magazine was a proponent of Norman Lindsay's aesthetic – a hotchpotch of ideas deriving from Plato, Nietzsche and other thinkers in the European symbolist tradition. According to Lindsay, art was transcendental and gave access to Life which was distinct from the humdrum, quotidian concerns of mere existence. In the highly decorative, even ornate, surfaces of Slessor's early poems one feels the strain of the poet's desire to escape into these magical realms of art and Lindsayan Life. But often the reader is struck by artifice rather than art – an exercise of skill rather than an expression of deep thought or feeling. In a few poems, however, 'The Night Ride', 'A City Nightfall', 'Winter Dawn' Slessor prefigures the direction of his later work. In these poems we have a sense of the world of lived experience, and also a sense of how this world is, for Slessor, threatened by death and meaninglessness.

The poems included in *Cuckooz Contrey* and *Five Bells* demonstrate a more refined diction than in the earlier work and a willingness to experiment with rhythm and rhyme, although it must be said that such experiment was conducted within well-defined parameters. Slessor never went as far as T.S. Eliot, say, in the disruption of conventional syntax and metre. There is some broadening of overt subject matter in the poems of the later 1920s and 1930s, but Slessor's obsessions remain recognisably constant. There is a penchant for evoking a romantic and decorative past that sits uneasily against the increasing bitterness with which Slessor regards the modern world. His famous poems, *Captain Dobbin* and *Five Visions of Captain Cook*, are essays in poetic portraiture which are concerned with the role of memory and imagination in the construction of myth. It is significant that both poems, despite their manifest charm, have elements in them which celebrate the past at the expense of the present, and more darkly intimate the defeat of all experience (including imagination and memory) by time. This latter theme finds its greatest expression in Slessor's most important poem, 'Five Bells'. This constitutes an elegy for Joe Lynch, drowned in Sydney Harbour, and explores yet again the equivocal relationship between art, time and death. Although through the operations of memory and imagination the poet can retrieve and express aspects of the dead man so that he becomes 'part of an idea', the poet also expresses his (and the poem's) failure to resurrect or even hear Joe's voice. It is no wonder that this poem was the herald of a poetic silence that was to last from 1944 to the poet's death in 1971, broken only by two further lyric poems which arose out of his experience during the war.

In 1939 Slessor was appointed as an official war correspondent and between 1940 and 1944 spent time with Australian troops in England, Greece, the Middle-East and New Guinea. His *War Diaries* and *War Despatches*, edited by Clement Semmler, were published in 1985 and 1987 respectively. 'Beach Burial', an elegy for dead sailors, plays on the obvious irony that death makes no distinction between the Allied and the Axis dead. More poignantly the poem intimates the vulnerability of memorials and the distance between the living and the dead. 'An Inscription for Dog River', Slessor's other war poem, is altogether slighter than 'Beach Burial' but nevertheless effectively satirises the vainglory of the Australian General Blamey.

This perhaps was the most political poem Slessor wrote in his adult career. It is a striking feature of his work that despite living through the 1930s, a decade of political turmoil in Australia and overseas, politics and social themes are never allowed to intrude into his poetry. Slessor shared Norman Lindsay's very conservative belief that art including poetry was 'above' politics. And even in Slessor's very accomplished light verse, where we sometimes glimpse some of the seedier aspects of Sydney, these are dealt with in tones which are devised to maximise fun and minimise critique. Like many of his 'serious' poems, the light verse also provides evidence of Slessor's highly ambivalent attitude towards women.

On resigning his position as a war correspondent, Slessor returned to the Sydney *Sun*, where he remained as leader-writer and literary editor until 1957. Thereafter he worked for the *Daily Telegraph* and *Sunday Telegraph* as a leader-writer and book-reviewer. Although he wrote no further poetry, he maintained his literary interests through various jobs as editor and adviser. He compiled the 1945 anthology *Australian Poetry* and co-edited *The Penguin Book of Australian Verse* (1958). In 1953 he became a member of the advisory board of the CLF and in 1968 a member of the National

Literature Board of Review. Between 1956 and 1961 he edited the literary magazine *Southerly*, typically insisting that it remain a purely *literary* periodical that did not dabble in politics. A *bon vivant*, Slessor relished his period as president of the Sydney Journalists Club 1956–65, a position which gave him considerable influence over the city's literary and journalistic scene.

Ironically in the years of his poetic silence his reputation steadily increased, and today this shows little sign of diminution. In 1991 Geoffrey Dutton published a biography of the poet, and John Tranter and Philip Mead chose to begin their *Penguin Anthology of Modern Australian Poetry* with selections from Slessor's work. In the same year Dennis Haskell provided a new selection of Slessor's writings including letters, journalism, light verse as well as some of the better-known poems, and in 1994 Haskell and Geoffrey Dutton edited his *Collected Poems*, including the casual Slessor verse that appeared in *Smith's Weekly*. Notwithstanding Slessor's limited output and the mixed quality of some of his early work, he remains undoubtedly one of Australia's most important poets.

ADRIAN CAESAR

SMITH, Vivian (1933–) was born and grew up in Hobart, Tasmania. He graduated with an MA in French from the University of Tasmania, where he taught French for ten years. After moving to Sydney he completed a Ph.D. in English at the University of Sydney, where he is now a reader in English. He has published five volumes of verse, *The Other Meaning* (1956), *An Island South* (1967), *Familiar Places* (1978), *Tide Country* (1982), which won the NSW Premier's Poetry Prize and the Grace Leven Prize, and *Selected Poems* (1985). He edited *Australian Poetry 1986* and *1988; Young St. Poets Anthology* (1981), and co-edited, with Margaret Scott, *Effects of Light: The Poetry of Tasmania* (1985) and, with Robert Gray, *Sydney's Poems* (1992). His edition *Nettie Palmer: Her Private Journal 'Fourteen Years', Poems, Reviews and Literary Essays* appeared in 1988. He has published monographs on James McAuley (1965) and Vance Palmer (1971) and critical studies, *Vance and Nettie Palmer* (1975) and *The Poetry of Robert Lowell* (1974). He also edited *Letters of Vance and Nettie Palmer 1915–1963* (1977) and wrote the poetry section of *The Oxford History of Australian Literature* (1981). Other publications include *Tasmania and Australian Poetry* (1984).

Smith's first poems were published in the *Bulletin* while he was still at school. His first volume, *The Other Meaning*, reveals Tasmania as the focal point of his work. This early poetry, seen by Kenneth Slessor as reflecting 'a gaunt, stony, achromatic landscape', is romantic in its symbolist imagery, linguistic musicality and melancholy pensiveness. Influenced by Judith Wright and Kenneth Slessor, it shares their preoccupation with landscape and sea, the latter 'an inescapable element' for a Tasmanian. Poems like 'Bird Sanctuary', 'In Summer Rain', 'Myth', 'Bedlam Hills' and 'Thylacine' are attractive lyrics fusing a personal inner world with a vividly evoked and precisely observed external scene.

An Island South, named for Tasmania, conveys the island's cold, still luminosity and searches 'for a vision in which contradictions are held in balance' and doubt and pain and fragmentation can be withstood. A group of savagely comic satires introduces a new detachment and toughness of tone. Longer lyrics ('Warmth in July', 'Hobart', 'Late April, Hobart') respond sensitively to the scenes and implications of autumn.

Familiar Places celebrates places that have become meaningful to the poet – Sydney ('Twenty Years of Sydney', 'Balmoral Summer') and Tuscany ('Il Convento, Batignano') joining with the first familiar place, Tasmania ('View from the Domain, Hobart' and 'Back in Hobart'); and the memory of three women (two of them Tasmanian artists, the third a Sydney refugee from Vienna), whose highly individual and isolated lives reflect wider human issues.

Tide Country brings together the two poles of Smith's imaginative world, Tasmania and Sydney. Les Murray writes of Smith as 'Slessor's natural successor in evocations of Sydney Harbour and its surrounds which few really match'. A new, less intimately congenial environment brings fresh imaginative alertness and a harder-edged quality to the verse. The book includes a section of translations ranging from the French Renaissance poet Maurice Sceve to the German modernist Paul Celan and continues Smith's main preoccupations with related notions of permanence and decreation, loss and endurance, decay and renewal.

Selected Poems contains a large group of new poems and shows Smith increasingly concerned with the scrutiny of modes and codes of behaviour, the odd, the unexpectedly poignant, observed in the animal as well as the human world ('Dung Beetles', 'At the Parrot House, Taronga Park'). The language becomes grittier, the rhythmic texture of the verse more complex. The book contains a series of prose poems of memories of Hobart in the 1940s, as well as many unrhymed free forms. At the same time the lyrical aspect of Smith's poetry continues with new controlled intensity ('Still Life', 'Tasmania').

Smith has commented on his own work:

> Looking back over my poems I find that they are concerned with various attitudes of mind – how to go on living fully and humanly without dogma or theory – on a provisional basis so to speak – but without becoming the victim of unstructured experience.

'Song of the Republic, A' was Henry Lawson's first published poem; a stirring appeal to the 'Sons of the South' (the original title) to bring about a new social order, it appeared in the *Bulletin* in October 1887. The circumstances of its composition, acceptance and publication are recorded in Lawson's 'A Fragment of Autobiography'.

Songs from the Mountains, Henry Kendall's final volume of verse, has an interesting publishing history. When first published in December 1880 it included a satirical poem, 'The Song of Ninian Melville', which heaped abuse upon the then member for Northumberland in the NSW parliament. Because the publishers feared a libel action by Melville the volume was hurriedly withdrawn, the satire replaced by a poem, 'Christmas Creek', and the volume reissued in January 1881. Kendall's best collection, *Songs from the Mountains*, contains the autobiographical lyrics 'Mooni' and 'Narrara Creek', and the well-known character pieces 'Bill the Bullock Driver' and 'Jim the Splitter'. The dedicatory poem of the volume, 'To a Mountain', reveals Kendall's understanding and acceptance of the problems that had so embittered his early life and his new sense of self-reconciliation.

Songs of a Sentimental Bloke, The (1915), the colloquial verse narrative that bestowed on C.J. Dennis the title 'Laureate of the Larrikin', tells of the courtship and marriage of Bill, a larrikin of the Melbourne streets, much given to 'gettin' on the shick', and his 'ideal tart', Doreen, whose 'lurk' was 'pastin' labels in a pickle joint'. Other characters in the story, Ginger Mick and Rose of Spadgers, were used by Dennis in later volumes to continue the series. An immediate best-seller, the book went through five printings in three months and has been frequently adapted for the stage, film and television. Although it has never recaptured its first popularity and has sometimes been accused of gross exaggeration in its vernacular style and unrealistic characterisation, it occupies a unique position in the folk-literature of Australia, immortalising and romanticising the city larrikin who was a feature of Australian urban life in the early part of the twentieth century.

SORENSEN, Jack (1907–49), born Kalgoorlie, WA, of mixed Danish, Irish and English heritage, was a WA boxing champion, shearer, newspaper representative and balladist whose poems appeared regularly in the *Bulletin* and in the newspapers of the

WA goldfields. His publications were *The Gun of Glindawor* (1932), *The Lost Shanty* (1939) and *The Collected Poems of Jack Sorensen, 1907–1949*, published posthumously in 1950. *The Collected Poems*, with such segments as 'Shearing Ballads and Rhymes of the North-West', 'Goldfields Verse' and 'Songs of the Kimberleys', illustrates the themes of Sorensen's verse. A new collected edition, *The Ghosts of Bayley Street*, was published in 1992.

SOUTER, C.H. (Charles Henry) (1864–1944), born Scotland, came to Australia in 1879 and spent three years in the bush before returning to Scotland to train as a doctor. After a journey to China as a ship's surgeon and some years in NSW he settled in a practice in SA. He began to contribute ballads to the *Bulletin* in 1896, sometimes using the pseudonyms 'Nil' and 'Dr Nil', and published four collections of verse, *Irish Lords and Other Verses* (1912), *To Many Ladies and Others* (1917), *The Mallee Fire and Other Verses* (1923) and *The Lonely Rose and Other Verses* (1935). Souter wrote bush ballads and sea shanties as well as lyrical verse. His bush ballads, which reflect the daily life of the small farms of SA, are sensitive to the experience and idiom of a wide range of personalities, both male and female. Some of his most memorable are 'Irish Lords', 'Pump'kin Time', 'When the Missus Is Away' and 'Harvestin'. His rhythmic, suitably salty, sea shanties, such as 'What the Red-Haired Bo'sun Said' and 'Blue Peter', are less individual and distinctive but found a ready audience.

'South of My Days', published in *The Moving Image* (1946), is the poem that chiefly characterises Judith Wright as the poet of the New England countryside. The poem echoes her affectionate memories of the 'clean, lean hungry country' in which she was born and grew up. It contains, too, fragments of stories from that countryside's pioneer past – drovers and bushrangers, desperate droughts and starving cattle, and the legendary coaches of Cobb & Co.

Southerly, the quarterly journal of the Sydney branch of the English Association, was founded in 1939 under the editorship of R.G. Howarth and A.G. Mitchell; Howarth was sole editor 1945–55 and subsequent editors have been Kenneth Slessor (1956–61), Walter Stone (1962), G.A. Wilkes (1963–87) and Elizabeth Webby (1988–   ). In its early years it gave coverage to English and American literature but from 1944, when Angus & Robertson (publishers 1944–71) became involved in its production, it gave increasing attention to Australian writing; from Slessor's editorship it has been subtitled *A Review of Australian Literature. Southerly* publishes creative work, chiefly short stories and poetry, as well as criticism and reviews. Apart from 1960, when no issues appeared, *Southerly* has continued to play a significant part in the study of Australian literature, particularly through its contribution to the establishment of a body of criticism on significant Australian writers such as C.J. Brennan and Patrick White. Its fiftieth anniversary issue (1989) includes many articles that illustrate its importance to Australian literature over half a century, including S.E. Lee's history of *Southerly* 1942–89.

SPENCER, T.E. (Thomas Edward) (1845–1911), born London, visited Australia at 18 and returned in 1875 to settle in Sydney, where he became a building contractor and a prominent figure in industrial arbitration. He is best known for his humorous ballads, several of which, e.g. 'How M'Dougall Topped the Score', 'Why Doherty Died' and 'O'Toole and McSharry', have become familiar recitation pieces. His ballads, frequently contributed to the *Bulletin*, appeared in two collections, *How M'Dougall Topped the Score and Other Verses and Sketches* (1906) and *Budgeree Ballads* (1908), reprinted in 1910 as *Why Doherty Died*. He also published a novel, *Bindawalla* (1912), and short stories.

SPENCER-BROWNE, Reginald (1856–1943), born Appin, NSW, joined the staff of the *Brisbane Courier* in 1882. He encouraged the work of the poet George Essex Evans. Commissioned in the Queensland Mounted Infantry in 1887, he had risen to major before the outbreak of the Boer War, in which he served with distinction. He later devoted much of his time to Queensland's light horse regiments, and in 1915 joined the AIF as colonel and saw action at Gallipoli, before being 'retired' to command of the Australian training depots in Egypt and England. He was formally retired in 1921 as honorary major-general and in his later years became a famous Queensland identity. He published a series of bush and mining yarns, *Romances of the Goldfield and Bush* (1890); two collections of poetry, *Shadow and Shine* (1874) and *The Last Ride* (1875); and reminiscences, *A Journalist's Memories* (1927).

Spinner (1924–27), a monthly poetry magazine, was published in Melbourne, edited by R.A. Broinowski. Numerous poets of the time, including Dorothea McKellar, Zora Cross, Mary Gilmore, Louis Lavater and 'Furnley Maurice', were contributors to the magazine, which also included brief reviews, biographical notes and photographs. Issues of *The Spinner* were also reprinted as annual volumes 1925–27, titled *Poetry in Australasia*.

STASKO, Nicolette (1950–), born Pensylvania, USA, came to Australia in 1979 and has lived in Canberra and Sydney. *Abundance* (1992) won the Anne Elder Award for the best first collection of poems that year. Her second volume, *Black Night with Windows*, was published in 1994. The title poem in *Abundance* contains the outraged musings of a Roman bureaucrat about the decadence of the Etruscans. One of the longer poems in the first book, it displays Stasko's ability to maintain the high quality of language and insight evident in such shorter poems as 'Hyperdome' and 'Last Rites'. The restrictions of domesticity surface in 'Lumeah Street' and 'Place and Landscapes'. In both volumes, however, the joy, wonder and, ultimately, the heartache of motherhood provide the deepest source of emotion, The little poem in the second, in which a widower and his dead wife present contrasting views, is a deft disclosure of the archetypal difference between the sexes.

STAUNTON, Madge (1917–), born Coolangatta, Queensland, taught and practised in the visual arts for many years. She did not begin writing until the early 1970s but has contributed poetry to numerous periodicals and has won the Henry Lawson Festival Award twice and the Silver Jubilee Henry Lawson Festival Award in 1982. She has published two collections, *The Cleaving Edge* (1982) and *Heritage of Air* (1984).

STEELE, Peter (1939–), born Perth, was educated there and in Melbourne. A Jesuit priest, he has been provincial superior of the Society of Jesus in Australia and now holds a personal chair in English at the University of Melbourne, where he has taught since 1966. He has published poetry extensively in periodicals and in two collections, *Word from Lilliput* (1973) and *Marching on Paradise* (1984). He has also written several critical works including *Jonathan Swift: Preacher and Jester* (1978), *Expatriates: Reflections on Modern Poetry* (1985), *The Autobiographical Passion: Studies in the Self on Show* (1989) and a study of Peter Porter in the Australian Writers series (1992). A poet with a strong sense of order and balance, Steele links worship of God with passion for language, and poetry with celebration of the divine.

STEPHENS, A.G. (Alfred George) (1865–1933), born and educated at Toowoomba, Queensland, was in 1880 apprenticed to a Sydney printer and in 1886 admitted to membership of the NSW Typographical Association. In 1888 he returned north to take up an appointment as editor of the *Gympie Miner*. Stephens became a leading member of the Gympie Literary Circle.

At the end of 1890 Stephens went to Brisbane and became sub-editor of the radical

Boomerang, to which he contributed leaders, features, social jottings, *faits divers* and a regular column, 'The Magazine Rifler', which surveyed the latest numbers of the English and American journals. When he left the *Boomerang* in October 1891 it was in the hands of a liquidator and Stephens received the office bible in lieu of wages. He then joined the staff of the Cairns *Argus*, becoming editor by the end of 1891 and part-owner in 1892. He instituted a literary supplement and ran an essay competition as he had done on the *Miner*. Stephens himself won the prize of £25 in a competition run in conjunction with the North Queensland Separation League for his essay 'Why North Queensland Wants Separation', later published as a pamphlet in 1893. Stephens left on a trip overseas, using funds from the sale of his interest in the *Argus* at the end of 1892. He travelled in America, Canada and Europe. *A Queenslander's Travel Notes*, published on his return to Sydney in 1894, criticised the pretensions and decorums of traditionalist Europe, and in the half of the work devoted to America used the high divorce rate, drug abuse, poverty and crime, side by side with American 'progress' and smugness about its achievements, to define what he saw as the peculiar and contrary American character. At the end of 1893 Stephens was working in Fleet Street for the *Daily Chronicle* when J.F. Archibald offered him a sub-editorship on the Sydney *Bulletin*, which he took up in 1894. By that time the *Bulletin* was a major intercolonial publication, and with Archibald's return to the editorship in 1886, it entered a period of high literary consciousness. It encouraged local authors, advocated literary nationalism and promoted a distinctive model of the short story. From the time of his arrival Stephens contributed literary notices and comments. In August 1896 the first Red Page appeared, a full-page literary section. Stephens continued his cosmopolitan interests, dividing comment among Australian, American, English and European writers. He frequently called for a greater awareness of overseas trends and standards. 'Is there a single Australian', he asked in January 1897, 'who could pass an examination in Huysmans, Maeterlinck, or Verhaeren?' Stephens's broad views on politics and his international literary tastes were consistent with his favourite critical yardstick, the concept of 'universality'. The concept recurs throughout his writings and indicates an absolute standard of critical appraisal beyond mutable and transitory criteria such as a work's national or moral value.

Stephens was, however, a nationalist critic in that he encouraged and welcomed new *Bulletin* writers as signs that Australian literature was growing toward maturity. Joseph Furphy, Shaw Neilson, Hugh McCrae, Mary Gilmore, Miles Franklin and Roderic Quinn all acknowledged his personal encouragement and guidance, and as controller of the *Bulletin's* publishing division from 1897 Stephens saw most of these writers into print in book form for the first time. Under Stephens the *Bulletin's* publishing activities were greatly expanded, beginning with Barcroft Boake's *Where the Dead Men Lie and Other Poems* in 1897 and producing twenty-five further volumes over the next nine years. Stephens acted as editor, literary agent and book designer. His editorship saw the publication of the classics *On Our Selection* (1899) by 'Steele Rudd' and *Such Is Life* (1903) by Furphy; the *Bulletin* anthologies *The Bulletin Reciter* (1901), *The Bulletin Story Book* (1901) and *A Southern Garland* (1904); and the first volumes of verse by Will Ogilvie, Arthur Adams, Louise Mack, E.J. Brady, W.T. Goodge and Bernard O'Dowd. Stephens's role as editor of the *Bulletin's* book division alone guarantees him a place of permanent importance in the history of Australian literature.

In 1902 Stephens's own volume of poems, *Oblation*, was published privately, with illustrations by Norman Lindsay. In 1904 he saw through the press a selection of his own essays from the *Bulletin* on social and literary topics, *The Red Pagan*. The volume expresses some of Stephens's characteristic literary attitudes, including the criterion of universality, the emotional impact necessary in great art, the sexual and racial conditioning of artistic creativity, and the correlation of artistic genius with insanity.

Stephens believed that the emotive qualities of poetry derived from a 'female' species of creativity. It has been argued that this made Stephens's poetic preferences lachrymose and led to bias in his selections of the work of Daley and Neilson. His views about the psychopathological origins of artistic creativity were derived from the writings of Havelock Ellis and through the latter from Francis Galton's *Hereditary Genius* (1869) and Cesare Lombroso's *L'Uomo di Genio* (1888). These views underpinned Stephens's emphasis on biography in his criticism and sometimes precluded from high praise writers who lacked the correct racial or temperamental qualifications.

In 1906 Stephens left the *Bulletin*. Archibald had stood down as editor in favour of James Edmond in 1902, and Stephens's relations with William Macleod, its former artist and now business manager, were prickly. He had also fallen out with Henry Lawson and Norman Lindsay. Stephens had a bluff, dogmatic side to his personality which sometimes irked acquaintances and which, according to Lindsay in *Bohemians of the Bulletin* (1965), was the reverse side of his emotional temperament. Stephens may also have been dissatisfied with the conditions and limitations of his role at the *Bulletin*. On 1 November 1906 the Red Page announced his departure and the establishment of his business venture, the Bookfellow, a literary bookshop named after the monthly literary magazine he had run for five issues from January 1899. In 1907 Stephens revived the *Bookfellow*. Its files contain a high standard of discussion of Australian, English and European contemporary writers and artists. By 1907, however, the magazine and the shop were in trouble, and in June the shop's stock and much of Stephens's own library were auctioned 'without any reserve'. In 1894 Stephens had married Constance Smith; the couple now had six dependent children, and financial necessity compelled a move to NZ, where Stephens accepted an offer from his old editor, Gresley Lukin, of a job on the Wellington *Evening Post*. Stephens maintained an aloof demeanour at the *Post* and in 1909 returned to Sydney, reviving the *Bookfellow* and working as a freelance journalist. The magazine lasted intermittently until 1925 (partly supported by Mary Gilmore) and fulfilled an important literary role. It provided an outlet for Shaw Neilson, Hugh McCrae and Mary Gilmore, and as he had done at the *Bulletin* Stephens also published books under the paper's imprint. In his last years the stream of Stephens's work hardly abated. He published another volume of verse, *The Pearl and the Octopus and Other Exercises in Prose and Verse* (?1911) and several pamphlets of his own poems, wrote a novel, *Bill's Idees* (1913), two plays, *The Australian Flower Masque* (1924) and *Capturing the Bushranger* (1924), and edited textbooks and anthologies for Australian schools, as well as producing significant critical studies of Henry Kendall and Christopher Brennan (1928, 1933). Rated by many as Australia's most influential pioneer man of letters, Stephens, especially through his editorial work and his steady stream of authoritative criticism, stimulated the development of Australian writing to a marked degree in the decades spanning the nineteenth and twentieth centuries. Leon Cantrell has edited *A.G. Stephens: Selected Writings* (1978). P.R. Stephensen and Vance Palmer wrote, respectively, the biographical works *The Life and Works of A.G. Stephens* ('The Bookfellow') (1940) and *A.G. Stephens: His Life and Work* (1941).

DOUG JARVIS

STEPHENS, James Brunton (1835–1902), born Bo'ness near Edinburgh, received a sound Scottish education, including a period at the University of Edinburgh. He was a private tutor and schoolmaster both before and after his migration to Queensland in 1866. Following the publication of several volumes of verse, and to acknowledge his growing literary stature, he was appointed to the civil service, ultimately becoming acting under-secretary to the colonial secretary in Brisbane. After the death of Kendall in 1882 Stephens became the leading literary figure of the period. He contributed both creative works and literary comment to important newspapers and journals, including the *Bulletin;* his poetry appeared in contemporary anthologies such as Douglas Sladen's *A Century of Australian Song* (1888); and he figured prominently in contemporary critical works such as H.G. Turner and Alexander Sutherland's *The Development of Australian Literature* (1898). He attempted fiction, publishing two novels in Scotland as well as *A Hundred Pounds* (1876), an Australian story; he wrote an ineffective drama, *Fayette: Or, Bush Revels* (1892); but his major successes were the poetry *Convict Once* (1871), *The Black Gin* (1873), *The Godolphin Arabian* (1873) and *My Chinee Cook* (1902). Despite the contemporary respect for him and the present-day acknowledgment of his undoubted influence on the literary scene during the two decades prior to the end of the nineteenth century, his own poetry now arouses little enthusiasm among readers and critics. He is extensively discussed in H.A. Kellow's *Queensland Poets* (1930); Cecil Hadgraft wrote the biographical study *James Brunton Stephens* (1969). He is the poet featured in Rosa Praed's reminiscences, *My Australian Girlhood* (1902).

STEVEN, Alexander Gordon (1865–1923), born London, came to Australia in infancy. He studied medicine at the University of Melbourne, but was prevented by ill health from completing the course. His lyrical, introspective verse appeared in five volumes during his lifetime, *The Witchery of Earth* (1911), *Wind on the Wold* (1914), *Poems* (1918), *Revolt* (1919) and *Lures* (1923), and in a posthumous collected edition, *Collected Poems* (1925), with a foreword by Hugh McCrae.

STEVENS, Bertram (1872–1922), born Inverell, NSW, became a solicitor's clerk in Sydney but abandoned law to become a prolific editor of works on Australian literature and art, in which role he exerted a considerable influence on the development of Australian culture in the first quarter of the twentieth century. Stevens's first editorial venture was John Farrell's *My Sundowner and Other Poems* in 1904. He then edited George Essex Evans's *The Secret Key and Other Verses* (1906) and *An Anthology of Australian Verse* (1906), which was revised and enlarged in 1909 as *The Golden Treasury of Australian Verse*, one of the first significant Australian anthologies. In 1911 he edited, with a memoir, Victor Daley's *Wine and Roses*, and in 1920 an edition of the poems of Henry Kendall. His other editorial works include *The 'Bulletin' Book of Humorous Verses and Recitations* (1920), several anthologies of verse for children, anthologies of verse in collaboration with George Mackaness, and critical and illustrative art works on Norman Lindsay, Arthur Streeton, Conrad Martens, Hans Heysen and others. In 1909–10 Stevens edited the Red Page of the *Bulletin*. One of the founders in 1916 of *Art in Australia*, he was involved editorially in it until his death; he was also connected editorially with the journals, *Commerce*, from 1918, and *Home*, from 1920. A founding member of the Dawn and Dusk Club and the Casuals Club, Stevens helped numerous writers in financial and other ways; he attempted with others to rehabilitate Henry Lawson.

STEWART, Douglas (1913–85), born Eltham, Taranaki Province, NZ, came to Australia in 1933, expecting to take up a position as light-verse writer on the *Bulletin* staff. When that position did not eventuate he returned to NZ in 1934, visited England in 1937, then came back to Australia in 1938 to become assistant to Cecil Mann, editor of the Red Page. In 1940 he took over the Red Page and remained its editor until 1961. With the *Bulletin* change of ownership Stewart joined Angus & Robertson as literary editor. He retired from Angus & Robertson in 1971 but actively continued his own literary career, consolidating his reputation as writer and critic.

Stewart's first publications were two volumes of poetry, *Green Lions* (1936) and *The White Cry* (1939). This early poetry is characterised by a delight in the beauty and colour of the NZ landscape and by an exuberance of language. Two small books of wartime verse, *Elegy for an Airman* (1940) and *Sonnets to the Unknown Soldier* (1941), followed. The title poem of the earlier volume commemorates Stewart's boyhood friend Desmond Carter, who was killed in action with the RAF in 1939. Stewart's first 'Australian' book of verse, *The Dosser in Springtime* (1946), contains both lyrics and ballads. The title poem, with its humorous account of an old cave-dweller's arousal by the sight of a girl bathing in a creek, sees Stewart giving expression for the first time to the gently ironic and whimsical strain that became characteristic of his later writing. 'The River' (from *The Dosser*), a poetic meditation on the spiritual and intellectual influences of his NZ boyhood, is one of Stewart's best poems. *Glencoe* (1947) is a sequence of twenty-six ballads based on the infamous slaughter of the Macdonald clan by the Campbells in 1691. *Glencoe* has been praised for its sustained and dramatic balladry, and applauded for its theme, a protest against barbarity, cruelty and violence in any age. *Sun Orchids* (1952), in addition to numerous small nature pieces, also contains 'Worsley Enchanted', a sequence of seventeen poems based on Shackleton's Antarctic expedition of 1914. This sequence indicates, as does his verse drama *The Fire on the Snow*, his attraction to Antarctic exploration and the explorer-figure. 'Terra Australis', also in *Sun Orchids*, describes a chance meeting between, and a comparison of notes by, two explorer/adventurer idealists, Pedro Fernandez de Quiros, a six-teenth-century Portuguese seaman, and William Lane, the founder of the Utopian socialist colony New Australia in Paraguay. That meeting allows Stewart to reflect, ironically but not too destructively, on the way in which human idealism is often thwarted by the weaknesses of human nature. Commissioned in 1954 to produce a script for a projected film, *Back of Beyond*, Stewart travelled along the Birdsville Track and published his reaction to the desolate Australian interior in a poem sequence of that title. The sequence begins at Marree in SA, 'the corrugated-iron town/ In the corrugated-iron air'; describes such identities as 'The Whipmaker', 'The Afghan', 'The Dogger', and an Aboriginal rainmaker; casts sidelong glances at red desert grass-hoppers, dingoes, wild mules, and bicycle lizards; and concludes, 300 miles north, at Birdsville, an undistinguished little desert town, whose glory lies in the fact that Leichhardt and Sturt once trod its dusty street. *The Birdsville Track* (1955) also contains Stewart's customary meticulous observations on small birds, animals, flowers and landscapes. The best of these lyrical re-creations of his visual and spiritual experiences in the Australian landscape are 'Brindabella', 'Spider Gums' and 'The Snow-gum'. Stewart's final volume of poetry, *Rutherford* (1962), emphasises, in Leonie Kramer's phrase, 'intellectual voyagers' rather than the physical explorers of earlier volumes. In the title poem the NZ atomic scientist Rutherford is addressed as 'the great sea-farer of science'. The most ambitious of Stewart's poems, 'Rutherford' examines the problem of the human need to extend the spirit and intellect to their fullest, even when the consequences are unforeseeable. The poem decides that there is no choice but to accept the destiny inherent in searching, restless human nature. 'The Silkworms', from *Rutherford*, is widely regarded as Stewart's finest individual poem, both for its sensitive and imaginative insight and for its perfect fusion of technique and theme. Stewart's *Selected Poems* was published in 1963 as *Australian Poets: Douglas Stewart*, other editions appearing in 1966 and 1973, the 1973 edition in A & R Modern Poets (reprinted 1993) differing from the earlier two in the Australian Poets series. *Collected Poems 1936–1967* (1967), which Stewart arranged in reverse chronological order, begins with a section 'The Flowering Place' that includes numerous satirical and explorer poems written since *Rutherford* or unpublished in earlier volumes.

Stewart also wrote six verse dramas, four of which were intended as radio plays. *The Fire on the Snow*, his greatest literary success, deals with Captain Robert Scott's tragic expedition to the South Pole in 1912. It was performed on radio by the ABC in 1941, was published in 1944, has been produced and published in many countries, and has been studied by countless Australian schoolchildren. *Ned Kelly*, written as a stage play during 1940, had its first performance in an abbreviated form as a radio play in 1942. Stewart's published fiction consists of one collection of short stories, *A Girl with Red Hair* (1944), and a handful of other stories in the *Bulletin* and *Coast to Coast*.

Stewart's greatest contribution to Australian literature, however, came from his twenty years' editorship of the Red Page, his ten years as publishing editor with Angus & Robertson, and his lifetime encouragement of Australian writers. In the Red Page, Stewart adopted encouragement and enthusiasm as his editorial philosophy, largely to counteract the apathy with which local writing was usually met. Although occasionally over-generous, he not only gave continued encouragement to established writers but accurately assessed the potential, and assisted in the development, of such major new writers as Judith Wright, James McAuley, Francis Webb, David Campbell, Rosemary Dobson and John Blight. Stewart's critical judgments on the literature of his editorial years are included in his two books *The Flesh and the Spirit* (1948) and *The Broad Stream* (1975). His publications as anthologist and editor include *Australian Bush Ballads* (1955), *Old Bush Songs and Rhymes of Colonial Times* (1957) and *The Pacific Book of Bush Ballads* (1967), all in collaboration with Nancy Keesing; *Voyager Poems* (1960); *Kenneth Mackenzie: Selected Poems* (1961); *Modern Australian Verse* (1964), with an introduction that stresses his belief that literature should provide joy; *Hugh McCrae: Selected Poems* (1966); *Short Stories of Australia: The Lawson Tradition* (1967); and *The Wide Brown Land* (1971), Australian verse. His suggestion that there should be annual anthologies of Australian poetry and short stories led to the introduction in the early 1940s of the *Australian Poetry* and *Coast to Coast* series. He also published reflections on some of Australia's famous literary figures, *Norman Lindsay: A Personal Memoir* (1975), *A Man of Sydney* (1977) on Kenneth Slessor, and *Writers of the Bulletin* (1977). In 1955–70 Stewart was a member of the advisory board of the CLF; in 1960 he was made OBE for his services to Australian literature and later AO; in 1967 he received the Sydney Myer Award for the best volume of poetry in that year. *Springtime in Taranaki* (1983), in the typically sensitive Stewart mode, is his autobiographical account of his first twenty-five years. *Douglas Stewart's Garden of Friends* (1987) consists largely of excerpts from his diaries relevant to his association with Australian writers and literature. Nancy Keesing wrote *Douglas Stewart* (1965) in the Australian Writers and Their Work series and Clement Semmler the 1974 volume on him in the Twaynes World Author series.

STEWART, Harold (1916–   ), born Drummoyne, Sydney, studied briefly at the Conservatorium of Music and the University of Sydney, and was a member of the Australian Army's Directorate of Research and Civil Affairs 1942–46, as also was James McAuley. In 1944 Stewart and McAuley perpetrated the famous Ern Malley hoax; Stewart's role in this affair and its subsequent effect on him is examined in Michael Heyward's *The Ern Malley Affair* (1993). After the war Stewart was a journalist, lecturer, bookshop salesman and radio broadcaster for the ABC. His first books of verse were *Phoenix Wings: Poems 1940–46* (1948) and *Orpheus and Other Poems* (1956). The poems of *Phoenix Wings*, many of them drawing on Chinese literature and culture, reveal Stewart's deep interest in the Orient, an interest that took him to visit and, from 1966, to live permanently in, Japan, where he studied under Bando Shojun, a Shin Buddhist priest and scholar at the Shin-shu Buddhist University, and where he ultimately became a member of the Shinshu Buddhist sect. In Kyoto he has eked out a frugal existence by teaching English, and publishing the popular volumes of translations of Japanese haiku, *A Net of Fireflies* (1960), *A Chime of Windbells* (1969) and *The Exiled Immortal: A Song Cycle* (1980).

Stewart's poetry has attracted a devoted following. *Phoenix Wings* and *Orpheus* have been praised for their observation and understanding of a culture other than Australian, and for the fine descriptive and narrative qualities of poems such as 'A Flight of

Wild Geese' and 'The Ascension of Feng'. As an expatriate, his more recent work has not been well known in Australia. The haiku translations, which are accompanied by his essays on the history, philosophy and technique of haiku, have been criticised by experts on the culture and language of Japan as too idiosyncratic in approach. The haiku, however, which allows, in Stewart's view, the achievement of 'perfection in little things', is a suitable vehicle for combining his own predilection for sensuous imagery with epigrammatic succinctness. *By the Old Walls of Kyoto*, subtitled *A Yearly Cycle of Landscape Poems*, Stewart's most recent verse (1981) and his *magnum opus*, is a long poem in twelve parts, which celebrates the beauty and significance of Kyoto and pays personal homage to it. Stewart has declared it 'his spiritual autobiography'. He has been awarded an emeritus fellowship of the Literature Board of the Australia Council.

STEWART, Kathleen , (1958–), born Sydney, has lived in Europe, the south coast of NSW and, latterly, Melbourne. The author of several works of fiction, *Waiting Room, Victim Train* and *Louis: A Normal Novel*, she published her first volume of poems, *Snow* in 1994. In an early poem, 'Teacher's College', she writes 'I wrestle with the pattern of my life'. Much of this first book depicts that pattern, an emphatically depressing one if 'The Long Shaft of Silence' is to be interpreted autobiographically. There are many echoes of lost love – 'Waving', 'Over You', 'Farewell to Romantic Love', 'Weedkiller' and 'The Sea of Stars'. Stewart's imagery is notably stark – 'a sky of dirty coddled cream', 'the dirty sheet of the sky', 'the city fogs over with sighs', 'beautiful as a cemetery in rain'. Acute insight combines with spare language to produce several effective epigrammatic cameos: 'Sunday Drive', 'The Sexes', 'Repeating'.

'Still Life', one of the best-known of Rosemary Dobson's painting poems, was first published in the *Bulletin*, 1946. It describes a painting by an unknown seventeenth-century artist of a table set for a simple, sacramental meal of bread and wine. The never-to-be-consumed meal is one of the many examples in Rosemary Dobson's poetry of the permanence of art. A belated sharer in the meal (as all are who have gazed at the painting down the centuries), the poet involuntarily reaches out to break the loaf and pour the wine that awaited the arrival of an unknown guest 300 years ago.

STONEHOUSE, Ethel (1883–1964), born Nhill, Victoria, contributed verse early in life to the *Bulletin* and the *Australian Journal*. She published two volumes of verse, *The Road of Yesterday* (1916) and *The Caravan of Dreams* (1923), and fifteen novels. In 1914 she married a Harley Street specialist, John McNaught Scott, but appears to have found the relationship oppressive and creatively deadening. After her husband's death she maintained a solitary existence at Mortlake, Victoria, and spent the last years of her life as a patient of Royal Park psychiatric hospital. Her novels are *Smouldering Fires* (1912), *Love Letters of a Priest* (1912), *Kathleen Mavourneen* (1913), *Sands o' the Desert* (1913), *Souls in Pawn* (1913), *The Years of Forgetting* (1914), *The Eternal Triangle* (1915), *The Gates of Silence* (1915), *The Interior* (1916), *The Woman Who Lived Again* (1916), *Sons of Iscariot* (1916), *That Woman from Java* (1916), *The Gates of Kut* (1917), *Land o' the Dawning* (1917) and *Earthware* (1918).

STOW, Randolph (1935–), born Geraldton into a long-established WA family, was educated at the University of WA. His varied career has included periods of lecturing in English literature at the universities of Adelaide, WA and Leeds, eighteen months of intensive travel in the USA, work on an Aboriginal mission and as an anthropologist and cadet patrol officer in New Guinea. Since 1966 he has lived permanently in England. His novels are *A Haunted Land* (1956), *The Bystander* (1957), *To the Islands* (1958, rev. edn 1982), *Tourmaline* (1963), *The Merry-Go-Round in the Sea* (1965), *Visitants* (1979), *The Girl Green as Elderflower* (1980), and *The Surburbs of Hell*

(1984). He has also written an outstandingly popular novel for children, *Midnite* (1967), and two libretti for operas with music by Peter Maxwell Davies, *Eight Songs for a Mad King* (1969) and *Miss Donnithorne's Maggot* (1974). He has published collections of poetry including *Act One* (1957), *Outrider* (1962), *A Counterfeit Silence* (1969) and *Randolph Stow Reads from His Own Work* (1974) and has edited *Australian Poetry* (1964). Anthony J. Hassall has edited *Randolph Stow* (1990) in the Portable Australian Authors series, which includes *Visitants*, episodes from other novels, poems, stories, interviews and essays. Stow's work, which won recognition early, has received several prizes including the 1958 Miles Franklin Award, the Gold Medal of the Australian Literature Society in 1957 and 1958, the Britannica-Australia Award in 1966, the Grace Leven Poetry Prize in 1969 and the Patrick White Literary Award in 1979. The Randolph Stow Fiction and Poetry Award was established in WA in 1987.

Stow's small volume of poetry reflects, like his fiction, his Australian experience, his feeling for landscape, his wide reading and interest in myth and folklore, his sense of dynasty and preoccupation with time, transience and isolation. Technically assured and traditional in form, his verse achieves, at its best, a simple, spare lyricism. Stow's work is the subject of monographs by Ray Willbanks (1978) and Anthony J. Hassall (*Strange Country*, 1986).

STRAUSS, Jennifer (1933–), born Heywood, Victoria, was educated at the Universities of Melbourne and Glasgow and Monash University (Ph.D.). She has taught at the universities of New England and Melbourne and since 1964 at Monash where she is currently associate professor in the Department of English. Her poetry has appeared widely in anthologies and she has published several collections, *Children and Other Strangers* (1975), *Winter Driving* (1981) and *Labour Ward* (1988). Especially sensitive to the experience and predicaments of women, she writes with wit, irony and pathos of such subjects as the passage of time, the presence of death, motherhood and love. She often examines the past to reveal how the lives of women have been limited and diminished by the role that history has allotted them. Personal poems based on experience – e.g. 'An End to Innocence', 'Et Ego in Arcadia', 'The Snapshot Album of the Innocent Tourist', 'Pine Cones', 'My Grandmother' and 'Tending the Graves' – are sensitive combinations of emotion, wit and realism. 'Tending the Graves', a particularly effective poem, shows that not even with death do the dead release their hold on the living. She won the *Westerly* Sesquicentenary Prize in 1979. Jennifer Strauss, as critic, has published *Stop Laughing! I'm Being Serious: Three Studies in Seriousness and Wit in Contemporary Australian Poetry*, lectures on Judith Wright, John Forbes and Chris Wallace-Crabbe. She has also published *Boundary Conditions: The Poetry of Gwen Harwood* (1992) and *Judith Wright* (1995), in Oxford's Australian Writers series. She edited *The Oxford Book of Australian Love Poems* (1993) and is preparing the Collected Poems of Mary Gilmore.

'Stroke', a seven-poem sequence by Vincent Buckley, was first published in *Quadrant* (1965). The poem describes the familiar events associated with the death of a parent: the hospital bedside, where the embarrassed visitors ('voyeurs of decay') engage in stiff, platitudinous conversation; the son's guilt over the lifetime lack of communication between himself and his father; and memories of the father in his prime compared with his present state. In the 'life studies' genre, which Buckley was one of the first Australian poets to employ, 'Stroke' conveys, in spite of its calm, almost detached phrasing, the anguish that the son feels, not simply because of the imminent death of his father, but because of the gulf between them that even at the end seems unbridgeable.

STRONG, Sir Archibald Thomas (1876–1930), born Melbourne, the son of Herbert Augustus Strong (1841–1918), professor of classics at the University of

Melbourne, was taken to England in 1883 and was educated at Liverpool, Oxford, and in Germany. In 1901 he returned to Melbourne, where he edited the short-lived *Trident* and was for many years literary critic for the *Herald* and lectured in English at the University of Melbourne. He also served as president of the Melbourne Literature, the Melbourne Shakespeare and Mermaid societies. From 1922 to 1930 he was professor of English at the University of Adelaide and was knighted in 1925. One of the founders and trustees of the Melbourne Repertory Theatre under Gregan McMahon, he was also vice-president of the Adelaide Repertory Theatre. He published three collections of conventional verse, *Sonnets and Songs* (1905), *Sonnets of the Empire* (1915) and *Poems* (1918); three collections of essays, *Peradventure* (1911), *Three Studies* (1921) and *Four Studies* (1932); *A Short History of English Literature* (1921) and a translation of *Beowulf* (1925). He also contributed the chapter on Australian literature to the first edition of the *Australian Encyclopaedia* (1925). He was chief Commonwealth film censor 1919–22.

STUART, Julian (1866–1929), born Eagleton, NSW, of Scottish ancestry, worked on his parents' farm in the Hunter Valley until 18, then went to Sydney where in 1887 he joined the civil service. In 1888 he went to the upper Dawson Valley in Queensland and became interested in the Shearers' Union, which had been established by W.G. Spence in 1886 at Ballarat, Victoria. In 1890 he was at Barcaldine when the shearers' strike was brewing; in 1891 he was elected chairman of the Central Queensland Labourers' Union at Clermont. Arrested in March 1891, he was convicted of conspiracy under an old law which had already been repealed in England and sentenced to three years' gaol. On his release he went to WA, where he took up journalism, wrote radical poetry and remained active in politics. His verses were already known in the *Bulletin* under the pseudonym 'Curlew'; much of his poetry in the *Geraldton Express* and the *Coolgardie Miner* appeared under the pseudonym 'Saladin'. In 1903–6 he edited the *Westralian Worker* and was a member of the WA parliament. He was later a clerk in the WA public service but retained his interest in the bush, the goldfields and the working class. Stuart was prominent in the halcyon days of bush balladry and radical poetry that flourished in WA newspapers at the turn of the century. His radicalism is succinctly expressed in the lines

> I am deformed by labor
> I am the working man
> Cursing the fate that holds me
> A dull-browed Caliban.

Lyndall Hadow, Stuart's daughter, published *Part of the Glory: Reminiscences of the Shearers' Strike, Queensland 1891 From the Pen of Julian Stuart* (1967). The novelist Donald Stuart was his son.

SYKES, Roberta (Bobbi) (1943–), born Queensland, a prominent activist for Aboriginal rights, left school at 14 and has had numerous occupations. She was the first executive secretary of the Aboriginal Embassy erected on the lawns in front of Parliament House, Canberra, in 1972; has written and lectured widely on race relations in Australia, the USA, Great Britain, Jamaica and NZ; was the first person of Aboriginal descent to graduate from Harvard University, where she earned first a master's degree and then a doctorate in education. She has written an analysis of twenty-one years of Black Australian experience, *Black Majority* (1989) and an account of the nature and consequences of non-Aboriginal educational systems for the Black community, *Incentive, Achievement and Community* (1986); helped Colleen Shirl Perry, one of the founders of the Aboriginal medical and legal services, to compose her autobiography, *Mum Shirl* (1981); and published a collection of poems, *Love Poems and Other Revolutionary Actions* (1979). She was awarded the 1981 Patricia Weickhardt Award for an Aboriginal writer.

TALBOT, Colin (1948–) has worked as a journalist and in radio and has spent some time in the USA. He has published two novels, *Massive Road Trauma* (1975) and *Sweethearts* (1978); a collection of his journalism, *Colin Talbot's Greatest Hits* (1977); a collection of verse, *Creek Roulette* (1973); and has compiled, with Robert Kenny, an anthology of poetry, *Applestealers* (1974). He has been a director of Outback Press and was involved in *Tabloid Story*.

TALBOT, Norman (1936–), born Suffolk, England, has taught English at the University of Newcastle since 1963 and has published several collections of verse, *Poems for a Female Universe* (1968), *Son of a Female Universe* (1971), *The Fishing Boy* (1973), illustrated by John Montefiore), *Find the Lady* (1977), *Where Two Rivers Meet* (1980), *The Kelly Haiku & Other Widdershin Tracks* (1985) and *Four Zoas of Australia* (1992, introduced by Gwen Harwood). A strong supporter of the arts in the Newcastle area, Talbot was founder and president of Nimrod publications, which has published the work of more than 200 Hunter Valley writers as well as collections of writing by disabled people. A colleague of the Welsh-born poet T. Harri Jones, Talbot published the poem *The Seafolding of Harri Jones* (1965), after Jones's death by drowning.

TATE, Henry (1873–1926), born Prahran, Melbourne, was a successful musician, composer and music critic for the *Age* (1924–26), as well as a poet and short-story writer. His ideas for an individual and distinctive Australian music are contained in *Australian Musical Possibilities* (1924). An active participant in the Australian Institute of Arts and Literature, Tate worked with Louis Esson, William Moore and Bernard O'Dowd. He composed musical settings for the poems of 'Furnley Maurice', titled *Songs of Reverie*. His verse included *The Rune of the Bunyip (Four Grotesques)* (1910), *Lost Love* (1918) and a collected edition, *The Poems of Henry Tate* (1928).

TAYLOR, Andrew (1940–), born Warrnambool, Victoria, studied arts and law at the University of Melbourne, where Vincent Buckley encouraged his interest in poetry. He graduated MA from Melbourne and studied and travelled in Europe and the USA, returning to Australia in 1965. From 1971 he taught in the English Department of the University of Adelaide and is now professor at Edith Cowan University, WA. Active in the Australian literary scene, Taylor has been involved in various writers' organisations and has officiated as chairperson of Writers' Week at the Adelaide Festival of the Arts. He has also been a member of the Literature Board of the Australia Council and was made AM for his services to literature. He took part in the poetry readings at La Mama in 1968 and was active in SA's Friendly Street poetry group, editing, with Ian Reid, the second Friendly Street anthology in 1978. His numerous collections of poetry began with *The Cool Change* (1971). Then followed *Ice Fishing* (1973), *The Invention of Fire* (1976), *The Cat's Chin and Ears* (1976), *Parabolas:*

Prose Poems (1976), *The Crystal Absences, The Trout* (1978), *Selected Poems 1960–1980* (1982, updated *1960–1985*, 1988), *Travelling* (1986, regional winner of the British Airways Commonwealth Poetry Prize) and *Folds in the Map* (1991). He has edited with Judith Rodriguez *Poems Selected from the Australian's 20th Anniversary Competition* (1985); translated with Beate Josephi selected poems from four German writers in a collection titled *Miracles of Disbelief* (1985); written a book for children, *Bernie the Midnight Owl* (1984); and the first full-length deconstructive study of the Australian poetic tradition from Lawson to Tranter, *Reading Australian Poetry* (1987). He has also written the libretti for two operas, *Letters of Amalie Dietrich* (1988) and *Barossa* (1988). The two *Selected* volumes offer a good sample of Taylor's poetry. The 1988 edition adds a substantial group from *Travelling. Parabolas*, short, often anecdotal, prose pieces that Taylor wrote while visiting Berkeley and Yale in 1975, are part of both books. Taylor has omitted *The Crystal Absences, The Trout* because it was conceived as a single poem and would not, he felt, benefit by division. That omission is unfortunate because *The Crystal Absences*, poems written on a regular basis while his wife Beate was visiting her parents in Germany, are sensitive and appealing love poems.

Because of his Melbourne academic background Taylor's early poetry has sometimes been regarded as based upon and influenced by the Melbourne University writers of the 1960s and 1970s, *The Invention of Fire*, for example, being linked to Chris Wallace-Crabbe. Taylor is, however, an innovative, individual and experimental poet. Athough his poetry is wide-ranging in reflecting his extensive travels, it is also narrowly and finely focused, contemplative and inward. Open-ended and unemphatic, his poems are frequently meditations which record the irresolutions and disconnections of living and are receptive to the contradictions and ambiguities of an indefinite self: 'Better to choose what isn't you/ if you is what you want to find.' Both landscape and language figure prominently, often as persistent testimonies to the gulf between human need and actuality. Concerned with the substance, solidity and endurance of landscape, compared with the transience of human experience, Taylor is also preoccupied with landscape's unreliability and the way that its existence defies appropriation by ideas even as it is determined by them: 'Landscape without ideas of it/ hasn't been seen.' Writing a 'difficult' poetry, especially in earlier collections, Taylor seeks to transcend the imposed difficulties of language: 'there are times/ words have to be trodden on/ and ridden across and scraped over/ before they'll reveal the reticence/ that knows how to speak/ if you know how to listen' ('Yugoslav Triptych').

Travelling has three sections: a sequence of poems 'Parts of the World', where the landscape is seen as, above all, a landscape of the mind, whose true meaning lies not in its physical self but in the meaning and significance that the poet brings to it; a second section of lyrics on various themes; and a long poem of eighteen sections, 'Travelling to Gleis-Binario', based on Taylor's travels through Europe. To the uninitiated 'Gleis-Binario' might appear to be a geographical locality; Taylor explains that it, too, is a locality of the mind, conjured up by combining the German and Italian words for that part of a railway station where one boards the train. *Travelling* is Taylor in his characteristically wry, meditative, polished poetic mode. *Folds in the Map* (1991) has some droll, enigmatic and clever poems, mixing prosaic subjects such as 'Spoons' ('I count them, like my friends'), 'Radio', 'Dish Drainers', 'Wineglass', 'Letterboxes' with pertinent philosophic comments. In the final section the importance of relationships both to places and people, a regular characteristic of his poetry, notably in *The Crystal Absences*, is reaffirmed. 'Walluf am Rheim', a fine poem that integrates intellect and emotion, affirms the sanctity of family.

TAYLOR, G.A. (George Augustine) (1872–1928), born Sydney, first became known as an artist and cartoonist, a contributor of drawings to the *Bulletin*, the *Worker*, the *Sunday Times*, the *Referee* and the London *Punch*. A member of the Dawn and Dusk Club, and a particular friend of Victor Daley, he wrote his reminiscences of its personalities, *Those Were the Days* (1918), which is also valuable as a record of Sydney in the 1890s. In 1898 he launched a highly original comic paper, *Ha-Ha*, although it survived for only three issues. Subsequent periodicals that he founded and edited fared better and reflected his fervent nationalism. He achieved original work in aviation and radio, constructing and successfully flying in 1909 a full-size biplane, the first flight in Australia of a manned heavier-than-air machine; his son, P.G. Taylor, flew with Charles Kingsford Smith. A prolific journalist, Taylor also published two collections of verse, *Songs for Soldiers* (1913) and *Just Jingles* (1922). J.M. Giles has written *Some Chapters in the Life of George Augustine Taylor* (1957).

TAYLOR, Ken (1930–   ), born Ballarat, Victoria, trained and worked as a journalist before travelling in Europe 1949–51. He later farmed in Queensland then joined the ABC as a radio drama producer in 1962. Interested in South-East Asia studies, he took up a Harkness Fellowship to study in the USA in 1965 but switched his interest to literature, studying at Cornell University. Back in Australia in late 1967 he became active in the emerging La Mama poetry workshops, and returned again in the 1980s to La Mama Poetica. His first poetry was published in *Two Poets* (1968, shared with Kris Hemensley). During the 1970s he became a well-known documentary film-maker specialising in natural history. His first major book of verse was *At Valentines*, published in 1975 but containing numerous poems written in the 1960s at Cornell and in Australia. 'At Valentine's – part one' was read at La Mama as early as 1969. A long poem with extremely short lines, it is based on Taylor's boyhood memories of holidays spent with his grandparents; a pot-pourri of sights, sounds and atmospheres, it conjures up countless echoes of the past – an Australian bushfire; old gramophone records that sent forth their music 'from a verandah to the bush'; 'bottles by the thousands'; tins by the tonne; card games; rainy days and nights; Miss Howell and her cottage, which smelt 'of sour milk on old stones'; the ever-present desiccating Australian sun; old-style cars with 'side running boards' and many other pieces of flotsam, stored up in countless similar Australian homes and sheds of the period. Somewhat similar in its montage effect is the impressive 'Pictures from the Sea', a kaleidoscope of colour and action with a long string of vivid images of bird and marine life, and scenes of maiming and killing by man and animal, all associated with the sea and its environs. *A Secret Australia* (1985), Taylor's second major book of verse, contains, in the 'Selected Poems' section, the best of his earlier work as well as a group of new poems and an essay on Taylor and his poetry by Robert Kenny. The 'new poems' include the laconic but precise 'Flying into Meekatharra', 'John Olson at Lake Eyre 1977' and 'The Twelve Apostles' poem as well as the nostalgic 'Old Songs', 'The Modern World' and 'The Alexandria Tea Rooms – Ballarat'. Taylor also wrote 'At Valentine's – part two', which, with its emphasis on modern ugliness, draws the contrast between his 'secret Australia' (comparable to Les Murray's 'vernacular republic') and today's Australia which 'we own . . . the way a cripple owns a street'. A poet of deft and attractive images, Taylor often strikes an elegiac note.

'Teams, The', Henry Lawson's well-known ballad celebrating the bullock wagons that helped to open up the country in pioneering times, was first published in 1889; it is a popular anthology and recitation piece. Renowned for their strength, the bullock teams became the subject of many tall stories, notable among which was the occasion when one team became stuck in the river and was pulled out when another team was hitched on. In the process the bends in the river were straightened. The most famous account of the feats of the horse-drawn wagons is Will Ogilvie's poem 'How the *Fire Queen* Crossed the Swamp'.

THATCHER, Charles (1831–78), born Bristol, England, was a flautist in theatre orchestras in London before seeking his fortune on the Victorian goldfields in 1852. Failing as a digger, Thatcher became a favourite goldfields entertainer, composing and singing catchy songs with topical local subjects. After several years in NZ (1861–66) he returned to Victoria, resuming his career as an entertainer, before leaving the Colony in 1869 to live again in England. Thatcher's songs, usually represented in anthologies of Australian folk-songs and ballads, were published as broadsheets in contemporary newspapers, and in such collections as *Thatcher's Victoria Songster* (1855), *Thatcher's Colonial Songster* (1857) and *Thatcher's Colonial Minstrel* (1859). Hugh Anderson compiled a selection of Thatcher's songs, *Goldrush Songster* (1958), and wrote the biography *The Colonial Minstrel* (1960). In Eric Lambert's novel *The Five Bright Stars* (1954) Thatcher engages in a singing contest with another character.

'They'll Tell You About Me' is the title of Ian Mudie's celebrated pot-pourri of Australian myth, legend, tall tales, folklore and history. In ironic, colloquial language and spiced with the good-natured braggadocio that has come to be recognised as the stock-in-trade of the brash Australian male, the poem is a treasure chest of such Australiana as Eureka, Ned Kelly, the Man from Snowy River, Waltzing Matilda, the Dog on the Tuckerbox, Lasseter's Lost Reef, the Sydney Harbour Bridge, and Gallipoli.

THIELE, Colin (1920–), born Eudunda, SA, graduated from the University of Adelaide in 1941 and served with the RAAF in the Second World War. He taught in SA high schools 1946–56, before joining Wattle Park Teachers College of which he was principal 1965–73 and director 1974–80. A prolific writer of verse, fiction, children's books, radio plays, historical, environmental and educational texts and an editor of verse anthologies, short stories and one-act plays, Thiele has published more than ninety books. A leading literary figure, especially in SA, he is the author of numerous radio features and documentaries and has been active in numerous bodies associated with literature and education. He was made AC in 1977.

Thiele's strongly nationalistic poetry comprises *Progress to Denial* (1945), an elegy to a soldier killed in the Second World War, which won the W.J. Miles poetry prize; *Splinters and Shards* (1945), also largely war poems; *The Golden Lightning* (1951); *Man in a Landscape* (1960), which won the Grace Leven Prize for poetry; *In Charcoal and Conté* (1966); *Selected Verse* (1970); and *The Best of Colin Thiele* (1980), a combined selection of prose and verse. Although he has written novels and short stories for adults, Thiele's most successful fiction has been for children. *Storm Boy* (1963), Thiele's classic children's novel set on the Coorong, was made into a successful film in 1976. Thiele also wrote the biography *Heysen of Hahndorf* (1968).

THOMPSON, John (1907–68), born Melbourne, was a war correspondent in New Guinea and Java 1945–46, and subsequently made a career as a broadcaster with the ABC. He was well known as an interviewer and published a series of interviews with prominent Australian poets in *Southerly*, as well as two collections of profiles of famous Australians, based on interviews, *On Lips of Living Men* (1962) and *Five to Remember* (1964). He also published four collections of his own poetry, *Three Dawns Ago* (1935), *Sesame and Other Poems* (1944), *Thirty Poems* (1954), winner of the Grace Leven Poetry Prize, and *I Hate and I Love* (1964); edited *Australian Poetry 1965* (1965) and, with Kenneth Slessor and R.G. Howarth, *The Penguin Book of Australian Verse* (1958); and compiled *Alfred Conlon: A Memorial* (1963). His wife, Patricia Thompson, describes his personality and achievements in her autobiography, *Accidental Chords* (1988).

THOMPSON, Tom (1953–), born Parkes, NSW, was educated at Macquarie University and has worked as a bookshop manager and freelance journalist and publisher. He has also edited the magazines *Dodo*, *Leatherjacket* and *Australasian Small Press Review*. He has published two collections of verse, *The Island Hotel Dreams* (1977) and *From Here* (1978), and one of short stories, *Neon Line* (1978). He selected and introduced two selections from Lennie Lower's writings, *Here's Lower* (1983), and *The Legends of Lennie Lower* (1988). He has also written *Growing Up in the 60s* (1986), an account of his childhood in Wagga Wagga, Broken Hill and Wollongong, and *Between Dark and Daylight* (1988).

THORNBURN, Hannah (1878–1902) was a bookkeeper and clerk when she met Henry Lawson around 1897. Lawson became infatuated with her, may have planned to leave his wife Bertha for her and was shattered by her death just before he arrived back from England in 1902. The subject of the poems 'To Hannah' and 'Hannah Thomburn' (*sic*), Hannah has also been identified in such other Lawson poems as 'Ruth', 'The Lily of St Leonards', and 'Do They Think That I Do Not Know?'.

THORNE, Tim (1944–), born Launceston, Tasmania, was educated at the University of Tasmania. During the 'poetry revolution' of the 1960s he lived briefly in Sydney (1967–68) and was associated with *Poetry Magazine*, later *New Poetry*. He won a writing scholarship to Stanford University in California in 1971–72 and in 1978 the Marten Bequest Travelling Scholarship for poetry. He has worked as a teacher of modern languages, an editor and full-time writer. Keenly involved in the development of literature within the Tasmanian community, he organises Launceston's annual Poetry Festival. He edited *Civil War/North* (1989), a small collection of poetry from northern Tasmania, and *Lozenge* (1992), poems by Kathy Allen and others. His own published works include *Tense Mood and Voice* (1969), *The What of Sane* (1971), *New Foundations* (1976), *A Nickel in My Mouth* (1979), *The Atlas* (1982) and *Red Dirt* (1990). Thorne's poetry is critical of the corruption and inhumanity of an unfeeling world, of the phoney and second-rate in modern society and culture. Wry and ironic rather than explosively angry, Thorne probes with precision and wit. His poems incorporate, at times, events and episodes of his own life and of Tasmanian history as well as occurrences in the wider contemporary world. The personal poems of 'White Diamond Gloom', for example, from *Red Dirt* are courageous and moving; those concerned with places, especially the Tasmanian scene, are sensitive and responsive. Tough, witty, technically innovative and confident, Thorne's is a distinctive poetic voice.

'Thousand Miles Away, A' is an Australian folk-song dating from the last decades of the nineteenth century which celebrates the overlanders travelling westwards in Queensland to muster cattle 'On the far Barcoo, where they eat nardoo, a thousand miles away'; the song was included as an anonymous composition in A.B. Paterson's *Old Bush Songs* (1905), but Charles Augustus Flower has been identified as the author by some writers. The 'Ten Thousand Miles Away' tune formed the basis for the popular theme-song of the 1970s television series *Rush*.

THWAITES, Michael (1915–), born Brisbane, won a Rhodes Scholarship to Oxford and served with the Royal Naval Volunteer Reserve 1939–45. He lectured in English at the University of Melbourne for three years, served with ASIO 1950–71, and was deputy head of the Parliamentary library 1971–76. Winner of the Newdigate Prize, Oxford, in 1938 and the King's Medal for poetry in 1940, he has contributed verse to numerous anthologies and has published four collections, *Milton Blind* (1938), *The Jervis Bay and Other Poems* (1942), *Poems of War and Peace* (1968) and *The Honey Man* (1989). He has also written *Truth Will Out* (1980), an account of the defection of the Russian diplomat Vladimir Petrov in 1954. Traditional in rhetoric and theme, Thwaites's poetry reflects his commitment to the Moral Rearmament movement and his admiration for such poets as John Masefield.

TIPPING, Richard Kelly (1949–), born Adelaide, studied literature, media and philosophy at Flinders University in 1968 and 1970–72. He lived in Balmain in the period of the New Poetry movement, has travelled widely both abroad and in Australia and has worked as a psychiatric nurse and in the film industry. He has also been active in sculpture, graphics and photography. He now lectures in communication and media arts at the University of Newcastle. He is also a performance poet and often accompanies his poetry with his own music, on the banjo-ukulele, jaw harp and didgeridoo. He edited the first *Friendly Street Poetry Reader* in 1977 and co-edited *Mok* (1968–69) and *News and Weather* (1973). His sculptures and graphics are in the collections of many public galleries. During five years of travelling around Australia he photographed a variety of interesting sights, which are included in *Signs of Australia* (1982) and are described by him as 'photo-poems'. He has also written for film – *Long Time Journey* (1979) – and the word works and ideographics, *The Sydney Morning* (1989). In 1986 Tipping began production of *Writers Talking*, a series of documentary portraits (films) of Australian writers who have spent considerable parts of their working lives overseas, e.g., Peter Porter, Randolph Stow, David Malouf. He has published three main books of verse, *Soft Riots* (1972), *Domestic Hardcore* (1975) and *Nearer by Far* (1986), but other poems are in manuscript form at the National Library. Listed among his other publications are *Airpoet* (1979), *Living on the Edge* (1984), *Headlines to the Heart* (1985), *The Diverse Voice* (1986), *Five O'Clock Shadows* (1979) and the play *Skinny and the Windowcleaner* (1975). *Soft Riots*, which contains, in Tipping's words, 'rhythms from my own breathings', has two sections, 'Balmain' and 'Stirling'. Many of the poems are of short lines, often single words, giving a fractured visual appearance and conveying, when read, a staccato effect. Often too, they are of strange shapes (e.g., 'the poster said'). The two frequently discussed poems of 'Stirling' are 'Multiple 1' and 'Multiple 2'. The girl who is their subject is of such quality that 'her beauty doesn't need/ the painted flourish of this praise'. Tipping's poetry is a far cry from 'painted flourish', the spareness and cryptic quality of the language carrying no flourish whatsoever. *Domestic Hardcore* also has two sections, 'Stirling and Beyond' and 'Mostly Balmain'. Notable poems include the 'Images' series and the long 'Soursobs'. *Nearer by Far* contains poems selected from a large body of work accumulated over the ten years after *Domestic Hardcore*. It is Tipping's best collection with some trenchant political and satirical poems allied to fine landscape verse. As always with Tipping the result is witty, inventive and lively writing.

TISHLER, Joseph (1871–1956), born NZ but resident most of his life in Victoria, was a fanatical contributor of atrocious, but distinctive and often unconsciously funny, verse to the *Bulletin* under the pseudonym 'Bellerive'. Most of his naive, unrhythmic outpourings were printed in the answers to correspondents column over a period of forty years. *The Book of Bellerive* (1961) is a selection of his verse, edited by Douglas Stewart, who dubbed him 'Australia's Worst Poet'.

'To God: From the Warring Nations', a poem by 'Furnley Maurice', first appeared in the *Book Lover* in 1916, with the word 'weary' in the title instead of 'warring'. It was published with the new title in *Eyes of Vigilance* (1920). The poem's theme is humanity's general guilt for war and its horror. In 1916 it met a mixed reception; its pacifist plea angered patriots, who saw it as an attack on the nation's will to fight, but it echoed the mood of the anti-war faction of the time.

TOMASETTI, Glen (1929–), born Melbourne, has travelled widely in Australia and overseas. She has written poetry, songs, radio and stage plays and works frequently as a contemporary troubadour, playing her own songs on the guitar. She has published a collection of her songs, *Songs from a Seat in the Carriage* (1970), and two novels, *Thoroughly Decent People* (1976) and *Man of Letters* (1981).

'Tomb of Lt. John Learmonth, A.I.F., The', an elegy by J.S. Manifold in memory of a school friend who had been captured in Crete in the Second World War and later died in a German prison camp, was first published in *New Republic* in 1945. Written while Manifold himself was involved in the German offensive in the Ardennes in 1944, the poem is both a tribute to the unpretentious quality of common human heroism as exemplified in John Learmonth's hopeless stand against the Germans in Crete and a linking of that courage to 'the old heroic virtues' that are part of Australia's past, as exemplified in the 'die hard, die game' attitude of such outback characters as the swagmen and the bushrangers.

TOMPSON, Charles (1807–83), born Sydney, tried farming before beginning a career in the public service, ultimately rising to be clerk of the Legislative Assembly. Tompson's chief work is *Wild Notes, from the Lyre of a Native Minstrel* (q.v, 1826). A 'currency lad', he was the first poet to attempt an appreciation of the beauty of the local landscape. His verse invests it with an arresting, picturesque quality and an aura of romantic sadness. One of the earliest conservationists, Tompson adopts a condemnatory tone towards the destructive effects of progress on both nature and the Aboriginal people. Although occasionally attractive with fresh and original imagery, his polished verses, heavily apostrophic, ponderous in tone and ornate in language, belong largely to the poetic tradition of the eighteenth century; *Wild Notes* was the first volume of poetry, written by a poet born here, to be published in Australia.

Tower of the Dream, The, published by Charles Harpur in a pamphlet in 1865, is a long poem in blank verse, interspersed with songs. Highly symbolic, the poem, which delves into the division between conscious knowledge and unconscious forces in the life of man, uses allegorical devices such as a monster, a lake, a tower and a maiden. Apart from fellow poet Henry Kendall's obsession with it ('the greatest of Australian poems') the poem aroused little contemporary interest. More recent critical opinion sees it, and Harpur's other philosophical verse, as evidence of a wider poetic talent than the corrupt 1883 collection of his poetry indicates.

TRAINOR, Leon (1945–), born Geraldton, grew up in Perth and was educated at the University of WA. He now lives in Canberra, where he works in the public service. He has published two volumes of poetry, *Memory's Apprentice* (1977) and *Benediction* (1979); and a novel, *Livio* (1988).

Translations from the Natural World (1992), a book of poems by Les Murray, won the NSW Literary Award, the Victorian Premier's Award and the NBC Turnbull Fox Phillips Award, all in 1993. The first of its three sections contains the long poem 'Kimberley Brief', Murray's verse travelogue of his trip from Broome up to the Kimberley region. The second section, 'Presence', contains the 'translations from the natural world'. The forty mostly brief poems, many of which, by presenting the complex of external characteristics that together illuminate the inner nature of a particular object – a cockspur bush, a mollusc, pigs, stone fruit, sunflowers, cuttlefish – re-create something of the essential 'inscape' of Gerard Manley Hopkins. The 'translation' of these objects into the 'poetic' world is striking in its verbal brilliance. 'The Wedding at Berrico' of the third section is, by contrast, unembellished, characterised by the quiet cadences of 'may you/ always have each other, and want to' and the calm recognition that the marriage vows of a daughter move her 'to the centre of life/ and us gently to the rear'.

TRANTER, John (1943–), born Cooma, NSW, grew up in an isolated farming district of the State's south-east coast. He studied arts at the University of Sydney for two years then left to work casually and travel overseas in 1967. Back in Australia he resumed his course, graduating in 1970. He was Asian editor (in Singapore) for A & R 1971–73, then worked as an editor and producer for the ABC in Brisbane until 1977. He has since been a publisher (Transit Poetry, 1981–83), editor (NSW Department of TAFE, 1983–84), teacher of communication, and writer-in-residence (NSW Institute of Technology, Macquarie University and ANU). He travelled through the USA and Europe (1985–86), reading his own and other Australian poetry and lecturing on Australian literature. He was arts coordinator for the ABC 1987–88, and was in charge of Radio Helicon, the ABC's weekly Radio National cultural and arts programme. Well known as a literary reviewer, he has also been poetry editor of the *Bulletin*.

Tranter has named his chief recreation as 'work' and his long list of publications substantiates that claim. His books of poetry are *Parallax* (1970), *Red Movie* (1972), *The Blast Area* (1974), *The Alphabet Murders* (1975), *Crying in Early Infancy: 100 Sonnets* (1977), *Dazed in the Ladies Lounge* (1979), *Selected Poems* (1982), *Gloria* (1986), *Under Berlin: New Poems 1988* (1988), *The Floor of Heaven* (1992), *Days in the Capital* (1992) and *At the Florida* (1993). He edited *Poetry Australia's Preface to the 70s* issue (1970); the anthologies *The New Australian Poetry* (1979), *The Tin Wash Dish* (1989), *The Penguin Book of Modern Australian Poetry* (1991, with Philip Mead) and *Martin Johnston: Selected Poems and Prose* (1993).

In the Introduction to *The New Australian Poetry* Tranter trenchantly argued the cause of post-modernism (he used the term 'modernism' at that time) and illustrated in the anthology the work of poets who had been attempting to practise it during the 1960s and 1970s. In rejecting the traditional, humanist-based dicta of poetry's methodology and function, he formulated such tenets for the 'new' poetry as:

'words – the fragments of language the poet places in the special framework of a poem – have a reality more solid and intense than the world of objects and self-perception'; 'self signature – the work validates its own technical innovations'; 'self-reference – the method is reflected consciously in the medium'; 'emphasis on individualist values as against an agreed social value'; 'fragmentation as against synthesis and harmony'; 'an intention to disrupt the canons of the art form and the preconceptions of the consumer'.

Because many 'consumers' have not been prepared to abandon their 'preconceptions' of poetry, post-modernism has not subsequently had the total flowering that Tranter and others had hoped for. The pages of Australia's literary journals during the 1970s and 1980s have seen the arguments for and against aired on many occasions. In much of his own poetry John Tranter has observed the Nietzschean maxim, 'the apparent world is the only true one' and the Wallace Stevens insistence that 'poetry should resist the intelligence/ Almost successfully'. Yet he has also, as Kate Lilley has indicated, 'embedded in his poetry a gesturing towards the reader' that falls somewhat short of post-modernism; he creates, in fact, a pact with the reader which, while it may sometimes result in mutual disappointment, often leads to 'mutual investment'.

Tranter's first collection, *Parallax and Other Poems*, published in 1970 as a special issue of *Poetry Australia*, indicated his remarkable technical ingenuity. *Red Movie* is notable both for its profusion of eccentrics and derelicts ('a landscape/ built with dust and vomit') and its succession of brilliantly effective cameos ('morning hunches, like a gathering of men/ in damp overcoats, waiting for something to happen'). The title section is prefaced by the words:

that which can be studied is the pattern of processes which characterize the interaction of personalities in particular recurrent situations or fields which 'include' the observer.

The title section contains five pieces, 'The New Field of Knowledge', 'Extract from the Ice Diary', 'The Death Circus', 'The Failure of Sentiment and the Evasion of Love' and 'The Knowledge of Our Buried Life'. Their obscure references, ambiguous syntax, disjointedness, fragmentary discourse and esoteric asides do little, however, to include the reader.

Crying in Early Infancy is a collection of one hundred sonnets, about seventy of which are included in Tranter's *Selected*. The traditional sonnet is among the most formal (in terms of theme and structure) of all poetry but Tranter revels in setting that tradition on its ears. His sonnets are lively, often colloquial, conversation pieces, their easy idiomatic fluency scurrying them along in verse paragraphs that appear to have slipped the authorial leash. They often begin with emphatic yet enigmatic statements:

> 'Yeats rises in the breathless air/ as simple as a spelling error';
> 'It's easy to be awfully sick,/ though difficult to do it well';
> 'Giving up women is worse than animal laxatives';
> 'They burn the radio and listen to the blues';
> 'It's bad luck with a coughing baby';
> 'My daughter's playing with her bloodstained doll again'.

Throughout the series there is a succession of brilliant images which, although often apparently disparate and unconnected, complement the sonnet's tone and atmosphere. Fellow poet Andrew Taylor sees many of these sonnets intelligible in terms of a 'conventional expectation of meaning in poetry'. *Dazed in the Ladies Lounge* contain several poems which have been singled out by critics to indicate the post-modernist penchant for concealing meaning behind a curtain of obscure references, symbols and thematic culs-de-sac. They include (and they are among Tranter's 'chosen') 'Leavis at the London', 'Sartre at Surfers Paradise', 'Foucault at Forest Lodge', 'Roland Barthes at the Poets Ball', 'Enzenberger at "Exiles"'. They conform, with striking stylishness, to the post-modernist belief that the language of the poem has a 'reality more solid and intense than the world of objects and self-perception'. In *Under Berlin: New Poems 1988* (which won the Grace Leven Poetry Prize in 1988) the word 'new' in the title presages a different newness from the same word in the 1979 *The New Australian Poetry*. The early poems of *Under Berlin* are 'new' in that Tranter drops into the traditional role of poet-as-communicator. He does it with such natural ease that, attractive and pleasing though it is, the suspicion arises that he is merely illustrating that writing in this manner is rather like riding a two-wheeled bicycle with trainer wheels – simple enough but unexciting. Yet Tranter's admission (in an interview after *The Floor of Heaven* was published) that 'poetry is meant to be read by other people' seems to place a new emphasis on the consumer.

Such poems as 'Country Veranda' ('Dry Weather' and 'Rain'), 'North Light', 'Widower' and 'South Coast After Rain, 1960' are graceful, lucid and nostalgic. Equally effective are those where the ugliness of modern life predominates – the 'Letter to America' series, 'Glow-Boys', and 'Those Gods Made Permanent', which indicts the entertainment industry for its worship of crime, violence, war and pornography. Although accepting the inevitable future – 'at the end of the show/ death knocks us down' – the poet opts for pleasing while there is still a little time left to please and be pleased: 'I want to be gentler, teasing the audience so they chuckle not sob.' The later poems of *Under Berlin* ('Sex Chemistry') return to post-modernist style – multi-voiced, multi-personed, multi-puzzled – and couched in the familiar Tranter onrush of colloquial idiom that always suggests, but is never really intent on, explication. *The Floor of Heaven* taps the rich vein of long verse narratives which seem to fascinate contemporary writers. Tranter's four story-poems 'Gloria', 'Stella', 'Breathless' and 'Rain' share some of the same characters and much of the same setting – the scenario of lives blighted by anger, greed, passion, betrayal, mischance and character flaws. Brutalities abound – the son who carves up his father's face so that his eyes are 'chopped up like soft-boiled eggs'; the disfigured Vietnam veteran who tries to blow up his brother with a grenade and becomes himself 'just pieces everywhere'; the

Porsche driver who crashes his car through a metal fence and ends up with a metal pole through his neck. Alcohol, drugs and sex – all misused – become ineffectual crutches for their hapless victims. Despite the long catalogue of horrors the narrative tone is only occasionally sensitive and sympathetic (as in the first story, 'Gloria'). In the main it is as chillingly indifferent as the reaction of those to whom the stories are told. Language, as always in Tranter, is expertly manipulated, juxtaposing wonderfully innocent lyricism and flatly brutal colloquialisms. Judged a *tour de force*, *The Floor of Heaven* sets the seal on Tranter's literary achievements to this point, confirming his position as one of Australia's most impressive, and influential, writers.

At the Florida, which won the 1993 *Age* poetry award, has three sections, the last of which is technically interesting. Section 3 contains thirty poems which provide a variation, as Tranter explains, of the 'haibun', a form developed in seventeenth-century Japan, consisting of a mixture of prose and verse, usually a short prose passage followed by a haiku. Tranter reverses the order, a twenty-line stanza of free verse followed by a paragraph of prose. The 'haibun' variations are yet another indication of Tranter's still-questing, still-probing poetic psyche. As many of the poems of *At the Florida* reveal, time has done little to clarify for Tranter the enigmas contained in such *curriculum vitae* entries as childhood, schooldays, family life, love, unfulfilment, ageing and death. No matter how finely life is filtered through the mind and soul, and scrutinised ultimately in the poetry, understanding seems always just beyond reach.

Tranter's considerable poetic achievements over more than a quarter of a century have been recognised by the Australia Council (a Creative Arts Fellowship in 1990) and by fellow poets who acknowledge his role as innovator and experimentalist.

TRITTON, 'Duke' (Harold Percy Croydon) (1886–1965), born Five Dock, Sydney, was well known as a folk-singer and source of Australian folk-songs and stories. Tritton had a scanty education and a series of labouring jobs before going off in 1905 to try his luck in the shearing sheds. He spent his last years in Sydney, where he became a popular performer of bush songs. The story of his four years battling round the bush was told much later as a serial in the *Bulletin* (1959) and then published as *Time Means Tucker* (1964). John Meredith wrote the biographical *Duke of the Outback* (1983).

TSALOUMAS, Dimitris (1921–   ), born on the island of Leros, grew up there under the Italian occupation and experienced at first hand a German attack on the island. He came to Australia in 1952, studied at the University of Melbourne and later taught modern languages and English. After moving to Australia he ceased writing poetry until 1974, but has since published several collections in his native language. By 1983 he had established the reputation in Greece as an important poet of the post-war period, and the first selection of his poetry in English, *The Observatory* (1983), mostly translated by Philip Grundy, won the 1983 NBC Award. His second book of English verse, *The Book of Epigrams* (1985), also consists of translations by Grundy in association with Tsaloumas, but since then three collections of poetry written directly in English have appeared, *Falcon Drinking* (1988), *Portrait of a Dog* (1991) and *The Barge* (1993). Tsaloumas has also translated a selection of Australian poetry into Greek in the collection *Contemporary Australian Poetry* (1985) and has edited the selected poems of Manfred Jurgensen (1987). Tsaloumas has disclaimed the description 'ethnic' writer, with its implications of a cultural ghetto, preferring to be described as an Australian Greek writer. Drawing on traditional Greek forms and techniques, his poetry in English is a conscious attempt to wed what is essentially Greek with the idioms and texture of Australian English. Densely metaphoric and technically assured, it draws on a range of styles from epigrammatic simplicity to Byzantine lushness, all modulated by a distinctive, authoritative voice which is by turns humorous, sardonic and deftly witty. Con Castan has written a critical account of his work, *Dimitris Tsaloumas, Poet* (1990). In 1994 Tsaloumas received the Patrick White Literary Award as well as the Wesley Michel Wright Poetry Prize.

TURNBULL, Clive (1906–75), born and educated in Tasmania, worked as a journalist on the staff of the *Mercury*, the *Argus* and the Melbourne *Herald*. His publications include two collections of verse, *Outside Looking In* (1933) and *14 Poems* (1944); several books on Australian art; a history of the destruction of the Tasmanian Aborigines, *Black War* (1948); a biography, *Essington Lewis* (1963); a concise history of Australia (1965); and a number of biographical sketches of Australian personalities.

TURNER, Walter James (1884–1946) was born and educated in Melbourne. He left Australia in 1907 to study in Europe, and served in the First World War, during which he published his first volume of poetry, *The Hunter and Other Poems* (1916). In London he was music critic for the *New Statesman* (1915–40); drama critic for the *London Mercury* (1919–23) and the *New Statesman* (1928–29); literary editor of the *Owl* (1919), the *Daily Herald* (1920–23) and the *Spectator* (1941–46). His range of interests, lively intellect and unconventional personality made him a significant member of the cultural groups of Bloomsbury and Garsington. He was acquainted with W.B. Yeats, who greatly admired his poetry and later collaborated with him in BBC poetry programmes. His uninhibited speech and writing nevertheless made him many enemies and Lady Ottoline Morrell, in particular, never forgave him for his representation of her in *The Aesthetes* (1927). Turner's poetry first won admiration as belonging to the Georgian school, but he later rejected the Georgians and experimented with more symbolist forms. He published sixteen volumes of poetry, two plays, including the successful comedy *The Man Who Ate the Popomack* (1922), and several critical works on music, painting and literature. He also published several comic, semi-autobiographical works of fiction, of which one, *Blow for Balloons* (1935), includes references to his Australian experience. Turner is the author of the familiar lines 'Chimboroso, Cotopaxi, They have stolen my heart away' often quoted in English verse anthologies. Wayne McKenna has written an account of his life and work, *W.J. Turner* (1990), and edited his *Selected Poetry* (1989).

Two Fires, The (1955), a volume of poetry by Judith Wright written at the time of the Korean War, sees, in the title poem, mankind threatened by a nuclear holocaust. The poem reflects the uncertainty that worried people as they witnessed the brinkmanship of statesmen prepared to run unimaginable risks to achieve their objectives. Poems such as 'For Precision', 'The Man beneath the Tree' and 'Gum Trees Stripping' also show humankind baffled in the painstaking search for things that should come effortlessly, e.g. love and truth, and indicate that in the natural world there are modes of existence whose simplicity and completeness deflate the human ego.

[U]

Ulitarra, launched in 1992 at the Harold Park Hotel, is a literary magazine, published twice yearly. It was launched by Michael Wilding and Les Murray and its inaugural issue included an extract from a Les Murray verse novel in progress. *Ulitarra* is published by Kardoorair Press, Armidale. One of its chief aims is to promote Aboriginal writing. Its first poetry competition in 1993 was won by Lola Stewart. Michael Sharkey is its poetry editor. *Ulitarra* will also award, from 1995, an annual prize in memory of Robert Harris.

Under Aldebaran (1946), the first volume of poetry published by James McAuley, is a mixture of introspective and philosophical poems which represent, in Vincent Buckley's words, 'an affirmation of the values which give real life and real stability to society'. One of the chief poems in the volume is 'The Blue Horses', which is inscribed in honour of Franz Marc, one of the founders of the Blue Rider expressionist movement in Germany and creator of the famous painting *The Tower of the Blue Horses*; the poem seeks to find in art a panacea for the 'malice, fraud and guile' of the modern world 'gone bad' as well as an escape for the individual to 'spaces infinite'. 'The Incarnation of Sirius' is a warning that the forces of revolution bring not the desired changes but a 'bloody and aborted' vision, a world of bestiality and chaos; 'Henry the Navigator' praises men of foresight and courage who, like the Portuguese prince who 'saw no distant seas, yet guided ships', are vital to the realisation of mankind's full potential; and 'The Family of Love' reflects McAuley's own incertitude and inner turmoil. Other notable poems of the volume are the epithalamium 'Celebration of Love', and the trio 'Terra Australis', 'Envoi', and 'The True Discovery of Australia'; the last reflects both McAuley's frustration with Australian attitudes ('the faint sterility that disheartens and derides'), and his indissoluble link with the environment ('there you come home').

Unspoken Thoughts, a volume of poems by Ada Cambridge, was published anonymously in London in 1887. A.G. Stephens appears to have been the originator of the myth that Cambridge withdrew the collection three days after publication, no doubt because some poems embarrassed her clergyman husband George Cross. Recent research has revealed that Cambridge withdrew the collection five years after publication, probably for professional and artistic reasons. Remarkably outspoken for their time, the poems in *Unspoken Thoughts* question faith, marriage and the social order. *The Hand in the Dark*, Cambridge's later collection, contains revised versions of many of the poems in *Unspoken Thoughts*. Patricia Barton has edited and introduced a recent edition of *Unspoken Thoughts* (1988).

USHER, Rod (Roderick Macleod) (1946–   ), born in the USA, has lived for extended periods in Britain and Spain. A journalist for twenty-five years, he is a former literary editor of the *Age* and has also worked for the London *Sunday Times* and *Time* magazine. He has written two non-fiction books and two novels, *A Man of Marbles* (1989) and *Florid States* (1990) and has published two collections of poetry, *Above Water* (1985) and *Smiling Treason* (1992). Wide-ranging in subject and style, his poetry includes ballads, love poems and humorous reflections on aspects of natural and man-made worlds.

VALLIS, Val (1916–), born Gladstone, Queensland, was educated at the University of Queensland (MA) and London University (Ph.D.) and served with the AIF 1941–46, spending some time in New Guinea. He taught at the University of Queensland, becoming reader in English, and has been involved in opera, both as critic for the *Australian* and as a lecturer at the Queensland Conservatorium of Music. His poetry has appeared in the collections *Songs of the East Coast* (1947) and *Dark Wind Blowing* (1961). He also edited, with R.S. Byrnes, *The Queensland Centenary Anthology* (1959), and, with Judith Wright, *Witnesses of Spring* (1970) by Shaw Neilson. Vallis delivered the 1988 Colin Roderick lectures for the Foundation for Australian Literary Studies, *Heart Reasons, These*, on poets Neilson, R.D. FitzGerald, Elizabeth Riddell, Ray Mathew and Eve Langley.

Van Diemen's Land Warriors: Or, the Heroes of Cornwall, The, the first book of Tasmanian verse, was published in 1827. A satire on the ineffectual attempts to capture the bushranger Matthew Brady, it narrates the misadventures of a group of citizens who, contemptuous of the failure of Governor Arthur and his soldiers to capture Brady, decide to do the job themselves. In the first of the poem's three cantos, each of ten tradesmen displays his bravado in punning couplets applicable to his trade. In the second, the Tailor is elected leader and the party sets out, but has to retrace its steps when it is discovered that the gunpowder has been forgotten; when they start again and stumble across what they think to be the gang, they flee in fright. In the final canto, Snip explains that he has run away to cover the gang's retreat; they return and discharge their firearms, only to discover that the 'gang' is a herd of donkeys. The noise awakens two soldiers, who arrest Snip and his associates on suspicion that they are the bushrangers; released by a magistrate, they eventually meet Brady, who has them all flogged, relieves them of their trousers and forces them to return in shame to their homes. *The Van Diemen's Land Warriors* is a rare work, possibly because it was suppressed. Its author, 'Pindar Juvenal', has been tentatively identified as Robert Wales, an officer of the Tasmanian courts.

Verse, a bi-monthly poetry magazine published in Melbourne and edited by Louis Lavater, succeeded the *Spinner* and appeared 1929–33. Although *Verse* generally published poetry that was conventional and nondescript, the magazine also attracted such contributors as 'Furnley Maurice', Mary Gilmore, Paul Hasluck, and Hal Porter.

Verses Popular and Humorous, Henry Lawson's second book of verse, was published in 1900, just before his departure for London. The volume included early work such as 'The Captain of the Push', and 'The Grog-an'-Grumble Steeplechase', a parody of A.B. Paterson, but most of the poems, e.g. 'The Lights of Cobb and Co.', 'The New Chum Jackaroo', 'The Uncultured Rhymer to His Cultured Critics' and 'Reedy

River', had been written after the publication of Lawson's *In the Days When the World Was Wide* (1896). *Verses Popular and Humorous* was reissued several times in two parts, *Popular Verses* and *Humorous Verses*, although in the volumes published under those two titles in 1924 the selection and arrangements are significantly different.

VIIDIKAS, Vicki (1948-   ), born Sydney of an Australian mother and Estonian father, left school at 15 and worked in various occasional jobs. At 16 she began writing poetry for reasons she termed 'therapeutic' and 'confessional', and had her first poem, 'At East Balmain', published when she was 19. She has published three books of verse, *Condition Red* (1973), *Knäbel* (1978) and *India Ink* (prose poems, 1984), and a volume of short prose, *Wrappings* (1974). As a result of several prolonged visits to India and the East she became interested in Indian life and the Hindu religion, an interest that is reflected in her poetry. *Indian Ink* captures more successfully perhaps than any Australian writer before her the spirit and ambience of the Asian subcontinent. Viidikas's aim in both poetry and prose has been to write about the realities, as she sees them, of such subcultures as those centred on drugs, crime, alternative sexualities, or general non-conformist attitudes. The poems of *Condition Red* and *Knäbel* are written mainly from experiences of love and sexuality. In her search for authenticity Viidikas has insisted that the spontaneity and immediacy of emotion, however chaotic and disturbed, should be reflected in the poetic form.

Vision (1923-24), a periodical edited by Jack Lindsay, Kenneth Slessor and Frank C. Johnson, was published in Sydney. It lasted only four issues but was of major importance. Jack Lindsay was the main force behind the magazine's production, but its inspiration derived chiefly from Norman Lindsay, who also provided the title and contributed illustrations and essays. The editors, who looked forward to a 'Renaissance' of 'creative passion' beginning in Australia, opposed both European modernism and the nationalist strain in Australian writing. Looking back to the Greeks and such European writers as Shakespeare, Byron, Burns, Villon, Browning, Rabelais and Nietzsche, they espoused a romantic, vitalist credo. Contributors to *Vision* included Kenneth Slessor, Jack Lindsay, Hugh McCrae, Adrian Lawlor, Dorothea Mackellar, R.D. FitzGerald, Dulcie Deamer, Louis Lavater, Philip Lindsay and Blamire Young. An important dispute between Jack Lindsay, Kenneth Slessor and Norman Lindsay on the circumstances of the magazine's publication and its influence later took place in *Southerly* (1952 and 1953).

Vision of Ceremony, A (1956), James McAuley's second collection of poetry, published after his conversion to Roman Catholicism, reflects his personal certainty and joy in his new faith and confidence that its 'vision of ceremony', ritual, order and beauty, can transfigure the material world. The central poem of the volume, 'Celebration of Divine Love' (one of the 'Black Swan' lyrics), affirms that creation, 'grown timeless and distraught', can be renewed by the love of God in whom 'are all things in perfection found'. Other 'Black Swan' lyrics include 'Invocation', 'To the Holy Spirit', 'To a Dead Bird of Paradise' and 'Canticle'. 'New Guinea', subtitled 'In Memory of Archbishop Alain de Boismenu, M.S.C'., expresses both the impact of New Guinea upon McAuley and his wonder at the noble faith of de Boismenu, a faith that makes 'life become authentic'. The mythological tales of the Prometheus legend, 'The Hero and the Hydra', 'A Leaf of Sage', a brief and highly effective rendering of a tale from the *Decameron*, and the long and discursive 'Letter to John Dryden', add variety to the volume which won the Grace Leven Prize for poetry in 1956.

'Vision of Melancholy, A Fragment, The', by 'C.S'., the first poem published in Australia, appeared in the *Sydney Gazette* 4 March 1804.

Voice from Tasmania, A, a verse satire written by Edward Kemp, was published in

1846. The major target of the poem is the governor of Van Diemen's Land, John Eardley-Wilmot, although there are attacks on Kemp's fellow littérateurs, including David Burn, Nathaniel Lipscomb Kentish and R.L. Murray. *A Voice from Tasmania* has some historical interest as the first book by an Australian-born author to be published in Tasmania; the racing description included in the poem is an early specimen of the genre, preceding the better-known work of Adam Lindsay Gordon by almost two decades.

Voices, the quarterly journal of the National Library of Australia, began in 1991, edited by Paul Hetherington. It presents information relating to the collections and services of NLA and publishes material based on research by the library's Harold White fellows (e.g. Dennis Haskell on Kenneth Slessor's poetry) as well as poetry, short fiction and book reviews. Its poetry, fiction and reviews editors are appointed annually and have included Peter Rose, Elizabeth Jolley, Nick Jose and Jan Owen. NLA also sponsors the Australian Voices Essay series published in *Australian Book Review*.

VOWLES, George (1844–1928), born Ipswich, became a schoolteacher in NSW and Queensland and published *Sunbeams in Queensland* (1870), the first book of verse by a Queenslander. H.A. Kellow's *Queensland Poets* (1930) devotes a chapter to Vowles, but his disharmonious, anglicised imitations of Romantic models have been neglected by other critics.

Voyager. The voyager theme in Australian poetry is recognised and illustrated in Douglas Stewart's anthology *Voyager Poems* (1968). The theme embraces all adventurers and discoverers down the centuries, but it concentrates on particular voyagers such as William Dampier, James Cook and Abel Tasman, who discovered the Australian continent, or others like George Bass, Matthew Flinders, Ludwig Leichhardt and Charles Sturt, who explored it. The poetry applauds the results of their efforts – colonisation and settlement – but, more importantly, emphasises their vision, skill and courage in battling against the unknown. The voyager theme is present in early colonial literature, as the titles 'Dampier's Dream' and 'The Story of Abel Tasman' and eulogies on the lost explorers Burke and Wills testify, but its unusually strong appeal in this century for Australian poets is demonstrated in such poems as Kenneth Slessor's 'Five Visions of Captain Cook', R.D. FitzGerald's 'Heemskerck Shoals', William Hart-Smith's 'Christopher Columbus', Francis Webb's 'Leichhardt in Theatre' and Alan Gould's 'The Great Circle' in *Years Found in Likeness* which deals, as does Slessor's 'Five Visions', with the life and explorations of Cook.

'VREPONT, Brian' (Benjamin Arthur Truebridge) (1882–1955), born Melbourne, where he eventually became a teacher of violin at the Melba Conservatorium, also lived in Queensland and WA and tried a variety of occupations, including that of masseur. He began publishing serious poetry late in life and in 1939 won the C.J. Dennis Memorial Prize for his poem on soil erosion, 'The Miracle'. Apart from some ephemeral writing for children, his publications are *Plays and Flower Verses for Youth* (1934), *The Miracle* (1939) and *Beyond the Claw* (1943). 'Vrepont's' best verse, simple and Wordsworthian in tone, reveals a strong but unsentimental response to nature. Surprisingly experimental for his generation, he uses some unusual, idiosyncratic forms that are clearly influenced by his musical interests.

WAKELING, Louise Katherine (1950–), born Sydney, was educated at the universities of NSW and Adelaide. She has published poetry in numerous periodicals and is the author of a novel, *Saturn Return* (1990). With Margaret Bradstock she edited an edition of Ada Cambridge's autobiography *Thirty Years in Australia* (1989) and collaborated with her in a biography of Cambridge, *Rattling the Orthodoxies* (1991). A joint collection of their poetry, *Small Rebellions*, was published in 1984.

WALFORD, Frank (1882–?) was educated in Sydney and tried various occupations including crocodile-hunting, buffalo-shooting, droving and fishing in northern Australia before turning to journalism. He published two booklets of verse, *Starlight and Haze* (1919) and *The Eternal Ego* (1921); a collection of short stories, *The Ghost and Albert and Other Stories* (1945); and five novels, several of which proved popular, *Twisted Clay* (1933), *The Silver Girl* (1935), *And the River Rolls On* (1939), *The Indiscretions of Iole* (1940) and *A Fool's Odyssey* (1942). He also edited various small short-lived periodicals, including *Walford's Weekly* (1918).

WALKER, Kath, see **NOONUCCAL, Oodgeroo**

WALKER, Lyndon (1951–), born Townsville, Queensland, had an itinerant childhood as the family followed his meteorologist father around Australia and to Papua New Guinea. He graduated in psychology from La Trobe University in 1983 and has published his poems in Australian anthologies and overseas. The best of his poetry is in *Singers and Winners* (1984). A keen observer of contemporary life and insistent on the need for 'emotional truth' in his (and all) writing, Walker is a talented poet who excels in the short lyric. In 1976 he shared (with twenty poems) a small Cochon publication, *Adam Scolds*, with Graham Rowlands and Grahame Pitt. *The Green Wheelbarrow*, another small poetry collection, was also published in 1976.

WALKER, William (1828–1908), born Glasgow, Scotland, came to Australia in 1837. A solicitor and member of the NSW parliament 1860–69, he was appointed to the Legislative Council in 1887 and was also prominent in civic, charitable and educational affairs. He published a collection of lectures and articles, *Miscellanies* (1884), which includes his lecture *Australian Literature* (probably 1864), the first separate work of Australian criticism. His other published works include the poem *The Flood, 1850* (1860) and *Poems Written in Youth* (1884).

'Walking to the Cattle-Place: A Meditation', a sixteen-poem sequence by Les Murray, was first published in *Poetry Australia* (1972). In the opening poem, 'Sanskrit', the poet, listening to the familiar sounds of cattle nearby in the night, repeats to himself the Sanskrit words for the various stages of a cow's life and vows that for the coming day he 'will follow cattle'. In the following sequence, 'Birds in Their Title

Work Freeholds of Straw', the dairy-farm children bring in the cows for the morning milking, a detested chore in 'the child-labour districts' that leads inevitably to the late-morning schoolroom scene of 'children dead beat at their desks'. 'The Names of the Humble' shows the cows at eyeball range and as he watches the regular circling movement of champing jaws the poet joins the ruminants by pondering on the vast ingestion of grass by cows down the ages. If he envies the cow one thing it is her stolid, cud-chewing indifference, 'her ease with this epoch'. 'The Artery' sees the herd disturbed by a passing 'beef mob' being driven to the abattoirs where, ultimately, 'out of cool rooms they crowd into our veins'. 'Death Words' reflects on the cows' habit of stampeding at the death of one of their number. The sequence then becomes extremely complex, breaking into fragments which contain Hindu and Krishna motifs. With 'Boopis' it returns to the cows, the opening lines, 'Coming out of reflections/ I find myself in the earth', indicating the meditative digression of the previous verses. The long concluding poem, 'Goloka', takes its title from the cow heaven of Krishna on Mount Maru.

Labelled by Murray as 'cow' poems, the Cattle-Place verses are among his most controversial and complex. The cattle, often set against historical and allegorical backgrounds, are used to carry deeply symbolic interpretations of the actual world.

WALLACE-CRABBE, Chris (1934–   ), born Richmond, Melbourne, was educated at Melbourne and Yale universities. In 1961–63 he was Lockie fellow in Australian literature and creative writing at the University of Melbourne and in 1965–67 Harkness fellow in the USA. From 1968 he has lectured in English at the University of Melbourne where he holds a personal chair. In 1989 he became the inaugural director of the Australian Centre at that University. In 1987–88 he held the visiting chair of Australian Studies at Harvard. He is general editor of the new OUP Australian Writers Series. Wallace-Crabbe's published volumes of verse are *The Music of Division* (1959), *Eight Metropolitan Poems* (1962), *In Light and Darkness* (1963), *The Rebel General* (1967), *Where the Wind Came* (1971), *Selected Poems* (1973), *The Foundations of Joy* (1976), *The Emotions Are Not Skilled Workers* (1979), *The Amorous Cannibal* (1985), *I'm Deadly Serious* (1988), *For Crying Out Loud* (1990), *Rungs of Time* (1993) and *Selected Poems 1956–1994* (1995). He has edited the poetry anthologies *Six Voices* (1963), *Australian Poetry* (1971), *The Golden Apples of the Sun* (1980), *Clubbing of the Gunfire: 101 Australian War Poems* (1984, with Peter Pierce) and *From the Republic of Conscience* (with Kerry Flattley, 1992). He has compiled two selections of critical essays by various writers, *The Australian Nationalists* (1971) and *Multicultural Australia: The Challenges of Change* (1991, with David Goodman and D.J. O'Hearn) and several selections of his own articles, reviews and lectures, *Melbourne or the Bush* (1974), *Toil & Spin* (1979), *Three Absences in Australian Writing* (1983) and *Falling into Language* (1990). He has also written a novel, *Splinters* (1981). His *Poetry and Belief* (1990) is the text of the 1989 James McAuley Memorial lecture.

Wallace-Crabbe's early poetry in *The Music of Division* and *In Light and Darkness* is, by his own admission, 'four square and syllogistic . . . written by a Lockean rationalist'. In the middle of unemphatic glimpses of the limited possibilities of life ('Ancient Historian', 'Fog at Midnight' and 'In Light and Darkness') there is a remarkable poem, 'The Wintry Manifesto', which is an affirmation of the potentialities of the here and now: 'our greatest joy to make an outline truly/ And know the piece of earth on which we stand.' The early volumes also reveal Wallace-Crabbe as a poet of the Melbourne suburbs, whose chief reaction is compassion for the shabby and often bewildered participants of modern city life, tempered by gentle irony. With his third volume, *The Rebel General*, Wallace-Crabbe turned towards more public and political themes, a trend accentuated in later volumes. The title poem, a portrait of failure and futility, is the centre-piece of a group of poems titled 'Brief Lives', mostly sardonic character sketches of figures such as Noah, King David and the young concubine Abishag. Wallace-Crabbe's changing poetic ambitions are reflected in his statement before the publication of *Where the Wind Came:* 'After stoical-formalist beginnings, I seek a poetry of Romantic fullness and humanity. I want to see how far lyrical, Dionysian impulses can be released and expressed without a loss of intelligence.' *Where the Wind Came* opens with the long poem 'Blood Is the Water', which concerns a Latin-American military dictator who has engineered power through a well-planned coup; the poem examines the motives and consequences of such dictatorial seizures of power. Wallace-Crabbe's freer approach to form is evident in the sequence 'Going to Cythera', where a thin line separates poetry from prose. His *Selected Poems*, a severe pruning of the first four volumes, is unusual in its grouping of seven poems from various volumes under the heading 'Meditations'. Wallace-Crabbe saw these meditative poems as a 'recurring series', part of a 'continuous landscape of debate'. The poetry of *The Emotions Are Not Skilled Workers*, is, in spite of a sometimes debonair and breezy tone, philosophically grave, even sombre. In 'The Shapes of Gallipoli' he joins the long line of Australian poets who have written on a subject rooted in Australian history. That Wallace-Crabbe could express greater satisfaction with 'The Shapes of Gallipoli', set though it is in 'mundane local conditions', than with 'Blood Is the Water', which is set in a 'laboriously constructed but finally metaphysical banana-republic', is a measure of his liberation from his 'stoical-formalist beginnings'.

The Amorous Cannibal also has as its centre Wallace-Crabbe's Melbourne, including the university campuses, suburbia with its gardens and houses and works of art. With consummate ease he handles both satirically clever lyrics and longer, more extended discourses, all characterised by an essential humanity and free-ranging wit and manifesting his philosophy: 'I believe it our duty to manage joy. We were put on this earth to be joyous.' In *For Crying Out Loud* that joy is partly tempered by an elegiac note, a sombre consideration of the loss that death has brought. Notable poems include 'The Shining Gift', 'Air Force, Burma 1942', 'The Otways' and 'The Ibis'.

With *Selected Poems 1956–1994* (1995), Wallace-Crabbe became (with Gwen Harwood and Peter Porter) the third Australian to publish a *Selected Poems* in the international Oxford Poets series. The new *Selected* contains poems from all his earlier volumes; they bear witness, in his own words, 'to past selves'. Encapsulating as it does the greater part of a poet's life, the new *Selected* is timely, providing a vauable record for present admirers and a fine opportunity for a new generation of readers. Two of the new poems, 'What Are These Coming to the Sacrifice' (with its echoes of Keats) and 'Why Do We Exist?', reveal that life continues to work its magic on him.

One of a group of so-called Melbourne University poets who emerged in the late 1950s (e.g. Vincent Buckley, Evan Jones, A.R. Simpson), Wallace-Crabbe took a stance somewhere between the mainstream poetry of the late 1940s and 1950s and the 'New Poetry' of the 1960s and 1970s. He has continued to be his own voice – not (in his words) a 'Tranterite' (John Tranter, the standard-bearer of the post-modernists) nor a 'Bushie' nor a 'Squatter'.

His poetry has won numerous awards including the John Masefield Award in 1956, Farmer's Prize for Poetry 1974, the Grace Leven Poetry Prize for 1985 and the Dublin Prize for 1987.

Some of Wallace-Crabbe's views on Australian literature and critical theory are included in *Three Absences* and *Falling into Language*. Australian writing is deficient, he believes, in romantic love, in fully developed metaphysical views and in radically new poetic or prose forms. *Falling into Language* is a collection of essays on language, poetry, autobiography, memory and dreams. Especially interested in autobiography's construction of self, he argues for its centrality in literature.

'**Waltzing Matilda**' is the title of Australia's most famous song. The phrase 'to waltz Matilda', meaning to carry a swag on one's travels, was in existence by the 1890s and probably derived from two German words: *walzen*, which was applied to apprentices travelling around from master to master; and *Mathilde*, a girl's name which became generic for a female travelling companion and then for a bedroll. The song chronicles the experiences of a swagman waltzing his Matilda who has camped by a billabong or waterhole; as he is boiling his billy, a jumbuck (sheep) comes to drink at the billabong, and is captured by the swagman for food. The swagman is then accosted by the owner of the sheep, a squatter, who is accompanied by three mounted policemen; to escape arrest the swagman jumps into the billabong and is drowned near the coolibah tree shading the billabong. 'Waltzing Matilda' became enormously popular, particularly among Australian troops, has assumed the status of an unofficial national anthem, and remains the song most closely identified with Australia among overseas people. Its anti-authoritarian sentiments probably prevented its selection as the national anthem in a 1977 national poll (28 per cent of the vote compared with 43 per cent for 'Advance Australia Fair'), although its sympathy for the underdog has been seen as characteristically Australian and as a significant reason for its continuing appeal.

The provenance and transmission of 'Waltzing Matilda' have been the subject of some dispute. The most generally accepted version is that the words were written early in 1895 by A.B. Paterson at Dagworth station near Winton. Paterson was on a visit to western Queensland and while staying at Dagworth heard Christina Macpherson, the sister of the owner, Robert Macpherson, play 'Craigielea', a march adapted from the Scottish song 'Thou Bonnie Wood of Craigielea', which she had first encountered at the Warrnambool races the previous April. In putting the words to the tune Paterson drew on several experiences during his three weeks at Dagworth: the discovery while riding of a dead sheep with a forequarter missing; a picnic at Combo waterhole, near where a suicide had taken place; and the casual after-dinner use of the phrase 'Waltzing Matilda', which took the fancy both of Paterson and Macpherson. The song was performed publicly for the first time in Winton in April 1895 and spread quickly in Queensland. A wider audience was reached after 1903 when Marie Cowan adapted Paterson's words and the 'Craigielea' tune as remembered by Macpherson to produce the version that has become the standard popular one. This audience was enlarged further by its inclusion in Thomas Wood's *Cobbers* (1934). Paterson, whose own 'Waltzing Matilda' was first published in his *Saltbush Bill, J.P.* in 1917, approved the adaptation, which was printed as part of an advertising leaflet wrapped around Billy Tea, and later in music broadsheet form. The Matilda Highway was the name given to a new sealed tourist trail that crosses the land of the pioneers – from Burke and Wills to Banjo Paterson – and passes through such outback towns as Barcaldine, Blackall and Winton.

WALWICZ, Ania (1951–   ), born Swidnica, Poland, arrived in Australia in 1963. A visual artist, she is a graduate of the Victorian College of the Arts, Melbourne, and has had several exhibitions. Her prose and poetry has been published very widely in anthologies and periodicals in Australia and Europe and she has published the collection *Writing* (1982, reprinted in 1989 in *Travel/Writing*) and the novels *Boat* (1989), which won the New Writing Prize in the Victorian Premier's Literary Awards, and *Red Roses* (1992). A performance poet, she has performed in Australia, England, Switzerland and France and has been writer-in-residence at several tertiary institutions. She has also written plays, including 'Girlboytalk' (1986), 'Dissecting Mice' (1989) and 'Elegant' (1990). Incantatory and repetitious, Walwicz's prose poems exploit the subconscious effects of language, often exposing the reader to the linguistic alienation suffered by the non-English-speaking migrant and deconstructing familiar linguistic affirmations of 'normality'. A group of poems (for example, 'So Little', 'Poland', and

'New World') focus on the first encounters with the new culture: in the old country the family was 'big and big time' but 'Here we were so little. We were nothing. We were none and naught and no money. We were no speak.' After travelling in the white snow 'that was nowhere' and 'in the blue ocean that was nowhere', the family gets to 'a place where we were less and had less and were less and less and grew smaller every day'. Others, such as 'wogs', which view the immigrant from the perspective of the settled, explore all the familiar anxieties of racism. In all Walwicz's work, however, feminism intersects with the immigrant experience, concentrating on the struggle to reclaim the self from smallness and even invisibility, which is also a struggle with the claims of the past. Registering and resisting the constructions of gender which increasingly imprison the growing girl-self, Walwicz's novels adopt a repetitious, unconventional language which disowns normal syntax and the artificial rules of grammar to deconstruct the imprisoning social constructions; at the same time, and notwithstanding passages reflecting frustration, intense struggle and even paralysis, a fluid, serial, many-layered identity is claimed which is an exultant realisation of creative strength: 'I am here. This is where I now am. This is my place. On my page. This is here for me. This place is a dot in my space. I choose to place myself where I am.' Self-conscious not just about the writing process but about the processes of thinking and feeling, Walwicz's original writing seeks to break normative and restrictive codes of being and challenge the ideologies of power and authority, whether of gender, nationality, status or language.

WANNAN, Bill (William Fielding Fearn-Wannan) (1915–   ), born Victoria, has travelled widely in Australia and abroad and served in the Pacific with the AIF in the Second World War. His first published work was a poem, *The Corporal's Story* (1943). Now widely known as a leading collector of, and authority on, Australian folklore and humour, especially of the sort of humour that was the staple of such periodicals as *Smith's Weekly* and the *Bulletin*, Wannan has compiled numerous collections of ballads, yarns, anecdotes and legends. He is also well known for his column 'Come In, Spinner!' contributed to the *Australasian Post* 1955–80.

'Ward Two', a poem sequence in eight parts by Francis Webb, was first published in its entirety in Webb's volume *The Ghost of the Cock* (1964), although separate parts had been published in the *Bulletin* and *Meanjin* in 1962. The sequence is probably set in the male ward of the Parramatta Psychiatric Centre, where Webb was a patient in 1962. The stark hospital setting, the poet's own well-known mental illness, and the deep compassion and sensitivity of the poem, have contributed to make it one of Webb's best-known works. Central to the poem is the acknowledgment that only in the real world, even if that world is the seemingly crippled world of Ward Two, can any individual make a meaningful existence. The opening segment, 'Pneumo-Encephalograph' (a device to locate brain tumours), counterpoises the cold, clinically beautiful, scientific apparatus of psychiatry and the human agony that has brought it into being and in the service of which it functions with magnificent precision. Other sections of the poem describe the ward's inmates through the sensitive and understanding eyes of a fellow sufferer: the moronic Harry, writing his letter; the 'Old Timer', the 'small grey mendicant man', whose wistful plea for communication melts the poet into instant compassion; the Homosexual; and the Old Women who visit the ward on Sunday afternoons. In the poem's final segment, 'Wild Honey', where the poet watches a girl combing her golden hair, the apprehension of the beauty of that ordinary everyday action brings the recognition that in 'the tiny, the pitiable, meaningless and rare' lie the stars themselves – in 'sacred dishevelment' perhaps, but the stars nevertheless.

WATKINS, Griffith (1930–69), born Christchurch, NZ, came to WA at the age of

6. Educated at the University of WA, he taught art at secondary school and at Claremont Teachers College. He also worked as a gold-miner and stockman. From the late
1950s he published poetry and short stories in numerous periodicals and won several
awards including the 1966 Henry Lawson Prize for poetry. In 1969 he took his own
life by drowning. In 1967 his novel *The Pleasure Bird* was published and in 1990 a
selection of his poetry and fiction, *God in the Afternoon*, selected and edited by Peter
Jeffery.

Ways of Many Waters, The (1899), the first volume of verse by E.J. Brady, established him as Australia's balladist of the sea. John Masefield praised the poems as 'the
best yet written about the merchant sailor and the man of war's man'. Notable poems
include 'Lost and Given Over', 'Tallow and Hides', 'The Great Gray Water' and the
title poem, 'The Ways of Many Waters'.

We Took Their Orders and Are Dead: An Anti-War Anthology (1971), edited
by Ros Cheney, David Malouf, Michael Wilding and Shirley Cass, includes work by
numerous Australian poets and prose-writers and was compiled as a protest at Australia's military involvement in the Vietnam War with the USA. The title is taken
from a line of A.D. Hope's poem 'Inscription for Any War'.

WEARNE, Alan (1948–   ), born Melbourne, has been part of the Australian poetry
scene since the late 1960s when he was involved in the Monash poetry readings which
helped formulate new directions for Australian poetry. Although he was included in
John Tranter's anthology *The New Australian Poetry* (1979), Wearne has not been as
widely anthologised as others in the New Poetry movement. He published two small
books of verse, *Public Relations* (1972) in the Gargoyle Poets series and *New Devil New
Parish* (1976) in the UQP Paperback Poets series. The latter included a verse novella,
Out Here, which indicated the literary path that Wearne was soon to follow with
conspicuous success. Commissioned in 1978 by Penguin to write a verse novel on the
strength of one chapter completed out of a projected ten, Wearne laboured for eight
years to produce the epic work *The Nightmarkets* (1986). An instant success, it won
both the NBC Banjo Award and the Australian Literature Society's Gold Medal in
1987. Although subtitled 'a novel', *The Nightmarkets* virtually defies plot summation.
The 'action' is presented in ten chapters – dramatic monologues by six of the major
characters of the book. Ian Metcalfe, in more central focus than most of the other
characters, is a pot-smoking, lazy, part-time public servant, student, lover, and so-
called 'investigative' journalist, who guides the reader into the Melbourne of the
middle 1960s and then through to 1980. In the opening chapter he recounts his
brother Robert's conscientious objection to the Vietnam War and his six months on a
prison farm; the euphoria of Labor's return under Whitlam in 1972; the sacking of the
Whitlam government in 1975; the nation 'post-Gough'; and the relapse of many of
the 1960s radicals into apathy, conservatism or overseas wanderings. Metcalfe tells
also of his two girl-friends – first Sue Dobson, then 18 and the pair of them 'apprentice
lovers', and, later, Allison. Metcalfe narrates two other chapters (2 and 4) and the
concluding one; his monologues thus provide the central theme around which the
other narrators and their stories ebb and flow. Sue Dobson, now a journalist, gives her
account of the same years, first in Chapter 2, 'The Bistro Variations', and then in
Chapter 6, 'Climbing up the Ladder of Love', the two longest chapters of the book.
Sue's 1960s radicalism and 1970s–80s feminism are the most deeply held attitudes of
all the characters but even they manage to get temporarily sidelined while she
becomes involved with John McTaggart, one-time federal Liberal MP and now
founder of the New Progress Party. McTaggart narrates one chapter, 'After the
Tribe', as does his mother, the tough, amiable old Liberal party campaigner Elise
McTaggart. Ian's brother Robert, seeking a political career as Labor member for

O'Dowd, also has a chapter. The prostitute hostess Terri, from the Crystal Palace Health Spa and Businessman's Club, is also a narrator and central to the action. The most honest, likeable and realistic of all the characters, she exposes the shortcomings of the others. Deliberate stereotypes of the period, the characters are exuberantly portrayed, especially by means of their speech patterns – 'strine', colloquial Australianisms, drug and dope 'lingo'. Intensely familiar with the personality of Melbourne, *The Nightmarkets* has been likened to Joyce's *Ulysses*, not only because of its stream-of-consciousness technique but also because of its sense of place and its linking of locality, history, language and social mores.

WEBB, Francis (1925–73) was born Francis Charles Webb-Wagg in Adelaide; after the death of his mother in 1927 he was raised in Sydney by his paternal grandparents (Webb) from whom he gained his interest in books, music, sailing and the seas. He had a reasonably happy and trouble-free childhood and adolescence and served with the RAAF 1943–45. He trained as a wireless air gunner in Canada but did not see action in the war. In 1946 he began an arts course at the University of Sydney but abandoned it in 1947 to return to Canada, where he was employed as a publisher's reader. In 1949 he went from Canada to England, where he suffered his first mental breakdown. He returned to Australia in 1950, spent the years 1953–59 in England, much of the time in hospitals in Birmingham and Norfolk, and came back to Australia in 1960. Throughout the 1960s Webb struggled unavailingly against schizophrenia and spent most of the decade in mental institutions in NSW and Victoria.

Webb's published works are *A Drum for Ben Boyd* (1948), *Leichhardt in Theatre* (1952), *Birthday* (1953), *Socrates and Other Poems* (1961), and *The Ghost of the Cock* (1964). His *Collected Poems* was published in 1969. 'A Drum for Ben Boyd', first published in the *Bulletin* (1946), is a long poem about the Scottish merchant-entrepreneur Benjamin Boyd. Webb also uses a heroic figure in the poem 'Leichhardt in Theatre', which was published in the *Bulletin* (1947), an abridged version appearing in his second volume of poetry in 1952. That volume, *Leichhardt in Theatre*, contains some of Webb's most significant shorter verse, e.g. 'Morgan's Country', 'Melville at Woods Hole', 'Dawn Wind on the Islands', 'On First Hearing a Cuckoo' and 'A View of Montreal'. *Birthday* (1953) takes its title from his radio verse play 'Birthday' about the final days of Adolf Hitler in the bunker in Berlin; it also contains the sequence of poems 'The Canticle', dealing with St Francis of Assisi, and several fine individual pieces, e.g. 'Galston' and 'End of the Picnic'. Most of the poems of Webb's next volume, *Socrates and Other Poems* (1961), had been written in Norfolk, England, following a long period of illness and recuperation during the late 1950s. Dedicated to Dr F.W. Klinghardt, who had supervised his recovery, and to the Australian poet David Campbell, who had much to do with his subsequent return to Australia, *Socrates* contains the most mature and assured of Webb's poetry, including his new concept of the artist's function (which W.D. Ashcroft has termed 'meditative purposefulness'). *Socrates* contains Webb's chief lyric poems, e.g. 'Bells of St. Peter Mancroft' and 'Five Days Old', and some of his most technically innovative and skilfully crafted verses, e.g. 'The Yellowhammer', 'Light' and 'Mousehold Heath'. *Socrates* also includes the fourteen-verse sequence 'Eyre All Alone', Webb's finest analysis of a heroic figure, in this case the Australian explorer Edward John Eyre. Webb's mental ordeals are revealed in such poems as 'The Brain-washers', 'Hospital Night' and 'A Death at Winson Green'. In the title poem, a dramatic monologue by Socrates just before his death, there is an unusual and impressive air of acceptance of the order of things; it reflects perhaps one of his few brief periods of remission.

> . . . I front the grieving
> Song of the long spear that is your lifted voice
> And coolly read the outcome in your eye, my star.

Webb's final volume, *The Ghost of the Cock* (1964), was compiled largely from his unpublished poems written before his admission to Callan Park hospital in the early 1960s. The title piece is a radio verse play in three acts, to be accompanied by the scherzos of Bruckner's ninth and seventh symphonies, in which Michael and Tobias descend to earth intending to 'ferry to eternity' the sole human survivors (a man and a woman) of a nuclear war. Accused by the surviving animal inhabitants of cruelty and selfishness, the humans are forgiven and saved only by the intercession of the cock. The last volume contains two of Webb's finest poetic achievements, 'Ward Two', a powerful and moving sequence set in the Parramatta psychiatric centre, and 'Around Costessy', a sequence centred on the Norfolk village of Costessy and conveying impressions of the Norfolk countryside. In the seventh part of 'Around Costessy', i.e. 'In Memoriam: Anthony Sandys, 1806–1883', Webb again defines the function of the creative artist. Webb's long-standing attraction to music, glimpsed in the earlier 'Tallis to Vaughan Williams' in *Birthday*, is indicated more strongly in this volume in 'Gustave Mahler' and 'Brahms at Bruckner's Funeral'. The *Collected Poems*, with a preface by Sir Herbert Read, adds a section 'Early Poems 1942–1948' to those volumes already mentioned. Important among Webb's uncollected poems is 'Lament for St. Maria Goretti', published in *Poetry Australia* (1973).

Francis Webb has drawn his greatest commendations from fellow poets: he was posthumously given the Christopher Brennan Award by the FAW. The most-publicised estimation of him is Sir Herbert Read's judgment that he is not inferior to Rilke, Eliot, Pasternak and Robert Lowell. Similar high opinions came from Douglas Stewart, who maintained that in his profoundly original writing Webb created 'a new language . . . a new imagery'. David Campbell insisted that Webb 'went higher than any other poet who has ever written in Australia'. Bruce Beaver sees the 'touch of genius' in Webb's capacity to 'take the earth-bound and spiritualise it, turning it into a holy fire of music'. Other reactions to the total body of Webb's poetry have been ambivalent. The earlier poetry, in which historical figures such as Boyd and Leichhardt are represented, has been generally well received, *A Drum for Ben Boyd* winning the 1948 Grace Leven Prize for poetry. In the later extremely complex poetry the obsessively religious nature of his personal response to experience, the brilliance of his language and intensity of imagery have combined to categorise him as an extraordinarily gifted, though esoteric and somewhat inaccessible poet. Something of a cult-figure since his death, Webb exercised considerable influence in the development of some of the new attitudes that spread through Australian poetry in the late 1960s and 1970s. The September 1975 number of *Poetry Australia* is a Francis Webb commemorative issue. Michael Griffith and James McGlade published an annotated collection of Webb's work, *Cap and Bells: The Poetry of Francis Webb* (1991) and Griffith also wrote *God's Fool: The Life and Poetry of Francis Webb* (1991). A collection of seminar papers which contains biographical information, *Francis Webb – Poet and Patient*, was published in 1983.

Westerly, a literary magazine but concerned also with historical, social and political issues, commenced publication in 1956 as a student-edited magazine of the arts union of the University of WA under the editorship of R.W. Smith. From 1963, when it was first assisted by a CLF grant, *Westerly* began quarterly publication. By contrast with its fellow journals *Meanjin*, *Overland* and *Quadrant*, *Westerly* began with neither a commitment to a particular ideology nor a well-known editorial identity. It thus became a forum magazine, although some continuity of editorial opinion and character was achieved in the late 1950s through the presence of Peter Cowan and John Barnes, and from 1975 when Cowan and Bruce Bennett became joint editors after publication of the magazine was transferred to the English Department of the University of WA. Dennis Haskell joined the editorial team in 1985, and Delys Bird in 1993, following the departure of Bruce Bennett. Concerned from its beginnings to propagate local, national and international interest in Australian writing and culture, *Westerly* has sought a continuing discussion of the nature and character of Australian literature, and of the need for Australian studies in universities and schools. *Westerly 21: An Anniversary Selection* (1978), edited by Bennett and Cowan, is an anthology from the magazine's first twenty-one years of publication. Recognition of geographic and cultural links with the Asia-Pacific region has resulted in increasing contributions by and about that area, reflected in the anthology *Westerly Looks to Asia* (1993) edited by Bennett, Cowan, Haskell and Susan Miller.

'Where the Dead Men Lie', the best-known poem by Barcroft Boake and the title poem of his only volume of verse (1897), was published in the *Bulletin* (1891) under the pseudonym 'Surcingle'. In the poem Boake uses the contemptuous name 'Moneygrub' to denote the typical wealthy absentee landlord who lives in city luxury provided for him by the ordinary men and women of the outback; 'out on the wastes of the Never-Never' they give their lives in the one-sided struggle against poverty, privation and the harshness of the land.

WHITE, Gilbert (1859–1933), born Cape Town, South Africa, was successively bishop of Carpentaria and of Willochra and wrote numerous theological works as well as the descriptive accounts *Round about the Torres Straits* (1917) and *Thirty Years in Tropical Australia* (1918). He also published six volumes of verse, *Melchior and Other Verses* (1893), *Night* (1897), *The World's Tragedy* (1910), *Australia* (1913), *The Poems of Gilbert White* (1919), *The Later Poems of Gilbert White* (1930) and *Selected Poems of Gilbert White* (1932). A biography by J.W.C. Ward, *White of Carpentaria*, was published in 1949.

'WICKHAM, Anna' (Edith Hepburn) (1884–1947), born London, came to Australia in infancy and was educated in Brisbane but returned to England in 1904 to pursue a literary career. From 1905, when she married Patrick Hepburn, she lived in London and was the friend of numerous writers, including Natalie Barney, Kate O'Brien, Dylan Thomas, Malcolm Lowrey, Ezra Pound, David Garnett and D.H. Lawrence. A compulsive writer of poetry, she was encouraged by Harold Munro and Louis Untermeyer. Her publications include two minor plays for girls, *The Seasons* (1902) and *Wonder Eyes* (1903); the volumes of poetry, *Songs* (1911), by 'John Oland'; *The Contemplative Quarry* (1915), *The Man with a Hammer* (1916) and *The Little Old House* (1921), all under the 'Anna Wickham' pseudonym. A combined volume, *The Contemplative Quarry* and *The Man with a Hammer*, was published in the USA in 1921 and her *Selected Poems* in 1971. In 1984 R.D. Smith edited a collection of her poetry and prose, *The Writings of Anna Wickham*, which includes her 'Fragment of an Autobiography' and extensive biographical information. Much of Wickham's verse reflects her ambivalence about marriage, social convention and the conflicting claims of family and art.

WILCOX, Dora (1873–1953), born Christchurch, NZ, worked as a teacher in NSW and with the VAD in England during the First World War. Her second husband was Australian art historian William Moore. Some of her poems appeared in Australian magazines and in 1927 she won a *Sydney Morning Herald* prize for an ode celebrating the opening of the Commonwealth parliament. Two of her plays were published, *Commander Capstan* (1931) and *The Fourposter* in *Best Australian One-Act Plays* (1937), edited by William Moore and T. Inglis Moore. She also published three volumes of poetry, *Verses from Maoriland* (1905), *Rata and Mistletoe* (1911) and *Seven Poems* (1924), although only the last collection contains poems drawn from her Australian experience.

'Wild Colonial Boy, The', one of Australia's best-known folk-songs, tells the story of an Irish-born bushranger, named Jack Doolan, who terrorises the squatters, holds up the Beechworth mail coach in the 1860s, robs Judge MacEvoy, and is eventually killed when surrounded by three troopers, Kelly, Davis and FitzRoy, to whom he refuses to surrender. Several versions of 'The Wild Colonial Boy', which is often sung to the Irish tune 'The Wearing of the Green', e.g. by Ned Kelly at Glenrowan, have survived: in some of them MacEvoy is called Macaboy, and Jack Doolan is variously Jim or John Dowling/Duggan/Dublin/Dolan/Davis. That the hero of the song always has the initials 'JD' has led many folklorists to argue that the Wild Colonial Boy was a fictitious character and that the song is an 1860s variant of the 'Bold Jack Donahoe' cycle of songs and ballads, which, as a result of oral transmission, acquired a new set of characters and events. The argument is strengthened by a chorus beginning 'Come along, my hearties, we'll roam the mountains high,/ Together we will plunder, together we will die', which is common to versions of both ballads, and by the fact that the songs are traditionally linked in Irish folk-music. John Manifold, however, in *Who Wrote the Ballads?* (1964), speculates that there was a bushranger of the 1860s named Jack Doolan and that his experiences were celebrated by taking over the existing Bold Jack Donahoe songs. Whatever the origins of the song, 'The Wild Colonial Boy' is well known overseas and is sung by John Wayne in the film *The Quiet Man*. In Australia, its popularity is such that 'wild colonial boys' became a phrase describing the bushrangers in general, as in Frank Clune's book *Wild Colonial Boys*, and, indeed, any Australian sharing their bravado and daring. In contrast, the heroic image of the bushranger is satirised in David Martin's novel *The Hero of Too* (1967). In 'Steele Rudd's' stage play *Gran'dad Rudd* (1918) a recalcitrant cow is encouraged to give milk by a rendition of 'The Wild Colonial Boy'.

Wild Notes, from the Lyre of a Native Minstrel (1826), by Charles Tompson, was the first volume of poems by an Australian-born writer to be published in Australia. The volume, containing the long poem 'Retrospect', together with odes, elegies, and miscellaneous verses, gives a picture of the foundation of the Colony and a description of the landscape from the well-disposed 'currency' viewpoint. Contrary to the title, the 'wild notes' are well-polished verses, strikingly ornate in a stereotyped, traditional style.

Wild Swan, The (1930) is the most significant book of verse by Mary Gilmore, including her favourite themes – nature, the Aborigines, wholehearted commitment to life, and love. She mourns, in several poems, the passing of the wild swans, a beloved feature of the landscape of her youth.

'William Street', a brief poem by Kenneth Slessor published in *One Hundred Poems 1919–1939* (1944), describes the main traffic artery that runs from the city up to Kings Cross (Sydney) as it would have appeared in all its garish flamboyance in the 1930s. The poem is part of Slessor's defence of his 'patch' – 'you find it ugly, I find it lovely.'

WILLIAMS, Justina (1916–   ), born Coolgardie, WA, has been a journalist on the *West Australian* and the *Daily News*, and an active supporter of radical and feminist causes over many years. Active also in the FAW, she has published three collections of poetry, *The Dreaming Vine* (1970), *By All the Clocks* (1975) and *People and Peace* (1986); a book of short fiction, *White River and Other Stories* (1979); two socio-political histories, *The First Furrow* (1976) and *Trade Unionism* (1978); and a children's story, *The Bird Girl* (1984). She also edited *Tom Collins and his House* (1973). Her autobiography, *Anger and Love* (1993), chiefly concerns her support for the left-wing movement in WA in the face of concerted opposition.

WILLIAMS, Lauren (1958–   ), born Melbourne where she still lives, published her first collection, *Live Sentences*, in 1991. Many of these poems, with their strong, incisive language and ironic observations, were regarded largely as performance poetry. *The Sad Anthropologist* (1994) is equally ironic and perceptive but the delivery is more muted, the message more subtle. The defeat of conservatism, artificiality, convention, greed and gender remains the aim of much of the poetry – of romance in 'Love Story', of convention in 'Ballet Girls', of male chauvinism in 'One Dick Poem Too Many', and of man's destructiveness in 'The Sad Anthropologist', where the anthropologist's (the poet) gloom is because of 'The work of my species'. As Jill Jones belongs to Sydney, Lauren Williams ('Dad', 'Cranes') is a poet of the Melbourne scene.

WILLIAMS, Max, born Redfern, Sydney, where he spent a very deprived childhood during the 1930s Depression, had his first brush with the law at the age of 5 and at the age of 10 was committed to an institution for wayward boys. He spent most of the next thirty years in prison. He has contributed to *Poems from Prison* (1973) and *Australians Aware* (1975), both edited by Rodney Hall, and to *Poet's Choice*. He has also published three collections, *The Poor Man's Bean* (1975), *Hard Is the Convict Road* (1977) and *Baronda* (1977), and has written an autobiography, *Dingo! My Life on the Run* (1980).

WILLIAMS, Victor (1914–   ), born Perth, was a farm worker and schoolteacher in WA before serving with the Australian Army in the Second World War. He has written four books of verse, *Harvest Time* (1946), *Into Battle With a Song* (1953), *Hammers and Seagulls* (1967) and *Three Golden Giants* (1977), as well as *The Years of Big Jim* (1975), a biography of Jim Healy, waterfront union official.

WILMOT, Frank, see **'MAURICE, Furnley'**

WILSON, Edwin (1942–   ), born Lismore, NSW, was educated at the University of NSW. He has taught science in secondary schools, and worked for a period as a lecturer at Armidale Teachers College and as education officer at the Australian Museum, Sydney. Since 1980 he has worked in Community Programs at the Royal Botanic Gardens, Sydney. He has contributed verse to numerous periodicals and anthologies and has published the collections *Banyan* (1982), *The Dragon Book* (1985), *Songs of the Forest* (1990), *The Rose Garden* (1991) and *The Botanic Verses* (1993). Reflecting his interest in plants, his delicately worked poems often use the vegetable world as a starting point for subtle, wry meditations on the human condition. He has also published the novels *Liberty, Egality, Fraternity!* (1984) and *Wild Tamarind* (1987), as well as pictorial histories and guides to Sydney's major public gardens and parks.

WILSON, Helen Helga (1902–91), born Mayne at Zeehan, Tasmania, spent her early years in the WA goldfields area, where her father was a mining engineer. A graduate of the University of WA, she published several anecdotal, historical accounts of the goldfields; the novels *The Golden Age* (1959), *Quiet, Brat!* (1958), *Where the Wind's Feet Shine* (1960), *If Golde Rust* (1961), *Island of Fire* (1973), *Bring Back the Hour* (1977), *The Mulga Trees* (1980) and *The House at Hardie's Corner* (1984); two collections of short stories, *A Show of Colours* (1970) and *The Skedule and Other Australian Short Stories* (1979); and three of verse, *Songs of Empire* (1941), *Occasional Verse, 1942–1943* (1943), and *The Letters of Huang Hu* (1946). In 1980 she was awarded the OAM.

'Wind at Your Door, The', a poem by R.D. FitzGerald, was first published in the *Bulletin* (1958). It is based on the uprising of Irish rebel convicts at Castle Hill in 1804 although the incident of the flogging depicted in the poem took place at Toongabbie in 1800. The poem has two central characters: the poet's ancestor, Martin Mason, surgeon, magistrate, and seemingly callous overseer of the brutal flogging of a convict; and the poet's namesake, Morris Fitzegarrel, the stoic convict victim. In these two figures and their history, FitzGerald sees the continuing problem, on both the national and the individual level, of the Australian identity. On the general level is the problem of the nation adapting to its development from a 'jailyard'; on the personal level is the problem of individual Australians (in this case the poet himself) adapting to both sides of their ancestry, authoritarianism and rebellion against authority. The poem indicates that the wind that blows the blood and flesh from the lacerated back of the convict Fitzegarrel into the faces of the bystanders will continue to blow the memory and the impact of that event, and scores of similar events, into the present and future Australian consciousness. FitzGerald's personal compromise is to accept that both the characters in the poem and others like them are equal victims. The convict Fitzegarrel also appears in Thomas Keneally's novel *Passenger* (1979).

'WITTING, Amy' (Joan Levick) (1918–), born Joan Fraser at Annandale, Sydney, attended the University of Sydney, where she was a member of the group of intellectuals and poets which included James McAuley and Harold Stewart. She later taught French and English at secondary level. She has contributed short stories and poems to such magazines as *Quadrant, Overland, Westerly* and the *New Yorker* and has published three novels, *The Visit* (1977), *I for Isobel* (1989) and *A Change in the Lightning* (1994); a short-story collection, *Marriages* (1990); and two collections of poetry, *Travel Diary* (1985) and *Beauty is the Straw* (1991). She has also written textbooks on language. Witting's poetry, diverse in range, tone and voice, is cerebral, sensual, witty and, like her fiction, often deftly ironic. Uniting the diversity as a thematic undercurrent is a tempered response to time, change and the certainty of death, an Auden-like awareness that 'The moment of our desolation/ Will be some other's consolation'. Witting received the Patrick White Award in 1993.

Woman to Man (1949), the second volume of poems published by Judith Wright, takes its title from the opening poem, a delicate, sensitive, yet forthright statement of the special relationship between man and woman as sharers in the act of conception. The sequential poems 'Woman's Song' and 'Woman to Child' are equally compelling statements of woman as mother. The poet's preoccupation with time is evident in 'Letter to a Friend', 'Spring after War' and 'The Bones Speak', but echoing as they do the optimism of her earlier poem 'The Moving Image', they indicate time's regenerative as well as destructive power.

WOODHOUSE, Jena (1949–), born Rockhampton, has worked as a teacher of creative writing and of English as a second language and as a freelance editor and writer. Winner of the FAW John Shaw Neilson Award for poetry in 1986, of the Rothmans Foundation Prize in 1988 and of an Australian-Greek Travel Award in 1987, she has published poetry in numerous periodicals and anthologies. She has also published the collection *Eros in Landscape* (1989) and the novella *Metis, the Octopus and the Olive Tree* (1993).

WOOLLS, William (1814–93), born Hampshire, England, came to Australia at the age of 17 and subsequently became a schoolmaster and an Anglican clergyman. His personality is described by one of his students, 'Rolf Boldrewood', in *In Bad Company and Other Stories* (1901). Woolls was one of Australia's first essayists, his *Miscellanies in Prose and Verse* appearing in 1838. An authoritative botanist, whose work was useful to Ferdinand von Mueller, he wrote several scientific books as well as articles published in proceedings of the Linnean Society. He also published three booklets of verse, *The Voyage* (1832), *Australia* (1833) and *In Memory of R.D. FitzGerald* (1892), grandfather of the prominent Australian poet of the same name.

WRIGHT, David McKee (1869–1928), born Ireland, was educated in Ireland and London, and in 1887 migrated to NZ. There he worked on sheep stations, studied for the Congregational ministry and from 1890 contributed to many NZ journals. In 1905 he gave up the ministry and in 1907 began work as a journalist on the *New Zealand Mail*. Four of his volumes of verse were published in NZ, *Aorangi and Other Verses* (1896), *Station Ballads* (1897), *Wisps of Tussock* (1900) and *New Zealand Chimes* (1900), and some of his poems appeared in Australian periodicals. In 1909 he moved to Sydney, where he worked as a freelance writer for the *Bulletin* and other newspapers before succeeding Arthur H. Adams as editor of the *Bulletin*'s Red Page. He continued to write prolifically in prose and verse, often using such pseudonyms as 'Curse O' Moses', 'Pat O'Maori', 'George Street' and 'Mary McCommonwealth'. In 1918 he published his most substantial collection of verse, *An Irish Heart*, and in 1920 was awarded a prize for a poem commemorating the visit of the Prince of Wales, as well as the Rupert Brooke Memorial Prize for a long poem titled 'Gallipoli' (published in 1920 in the *Bulletin*). Wright also wrote some plays, although these, with much of his verse and prose writings, are uncollected. Like Victor Daley, Wright was strongly influenced by Irish history and legend, although his verse is generally thinner and less striking. The best-known characteristics of his prolific output are an indistinct but pervasive nostalgia for Ireland, visual, general imagery, firmly handled rhythms and a generally optimistic content. But Wright also published a great deal of work which had nothing to do with Ireland and which included satirical verse on political and social life in Australia and NZ. His longest satire, 'Apollo in George Street', written under the pseudonym 'Gillette', includes shrewd observations on contemporary poets, artists, editors and novelists. Regarded as a minor figure in Australia's Celtic tradition, Wright was in fact a more varied, innovative writer, sensitive to intellectual movements and well versed in different cultures and genres. It has been suggested that his disputes with Hugh McCrae and Norman Lindsay over their interpretation of classical art and literature may have led to his continuing disparagement. An influential, sometimes controversial, editor of the Red Page, Wright also edited *Poetical Works of Henry Lawson* (1925). Wright, who had been previously married in NZ, lived 1912–18 with the writer Margaret Fane, who was the mother of four of his sons, and with Zora Cross from 1918 until his death; they had two daughters.

WRIGHT, Judith (1915–   ) was born at Thalgaroch Station, near Armidale, NSW, into a pastoralist family whose roots go back on her paternal grandmother's side to the original settlement of the Hunter Valley in the 1820s. Her father, Phillip Arundell Wright (1889–1970), prominent New England pastoralist, and benefactor of New England University, wrote the autobiographical *Memories of a Bushwacker* (1971). She grew up on the family property Wollomombi (Wallamumbi), near Armidale, in the heart of the New England tableland, and her love for that countryside, her 'blood's country', runs through much of her early poetry. Educated at New England Girls School, she read English at the University of Sydney, and visited England and Europe, 1937–38 before settling in Sydney to work and write. She published an occasional modest, thoughtful poem, e.g. 'The Hanging Avalanche of Days' in *Southerly* (1940), but with the entry of Japan into the war she returned to help out at Wollomombi, then badly beset by manpower problems. The homecoming, which brought the rediscovery and reassessment of her attachment to the countryside and the opportunity to think deeply about her art, led to her first intensive creative period. From the old stockman Dan's tales of the early days of the district and later from the diaries of her grandfather, Albert Wright, came material that filled much of her early writing, stories that in her own words at the time, 'still go walking in my sleep'. Several fine poems about the war, 'The Trains', 'The Company of Lovers', 'To A.H. New Year, 1943', were written at this time. In 1943–47 she worked at the University of Queensland, where she met and married J.P. McKinney, philosopher and writer whose influence, some believe, has been emphatic in her poetry. Since Wright's publication of *The Moving Image* (1946), she has been a prolific poet, literary critic, anthologist, editor, children's writer, short-story writer, supporter of the Aboriginal land rights cause and active conservationist. She has received honorary D.Litts from seven Australian universities, and many awards for her writing, e.g. the Grace Leven Prize twice, the Britannica-Australia Award, the Christopher Brennan Award of the FAW and the ASAN World Prize for Poetry. In 1970 she was elected a foundation fellow of the Australian Academy of the Humanities; she has been a member of the governing body of the Australia Council and a creative arts fellow of the ANU. In her role as conservationist and activist she was for a number of years president of the Wildlife Preservation Society of Queensland, a member of the Committee of Enquiry into the National Estate, secretary of the Aboriginal Treaty Committee and life member of the Australian Conservative Foundation. In 1992 she received the Queen's Gold Medal for Poetry, the first Australian to receive the award. She was earlier awarded an emeritus fellowship of the Literature Board of the Australia Council.

Her chief volumes of poetry after *The Moving Image* have been *Woman to Man* (1949); *The Gateway* (1953); *The Two Fires* (1955); *Birds* (1962); *Five Senses* (1963), (her first selected volume); *Judith Wright* in the Australian Poets Series (1963); *City Sunrise* (1964); *The Other Half* (1966); *Alive: Poems 1971–1972* (1973), *Fourth Quarter and Other Poems* (1976) and *Phantom Dwelling* (1985). Her *Collected Poems 1942–1970*, *The Double Tree: Selected Poems 1942–1976* and *A Human Pattern: Selected Poems* were published in 1971, 1978 and 1990 respectively. A further more substantial collection, 1942–85, was published in 1994 as well as a bilingual work, *The Flame Tree*, fifteen poems translated into Japanese by Nobuo Sakai and Wright's daughter Meredith McKinney. She has written children's fiction, including *Kings of the Dingoes* (1958), *The Day the Mountains Played* (1960) and *The River and the Road* (1966), and a book of short stories, *The Nature of Love* (1966); edited several anthologies, including *A Book of Australian Verse* (1956), *New Land, New Language* (1957) and *The Poet's Pen* (1965), and two selections of John Shaw Neilson's poetry (1963 and 1970); written monographs on Charles Harpur and Henry Lawson; narrated her family's history in *The Generations of Men* (1959) and its sequel, *The Cry for the Dead* (1981); published a selection of her essays and reviews, *Because I Was Invited* (1975); written a seminal book of Australian poetic criticism, *Preoccupations in Australian Poetry* (1965); and, in her role as conservationist, has published *The Coral Battleground* (1977) and a book of essays, *Going on Talking* (1992), the second half of which focuses on her anxiety about the environment. Her struggle for the welfare of the Aborigines is given expression in *The Cry for the Dead*, *We Call for a Treaty* (1985) and *Born of the Conquerors* (1991). In an essay for the Tasmanian Wilderness Calendar (1981) she sums up the basis of her desire to fight the Aborigines' cause:

> Those two strands – the love of the land we have invaded and the guilt of the invasion – have become part of me. It is haunted. We owe it repentance and such amends as we can make ...

The appearance of *The Moving Image* in 1946 brought a sense of excitement and anticipation to the Australian literary world of the time; its impact was summed up in Douglas Stewart's *Bulletin* review: 'These poems promise anything, everything, the world.' The poems were acclaimed for their lyric beauty, brilliant craftsmanship and emotional honesty. The volumes following *Woman to Man*, except for the whimsical *Birds*, were received with less general enthusiasm. Wright herself has often expressed discomfiture by the view that those early poems, which she recently described as having 'dropped off several incarnations back', should be the yardstick of all her work. She has been supported by some critics who see that in her later poetry 'she made the harder choice of seeking, through private struggle, to wring from poetry a new vision of the world' (H.P. Heseltine). In the later volumes she reached beyond the easily perceived world of the senses in a search for an ultimate reality, perception or self-knowledge. In *The Gateway* she refers to 'the Traveller', and many of the poems in that collection and following volumes are a record of her 'travelling', her pilgrimage towards that reality and knowledge. Her initial view of the poet as the creative interpreter of the universe and its eternal processes of change still remains, however, at the centre of her poetry. Her recognition of 'the continuity of experience through time' leads her to accept the world as an interdependent community of all living things (human, animal, plant) and her use of nature as a stepping-stone to a deeper exploratory probing of universal human questions is still a satisfying basis from which the reader can proceed to an understanding and appreciation of her total work. In later volumes, especially in 'Shadow' (1970), the closing section of her *Collected Poems 1942–1970*, she attacks the evils of modern society, especially its abnegation of responsibility for the brutality that daily characterises world affairs. Her next three volumes, *Alive, Fourth Quarter* and *Phantom Dwelling*, chart yet another watershed in her poetic and philosophical approach. Shirley Walker has described *Alive* as 'a period of stasis', the poetry seeking through meditation 'the pattern of past experience'. Thus Walker sees the poems emphasising, in an elegiac tone, the significance of continuity, the importance of memory. From *Fourth Quarter* on, however, there is a resurgence of energy, as if the limitations of physicality are now dismissed and creative power, undiminished by increasing age, remains as ample recompense. *Phantom Dwelling* goes a step further, reinforcing, with its freshness, strength and clarity, that sense of limitless poetic power still available to her. Many *Phantom Dwelling* poems are familiar in theme – nature, love, her family and its pastoral links (past and present). The six poems of 'For a Pastoral Family' give a partly nostalgic but judicious assessment of the past viewed from the present, and a present still much aligned in attitude and outlook to the past. The things of nature – flora, fauna, the land itself – are still paramount to her, still retain their own 'thisness' ('The remnant of a mountain has its own meaning'). *Phantom Dwelling* ends with twelve short poems titled 'The Shadow of Fire: Ghazals' (Ghazals being a species of Oriental lyrics), in which the interface between ageless natural phenomena (a rockface, a rockpool, a flowering heath) and impermanent individual human life (our 'phantom dwelling') is again lovingly and carefully explored but with an increased, and seemingly new-won, equanimity. *A Human Pattern*, the Selected Volume of all her poetry to that point (1990), reveals the extraordinary substance, or as one critic called it, the 'nobleness', of Judith Wright's overall poetic achievement.

W.N. Scott wrote the biographical *Focus on Judith Wright* (1967), A.K. Thomson edited *Critical Essays on Judith Wright* (1968), A.D. Hope wrote the monograph *Judith Wright* (1975) and Shirley Walker, *The Poetry of Judith Wright: A Search for Unity* (1980), updated as *Flame and Shadow: A Study of Judith Wright's Poetry* (1991, in the UQP Studies in Australian Literature).

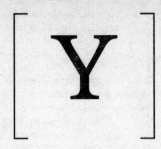

YARRINGTON, W.H.H. (William Henry Hazell) (?-1920), a clergyman with numerous literary friends, published several volumes of verse in book and pamphlet form 1880–1919. They include *University Prize Poem and Other Verses* (1880), *Coelestia* (1882), *Turning to the East* (1890), *Australian Verses* (1892), *Sonnets on Ritualism* (1901), *The Man of Principle* (?1904), and *Crossing the Mountain* (1919). He also edited the anthology *Prince Alfred's Wreath* (1868), which includes poetry by Henry Kendall and J. Sheridan Moore. Yarrington is one of the minor targets of Kendall's satiric poem *The Bronze Trumpet*.

ZILLMANN, John Herman Leopold (1842–1919), an Anglican minister, born Brisbane and resident in Queensland, published two novels which are mainly religious in tone, *In the Land of the Bunya: Or, the Convict and the Boy* (1899) and *From Old to New: Or, Mitre Versus Gown* (1901); four collections of religious verse and one of hymns; a prose meditation on the supernatural, *Two Worlds Are Ours* (1885); and two works which mingle history, description and personal reminiscence, *Past and Present Australian Life* (1889) and *Career of a Cornstalk* (1914).

ZWICKY, Fay (1933–   ), born Melbourne, began writing as an undergraduate at the University of Melbourne and has published short stories and poems in anthologies and periodicals. A concert pianist for some years before teaching English at the University of WA 1972–87, she has published the collections of verse *Isaac Babel's Fiddle* (1975), *Kaddish and Other Poems* (1982, winner of the NSW Premier's Award), *Ask Me* (1990, winner of the 1991 WA Premier's Award for poetry), *A Touch of Ginger* (1991, with Dennis Haskell) and *Fay Zwicky: Poems 1970–1992* (1993). She has also edited *Quarry* (1981), a selection of contemporary WA poetry; *Journeys* (1982), an anthology of poems by Judith Wright, Rosemary Dobson, Gwen Harwood and Dorothy Hewett; and *Procession* (1987), a collection of poetry by members of the group known as the Young Street poets. Her first collection of short stories, *Hostages*, was published in 1983. A well-known critic, Zwicky has published a substantial collection of her essays, reviews and articles in *The Lyre in the Pawnshop* (1986).

Zwicky writes an individual, emotionally direct and densely textured poetry which is concerned with division, conflict and dispossession, the paradoxes of experience, the ambivalences of relationships and the relation between artist and art. One of the most marked characteristics of her poetry is a challenging of patriarchal myth and its implicit silencing of the language and experience of women. Resisting traditional values, structures and perceptions as they are represented both by myth and by linguistic convention, Zwicky's is an original, confident voice which can move easily from elegy to satire to parody. One of her most admired poems, 'Kaddish', is a lament for the death of her father, which is also a vivid, funny/sad evocation of life in a Melbourne Jewish family. Four of the stories of *Hostages* also draw on her youthful experience in Melbourne and evoke the pains, humiliations and enlightenments of growing up; others use a range of narrators to explore various aspects of contemporary Australian life.